CISA®
Certified Information Systems Auditor™
Study Guide
Second Edition

CISA®
Certified Information Systems Auditor™

Study Guide

Second Edition

David L. Cannon

Wiley Publishing, Inc.

Acquisitions Editor: Jeff Kellum
Development Editor: Lisa Bishop
Technical Editor: Brady Pamplin
Production Editor: Rachel McConlogue
Copy Editor: Sharon Wilkey
Production Manager: Tim Tate
Vice President and Executive Group Publisher: Richard Swadley
Vice President and Executive Publisher: Joseph B. Wikert
Vice President and Publisher: Neil Edde
Media Project Manager: Laura Atkinson
Media Assistant Producer: Angie Denny
Media Quality Assurance: Josh Frank
Book Designer: Judy Fung and Bill Gibson
Compositor: Craig Woods, Happenstance Type-O-Rama
Proofreader: Jen Larsen, Word One
Indexer: Ted Laux
Cover Designer: Ryan Sneed

Copyright © 2008 by Wiley Publishing, Inc., Indianapolis, Indiana

Published simultaneously in Canada

ISBN: 978-0-470-23152-4

Sybex®
An Imprint of
⊛WILEY

Dear Reader,

Thank you for choosing *CISA: Certified Information Systems Auditor*. This book is part of a family of premium quality Sybex books, all written by outstanding authors who combine practical experience with a gift for teaching.

Sybex was founded in 1976. More than thirty years later, we're still committed to producing consistently exceptional books. With each of our titles we're working hard to set a new standard for the industry. From the paper we print on, to the authors we work with, our goal is to bring you the best books available.

I hope you see all that reflected in these pages. I'd be very interested to hear your comments and get your feedback on how we're doing. Feel free to let me know what you think about this or any other Sybex book by sending me an email at nedde@wiley.com, or if you think you've found a technical error in this book, please visit http://sybex.custhelp.com. Customer feedback is critical to our efforts at Sybex.

Best regards,

Neil Edde
Vice President & Publisher
Wiley Publishing, Inc.

This book is a tribute to the students who attended our classes. Their infinite questions were instrumental in the creation of this Study Guide. I wish to express my appreciation to my past employers and clients for the opportunities that led me down this path.

I would like to express a special appreciation to the following people for their years of encouragement: Kristine Lindamood, Carl Adkins, Thomas Carson Jr., Jeff Kellum, Reno Marsh, Toni Spray, Dewayne Neagle, Scott Barber, Richard Darrell, William "Bill" Giles, Tim and Cynthia McDonald, Pat Cathey, Lori Martin, Gary Sprague, Lori Acree, Terry Perkins, Mike English, Sean Burke, Mike Pratt, Dianna Pickens, David Bassham, Timothy S. Bergmann, Brady Pamplin, Mark and Kris Herber, Wendy Stevens, Brian Wrozek, Frank Carter, Kris Lonborg, Joe Moore, Danney Jarmon, Bob Mahlstedt, Chris and Tammy Stevens, Daryl Luthas, Stephen Harding, Kirk Pingel, Darlene Miller, Matt Gair, Nan Robinson, Tarik Nasir, Gary and Michelle Ames, Mitch and Cindy Waters.

I thank my family–Del, Martha, Rose Ann, John, Joann, and my grandmother Josephine–for their support. In addition, I have been blessed to work with the best staff on this planet: Joe DeVoss, Melissa Robinson, Tom Kormondy, Kayla McGee, Alan Yue, Jon Murphy, and Steve Lineberry.

Semper Fidelis
—Dave Cannon

Acknowledgments

We would like to thank our Acquisitions Editor Jeff Kellum and Development Editor Lisa Bishop for their vision and guidance. Our Technical Editor Brady Pamplin was very helpful in providing his expert assistance during the writing of this book. We wish to thank Production Editor Rachel McConlogue for keeping the book on track, and for her tireless effort in ensuring that we put out the best book possible. We would also like to thank Copy Editor Sharon Wilkey, Compositor Craig Woods, Illustrators Mike Park and Jeffrey Wilson, Proofreader Jen Larsen, and Indexer Ted Laux for their polished efforts to make certain this second edition became a reality.

Contents at a Glance

Contents

Chapter   6   IT Service Delivery   323

Introduction

This book is designed for anyone interested in taking the Certified Information Systems Audit or (CISA) exam. The CISA certification is one of the hottest in the market, with annual growth in excess of 28 percent, according to the Information Systems Audit and Control Association (ISACA), the administering organization.

It is a trend worldwide for organizations to have to implement and prove the existence of strong internal controls. You may have heard of a few of these, such as the following:

- Basel II accord for risk management in banking
- Sarbanes-Oxley Act (SOX) for public corporations
- Federal Information Security Management Act (FISMA)
- Payment Card Industry (PCI) standards for credit card processing
- Health Insurance Portability and Accountability Act (HIPAA)

These are just five of more than twenty high-profile regulations that demand audited proof of internal controls. Frankly, these result in a long list of opportunities for a CISA. This may be the opportunity that you have been looking for, especially if you come from a background of finance or technology.

What is the Job Market for Certified IS Auditors?

The CISA world is exploding. Corporations are hiring more consultants than ever before in an effort to obtain compliance before they get caught short. Consulting companies are hiring as many people as they can represent as qualified in an effort to service the same corporations. Small organizations are finding themselves at a competitive disadvantage if they're unable to demonstrate the same level of internal controls to their larger customers. One of the fundamental rules of auditing is that participating in the remediation (fixing) of problems found during the audit would compromise the auditor's independence. Under the rules of independence, the independent auditor must remain independent to certify the results as valid. A second, unrelated auditor should work on the remediation. The requirements for regulatory compliance are ongoing, and that means remediation at some level will be ongoing too. In other words, the auditor requirement is actually doubled. The opportunity for you is available right now.

For many years, organizations have undergone the scrutiny of financial audits. As financial systems have become more and more complex, automation has introduced a situation in which the integrity of financial records may be in question. An organization would hire a certified public accountant to review their financial records and attest to their integrity. Larger organizations would hire certified internal auditors to assist with normal internal controls of the business. Now, the long list of regulations requiring internal controls has focused attention on the information systems. Computers are now the house in which the financial records live. The CISA is the top credential for auditing IS and related internal controls.

This book is designed to help you become a well-respected CISA. We have been teaching CISA classes for several years and have some truly outstanding success stories. The test alone is a stepping-stone in your career. Our goal is to take you through the CISA test better than anyone else by showing you the "how and why" of IS auditing. If you are familiar with technology, this book will help you understand how the auditor must act to be successful. If you come from a financial background, we're going to take you through an introductory tour of technology. The explanations in this book are technically correct and designed to be simple to understand.

Many opinions exist about how the information systems audit should be performed. This book covers the official auditing standards necessary for you to be successful. You'll find that this book contains the valuable information necessary to operate a successful consulting practice. Initially our focus is on helping you pass your exam. However, this information will help you earn a great deal more than just a paper certificate, if you apply it.

Each chapter in this book has been arranged in a logical sequence focusing on a practical application. ISACA produces fine materials written by committees of authors. We have chosen to take a different route. We have written the material in this book in the sequence that we would use to teach you prior to an audit engagement. Every point that you read will carry through to the subsequent pages of this Study Guide. The analogy is comparable to building a pyramid. You'll start with gaining a firm understanding of the basics and build your way up to the advanced material. We strongly suggest that you read the book in sequence, without skipping ahead.

One of our complaints about other study material is that it simply represents a brain dump of answers or contains excessive redundancy. We have tried our best to present the material in an orderly fashion and to provide supporting examples.

What Is the CISA Certification?

ISACA offers the most recognized certification in the world for IS auditors: the Certified Information Systems Auditor (CISA) certification. It is recognized worldwide by all corporations and governments. ISACA has members in more than 140 countries and is recognized as the leader in IT governance, control, and assurance. This association was founded in 1969 as the Electronic Data Processing Auditors Association, with an objective to develop international IS auditing and control standards. As a result, it has created the number one information systems audit certification in the world, the CISA.

ISACA controls and administers the CISA exam worldwide. More than 50,000 professionals have earned their CISA to date. Still, the demand exceeds the supply.

Why Become a CISA?

So, why become a CISA? The answer: credibility and opportunity. Many people proclaim themselves to be IS auditors. The majority of uncertified auditors are no more than well-meaning individuals who habitually violate the official audit standards. Here is a short list of the benefits associated with becoming a CISA:

Demonstrates proof of professional achievement   The CISA certification provides evidence that you have prior experience and are able to pass a rigorous certification exam. The exam tests your knowledge of auditing practices related to information systems. The test itself is loaded with technical challenges that require a significant understanding of technology. The

CISA certification shows that you understand the audit requirements and are able to lead a successful audit in accordance with widely accepted audit practices. The certification demonstrates to the world that your experience represents a significant value.

Provides added value to your employer   Today's employers are savvy to the value of training. Your CISA study is expected to illuminate new methods to improve your skills on the job. It's fairly common for individuals to start their career by mimicking a more senior person performing a similar job (as the saying goes, monkey see, monkey do). Our goal is to shine the light on specific practices that you should have been following, even if you never heard of them before. Your job performance will improve after you learn the proper foundation and CISA resources.

Provides an assurance of quality to your clients   Audit clients are a demanding breed of individuals. The fate of the client's organization may rest on the findings detailed in the auditor's report. There is little room for mistakes. The CISA credential indicates that you are a person who can be trusted to deliver accurate results. Who would you trust to represent you: a person with no proof, or someone who can demonstrate a measure of credibility? The person reading the audit report needs to understand that your work is accurate. The client will direct capital and resources to be expended according to the report you provide. The CISA certification represents a third-party audit of your personal knowledge. It helps prove your credibility.

Increases your market value   The IS audit market is exploding at a phenomenal rate. The CISA credential helps separate you from the mass of self-proclaimed auditors. Many organizations regard the CISA as the hallmark of professionalism. There is no better way to attract the favorable attention of management. It does not matter whether you're internal or external to the organization—the credential speaks for itself. The requirements called for in government regulations are becoming a growing concern for executives. Your customer may not understand all the details necessary to describe the job of an auditor; however, your client will recognize that an auditor with the CISA certification should be able to fulfill their needs. In addition, audit firms can bill more money for certified professionals.

Provides a greater opportunity for advancement   Every organization strives to hire good people who are motivated. What does the lack of certification say about someone? Is it that they are unmotivated? Could it be that they are not capable? Or is it simply that they are afraid to try? No manager in their right mind would promote an individual who has not proven their value. Taking the time to get trained and certified shows the world that you are motivated, that you are somebody who wants to get things done. That trait alone can get you promoted. Instead of using words to describe your ability, you can prove it with your CISA credential. People will know that you're serious about your job and will treat you accordingly.

Builds respect and confidence from other people   The world today is extremely specialized. Consider that many things of premium value in today's world are certified. We have certified used cars, certified mail, certified public accountants, certified travel agents, certified lawyers, and even certified Subway sandwich artists. The people you meet may not completely understand what is involved in being a CISA. However, they will understand that you have expended time and energy to obtain the certification. You will gain their respect because of the effort you've demonstrated. If given the choice, almost everyone would choose to use a person who is certified. The CISA is a major step toward the widespread credibility that you desire.

How to Become a CISA

The CISA designation is given to individuals who have demonstrated their ability to fulfill the following five requirements:

Pass the CISA exam   The CISA examination is offered two times a year, once in June and again in December. You have to register for the test three months before it is administered. You can register online at www.isaca.org or by mail. You take the test with pencil and paper in front of a live test proctor. The examination is 200 multiple-choice questions that will take approximately 4 hours. A grade of 75 percent is required to pass the CISA examination. There is a 4-hour time limit.

Professional experience in information systems auditing, control, or security   To qualify for certification, you must demonstrate five years of IS auditing experience. ISACA will accept up to two years of substitution toward the work experience requirement, as follows:

Related experience substitution   You can substitute a maximum of one year of experience from financial or operational auditing, or from information systems experience.

College credit hour substitution   The equivalent of an associate or bachelor's degree can be substituted for one or two years, respectively (60 hours or 120 hours).

University instructor experience substitution   A full-time university instructor can substitute two years of on-the-job experience toward one year of the IS auditing control or information security experience.

Your CISA test results are valid for five years from the examination date. Even without any experience at this time, you can take the examination. Certification will be awarded only after you have provided verification of desired work experience (of five years or the equivalent). ISACA limits acceptable experience to that which has occurred within 10 years prior to your application date.

Continuous adherence to ISACA's code of professional ethics   Trust and integrity are paramount to the auditor's profession. You will be required to pledge your ongoing support for adherence to the IS auditor's code of professional ethics.

Continuing education in the profession   You are required to continuously improve your skills. Continuing education is the best method of maintaining an individual's competency. Learning new skills with new certifications will improve your professional abilities. Demonstrating a commitment to continuing education differentiates qualified CISAs from those who have not fulfilled their professional responsibilities. You will be required to demonstrate a minimum of 20 contact hours of training each year, which must total 120 contact hours in a three-year period.

Adherence to well-established IS auditing standards   The purpose of auditing standards is to ensure quality and consistency. An auditor who fails to meet the standards places themselves and the profession in peril. ISACA provides excellent information to guide auditors through their professional responsibilities. The auditing standards are based on well-recognized professional practices applied worldwide.

Why Should I Buy This Book?

If you're serious about becoming a professional CISA auditor, you should buy this book to study for your exam. If you're curious about becoming an auditor, you should buy this book to learn how the job is actually done.

The people entering the CISA profession are usually one of the following:

- IT professionals with a desire to expand into the lucrative world of consulting

- Financial professionals looking for upward mobility with new challenges

- Internal auditors seeking to demystify the control issues within IT

This book is unique in the field of IS auditing. You will benefit from this book by learning the methods necessary to be a successful auditor. Each chapter builds step-by-step toward obtaining your goal. This book provides important details about how to accomplish your job, the exam objectives for each chapter, and all of the most important auditing concepts.

How to Use This Book and CD

This book is organized into eight chapters. Each begins with a list of chapter objectives that relate directly to the CISA exam.

An "Exam Essentials" section appears near the end of every chapter to highlight the topics that you're likely to encounter during your exam. These exam essentials are intended to provide guiding thoughts rather than a laundry list of details. Our goal is to help you focus on the higher-level objectives from each chapter as you move into the next chapter.

At the end of every chapter are approximately 35 review questions with explanations. You can use these review questions to help gauge your level of understanding and better focus your study effort. As you finish each chapter, you should review the questions and check whether your answers are correct. If not, you should really read the section again. Look up any incorrect answers and research why you may have missed the question. It may be a case of failing to read the question and properly considering each of the possible answers. It could also be that you did not understand the information. Either way, going through the chapter a second time would be valuable.

We have included several other testing features in the book and on the companion CD. Following this introduction is an Assessment Test that will help you gauge your study requirements. Take this test before you start reading the book. It will help you identify areas that are critical to your success. The answers to the assessment test appear after the last question. Each question includes a short explanation with information directing you to the appropriate chapter for more information.

Included on this book's CD are two bonus exams of 80 questions each. In addition, there are more than 300 flash cards. You should use this Study Guide in combination with your other materials to prepare for the exam.

Take these practice exams as if you were taking the real exam. Just sit down and start the exam without using any reference material. We suggest that you study the material in this book in conjunction with the related ISACA references on IS auditing standards. The official CISA exam is very challenging. Most individuals will barely finish the exam before time runs out. Fortunately for you, our students have a high success rate. You have it within you to become the next certified CISA.

You are ready for your CISA exam when you score higher than 90 percent on the practice examinations and chapter reviews.

A copy of this book is on the CD in Adobe Acrobat PDF format for easy reading on any computer.

 The practice exams included on the CD are timed to match the pace of your actual CISA exam.

What to Expect on the CISA Exam

Certainly you are curious about the types of questions you will encounter on the exam. ISACA is very protective of the actual test questions. Let's look at how the test is designed:

- The CISA exam is not an IT security test. Candidates will be expected to understand the basic concepts and terminology of what they will be auditing. However, security knowledge alone will not help candidates pass the test.

- The CISA exam is not a financial auditor exam. Candidates are not expected to be accounting technicians or to perform complex financial transactions.

- The CISA exam is not a computer technician exam. Candidates are not expected to build computers or to configure network devices. They are expected to understand the common terminology.

- The entire focus is on how to apply the structured rules of financial auditing to the abstract world of managing information technology.

By properly studying this book, you will better understand the hows and whys of being a successful CISA. Just remember, the IS auditor is a specially trained observer and investigator. We don't actually fix problems; we report findings after using a structured process of investigation. Understanding how to get the right evidence is the key.

How to Fail your CISA Exam

The CISA exam is based on ISACA's auditing standards and the application of the Statement on Auditing Standards (SAS). Abstract concepts of IT require the auditor to use a different approach to auditing. Adults learn by direct experience or by speaking with other people. Here are the two ways to fail your exam:

Rehearsing practice questions more than twice   One bad habit is to rehearse by using practice questions. The brain stops learning after the second pass over the same question, and then it starts memorizing the wording. This causes the brain to record the answer as rote memory rather than to learn the information. As a result, you will likely miss the correct answer on your exam because of the different way ISACA presents the questions and answer choices. Another problem is using questions from the Internet that cannot be traced to an official source. Bad questions make the seller money while programming your mind with the wrong information. Beware of ghostly sellers hiding behind websites without full contact information prominently displayed. I suggest you stick to the questions in this book or use the ISACA official practice questions. Stop rehearsing the same question after two passes. Instead, reread the corresponding section in the book.

Improper study preparation   The CISA exam is designed to prevent cram study. You will discover that the structure of the exam questions is rather convoluted. Some of the answer choices will barely fit the question. Just select the best choice that honors the spirit and intent of our audit objectives. It's possible that the best answer is only 51 percent correct. Go with the 51 percent answer if that is the best choice available. This confusion is intentional, to prevent the test taker from using rote memory. The best study technique is to read about 1 hour per night while taking manual notes. Be sure to read all the sections—every page. Previous CISA candidates were quite perturbed to discover that the area they assumed to be their strongest was instead where they scored poorly. You may have many years of experience in the subject, but what matters is that your view agrees with ISACA's exam. I have not heard of a single person getting a better score after protesting an official exam question. ISACA uses a professional testing company to run their exam. Protest a question if you must, but I'll wager that you lose the protest and your protest fee in the end.

Test Taking and Preparation

The CISA examination is quite difficult unless you are prepared. Preparation requires good study habits and a well-planned schedule. You should review your notes at least 30 minutes per night, but not more than 2 hours per day. As we said, cramming for this examination will not work.

Let's discuss preparations leading up to test day—specifically, the best method to arrange your schedule for that ace grade.

10-Day Countdown

Review each chapter in your Study Guide. Give extra attention to the subjects that you may have skimmed over earlier. The test is written from the viewpoint of an auditor, using directives from ISACA's world.

 Number one hint: Make sure you are reading from the auditor's perspective.

You should review the flash cards on the accompanying CD. It is also an excellent technique to make your own flashcards by using $3'' \times 5''$ index cards. Take a dozen or two dozen to the office each day for random practice between meetings.

Be sure to run through the Bonus Exams on the CD. They are less difficult than the real test, but still a good resource to see where you stand. The value of these tests is in improving your resilience and accuracy.

Be sure to request a day of rest. Ask your boss for personal time. Use vacation time if necessary. Most employers will understand after you remind them of the limited testing dates.

3-Day Countdown

The exam location may be in a hotel, college, or convention center. It will save you a great deal of time and stress to drive over to visit the test site. You should do this even if you have been there recently. The room number for your test will be printed on your exam acceptance letter. Make it a point to locate the meeting room and physically walk up to touch the door. In colleges, it is possible that room 300 is a significant walk away from room 302. Arriving at the wrong building can ruin your day if it makes you late to the exam.

Convention centers are worse. Unknown to you, there may be a big trade convention over the upcoming weekend. Such an event will change the availability of parking in the area. It will also affect the long route you may have to walk in order to enter the examination room.

The best suggestion is to scout the area for a nearby place to eat breakfast. Plan to eat healthy before the exam begins.

1-Day Countdown

The best aid to a high score is to take off early on Friday. Remember, the exam is early on Saturday morning. Make a pact with your friends and family to leave you alone all day Friday. You may consider limiting your diet to simple foods, avoiding anything that is different than usual. This is not the time to experiment.

Make a pact with yourself: There are no errands or chores more important than passing the exam.

Go to bed earlier than usual. Do whatever it takes. You will need to be up and totally focused by 6 a.m. Try to go to bed by 10 p.m. Set two alarm clocks to get up on time. Put your favorite study materials together in a carrying bag. You will take them with you to the exam for a final glance before being seated for the test. The exam is a "closed book" test.

Do not attempt to cram on Friday night; it will work against you in a long test like the CISA. Just review your notes again. Be sure to run through the flash cards and chapter review questions.

We suggest people with a technical background review Chapter 2, "Audit Process," and Chapter 3, "IT Governance," twice. If you have a financial background, the best advice is to reread Chapter 4, "Networking Technology," and Chapter 7, "Information Asset Protection." Practicing drawing the diagrams and models on a separate sheet of paper will help you understand the specific wording of questions and make it easier to select the correct answer. Be prepared to redraw the models from memory during your exam.

Test Morning

Time to get up and get yourself moving. Be sure to arrive at the exam early. Test room locations have been known to change overnight, especially at college locations.

After arrival, you can sit in the hallway while you wait. This is an excellent time to make a final review of your notes. There is no advantage to being seated before 7:30 a.m. Just park yourself within a few feet of the door to ensure that you are not forgotten or missed. You can expect a long line at some test locations. Major cities may have 200–300 people sitting in different rooms.

Upon entering the room, ask if you can draw inside the test booklet. Tell the proctor you like to make longhand notes when solving problems. Usually the booklet will never be reused, so you can mark in it all day long.

You can make notes to yourself in the booklet and mark your favorite answer, and then just transfer the answer from the test booklet to the answer sheet. This technique really helps if you start jumping around or choose to skip a question for later. Consider drawing useful diagrams such as the OSI model on the inside back cover of the booklet. The proctor will tell you that only answers on the answer sheet will count toward your score.

Plan on Using All 4 Hours

You should expect the test to take the entire 4 hours. Manage your time carefully to avoid running out of time before finishing the test. It is advisable to plan ahead for both pace and breaks. The exam proctor will usually allow you to take restroom breaks as long as you do not talk to anyone about the exam while out of the room. You might find it helpful to reduce fatigue by just taking a walk to the restroom and then splashing water on your face. One trip per hour seems to work fine. Most test takers will finish in the last 10 minutes before time is called by the proctor.

Read the Question Carefully

Read each question *very* carefully! The questions are intentionally worded differently from this Study Guide. For overly confusing questions or ones that you are not sure of, try reading them twice or even three times.

On the first pass, circle the operative points in the question, such as the words *not*, *is*, *best*, *and*, *or*, and so on. Next, underline the nouns or the subject of the question. For example, if the question is "The purpose of controls is to…," you would underline *purpose* and circle the word *is*.

On the second pass, ensure that you understand the implied direction of the question and its subject. Is the question a positive (*is*) or negative (*is not*) implication? Watch for meanings that are positive, negative, inclusive, or exclusive. A common technique used for writing test questions is to imply terminology associations that should not exist or vice versa. Do not violate the intent of the question or answer. Most people fail a question by misreading it.

On the third pass, dissect the available answers by using a similar method. Watch for conflicting meaning or wrong intent.

Place a star next to any question in the booklet when you have doubts about your answer. You can return to the question before turning in your answer sheet. (This keeps your answer sheet clean of any stray marks.)

For your final check, you can compare the answers marked in the test booklet to your answer sheet. Remember that there is no penalty for wrong answers. Do not leave any blank. Just take a guess if you must.

Done! The Exam Is Over

Plan for a relaxing activity with your family or friends after the exam. We suggest you plan something that is fun and doesn't require mental concentration; you will be mentally worn out after the exam. Do not punish yourself by looking up the answers for a particular test question. The test is over.

You should receive your score from ISACA in about five to seven weeks. It may be by email or a simple one-page letter.

We wish you all the best. Good luck on your exam.

Getting Your CISA Awarded

A notice of your official score will be mailed or emailed to you six to eight weeks after the exam. You should expect the mailed letter to be two pages stating that you either failed or passed. ISACA will inform you of your score. Contesting a score is usually a waste of effort.

After you pass, the next step is to complete ISACA's application to be certified. You will need to provide contact names, email addresses, and phone numbers for each of your references. ISACA will verify your claim prior to awarding you the CISA credential. No reference = no credit. So, contact your references in advance so they are ready to respond to ISACA's reference check. It's a good idea to have lunch with your references in advance. Give them a copy of your CISA application to discuss together in person. You can expect to be an official CISA 10 to 12 weeks after the exam—*if* you are prompt in filing the application and do a good job of managing the response time of your references.

Related Professional Certifications

Although this book focuses on ISACA's CISA certification, there are many more certifications you should consider for your professional advancement. This section offers a sampling of the more commonly known professional certifications that cover many of the same topics that the CISA does. This list is not inclusive of all certifications. It focuses only on vendor-neutral certification, which provides an unbiased view of the issues facing all vendors and customers.

It is important to be able to separate performance claims (smoke) from truly effective function (results). Results are measured by highest effect on the ultimate need and not by the use of a particular computer software package. There is a big difference between managing and just being an application operator. Persons with the following certifications should be versed in the basics for success in their field.

Information Systems Security Practices

The following certifications are focused on IS security topics:

Certified Information Systems Security Professional (CISSP)   This exam, administered by the International Information Systems Security Certification Consortium, or (ISC)^2, covers the 10 knowledge areas of information security. Certification requires passing the exam plus five years of IS security experience.

Systems Security Certified Practitioner (SSCP)   This exam, administered by (ISC)^2, covers 7 of the 10 knowledge areas of information security. Certification requires passing the exam plus two years of IS security experience. SSCP is a subset of the CISSP subject material. CertTest recommends that you attend the CISSP course to ensure that you receive all the training necessary for your future.

Certified Information Security Manager (CISM)   CISM is intended for managers. The CISM certification provides a different level of practices when compared to the CISSP. This exam is administered by ISACA. CISM covers the more advanced areas of risk management, specific management controls, and governing IS security. Certification requires passing the exam plus five years of experience in IS auditing, control, or security. Your CISA experience can count toward the work experience.

Security+   This exam, administered by the Computing Technology Industry Association, or CompTIA (www.comptia.org), is an entry-level security certification. It covers a fraction of the topics covered in the CISSP certification. Security+ is not intended to be a prerequisite for CISM or CISSP. Security+ is good for beginners and individuals who would not be able to meet the work experience of the other certifications.

Auditing

In addition to the CISA, a few of the other certifications focus on auditing, including the following:

Certified Internal Auditor (CIA)   This certification, administered by The Institute of Internal Auditors (www.theiia.org), requires passing a four-part exam. The exams may be taken separately or combined in any order. Each part is 125 multiple-choice questions. In addition, candidates must have a bachelor's degree or equivalent, plus 24 months of internal auditing experience.

Certified Fraud Examiner (CFE)   This certification, administered by the Association of Certified Fraud Examiners (www.acfe.org), requires passing the exam plus a bachelor's degree and two years of fraud detection–related work experience in the areas of accounting, auditing, fraud investigation, criminology, loss prevention, or law.

Information Assessment Methodology (IAM)   This certification, administered by the U.S. National Security Agency (www.nsa.gov), requires U.S. citizenship with at least two years of experience in information system security and/or IS auditing. This certification was originally created by presidential executive order and is now mandated by U.S. Homeland Security Directive/HSPD-7. IAM certification is designed for system administrators and auditors working on government systems, critical infrastructure, and commercial systems.

Information Evaluation Methodology (IEM)   IEM is a new certification that extends the IAM to include hands-on technical testing and formal evaluation of IS systems by using the NSA's official evaluation methodology. Certification is administered by the U.S. National Security Agency. The only way to get certified is to attend the actual class and perform the labs in person under the supervision of the NSA's official instructor. You must complete all the labs in person, just like taking your driving test to get a driver's license.

Disaster Recovery and Business Continuity

The following certifications focus on disaster recovery and business continuity topics:

Associate Business Continuity Professional (ABCP)   This certification, administered by the Disaster Recovery Institute International, or DRII (www.drii.org), covers the 10 best practices of disaster recovery and business continuity. The Associate covers the same material as the CBCP, but does not require any work experience.

Certified Business Continuity Professional (CBCP)   This certification, also administered by DRII, requires passing the CBCP exam, plus you must have two years of experience as a business continuity/disaster recovery planner.

Master Business Continuity Professional (MBCP)   This certification, also administered by DRII, requires participation in the DRII Masters program along with passing a qualifying exam and then the MBCP exam. You must also have five years of practical experience.

Fellow of the Business Continuity Institute (FBCI)   This certification, administered by the Business Continuity Institute (www.thebci.org), is based on a points-scoring system.

Project Management

The following certifications focus on project management:

Certified Associate in Project Management (CAPM)   This certification, administered by the Project Management Institute (www.pmi.org), requires passing the CAPM exam plus 23 hours of formal PMI training or 1,500 hours of project management–related work experience. The CAPM test covers a reduced version of the PMP content areas. CertTest recommends that all CAPM candidates follow the complete PMP study curriculum to ensure you receive the full training necessary for a leadership role. The secret is to show your boss that you have been trained with as much knowledge as a PMP. This will help you advance, even though you are still building your hours of experience.

Project Management Professional (PMP)   This certification, also administered by the Project Management Institute, covers 44 process areas of project management. Certification requires 35 hours of formal PMI training with 4,500 hours of project management–related work experience if you have a four-year college degree. Alternatively, you can qualify with 7,500 hours of experience and a high school diploma. PMI will check your work references before you can schedule your exam. The PMP exam is a 4-hour computer-based test that you must take in person at your nearest Prometric testing center. You are officially a PMP after your experience is accepted and you pass your exam.

Project+   This entry-level certification is administered by CompTIA. Certification is obtained via a computer-based exam at your nearest Prometric test center. No work experience is required. Project+ is not intended to be a prerequisite for CAPM or PMP.

Physical Building Security

The following certifications focus on physical building security topics:

Physical Security Professional (PSP)   This certification is administered internationally by ASIS International (www.asisonline.org). Certification requires passing the exam plus a high school diploma and five years of verified security-related work experience.

Certified Protection Professional (CPP)   This certification, also administered internationally by ASIS International, requires passing the exam plus a bachelor's degree and nine years of verified security-related work experience. A minimum of three years of your experience must be in security management.

 CertTest Training Center, the training center we teach at, offers many classes for a number of these certifications. In addition, we offer a SuperHERO course, which covers project management, CISM/CISSP for IS security, and business continuity. For more information, visit our website at www.certtest.com.

Assessment Test

1. What are the qualifications of the incident commander when responding to a crisis?
    - **A.** Member of management
    - **B.** First responder
    - **C.** Trained crisis manager
    - **D.** First person on scene

2. Which of the following would be a concern that the auditor should explain in the audit report along with their findings?
    - **A.** Detailed list of audit objectives
    - **B.** The need by the current auditor to communicate with the prior auditor
    - **C.** Undue restrictions placed by management on evidence use or audit procedures
    - **D.** Communicating results directly to the chairperson of the audit committee

3. What are the different types of audits?
    - **A.** Forensic, accounting, verification, regulatory
    - **B.** Financial, compliance, administrative, SAS-74
    - **C.** Information system, SAS-70, regulatory, procedural
    - **D.** Integrated, compliance, operational, administrative

4. What indicators are used to identify the anticipated level of recovery and loss at a given point in time?
    - **A.** RTO and SDO
    - **B.** RPO and ITO
    - **C.** RPO and RTO
    - **D.** SDO and IRO

5. What is the principal issue surrounding the use of CAAT software?
    - **A.** The capability of the software vendor.
    - **B.** Documentary evidence is more effective.
    - **C.** Inability of automated tools to consider the human characteristics of the environment.
    - **D.** Possible cost, complexity, and the security of output.

6. Which is *not* a purpose of risk analysis?
    - **A.** Supports risk-based audit decisions
    - **B.** Assists the auditor in determining audit objectives
    - **C.** Ensures absolute safety during the audit
    - **D.** Assists the auditor in identifying risks and threats

7. Which of the following answers contains the steps for business process reengineering (BPR) in proper sequence?

  A. Diagnose, envision, redesign, reconstruct

  B. Envision, initiate, diagnose, redesign, reconstruct, evaluate

  C. Evaluate, envision, redesign, reconstruct, review

  D. Initiate, evaluate, diagnose, reconstruct, review

8. Which of the following functions should be separated from the others if segregation of duties cannot be achieved in an automated system?

  A. Origination

  B. Authorization

  C. Correction

  D. Reprocessing

9. At which layer of the OSI model does a gateway operate?

  A. Layer 6

  B. Layer 3

  C. Layer 7

  D. Layer 5

10. What is the purpose of the audit committee?

  A. To provide daily coordination of all audit activities

  B. To challenge and review assurances

  C. To govern, control, and manage the organization

  D. To assist the managers with training in auditing skills

11. What does the third layer of the OSI model equate to in the TCP/IP model?

  A. Network

  B. Internet

  C. Data-Link

  D. Transport

12. What are three of the four key perspectives on the IT balanced scorecard?

  A. Business justification, service-level agreements, budget

  B. Organizational staffing, cost reduction, employee training

  C. Cost reduction, business process, growth

  D. Service level, critical success factors, vendor selection

13. Which of the following statements is true concerning asymmetric-key cryptography?

  A. The sender encrypts the files by using the recipient's private key.

  B. The sender and receiver use the same key.

  C. The sender and receiver have different keys.

  D. Asymmetric keys cannot be used for digital signatures.

14. How should management act to best deal with emergency changes?

    A. Emergency changes cannot be made without advance testing.

    B. All changes should still undergo review.

    C. The change control process does not apply to emergency conditions.

    D. Emergency changes are not allowed under any condition.

15. What is one of the bigger concerns regarding asset disposal?

    A. Residual asset value

    B. Employees taking disposed property home

    C. Standing data

    D. Environmental regulations

16. Which of the following is the most significant issue to consider regarding insurance coverage?

    A. Salvage, rather than replacement, may be dictated.

    B. Premiums may be very expensive.

    C. Coverage must include all business assets.

    D. Insurance can pay for all the costs of recovery.

17. Which of the following is required to protect the internal network when a wireless access point is in use?

    A. Wireless encryption

    B. Wired equivalent protection

    C. Wireless application protocol

    D. Network firewall

18. Digital signatures are designed to provide additional protection for electronic messages in order to determine which of the following?

    A. Message deletion

    B. Message sender verification

    C. Message modification

    D. Message read by unauthorized party

19. What is the primary purpose of database views?

    A. Restrict the viewing of selected data

    B. Provide a method for generating reports

    C. Allow the user access into the database

    D. Allow the system administrator access to maintain the database

20. Which of the following indicates why continuity planners can create plans without a business impact analysis (BIA)?

   A. Management already dictated all the key processes to be used.

   B. Not possible—critical processes constantly change.

   C. Business impact analysis is not required.

   D. Risk assessment is acceptable.

21. Segregation of duties may not be practical in a small environment. A single employee may be performing the combined functions of server operator and application programmer. The IS auditor should recommend controls for which of the following?

   A. Automated logging of changes made to development libraries

   B. Procedures that verify that only approved program changes are implemented

   C. Automated controls to prevent the operator logon ID from making program modifications

   D. Hiring additional technical staff to force segregation of duties

22. The auditor is permitted to deviate from professional audit standards when they feel it is necessary because of which of the following?

   A. Standards are designed for discretionary use.

   B. The unique characteristics of each client will require auditor flexibility.

   C. Deviating from standards is almost unheard of and would require significant justification.

   D. Deviation depends on the authority granted in the audit charter.

23. What does the principle of auditor independence mean?

   A. It is not an issue for auditors working for a consulting company.

   B. It is required for an external audit to prevent bias.

   C. An internal auditor must undergo certification training to be independent.

   D. The audit committee would bestow independence on the auditor.

24. What are the five phases of business continuity planning according to ISACA, for use on the CISA exam? (Select the answer showing the correct phases and order.)

   A. Analyze business impact, develop strategy, develop plan, implement, test plan

   B. Analyze business impact, develop strategy, develop plan, test plan, implement

   C. Analyze business impact, develop plan, implement, test plan, write the plan

   D. Analyze business impact, write the plan, test strategy, develop plan, implement

25. Using public-key infrastructure (PKI) encryption, which key is used by the sender for authentication of the receiving party?

   A. Sender's private key

   B. Recipient's private key

   C. Sender's public key

   D. Recipient's public key

26. Which of the following audit tools incorporates dummy transactions into the normal processing on a system?

    A. Integrated test facility (ITF)

    B. Snapshot

    C. Program audit hooks

    D. Continuous and intermittent simulation (CIS)

27. Which sampling method is used when the likelihood of finding evidence is low?

    A. Discovery

    B. Cell

    C. Random

    D. Stop and go

28. Which of the following would represent the greatest concern to an auditor investigating roles and responsibilities of the IT personnel?

    A. An IT member is reviewing current server workload requirements and forecasts future needs.

    B. An IT member monitors system performance, making necessary program changes and tracking any resulting problems.

    C. An IT member tests and assesses the effectiveness of current procedures and recommends specific improvements.

    D. An IT member works directly with the user to improve response times and performance across the network.

29. When auditing the use of encryption, which of the following would be the primary concern of the auditor?

    A. Management's control over the use of encryption

    B. Strength of encryption algorithm in use

    C. Key sizes used in the encryption and decryption process

    D. Using the correct encryption method for compliance

30. Which method of backup should be used on computer files prior to starting a forensic investigation?

    A. Bit stream

    B. Logical

    C. Differential

    D. Full

31. Which of the following represents the hierarchy of controls from highest level to lowest level?

    A. General, pervasive, detailed, application

    B. Pervasive, general, application, detailed

    C. Detailed, pervasive, application, detailed

    D. Application, general, detailed, pervasive

32. What is the purpose of using the ACID principle with database applications?

   A. Write the entire transaction to the master file or discard without making any changes.

   B. Environmental protection to safeguard the server to ensure maximum uptime.

   C. Each data transaction is step-linked to ensure consistency.

   D. Unnecessary data is removed from the database for better performance.

33. Which key is used for decryption in public key cryptography to provide authentication of the person transmitting the message?

   A. Sender's private key

   B. Recipient's private key

   C. Sender's public key

   D. Recipient's public key

34. What is the principle purpose of using Function Point Analysis?

   A. Verify the integrity of financial transaction algorithms in a program

   B. Estimate the complexity involved in software development

   C. Review the results of automated transactions meeting criteria for the audit

   D. Provide system boundary data during the Requirements Definition phase

35. Which of the following is not one of the three major control types?

   A. Preventative

   B. Detective

   C. Deterrent

   D. Corrective

36. What is the primary objective in the third phase of incident response?

   A. Containment

   B. Lessons learned

   C. Eradication

   D. Analysis

37. After presenting the report at the conclusion of an audit, the lead auditor discovers the omission of a procedure. What should the auditor do next?

   A. Log on to www.monster.com and change your current employment status to available. ☺

   B. Cancel the report if audit alternatives cannot compensate for the deficiency.

   C. File an incident disclosure report with the audit association to minimize any liability.

   D. No action is required as long as the omitted procedure is included in the next audit.

38. Which of the following management methods provides the most control rather than discretionary flexibility?

   A. Distributed

   B. Centralized

   C. In-house

   D. Outsourced

39. Executing the verify function during a tape backup is an example of which type of the following controls?

   A. Corrective

   B. Administrative

   C. Preventative

   D. Detective

40. Which of the following is the best representation of a soft token used for two-factor authentication?

   A. Digital certificate

   B. Key fob

   C. Hash file

   D. Strong password

41. In regards to the IT governance control objectives, which of the following occurrences would the auditor be least concerned about during execution of the audit?

   A. Using the practice of self-monitoring to report problems

   B. Using proper change control

   C. Conflict in the existing reporting relationship

   D. Production system without accreditation

42. Which of the following is *not* one of the primary methods used to implement physical controls, detective controls, and corrective controls?

   A. Legal

   B. Logical

   C. Physical

   D. Administrative

43. Which the following statements is true concerning a software worm?

   A. Must be executed by opening a file

   B. Is a synonym for a virus

   C. Freely travels across the network to infect other systems

   D. Attaches itself to programs and data by the opening and closing of files

44. What is the purpose behind the system accreditation?

  A. Hold management responsible for fitness of use and any failures

  B. Provide formal sign-off on the results of certification tests

  C. Improve the accuracy of forecasting in IT budgets

  D. Make the user responsible for their use of the system

45. Which of the following techniques is used in the storage and transmission of a symmetric encryption key?

  A. Key rotation

  B. Generating a unique encryption key

  C. Key wrapping

  D. Generating a shared encryption key

46. Which of the following statements is true concerning the auditor's qualified opinion?

  A. The auditor has reservations about the findings.

  B. The auditor is professionally qualified to give an opinion.

  C. The auditor has no reservations about the findings.

  D. The auditor has prior experience working in the IT department.

47. Which of the following situations should the auditor consider if the auditee has implemented six phases of the System Development Life Cycle (SDLC)?

  A. The auditee is probably doing a good job with no concerns at this time.

  B. The IT governance model has been implemented.

  C. The auditee may be missing a critical function.

  D. There are only five phases to the System Development Life Cycle.

48. Which backup method will copy only changed files without resetting the archive bit (archive flag)?

  A. Physical

  B. Incremental

  C. Full

  D. Differential

49. In using public-key infrastructure (PKI) encryption, which key is *not* used by the recipient for decrypting a message?

  A. Sender's private key

  B. Recipient's private key

  C. Sender's public key

  D. Recipient's public key

50. Which of the following situations does *not* represent a reporting conflict?

  A. Information security manager reporting to internal auditors.

  B. Employee reporting violations to their boss, who is also in charge of compliance

  C. IT security reporting to the chief information officer

  D. Self-monitoring and reporting of violations

51. What is the purpose of a digital signature?

  A. Electronic marker showing the recipient that a sender actually sent a document

  B. Provides the recipient with a method of testing the document received from a sender

  C. Cyclic redundancy check to prove document integrity

  D. Provides a copy of the sender's public key along with the document

52. Which of the following is the best way to protect encryption keys from being compromised?

  A. Storing the keys in a key vault rated server

  B. Using a physically isolated system to generate the keys

  C. Changing the encryption keys every four months

  D. Limiting the use of individual keys

53. Which of the following statements is true concerning the role of management and the role of the auditor?

  A. Management uses the auditor's report before making their assertions.

  B. Management must make their assertions prior to the auditor's report.

  C. The auditor is able to view only evidence that has been predetermined by management.

  D. The auditor's opinion will be based on the desire of management.

54. During a business continuity audit, it is discovered that the business impact analysis (BIA) was not performed. What would this indicate to the auditor?

  A. The business continuity plan is likely to be a failure.

  B. The customer was able to get their plan in place without using the BIA technique.

  C. Risk analysis and their selection of the strategy fulfill their most important objectives.

  D. It is not necessary to perform a business impact analysis.

55. What is the functional difference between *identification* and *authentication*?

  A. Authorization is a match; identification is only a claim until verified.

  B. Authentication is only a claim; identification is a verified match.

  C. Identification is only a claim until verified; authentication is a match.

  D. Identification is only a claim; authorization is a match.

56. Which of the following is the best way for an auditor to prove their competence to perform an audit?

    A. Prior experience working in information technology

    B. Citing each point in a regulation with an audit objective and specific test

    C. Obtaining auditor certification with ongoing training

    D. Prior experience in financial auditing

57. What is the primary objective of the ISACA audit standards and professional ethics publication?

    A. Provide consistency without embarrassing you or our profession

    B. Explain the professional duties you could follow when building your practice

    C. Provide a comprehensive audit toolkit

    D. Provide a sample reference the auditor may use during their audit without copyright restrictions

58. Complete the following statement: A Certified Information Systems Auditor will lose their certification if they _____.

    A. Advise and educate the auditee about what the auditor is looking for

    B. Continue to participate in professional education

    C. Share blank audit checklists with the auditee

    D. Possess or use materials for which they do not hold a valid copyright license

59. Portfolio management includes all of the following, except:

    A. Selection of projects based on the best return on investment

    B. Centralized control of priorities across the projects

    C. Management of concurrent projects

    D. Method of controlling changes in the work breakdown structure

60. What function does the auditor provide?

    A. Second set of eyes, which are external from the subject under review

    B. Independent assurance that the claims of management are correct

    C. Assistance by fixing problems found during the audit

    D. Adapting standards to fit the needs of the client

61. Complete the following statement with the best available answer: The _____ file is created when the system shuts down improperly. It usually contains _____ that is/are useful in forensic investigations.

    A. Dump, contents from RAM memory

    B. Abend, a history of all the user transactions processed

    C. Diagnostic, system startup settings

    D. Abort, all user account information

62. Which of the following systems uses heuristic techniques to make decisions on behalf of the user?

   A. Associate decision mart

   B. Expert system

   C. Decision support system (DSS)

   D. Data warehouse

63. Where should the computer room be located?

   A. Secure basement

   B. First floor

   C. Middle floor

   D. Top floor

64. Which of the following nonstatistical audit samples is also known as a judgmental sample?

   A. Unstratified mean

   B. Haphazard

   C. Attribute

   D. Random

65. Select the best answer to finish this statement: A _____ is strategic in nature, while the _____ is tactical.

   A. Policy, procedure

   B. Standard, procedure

   C. Procedure, standard

   D. Policy, standard

66. Which of the following processes would be the best candidate for business process reengineering?

   A. Excluded process

   B. Working process

   C. Nonworking process

   D. Marginal process

67. Which step is necessary before moving into the next phase when using the System development Life Cycle?

   A. Review meeting

   B. Formal approval

   C. Change control

   D. Phase meeting

68. Complete the following statement. A _____ must be used to prevent _____ of the hard-disk evidence during the collection phase of forensic investigations.

    A. Forensic specialist, analysis

    B. Data analyzer, destruction

    C. Write-blocker, contamination

    D. Immunizer, corruption

69. What is the primary objective for using a system with a Redundant Array of Independent—or Inexpensive—Disks (RAID)?

    A. Prevent corruption

    B. Increase availability

    C. Eliminate the need for backups

    D. Increase storage capacity

70. What is the primary purpose of the audit charter?

    A. Grant the auditor responsibility, authority, and accountability

    B. Specify the mutually agreed upon procedures that will be used during the audit

    C. Serve as a record for the agreed upon terms of the engagement with external auditors

    D. Specify the scope of the audit

71. What is the primary purpose of using the root kit?

    A. System administration tool used by the super user, also known as the server administrator

    B. Method for tracing source problems in determining cause-and-effect analysis

    C. Covert method of remotely compromising the operating system kernel

    D. Camouflage technique designed to hide certain details from view.

72. Which of the following statements is true regarding use of the Rapid Application Development (RAD) methodology in software programming?

    A. Automates the entire software development process, starting from phase 1

    B. Eliminates the need for using traditional planning techniques for project management

    C. Automates the software development process from feasibility through implementation

    D. Still requires the use of traditional project management techniques

73. What is the best definition of *auditing*?

    A. Review of past history using evidence to tell the story

    B. Forecasting compliance generated by a new system preparing to enter production

    C. Precompliance assessment based on management's intended design

    D. Certification testing of the system benefits or failures

74. Who is responsible for designating the appropriate information classification level?

    A. Data custodian

    B. Data user

    C. Data owner

    D. Security manager

75. Which of the following is the best example of implementing a detective control via administrative methods?

    A. Auditing of system configuration and log files

    B. Running a verification of the backup tape for integrity

    C. Using an intrusion detection and prevention system (IDPS)

    D. Restoring a damaged file using a copy from the vendor's installation CD.

76. Which of the following firewall setups would *not* be a concern to the auditor?

    A. Source routing enabled

    B. Backup media left in the drive

    C. Remote login or file sharing enabled

    D. Firewall not backed up nightly

77. A member of the auditee staff offers to loan you an unauthorized copy of software that you need for a short time. What should you, as the auditor, always remember?

    A. It's okay to borrow the software for one-time use.

    B. The auditee is not acting in an ethical manner.

    C. The auditee will usually get amnesty for turning in the auditor or discrediting the auditor.

    D. Odds of getting caught on this are very low.

78. Who should the auditor notify if an illegal or inappropriate act involves the persons responsible for governance of controls?

    A. Law enforcement

    B. Federal regulators

    C. Audit committee

    D. Whistle-blower hotline

79. What is the primary purpose of the agile programming methodology?

    A. Automate the tedious administrative portions of the System Development Life Cycle

    B. Rapidly create prototypes within a very short time

    C. Create flexible internal controls that are easy to keep up-to-date

    D. Improve the quality of traditional planning with better documentation of requirements

80. Which of the following is true concerning reporting by internal auditors?

    A. Results can be used for industry licensing.

    B. The corresponding value of the audit report is high.

    C. Results can be used for external reporting.

    D. The corresponding value of the audit report is low.

Answers to Assessment Test

1. D. The first person on the scene is the incident commander, regardless of rank or position. The incident commander may be relieved by a person with more experience or less experience, according to the situation. The incident commander will change throughout the crisis. For more information, see Chapter 8.

2. C. Undue restrictions on scope would be a major concern as would a lack of time or the inability to obtain sufficient reliable evidence. For more information, see Chapter 2.

3. D. All of the audit types are valid except procedural, SAS-74, verification, and regulatory (which are all distracters). The valid audit types are financial, operational (SAS-70), integrated (SAS-94), compliance, administrative, forensic, and information systems. A forensic audit is used to discover information about a possible crime. For more information, see Chapter 1.

4. C. The recovery point objective (RPO) indicates the fallback position and duration of loss that has occurred. A valid RPO example is to recover by using backup data from last night's backup tape, meaning that the more recent transactions would be lost. The recovery time objective (RTO) indicates a point in time that the restored data should be available for the user to access. For more information, see Chapter 8.

5. D. Computer assisted audit tools are able to perform detailed technical tasks faster than humans and produce more-accurate data during particular functions such as system scanning. Cost, training, and security of output are major considerations. For more information, see Chapter 2.

6. C. The risk analysis does not ensure absolute safety. The purpose of using a risk-based audit strategy is to ensure that the audit adds value with meaningful information. For more information, see Chapter 2.

7. B. According to ISACA, the general steps in business process reengineering are envision the need, initiate the project, diagnose the existing process, redesign a process, use change management to reconstruct the organization in transition, and evaluate the results. For more information, see Chapter 3.

8. B. Authorization should be separate from all other activities. A second person should review changes before implementation. Authorization will be granted if the change is warranted and the level of risk is acceptable. For more information, see Chapter 3.

9. C. According to ISACA, the gateway operates at application layer 7 in the OSI model. The function of the gateway is to convert data contained in one protocol into data used by a different protocol. An example is a PC-to-mainframe gateway converting ASCII to mainframe Extended Binary Coded Decimal Interchange Code (EBCDIC). For more information, see Chapter 4.

10. B. The purpose of the audit committee is to review and challenge assurances made, and to maintain a positive working relationship with management and the auditors. For more information, see Chapters 2 and 3.

11. B. The third layer of the OSI model is the Network layer. Use the memory tool of "Nor Do I Throw Apples" to remember the layers of the TCP/IP model. The third layer of the TCP/IP model is the Internet layer. For more information, see Chapter 4.

12. C. The four perspectives on the IT balanced scorecard are the customer perspective, business process perspective, financial perspective, and the growth perspective. Each of these seek to define the highest return by IT. For more information, see Chapter 6.

13. C. The sender and receiver each have their own public and private (secret) key pair. All the other statements are false. Asymmetric keys are definitely used for creating digital signatures. The sender would never use the recipient's private key, only the recipient's public key. For more information, see Chapter 7.

14. B. All emergency changes should still undergo the formal change management process after the fact. The review determines whether the change should remain in place or be modified. For more information, see Chapter 6.

15. C. Any standing data should be purged from the equipment prior to disposal. *Standing data* refers to information that can be recovered from a device by using any means. For more information, see Chapter 6.

16. A. The insurance company may dictate salvage to save money. Salvage will increase the delay before recovery. Any replacement purchases by the organization may not be covered under reimbursement. For more information, see Chapter 8.

17. D. The wireless network may be using wired equivalent protocol (WEP); however, a firewall is still required to protect the internal network. The WEP design has been broken and is considered insecure under all conditions. In addition, new CISP regulations of the Senate Banking Committee with VISA, MasterCard, American Express, and Discover place $100,000 penalties per occurrence for any loss due to noncompliance.

18. B. Digital signatures provide authentication assurance of the email sender. Digital signatures use the private key of the sender to verify identity. For more information, see Chapter 7.

19. A. Database views are used to implement least privilege and restrict the data that can be viewed by the user. For more information, see Chapter 7.

20. B. It is not possible to create business continuity plans without a current Business Impact Analysis (BIA). The BIA identifies critical processes and their dependencies. The critical processes will change as the business changes with new products and customers. For more information, see Chapter 8.

21. B. Procedures should be implemented to ensure that only approved program changes are implemented. The purpose of separation of duties is to prevent intentional or unintentional errors. A logical separation of duties may exist if a single person performs two job roles. The ultimate objective is to ensure that a second person has reviewed and approved a change before it is implemented. For more information, see Chapter 3.

22. C. Standards are mandatory, and any deviation would require justification. Exceptions are rarely accepted. For more information, see Chapter 2.

23. B. The auditor must be independent of personal and organizational relationships with the auditee, which could imply a biased opinion. The auditor is not permitted to audit a system for which they participated in the support, configuration, or design. An auditor may not audit any system that they helped to remediate. For more information, see Chapter 1.

24. A. Notice that analyzing the business impact is always the first step. Then criteria are selected to guide the strategy selection. A detailed plan is written by using the strategy. The written plan is then implemented. After implementation, the plan and staff are tested for effectiveness. The plan is revised, and then the testing and maintenance cycle begins. For more information, see Chapter 8.

25. D. The sender uses the recipient's public key to encrypt a file that only the recipient can read (decrypt). The sender's private key provides authenticity. The sender's public key provides integrity. The role of the keys is based on the direction of the transaction. The roles reverse when the original recipient replies with another message, thereby assuming the sender's role. For more information, see Chapter 7.

26. A. The auditor can use an embedded audit module, also known as an *integrated test facility*, to create a set of dummy transactions that will be processed along with genuine transactions. The auditor compares the output data against their own calculations. This allows for substantial testing without disrupting the normal processing schedule. For more information, see Chapter 2.

27. A. Discovery sampling is known as the 100 percent sample. All available sources are investigated to find any evidence that may exist. Discovery sampling is commonly used in criminal investigations. It's also the best way to find possible correlations when an event cannot be explained. For more information, see Chapter 2.

28. B. The separation of duties is intended to prevent an individual from monitoring their own work or authorizing their own changes. Self-monitoring and self-authorization would be a problem warranting serious concern because it violates the intention of IT governance. The auditor would want to investigate whether changes were formally reviewed and approved by the change control board prior to implementation. For more information, see Chapter 6.

29. A. The most important concern is how management controls the use of encryption. Is the encryption managed under a complete life cycle that governs creating the keys, storing the keys, providing proper authorization to use the keys, using the keys correctly with the appropriate algorithm for maximum confidentiality, tracking the use of the keys, archiving or reissuing keys, retiring the keys, and ultimately destroying the encryption keys after all legal obligations have been met? For more information, see Chapter 7.

30. A. Bit stream imaging is the only backup method that records the deleted files along with the contents of the swap space and slack space. Bit stream backup is also referred to as *physical imaging*. All of the other choices would miss these important files that are necessary as evidence. For more information, see Chapter 7.

31. A. General controls represent the highest class of controls that apply to everyone within the organization. Pervasive controls represent the protection necessary when using technology. IS controls are pervasive in all departments using computers. No matter who is in charge, the IS controls must be used to ensure integrity and availability. Detailed controls specify how a procedure will be executed. Application controls are the lowest-level controls that are usually built into the software or that govern its use. Application controls will be compromised if the higher-level controls are not present. For more information, see Chapter 3.

32. A.   The ACID principle says to write the entire transaction or back it completely out. *A* stands for *atomicity* (all or nothing), *C* for *consistency* (restore data if the write fails), *I* for *isolation* (separation between transactions), and *D* for *durability* (retain the data). For more information, see Chapter 5.

33. C.   The sender's public key provides authentication that the message came from that specific individual. A private key provides confidentiality. For more information, see Chapter 7.

34. B.   Function Point Analysis is used by highly experienced programmers to estimate the complexity involved in writing new software. It starts by counting the inputs, outputs, inquiries (searches), data structure, and external interfaces. For more information, see Chapter 4.

35. C.   The major control types are physical (stops), detective (finds), and corrective (fixes). A deterrent control is simply a very weak form of preventative control. For more information, see Chapter 3.

36. A.   The phases in incident handling are 1) preparation, 2) detection and analysis, 3) containment eradication and recovery, and 4) postincident activity, including lessons learned. For more information, see Chapter 6.

37. B.   The auditor needs to review the audit alternatives to determine whether the alternatives could sufficiently compensate for the omission. The auditor should cancel their report if the omitted procedures would change the outcome and if audit alternatives cannot compensate for the deficiency. For more information, see Chapter 2.

38. B.   Centralized management always provides the most control. Distributed management is also known as discretionary because the decision is made locally and is based on a variety of factors. Distributed methods provide the lowest overall control. For more information, see Chapter 7.

39. D.   Creating a tape backup is a preventative control to prevent the loss of data. However, the verify function is a detective control intended to detect any discrepancies between the tape and the hard disk. It's a detective control because it still requires the operator to manually fix the problem after it is found. Verification and audits are always detective controls. For more information, see Chapter 7.

40. A.   Digital certificates (also known as a soft token) can be used for two-factor authentication. The key fob is also known as a hard token because of its physical nature. Passwords do not provide for two-factor authentication unless coupled with hard tokens, soft tokens, or biometrics. For more information, see Chapter 7.

41. B.   Use of proper change control would represent the least concern for the auditor. Auditors want to see change control procedures being used for separation of duties. All of the other choices represent violations warranting further investigation. For more information, see Chapter 6.

42. A.   Legal is not one of the primary implementation methods. Controls are implemented by using physical methods, logical methods (technical), and administrative methods. Administrative methods include laws, policies, procedures, and contracts. The combination of physical, logical, and administrative methods is used to obtain legal compliance. For more information, see Chapter 3.

43. C.   Unlike a virus, a worm can freely travel across network connections to infect other systems. Worms can infect files without the file being opened or closed by the user. For more information, see Chapter 7.

44. A.   System accreditation is a formal sign-off witnessing management's acceptance of fitness for the system's intended use and full responsibility for any failures. System accreditation is for a period of 90 days, 180 days, or 365 days (annual). The system must be reaccredited by the expiration date. For more information, see Chapter 5.

45. C.   Key wrapping is used to protect encryption keys during storage and transmission of the keys. Encryption keys should never be directly accessible to the user. For more information, see Chapter 7.

46. A.   A qualified opinion means the auditor has reservations about the scope of the audit, concerns with the available evidence, or concerns that the findings may not represent the true story. Audit reports containing a qualified opinion will have limitations on the use of the report. For more information, see Chapter 2.

47. Answer: C.   The complete System Development Life Cycle contains seven phases, not six. The auditee may have a control failure because the postimplementation (phase 6) or disposal process (phase 7) may not have been formally adopted. Using fewer than seven phases would indicate that shortcuts have been taken. For more information, see Chapter 5.

48. Answer: D.   The differential backup method will copy all files that have changed since the last full backup but will not reset the archive bit. Files can be restored in less time by using just the last full backup with the last differential backup tape. For more information, see Chapter 6.

49. A.   The sender's private key is never used by the recipient. It takes only three keys to decrypt the message: the sender's public key, the recipient's public key, and the recipient's private key. For more information, see Chapter 7.

50. A.   IT security managers should report problems to internal auditors. It's a reporting conflict if an IT-related employee is required to make violation reports directly to their manager. There may be job pressures to cover up problems. A built-in reporting conflict exists when your job requires you to report violations to your superior, when the same person is responsible for ensuring compliance. For more information, see Chapter 6.

51. B.   An electronic signature is worthless unless the recipient actually tests the signature by decrypting it. Electronic signatures should never be trusted by their presence. Digital signatures must be tested by the recipient to verify their authenticity. For more information, see Chapter 7.

52. D.   Limiting the use of encryption keys is the best available choice to protect them from compromise. Separation of duties also applies to encryption keys. Each encryption key should have a special purpose without reusing the same key on different tasks. For more information, see Chapter 7.

53. B.   Management must make their assertions independent of the auditor's report. The role of the auditor is to determine whether management claims can be verified as correct by the available evidence. For more information, see Chapter 1.

54. A. The business continuity (BC) plan is likely to fail. It would be nearly impossible for a BC plan to work without first performing a business impact analysis (BIA). Nobody can protect business processes that they were unable to define in a formal specification (BIA report). For more information, see Chapter 8.

55. C. Identification is simply a claim that must be verified. Authentication is when the claim matches the reference, thereby indicating that the identity is correct. For more information, see Chapter 7.

56. B. Every auditor should build a list of all the individual points contained in a regulation, citing each point by page, paragraph, and line number. This detailed specification will be used to explain how the audit meets the objective. Specific tests should be created for each item. If the audit test must be rerun, the subsequent auditor should always find similar results by using your documentation. For more information, see Chapter 2.

57. A. ISACA audit standards of professional ethics are intended to provide consistency. We do not want you to cast any disgrace upon our profession. We hope that by following the standards, you will not embarrass yourself or fail to understand the duties of an auditor. For more information, see Chapter 1.

58. D. CISAs can lose their credentials by possessing or using materials for which they do not hold a valid copyright license. Violating copyright restrictions is a violation of law and ethics. For more information, see Chapter 1.

59. D. Portfolio management is similar to trading stocks or baseball cards. The objective is to get the highest possible value for your collection of projects. Each project is judged on which ones represent the best return on investment; all other projects are cancelled or ignored. Changes to the work breakdown structure (list of project tasks) will occur within the project itself. For more information, see Chapter 1.

60. A. Whether conducting an internal or external audit, the auditor is a paid impartial observer. None of the other statements are true. The auditor never takes ownership of problems found. Standards are either met by the client (compliant) or not met by the client (not compliant). For more information, see Chapter 1.

61. A. A crash dump file is created when the system crashes abruptly. This file contains the contents of working memory (RAM) and a list of tasks that were being processed. This special diagnostic file is extremely helpful during forensic investigations. For more information, see Chapter 6.

62. B. Expert systems make decisions for the user by using weighting rules against data points in the database (heuristics) to build correlations. Expert systems frequently contain more than 100,000 discrete points of data. All the other choices expect the user to make their own decision based on available information. For more information, see Chapter 5.

63. C. Middle floors. ISACA states that the computer room should never be in the basement because of the risk of flooding. The first floor is susceptible to break-ins. The top floor is susceptible to roof leaks and storm damage. In this book, we discuss the details of how the basement decision occurred. For more information, see Chapter 7.

64. B. A haphazard sample is also known as a judgmental sample. For more information, see Chapter 2.

65. D.   A policy is strategic, standards are tactical, and procedures are operational. For more information, see Chapter 1.

66. C.   A nonworking process would be the best candidate for reengineering. The actual decision is based on the best return on investment. There is no need to reengineer something that fails to generate a positive return. For more information, see Chapter 3.

67. B.   Formal approval is necessary before moving into the next phase. A review meeting is held with the stakeholders, project manager, and executive chairperson. All of the projections and open issues are discussed. Each item is approved, rejected, or cancelled. The project may advance to the next stage with formal approval. The auditor should look for evidence of formal approval and how the decision was made. For more information, see Chapter 5.

68. C.   A write-blocker is used to prevent any changes from being written to the hard disk during the collection of evidence. The simple act of booting up the computer will cause changes that taint the evidence. Any changes, no matter how small, will be used by defense lawyers to prove that evidence tampering occurred. Any claim of evidence tampering that cannot be disproved will destroy the value of the evidence. For more information, see Chapter 6.

69. B.   Using a system with a Redundant Array of Independent—or Inexpensive—Disks (RAID) will increase availability. RAID does not prevent data corruption; therefore, backups are still required. RAID systems use more disk space for redundancy but provide less available storage capacity. For more information, see Chapter 4.

70. A.   Audit charters are high-level documents used to grant authorization to the auditor responsible for conducting an audit, and to specify that the auditor will be accountable for their behavior. For more information, see Chapter 2.

71. C.   Root kits are used by hackers to remotely subvert the operating system security and compromise the kernel. Root kits can be installed without the knowledge of the user and use stealth techniques to hide their existence from monitoring software. For more information, see Chapter 7.

72. D.   Rapid Application Development (RAD) methodology automates only a portion of phase 2 requirements, phase 3 design, and phase 4 development. RAD does not provide the planning and documentation necessary in feasibility, requirements, implementation, and postimplementation. For more information, see Chapter 5.

73. A.   Auditing is a review of past history. We use evidence and testing to determine the story. It's not possible to use an audit to forecast compliance benefits before entering production. Every system creates unforeseen consequences that can be fully realized only after that system enters production. You can audit the system attributes during design and development, not the unrealized operating issues impacting its compliance. Compliance requires an audit after it enters production to include the way the system is actually used and managed. For more information, see Chapter 5.

74. C.   The data owner is responsible for designating the appropriate information security level and appointing the custodian. The data owner is usually a vice president or higher, up to an agency head. The data owner also specifies the controls to be used. The audit committee and management can change the security level if the data owner fails to properly classify the data. For more information, see Chapter 3.

75. A. Auditing of the system configuration and reading system logs are examples of detective controls implemented by using administrative methods. Auditing is always a detective control. Auditors may use computer assisted audit tools, but auditing is still an administrative process. For more information, see Chapter 2.

76. D. Firewalls do not need to be backed up except after changes to the system. Backups of the firewall must be full backups on stand-alone devices, also known as a zero day restore. An auditor should be seriously concerned if source routing is enabled (major hazard), backup media is left in the drive (covert storage for attackers), remote login or file sharing is enabled (open to remote access). For more information, see Chapter 7.

77. C. The auditee will usually get amnesty for turning you in. Copyright violations are always illegal and unethical. You can bet that the auditee will later boast about how they helped you, or blast you for issuing an unfavorable report after they did you a favor. Never use unauthorized software under any condition; besides breaking the law, it will make you look bad. No honest person or organization wants to use an auditor who violates the law. For more information, see Chapter 1.

78. C. The auditor should contact the audit committee, never law enforcement or the regulators. If necessary, the auditor's lawyer will handle contacting the authorities. For more information, see Chapter 2.

79. B. Agile programming is used to create prototypes via time-box management techniques to force new iterations within short periods of time. Traditional administrative planning and documentation is forfeited in favor of the undocumented knowledge contained in a person's head. For more information, see Chapter 5.

80. D. Reports by internal auditors have a low corresponding value due to the built-in reporting conflict that may exist. This is why external independent audits are required for regulatory licensing. For more information, see Chapter 2.

Secrets of a Successful IS Auditor

THE OBJECTIVE OF THIS CHAPTER IS TO ACQUAINT THE READER WITH THE FOLLOWING CONCEPTS:

- ✓ Understanding the foundation of IS audit standards
- ✓ Understanding the auditor's professional requirements
- ✓ Familiarity of auditor skills necessary for a successful audit
- ✓ Understanding mandatory versus discretionary wording of regulations
- ✓ Knowing the various types of audits
- ✓ Knowing how to communicate with the auditee
- ✓ Understanding auditor leadership duties, including planning and setting priorities
- ✓ Understanding the organizational structure of corporations and consulting firms
- ✓ Understanding the methods of managing projects, including audit projects

Welcome to the world of information systems (IS) auditing. We congratulate you for having the foresight and ambition to enter one of the most challenging careers in the world. The business issues in our global economy have created tremendous opportunities for individuals such as yourself.

Imagine what the world would be like without the Internet. A world without electronic systems would feel prehistoric. The days of manual systems of bookkeeping are gone. All organizations, regardless of size, are being driven toward increasing levels of automation. This increasing dependency on electronic information systems has created the need for a new type of auditor: the information systems auditor.

Just as financial auditors verify monetary balances and bookkeeping practices, the IS auditor verifies the integrity of the electronic system. Information systems are used to maintain customer data, company files, inventory, and records of transactions. IS auditing can provide a fabulous opportunity for people with financial or information technology backgrounds.

You may be asking yourself whether this opportunity would work for you. Becoming an IS auditor will expand your career options.

In this chapter, you will study the foundation of IS audit standards. The Certified Information Systems Auditor (CISA) establishes professional requirements and defines the auditor skills necessary for a successful audit.

The CISA candidate is expected to know the different types of audits. There is an established process for communication with the auditee. Every successful auditor must understand their leadership duties, including planning and setting priorities. Every IS auditor is expected to recognize the difference between mandatory versus discretionary wording in regulations.

We will discuss the organizational structure of corporations and consulting firms. The auditor will need to evaluate the organization's governance structure to determine whether IT objectives are aligned to organizational goals. This chapter reviews methods for managing projects, including audit projects.

This chapter is a foundation for the next chapter, which is about the IS audit process. Each concept we discuss will be in effect from now through to the end of this Study Guide to progressively build your knowledge.

Understanding the demand for IS Audits

For decades, the dominant control placed upon an organization was the financial audit. Although theft and fraud have always existed, the general expectation was that almost all organizations could be trusted without additional regulations. We expected management to be honest. Well, those naive days are over. Welcome to the new world, which has a growing number of intrusive regulations. Modern business culture is moving rapidly to less trust and more testing.

Let's reflect on a few of the great people who created this wonderful job opportunity for us. Mom always said to give special recognition to those deserving people who help you further your career opportunities:

- Italy's Parmalat dairy scandal occurred in 2003, when executives admitted that an account that was supposed to be holding 4 billion Euro dollars of assets in the Cayman Islands did not exist. The 14 billion Euro organization collapsed into bankruptcy. According to industry news, four of the world's leading banks were indicted in June 2007 for their participation.

- Adelphia Communications Corporation executives John Rigas and son Timothy Rigas were convicted of securities fraud, bank fraud for misrepresenting the source of $1.6 billion of funds used in company stock, and stealing $51 million in cash advances. Rigas's illegally misrepresented $2.6 billion of off-balance sheet loans, which led to the company's collapse in 2002. In July 2006, Comcast and Time Warner purchased the failed company and relocated it to Colorado.

- American International Group (AIG) former CFO Howard Smith overstated income by $3.9 billion (10 percent of income) and loss reserves by $500 million to quiet analyst complaints about AIG's declining financial reserves. Executives at the world's largest insurer are struggling to recover. Securities and Exchange Commission agreed to settle after AIG agreed to pay over 1.6 billon in damages. SEC did not release Mr. Smith from prosecution as the case continues to progress. *— Complete bankruptcy and takeover by U.S. government in 2008/9*

- Arthur Andersen executive David Duncan violated his independence with his client, CFO Andrew Fastow of Enron. Duncan participated in improper, biased activities for Enron by ordering his staff to shred documents to obstruct the Enron investigation.

- Cendant Vice Chairman E. Kirk Shelton was convicted of fraud in an accounting scandal for falsely inflating income to drive up the stock price.

- Converse Technology CEO Jacob "Kobi" Alexander was captured by Federal authorities after fleeing the country in an attempt to avoid prosecution for orchestrating a fraudulent scheme of backdating options while running a secret stock options slush fund. This illegal scheme made millions of dollars. CFO David Kreinberg and General Counsel William Sorin voluntarily surrendered to authorities for their participation in the scheme. All three are currently in jail awaiting prosecution.

- Enron executives Ken Lay, Jeffrey Skilling, Andrew Fastow, Lea Fastow, Ben Glisan Jr., and Dan Boyle were proven guilty for running the world's largest scam of off-balance sheet (OBS) transactions.

- International Product Investment Corp. (IPIC) CEO Gregory Earl Setser was convicted of conspiracy, securities fraud, and money laundering Mr. Setser has been sentenced to 40 years in prison without parole and ordered to pay approximately $62 million in restitution for running an investment pyramid scam.

- ImClone Systems CEO Samuel D. Waksal was sentenced to more than 7 years in prison and ordered to pay $4.2 million for insider trading in his attempts to sell off his shares of stock after learning that the Federal Drug Administration was planning to reject ImClone's application for Erbitux, a new cancer drug. In a twist of irony, the FDA granted tentative approval for Erbitux the day after Waksal was sentenced.

- Former HealthSouth CFO Weston Smith was sentenced to 27 months in prison for his participation in the $2.7 billion accounting fraud at the company. Smith was one of five ex-CFOs who agreed to plead guilty and testify against former CEO Richard Scrushy. Ultimately Scrushy was acquitted on all counts of the accounting fraud charges.

- Tyco ex-CEO Dennis Kozlowski is serving 8–25 years in prison for stealing $134 million from the company. Ex-CFO Mark H. Schwartz was given the same prison sentence. The scheme involved grand larceny, conspiracy of falsifying business records, and inflating statements of operating income by at least $500 million by using improper accounting practices.

- Patterson-UTI Energy CFO Jody Nelson was sentenced to 25 years and $77 million restitution for a phony invoice scheme of embezzling $77 million for personal use. (Criminal filing took only two weeks to freeze accounts and assets.)

- Lincoln Savings and Loan CEO Charles Keating was found guilty of causing the $2.6 billion collapse of the savings and loan industry in 1988. So far the estimated cost of the bailout is said to be over $110 billion ($10 from every person in America). Mr. Keating accused the auditor of having a vendetta against him for bringing the evidence to the attention of regulators.

- WorldCom ex-CEO Bernard Ebbers is serving 25 years for securities fraud and filing false reports concerning an $11 billion accounting fraud. WorldCom triggered the creation of the U.S. Sarbanes-Oxley Act of 2002 (a corporate governance law for internal controls). CFO Scott Sullivan testified against Ebbers to get a reduced sentence. Controller David Myers admitted he told the accounting staff to make billions of dollars in adjustments to financial statements so their stock price would rise. Former accounting director Buford Yates went to prison for following the orders of his superiors to make billions of dollars of unexplained adjustments in financial records.

- More than 1,000 successful corporate fraud convictions by the U.S. Securities and Exchange Commission (SEC) from 2002–2005 include the following:
  - 92 corporate presidents
  - 86 chief executive officers (CEOs)
  - 40 chief financial officers (CFOs)
  - 14 chief operating officers (COOs)
  - 98 vice presidents (VPs)
  - 17 attorneys (lawyers serving as corporate council)

Times are rapidly changing worldwide. These global businesses were damaged by bad executive decisions. Even some common business practices that were acceptable five to ten years ago are now illegal. No one in their right mind would want to suffer the fate of those poor souls.

New regulations for more-stringent financial and internal controls are driving business leaders into a controlled frenzy. You may have heard of the following: Sarbanes-Oxley Act (SOX, for corporations), Gramm-Leach-Bliley Act (financial transactions), Federal Information Security Management Act (FISMA, for government), Health Insurance Portability and Accountability Act (HIPAA), Supervisory Control and Data Acquisition (SCADA, for utilities), Fair and Accurate Credit Transactions Act (credit processing), Federal Financial Institutions Examination Council regulations (FFIEC), Payment Card Industry (PCI), and numerous privacy laws worldwide. These are just a sample of the regulations and regulators facing today's businesses.

All of these regulations require businesses to possess two simple components:

- Evidence of business integrity
- Evidence of internal controls to protect valuable assets

An *asset* is defined as anything of value, including trademarks, patents, secret recipes, durable goods, data files, competent personnel, and clients. Although people are not listed as corporate assets, the loss of key individuals is a genuine business threat. We can define a *threat* as a negative event that would cause a loss if it occurred. The path that allows a threat to occur is referred to as *vulnerability.* Your job as an IS auditor is to verify that assets, threats, and vulnerabilities are properly identified and managed to reduce risk.

see pg 570 464, 476

In the past, businesses were allowed to operate with fewer restrictions. The problem with past regulation (or lack thereof) was that many organizations were taking risks that would have been unacceptable to investors and business partners had they been fully informed of corporate actions. Financial auditors were focused on bank balances and transaction totals proving to be correct. Increasing automation enables little mistakes to cascade into massive catastrophes. Stockholders, customers, and the government are looking for reassurance that management has taken the necessary precautions to prevent loss or corruption.

Our economy is founded on banking and investment. The majority of our global economy invests directly or indirectly in stock and financial markets. You may be an indirect investor through pension funds or bank investment portfolios. Unfortunately, there exists a group of individuals who view stock as their own private monetary system. How wonderful it must be to have our money at their disposal, without any terms of repayment, without interest or consideration, and without the requirement to ever pay the money back. Sounds ridiculous, doesn't it? But frankly, that is exactly how the stock market operates. You invest money with the hope that one day you will see something in return, knowing that you could lose it all.

One of the purposes of a controls audit is to ensure that there is reason to believe investors' money is protected from stupid mistakes. Our free enterprise strives to prevent another market collapse and protect the world banking system from crashing. We expect management to specify policies and to create procedures, processes, and safeguards to prevent loss and corruption. It is the job of management to design a solution that effectively protects corporate assets.

As an IS auditor, you must be familiar with the various policies, standards, and procedures of any organization or company that you are auditing. In addition, you must understand the purpose of your audit. You will look at those topics in this section.

An "incident" is a negative or harmful event that involves people, property, or assets.

Understanding Policies, Standards, Guidelines, and Procedures

A plethora of documentation exists in the operation of any organization. Management uses this documentation to specify operating and control details. Consistency would be impossible without putting this information into writing.

Organizations typically have four types of documents in place:

Policies   These are high-level documents signed by a person of significant authority (such as a corporate officer, president, or vice president). The policy is a simple document stating that a particular high-level control objective is important to the organization's success. Policies may be only one page in length. Policies require *mandatory* compliance.

- The highest level of people in charge is the officers of upper management. Chief executives, financial officers, and operating officers are the principal issuers of policies.

Standards   These are mid-level documents to ensure uniform application of a policy. After a standard is approved by management, compliance is *mandatory*. All standards are used as reference points to ensure organizational compliance. Testing and audits compare a subject to the standard, with the intention of certifying a minimum level of uniform compliance.

- Public standards include the International Organization for Standardization (ISO), Sarbanes-Oxley, and most government laws.

Guidelines   These are intended to provide advice pertaining to how organizational objectives might be obtained in the absence of a standard. The purpose is to provide information that would aid in making decisions about intended goals (should do), beneficial alternatives (could do), and actions that would not create problems (won't hurt). Guidelines are often *discretionary*.

Procedures   These are "cookbook" recipes for accomplishing specific tasks necessary to meet a standard. Details are written in step-by-step format from the very beginning to the end. Good procedures include common troubleshooting steps in case the user encounters a known problem. Compliance with established procedures is *mandatory* to ensure consistency and accuracy. On occasion a procedure may be deemed ineffective. The correct process is to update the ineffective procedure by using the change control process described later. The purpose of a procedure is to maintain control over the outcome.

Figure 1.1 illustrates the hierarchy of a policy, standard, guideline, and procedure.

Understanding the ISACA Code of Professional Ethics

The Information Systems Audit and Control Association (ISACA) set forth a code governing the professional conduct and ethics of all certified IS auditors and members of the association. As a CISA, you are bound to uphold this code. The following eight points represent the true spirit and intent of this code:

- You agree to support the implementation of appropriate policies, standards, guidelines, and procedures for information systems. You will also encourage compliance with this objective.

FIGURE 1.1   The relationship between a policy, standard, guideline, and procedure

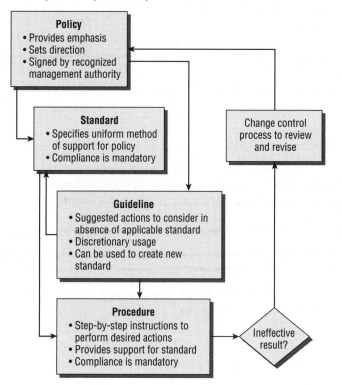

Policies, Standards, Guidelines, and Procedures

- You agree to perform your duties with objectivity, professional care, and due diligence in accordance with professional standards. You will support the use of best practices.

- You agree to serve the interests of stakeholders in an honest and lawful manner that reflects a credible image upon your profession. The public expects and trusts auditors to conduct their work in an ethical and honest manner.

- You promise to maintain privacy and confidentiality of information obtained during your audit except for required disclosure to legal authorities. Information you obtain during the audit will not be used for personal benefit.

- You agree to undertake only those activities in which you are professionally competent and will strive to improve your competency. Your effectiveness in auditing depends on how evidence is gathered, analyzed, and reported.

- You promise to disclose accurate results of all work and significant facts to the appropriate parties.

- You agree to support ongoing professional education to help stakeholders enhance their understanding of information systems security and control.

- The failure of a CISA to comply with this code of professional ethics may result in an investigation with possible sanctions or disciplinary measures.

Ethics statements are necessary to demonstrate the level of honesty and professionalism expected of every auditor. Overall, your profession requires you to be honest and fair in all representations you make. The goal is to build trust with clients. Your behavior should reflect a positive image on your profession. All IS auditors are depending on you to help maintain the high quality and integrity that clients expect from a CISA.

 Every CISA should have a strong understanding of these objectives and how each would apply to different audit situations.

Preventing Ethical Conflicts

Auditors are bombarded by certain people attempting to sway us from our straight and narrow course of honesty. Seemingly simple violations can become uncontrollable career killers. Do not allow yourself to participate in any situation that could tarnish your image as an auditor. Just having a false reputation of dishonest activity will quash your career like a black plague. Let's look at a few common examples:

- Copyright violations. The possession, purchase, or distribution of bootleg materials will lead to forfeiting your CISA certification along with any other certifications requiring an ethics statement. You don't have to be convicted of a crime to lose your certification. Make sure that you purchase only genuine software and commercially licensed copies of printed material. Don't use anything except your own copies of materials that were rightfully obtained from the license holder. This includes copies of the ISO standards, software tools, special reports, and even this book or CD. Always be prepared to show the receipt and original product to prove you are honest and ethical. Lack of evidence implies guilt. Vendors' shipping records are an excellent source of proof. Trafficking in bootlegs provides an excellent route to living in jail.

- Guilty people get amnesty for turning you in. It's unfair, but the guiltiest will typically get amnesty for turning someone else in for participation. So the person who says, "don't worry" is not worried. They secretly know that you will become their scapegoat at the first sign of trouble. Beware of any special deal or exception that can be used against you. The truth never stays secret.

- Failing to follow your own rules. Make sure that you uphold the spirit and intent of the audit profession. The worst thing you could do to kill your career is to give the perception that you violate the rules yourself. It's necessary to "walk the talk" by doing everything right, just as you expect from your customer. By doing this religiously, you will become almost bulletproof.

- Review the beginning of this chapter again if you need any examples of executives and auditors being "burned at the stake" for violating the public's trust.

- Avoid violating the law. Being associated with a suspected scam is nearly as damaging as being convicted in the courtroom. The best way to stay out of trouble is to avoid questionable deals. Never accept a free or loaner copy of software from IT workers. It's a trap that usually involves someone bragging about how they helped you out by violating the law, ethics, or company policy.

- Report violations promptly. Remember, the person reporting (in this case, you) will usually get amnesty, unless someone else turns you in first. You need to be prepared to turn over evidence unless you want to join others in their convictions. Honest auditors always report the truth. It's what keeps us in business.

Understanding the Purpose of an Audit

An *audit* is simply a review of past history. The IS auditor is expected to follow the defined audit process, establish audit criteria, gather meaningful evidence, and render an independent opinion about internal controls. The audit involves applying various techniques for collecting meaningful evidence, and then performing a comparison of the audit evidence against the standard for reference.

If the assertions of management and the auditor's report are in agreement, you can expect the results to be truthful. If management assertions and the auditor's report do not agree, that would signal a concern warranting further attention.

Your key to success in auditing is to accurately report your findings, whether good or bad or indifferent. A good auditor will produce verifiable results. No one should ever come in behind you with a different outcome of findings. Your job is to report what the evidence indicates.

Classifying Basic Types of Audits

We can classify audits into three basic categories. Each of these represents a slightly different level of trust and unique objectives. The purpose is always to determine the truth.

Internal audits and assessments   This involves auditing your own organization to discover evidence of what is occurring inside the organization (self-assessment). These have restrictions on their scope, and the findings should not be shared outside the organization. The findings cannot be used for licensing.

External audits   External audits involve your customer auditing you, or you auditing your supplier. The business audits its customer or supplier, or vice versa. The goal is to ensure the expected level of performance as mutually agreed upon in their contracts.

Independent audits   Independent audits are outside of the customer-supplier influence. Third-party independent audits are frequently relied on for licensing, certification, or product approval. A simple example is independent consumer reports.

So what will the CISA be asked to look at during an audit? Auditors are called to audit products, processes, and systems. Each of these requires a different approach. Let's review the basic approach required for each of these audits to be successful:

Product audits check the attributes against the design specification (size, color, markings). The 2007 hazardous toy recall of over a million Chinese-manufactured toys for Mattel is an example of using a product audit. The lead-based paint used on the toys was in violation of the design specifications. You can expect that CISAs will audit more software products than toys.

Process audits evaluate the process method to determine whether the activities or sequence of activities meet the published requirements. We want to see how the process is working. This involves checking inputs, actions, and outputs to verify the process performance. /effective- ness

System audits seek to evaluate the management of the system, including its configuration. The auditor is interested in the team members' activities, control environment, event monitoring, how customer needs are determined, who provides authorization, how changes are implemented, preventative maintenance, and so forth, including incident response capability.

Financial audit verifies financial records, transactions, and account balances. This type of audit is used to check the integrity of financial records and accounting practices compared to well-known accounting standards.

Operational audit verifies effectiveness and efficiency of operational practices. Operational audits are used frequently in service and process environments, including IT service providers. An operational audit is detailed in Statement on Auditing Standard 70 (SAS-70).

Integrated audit includes both financial and operational controls audits. An integrated audit is detailed in SAS-94.

Compliance audit verifies implementation of and adherence to a standard or regulation. This could include ISO standards and all government regulations. A compliance audit usually includes tests for the presence of a working control.

Administrative audit verifies that appropriate policies and procedures exist and have been implemented as intended. This type of audit usually tests for the presence of required documentation.

Information systems certification and/or accreditation. Certification usually involves system testing against a reference standard, whereas accreditation represents management's level of acceptance.

Now we need to move on to the different roles people play in the audit.

Understanding the Auditor's Responsibility

As an auditor, you are expected to fulfill a fiduciary relationship. A *fiduciary relationship* is simply one in which you are acting for the benefit of another person and placing the responsibilities to be fair and honest ahead of your own interest. An auditor must never put the auditee interests ahead of the truth. People inside and outside of the auditee organization will depend on your reports to make decisions.

The auditor is depended on to advise about the internal status of an organization. Audits are different from inspections or assessments because the individual performing the audit must be both objective and impartial. This is a tremendous responsibility.

Comparing Audits to Assessments

As stated earlier, the audit is a formal process performed by a qualified independent auditor. To clarify, the following provides a comparison of an audit and assessment:

Audit An audit generates a report considered to represent a high assurance of truth. Audits are used in asset reporting engagements.

Assessment   An assessment is less formal and frequently more cooperative with the people/objects under scrutiny. Its purpose is to see what exists and to assess value based on its relevance. The assessment report is viewed to have lower value (moderate-to-low value) when compared to an audit.

The primary goal of an assessment is to help the user/staff work toward improving their score. However, the audit is the score that actually counts for regulatory compliance purposes.

Remember that the basic control requirement is to separate the worker from the person providing *authorization* (separation of duties). Assessments are considered biased because the separation is not clean as it would be under a formal independent audit.

Auditor Role versus Auditee Role

There are only two titles for persons directly involved in an audit. First is the *auditor*, the one who investigates. Second is the *auditee*, the subject of the audit. A third role exists which is normally outside of the audit, known as the *client*. ISACA refers to these as audit roles versus nonaudit roles.

Let's clarify the titles and basic roles of these people by their relationship to the audit. We can refer to them as members of the following categories:

Auditor   The auditor is the competent person performing the audit.

Auditee   The organization and people being audited are collectively called the auditee.

Client   The client is the person or organization with the authority to request the audit. A client may be the audit committee, external customer, internal audit department, or regulatory group. If the client is internal to the auditee, that client assumes the auditee role.

typically the Audit Committee - pg 139

Everyone else is considered outside of the audit roles. Audit details should be kept confidential from persons not directly involved as auditee or the client.

Your purpose as an auditor is to be an independent set of eyes that can delve into the inside of organizations on behalf of management or can certify compliance on behalf of everyone in the outside world. *Independent* means that you are not related professionally, personally, or organizationally to the subject of the audit. You cannot be independent if the audit's outcome results in your financial gain or if you are involved in the auditee's decisions or design of the subject being audited.

When determining whether you are able to perform a fair audit, you should conduct an independence test. In addition, you must remain aware of your responsibility as an auditor under the various auditing standards.

Applying an Independence Test

Here is a simple self assessment to help you determine your level of independence:

- Are you auditing something you helped to develop?
- Are you free of any conflicts, circumstances, or attitudes toward the auditee that might affect the audit outcome?

- Is your personal life free of any relationships, off-duty behavior, or financial gain that could be perceived as affecting your judgment? *You can't audit a co. you used to work for.*
- Do you have any organizational relationships with the auditee, including business deals, financial obligations, or pending legal actions?
- Do you have a job conflict? Does the organizational structure require your position to work under the executive in charge of the area being audited?
- Did you receive any gifts of value or special favors?

If any answer is "yes," you are not independent. Any conflicts will place a shadow of doubt on the objectivity of the audit findings. Only internal auditors (whose aim is to improve internal performance) can answer yes and still possibly continue the audit. External auditors are required to remain independent during an independent audit. Any potential conflicts should be disclosed immediately to the lead auditor. You may be reassigned to eliminate the conflict. The lead auditor may determine that the impact is low enough that you can remain in the role as long as the client sponsor is aware of the situation. Attempting to hide the truth is a bad idea. No conflict means you are cleared to proceed.

🌐 Real World Scenario

Being Fair and Objective

Early in my career, I learned a slogan that helped guide me through some difficult decisions: "The truth is the truth until you add to it." As an auditor, you are expected to report findings that are fair and objective. It is presumed that the auditor will ask the right questions during the audit. In this book, we intend to teach you a practical application of the audit standards, including the right questions to ask.

What if the client asks you to provide advice to their design staff while you are engaged as their external auditor? The unknowledgeable auditor could create a conflict or lose the client's respect. A good auditor would remind the client of the need for auditor independence. Imagine the power of the following statement that you, as a professional auditor, could make:

Sir/Madam, In my role as external auditor, I must remain independent of design decisions; otherwise, I would not be able to provide you the independence and objectivity required. Providing design advice would be a violation of several standards governing auditor independence, including public corporation audit standard AS-1, GAAP audit practices, ISACA professional standards, and Statement on Auditing Standards 1, 37, and 74 (SAS-1, SAS-37, and SAS-74).

You are encouraged to explain what an auditor looks for during an audit. You must be careful not to participate in design decisions, detailed specification, or remediation during your role as the auditor. You may be hired to help with remediation; however, you will be disqualified from auditing any related work. The same principle applies to design work and system operation.

Auditors have the luxury of being able to rely on well-known accounting standards that have been accepted worldwide. The standards were originally developed for financial audits, but their spirit and intent also apply to IS auditing. Frequently, a minor adaptation will provide the foundation and detail necessary for use in IS audits. These standards allow you to render a fair opinion without fear of retribution or liability.

Understanding the Various Auditing Standards

Understanding the basic types of audits: audits either verify compliance (_compliance test_) or check the substance and integrity of a claim (_substantive test_). Just how does an auditor know what to do in these audits? As an IS auditor, you are fortunate to have several credible resources available to assist you and guide your clients.

Among these resources are standards and regulations that direct your actions and final opinion. It would be quite rare to depart from these well-known and commonly accepted regulations. In fact, you would be in an awkward situation if you ever departed from the audit standards. By following known audit standards, you are relatively safe from an integrity challenge or individual liability. By adhering to audit standards, a good auditor can operate from a position that is conceptually equal to Teflon nonstick coating. Nothing negative or questionable could stick to the auditor.

You can learn more about auditing standards by reading and then implementing information provided by the following:

- American Institute of Certified Public Accountants (AICPA) and International Federation of Accountants (IFAC).

- Financial Accounting Standards Board (FASB) with Statement on Auditing Standards (SAS), standards 1 through 114, which are referenced and applied by the AICPA and IFAC.

- Generally Accepted Accounting Principles (GAAP).

- Committee of Sponsoring Organizations of the Treadway Commission (COSO), providing the COSO internal control framework that is the basis for standards used in global commerce. COSO is the parent for the standards used by governments around the world.

- Public Company Accounting Oversight Board (PCAOB) of the Securities and Exchange Commission, issuing audit standards AS-1, AS-2, AS-3, AS-4, and AS-5. PCAOB is the standards body for Sarbanes-Oxley, including the international implementation by the Japanese government and European Union (US-SOX, J-SOX and E-SOX).

- Organization for Economic Cooperation and Development (OECD), providing guidelines for participating countries to promote standardization in multinational business for world trade.

- International Organization for Standardization (ISO), which represents participation from more than member governments.

- U.S. National Institute of Standards and Technology (NIST), providing a foundation of modern IS standards used worldwide. When combined with British Standards/ISO (BS/ISO), you get a wonderful amount of useful guidance.

- U.S. Federal Information Security Management Act (FISMA), which specifies minimum security compliance standards for all systems relied on by the government, including the military and those systems operated by government contractors. (The U.S. government is the world's largest customer.)

- IS Audit and Control Association (ISACA) and IT Governance Institute (ITGI) issue the Control OBjectives for IT (CObIT) guidelines which are derived from COSO with a more specific emphasis on information systems.

- Basel Accord Standard II (Basel II), governing risk reduction in banking.

Although this list may appear daunting, it is important to remember that all these examples are in fundamental agreement with each other. Each standard supports nearly identical terms of reference and supports similar audit objectives. These standards will have slightly different levels of audit or audit scope. ITGA and ISACA have developed a set of IT internal control standards for CISAs to follow. These incorporate several objectives of the COSO internal control standard that have been narrowed to focus on IT functions. Let's look at a brief overview of the ISACA standards.

ISACA IS Audit Standards

The members of ISACA are constantly striving to advance the standards of IS auditing. CISAs should check the ISACA website (www.isaca.org) for updates on a quarterly basis. ISACA added five new standards during 2006–2007 to clarify our minimum level of performance. The current body of ISACA Audit Standards is organized using a format numbered from 1 to 16:

S1 Audit Charter   The audit charter authorizes the scope of the audit and grants you responsibility, authority, and accountability in the audit function.

S2 Independence   Every auditor is expected to demonstrate professional and organizational independence.

S3 Professional Ethics and Standards of Conduct   The auditor must act in a manner that denotes professionalism and respect.

S4 Professional Competence   The auditor must have the necessary skills to perform the audit. Continuing education is required to improve and maintain skills.

S5 Planning   Successful audits are the result of advance preparation. Proper planning is necessary to ensure that the audit will fulfill the intended objectives.

S6 Performance of Audit Work   This standard provides guidance to ensure that the auditor has proper supervision, gains the correct evidence to form conclusions, and creates the required documentation of the audit.

S7 Audit Reporting   The auditor report contains several required statements and legal disclosures. This standard provides guidance concerning the contents of the auditor's report.

S8 Follow-up Activities   The follow-up activities include determining whether management has taken action on the auditor's recommendations in a timely manner.

S9 Irregularities and Illegal Acts   This standard outlines how to handle the discovery of irregularities and illegal acts involving the auditee.

S10 IT Governance   This standard covers the authority, direction, and control of the information technology function. Technology is now pervasive in all areas of business. Is the auditee properly managing IT to meet their needs?

S11 Use of Risk Analysis in Audit Planning   This standard provides guidance for implementing a risk-based approach in audit planning. Risk planning is used to determine whether an audit is possible. Auditors always weigh our level of competency to conduct the audit. Audit plans should be structured for the maximum return on investment when designing specific audits, aka *impact for the dollar spent.*

S12 Audit Materiality   Auditors must use evidence that portrays the most accurate story. The absence of controls or a potential weakness may cumulatively result in unacceptable risk to the organization. Ineffective controls, absence of controls, and control deficiencies should be disclosed in the audit report.

S13 Using the Work of Other People   It's impossible for the auditor to perform all the work alone. The work of other experts may be included in the audit, provided the auditor is satisfied with their competencies, relevant experience, professional qualifications, independence, and quality control. A scope limitation may be required in the final audit opinion if the other experts do not provide appropriate and sufficient evidence. An expert working in the same area as the one being audited should not be relied on.

S14 Proper Audit Evidence   Appropriate evidence includes the written procedures performed by the auditor, source documents, corroborating records, samples, and corresponding test results. Reliable evidence is based on its source, natural state, and authenticity. Audit evidence must be specifically identified, cataloged, and cross-referenced in the audit documentation, via auditor notes and working papers.

S15 Effective IT Controls   Working IT controls represent an integral foundation in the organization's overall internal control environment. IS auditors should monitor and evaluate the effect or absence of IT controls. It's necessary to help management understand the IT controls' design, implementation, and methods of improvement. The level of effective controls provided by outsourcing, or their absence, may help or hurt the organization.

S16 Electronic Commerce Controls   E-commerce allows the business to conduct electronic transactions with other businesses (business-to-business, or B2B) and directly to consumers (business-to-consumer, or B2C) over the public Internet. E-commerce requires the auditor to implement risk-based audit plans with data-gathering techniques for continuous assurances regarding the security and integrity of the environment. ISACA standard S16 excludes non-Internet-based private networks such as Electronic Data Interchange (EDI) and Society for Worldwide Interbank Financial Telecommunication (SWIFT).

NOTE   This chapter, as well as Chapter 2, "Audit Process," thoroughly discusses all the objectives contained in ISACA's audit standards.

During the audit process, you will find clients are more receptive when your audit goals are linked to specific citations in the audit standards. You should aim to fill a known and defined point of compliance rather than provide a vague statement relating to something you may have read in a textbook. Don't make the mistake of trusting your job to misinformation, rumors, or free advice on the Internet.

Most of the IT controls originated from demands imposed by a government agency. Security started in the military. Budgets and financial tracking were introduced by the banking industry. In fact, the first internal control in business was the budget. Since 1998, additional internal controls have been added each year. Figure 1.2 demonstrates the relationship of these various sources.

FIGURE 1.2   Where I.T. control standards originate

Specific Regulations Defining Best Practices

Let's review the basic purpose of several major regulations (see Figure 1.3). These are predominantly U.S. regulations with worldwide compliance implications due to global outsourcing.

Every regulation is designed to mandate the minimum acceptable requirements when conducting any form of business within that specific industry. The auditor must remain aware of two types of statements contained in all regulations:

Recommended (discretionary)   These are actions that usually contain statements with the word *should*—for example, suggested management responsibilities, staffing, control mechanisms, or technical attributes.

FIGURE 1.3 Sample of regulations defining best practices

Sample of Regulations	Intended Purpose	Application
SOX U.S. Sarbanes-Oxley Act of 2002	· Integrity in public corporations. · Mandates full disclosure of potential control weaknesses to audit committee. · Creates officer liability.	· 906 Act, signed attestation of integrity in financial statement. · 302 Act, signed attestation of full disclosure to audit committee every 90 days of any potential control weaknesses. Management commitment to find and remediate weaknesses. · 404 Act, recommended internal controls.
GLBA U.S. Gramm-Leach-Bliley Act 2002	· Minimum processing performance requirement for financial institutions, collection agencies, mortgage and real estate companies. · Privacy & data protection controls in banking. · Creates officer liability.	· Sets maximum service outages at 59 minutes for basic account functions. · Public disclosure of security breaches. · Mandatory verification of continuity plans by quarterly testing.
Basel II Basel Accord Standard II	· Risk management controls in banking.	· World banking consortium of the G-10 member countries to safeguard international banking.
PCI Payment Card Industry Security Act of 2005.	· Information security requirements for merchants and card processors to reduce fraud and identity theft	· More-restrictive data retention. · Prohibit storage of account numbers. Violation if IT system fails to comply. · Data destruction requirements.
FFIEC U.S. Federal Financial Institutions Examination Council	· Multiple government authorities. · Uniform principles, standards, and report forms. · Mandatory federal examination of financial institutions.	· Financial institutions. · Banks. · Non-banks, credit unions, & thrifts. · Subsidiaries. · Holding & edge companies. · Foreign banks and non-banks operating in U.S. jurisdictions. · Officers, employees, and certain individuals.
HIPAA U.S. Health Insurance Portability and Accountability Act of 1996	· Privacy for records in healthcare organizations and benefit managers. · Combat fraud, waste and abuse in healthcare.	· Insurance companies. · Insurance processors. · Healthcare providers. · Custodian of records. · Patient record handling.
FISMA U.S. Federal Information Security Management Act of 2002	· Security controls in all systems and information relied upon by the U.S. government. · Designed to unite Federal Information Processing Standards (FIPS).	· All U.S. government federal systems including military. · IT systems for U.S. critical. · Infrastructure in commerce.
SCADA U.S. Supervisory Control and Data Acquisition	· Security for automated control systems in U.S. critical infrastructure.	· Utility industry, power generation & transmission, water, gas, communications. · Research facilities. · Traffic control. · Manufacturing. · Other automated control.

Required (mandatory)   These are actions that contain the word *shall*. *Shall* indicates that statement is a commandment of compliance. *Shall* is not optional. The auditor must remember that failing to meet a required Shall objective is a real concern. The regulations serve to protect the citizens at large.

Incredible justification would usually be required to prove the organization's actions do not fall under the jurisdiction of the regulation. The regulator will accept no excuses without a major battle and on almost every occasion will win any potential disputes. Most juries comprise individuals who will interpret claims by using a basic commonsense approach without detailed knowledge of a particular industry. Almost all excuses for violating the regulatory objective have failed in court battles.

Each organization in that market is required to meet the objective in spite of cost or revenue issues. In other words, the organization must comply even if it means that compliance will cause the organization to lose money. Failure to make a profit is not a valid exception from the law. The organization must strive to obtain compliance or can be forced to exit the industry with fines and sanctions. The auditor may need to consult a lawyer for advice upon discovery of significant violations.

SHOULD

SHALL

vs.

Recommendation of
actions to take

Mandatory actions,
or suffer dire consequences

Identifying Specific Types of Audits

IS auditors may be engaged in a variety of audits. The only fundamental difference between internal and external audits is auditor independence. Although the focus and nature of the audit may vary from time to time, your audit function and responsibilities will remain constant.

Medium-to-large businesses undergo a quarterly audit for their financial statements. IS auditors are called upon to determine whether the systems used for financial reporting are trustworthy. The goal is to ensure that the executives are held accountable for the accuracy of financial reports. A common defense is to claim someone else committed any offenses creating misrepresentation. However, a well-managed IS environment prevents and detects unauthorized modifications. This connects the integrity of the financial statement to the integrity of the IS environment. With this level of combined control, you will have integrity.

Government interpretation of laws and regulations has determined that financial audits and internal controls are interrelated. You could not ensure the integrity of one without verifying the other. As an example, consider the requirements specified under SOX for public corporations. There are two critical reporting functions that management must fulfill under SOX:

- SOX Act section 906 statement, in which management attests to the integrity of financials and indicates that no hidden or questionable transactions exist.
- SOX Act section 302 statement, in which management attests that full disclosure of the section 401–404 internal controls has been made to the audit committee, and that no deficiencies or weaknesses were withheld.

Management must make their assertions of compliance without reliance on the auditor. The intention of these two statements is to bind management with liability. SOX is essentially a disclosure law. Its purpose is to provide government authorities with a method of ensuring criminal prosecution of corporate officers if management misrepresents the truth.

As an IS auditor, you should remain aware of your leadership responsibilities.

Auditor Is an Executive Position

Many people are envious of the CISA's position. They see nice cars, lunches with important people, expensive suits, and comfortable expense accounts. Nobody seems to pay attention to the humorous situation of six auditors sharing one folding table while sitting in a closet, balancing laptop computers with only one network jack and one telephone to share. Frankly, the auditor position grants you the luxury of being well-paid observers with professional benefits. Occasionally, your office and travel accommodations may not be the best. However, the reality is that most people look up to auditors with respect.

Your clients expect you to be authoritative and professional regardless of the circumstances. Your office is mobile, so you are depended on to handle decisions in the field. Your clients include the highest levels of management within an organization. Those clients expect you to assist them with your observations and occasional advice. You will deal with the challenges of providing advice in a manner that does not interfere with the independent audit. Remember the independence question raised earlier in this chapter?

Personnel at every level of your client's organization have an expectation of your appearance. You are going to be judged by your speech, mannerisms, clothing, and grooming. You should always wear professional attire to a level more formal than the attire of your client. Your neat and pressed appearance instills respect and confidence. Your courtesy of manner and speech dictates that you should use reassuring words. Any humor by the auditor should always be restrained and professional.

Understanding the Importance of Auditor Confidentiality

The client entrusts the auditor with sensitive information. A good auditor would never betray that confidence nor allow sensitive information to be revealed at any time. Any breach of confidentiality would be unforgivable. It is conceivable that during your audit, you may discover information that could cause some level of damage to the client if disclosed. You should prepare for the possibility of detecting irregular or even illegal acts that have occurred.

To protect yourself, you must exercise caution and least privilege in all activities. The concept of *least privilege* refers to providing only the minimum information necessary to complete a required task. It is the auditor's responsibility to implement security controls to maintain confidentiality. An auditor's working papers contain details and secrets that need to be protected. The information you're privy to may be alarming to some, damaging to others, or trigger additional actions by a perpetrator.

To ensure confidentiality, the auditor should adopt the following operating principles:

- Sensitive information is the property of the owner and should not be removed from their office by the auditor.

- The auditor should contact legal counsel for advice concerning confidentiality and laws that would dictate disclosure to authorities. You should follow basic principles of confidentiality at all times.

- Many auditors use automated *working papers (WPs)* during an audit. Spreadsheets and report-writing templates are common tools to increase efficiency. We refer to audit checklists, procedures, computer-generated output, templates, and databases as working papers. The next level of automation is entering our workplace to aid even the smallest auditor. This includes more-advanced database automation, evidence tracking, and report-generation tools. The data must be protected with access control and regular data backup. Make sure to back up your work. It would be unforgivable to lose your audit work and client data by failing to implement your own controls.

- Every auditor should seriously consider using locking security cables and privacy viewing screens for laptops. You will gain respect by demonstrating your concern for maintaining confidentiality while protecting assets. The laptop could still be stolen with broken parts lying on the floor, but at least you would have some evidence that the theft was not completely your fault. At prior audit firms where I worked, these controls were mandatory for continued employment.

- A document file archive is created during each audit. The archive is subject to laws governing records retention. Every auditor is advised to leave all records in the custody of the client unless criminal activity is suspected. The client shall maintain sole responsibility for the safe retention of the archive.

Working with Lawyers

There is much discussion concerning who should hire the auditor. Is it the client or is it their lawyer? At stake is the legal argument of confidentiality under attorney-client privilege. Most communication between lawyers and the client may be exempt from legal discovery (disclosure).

We suggest that you ask the client. If necessary, the lawyer could issue a letter authorizing the auditor's work on their behalf. As an auditor, you have to be able to do your job without intimidation in order for it to be fair and honest work. This should be spelled out in the audit charter or your engagement letter. A good auditor will leave the legal issues to the lawyers and focus on their job of performing a good audit. Truth often serves as an excellent defense.

Retaining Audit Documentation

In most cases, the archive of the integrated audit may need to be kept for seven years. Each type of audit may have a longer or shorter retention period, depending on the regulations identified during audit planning. If the client loses the files, that would be their problem and not yours.

When I hear that a client does not have a complete archive, the first sound in my head is *chi-ching*! I get to charge them extra money for re-creating the missing documentation.

During an audit, you will be preparing reports and documentation on laptops belonging to members of your audit staff. All members of the audit team should practice good physical security, including using physical cable locks on the laptops and locking up sensitive files each evening or when not in use. You must be wary of prying eyes and big ears. It is advisable for the audit team to implement a designated "war room" as a secure work location. Meetings and interviews with all other persons should occur in a different location that is also safe from prying eyes and ears.

Providing Good Communication and Integration

Have you ever felt nervous, threatened, or intimidated? What are your own feelings when you're told an auditor is coming to visit? Nothing launches a person's defensive attitude faster than the threat of an audit. A good auditor understands client expectations and realizes it is necessary to take time to speak with customers who may be curious or nervous.

It is a good idea to alleviate fear and anxiety by implementing the following objectives with your client:

- The auditor's job is to be a second set of eyes and ask the right questions.
- Establish mutual respect. To be successful, mutual respect must exist between the auditees and auditor. When you find a problem, do not place blame on a specific individual, because the very person you are speaking with could be the one who made the poor decision. Do not insult your client; just stick to the facts. You could say the following: "Based on the information available at the time, it may have looked like an acceptable idea; however, it is time for you to consider…" A good auditor is always respectful of other people and their feelings.

As a former auditee, I always appreciated an auditor who took the time to explain to me what the audit would entail. Please keep in mind that the auditee feels at a disadvantage. It will be helpful to simplify your explanations. You can measure your own performance by the general attitude toward you at the auditee site. You are doing a good job if the client shows interest and is forthcoming with truthful answers.

Understanding Leadership Duties

A good auditor spends time planning and setting priorities before commencing an audit. You will need to make plans on how you will be working with your own team. Develop the leadership style you want to implement. The days of Captain Bligh shouting orders "lest ye be flogged" are gone.

Let's look at the characteristics of good leadership:

- Your leadership style needs to clearly identify when your directions are mandatory and when they are open to feedback and comments. Team members should feel comfortable making comments and asking questions.

- A good leader will develop specific requirements for success and then share those plans. A good leader will strive for the buy-in and cooperation of the staff. You cannot lead those who do not want to be led or those who do not understand the objectives.

- An old and still valuable leadership lesson states that the staff holds the fate of their manager in their hands. The manager will be promoted or disgraced by the performance of their staff. If your people believe the work is good, you will usually get good results. If they do not believe in what you're doing, it will become a failure. Your personal opinion of good or bad is not the pinnacle factor. What matters is what the staff believes. True believers can generate exceptional results. Making time to educate your staff and demonstrating a willingness to take criticism are traits of a good leader.

The audit manager is responsible for creating clearly defined responsibilities and authority. There can be only one boss in order to prevent confusion. It is the responsibility of this one boss to make the hard decisions and answer for the choices made.

A regular schedule of briefings for both the auditee and the audit team are required. All client communication should be vetted before it is shared. *Vetting* is the process of evaluating and editing words to obtain the desired outcome.

Planning and Setting Priorities

Good auditing is the result of proper planning, not magic or luck. Every audit starts with an audit charter or engagement letter. The customer will define the focus and scope of the audit. It is the auditor's responsibility to gather pre-audit information and develop a schedule integrating the audit team functions with the customer's schedule. To be successful, a project management methodology should be used.

Let's look at a few of the auditor's responsibilities during the planning phase:

- Gaining an understanding of the customer's business

- Respecting business cycles (monthly, quarterly, seasonal, and annual)

- Establishing priorities

- Selecting an audit strategy based on risk and information known or observed

- Finding the people for your audit team

- Coordinating the logistics prior to the audit for resources, work space, and facilities

- Requesting documents (discovery requests) *~ see btm of pg 140*
- Scheduling people's time and availability
- Arranging travel and accommodations
- Planning for delays or nonperformance
- Considering rescheduling if recent downtime or risks warrant it
- Developing alternative strategies
- Developing a briefing schedule

> **NOTE** We will be spending a significant amount of time on the subject of audit planning in the next chapter.

A professional auditor provides the auditee with a list of basic requirements and necessary resources well in advance of the audit team arrival.

A good auditor gives plenty of notice as to what they need to perform their job. This includes documentation requests for manuals, policies, and procedures that will be included in the subject of the audit.

> **NOTE** We are astounded by how many times auditors fail to request sufficient desk space and access to IT resources prior to an audit team's arrival.

Providing Standard Terms of Reference

The auditor needs to remain fair and objective when executing an audit. As an auditor, you should be consistent and courteous to your clients. *Standard terms of reference* can be developed to promote respectful and honest interpretation. As an auditor, you should try using the following terms, or something similar:

- Auditee claim/statement   *~ assertions = claims*
- Present
- Not present
- Planned
- Tested (how)
- Not tested (why)
- Observed
- Verified (how)
- Not verified
- New requirement

- Requirement changed
- Requirement cancelled
- Failed to meet requirement
- Resource not available
- Insufficient evidence
- Access denied
- Personnel unavailable
- Lack of time

Dealing with Conflicts and Failures

A good auditor recognizes that some degree of conflict is inevitable and failures are always possible. IS auditors face the challenges of time, money, resources, and attitudes.

These challenges may be with the client or with the auditor. The auditor must always demonstrate professionalism. An exceptional auditor will exercise common sense with a quick response. An exceptional auditor uses past experiences and makes the job look effortless, especially when dealing with change or conflict.

🌐 Real World Scenario

What Exactly Does *Addressed* Mean?

A genuine pet peeve of many practitioners is the term *addressed*. Just what does it mean? Does it mean that we are working on it? Does it mean that we scheduled it for a future meeting and nothing is happening at this time? Does it mean that you wrote down the details and put it in an envelope with the name of the person who should look at it?

Imagine how satisfied a mortgage company would be if you told them your payment has not been made yet, but it's in an envelope and addressed. That envelope is in your pocket, and you intend to mail it someday, but it's been addressed! A more specific explanation is required. Hopefully we can find something better than the word *addressed*.

Identifying the Value of Internal and External Auditors

In this Study Guide, we as authors are often implying an external auditor position. This is intentional in order to emphasize auditor independence. However, substantial opportunities exist for both internal and external auditors.

External auditors are paid to be independent reviewers for an organization. *Internal auditors* can add enormous value to an organization by providing ongoing efforts that help prepare the organization for an external audit. The internal auditor could approach the situation with an attitude of independence even though they will be unable to certify or attest final results. Their expert audit skills could help guide design and remediation efforts at a substantially lower cost than that of their external counterparts.

In the internal auditor position, I would focus my efforts on reducing a four-week external audit to only ten days. Depending on the organization, it may take a few years to reach this noble objective. In the meantime, my auditing services will definitely be adding value to the organization through emphasis and cost reduction. Internal auditors can aid every organization by improving evidence collection.

Understanding the Evidence Rule

The audit world revolves around the collection and review of reliable evidence. Without evidence, a claim or assertion is unverifiable and an auditor cannot separate fact from fiction. Good evidence is intended to substantiate a claim or prove the existence of something you have interest in knowing.

A good auditor will use sufficient evidence to formulate their *auditor's opinion*. No opinion can be formed when you lack evidence of acceptable quantity, relevance, and reliability. Your job is to be a professional skeptic and demand proof in the form of evidence you can verify. The best evidence will need little explanation to interpret. When more judgment is required to understand the evidence, that evidence has decreased value. Your job is to render a score based on the evidence captured during the audit. Having no evidence would warrant a zero score.

Let's suppose you are looking for evidence concerning an existing corporate policy. First, you would look for the policy itself. Is it a paper or electronic document? Documents that cannot be located within a couple of hours could be assumed not to exist. Inability to find the policy would indicate it is not actively used. Now assume the client has found a copy of the policy. Was it easily accessible or covered with dust?

The next step is to verify that you have the current edition. Your audit charter may or may not ask you to review (test) the contents of the policy. Either way, you will need to verify that the policy is actually in use by the client's organization. You might conduct a random survey of workers, asking whether they can show you a current copy of the policy.

Next, you would ask questions to see whether the workers had actually read the document.

It is not uncommon for an auditee to respond that the policy is on their website. You should ask the person to show you the link and open the page. You want to know if the client can successfully demonstrate an ability to find the document.

However, existence of the policy alone does not meet the evidence rule. The auditee's score would improve as more persons demonstrate that they read the document.

Another method would be to look for notes containing the minutes of meetings where the policy was discussed. It is rare for a policy to exist without some form of questions being raised or argued. Challenges to the policy may exist in emails. You may also ask for a person to perform the tasks related to the policy and observe their actions. Direct observation is powerful evidence. Simply ask the client to reperform a task whenever you want to cut to the heart of a claim. The words *show me* can invoke either fear or pride depending on the truth of the situation. Once again, no evidence equals no score.

We will discuss evidence again in Chapter 2.

Identifying Who You Need to Interview

As an IS auditor, it is important for you to be cognizant of whom you should be interviewing, and how long those interviews should take. Every auditor will frequently face a time crunch due to the customer's schedule or other issues. You will need to pay particular attention to the value of the others' time. Consider the work outage created when you take someone out of their job role to spend time with you. Will it be necessary to backfill their position by providing a substitute during this time away?

Think for a moment of what it would cost the organization for a key executive to spend 15 minutes with you. This executive's time may be measured in personal compensation or by the revenue they generate for the organization. Top executives, such as the CEO, will have compensation packages that include both money and substantial shares of stock. Based on total compensation, the CEO may be receiving several thousand dollars per hour or more.

Former Walt Disney CEO Michael Eisner received compensation equal to $27,000 per hour, which was equivalent to approximately .01 percent of the revenue generated under his leadership during the same time period.

The moral is that to justify 15 minutes of somebody's time, you better have something to discuss that is of greater value than his prorated value to the organization (greater than prorated revenue + compensation). Consider the cost for a meeting of high-level executives. You need to ensure that the time spent is relevant and remains focused on the audit objectives. The savvy auditor respects the value of a person's time.

Every system will have an inherent need for controls. The auditor needs to ensure that discussions occur with the correct individuals concerning appropriate controls. Three basic IT-related roles exist for every system: owner, user, and custodian. Table 1.1 shows examples of individuals with their associated roles and responsibilities.

TABLE 1.1   Responsibilities of Data Owner, User, and Custodian

Role	Example	Basic Responsibilities
Data owner	Vice president	Determine classification Specify controls Appoint custodian
Data user	Internal business user Business partner Business client (web)	Follow acceptable usage requirements Maintain security Report violations
Data custodian	Database administrator Production programmer System administrator	Protect information Ensure availability Implement and maintain controls Provide provisions for independent audit Support data users

These individuals don't have to work in the IT department. On the contrary, these roles exist regardless of the individual department boundaries. If someone performs the function, the responsibility of the role applies to that person. No exceptions. If a person performs two roles, two sets of responsibilities apply. If someone performs all three roles, either it's a one-person operation or you need to have a talk about separation of duties and the value of their data.

Understanding the Corporate Organizational Structure

It is always helpful for the auditor to clearly understand the relationships and responsibilities at different levels of an organization. The auditor needs to understand who holds the authority. Let's focus on some basics that will be pervasive throughout this book.

Identifying Roles in a Corporate Organizational Structure

Businesses are focused on generating money for investors. There will always be some type of management hierarchy in order to maintain control. Government and nonprofit organizations will use a similar control hierarchy; however, the titles will be different. For government and nonprofit organizations, the term *mission objectives* would be substituted for the term *revenue*.

Figure 1.4 illustrates a typical business *corporation*. Let's start at the top of the diagram and work our way down:

Board of directors   The board of directors usually comprises key investors and appointed advisers. These individuals have placed their own money at stake in the hopes of generating a better return than the bank would pay on deposits. Board members are rarely—usually never—involved in day-to-day operations. Some members may be retired executives or run their own successful businesses. Their job is to advise the CEO and the CFO. Most organizations indemnify board members from liability; however, government prosecutors will pursue board members if needed.

FIGURE 1.4   A typical business organizational chart

Audit and oversight committee   The members of the board will have a committee comprising directors outside of the normal business operations. Executives from inside the organization can come to the committee for guidance and assistance in solving problems. This committee has full authority over all the officers and executives. They can hire or fire any executive. Each audit committee has full authority with a charter to hire both internal and external auditors. Auditors are expected to discuss their work with the audit committee. An auditor has the right to meet in private to discuss issues with the audit committee once a year without the business executives present. If auditors discover certain matters that stockholders should be informed about, the auditor shall first bring it to the attention of the audit committee. Regulations such as SOX require that all significant weaknesses be disclosed to the audit committee every 90 days.

Chief executive officer (CEO)   The CEO is primarily focused on generating revenue for the organization. The CEO's role is to set the direction and strategy for the organization to follow. The CEO's job is to find out how to attract buyers while increasing the company's profits. As a company officer, the CEO is liable to government prosecutors. Corporate officers have signing authority to bind the organization.

Chief operating officer (COO)   The COO is dedicated to increasing the revenue generated by the business. This is a delegate in charge of making decisions on behalf of the CEO with assistance from the CFO. COOs are often found in larger organizations. As a company officer, the COO is liable to government prosecutors.

Chief financial officer (CFO)   The CFO is in charge of controls over capital and other areas, including financial accounting, human resources, and IS. Subordinates such as the CIO usually report to the CFO. As a company officer, the CFO is liable to government prosecutors.

Chief information officer (CIO)   The CIO is subordinate to the CFO. The CFO is still considered the primary person responsible for internal control. A CIO might not be a true company officer, and this title may bear more honor than actual authority, depending on the organization. An exception may be the CIO in the corporate headquarters. The CIO has mixed liability, depending on the issue and their actual position in the organization.

President/general manager   The president, sometimes referred to as the general manager, is the head of a business unit or division. As a company officer, the president/general manager is usually liable to government prosecutors. Regulations such as SOX encourage management to require all divisional presidents and controllers to sign the integrity statements in an effort to increase divisional officer liability.

Vice president (VP)   The vice president is the second level of officer in a business unit or division. As a company officer, the vice president is usually liable to government prosecutors.

Department directors (line management position)   Typically directors are upper-level managers supervising department managers and do not have company officer authority. In large organizations, you may encounter a major-level director and minor-level director.

Managers and staff workers   Managers are responsible for providing daily supervision and guidance to staff members. Staff members may be employees or contractors working in the staff role. Managers and staff members are seldom held responsible for the actions of a company unless they knowingly participate in criminal activity.

Identifying Roles in a Consulting Firm Organizational Structure

Now we will look at the structure of a typical consulting firm. A *consulting firm* is a hybrid organization. Internal clerical and support functions are similar to those in a typical business. The consulting side of the firm uses functional management positions. The staff is allocated according to temporary project assignments. At the end of each engagement, the staff will be reallocated by either returning to the available resource pool or by becoming unemployed until the next engagement.

Figure 1.5 illustrates the organizational structure of a typical audit firm. We'll review the structure here:

FIGURE 1.5   A typical auditing firm organizational chart

Managing partner   A managing partner refers to a C-level executive in the consulting practice. This could be a position equal to a corporate president. Managing partners have the responsibility and authority to oversee the business divisions. Various partners in the firm will report to the managing partner.

Partner   A partner is equivalent to a divisional president or vice president and is responsible for generating revenue. Their role is to represent the organization and provide leadership to maximize income in their market segment. Partners are required to maintain leadership roles in professional organizations and to network for executive clients. Most partners have made financial commitments to produce at least $15 million in annual revenue along with supporting other business management functions. The partner and all lower managers are responsible for professional development of the staff.

Engagement manager   This is a director-equivalent position with the responsibility of managing the client relationship. The engagement manager is in charge of the audit's overall execution and the audit staff. The engagement manager is responsible for facilitating the generation of new income opportunities from the client.

Senior consultant   This is a field manager whose responsibilities include leading the daily on-site audit activities, interacting with the client staff, making expert observations, and managing staff assigned to the audit.

Consultant   This is a lead position carrying the responsibility of interacting with the client and fulfilling the audit objectives without requiring constant supervision. A consultant is often promoted by demonstrating an ability to fulfill the job of senior consultant or supporting manager.

Systems analyst   This is usually an entry-level position. Often the individual is selected for their ambition and educational background and may be fresh out of college. Systems analysts perform some lower-level administrative tasks as they build experience.

Managing Projects

A typical IS audit has many elements in common with projects and project management. We believe that the two disciplines go hand in hand. To excel in auditing, you must excel at project management. Through project management, you define what you strive to accomplish and the actions that will be taken as part of the project.

> During our careers, we have worked with organizations using each of the different models for managing projects and quality. The project models are used for unique events or to refresh quality-control programs. The quality-control programs require every person in the organization to be trained and participate in support of every quality effort. Projects are typically run with less overhead, using smaller groups of people focused on a particular goal.

Table 1.2 shows the most common models for either managing projects or ensuring quality.

TABLE 1.2   Project Management and Quality-Control Models

Source	Focus	Structure
Project Management Institute (PMI)	Projects (international) Unique or repeating for everyone	44 process areas Well defined, especially initiating solid projects
Prince2	Projects (UK) Unique or repeating for the British government	9 process areas Less defined than PMI
Total Quality Management (TQM)	Quality control Repeating process control	Zero defects program Statistical process control Invented by William Shewhart (1930) and better known from works by Phillip Crosby and Edwards Deming

TABLE 1.2   Project Management and Quality-Control Models *(continued)*

Source	Focus	Structure
Six Sigma	Quality control Repeating process control	Reduce defects from 16,000 to 3.4 per million Motorola derivative of TQM for widget-type mass production.
ISO 9001	Quality control Repeating process control	Revision of ISO 9000 quality standards International derivative of TQM

The Project Management Institute (PMI) is one organization that stands above all others for defining project management and commercial project management processes.

PMI has created a definitive standard for managing projects. This standard is called *A Guide to the Project Management Body of Knowledge (PMBOK)*, detailing a complete process framework and recipe for successfully managing a project. The first version was published in 1987. This guide is now updated every four years. The third edition was released in 2004, with a revised fourth edition expected in 2008. The PMBOK provides project managers a framework of processes to professionally manage both large and small projects.

In this section, you will learn some basic information about using the *PMBOK* standard to help you manage your audit. It would be a very good idea to acquire additional knowledge about project management and how to manage specialized projects. We suggest two sources for additional information:

- CertTest Training Center (`www.certtest.com`)—the company we work for—for training courses in project management. CertTest is a PMI global Registered Education Provider (REP). In addition to CISA training, we teach people how to become exceptional project managers.

- PMI (`www.pmi.org`) for additional information about the project management standard, ordering copies of the *PMBOK*, or information about becoming a certified Project Management Professional (PMP).

What Is a Project?

The purpose of a *project* is to create a better result than would naturally occur. If you have so much money that you can just write a check for whatever you want, that would not be a project, only an expense. The purpose of a project is to help overcome the limitations of time, resources, and quality. All projects have three characteristics that define it as a project rather than a perpetual ongoing program.

A project is temporary.   The project has a defined start (beginning) and a definite end (stop). The project is *not* an ongoing operation of the company. It lasts for only a specific time period.

A project is unique.   All projects are run for a unique purpose. The project will create a product or service with unique characteristics. It may be used to fix something broken or to add new features.

A project is progressively elaborated.   The project starts out with simple high-level ideas that are polished and becomes defined into more and more detail during planning. Each successive version of the plan adds details about the definition of work and the purpose. Interrelated processes are used to further define and control the project.

Let's discuss each of these project characteristics as they relate to auditing:

What defines a project as temporary?   Your project must have a start date and an end date. For example, SOX requires the organization to report their status of internal controls on an annual basis with their annual financial filings. The SOX regulation also requires weaknesses to be assessed and disclosed to the organization's audit committee every 90 days (quarterly). Performing multiple internal security control audits in multiple departments over the calendar year is an ongoing business operation, yet each individual audit is a separate entity with separate definitions (scope) and goals. The individual audits with specific scope are projects.

Each little audit project adds up to create the overall compliance program.

What defines your project as unique?   You are probably using the same processes and similar procedures for each audit. Auditing a new functional area that has never been audited before will have unique goals or outcomes. This is certainly a project. Performing the audit again next year will have to include changes to match the differences in the environment since last year. Its evolutionary successor audit is a unique project as well. Each audit uses similar processes and has similar goals, but the data, new tests, samples, and outcome will be unique. It never fails that the software version or the people involved have changed since the last time. You will be revising your plans before each audit.

Projects are always unique events of limited duration. Programs are simply a series of smaller projects tied together to keep things running.

How do we define *progressively elaborated*?   The *PMBOK* defines 5 major process groups and 44 specialized processes for managing a project. These processes take a project from a high-level vision down into more and more detail to create your final product. The processes flow from one process to the next and act as a framework to guide proper definition with built-in control.

All of the processes interrelate to manage your efforts and to generate the final outcome. PMI set forth standards of planning that will help you convert a good idea into a deliverable product. It is not a magic spell that converts a bad idea or poor decisions into a good product.

Let's apply this to an example for auditing. The first step of a project is to get a signed <u>project charter.</u> The project charter is signed by the client sponsor to give the project manager responsibility, authority, and accountability for the project (exactly the same as an audit charter). This charter authorizes the project and provides the money necessary to begin.

Next you use the project charter as input for developing your <u>preliminary scope statement.</u> Your preliminary scope statement adds more details to describe the high-level project activities. You will use this as input (along with the project charter) to create a <u>scope plan.</u> In scope planning, you further define how the scope will be controlled—with a scope management plan.

You continue to use the information in the previous documents as more input for the <u>Scope Definition</u> process. The objective is to elaborate and document the total scope of the project in the final scope statement. After the scope is complete, you can move down into more and more detailed planning. It may seem like a lot of work, but this is the best way to cut through politics. Besides, good planning with clear definition is the way you avoid stupid mistakes. It's impossible to delegate work when people don't agree on what the work entails. The better your planning definition, the more likely you will get to actually enjoy a peaceful vacation or day off.

We can relate this portion of the process to a security audit: getting authorization to audit (*project charter*), defining a high-level need (*preliminary project scope*), planning how to handle change to the audit scope (*scope planning*), and then setting the goals and objectives as well as documenting all items to be audited (*scope definition*).

This describes just the first four processes and their relationship. There are 40 more processes available to help us make every project a success.

What Is Project Management?

Project management is defined in the *PMBOK* as the application of knowledge, skills, tools, and techniques to perform the activities needed by your project requirements. A good project manager will use their knowledge of the subject, their knowledge of project management, and all available processes to fulfill the goals of their project.

A simple definition of project management is to balance competing demands. These demands are referred to as the *triple constraint*. We can define them as competing values of

- Scope
- Resources (cost, time)
- Quality

Think about it: Could you ever satisfy all the items on your to-do list within the budget and available time? Maybe if the scope is small or you win the lottery. Could you finish the project in the time allotted and not fulfill all the to-dos? What effect will time or scope have on your project's objective? Managing competing demands determines whether a security audit is complete when it is due or when all necessary items have been properly audited. The project scope document will help you defend your decision. Project managers and audit managers will have to work with multiple stakeholders while managing the project and the competing demands. *Stakeholders* are defined as anyone with viable interest in the project. Stakeholders can be above the project manager in the organization, below the project manager, or peers. Stakeholders can also be outside the organization.

It is stressed that the project manager should concentrate on the defined scope of the project. Our motto is that "all the scope and only the scope" should be done. Sometimes the project manager will be required to make difficult decisions to balance the competing demands of scope, time, and cost. This will require negotiation skills or leadership skills to "sell" an unpopular decision.

> The CISA exam will expect you to understand project management. You need to be prepared to explain project management terminology and objectives. As practitioners, we have found that the PMI reference information provides an excellent fit in the audit world.

Identifying the Requirements of a Project Manager

A project manager must have several levels of knowledge and skills to be successful:

- Project management knowledge and skills. (Know how to lead and control projects.)
- General management knowledge and skills. (Understand the business details.)
- Interpersonal skills. (Be nice yet convince people to agree.)
- Application area knowledge and skills. (Know how this darn thing actually works.)

Without all of these elements, the project manager has problems leading to an unsuccessful end. Many times we need some form of "expert judgment" to define our needs. The problem is compounded by a misunderstanding of who is qualified to be an expert.

> Real experts will have more experience than anyone else, or special training with direct experience. A real expert will form the correct conclusion when others will not. For example, Burt Rutan could be considered an expert on building low-cost spacecraft because of his direct experience in successfully developing the SpaceShipOne reusable fiberglass spacecraft. He is the winner of the scientific industry Ansari X Prize, as the first commercial venture to successfully launch a privately owned, manned spacecraft into orbit and return safely back to earth.

Without specialized application knowledge and skills, the project manager would not know what specific requirements were needed or specific tasks must be accomplished to fulfill the project goals.

To translate this into controls auditing, the auditor must have the following:

- Security auditing skills (and certification)
- Specialized application knowledge of the company processes and procedures
- Specialized application knowledge of the functional area being audited

- General management knowledge and skills
- Interpersonal skills

Identifying a Project Manager's Authority

Project managers are not created equal. Their level of authority and influence is dictated by the organizational structure and culture. The same issues exist in managing the audit as would exist when clients are managing their own projects.

Table 1.3 demonstrates the basic differences among management structures and cultures. Every auditor needs to understand the advantages and disadvantages of each.

TABLE 1.3   Differences in Project Manager Authority and Organizational Structure

Organization Type	Advantages	Disadvantages
Functional (Weak matrix)	Functional manager remains in charge. Project manager has no real authority. Good for recurring operations-oriented projects in which change is very small.	Project manager has no formal authority. Project manager is a low-level staff function that needs to beg for resources or rely on personal influence. Common titles are project leader, coordinator, or expediter.
Balanced matrix	Project manager shares authority with functional managers. Staff members are dedicated to the project manager. Functional department manager provides HR support and paychecks. Allows for efficiency in resource use.	Project manager and functional manager usually wind up arguing over resources. Without clear direction, team members may feel torn between two bosses.
Projectized (Strong matrix)	Project manager holds formal authority and has the ability to decide project direction with little second guessing or interference. Authority level improves team dynamic and communications.	Project manager's success or failure is based on project results. This encourages hoarding of resources with competition toward other groups. Jobs in the project will end upon project completion. Expect a lack of focus toward the end as people search for employment.

Understanding the Project Management Process Framework

The PMI standard for project management as defined in the *PMBOK* is intended to be applied to all sorts of projects in all sorts of environments. The project manager may use all or some of the processes along with their inputs, tools, and techniques, and outputs for the project they are managing. The use of these processes is need based. The PMI processes provide an excellent checklist to prevent errors and omissions in the project management of any specific project.

As previously stated, we look upon the PMI standard as a framework for project management. You and your company define specific specialized processes and procedures to be used for project management within your enterprise. PMI provides this standard for you to measure your internal processes against.

The *PMBOK* provides a reference for defining the project life cycle. Your organization may decide to modify this life cycle to meet the unique challenges facing your needs. There is also specific definition of a project phase. Consider that each phase:

- Is defined by the organization
- Is part of the life cycle
- Is a subset of the overall project
- Has a measurable deliverable
- Ends with a review

PMI places the project management framework as defined in the *PMBOK* into the specialized life cycle and phases that are defined by the organization. The *PMBOK* focuses on process groups, processes, inputs to processes, tools and techniques used in processes, and outputs from processes.

A simple outline of this framework would look something like this:

```
 –  Project life cycle          (as defined by the organization)

    o  Phases                   (as defined by project need)

       ▲ Process groups         (initiate, plan, execute, control)
        · Processes             (procedures)
         o  Inputs              (requirement date)
         o  Tools               (technique or formula)
         o  Outputs             (reports)

           ▲ Actions or tasks   (unique to project)
```

The five process groups as defined by PMI are as follows:

- Initiating
- Planning
- Executing
- Monitoring and Controlling
- Closing

Each process group has a general function and contains processes that have specific functions to be accomplished. The process groups are interdependent; changes made in one process group can generate cascading change into another group. Each process group performs the functions indicated by its name:

Initiating   This process group begins the project or a phase of the project. This group contains two processes. One component sets the scope; the second component authorizes the project to begin.

Planning   This process group contains almost half of the 44 processes. Planning is where the project scope, goals, and objectives are detailed.

Executing   The largest portion of resources is used during executing activities. The processes within this group are used to create the project deliverables.

Monitoring and Controlling   This is where you control the project. These 12 processes are used to measure performance and control changes. Examples include review meetings, dealing with substitutions, and schedule changes. You might fire a vendor and hire a replacement.

Closing   When a phase or the project is completed, this process group will pay vendors and put the files in an archive to close out the project.

PMI defines 44 processes that fit into these 5 process groups. As the project runs, changes will be discovered that create a revision in the planning and execution phases. Figure 1.6 illustrates the relationship of each process group.

FIGURE 1.6   Relationship of process groups

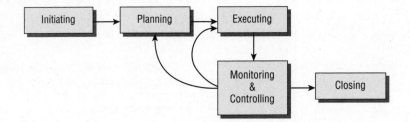

Changes in scope or poor results will force the project manager to loop backward to the sponsor from the initiation phase. Sometimes a project exceeds the scope or needs revision before it can continue. Your sponsor may help or decide to cancel it.

Applied Project Management Quick Reference

The following information is a quick reference describing the knowledge areas and associated processes. You'll learn where each process fits in to a process group, the actions taken in the process, and the main output or result from the process.

For further reference, refer to *A Guide to the Project Management Body of Knowledge* (current edition).

Project Integration Management

Project Integration Management is the knowledge area containing processes that tie all of the other processes together. Each process can feed iterative changes into the next process. This is why project management is referred to as an *iterative management process*. A change in scope or deadlines, for example, will trigger changes throughout the entire plan. As a result, each process would need to be updated to remain synchronized. Therefore, another iteration of the plan is created.

Table 1.4 shows the various processes of the Project Integration Management knowledge area.

TABLE 1.4   The Project Integration Management Processes

Process	Process Group	Action Taken	Main Output
Develop Project Charter	Initiating	Documenting intent of project and obtaining approval	Project charter
Develop Preliminary Scope Statement	Initiating	Elaborating project definition	Scope statement
Develop Project Management Plan	Planning	Combining all of the other project outputs into one collection of documents that defines the project	Project management plan
Direct and Manage Project Execution	Executing	Obtaining work results and identifying changes	Deliverables
Monitor and Control Project Work	Monitoring and Controlling	Identifying actions required to create work results	Recommended corrective actions, change requests
Integrated Change Control	Monitoring and Controlling	Updating project definition	Approved change requests
Close Project	Closing	Obtain final approvals	Project archives

Project Scope Management

Project Scope Management contains processes that define the product created by the project and the work to be performed on the project. During this process, a structure is created that breaks each task into itemized details of work to be performed. This is an excellent method for defining your audit plans to get better funding with higher sponsor satisfaction.

Table 1.5 shows the various processes of the Project Scope Management knowledge area.

TABLE 1.5   The Project Scope Management Processes

Process	Process Group	Action Taken	Main Output
Scope Planning	Planning	Documenting intent of project to define the scope	Scope management plan
Scope Definition	Planning	Elaborating preliminary project scope statement	Scope statement *Statement of Work*
Create Work Breakdown Structure (WBS)	Planning	Decomposing the scope statement into a work breakdown structure	Work breakdown structure and dictionary
Scope Verification	Monitoring and Controlling	Obtaining work results and acceptance of work	Accepted deliverables
Scope Control	Monitoring and Controlling	Identifying changes to project scope	Project scope updates

Project Time Management

Project Time Management contains processes that define and control the activities required to complete the project as well as resources for the project. In this knowledge area, the project manager defines the baseline schedule for the project. You can use this to organize your audit activities into a high-impact plan.

Table 1.6 shows the various processes of the Project Time Management knowledge area.

TABLE 1.6   Project Time Management Processes

Process	Process Group	Action Taken	Main Output
Activity Definition	Planning	Decomposing WBS to create an activity list	Activity list
Activity Sequencing	Planning	Identifying interactivity in logical relationships	Network diagrams (PERT or Gantt chart)
Activity Resource Estimating	Planning	Determining resource requirements for activities	Resource requirements

TABLE 1.6   Project Time Management Processes *(continued)*

Process	Process Group	Action Taken	Main Output
Activity Duration Estimating	Planning	Estimating a time duration for each task	Activity duration estimates
Schedule Development	Planning	Calendaring activity durations and sequences	Project schedule
Schedule Control	Monitoring and Controlling	Identifying schedule changes and variances	Schedule updates

Project Cost Management

Project Cost Management comprises three processes that define, specify, and control costs for the project. This knowledge area uses earned value technique to measure cost performance for the project. *Earned value (EV)* is the current value of work that has been performed in the project.   *see pg 43*

Table 1.7 shows the various processes of the Project Cost Management knowledge area.

TABLE 1.7   Project Cost Management Processes

Process	Process Group	Action Taken	Main Output
Cost Estimating	Planning	Using task estimates and resource estimates to create a cost estimate	Cost estimate
Cost Budgeting	Planning	Assigning cost estimates to work packages (from WBS)	Cost baseline
Cost Control	Monitoring and Controlling	Identifying changes and variances to baseline	Budget updates

Project Quality Management

Quality is just as relevant in audit planning as it is in manufacturing. The *Project Quality Management* knowledge area comprises three processes that define the level of quality applied to the project's product and performance. Project team members audit the performance of their project. Next, the product created by the project is inspected for conformance to the design objectives. Inspection tests determine whether the product created will live up to its intended fitness for use. Any necessary changes are cycled into plan revisions. The entire process repeats until the product is acceptable or the project ends.

Table 1.8 shows the various processes of the Project Quality Management knowledge area.

TABLE 1.8   Project Quality Management Processes

Process	Process Group	Action Taken	Main Output
Quality Planning (plan, design)	Planning	Documenting intent of project and product quality	Quality management plan
Perform Quality Assurance (do, monitor)	Executing	Performing project audits to determine project quality	Quality improvement
Perform Quality Control (check, act)	Monitoring and Controlling	Inspecting outputs to ascertain quality	Acceptance or rejection of work results

We will cover the complete quality model of Plan, Do, Check, Act (PDCA) in Chapter 2, "Audit Process".

Project Human Resource Management

Project Human Resource Management facilitates planning the organizational structure, job roles, specific responsibilities, and acquisition of staff for the project. This is the best technique to get the skilled people needed for your project. Use the work breakdown structure (WBS) from scope management planning to build a *skills matrix*. The skills matrix documents special skills needed to perform each task. This technique can eliminate problems of being assigned an unskilled person who is simply a "warm body" on your team. Unskilled team members create an undesirable drain of valuable project money.

 A comprehensive staff management plan is a key tool for managing resources and controlling project costs and schedules. A skills matrix is required for audit projects.

Table 1.9 shows the various processes of the Project Human Resource Management knowledge area.

TABLE 1.9   Project Human Resource Management Processes

Process	Process Group	Action Taken	Main Output
Human Resource Planning	Planning	Determining human resources required to complete the project	Roles and responsibilities, skills matrix

TABLE 1.9   Project Human Resource Management Processes *(continued)*

Process	Process Group	Action Taken	Main Output
Acquire Project Team	Executing	Negotiating or procuring staff	Project staff
Develop Project Team	Executing	Developing team competency, training	Performance improvement
Manage Project Team	Monitoring and Controlling	Obtaining work results and identifying corrective actions	Change requests, corrective action

Project Communications Management

Project Communications Management defines the communications needs of the project stakeholders, and then facilitates and controls communications distribution during the life of the project. Audit projects need this level of planning to clarify what is discussed or reported to our stakeholders. Consider the different conversational needs to communicate with our auditees, clients, and our own audit team members. A calculation of EV is used to show stakeholders the value of work performed in the project. EV provides a financial measurement of the value created to date.

Table 1.10 shows the various processes of the Project Communications Management knowledge area.

TABLE 1.10   Project Communications Management Processes

Process	Process Group	Action Taken	Main Output
Communications Planning	Planning	Documenting communications needs of project stakeholders	Communications management plan
Information Distribution	Executing	Sending out info as per plan	Project records
Performance Reporting	Monitoring and Controlling	Measuring performance using EV	Performance reports
Manage Stakeholders	Monitoring and Controlling	Managing stakeholder communication	Resolved issues

Project Risk Management

Project Risk Management comprises six processes that define the risk methods to be used, define the risks of the project, analyze the risks, and document responses to identified risks. Through these processes, managing the risk becomes a high priority for the project and remains in the forefront of project activities.

Table 1.11 shows the various processes of the Project Risk Management knowledge area.

TABLE 1.11   Project Risk Management Processes

Process	Process Groups	Action Taken	Main Output
Risk Management Planning	Planning	Documenting intent of project regarding risk management	Risk management plan
Risk Identification	Planning	Reviewing project to identify risks	Risk register
Qualitative Risk Analysis	Planning	Analyzing risk impacts and probabilities	Risk register updates
Quantitative Risk Analysis	Planning	Analyzing risks numerically to predict outcomes	Risk register updates
Risk Response Planning	Planning	Identifying actions to respond to prioritized risks	Risk register updates
Risk Monitoring and Control	Monitoring and Controlling	Monitoring for identified risks and symptoms, looking for new risks	Risk register updates

Risk management is an area of major focus during the audit planning process described in Chapter 2.

Project Procurement Management

Project Procurement Management defines the processes that are required to purchase resources. All projects need to procure people, equipment, and materials from outside the organization. Advance planning in procurement creates an orderly, documented method for contracting with vendors. Special handling procedures need to be honored in the bid process as well as in government-awarded projects. Mishandling will create legal problems.

Table 1.12 shows the various processes of the Project Procurement Management knowledge area.

TABLE 1.12   Project Procurement Management Processes

Process	Process Groups	Action Taken	Main Output
Plan Purchases and Acquisitions	Planning	Deciding whether to make or purchase.	Procurement management plan
Plan Contracting	Planning	Determining type of procurement document. Decision 1: Offer fixed price, cost reimbursable, or time and material. Decision 2: Use request for proposal (RFP), request for information (RFI), or invitation to tender (ITT). Controlling communications and visitation with bidders to prevent accusation of bias.	Procurement documents
Request Seller Responses	Executing	Sending out procurement documents, holding bidders conferences.	Procurement packages
Select Sellers	Executing	Negotiating a contract.	Signed contract
Contract Administration	Monitoring and Controlling	Managing sellers work.	Contract documentation
Contract Closure	Closing	Giving seller formal acceptance.	Closed contract

Using Project Management Diagramming Techniques

Effective project management requires a significant level of communication and integration. Two of the more common diagramming techniques include Gantt charts and PERT network diagrams. All projects have a critical path of tasks. This *critical path* represents the minimum steps necessary to complete a successful project. This path is the longest route in the diagram and the shortest time estimate for project completion

Gantt charts (see Figure 1.7) are used to schedule and sequence activities in a waterfall-type representation. Planned activities are shown flowing downward to completion. The figure shows both sequential and concurrent activities in a linear bar-chart-style presentation. Milestones will be identified and progress reported against planned activities. Gantt charts are more simplistic than PERT diagrams. In a typical Gantt chart, the bars show tasks, and diamond symbols indicate milestones. The long, dark overhead bars depict a phase or a section of the schedule. Unfortunately, Gantt charts fail to illustrate the relationships between activities and the most important activities (critical path). Only an idiot would try to manage projects by using a Gantt chart without the critical path clearly identified. To be successful, every Gantt chart should have a matching PERT chart in use.

Program Evaluation Review Technique

Real World Scenario

Why Is This Important?

Managing projects can become complex and exceed the ability of some individuals. The goal of the project management framework is to ensure proper control during the project life cycle. An organization will be able to avoid costly mistakes by understanding and following these techniques.

Proper training will improve a person's understanding of the project management process. The next goal after training is to obtain proficiency. You can achieve proficiency by practicing the process. CISAs should exercise every opportunity to improve their skills and proficiency in project management.

We strongly advise every IS auditor to update their project management skills because major changes are added every three to four years. Your success in auditing is directly related to your ability to manage projects. It will help you advance in your career.

The better projects are run by a PERT chart. Gantt charting makes it look like all the tasks are going to be accomplished, usually in a serial sequence. In reality, the tasks outside of the PERT's critical path may be eliminated from the project.

FIGURE 1.7   A Gantt chart

CISA 2006 Guide

ID	Task Name	Week 1	Week 2	Week 3
1	**MDPM Project**			
2	Discovery Phase			
3	*Document scope*	Project Mgr		
4	*Create functional process map*	1/3		
5	*Review competitive offerings*		Marketing Mgr	
6	*Create initial marketing plan*			MM
7	Design Phase			
8	*Finalize equipment requirement*			
9	*Procure hardware and software*		OM, AM	
10	*Revise operation plan as required*		OM	
11	Development Phase			
12	*Receive and test hardware*	OM		
13	*Install office infrastructure*		AM	
14	*Test operations plan*		1/8	
15	Deployment PhaseID			

Program Evaluation Review Technique (PERT) is used to illustrate the relationship between planned activities (see Figure 1.8). PERT diagramming shows multiple routes through the project activities, as necessary for accomplishing the goal. PERT has two major advantages. First is the ability to demonstrate a critical path. The second advantage is that PERT provides a quantitative measurement tool for risk analysis. It can help measure the risk of delays, failure, and likely completion. The most successful project managers use both Gantt and PERT—Gantt to display resource detail, and PERT to show the current and most up-to-date critical path.

FIGURE 1.8   A PERT diagram

ES = Early Start
EF = Early Finish
LS = Late Start
LF = Late Finish

You can use the critical path method for planning your audit. This is an excellent technique to show your sponsor the effects of any changes or delays in your project activities:

1. Make a list of all your planned activities.

2. Group the related activities into boxes.

3. Calculate the duration of each activity by using three estimates (optimistic, most likely, pessimistic).

4. Pick the most important activity boxes, and then use arrows to construct a sequence diagram.

5. Adjust your plans to fit the available time. If your plans don't fit, request a change in scope.

Beginners in project management will often use Microsoft Project to build project plans with primitive Gantt charts. Unfortunately, it is almost impossible to persuade sponsors by using Gantt reports because of the report's serial nature and lack of dependency analysis. PERT analysis is the best method to show the effect of dependencies with quantitative measurement. Advanced project managers use software such as that from Primavera Systems, which provides fabulous reporting features not found in MS Project. If you are an MS Project user, your best chance of survival is to use a PERT reporting add-in such as PERT chart Expert from Critical Tools. This nifty tool will automatically create several of the basic PERT reports using your MS Project activity list.

Summary

In this chapter, we covered the pervasive foundation of knowledge necessary for you to be a successful IS auditor. Our goal is to provide basic auditor knowledge to help guide your decisions. The secret of a successful auditor is to understand who to believe and their motivation. A successful IS auditor will follow industry-accepted practices while dealing with conflict and change in a manner that generates admiration from their clients. It is your responsibility as an IS auditor to demonstrate effective leadership skills in the pursuit of your work. A good leader will take control of the situation to direct all effort toward fulfilling the desired objective.

In the next chapter, we will discuss the audit process in detail.

Exam Essentials

Know the purpose of policies, standards, guidelines, and procedures.   Policies are high-level objectives designated by a person of authority, and compliance to policies is mandatory. Standards ensure a minimum level of uniform compliance to a policy, and compliance to standards is mandatory. Guidelines advise with preferred objectives and useful information in the absence of a standard. Guidelines are often discretionary. Procedures are a cookbook recipe of specific tasks necessary to implement a standard. Compliance to procedures is mandatory.

Know the ISACA standards governing professional conduct and ethics.   The auditor is expected to perform with the highest level of concern and diligence. Each audit should be conducted in accordance with professional standards and objectivity, and should implement best practices.

Understand the general purpose of the audit and the role of the IS auditor.   The purpose of auditing is to challenge the assertions of management and to determine whether evidence will support management's claims.

Understand an audit role versus a nonaudit role.   There are only two roles in an audit. The first role is that of the auditor who performs an objective review, and the second is the role of everyone else. A person cannot be an auditor and also involved in the design or operation of the audit subject.

Understand the importance of IS auditor independence.   It is unlikely that an auditor could be truly independent if the auditor were involved with the subject of the audit. Auditor independence is an additional assurance of truth.

Know the difference between discretionary and mandatory language.   In regulatory language, the word *shall* designates a mandatory requirement. The word *shall* indicates that there is no excuse for failing to meet the stated objective, even if compliance would cause a financial loss. The word *should* indicates a recommendation that could be optional, depending on the circumstance.

Know the different types of audits.   The types of audit are financial, operational (SAS-70), integrated (SAS-94), compliance, administrative, and information systems.

Understand the importance of IS auditor confidentiality.   The IS auditor shall maintain confidentiality at all times to protect the client. Sensitive information should not be revealed at any time. Your client expects you to protect their secrets whenever legally possible.

Understand the need to protect audit documentation.   The data must be protected with access controls and regular backup. Sensitive information is the property of the owner, and its confidentiality shall be protected by the auditor. A document archive is created during the audit and is subject to laws governing record retention.

Know how to use standard terms of reference.   The auditor should communicate by using standardized terms of reference to avoid misunderstanding or confusion. The standard terminology should be defined through a mutual agreement at the beginning of the audit.

Understand application of the evidence rule.   Audit evidence needs to be confirmed or verified to ensure that it is actually used in the production process.

Identify who the auditor may need to interview.   The IS auditor needs to consider the roles of data owner, data user, and data custodian when selecting persons to interview. Data owners specify controls, data users are to follow acceptable usage requirements, and custodians protect the information while supporting data users.

Understand the organizational structure.   Officers of an organization are usually persons with the title of vice president or higher, up to the board of directors. Department directors, managers, and staff workers are seldom liable for the organization, unless criminal activity is involved.

Understand how to manage projects, including the audit project.   The IS auditor is expected to manage audit projects and be cognizant of project management techniques. The auditor is expected to be competent in evaluating the client's management of projects. Every project contains the three competing values of scope, cost, and time. A project manager in the projectized, or strong matrix, organization has more authority than a project manager in a weak matrix, or functional, organization.

Review Questions

1. What is the difference between a policy and a procedure?

   A. Compliance to a policy is discretionary, and compliance to a procedure is mandatory.

   B. A procedure provides discretionary advice to aid in decision making. The policy defines specific requirements to ensure compliance.

   C. A policy is a high-level document signed by a person of authority, and compliance is mandatory. A procedure defines the mandatory steps to attain compliance.

   D. A policy is a mid-level document issued to advise the reader of desired actions in the absence of a standard. The procedure describes suggested steps to use.

2. Which of the following in a business organization will be held liable by the government for failures of internal controls?

   A. President, vice presidents, and other true corporate officers

   B. Board of directors, president, vice presidents, department directors, and managers

   C. All members of management

   D. Board of directors, CEO, CFO, CIO, and department directors

3. What does *fiduciary responsibility* mean?

   A. To use information gained for personal interests without breaching confidentiality of the client.

   B. To act for the benefit of another person and place the responsibilities to be fair and honest ahead of your own interest.

   C. To follow the desires of the client and maintain total confidentiality even if illegal acts are discovered. The auditor shall never disclose information from an audit in order to protect the client.

   D. None of the above.

4. What are the different types of audits?

   A. Forensic, accounting, verification, regulatory

   B. Integrated, operational, compliance, administrative

   C. Financial, SAS-74, compliance, administrative

   D. Information systems, SAS-70, regulatory, procedural

5. What is the difference between the word *should* and *shall* when used in regulations?

   A. *Shall* represents discretionary requirements, and *should* provides advice to the reader.

   B. *Should* indicates mandatory actions, whereas *shall* provides advisory information recommending actions when appropriate

   C. *Should* and *shall* are comparable in meaning. The difference is based on the individual circumstances faced by the audit.

   D. *Should* indicates actions that are discretionary according to need, whereas *shall* means the action is mandatory regardless of financial impact.

6. Highest authority for a project manager is in the _____ organizational structure.

pg 36

    A. Projectized

    B. Functional

    C. Cross-functional matrix

    D. Business corporation

7. Which of the following is *not* defined as a nonaudit role?

    A. System designer

    B. Operational staff member

    C. Auditor

    D. Organizational manager

8. Why is it necessary to protect audit documentation and work papers?

    A. The evidence gathered in an audit must be disclosed for regulatory compliance.

    B. A paper trail is necessary to prove the auditor is right and the auditee is wrong.

    C. The auditor will have to prove illegal activity in a court of law.

    D. Audit documentation work papers may reveal confidential information that should not be lost or disclosed.

9. Which of the following is a network diagram that shows the critical path for a project?

    A. Program Evaluation Review Technique *PERT chart*

    B. Gantt chart with activity sequencing

    C. Shortest Path Diagramming Technique

    D. Milestone reporting

10. What is the purpose of standard terms of reference?

    A. To meet the legal requirement of regulatory compliance

    B. To prove who is responsible

    C. To ensure honest and unbiased communication *clear, consistent, standards*

    D. To ensure that requirements are clearly identified in a regulation

11. What does the term *auditor independence* relate to?

    A. It is not an issue for auditors working for a consulting company.

    B. It is required for an external audit.

    C. An internal auditor must undergo certification training to be independent.

    D. The audit committee bestows independence upon the auditor.

12. Which of the following is true concerning the roles of data owner, data user, and data custodian?

    A. The data user implements controls as necessary.

    B. The data custodian is responsible for specifying acceptable usage.

    C. The data owner specifies controls.

    D. The data custodian specifies security classification.

13. What is the definition of a *work breakdown structure*?

    A. A detailed staffing plan

    B. Sequence of steps with milestones in support of the project scope

    C. The levels of authority delegated by the project manager

    D. Decomposition of tasks

14. What is the definition of a *standard* as compared to a *guideline*?

    A. Standards are discretionary controls used with guidelines to aid the reader's decision process.

    B. Standards are mandatory controls designed to support a policy. Following guidelines is discretionary.

    C. Guidelines are recommended controls necessary to support standards, which are discretionary.

    D. Guidelines are intended to designate a policy, whereas standards are used in the absence of a policy.

15. Who should issue the organizational policies?

    A. Policies should originate from the bottom and move up to the department manager for approval.

    B. The auditor should issue the policies in accordance with standards and authorized by the highest level of management to ensure compliance.

    C. Any level of management.

    D. The policy should be signed and enforced by the highest level of management.

16. The auditor's final opinion is to be based on:

    A. The objectives and verbal statements made by management

    B. An understanding of management's desired audit results

    C. The audit committee's specifications

    D. The results of evidence and testing

17. What is the purpose of ISACA's professional ethics statement?

    A. To clearly specify acceptable and unacceptable behavior

    B. To provide procedural advisement to the new IS auditor

    C. To provide instructions on how to deal with irregularities and illegal acts by the client

    D. To provide advice on when it is acceptable for the auditor to deviate from audit standards

18. How does the auditor derive a final opinion?

    A. From evidence gathered and the auditor's observations

    B. By representations and assurances of management

    C. By testing the compliance of language used in organizational policies

    D. Under advice of the audit committee

19. What are the three competing demands to be addressed by project management?

    A. Scope, authority, and money

    B. Time, cost, and scope

    C. Requirements, authority, and responsibility

    D. Authority, organizational structure, and scope

20. What is the difference between a threat and a vulnerability?

    A. Threats are the path that can be exploited by a vulnerability.

    B. Threats are risks and become a vulnerability if they occur.

    C. Vulnerabilities are a path that can be taken by a threat, resulting in a loss.

    D. Vulnerability is a negative event that will cause a loss if it occurs.

21. Which of the following statements is *not* true regarding the audit committee?

    A. Executives inside the organization oversee the audit committee and are responsible for keeping the committee busy working on compliance programs.

    B. Executives can be hired and fired by the audit committee because this committee is responsible for management oversight.

    C. The audit committee is composed of members from the board of directors. This committee has the authority to hire external auditors, and external auditors may meet with the committee on a quarterly basis without other executives present.

    D. The audit committee provides senior executives a method of bringing problems into a confidential discussion for the purpose of exploring a resolution.

22. What is the functional difference between managing a project by using Gantt charts as compared to PERT diagrams?

    A. Gantt charts show the sequence of project activities, and PERT diagrams display a more detailed work breakdown structure. The PERT diagrams provide valuable details necessary to create a skills matrix.

    B. PERT charts put work packages from the work breakdown structure in sequence to show multiple routes through the project, using time estimates of most likely, least likely, and optimistic for quantitative measurement.

    C. PERT diagrams follow a waterfall-type sequence to provide a bar graph diagram of details, milestones, and activities. PERT provides qualitative measurement of the work breakdown structure.

    D. Projects of any size can be effectively managed by using Gantt chart diagrams. PERT diagrams are optional reports.

23. How should the auditor assist in the remediation of problems found during the audit?

    A. Take ownership of the issue and participate in designing the plan for fixing the problem.

    B. The auditor should decide whether the problem is major or minor, and then advise the auditee with a specific solution after considering the impact to the business.

    C. The auditor should help the auditees. The auditor can add value by defining the specific steps necessary for remediation of the problem.

    D. The auditor should never take ownership of problems found. Auditors are encouraged to provide general advice to the auditee, including an explanation of what to look for during the audit.

24. The _____ type of audit checks attributes against the design specifications.

    A. Process

    B. System

    C. Compliance

    D. Product

25. Assessments and audits have several points in common. Which of the following statements provides the best description of an assessment compared to an audit?

    A. Audits are more formal than assessments.

    B. They are similar in nature; the difference is in wording.

    C. Both provide reports that can be used for licensing purposes.

    D. Assessment reports provide a high assurance of the situation.

26. The audit may uncover irregularities and illegal acts that require disclosure. The auditor is obligated to promptly disclose this information to the authorities.

    A. True

    B. False

27. Corporations can avoid compliance under the Sarbanes-Oxley Act by using which of the following strategies?

  A. Relocating the corporate headquarters offshore to a country such as Japan.

  B. Remediating their internal controls to fulfill the requirements of SOX section 404.

  C. Auditing their internal controls and reporting the findings to the audit committee at least once every 90 days.

  D. Applicable corporations in the United States and Japan are not able to avoid compliance.

28. Which of the following statements is true?

  A. The auditee is the person running the audit, and the client is the subject of the audit.

  B. The auditor is the person running the audit, and the client is the subject of the audit.

  C. The client is the person setting the scope for the audit, and the auditor performs the work.

  D. The client pays for the audit, and the auditor sets the scope of the audit that will follow.

29. What is the purpose of the skills matrix?

  A. Identify which person to interview during the audit

  B. Describe the person needed during the performance phase of the audit

  C. Identify the skills required by the auditee in order to complete the audit within scope

  D. Show the client how to save money during the audit engagement

30. Which of the following is the best description of an ongoing audit program for regulatory compliance?

  A. An audit is performed once for the entire year, and then repeated by using the same information for each successive year.

  B. An audit may be automated by using audit program software.

  C. An audit is a series of unique projects of short duration that add up to cover all the steps necessary for annual compliance.

  D. An audit is a set of assessments performed by the auditee for the purpose of licensing and regulatory compliance.

Answers to Review Questions

1. C. A policy is signed by the person of highest authority to ensure compliance by the members of the organization. Compliance to policies, standards, and procedures is mandatory.

2. A. Officers of the organization will typically hold the title of vice president or higher. A CIO might not be a corporate officer, unless the position is located in the parent organization. A division-level CIO may or may not be a true corporate officer. Those holding the position of department director and below are seldom held liable by the government for internal control failure. A department director is a supporting manager to the vice president.

3. B. Accountants, auditors, and lawyers act on behalf of their client's best interests unless doing so places them in violation of the law. It is the highest standard of duty implied by law for a trustee and guardian.

4. B. All of the audit types are valid except procedural, SAS-74, verification, and regulatory. The valid audit types are financial, operational (SAS-70), integrated (SAS-94), compliance, administrative, forensic, and information systems. A forensic audit is used to discover information about a possible crime.

5. D. *Should* represents discretionary information in a regulation. *Shall* indicates that compliance is mandatory regardless of profit or loss.

6. A. The highest level of authority is in the projectized organization, followed in decreasing authority by the balanced matrix, and weak matrix (functional). In functional organization the project manager has almost no authority and relies on begging and personal influence.

7. C. Every role except an auditor is a nonaudit role. Anyone in a nonaudit role is disqualified from being an independent auditor.

8. D. The auditor may discover information that could cause some level of damage to the client if disclosed. The information could trigger additional actions by a perpetrator. In addition, the auditor shall implement controls to ensure security and data backup of their work.

9. A. A Program Evaluation Review Technique (PERT) diagram is designed to show the critical path of a project. A Gantt chart shows activity sequences and milestones without identifying the critical path. Answers C and D are distracters.

10. C. Standard terms of reference are used between the auditor and everyone else to ensure honest and unbiased communication. Without standard terminology, it would be difficult to know whether we were discussing the same issue or agreed on the same outcome.

11. B. The auditor must be independent. Having a personal relationship with the organization being audited could result in a biased opinion. The business relationship is also an issue if the organization has influence over the auditor. The goal is to be fair, objective, and unrelated to the subject of the audit.

12. C. The data owner specifies controls, is responsible for acceptable use, and appoints the data custodian. The data users will comply with acceptable use and report violations. The data custodian will protect information and ensure its availability. The custodian will also provide support to the users.

13. D. A work breakdown structure is the decomposition of tasks necessary to perform the required work for the project.

14. B. A standard is implemented to ensure a minimum level of uniform compliance. Guidelines are advisory information used in the absence of a standard. Compliance to standards is mandatory; compliance to guidelines is discretionary.

15. D. Policies should be signed, issued, and enforced by the highest level of management to ensure compliance by the organization. It is the responsibility of management (not the auditor) to implement internal controls.

16. D. The auditor is to be a professional skeptic who tests assertions of management and renders an opinion based on the evidence discovered during the audit.

17. A. This statement specifies that IS auditors are expected to fulfill their duties with the highest standards of honest and truthful representation. It is unacceptable to violate the fiduciary relationship with your client.

18. A. A final opinion is based on evidence gathered and testing. The purpose of an audit is to challenge the assertions of management. Evidence is gathered that will support or disprove claims.

19. B. Scope, cost, and time are the three constraints in every project. Scope includes authority, while cost includes resources and personnel. Time affects both cost and scope of the project to be completed as planned.

20. C. Assets are anything of value. Threats are negative events that cause a loss if they occur. Vulnerabilities are paths that allow a threat to occur.

21. A. All of the answers except A are true. The audit committee is responsible for management oversight of the executives. The audit committee is usually composed of board members who provide executives a forum to discuss problems in order to rectify the situation. The audit committee can hire or fire anyone in the organization, usually focusing their attention on external auditors and senior executives.

22. B. A Program Evaluation Review Technique diagram provides a visual representation of the critical path. The critical path is the shortest route through the tasks necessary to accomplish the delivery of the highest-priority objectives in each project. Smart project managers will use Gantt chart data to build a PERT diagram for management of the project.

23. D. The auditor must never take ownership of the problems found. The auditor may provide general advice to the auditee and demonstrate what we are looking for during the audit. The auditee needs to design their own remediation plan. Auditors who participate in detailed remediation planning are no longer objective nor independent.

24. D. Product audits compare design specifications (feature, size, color, markings, and so forth) against the attributes of the finished product. The CISA may use this type of audit during certification of custom-built software programs or prior to software release from a development company.

25. A. An assessment is less formal than an audit. The purpose of an assessment is to determine value based on relevance. Assessments have a lower value because they are not independent or a regimented independent audit.

26. B. False. The auditor should contact one level of management above where the suspected activity took place. If the problem involved managers responsible for internal controls, the auditor should report it to the highest level of management available, which is usually the audit committee. Auditors should never contact the authorities directly unless advised to do so by their own attorney.

27. Answer: D. Corporations that fall under the Sarbanes-Oxley Act (SOX) are not able to avoid compliance if they are located in the United States or Japan. SOX is forcing the use of internal controls and now expanding into other countries, including the European Union. Foreign countries are implementing laws such as SOX to deter corporate corruption by holding the executives liable.

28. C. The client sets the scope of the audit. The auditee is the target (subject) of the audit. The auditor designs the audit plan according to the client's scope and then performs the audit in accordance with published audit standards and procedures.

29. B. A skills matrix is created during preplanning to identify the skills necessary to perform a competent audit. The purpose of the skills matrix is to justify the training of personnel or to describe the skills needed by members of the audit team. A skills matrix prevents the auditor from being stuck with an unskilled "warm body."

30. Answer: C. Projects are unique and usually of limited duration, for a fixed period of time with a definite start and stop date. The projects may be coupled together into a series of projects in order to fulfill an ongoing operational need, such as an annual audit program or perpetual quality program.

Chapter

2

Audit Process

THE OBJECTIVE OF THIS CHAPTER IS TO ACQUAINT THE READER WITH THE FOLLOWING CONCEPTS:

✓ Developing and implementing a risk-based audit strategy

✓ Understanding how to structure an audit

✓ Implementing the principles of quality into audit activities

✓ Planning required for specific audits

✓ Implementing risk management and control practices while maintaining independence

✓ Understanding qualifications and competence requirements

✓ Conducting audits in accordance with standards, guidelines, and best practices

✓ Knowing the types of controls and how they are implemented

✓ Understanding the effect of pervasive controls on audits

✓ Acquiring and using proper audit evidence

✓ Understanding the new challenge of electronic discovery

✓ Dealing with conflict, potential risks, and communicating to stakeholders

✓ Conducting audit documentation and reports

The auditing process is based on a series of generally accepted procedures. Your job as an IS auditor is to provide reasonable assurance that audit objectives are accomplished using applicable professional auditing standards.

During an audit, it is important to remember that all decisions and opinions will need to be supported by evidence and documentation. It is the auditor's responsibility to ensure consistency in the audit process. An *audit quality control plan* should be adopted to support these basic objectives.

There are 10 audit stages to be aware of when performing an audit. A CISA needs to be aware of their duties in each of these stages:

- Approving the audit charter or engagement letter
- Preplanning the audit
- Performing a risk assessment
- Determining whether an audit is possible
- Performing the actual audit
- Gathering evidence
- Performing audit tests
- Analyzing the results
- Reporting the results
- Conducting any follow-up activities

In this chapter, you will look at each of these stages in detail along with various procedures used during the audit. Figure 2.1 illustrates a simple flowchart of the audit process. The actual execution of the audit will be more complex.

We will begin with the process of establishing an audit charter in order to gain the authority to perform an audit.

Establishing and Approving an Audit Charter

The first audit objective is to establish an *audit charter*, which gives you the authority to perform an audit. The audit charter is issued by executive management or the board of directors.

 When we refer to management, we are referring to the auditee unless stated otherwise.

The audit charter allows the delegation of an audit to an external organization, via an engagement letter. — pg 63

FIGURE 2.1   Overview of the audit process

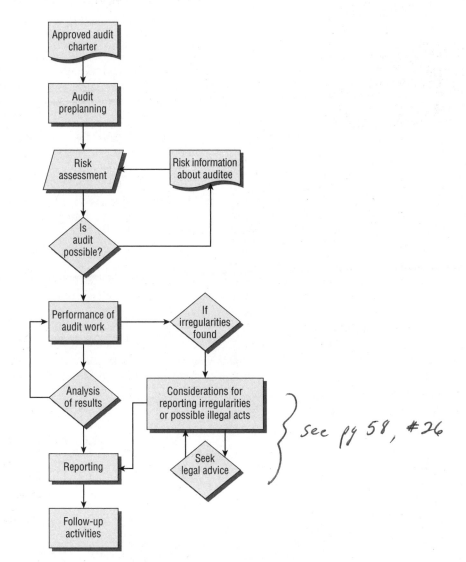

see pg 58, #26

The audit charter should clearly state management's assertion of responsibility, their objectives, and delegation of authority. An audit charter outlines your responsibility, authority, and accountability:

Responsibility   Provides scope with goals and objectives

Authority   Grants the right to perform an audit and the right to obtain access relevant to the audit

Accountability   Defines mutually agreed-upon actions between the audit committee and the auditor, complete with reporting requirements

The audit charter should be approved by the highest level of management as well as the audit committee. - pg 63

(handwritten margin note, top right) — To conduct perf. reviews of executives - pg 139

(handwritten margin note, top right) — T. challenge + review assurances - p 109

Role of the Audit Committee

Each organization should have an *audit committee* composed of business executives. Each audit committee member is required to be financially literate, with the ability to read and understand financial statements including balance sheets, income statements, and cash flow statements. The audit committee members are expected to have past employment experience in accounting or finance, and hold certification in accounting. A chief executive officer with comparable financial sophistication may be a member of an audit committee.

(handwritten margin note, left) Why? Because→

The purpose of the audit committee is to provide advice to the executive accounting officer concerning internal control strategies, priorities, and assurances. It is unlikely that an executive officer will know every detail about the activities within their organization. In spite of this, executive officers are held accountable for any internal control failures. Audit committees are not a substitute for executives who must govern, control, and manage their organization. The audit committee is delegated the authority to review and challenge the assurances of internal controls made by executive management.

(handwritten margin note, left) they retain/ terminate CPA firms (i.e. independent auditors) and oversee the co's financial reporting process and prepare for filing w/SEC

The audit committee is expected to maintain a positive working relationship with management, internal auditors, and independent auditors. The committee manages planned audit activities and the results of both internal and external audits. The committee is authorized to engage outside experts for independent assurance. Both internal auditors and external auditors will have escalation procedures designed to communicate significant weaknesses that have been identified. The auditor will seek to have the weaknesses corrected in order to give a positive assurance that the risk is appropriately controlled and managed. The head of the internal audit and the external audit representative should have free access to the audit committee chairperson. This ensures an opportunity to raise any concerns the auditor may have concerning processes, internal controls, risks, and limitations. This reporting relationship is shown in the following graphic.

(handwritten margin note, right) — According to SEC, Board members can also be audit committee members (non-employee)

The audit committee should meet on a regular basis, at least four times a year, to fulfill this requirement. The Sarbanes-Oxley Act of 2002 (SOX) requires executives to certify that all internal control weaknesses have been discovered, with full disclosure to the audit committee provided every 90 days.

The audit committee is responsible for issuing the audit charter to grant the authority for internal audits. The audit charter should be approved by the highest level of management as well as the audit committee. Authority also needs to be granted for an independent audit. A document called an engagement letter grants authority for an independent external audit.

Engagement Letter

The audit charter allows the delegation of an audit to an external organization via an engagement letter. The *engagement letter* helps define the relationship to an independent auditor for individual assignments. The letter records the understanding between the audit committee and the independent auditor.

> The primary difference between an engagement letter and an audit charter is that an engagement letter addresses the independence of the auditor.

Engagement letters should include the following:

- All points outlined in the audit charter
- Independence of the auditor (responsibility)
- Evidence of an agreement to the terms and conditions (authority)
- Agreed-upon completion dates (accountability)

Preplanning the Audit

Chapt 3 is loaded with suggestions for what to audit

The second audit objective is to plan the specific audit project necessary to address the audit objectives. Analysis should occur at least annually to incorporate the constant stream of new developments in both the industry and the auditing field.

Your audit objectives will include compliance to professional auditing standards and applicable laws. The IS auditor needs to be prepared to justify any deviation from professional audit standards. Deviation is a rare event.

As an auditor, you will need to consider the impact of the audit on the business operation. You will need to gain an understanding of the business, its purpose, and any potential constraints to the audit. Let's look at the questions an auditor could ask to gain insight of the business operation:

Knowledge of the business itself   What are their specific industry regulations? For example, are they governed by the U.S. Occupational Safety & Health Administration, any financial securities regulations, or the Health Insurance Portability and Accountability Act because of offering employee medical benefits?

- What are the business cycles? The retail industry operates on a schedule that begins Christmas holiday activities in September. Their busy season is at the end of the year, whereas the construction industry is busy from March through August.

- What are the reporting cycles? Is their year-end on September 30 or December 31?

- What are the critical business processes necessary for survival?

- Are reports available from prior audits?

- Will the auditors be able to tour the facilities? Which location and when?

- Who should be interviewed? Will those people be available?

- What are their existing plans? Are any new products, clients, or significant changes planned?

Strategic objectives   The top executive sets a strategy with supporting definitions for the entire organization. This strategy defines what the business will be doing over the next three to five years. It answers the question of what the business will be engaged in. Is it the same industry or is it branching out into another market?

- What is the direction and structure going forward?

- What is the organizational plan for integrating IS?

- What are the business objectives that IS will be expected to fulfill?

- What are the defined IS goals?

- What is the strategic plan for the next two to three years?

- What are the supporting tactical plan steps during the next one to two years?

- What work is occurring from now to the end of the year?

Financial objectives   Businesses use a portfolio approach to manage their investments, keeping those with the highest return and discarding underperformers. What is the return on investment (ROI) goal for the current capital investment and related expenses?

- How are assets managed?

- How are costs allocated to departments and projects?

- What is the budget and forecasting process?

- What are the financial reporting objectives? Will the client need an integrated audit for SOX reporting?

- What are the business continuity plans?

Operational objectives for internal control   Operational activities focus on running the business within a budget period, usually within a 12- to 14-month window. The focus is on what should be done today and this year.

- Should any policies or procedures be tested?

- Will this be an administrative audit?   − pg 10

- How is system administration managed?

- How are performance metrics managed?

- What is the method used for capacity planning?

- How have access controls been implemented?

- What is the strategy and status of business continuity and disaster recovery plans? How many exercise tests have occurred this year?

- What controls exist for managing network communications?

- What is the nature of the last system audit? Are self-assessments used?

- What are the staffing plans?

Figure 2.2 shows four basic areas related to the organization's business requirements.

FIGURE 2.2 Understanding the business requirements *(for planning an audit)*

Identifying Restrictions on Scope

Every IS auditor will need to provide details when significant restrictions are placed on the scope of an audit. You will need to review your audit objectives and risk strategy to determine whether the audit is still possible and will meet the stated objectives. The audit report should explain specific restrictions and their impact on the audit. If the restrictions preclude the ability to collect sufficient evidence, you should render no opinion or no attestation in the audit.

Examples of restrictions include the following:

- Management placing undue restrictions on evidence use or audit procedures that could seriously undermine the audit objective

- Inability to obtain sufficient evidence for any reason

- Lack of resources or lack of sufficient time

- Ineffective audit procedures

Auditors have been known to terminate an engagement if the client places restrictions that are too severe on the audit. It is not unheard of for a client to discharge an auditor after receiving accurate findings that are distasteful to the client. The replacement auditor may need to inquire why a prior auditor is no longer being used by the auditee.

In some instances, the auditee will need to establish a level of communication between the previous auditor and replacement auditor. The purpose of this communication is to ensure that the client is not trying to obstruct truthful findings. Blackouts, or missing audit periods, would be a concern shared by more people than just the auditor. Statement on Auditing Standard 84 (SAS-84) provides additional details if you ever encounter this situation.

Understanding the Variety of Audits

see pp 55,
30

see pp'
9, 10

Each audit is actually an individual project linked to an ongoing audit program. The IS auditor may be asked to perform a variety of audits, including the following:

Product or service   Efficiency, effectiveness, controls, and life-cycle costs

Processes   Methods or results

System   Design or configuration

General controls   Preventative, detective, and corrective

Organizational plans   Present and future objectives

To be successful, the auditor needs to engage in a fact-finding mission. You will need to take into consideration business requirements that are unique to the auditee or common to their industry. Each business has its own opportunities, challenges, and constraints. Remember, the purpose of an audit is to help management verify assertions (claims). Proper planning is necessary to ensure that the audit itself does not disrupt the business, or waste valuable resources, including time and money.

Gathering Detailed Audit Requirements

Every audit should have a set of requirements and objectives in support of the ongoing program—for example, the controls and efforts necessary to comply with regulations such as SOX. It is not possible to test all the requirements in one monolithic audit, so we break down (*decompile*) the larger compliance requirements into a series of smaller audits (*modular stages*):

Client duties   Every audit has a client who sets the scope, grants authority, and agrees to pay for the project. The client's duties include the following:

- Set the scope
- Specify the audit objectives
- Grant access to the auditee and resources
- Define the reporting structure and confidentiality requirements

Auditee duties   The auditee is responsible for working with the auditor to do the following:

- Confirm purpose and scope
- Identify critical success factors (CSFs) and measures of performance
- Identify personnel roles and responsibilities
- Provide access to information, personnel, locations, and systems relevant to the audit
- Cooperate with the gathering of audit evidence
- Provide access to prior audit results or to communication with prior auditors if necessary
- Specify reporting lines to senior management
- Make their assertion of controls and effectiveness independent of the auditor

Auditor duties   The auditor is responsible for the following:

- Plan each audit to accomplish specific objectives necessary for annual compliance.
- Identify specific standards used for the audit (such as PCI section 11, NIST 800-53 controls, ISO 27002 management objectives, SOX section 401 or 404, FIPS 142, and so forth).
- Use a risk-based audit strategy.
- Identify special requirements of confidentiality, security, and safety. The information encountered by the auditor may be sensitive because of competitive value or possible legal repercussions.
- Identify specific procedures to be used for the audit. All procedures must be in writing.
- Document how the audit procedures are linked with specific audit objectives.
- Create a list of the evidence needed to review in order to prepare the audit findings.
- Create a written project plan.
- Identify resources required, including people, areas for access, hardware, and software.
- Develop time and event schedules with estimated start and end times.
- Provide audit cost estimates.
- Specify a date when the auditee and client can expect to receive a final report.

Scheduling should be mutually agreed upon so there are no surprises. Surprise requests tend to damage the relationship rather than build confidence. Your auditee will wonder whether you are just an incompetent planner or if you have an ulterior motive. Surprises make the auditee leery, if not downright distrustful, of your intentions.

As an auditor, you need to understand the nature of the systems that your client desires to be audited. It would be nearly impossible to audit systems whose mission you do not understand.

During preplanning, it's important to review the capabilities of each member of the audit team. Is each member of the audit team up to the task? The engagement manager or lead auditor should be made aware if a member of the team is missing a certification or a clearance rating necessary to conduct the audit.

In addition, audit plans can change depending on whether the client is using a centralized or distributed system design. The location of IS facilities and personnel will need to be considered.

The auditor needs to demonstrate due care as a professional in both planning and execution. There are a number of definitions for the word *care*:

Basic care is defined as the bare minimum necessary to sustain life without negligence.

Ordinary care is better than basic and provides an average level of customary care in the absence of negligence.

Extraordinary care is defined as that which is dramatically above and beyond what a normal person would offer or a situation would entail.

Various degrees of care could fall under the definition of *due care*. The degrees of care are proportional to the level of risk or loss that could occur. *Negligence* is the absence of care. A conscientious person will exercise due care in the performance of their job. Failure to exercise due care would be negligence.

Using a Systematic Approach to Planning

Every audit is a systematic approach of testing samples of evidence to measure compliance against a designated standard. Anyone with the correct attitude has the potential to be a good auditor after proper training. Let's start with two foundation-level audit objectives:

- To test control implementation to see whether the auditee has implemented adequate safeguards

- To comply with legal requirements that specify procedures necessary to remain legal

It is not unusual to discover missing controls or the absence of formally documented legal requirements. Auditors may discover that the auditee's understanding of the requirements is quite vague—but no need to fear, because you can be the super auditor with a solution. You can use a special method called the *process technique*, invented by Walter Shewhart. Shewhart conceived the quality techniques used by Edwards Deming and Philip Crosby.

The purpose of the process technique is to guide a repeating cycle of constant improvement for a process or system. It can be used to identify specific action items necessary to accomplish vague requirements, such as "maintain adequate security." Let's implement the four basic steps used to perform Shewhart's process technique (Plan, Do, Check, Act):

Plan Is there a plan or a method?

Did management convey the importance of this objective by sponsoring a policy?

Has the auditee established what needs to be done by identifying specific tasks or procedures?

The auditor may find evidence including outlines, procedures, flowcharts, specifications, or notes.

Do Now you look to see whether the plan, procedure, or method is being followed according to their plan. Is the work output matching their plan?

Look for the existence of status reports, meeting records, employee training, or other documentation used in their work area.

Check Is anyone monitoring the process? Is there a quality control check or peer review being used? If so, what is the acceptable criterion?

How are problems discovered and reported? Look for compliance testing and evidence of non-compliance, such as rework or discards. What metrics are used? Look for deviation reporting.

Act   Inevitably, there are differences between what was expected in the plan and the actual outcome. This Act step refers to analyzing the differences, and then taking action to adjust the process so the problem is corrected. Action should always be taken to fix the problems as they are found.

Shewhart's famous graphic is shown next to illustrate the Plan-Do-Check-Act cycle. Using this cycle made Deming famous. It will help you too.

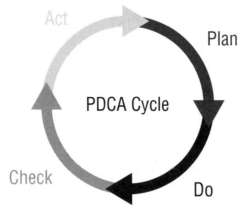

A really smart auditor will focus on situations that are not normal to determine how decisions are made. Auditors should always be curious about how a decision was reached. What evidence is available to justify the decision? Whose approval was required?

Comparing Traditional Audits to Assessments and Self-Assessments

A discussion of the audit process would not be complete without mentioning the specific differences between audits and assessments or control self-assessments. The auditee can work to improve their audit score between audits by using assessments and self-assessment techniques.

Traditional audits   To employ the formal skills of a professional auditor is considered a traditional audit. In a traditional audit, the auditor manages the audit through the entire audit process and renders a final opinion.

Audits are used to specifically measure auditee claims against a reference standard. The audit generates a report viewed to represent a high assurance of truth. Audits are used in attest reporting engagements (when the auditor attests that the auditee claims are true).

The audit results may be used for regulatory licensing and external reporting.

Assessments   Assessments are less formal and frequently more cooperative processes that scrutinize people and objects. A client may employ a professional auditor to work with the auditee. The goal is usually to "see what is out there." Assessments implement informal activities designed to determine the value of what may already exist. Value is based on relevance and fitness of use. An assessment report is viewed to have a lower value (moderate-to-low value) when compared to an audit. Assessments are excellent vehicles for training and awareness. The goal of an assessment is to help the staff create a sense of ownership while working toward improving their score.

Results of the assessment remain internal to the organization and are not eligible for use in regulatory licensing.

Control self-assessments (internal)   A control self-assessment (CSA) is executed by the auditee. With a CSA, the auditor becomes a facilitator to help guide the client's effort toward self-improvement. The auditee uses the CSA to benchmark progress with the intention of improving their score. A great deal of pride can be created by the accomplishment of CSA tasks and learning the detail necessary to succeed in a traditional audit. Therefore, the CSA process can generate benefits by empowering the staff to take ownership and accountability.

Control self-assessment will not fulfill the independence requirement, so a traditional audit is still required. CSAs can be used to identify areas that are high risk and may need a more detailed review later.

> Know the difference between audits and assessments. *Audits* are formal activities that are conducted by a qualified auditor and generate a high assurance of the truth. Audits can be used for licensing and regulatory compliance. *Assessments* are informal activities designed to determine the value of what may already exist. Value is based on relevance and fitness of use. The assessment is excellent for instilling a sense of ownership in the staff. Assessment results should remain internal to the organization.

As auditors, our goal is to report the truth and to educate our clients. Using traditional audits with a combination of lower-cost assessments will help our client become more successful. Now it's time to move forward into risk management.

Choosing a Risk Management Strategy

[handwritten: Part of the Act Phase of PDCA cycle]

After identifying a methodology for risk evaluation and control, the auditor will need to identify potential risks to the organization. The auditee will assist by providing information about their organization.

To properly identify risks, the auditor also needs to identify the following:

- Assets that need to be protected
- Exposures for those assets
- Threats to the assets
- Internal and external sources for threats
- Security issues that need to be addressed

[handwritten: See pg 464]

Part of documenting risk data is for the auditor to identify potential risk response strategies that can be used in the audit with each identified risk. The four risk responses are as follows:

Accept (de facto)   Take your chances. Ignoring a risk is the same as accepting it. The auditor should be concerned about the acceptance of high-risk situations. By not taking action, the management team has automatically accepted the risk. Not making a decision and taking action means management has already accepted the risk.

"self-insurance" is a term used for this – pg 119

Mitigate (reduce)   Do something to lower the odds of getting hurt. The purpose of mitigation is to reduce the effect of the potential damage. Most internal controls are designed to mitigate risk.

Transfer   Let someone else take the chance of loss by using a subcontractor or insurance. You can transfer the risk but not the liability for failure. Blind transfer of risk would be a genuine concern. This applies to outsourcing agreements and the reason for a *right to audit* clause in the contract.

Avoid   Reject the situation; change the situation to avoid taking the risk.

An assessment of risk will usually include a list of all possible risks that threaten the business and your evaluation of how imminent they are.

Toy manufacturer Mattel experienced the problem of inherited liability for distributing toys manufactured with hazardous lead paint (2007). Mattel was held responsible in the eyes of the public for failing to manage their subcontractor effectively. Unknown to Mattel, their subcontractor chose to ignore specifications in favor of using a lead-based paint. Mattel is under scrutiny for failing to detect the violation prior to shipping their toys. When you transfer risk, you still own the liability. Mattel is only one example of the inherited liability issue.

Other examples of inherited liability include the pet food recall of 2007 caused by tainted flour in the ingredients. The U.S. Food and Drug Administration placed a widespread ban on fish from Chinese suppliers because of questionable practices by the subcontractors using illegal growth hormones. A quick Google search will yield many more examples of liability inherited from subcontractors.

Figure 2.3 shows the basic process of responding to risks. A CISA is expected to understand the different types of responses. Risk management principles will apply to your audit planning. Your client will select from similar choices in their decisions about the risks faced by their organization.

4. part Risk Management Strategy:
(see pg 144)
- Identification (steps 1-3)
- Assessment (steps 4-6)
- Mitigation (steps 7, 8)
- Monitoring & Reporting (step 9)

FIGURE 2.3   Risk analysis process flowchart

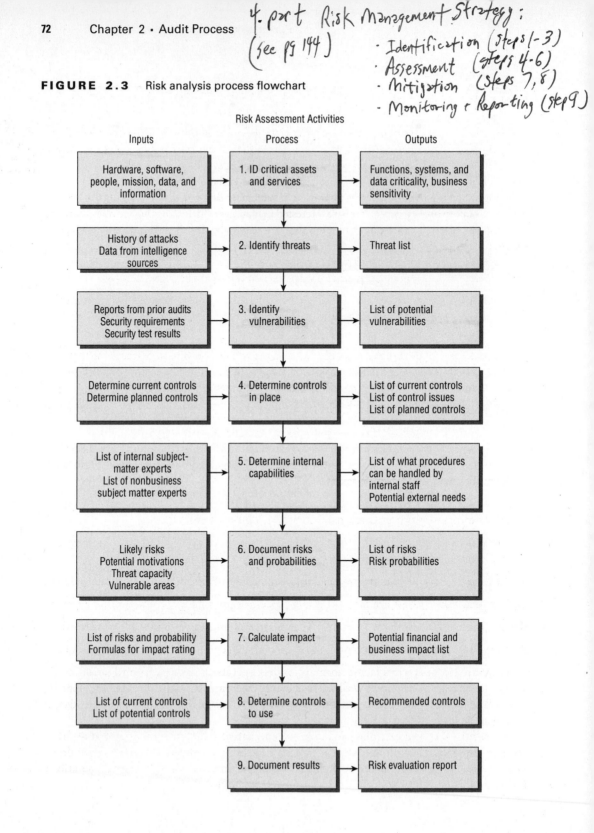

Performing an Audit Risk Assessment

Performing a risk assessment is the next step after the audit objectives have been identified. The purpose of a risk assessment is to ensure that sufficient evidence will be collected during an audit. We will add a new term to your auditor vocabulary: _materiality_. Materiality refers to evidence that is significant and could change the outcome.

While searching for evidence, it is important to remember that you are not looking for 100 percent of all conceivable evidence. You are interested in material evidence that will be relevant to the outcome of your audit. Please keep in mind that it is easy to be distracted during an audit. You should focus your efforts on material evidence that either proves or disproves your specific audit objective. Your findings and opinion will be based on this material evidence.

see pg 90

An audit risk assessment should take into account the following types of risks:

Inherent risks　These are natural or built-in risks that always exist. Driving your automobile holds the inherent risk of an automobile accident or a flat tire. Theft is an inherent risk for items of high value.

Detection risks　These are the risks that an auditor will not be able to detect what they are looking to find. It would be terrible to report no negative results when material conditions (faults) actually exist. Detection risks include sampling and nonsampling risks:

Sampling risks　These are the risks that an auditor will falsely accept or erroneously reject an audit sample (evidence).

Nonsampling risks　These are the risks that an auditor will fail to detect a condition because of not applying the appropriate procedure or using procedures inconsistent with the audit objective (detection fault).

failing to prevent or detect a material error

Control risks　These are the risks that an auditor could lose control, errors could be introduced, or errors may not be corrected in a timely manner (if ever).

Business risks　These are risks that are inherent in the business or industry itself. They may be regulatory, contractual, or financial.

Technological risks　These are inherent risks of using automated technology. Systems do fail.

Operational risks　These are the risks that a process or procedure will not perform correctly.

Residual risks　These are the risks that remain after all mitigation efforts are performed.

Audit risks　These are the combination of inherent, detection, control, and residual risks.

These are the same risks facing normal business operations. In the planning phase, an IS auditor is primarily concerned with the first three: inherent risk, detection risk, and control risk. All of the risks could place the business or audit in jeopardy and should be considered during some level of advance planning.

An auditor should create plans to allow for alternative audit strategies if an auditee has recently experienced an outage, service interruption, or unscheduled downtime. It would be unwise to pursue an audit before the business has ample time to restabilize normal operations. Plans should include an opportunity to reschedule without violating a legal deadline.

47,464 for Risk Analysis
see pg 144 for Risk Mgmt
158 for Risk Assessment

Determining Whether an Audit Is Possible

A good auditor remembers that setting priorities is their responsibility. You will need to assess the risk of the audit and ensure that priorities have been fulfilled. If you are unable to perform the necessary audit functions, it is essential that the issues be properly communicated to management and the audit committee. An audit without meaningful evidence would be useless.

The auditor will need to work with the auditee to define specific requirements and identify any third-party providers. You will need to review the auditee's organizational structure and to identify persons in areas of interest that are material to your audit.

Management has the ultimate responsibility for internal controls and holds the authority for delegation. Management may choose to delegate tasks to a third party (*outsource*). The outsource organization must perform the daily tasks as designated, but unfortunately management will still retain liability that cannot be delegated. Executive management will still be held responsible for any failures that occur with or at the outsource organization. The federal government has gone to great lengths to ensure that the decision maker (management) can be held fully accountable for their actions and liable for any loss or damage.

Organizations with outsourcing contracts and labor unions could be particularly difficult unless you have sufficient cooperation. In the case of labor unions, it is often necessary for the shop steward to be present and involved in all plans and activities. Failure to do so may result in an operational risk of the union workers walking off the job.

Outsourced activities will present their own challenges with potential restrictions on access to personnel and evidence. It would not be uncommon for a service provider to decline your request for an audit. Most outsource providers will attempt to answer such requests by supplying you with a copy of their latest SAS-70 report, which is a standard report format for service providers. Occasionally, when a client requests and receives the SAS-70 report from a service provider, the value of content in the SAS-70 report may be overstated.

The purpose of the SAS-70 is to eliminate multiple organizations from individually auditing the service provider. You can expect that several points of detailed evidence you requested will have been filtered or masked in the SAS-70 report. Your client's original outsource contract should have included a provision for the right to audit along with the service-level agreement. It must be clearly stated whether the SAS-70 is acceptable or if an individual audit is required. Performing your own audit adds cost but offers high levels of control. Be advised that some outsource providers run on a different business schedule than their clients.

Performing the Audit

The next objective in the audit is to perform the actual audit. Here you will need to make sure you have the appropriate staff, ensure audit quality control, define auditee communications, perform proper data collection, and review existing controls.

> ### Real World Scenario
>
> **Working in Labor Union Environments**
>
> We are acutely aware of how seemingly trivial actions can have significant consequences in a labor union environment. Plugging in our own computers to a client's network resulted in a complete work stoppage after our actions were observed by an unhappy union worker. Every union worker in the plant stopped what they were doing. We were immediately summoned by management to explain our actions. After several agonizing minutes of us begging forgiveness, the shop steward agreed that everyone could return to work. Your illustrious author received a dire warning not to do this again. Fortunately, the client agreed to cover the cost of the work stoppage, and we did not have the take money out of our own pocket.

Allocating Staffing

You will need to have personnel for the audit and to define the audit's organizational structure. You also will need to create a personnel resource plan, which identifies specific functions and skill sets necessary to complete your audit objectives. Individual skills and knowledge should be taken into consideration while planning your audit. Remember, it's impossible for the auditor to be an absolute expert in everything.

You will need to rely on the work of others, including your own audit team members, subcontractors, and possibly members of the client's staff. You should create a detailed staff training plan that is reviewed at least semiannually and before each audit. The time to train or retrain personnel is before the audit begins.

Creating a Skills Matrix

The auditor will lead persons with specialized skills, including the use of database scanners and other automated audit tools. A *skills matrix* should be developed, which indicates areas of knowledge, proficiency, and specialized training required to fulfill the audit. You use the skills matrix to identify members of the audit team according to the specific tasks each will perform. The purpose of the skills matrix is to ensure that the team has the right people with the right qualifications working on the right task. You use the matrix to demonstrate gaps and training needs. This discourages management from assigning you an unskilled "warm body." Table 2.1 shows a sample skills matrix.

TABLE 2.1   Sample Skills Matrix

Person	Training or Certification	Related Work Experience	Audit Task
M. Anderson	IA, CISA	Internal auditor	Audit task 8: Review of existing policies and records for PCI user training, all security, system configuration, and incident response.

TABLE 2.1   Sample Skills Matrix *(continued)*

Person	Training or Certification	Related Work Experience	Audit Task
J.T. Jennings	CISA, Network+, CCNA	PCI and PCI section 11 testing	Audit task 9: PCI section 11 network perimeter analysis.
R. Martin	CISA	XP admin, BSD Unix admin	Audit task 10: Conduct enumeration scan of network hosts and open ports. Exclude "Zeus" server and customer service computers. Audit task 14: Select logs for review. Supervise and assist in review with B. Goldfield performing task.
B. Goldfield	BS Computer Science	Intern, system analyst	Audit task 14: Catalog system log file data for analysis of past events to forensic-test the incident response.

Using the Work of Other People

Occasionally, finding a competent, independent expert in database administration for a particular vendor on your project may prove difficult. However, you might be able to train a member of the client's support staff to provide sufficient assistance to complete the audit.

Auditors frequently use the work of others as long as the following conditions are met:

- Assess the independence and objectivity of the provider.

- Determine their professional competence, qualifications, and experience.

- Agree on the scope of work and approach used.

- Determine the level of review and supervision required.

If these conditions are met, the auditor may choose to use the work of others. A CISA should have serious concerns if the work does not meet their audit evidence requirement for any reason. You can use only evidence of sufficient quality, quantity, and relevance. Failure to meet this requirement may require a change in the audit scope or canceling the audit.

Competence means having the right training, related experience, discipline, and qualifications for the job. Qualifications include recognized certification with the proper clearance for the job. Clearance may include having both permission to work the audit and a valid security clearance, especially in government auditing.

Ensuring Audit Quality Control

Quality does not happen automatically. It is a methodology that must be designed into your process and not just inspected afterward. Quality control is necessary in every audit.

Let's take a moment to define what quality is and how to recognize quality. We can do this by using three easy-to-remember points:

- _Quality_ is defined as conformance to specifications.
- Planning and prevention create quality. Quality does not occur by post appraisal.
- The standard of performance is zero defects, not by just getting "close enough." Sixth and seventh sigma do not reach zero defects. Quality can be measured by the price of failure (nonconformance).

Audit standards, guidelines, and procedures were developed to promote quality and consistency in a typical audit. The ISACA audit standards were developed to assist CISA auditors in performing audits. Additional guidance can be obtained by reading the ISACA audit guide at `www.isaca.org/standards`.

Your audit will need a variety of quality performance metrics to ensure success. When designing a quality control process, an auditor should consider doing the following:

- Use an audit methodology (documented plan and procedures).
- Gain an understanding of the auditee needs and expectations.
- Keep a checklist of the tasks to be accomplished.
- Respect business cycles and deadlines.
- Hold client interviews and workshops.
- Use customer satisfaction surveys.
- Agree to terms of reference used by client, auditee, and auditor (discussed in Chapter 1, "Secrets of a Successful IS Auditor").
- Establish audit performance metrics.
- Measure audit plan to actual performance.
- Respond to auditee complaints.

Quality can vary according to the requirements set forth by management. The auditor must take all the necessary steps to ensure that audit work is performed with very high standards of quality to generate a high assurance of the truth. Anything less will make you and the images of our profession appear questionable. High standards always bring respect.

Defining Auditee Communications

The auditor must work with management to define the auditee communication requirements.

As discussed in Chapter 1, the auditee often feels at a disadvantage to the auditor. Without effective communication, the auditee will feel disillusioned, confused, or disconnected from the audit. Each of these conditions would be undesirable; audits without client buy-in would be a major disaster.

Occasionally, the auditee may request to see information concerning the audit plan. Depending on your assignment, it may be acceptable to allow the auditee to view your blank checklists; however, the auditor's notes should remain confidential during the audit. It is usually not a good idea to give the auditee copies of your blank forms because doing so could provide the foundation for disputes or engineered answers.

It is your job as the auditor to be a "second set of eyes" in reviewing the present condition at the organization. You are responsible for reporting accurate findings to senior management and the audit committee. The audit charter should assist you by defining the required level of auditee communication.

To be effective in your communication, you need to consider several points, including the following:

- Describing the audit's purpose, service, and scope

- Dealing with problems, constraints, and delays

- Responding to client questions and complaints

- Dealing with issues outside the scope of this particular audit

- Understanding timing and scheduling—knowing when they expect the work to occur

- Following the reporting process—knowing when and how the client wants to hear from you

- Obtaining an agreement of your findings with your client

- Implementing confidentiality, implementing the principle of least privilege (need to know)

- Providing special handling for evidence of irregularities or possibly illegal acts

Nothing will replace the simple act of asking the client what level and frequency of communication they expect. The preceding points are simply a starting position. You should synchronize the auditee communication plan with your own internal audit team communication plans.

During the planning process, the auditor will need to gain approval from management for access to the appropriate staff personnel. A member of the audit team may be assigned to coordinate everyone's schedule.

Now is a good time to introduce some of the data collection techniques that auditors use in audits.

Using Data Collection Techniques

As part of the planning process, the auditor needs to determine how data will be gathered for evidence to support the audit report. To collect useful data, the savvy auditor will use a combination of techniques, including the following:

Staff observation You can observe staff in the performance of their duties. Auditor observation is a powerful form of evidence.

Document review Remember, the evidence rule will apply as you review existing documentation. Presence of a document does not mean it is actually in use. You should review the auditee documentation and any related legal documentation. Legal documentation may be either contracts or regulatory laws.

Interviews   You can interview selected personnel appropriate to the audit. Be sure to structure the timing and questions for the interview. You need to ensure that the questions are consistent and to allow extra time to discuss any interesting points raised.

Workshops   Workshops can generate awareness and understanding. The audit committee may be a good audience for a workshop. Well-executed workshops can save time compared to individual interviews.

Computer assisted audit tools (CAAT)   Newer auditing software does a fabulous job of checking configuration settings, user account parameters, system logs, and other time-consuming details.

Surveys   Conducting surveys is a tried-and-true method of obtaining cheap and easy answers. Unfortunately, the truthfulness of individual responses raises questions about the survey's consistency and resulting trustworthiness. People may answer the question using a skewed perspective, or just respond with answers they believe you want to hear, regardless of the truth. Overall reliability of the survey remains an ongoing concern.

Each technique has its advantages and disadvantages. For example, surveys offer an advantage of time but have the disadvantages of inconsistency and limited response. A survey cannot detect a personal mannerism such as hesitancy, surprise, or restlessness.

An auditor can observe an auditee during an interview and ask additional probing questions based on the auditee response. The auditor weighs each response in an attempt to create consistent scoring of answers by multiple interview subjects. Interviews consume more time but can gather additional information.

🌐 Real World Scenario

Familiarize Yourself with the Auditee's IT Environment

That old saying of "getting to know a person by walking in their shoes" certainly applies to IS auditing. You have to depend on the auditee to show you the design strategy and purpose of their IT environment. Their IT structure is supposed to be aligned to their business objectives.

Before you can determine whether that alignment exists, you will need to tour their facility. You should expect the client to provide a current network diagram. We prefer a schematic-level diagram rather than a high-level overview. The view from 3 feet away is a zillion times more informative than from 100 thousand feet. It does not matter whether the diagram is in digital format or hand drawn. What matters is that the diagram is accurate. We would accept a computer diagram with small handwritten changes, under the condition that the original document is updated before we finish the audit. Good detail would indicate that the auditee is actively working to manage their systems. We would ask the auditee to sign the document to certify that it is current and correct.

You should be particularly interested in understanding how transactions flow through the auditee's IS environment. You need to identify how transactions are authorized along with any potential routes for physical and logical access. Integrity cannot exist without access controls. A good auditor will take plenty of notes during a walk-through and will follow up with questions. Areas of significant interest to the auditor include the following:

- Hardware systems.

- Operating systems.

- Applications, database software, and special utilities.

- Monitoring and control systems (at the server, network, and application level).

- Relevant documentation, especially diagrams, flowcharts, and process diagrams.

- Personnel roles and specific duties. Job descriptions and a copy of the organizational reporting relationship will be helpful (*org chart*). Hopefully a skills matrix or training plan will exist.

- Relationship of the IT design to their higher-level business objectives. Is the design driven by strategic business requirements or technology favorites?

- Separation of duties pertaining to transaction authorization. This would apply to all significant transactions in the IT environment and within applications. The auditor would want to know who authorizes system access, changes, new transactions, deletions, and updates.

Surveys may execute quickly but carry extra administrative support burdens. It will take time and resources to create the survey, distribute the survey, track responses, provide answer assistance, ensure quality control, and tally the results. Because of human nature, people will seldom answer a survey in a manner that reduces their agenda and perceived value to an organization.

Most clients will be impressed if you demonstrate genuine interest and take good notes. It will help you obtain auditee buy-in and make them feel the audit report will contain statements of value. Just be sure to avoid the perception of an interrogation.

The hierarchy of internal controls

Every auditor should consider two fundamental issues concerning internal control:

Issue 1: Management is often exempt from controls. "**Ye who make the rules might try to avoid those rules.**"   Management has the responsibility of installing controls for the organization, yet some of the executives themselves are exempt from their own control. An excellent set of examples is noted at the beginning of Chapter 1, where multiple executives fraudulently altered records. One of the fundamental purposes of an audit is to determine whether executives are providing an honest and truthful representation based in fact.

Issue 2: How controls are implemented determines the level of assurance.   Implementing strong controls contributes to the level of assurance, which may be confirmed by the auditor. Strong assurance means it represents a 95 percent or greater degree of truth. Unsatisfactory implementation of controls compromises the overall objectives. No auditor can provide a satisfactory report if the controls are improperly implemented or insufficient for their objective.

Let's review the basic framework of controls according to the ISACA standards. ISACA based their standards on the common auditing guidelines for financial audits as well as the government guidelines for auditing and for the computer environment. Information systems controls are composed of four high level controls: general controls, pervasive IS controls, detailed IS controls, and application controls. This clarification is required because portions of the financial audit techniques may not be appropriate for some IS audits. Computer environments can be rather complex and abstract.

General controls (Overall)   This is the parent class of controls governing all areas of the business. Examples of general controls include separating duties to prevent employees from writing their own paychecks and creating accurate job descriptions. We expect management to implement administrative controls to govern the behavior of their entire enterprise. General controls also include defining an organizational structure, establishing HR policies, monitoring workers and the work environment, as well as budgeting, auditing, and reporting.

Pervasive IS controls (Technology)   A pervasive order or pervasive control defines the direction and behavior required for technology to function properly. The concept of pervasive control is to permeate the area by using a greater depth of control integration over a wide area of influence. Internal controls are used to regulate how the business operates in every area of every department.

The IS function uses pervasive controls in the same manner as a manufacturing operation, bank, or government office. Pervasive controls are a subset of general controls with extra definition focused on managing and monitoring a specific technology. For example, pervasive IS controls govern the operation of the information systems duties.

Pervasive IS controls are used across all internal departments and external contractors. Proper implementation of pervasive IS controls improve the reliability of the following:

- Overall service delivery
- Software development
- System implementation
- Security administration
- Disaster recovery and business continuity planning

The lack of pervasive IS controls, or weak controls, indicates the possibility of a high-risk situation that should draw the auditor's attention. Lower-level detailed controls will be compromised if the pervasive controls are ineffective.

At the pervasive control level, the auditor needs to consider the experience level, knowledge, and integrity of IS management. Look for changes in the environment or pressure that may lead to concealing or misstating information. This problem is prevalent when users manage their own departmental systems separate from the IT department. External influences include outsourcing, joint ventures, and direct relationships. Internal influences include flaws in the organizational structure or reporting relationship where a built-in conflict may exist.

Detailed IS controls (Tasks)   Specific tasks require additional detailed controls to ensure that workers perform the job correctly. Detailed controls refer to specific steps or tasks to be performed. In the finance department, a specific set of controls is practiced when creating a trial balance report. Detailed IS controls work in the same manner to specify how system security parameters are set, how input data is verified before being accepted into an application, or how to lock a user account after unsuccessful logon attempts. Detailed IS controls specify how the department will handle acquisitions, security, implementation, delivery, and support of IS services.

An auditor investigating the IS controls should consider findings from previous audits in the subject area. Give consideration to the amount of manual intervention required, the activities outside the daily routine, and the susceptibility of bypassing the IS controls. A smart auditor will always consider the experience, skills, and integrity of the staff involved in applying the controls.

Application controls (Embedded in programs)   This is the lowest subset in the control family. All activity should have filtered through the general controls, then the pervasive controls and detailed controls, before it reaches the application controls level. The higher-level controls help protect the integrity of the application and its data. Leaving an application exposed without the higher-level controls makes as much sense as leaving a child naked in the woods to fend for itself. Just like children, the application needs to be sheltered and protected from harm.

Management is responsible for having applications tested prior to production through a recognized test method. The goal is to provide a technical certification that each system meets the requirements. Management has to sign a formal accreditation statement granting their approval for the system to enter production based on fitness of use and accepting all responsibilities of ownership. Accreditation makes management accountable for system performance and liability of failure (who to blame or who to reward).

Reviewing Existing Controls

The next step in the planning process is to review the existing internal controls that are intended to prevent, detect, or correct problems. Management is responsible for designating and implementing internal controls to protect their assets. You can obtain initial information about existing controls by reviewing current policies and procedures, and later by interviewing managers and key personnel. The purpose of internal controls can be classified into one of three categories:

Preventative   Controls that seek to stop (prevent) the problem from occurring. A simple example is prescreening job applicants for employment eligibility. Synonyms for preventive controls include words such as *proactive* or *deterrent activities* designed to discourage or stop a problem.

Detective   Controls that are intended to find a problem and bring it to your attention. Auditing is a detective control for discovering information.

Corrective   Controls that seek to repair the problem after detection. Restoring data from a backup tape after a disk drive failure is a corrective control. _Reactive control_ is a synonym of _corrective control_.

Controls from the three mid-level categories are implemented by using one of the following three methods:

Administrative   Using written policies and procedures (people based)

Technical   Involving a software or hardware process to calculate a result (special technology)

Physical   Implementing physical barriers or visual deterrents (building design)

The auditor should be concerned with the attitude and understanding demonstrated by the auditee. An excellent exercise is to ask the auditee to which category their control would best apply. You may hear some unique and often incorrect responses. The process of reviewing the controls to prevent, detect, or correct is an excellent awareness generator with your auditee.

Table 2.2 lists some examples of these control types.

TABLE 2.2   Controls and Methods of Implementation

Control Type	Implementation Method	Some Examples
Preventative "stops"	Administrative	Hiring procedures, background checks, segregation of duties, training, change control process, acceptable use policy (AUP), organizational charts, job descriptions, written procedures, business contracts, laws and regulations, risk management, project management, service-level agreements (SLAs), system documentation
	Technical	Data backups, virus scanners, designated redundant high-availability system ready for failover (HA standby), encryption, access control lists (ACLs), system certification process
	Physical	Access control, locked doors, fences, property tags, security guards, live monitoring of CCTV, human-readable labels, warning signs
Detective "finds"	Administrative	Auditing, system logs, mandatory vacation periods, exception reporting, run-to-run totals, check numbers, control self-assessment (CSA), risk assessment, oral testimony

TABLE 2.2   Controls and Methods of Implementation *(continued)*

Control Type	Implementation Method	Some Examples
	Technical	Intrusion detection system (IDS), high-availability systems detecting or signaling system failover condition (HA failure detection), automated log readers (CAAT), checksum, verification of digital signatures, biometrics for identification (many search), CCTV used for logging, network scanners, computer forensics, diagnostic utilities
	Physical	Broken glass, physical inventory count, alarm system (burglar, smoke, water, temperature, fire), tamper seals, fingerprints, receipts and invoices
Corrective "fixes"	Administrative	Termination procedures (friendly/unfriendly), business continuity and disaster recovery plans, outsourcing, in sourcing, implementing recommendations of prior audit, lessons learned, property and casualty insurance
	Technical	Data restoration from backup, high-availability system failover to redundant system (HA failover occurs), redundant network routing, file repair utilities
	Physical	Hot-warm-cold sites for disaster recovery, fire-control sprinklers, heating and AC, humidity control

When you exercise this awareness game of preventative, detective, and corrective controls, it is interesting to notice how technology-oriented people will provide an overt emphasis on technology, while nontechnology-oriented people will focus on administrative and physical controls. If your background is technology, you will need to consider administrative or physical solutions to approach a reasonable balance of controls. Nontechnology-oriented people will need to force their emphasis to include technical controls and achieve a similar level of balance.

The Secret of Strong Controls

The secret to achieving strong controls is to implement layers. The minimum for an effective control is to have at least one point in each of the three areas: preventative, detective, and corrective. For example, a policy without a detective mechanism or a corrective mechanism is not enforceable. The strongest controls implement all nine layers (Preventative, Detective, Corrective implemented using administrative methods, physical methods and technical methods).

The preventative control, for example, would include an administrative policy with technical protection and physical signs or barriers. A corresponding detective control would be implemented with authorization to audit proper job descriptions and procedures. The detective control would include technical methods, such as intrusion, and detection and physical indicators, such as a video recording of people's activity in secure areas. The control would be coupled with corrective actions—such as manual procedures for isolation, and technical recovery using data restored from backup tapes or physical replacement. This is referred to as *depth of controls*.

Strong control = multiple preventive controls + multiple detective controls + multiple corrective controls

Weak control = shallow bare minimum control + implementation or no implementation

Now that we have covered the basic preventative, detective, and corrective controls, it is time to move on to the impact of pervasive controls.

Gathering Audit Evidence

Every good auditor understands the necessity of collecting tangible and reliable evidence. You read an introduction to the evidence rule in Chapter 1. Although you may really like or admire the people who are the subject of the audit, your final auditor's report must be based on credible factual evidence that will support your statements.

Consider for a moment something not related to IS auditing: police investigations or famous television courtroom dramas. Every good detective story is based on careful observation and common sense. A successful detective searches for clues in multiple places. Witnesses are interviewed to collect their versions of the story. Homes and offices are tirelessly searched for the minutest shred of relevant evidence. Detectives constantly ask whether the suspected individual had the motive, opportunity, and means to carry out the crime. The trail of clues is sorted in an attempt to determine which clues represent the greatest value and best tell the story. Material clues are the most sought after. From time to time, the clues are reviewed, and the witnesses reinterviewed. The detective orders a stakeout to monitor suspects. Ultimately, the suspects and clues of evidence are brought together in one place for the purpose of a reenactment. Under a watchful eye, the materially relevant portions of the crime are re-created in an attempt to unmask the perpetrator. In the movies, the detective is fabulously successful, and the criminal is brought to justice.

Unfortunately, IS auditing is not so dramatic or thrilling to watch. A CISA candidate needs to possess a thorough understanding of evidence, because IS auditing is centered on properly collecting and reviewing evidence. Let's start with a short discussion on the characteristics of good evidence.

Using Evidence to Prove a Point

Evidence will either prove or disprove a point. The absence of evidence is the absence of proof. In spite of your best efforts, if you're unable to prove those points, you would receive zero credit for your efforts. An auditor should not give any credit to claims or positive assertions that cannot be documented by evidence. No evidence, no proof equals no credit.

> All auditees start the audit with zero points and have to build up to their final score.

Types of Evidence

There are two primary types of evidence, according to legal definition:

Direct evidence   This proves existence of a fact without inference or presumption. *Inference* is when you draw a logical and reasonable proposition from another that is supposed to be true. Direct evidence includes the unaltered testimony of an eyewitness and written documents.

Indirect evidence   Indirect evidence uses a hypothesis without direct evidence to make a claim that consists of both inference and presumption. Indirect evidence is based on a chain of circumstances leading to a claim, with the intent to prove the existence or nonexistence of certain facts. Indirect evidence is also known as *circumstantial evidence*.

An auditor should always strive to obtain the best possible evidence during an audit. Using direct evidence is preferable whenever it can be obtained. Indirect evidence represents a much lower value because of its subjective nature. An auditor may find it difficult to justify using indirect evidence unless the audit objective is to gather data after detecting an illegal activity. An audit without direct evidence is typically unacceptable.

Typical Evidence for IS Audits

You will attempt to gather audit evidence by using similar techniques as a detective. Some of the data you gather will be of high value, and other data may be of low value. You will need to continually assess the quality and quantity of evidence. You may discover evidence through your own observations, by reviewing internal documentation, by using computer assisted audit tools (CAAT), or by reviewing correspondence and minutes of meetings.

Examples of the various types of audit evidence include the following:

- Documentary evidence, which can include a business record of transactions, receipts, invoices, and logs
- Data extraction, which mines details from data files using automated tools
- Auditee claims, which are representations made in oral or written statements
- Analysis of plans, policies, procedures, and flowcharts
- Results of compliance and substantive audit tests
- Auditor's observations of auditee work or reperformance of the selected process

All evidence should be reviewed to determine its reliability and relevance. The best evidence will be objective and independent of the provider. The quality of evidence you collect will have a direct effect on the points you wish to prove.

Using Computer Assisted Audit Tools

Computer assisted audit tools (CAAT) are invaluable for compiling evidence during IS audits. The auditor will find several advantages of using CAAT in the analytical audit procedure. These tools are capable of executing a variety of automated compliance tests and substantive tests that would be nearly impossible to perform manually.

These specialized tools may include multifunction audit utilities, which can analyze logs, perform vulnerability tests, or verify specific implementation of compliance in a system configuration compared to intended controls.

CAAT includes the following types of software tools and techniques:

- Host evaluation tools to read the system configuration settings and evaluate the host for known vulnerabilities

- Network traffic and protocol analysis using a sniffer

- Mapping and tracing tools that use a tracer-bullet approach to follow processes through a software application using test data

- Testing the configuration of specific application software such as a SQL database

- Software license counting across the network

- Testing for password compliance on user login accounts

Many CAATs have a built-in report writer that can generate more than one type of predefined report of findings on your behalf.

Numerous advantages may exist, but they come at a cost. These expert systems may be expensive to acquire. Specialized training is often required to obtain the skills to operate these tools effectively. A significant amount of time may be required to become a competent CAAT operator.

Some of the concerns for or against using CAAT include the following:

- Auditor's level of computer knowledge and experience

- Level of risk and complexity of the audit environment

- Cost and time constraints

- Specialized training requirements

- Speed, efficiency, and accuracy over manual operations

- Need for continuous online auditing

- Security of the data extracted by CAAT

WARNING A CISA may encounter individuals who are self-proclaimed auditors based solely on their ability to use CAAT software. You should consider this when using the work of others. The ability to use CAAT alone does not represent the discipline and detailed audit training of a professional auditor.

Using CAAT for Continuous Online Audit

The new audit tools offer the advantage of providing continuous online auditing. You should be aware of the six types of continuous online auditing techniques:

Online event monitors   Online event monitors include automated tools designed to read and correlate system logs or transaction logs on behalf of the auditor. This type of event monitoring tool will usually generate automated reports with alarms for particular events. A few examples include software that reads event logs, intrusion detection systems, virus scanners, and software that detects configuration changes, such as the commercial product Tripwire. (Low complexity.)

Embedded program audit hooks   A software developer can write embedded application hooks into their program to generate red-flag alerts to an auditor, hopefully before the problem gets out of hand. This method will flag selected transactions to be examined. (Low complexity.)

Continuous and intermittent simulation (CIS) audit   In continuous and intermittent simulation, the application software always tests for transactions that meet a certain criteria. When the criteria is met, the software runs an audit of the transaction (intermittent test). Then the computer waits until the next transaction meeting the criteria occurs. This provides for a continuous audit as selected transactions occur. (Medium complexity.)

Snapshot audit   This technique uses a series of sequential data captures that are referred to as *snapshots*. The snapshots are taken in a logical sequence that a transaction will follow. The snapshots produce an audit trail, which is reviewed by the auditor. (Medium complexity.)

Embedded audit module (EAM)   This integrated audit testing module allows the auditor to create a set of dummy transactions that will be processed along with live, genuine transactions. The auditor then compares the output data against their own calculations. This allows substantive integrity testing without disrupting the normal processing schedule. EAM is also known as *integrated test facility*. (High complexity.)

System control audit review file with embedded audit modules (SCARF/EAM)   The theory is straightforward. A system-level audit program is installed on the system to selectively monitor the embedded audit modules inside the application software. Few systems of this nature are in use. The idea is popular with auditors; however, a programmer must write the modules. (High complexity.)

Table 2.3 summarizes the differences between these CAAT methods.

TABLE 2.3   Summary of CAAT Methods

CAAT Method	Characteristics	Complexity
Online event monitors	Reads logs and alarms.	Low
Embedded program audit hooks	Flags selected transactions to be examined.	Low

TABLE 2.3   Summary of CAAT Methods *(continued)*

CAAT Method	Characteristics	Complexity
Continuous and intermittent simulation (CIS)	Audits any transaction that meets preselected criteria, waits for the next transaction meeting audit criteria.	Medium
Snapshot	Assembles a sequence of data captures into an audit trail.	Medium
Embedded audit module (EAM)	Processes dummy transactions along with genuine, live transactions.	High
System control audit review file with embedded audit modules (SCARF/EAM)	System-level audit program used to monitor multiple EAMs inside the application software. This is a mainframe class of control.	High

CAAT simplifies the life of an auditor by automatically performing the more menial, repetitive, detail tasks. The auditor needs to consider the CAAT reports while tempering them with some basic commonsense observations.

Electronic Discovery

New developments are occurring in legal procedures for courts. The increased use of computers has led to widespread reliance on electronic data records. In the old days, evidence could be discovered by rummaging through printed mail, business records, file cabinets, and the dusty storage warehouse. Electronic record keeping is a wonderful tool for automation, yet it can also perpetuate fraud, intentional omissions, or misrepresentation. *Electronic discovery* is the investigation of electronic records for evidence to be used in the courtroom.

The new legal standard for electronic discovery is referred to as *e-discovery*. These rules were created to aid auditors and investigators by requiring owners of electronic records to disclose their existence and to provide the data in a simple easy-to-read format (unencoded). Under e-discovery rules, the party who owns or possesses the data is required to perform the conversion and to certify that the contents are truthful and complete in their representation of the content. Put simply, the data owner is no longer permitted to use unintelligible or secret codes to keep database contents a secret from investigators.

State and federal courts are still debating the final rules for e-discovery. The law recognizes two parties: the producing party, which provides the evidence, and the receiving party, which receives the evidence. Here's what the auditor can expect until a final ruling is ratified:

- Discovery starts with a conference between the parties to plan the discovery process. Any issues related to disclosure of electronically stored information should be identified.

- The conference sets the scope to identify possible sources of information. The judge may be asked to include the decisions of the meeting in a court order.

- Limitations on scope may be identified based on undue cost or undue burden of production. Limitations will be determined by the judge after considering assertions of both parties and the nature of the case. Discovery may be ordered if the requesting party shows good cause in support of a claim or defense.

  - The scope may include data available online on any system.

  - The scope may include recovering deleted data.

  - The scope may include searching standing data from backup media and other offline sources.

  - The scope may include discovery of email and email records.

  - A search protocol will be agreed upon by the parties or ordered by the judge.

  - Unless the parties agree otherwise, the format shall be PDF or TIFF images without alteration of format or removal of revision history.

  - The judge may order the costs to be allocated equally, or unequally if good cause is shown why the other party should bear the cost.

- Sometimes portions of data, such as formulas and lawful business secrets, are protected by a claim of privilege. If privileged information is produced in discovery, it may be recalled for return, sequester, or destruction after notification is given to the receiving party with an explanation of the basis for privilege. The information may not be disclosed after notice is given, and the producing party must preserve the information until the claim is resolved.

- Under rule 37, the court may not impose sanctions on a party for failure to provide electronically stored information that was lost as a result of routine good-faith operations, if the records preservation was not mandated by regulation or exceptional circumstances.

E-discovery applies to criminal cases and civil lawsuits. The courts have determined that using encryption to hide or to cover illegal activities will result in multiple criminal penalties. Failure to cooperate with e-discovery requests can result in fines or prosecution. E-discovery requests include access to audit company records, HR files, database files, financial systems, and email correspondence.

 The management of every organization, as well as auditors, need to learn more about the impact of e-discovery on their business activities. Awareness can prevent future legal headaches.

Grading of Evidence

All evidence is graded according to four criteria. This grading aids the auditor in assessing the evidence value. It is important to obtain the best possible evidence. The four characteristics are as follows:

Material relevance   Evidence with material relevance influences the decision because of a logical relationship with the issues. Materially relevant evidence indicates a fact that will help determine that a particular action was more or less probable. The purpose of material evidence is to ascertain whether the same conclusion would have been reached without considering that item of evidence. Evidence is _irrelevant_ if it is not related to the issue and has no logical tendency to prove the issue under investigation.

Evidence objectivity   Evidence objectivity refers to its ability to be accepted and understood with very little judgment required. The more judgment required, the less objective the evidence. As you increase the amount of judgment necessary to support your claims, the evidence quickly becomes subjective or circumstantial, which is the opposite of objective. _Objective evidence_ is in a state of unbiased reality during examination, without influence by another source. Objective evidence can be obtained through qualitative/quantitative measurement, and from records or statements of fact pertaining to the subject of the investigation. Objective evidence can be verified by observation, measurement, or testing.

Competency of the evidence provider   Evidence supplied by a person with direct involvement is preferred. The source of their knowledge will affect the evidence value and accuracy. A secondhand story still holds value by providing information that may lead to the evidence the auditor is seeking.

An _expert_ is legally defined as a person who possesses special skill or knowledge in a science or profession because of special study or experience with the subject. An expert possesses a particular skill in forming accurate opinions about a subject; in contrast, a common person would be incapable of deducing an accurate conclusion about the same subject.

Evidence independence   Evidence independence is similar to auditor independence, meaning the provider should not have any gain or loss by providing the evidence. Evidence supplied by a person with a bias is often questionable. The auditor should ask whether the evidence provider is part of the auditee's organization. Qualifications of the evidence provider should always be considered. A person with a high degree of detailed understanding is vastly more qualified than an individual of limited knowledge. Evidence and data gathered from a novice may have a low value when compared to data gathered by an expert. A person who is knowledgeable and independent of the audit subject would be considered the best source of evidence.

Table 2.4 lists examples of evidence grading. An IS auditor should always strive to obtain the best evidence, which is shown in the far right column.

TABLE 2.4   Example of Evidence Grading

	Poor Evidence	Good Evidence	Best Evidence
Material Relevance	Unrelated	Indirect (low relation)	Direct (high relation)
Objectivity	Subjective (low)	Requires few supporting facts to explain the meaning	Needs no explanation

TABLE 2.4   Example of Evidence Grading *(continued)*

	Poor Evidence	Good Evidence	Best Evidence
Evidence Source	Unrelated third party with no involvement	Indirect involvement by second party	Direct involvement by first party
Competency of Provider	Biased	Nonbiased	Nonbiased and independent
Evidence Analysis Method	Novice	Experienced	Expert
Resulting Trustworthiness	Low	Medium	High

Evidence is analyzed by using a structured test method to further determine the value it represents. The audit process itself represents a major portion of preparation work to support the analysis of actual evidence.

> Every test procedure must be documented in writing to ensure that a duplicate test for verification will yield the same result. Tests may need to be repeated quarterly or annually to measure the auditee's level of improvement. Each test execution should be well documented with a record of time, date, method of sample selection, sample size, procedure used, person performing the analysis, and results.

It is often a good practice to use video recording to document the test process when the execution of the test method may be challenged—for example, to videotape a forensic computer audit if the results may be subject to dispute by individuals who are unfamiliar with the process.

The evidence grading effort aims to improve the resulting trustworthiness of the evidence. A competent IS auditor who can gather evidence and provide expert analysis with a high evidence trustworthiness rating is quite valuable indeed.

Timing of Evidence

An additional factor to consider in regards to evidence is timing. *Evidence timing* indicates whether evidence is received when it is requested, or several hours or days later. In electronic systems, the timing has a secondary meaning: Electronic evidence may be available only during a limited window of time before it is overwritten or the software changes to a new version.

We have discussed the character of evidence, evidence grading, and timing. The next section explains the evidence life cycle relating to the legal chain of custody.

Evidence Life Cycle

- Evidence handling Chain of Custody (handwritten)

The evidence will pass through seven life-cycle phases that are necessary in every audit. Every IS auditor must remain aware of the legal demands that are always present with regard to <u>evidence handling.</u> Failure to maintain a proper chain of custody may disqualify the evidence. Evidence handling is just as important for SOX compliance is it would be for suspected criminal activity. Evidence handling is crucial for compliance to most industry regulations.

WARNING   Mishandling of evidence can result in the auditor becoming the target of legal action by the owner. Mishandling evidence in criminal investigations could result in the bumbling auditor becoming the target of both the owner and the alleged perpetrator of a criminal activity.

The seven phases of the evidence life cycle are identification, collection, initial preservation storage, analysis, post analysis preservation storage, presentation, and return of the evidence to the owner. The entire set of seven phases is referred to as the *chain of custody.* Let's go down the list one by one:

Identification   The auditor needs to identify items that may be objective evidence lending support to the purpose of the audit. The characteristics of the evidence location or surroundings should be thoroughly documented before proceeding to the collection stage. All evidence shall be labeled, dated, and notated with a short description about its purpose or discovery. From this point forward, the evidence movements must be logged into a tracking record. Your client will not be happy if evidence is misplaced.

NOTE   It may be important to demonstrate how the evidence looked when it was discovered. Identification includes labeling and can include photographing physical evidence <u>in an undisturbed state</u> at the time of discovery.

Collection   The collection process involves taking possession of the evidence to place it under the control of a custodian. Special consideration should be given to items of a sensitive nature or high value. The IS auditor needs to exercise common sense during the collection process. Client records need to be kept in a secure location.

TIP   For most audits except criminal investigations, the IS auditor should be cognizant of the liability created by taking the client's confidential records out of the client's office. We strongly advise that all records remain within the client's facility to relieve the auditor of potential liability. The best way to prevent accusations is to ensure that you never place yourself in a compromising position. Allow the client to remain responsible for evidence security. Just be sure to lock up each evening before you leave.

Evidence of compliance is required for regulations such as SOX. A smart auditor recognizes that storage of any evidence in their own office is not acceptable. Records should be placed in a bonded record storage facility with the cost paid by your client. Consider the liability created by exposing records in your office to theft, destruction, or disclosure by a search order from an unrelated court subpoena.

Criminal evidence should not be disturbed until after proper identification and labeling. It may be beneficial to have a nonbiased observer present as a witness to attest to the investigator's actions as observed during the collection activity.

Initial preservation storage   A major problem with evidence is the challenge of preserving it in its original state. The preservation and storage process is a vital component in the chain of custody. The custodian of the evidence must be able to prove that the evidence has been protected and no alteration has occurred. The slightest change will transform the evidence without changing its identity. Electronic evidence requires special handling procedures to overcome future claims that the evidence has been altered (evidence tampering).

The chain of custody must remain unbroken to prevent evidence from being disqualified. In legal proceedings, a common method of disqualifying evidence is to argue that the custodian has failed the chain of evidence requirements. A related accusation is that evidence has been tampered with, which is often a plausible argument unless it can be proven that mishandling never occurred.

Analysis   In this phase, the evidence samples are examined by observation, scientific test, and qualitative and quantitative measurement. The entire process and results should be well documented. Individual tests may need to be rerun if errors are discovered with the test procedure, sample, or personnel executing the test.

In some instances, the test results may need to be duplicated by a second independent tester to validate the initial finding.

As you may recall, regulatory compliance is an ongoing requirement. The same internal controls will need to be tested at least once each year. The auditor should ensure that the testing process produces a reasonable degree of consistency in each subsequent audit.

Post analysis preservation storage   After testing, the evidence and samples must be returned to preservation and secure storage. The evidence will continue to stay in storage except during presentation or retesting. *(no evidence tampering)*

The auditor should be aware that proper handling is paramount for success in legal proceedings. Evidence used in legal trials may be retrieved and returned multiple times for use in court presentations prior to final release for return to the owner. The U.S. legal process allows for trials in at least three separate courts as the case progresses through to final appeal.

A bonded evidence storage facility might be used for storage when the evidence is used in legal cases lasting several years. An example would be a case of corporate fraud or theft.

Management may decide that the evidence used in routine compliance audits should be copied and bound into storage binders. Selected copies of those documents would be sent to storage with the client's financial records. This ensures the ability to demonstrate the evidence in a near original state for any future investigation by industry regulators. Initial evidence collection is a time-consuming process that might be difficult to duplicate in the future.

Presentation   The evidence and findings are to be presented in support of the auditor's report. A variety of details may be included or omitted depending on the nature of the report. Reports of system performance offer little detail when compared to reports of criminal activity.

Return to owner   The evidence is returned to the owner after the audit test results are successfully evaluated, or after legal proceedings are officially concluded by order of the final court. It is important to notice the distinction. In noncriminal activity, the evidence is promptly returned when the audit is concluded. Evidence may be held in preservation storage for several years if situations of suspected criminal activity exist.

Figure 2.4 demonstrates the logical flow through the entire chain of custody. A CISA is required to be competent in this evidence life cycle.

Now we will discuss examples of evidence that an IS auditor will typically use during an audit.

FIGURE 2.4   The evidence life cycle

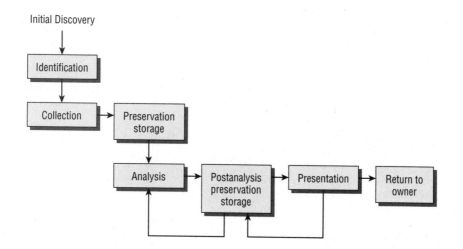

Preparing Audit Documentation

see btm
of pg
140

All auditors are required to prepare a thorough set of audit documentation at the start of each audit. This includes copies of the charter and scope, audit plans, policies, and specific procedures used during the audit. You should record both handling and test procedures. Audit reports are frequently used as evidence in lawsuits and criminal cases of embezzlement or fraud. As you recall, in Chapter 1 we mentioned several cases involving corruption perpetuated by dishonest executives. Professional auditors will need to demonstrate the extent to which they have complied with IS auditing standards.

Your job as an auditor is to provide consistency. All your findings should be repeatable by another auditor. Documentation should include auditor's working notes and evidence necessary to reperform the audit. The key to building a successful practice is to map each of your planned tasks and corresponding findings to a specific point of compliance in the standard or regulation. This mapping may require you to identify the page, paragraph, and line number in the regulation and for each item you will show as compliant or noncompliant. During the audit, you should be preparing records to answer the following questions:

- Who was involved?
- What was audited, how was the evidence obtained, and what specific test procedure was used?
- When did it occur?
- Where did it occur?
- Why (the purpose of the audit)?
- How were the audit plan and procedures executed?

Later, the auditor's final working papers should be placed into an audit documentation archive, including copies of any reports that were issued.

The auditor should always remember that records of each audit may be needed again in the future. Integrated audits such as SAS-94 will have documentation retention requirements equal to the financial statement, typically at least seven years. Financial and internal control records for an integrated audit serve as a matched pair that should not be separated. Records for certain systems or processes may have a retention requirement specified in their service-level agreement or contract. Very specialized systems used in aerospace, life safety, hazardous materials, or the military may be retained for decades.

Let's look at the selection method for your audit samples and begin the move toward actual testing.

Selecting Audit Samples

Audit samples are selected for the purpose of collecting representative evidence to be subjected to either compliance testing or substantive testing (which is defined later in this chapter). The auditor should consider a selection technique that will provide the most relevant evidence supported by appropriate analytical procedures.

Two basic types of audit samples can be designed by the auditor to fulfill their requirements: statistical and nonstatistical. Figure 2.5 shows the various audit samples, as well as their testing methods. Care is given to the selection process in order to avoid drawing the wrong conclusion from the wrong sample. This is referred to as a _sampling risk_. Let's look at each of these samples more closely.

FIGURE 2.5   Audit samples

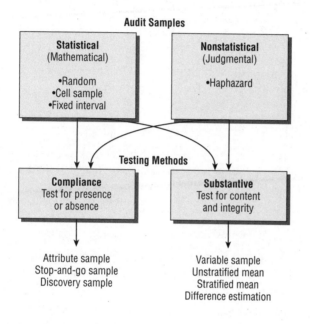

Statistical Sampling

Statistical sampling uses mathematical techniques that result in an outcome that is mathematically quantifiable. Statistical samples are usually presented as a percentage. The purpose of statistical sampling is to gain an objective representation. Samples are selected by an objective mathematical process. The auditor should be aware that if the client has strong internal controls, the sample sizes may be smaller because the odds of fraud or failure will be lower.

Examples of statistical sampling include the following:

Random sampling   Samples are selected at random.

Cell sampling   Random selection is performed at predefined intervals.

Fixed interval sampling   The sample existing at every $n +$ interval increment is selected for testing.

Nonstatistical Sampling

Nonstatistical sampling is based on the auditor's judgment (also referred to as _judgmental sampling_). The auditor determines the sample size, the method of generating the sample, and the number of items to be analyzed. The results of judgmental sampling are unlikely to represent the actual population. This is a subjective process usually based on elements of risk or materiality. An example of nonstatistical sampling includes *haphazard sampling*, in which the samples are randomly drawn for testing.

After the samples are selected, the next step is to perform compliance tests or substantive testing.

Conducting Audit Testing

As stated earlier, the basic test methods used will be either compliance testing or substantive testing. Appropriate audit samples will have to be generated for the test.

Compliance Testing

Compliance testing tests for the presence or absence of something. Compliance testing includes verifying that policies and procedures have been put in place, and checking that user access rights, program change control procedures, and system audit logs have been activated. An example of a compliance test is comparing the list of persons with physical access to the data center against the HR list of current employees.

Compliance testing is based on one of the following types of audit samples:

Attribute sampling   Generally popular in compliance testing. The objective is to determine whether an attribute is present or absent in the subject sample. The result is specified by the rate of occurrence—for example, the presence of 1 in 100 units would be 1 percent.

Stop-and-go sampling   Used when few errors are expected. Stop-and-go allows the test to occur without excessive effort in sampling and provides the opportunity to stop testing at the earliest possible opportunity. It is a simple form of testing to reinforce any claim that errors are unlikely in the sample population.

Discovery sampling   A 100 percent sampling used to detect fraud or when the likelihood of evidence existing is low. Forensics is an excellent example of discovery sampling. This is an attempt to discover evidence.

Precision, or expected error rate   The precision rate indicates the acceptable margin of error between audit samples and the total quantity of the subject population. This is usually expressed as a percentage, such as 5 percent. To obtain a very low error rate, it is necessary to use a very large sample in testing. Auditors are justified in using a smaller sample size when the total population is expected to be error-free. A larger sample is required when errors are expected to be present in the population. The larger sample can yield a higher average. When errors are expected, the auditor must examine more data to determine whether the actual errors are within a tolerable error rate (maximum errors you would accept).

Error levels may be determined by reviewing the findings of a prior audit and by considering changes in the organization's procedures. Use the risk-based audit strategy to determine whether your samples and tests are telling the truth about the auditee.

Substantive Testing

Substantive testing seeks to verify the content and integrity of evidence. Substantive tests may include complex calculations to verify account balances, perform physical inventory counts, or execute sample transactions to verify the accuracy of supporting documentation. Substantive tests use audit samples selected by dollar value or to project (forecast or estimate) a total for groups with related characteristics.

Substantive testing is based on one of the following types of audit samples:

Variable sampling   Used to designate dollar values or weights (effectiveness) of an entire subject population by prorating from a smaller sample. Consider the challenge of counting large volumes of currency by its weight. Variable sampling could be used to count currency by multiplying the physical weight of one unit by the total weight of the combined sample, and then multiplying by the face value printed on the bill or coin. A demonstration is a single $50 bill weighing 1.0 gram, with the entire sample of $50 bills weighing 61 grams altogether. The combined sample weight would indicate a total quantity of 61 bills for an estimated dollar value of $3,050. This is a common technique for forecasting quantity and value of inventory based on particular characteristics.

Unstratified mean estimation   Used in an attempt to project an estimated total for the whole subject population.

Stratified mean estimation   Used to calculate an average by group, similar to demographics, whereby the entire population is divided (stratified) into smaller groups based on similar characteristics. Examples are teenagers from the ages of 13 to 19, people from the ages of 20 to 29, people from the ages of 30 to 39, and those who are male or female, smokers or nonsmokers, and so on.

Difference estimation   Used to determine the difference between audited and unaudited claims of value.

Tolerable error rate

Used to indicate the maximum number of errors that can exist without declaring a material misstatement.

- For compliance tests, a tolerable error rate is the maximum deviation from a procedure that the auditor is willing to accept. Hint: If you want to remain an auditor, it had better be a very small deviation.

- In substantive testing, the auditor uses their judgment concerning material relevance and concludes whether the audit objective has been achieved. The test procedure and results should indicate a truthful pass or fail. A smart auditor will always lean toward the conservative side for safety in their measurement.

Regardless of the audit sample and test method used, the auditor is presumed to have a high degree of confidence when the audit coefficient is 95 percent or higher. The *audit coefficient* represents your level of confidence about the audit results. It is also referred to as a *reliability factor.*

Every good audit plan contains both collection plans and sampling plans. Be sure you know what you want to see and what samples you will need to test. A good sampling plan is required unless you want to conduct a 100% examination.

Record Your Test Results

Just like Leonardo DaVinci and Louis Pasteur, every auditor needs to keep logs documenting their tests, samples, results and observations. The auditor must trace all findings of conformity and nonconformity in their documentation of test results. Always remember your audit test results must be repeatable by another auditor.

Each finding of evidence can be classified into one of these common reporting statements, presented in order of most desirable to least desirable.

Noteworthy achievement   Auditee has demonstrated some aspect in the process or system is being done very well. Auditee's efforts are very effective and the auditor wants to bring recognition where credit is due. Auditee has exceeded the requirements.

Conformity   The testing of evidence proves the auditee is accomplishing their stated objectives. Minimum requirements have been met.

Opportunity for improvement   A specific item found is not in violation, but should be targeted as an opportunity for improvement. For example the level of work integration is low, therefore fixing this issue could reduce waste or the amount of manual effort required.

Concern   The evidence and auditor's observations indicate the possibility for future problems that need to be understood by management. Examples include over reliance, inefficiency, cascading problems and the likelihood of failure.

Nonconformity   Testing indicates a violation exists which needs to be corrected. The violation found may be minor or major significance. Nonconformities include system defects or missing control capabilities.

Analyzing the Results

Using your audit plan as a roadmap, it's time to analyze the evidence samples. The goal is to determine if the samples tested by the auditor indicate conformity (meets requirement) or nonconformity (fails requirement).

We have two concerns as auditors related to testing: sufficiency of evidence and contradictory evidence. Let's look into this further.

Sufficiency of evidence   Is there enough evidence of sufficient quantity and quality to fulfill the intended purpose and scope of the audit? If not, the auditor will not be able to prove conformity. The auditor should continue working the audit and report the limitations. Unless enough evidence can be found the auditee will fail to meet compliance or substantive goals.

Contradictory evidence   Let the evidence tell the story. Contradictory evidence suggests either the auditor is doing something wrong or you have discovered evidence proving a problem actually exists (nonconformity). The auditor needs to perform additional quality assurance checks and recheck the test results to determine the reason why this nonconformity has been detected.

Detecting Irregularities and Illegal Acts

It is management's responsibility to implement the controls and supervision necessary to detect irregularities and potentially illegal acts in their environment. Management is responsible for making written assertions as to their representation of internal controls. Audit plans should include provisions and procedures in the event an auditor encounters irregularities or possibly illegal acts.

Examples of illegal activities include the following:

Fraud   Any act of deception used to gain an advantage. Misrepresentation is a type of fraud. Examples include posting transaction records that are intentionally false and without genuine merit.

Theft   Taking or acquiring resources that are not rightfully yours. The legal term *conversion* is another name for theft. Embezzlement is a form of theft.

Suppression   Suppressing data or records and their effects in business transactions. This is related to *obstruction* and *willful omission*.

Racketeering   The process of repeated (pervasive) fraud or other crimes. Racketeering is governed by the Racketeer Influenced and Corrupt Organizations (RICO) Act, which carries dire consequences to those parties alleged to have participated.

Regulatory violations   Intentionally or unintentionally violating the law.

Indicators of Illegal or Irregular Activity

The IS auditor should understand that an organization's internal controls will not eliminate the possibility of irregular or illegal activity. Although it is not the auditor's job to detect these conditions, it is important to be alert to potential indicators. The auditor should be on the lookout for the following symptoms:

Questionable payments   Examples include fees that appear to be excessively high or low, failed account reconciliation, payments to government officials, and payments for unspecified services.

Unsatisfactory record control   Examples include poor record keeping in general, proper controls not in use, evidence of falsified documents, missing documentation, and the untimely shredding of documents in advance of corporate retention guidelines.

Unsatisfactory explanations   Examples include large or unusual transactions, and especially transactions with related companies at the end of the financial reporting period such as month-end or quarter-end. Other examples include overbooked or under booked sales, unexplained or unusual items, or unexplained funds held in suspense accounts.

Other questionable circumstances   These might relate to the lifestyles of the organization's executives and employees.

Responding to Irregular or Illegal Activity - *Seek legal advice before finishing the audit - pg 118* 114

If you discover any potentially irregular or illegal activity, the next step is to attempt to determine whether management is aware of the situation or has participated in the suspected activities. The auditor should document all information, evidence, findings, and conclusions that led to the discovery of the suspected activities:

- The auditor should consider any unusual or unexpected relationships that could lead to material misstatements or misrepresentations.

- The auditor should maintain a position of professional skepticism.

- Upon learning of material irregularities or illegal acts, the auditor should promptly notify one level of management higher than where the suspected activities may have taken place.

- If the activities involve a person charged with internal controls or governance, reporting should take place at the highest level possible.

- The auditor should not contact law enforcement or regulators until advised to do so by the auditor's legal counsel. Special handling procedures are usually required to protect the auditor.

- The auditor should never become a party to the suspected activity. The auditor should seek competent legal advice if unsure about what actions to take. You may be advised to prepare for termination of the audit.

Findings Outside of Audit Scope

Don't be surprised to discover something outside the scope of your audit; it happens all the time. Smart auditors recognize their obligation to stay within the mutually agreed-upon scope of their client. No respectable auditor would ignore problems found outside the original scope. The first objective is to determine whether the problem is major or just a minor nuisance. Here's what to do:

Minor problem   Report the discovery to the auditee and continue the audit within the original scope.

Major problem   Report the finding to your lead auditor or engagement manager. The audit team leader is responsible for reporting the discovery to the auditee's management. In addition, a decision needs to be made regarding whether this situation warrants additional investigation, and whether the audit should stop or continue within the original scope. Major problems outside of scope should be listed in your audit report. Be sure to ask your lead auditor whether the problem warrants reporting as a nonconformity within this particular audit or just mentioning it without marking as a nonconformity. The most successful auditors understand that the highest level of professionalism is necessary to handle this type of situation. Well-mannered professionals may gain additional audit work if the situation is handled correctly.

Reporting Your Audit Findings

see SAS-70 pg 74, 150

After performing your audit, the next step is to prepare a presentation to report your findings. Reporting is the process by which the auditor conveys to management their findings, including the following:

- Audit scope
- Audit objectives
- Methods and criteria used
- Nature of findings
- Extent of work performed
- Applicable dates of coverage

In addition, the final report should state any restrictions, reservations, or qualifications (concerns) that the auditor holds in relation to the audit. The auditor may provide a final opinion or no opinion based on these potential limitations. Auditors may issue qualified or unqualified opinions:

A **qualified opinion** means there are restrictions on the nature or the content of the findings.

An **unqualified opinion** has no restrictions on its use because the findings have no reservations.

Statement on Auditing Standards (SAS), the COSO internal controls framework, and the IT Governance Institute (ISACA-ITGI) publish several points of information that should be included in the final report. You should consult their publications for specific details. In summary, the recommendations include the following:

- A title that includes the word *independent* (for an external audit)
- The applicable date of the report
- Identification of the parties and subject matter
- An executive summary
- Any visual representations, charts, graphs, or diagrams
- A statement of the standards followed during the audit
- A statement of the procedures performed, and whether they were agreed to by the specified parties
- Any necessary disclaimers
- A statement of additional procedures, if performed
- A statement of restrictions on the use of the report
- A statement of any auditor concerns, reservations, or qualifications to the audit
- Detailed findings and the auditor's opinion
- Auditor signature and contact information

The IS auditor's signature attests that the audit report and stated findings are true and correct. *Attestation* is the act of providing your assurance via a signature that the contents of a document are authentic and genuine.

You should keep your report easy to read. Simple graphics, tables, and color coding will be appreciated by your client.

After producing the final report, you will need to meet with the auditee and management to review the findings. The primary purpose of this meeting is not to change your findings, but to obtain acceptance and agreement by the auditee. This is the final quality-control check before issuing your final report. You want to ensure that the facts are correctly presented in your report. A final copy of this report and of your working notes will need to be placed into the audit archive for document retention.

Identifying Omitted Procedures

On the rare occasion that an auditor determines after issuing a final report that one or more auditing procedures have been omitted, it may be necessary to review some of the audit alternatives to compensate for the omission. If the omitted procedures present material bearing on the outcome, and the audit alternatives cannot compensate for the deficiency, canceling the report and reissuing a new report (if appropriate) may be necessary. If the omitted procedures have tangible bearing on the outcome, the auditor should consult with their lawyer for advice concerning any possible avenues or potential legal actions.

Conducting an Exit Interview

After issuing a report, the auditor is required to conduct an exit interview with management to obtain a commitment for the recommendations made in the audit. Management is responsible for acknowledging the recommendations and designating whatever corrective action will be taken, including the estimated dates for the action.

In subsequent audits, you will check whether management honored their commitments to fix or remediate deficiencies found in a prior audit. Occasionally, the deficiencies are left uncorrected because changes in the organizational design or practice have eliminated the conditions of the prior control's weakness. Particular findings may apply to events that are no longer relevant. Otherwise, you expect management to act in a timely manner to correct the deficiency as originally reported.

The auditor should never take ownership of any problems found. This would violate your independence. All issues raised in your findings should be regarded as owned by the auditee. It's the job of their management to fix it.

Conducting Follow-Up Activities

Sometimes events of concern are discovered, or occur, after an audit has been completed. You would be concerned about the discovery of subsequent events that pose a material challenge to your final report. Accounting standards recognize these events and classify them as follows:

Type 1 events refer to those that occurred before the balance sheet date.

Type 2 events are those that occurred after the balance sheet date.

Depending on the type of audit, you may have additional reporting requirements or activities. These may require additional disclosures or adjustments to your report based on the nature of the event that was recently discovered or occurred.

 It is not the auditor's responsibility to detect subsequent events.

Summary

This concludes our review of the IS audit process. A CISA is expected to have a thorough understanding of the entire audit process. You will be expected to understand the issues and motivation behind each step.

A violation of the audit process would be a concern and would likely indicate that the outcome is meaningless. As an IS auditor, you should always strive to honor the spirit and intent of the audit process. Conduct audits in accordance with recognized audit standards, guidelines, and best practices. It is your job to plan the audit around the business requirements by using a risk-based approach and to collect meaningful evidence. You are expected to produce an objective report based on the evidence you obtained during the audit. The final report will be communicated to management with the goal of gaining their commitment to resolve any weaknesses found. Your actions should be well documented and reproducible by another auditor.

Chapter 1 covered how the auditor should look, act, and think. This chapter discussed how the auditor should carry out the audit. The next chapter presents the techniques used for IT governance.

Exam Essentials

Know how to develop and implement a risk-based audit strategy.   The auditor should focus on areas of high value. The risk assessment will help to determine whether the audit will yield meaningful information. Certain types of conditions may be difficult to audit. It is important that the audit is based on meaningful evidence that is materially relevant.

Understand how to conduct IS audits in accordance with published standards, guidelines, and best practices.   The auditor is expected to follow published audit standards to ensure thoroughness and consistency. Deviations from standards and guidelines is rare. Any deviation must be well documented, but results may not be accepted by the audit community. The purpose of best practices is to aid the auditor by identifying useful procedures and techniques. Every audit should be designed to adhere to standards.

Be familiar with how to plan for specific audits.   The CISA needs to understand the constraints and requirements of individual audits. It is the auditor's job to identify the resource requirements, sampling requirements, test methods, and procedures to be used. The auditor will identify appropriate personnel to be interviewed. The interview process must be scheduled and must implement predefined questions for the purpose of gathering data. An audit involving third-party personnel will present its own unique challenges.

Know the auditing practices and techniques.   Well-established IS auditing procedures ensure thoroughness and consistency necessary for a successful audit. Good audits will implement a well-thought-out sequence of procedures to evaluate materially relevant samples. ISACA provides the auditor with foundation knowledge that should be implemented during your audit. Effective sample selection of meaningful tests should yield materially relevant results.

Be familiar with IS control objectives and performing control assessment.   High-level controls are categorized as general controls, pervasive controls, detailed controls and application controls. Internal controls are intended to be preventative, detective, and corrective. Each control may be implemented using administrative methods, physical methods, and technical methods. The purpose of the controls is to prevent harm and protect an asset. The IS auditor is responsible for evaluating the effectiveness of controls.

Know some of the various types of computer assisted audit tools (CAAT).   Computer assisted audit tools are software tools that can provide detailed analysis of computer systems configuration, vulnerability, logs, and other information. The CAAT output should be kept confidential because of the potentially sensitive nature of its contents.

Understand the continuous auditing methods.   Continuous audit methods such as audit hooks or SCARF with embedded audit modules (SCARF/EAM) are used in environments where it is not possible to interrupt production.

Know the techniques to gather information and manage the evidence life cycle.   The auditor can collect information through traditional sources of business records, computer data files, and CAAT. Meaningful information can be obtained through personal interviews, workshops, and surveys. All information and evidence should be recorded and tracked. The evidence life cycle comprises identification, collection, preservation, analysis, safe storage, and finally its return to the owner. Evidence used for criminal prosecution must be handled with the highest degree of care. Evidence that is mishandled will void legal claims and may result in punitive legal action.

Know the types of evidence and evidence grading.   The best evidence will tell its own story. The best evidence will prove or disprove a point. The best evidence is both objective and independent. The timing of evidence must be considered when calculating its useful value. Evidence that is late and subjective will be of low value. Material evidence will have a bearing on the final outcome. Irrelevant evidence will not affect the final decision.

Familiarize yourself with the types of audit tests and sample selection.   Audit tests can be substantive or compliance based. It is important to select an appropriate sample in order to generate data to reflect the actual situation. Audit test procedures and sample selection methods must be well documented to ensure verifiable and reproducible tests. The sample may be selected based on physical characteristics, value, or size of population.

Understand how evidence is analyzed for reporting conformity or nonconformity.   The auditor must have sufficient evidence of quality and quantity in order to report a conformity. Test results are usually reported as noteworthy for special achievement, conforming to minimum requirements, opportunity for improvement, concern that's not a violation yet, and nonconformity.

Know how to deal with irregular and illegal acts.   It is possible that you could encounter evidence of irregular or illegal acts. The discoveries should be communicated to the next level of management higher than where the act occurred. Such a discovery involving persons responsible for internal controls must be reported to the absolute highest level of management. The auditor should consult their attorney for legal advice.

Know how to advise clients on implementing risk management and control practices while maintaining independence.   The auditor is encouraged to educate their client and help increase awareness of control issues. It is important that the auditor does not participate in specific discussions of design or architecture. The auditor must not work on fixing problems if the auditor is expected to be independent. A client may hire an auditor for remediation and use a separate, unrelated auditor for the audit. The auditor cannot be independent if they participated in the audit subject.

Be able to communicate issues, potential risks, and audit results.   The auditor is expected to communicate materially relevant issues to management through the audit reporting process. Issues of high significance should be communicated directly to the audit committee. The final results of each audit should be verifiable and reproducible. All communication must convey the facts without placing blame on individuals.

Understand the role of traditional audits compared to control self-assessment (CSA).   Control self-assessments are designed to empower the customer's staff. The intention is to generate awareness and ownership of problems. A control self-assessment is an excellent way to improve the performance of an organization between traditional audits. The traditional audit is still necessary to the independence requirement.

Review Questions

1. Failing to prevent or detect a material error would represent which type of risk?

    A. Overall audit risk

    B. Detection risk

    C. Inherent risk

    D. Control risk

2. Which term best describes the difference between audit sample and the total population?

    A. Precision

    B. Tolerable error rate

    C. Level of risk

    D. Analytic delta

3. Which is *not* a purpose of risk analysis?

    A. Support risk-based audit decisions

    B. Assist the auditor in determining audit objectives

    C. Assist the auditor in identifying risks and threats

    D. Ensure absolute safety during the audit

4. Which of the following is not a type of quantitative sampling model?

    A. Difference estimation

    B. Stratified mean per unit

    C. Unstratified mean per unit

    D. Qualitative estimation per unit

5. Which of the following is false concerning a control self-assessment?

    A. Empowers the user to take ownership and accountability

    B. Eliminates the need for a traditional audit

    C. May be used to identify high-risk areas for later review

    D. Will not have the level of independence provided by an external auditor

6. Which control classification attempts to repair the impact of a threat?

    A. Preventative

    B. Detective

    C. Corrective

    D. Deterrent

7. The two types of tests are referred to as _____ and _____ using _____ sampling methods.

   A. Substantive tests, compliance tests, variable and attribute

   B. Compliance tests, substantive tests, variable and discovery sampling

   C. Predictive tests, compliance tests, stop-and-go and difference estimation

   D. Integrity tests, compliance tests, stratified mean and unstratified mean

8. What is the purpose of the audit charter?

   A. To engage external auditors

   B. To grant responsibility, authority, and accountability

   C. To authorize the creation of the audit committee

   D. To provide detailed planning of the audit

9. Which of the following would be a concern of the auditor that should be explained in the audit report along with their findings?

   A. Detailed list of audit objectives

   B. The need by the current auditor to communicate with the prior auditor

   C. Communicating results directly to the chairperson of the audit committee

   D. Undue restrictions placed by management on evidence use or audit procedures

10. The concept of due care is best defined as which of the following?

    A. Proportional to the level of risk or loss that could occur

    B. Basic care providing a minimal level

    C. Ordinary care providing an average level

    D. Extraordinary care above and beyond average

11. What is the purpose of the audit committee?

    A. To assist managers with training in auditing skills

    B. To govern, control, and manage the organization

    C. To challenge and review assurances

    D. To provide daily coordination of all audit activities

12. What is the best data collection technique the auditor can use if the resources are available?

    A. Surveys that create a broad sample

    B. Review of existing documentation

    C. Auditor observation

    D. Interviews

13. Which of the following types of risk are of the most interest to an IS auditor?

    A. Control, detection, noncompliance, risk of strike

    B. Inherent, noninherent, control, lack of control

    C. Sampling, control, detection, inherent

    D. Unknown, quantifiable, cumulative

14. Which of the following best describes the early stages of an IS audit?

    A. Documenting the IS environment

    B. Testing for compliance to applicable regulations as agreed to

    C. Reviewing prior IS audit reports

    D. Commencing the planning process

15. Which of the following describes the relationship between compliance testing and substantive testing?

    A. Compliance testing checks for the presence of controls; substantive testing checks the integrity of internal contents.

    B. Substantive testing tests for presence; compliance testing tests actual contents.

    C. The tests are identical in nature; the difference is whether the audit subject is under the Sarbanes-Oxley Act.

    D. Compliance testing tests individual account balances; substantive testing checks for written corporate policies.

16. What is the principal issue surrounding the use of CAAT?

    A. The capability of the software vendor.

    B. Possible cost, complexity, and the security of output.

    C. Inability of automated tools to consider the human characteristics of the environment.

    D. Documentary evidence is more effective.

17. An IS auditor is performing a review of an application and finds something that might be illegal. The IS auditor should

    A. Disregard or ignore because this is beyond the scope of this review

    B. Conduct a detailed investigation to aid the authorities in catching the culprit

    C. Immediately notify the auditee of the finding

    D. Seek legal advice before finishing the audit

18. The auditor is permitted to deviate from professional audit standards when they feel it is necessary because of which of the following?

    A. Standards are designed for discretionary use.

    B. Deviation is almost unheard of and would require significant justification.

    C. Deviation depends on the authority granted in the audit charter.

    D. The unique characteristics of the client will require auditor flexibility.

19. What are the proper names of the four methods of risk response?

    A. Avoid, accept, transfer, and mitigate

    B. Mitigate, accept, transfer, and reduce

    C. Ignore, accept, assign, and mitigate

    D. Analyze, mitigate, reduce, and assign

20. Audits are intended to be conducted in accordance with which of the following ideals?

    A. Specific directives from management concerning evidence and procedure

    B. Reporting and communication

    C. Assessment of the organizational controls

    D. Adherence to standards, guidelines, and best practices

21. Which is the best document to help define the relationship of the independent auditor and provide evidence of the agreed-upon terms and conditions?

    A. Audit charter

    B. Annual audit plan

    C. Engagement letter

    D. Auditor's report

22. Who has the responsibility of setting the scope of the audit?

    A. Auditor

    B. Client

    C. Audit manager

    D. Auditee

23. What technique could the auditor use for planning an audit when the requirements and process to audit are vague?

    A. Monte Carlo

    B. Process technique

    C. Delphi technique

    D. Inverted straw-dog estimation

24. Which type of audit may be used for regulatory licensing or external reporting?

    A. Qualified audit

    B. Independent assessment

    C. Control self-assessment

    D. Traditional audit

25. What is the biggest issue with the decision to transfer risk to an outsourced contractor?

    A. There is potential for uncontrollable increase in operating cost over time.

    B. Outsourcing shifts the entire risk to the contractor.

    C. The company still retains liability for whatever happens.

    D. Outsourcing shields the company from intrinsic risks.

26. Why is the best practice in contracting to have a provision for the right to audit along with service performance metrics?   *P2 74*

    A. SAS-70 reports may be used to reduce the number of audits requested by clients.

    B. SAS-70 reports contain all the important details of interest for the client.

    C. SAS-70 reports may be used if agreed to by the client; however, the auditor producing the report is more important than the content.

    D. Performing your own audit bears a higher cost than accepting the SAS-70 report.

27. During audit planning, several documents are produced in support of the project. Which of these is used to identify the person responsible for specific tasks in order to gain funding and ensure quality?

    A. Skills matrix

    B. Procurement matrix

    C. Task matrix

    D. Activities matrix

28. Which of the following conditions is false in regard to using the work of other people during your audit?

    A. Ensure independence of the provider.

    B. Accept the work based on job position.

    C. Use agreed-upon scope and approach.

    D. Provide supervision and review.

29. What is the best reason why quality control planning techniques are important in auditing?

    A. To ensure that better products are manufactured.

    B. Quality inspection will improve the audit.

    C. Quality appraisal is the best metric for measuring success.

    D. Quality is measured by the price of nonconformance.

30. ISACA refers to testing for strong controls. What is the best description of a strong control?

    A. Effective implementation of multiple controls targeting the same objective

    B. Preventative controls that stop the problem from ever occurring

    C. Using at least one control in each of the three categories of preventative, detective, corrective

    D. Implementing comprehensive pervasive controls inside of an ERP application

31. Which of the following choices gives the best definition of controls focused on managing and monitoring inside a specific department?

    A. General controls

    B. Pervasive controls   *Pgs 82-85*

    C. Technical controls

    D. Application controls

32. Which of these statements is true regarding electronic discovery? *Pg 89*

   A. It provides access to data and systems, and may include recovering deleted data from any storage medium.

   B. If privileged information is unintentionally disclosed during discovery, there is no way to retrieve it.

   C. The data owner is liable if the stored information was lost during normal operations, even if the loss was not the result of negligence.

   D. Encryption can be used to prevent disclosing confidential information requested in the discovery process.

33. Auditors base their report on findings, evidence, and the results of testing. It's more of a score than an opinion. Which of the following types of evidence sampling refer to a 100 percent sample?

   A. Attribute

   B. Stop-and-go *Pg 98*

   C. Cell

   D. Discovery

34. Which of these types of computer assisted audit tools (CAAT) is designed to process dummy transactions during the processing of genuine transactions?

   A. Continuous and intermittent simulation

   B. Embedded program audit hooks *Pg 88*

   C. Embedded audit module

   D. Online event monitor

35. What does the term *unqualified opinion* refer to? *Pg 116*

   A. There are no restrictions on use.

   B. The auditor is not properly qualified to give an opinion.

   C. Evidence testing methods did not produce a conclusive answer.

   D. There are restrictions on use.

Answers to Review Questions

1. B. A detection risk is that you would fail to detect that a material error has occurred.

2. A. The compliance testing uses precision to describe the expected error rate of the sample compared to total population. Precision is usually expressed as a percentage. Depending on the consequence of error, higher rates above 5% may indicate the auditor needs to increase sampling and test more evidence.

3. D. Risk analysis does not ensure absolute safety. The purpose of using a risk-based audit strategy is to ensure that the audit adds value with meaningful information.

4. D. Difference estimation, stratified mean, and unstratified mean are valid sample types for substantive testing. Qualitative estimation is just a distracter.

5. B. All of the statements are true except B. A CSA is not a substitute for a traditional audit.

6. C. Corrective controls are designed to fix the damage caused by the threat's impact.

7. A. Answer B is incorrect because compliance testing uses discovery sampling to detect fraud. C and D are distracters.

8. B. The audit charter's purpose is to grant the right to audit and delegate responsibility, authority, and accountability.

9. D. Undue restrictions on scope would be a major concern as would the lack of time or the inability to obtain sufficient reliable evidence.

10. A. Due care is proportional to the level of risk or loss that could occur. Greater care is required for items of high value or greater impact due to loss.

11. C. The audit committee's purpose is to review and challenge assurances made, and to maintain a positive working relationship with management and the auditors.

12. D. Interviewing selected personnel is the best technique. Surveys, document review, and observations generate a lower yield.

13. C. The answers including risk of strike, lack of control, and unknown are distracters.

14. D. You start the planning process to identify objectives, resources, and the risk-based audit approach.

15. A. Substantive testing checks the substance or integrity of a transaction. Compliance testing looks for presence.

16. B. CAATs are able to perform faster than humans and produce more-accurate data in functions such as system scanning. Cost, training, and security of output are major considerations.

17. D. Seek competent legal advice. It is not the auditor's job to detect potentially illegal acts; however, the auditor should seek the aid of a lawyer concerning liability and reporting requirements.

18. B. Standards are mandatory, and any deviation would require justification.

19. A. The proper answer is avoid, accept, transfer to another party, and mitigate to reduce exposure. The other answers contain distracters.

20. D. Audits should adhere to standards, guidelines, and best practices. Answer A represents a restriction on scope. B and C are components of answer D.

21. C. The engagement letter is used with independent auditors to define the relationship. This letter serves as a record to document the understanding and agreement between the audit committee and the independent auditor. It provides the independent auditor the responsibility, accountability, and authority to conduct the audit.

22. B. Every audit is paid for and requested by a client, who is responsible for setting the scope, granting authority, and providing access to the auditee.

23. B. Shewhart's process technique of Plan-Do-Check-Act can be used to gather the requirements and refine the definition of any process. Repeat the cycle until you have enough information to conduct an audit. Findings can be used on the next cycle to improve the results.

24. D. Traditional independent audits are conducted with formality and adherence to standards necessary for regulatory licensing and external reporting. It's true that there is always a small shady accounting firm ready to lie for a client. The world expects an independent audit to be conducted by a qualified auditor representing a high degree of truth. Assessments are too informal and therefore can be used only internally in the organization.

25. C. The work can be outsourced; however, the liability for failure remains with the company. One example is the Firestone tire failure affecting Ford Motor Company. Another is the lead paint used by subcontractors forcing the giant toy recall of 2007. Liability cannot be outsourced.

26. C. Not all SAS-70 reports are created equal. The subcontractor will use the SAS-70 to reduce or eliminate audits by their customer. A poorly run SAS-70 audit is not worth the paper it's written on. In addition, the client may know details omitted or ignored by the SAS-70. Every contract must contain a clause granting right to audit at any time, and must specify who pays the expense.

27. A. A skills matrix is used to identify the skills of each person and to ensure that the right person is performing the task. Using a skills matrix in planning is an excellent method to justify proper funding for training or additional personnel.

28. Answer: B. The auditor should never base the decision on the job position of the other person. All of the other choices are vague but truthful. Always assess the independence of the provider, check their qualifications, agree on scope and procedures used, and supervise and review their work. Don't use it if the results are questionable or fail to follow very high adherence to audit standards.

29. D. Quality is measured by the added costs for failure (nonconformance). Planning, prevention, and conformance to specifications will create quality. This means that your audit needs to have a clear definition of requirements to be successful. The standard of performance is zero defects.

30. A. Strong controls will implement multiple types of preventative, detective, and corrective controls using a combined approach of administrative methods, physical methods, and technical methods. This is referred to as depth of control, hopefully using all nine layers. Using the bare minimum would be a weak control.

31. B. Pervasive controls define the direction and behavior of a department. The IS department uses pervasive controls that permeate their activities to create a cooperative environment of help desk, software support, security, and administration. General controls govern all the departments. Detailed controls focus on specific steps and procedures.

32. B. All the other options are false and contradict the laws of electronic discovery. You can't block disclosure of evidence during discovery unless the information is protected by the legal definition of privilege. Accidental disclosure may occur; therefore, the disclosing party can notify the other party to sequester, destroy, or return the information. The receiving party is prohibited from disclosing the information after notice of privilege is given.

33. D. Discovery sampling is used to find 100 percent of everything possible when fraud is suspected or the likelihood of finding evidence is low. All the other possible choices are valid sampling methods used in compliance testing.

34. C. Embedded audit module (EAM) processes dummy transactions during the processing of genuine transactions. The intention is to determine whether the system is functioning correctly.

35. A. A qualified opinion means the auditor had reservations about the results and the report is valid for only certain conditions. An unqualified opinion has no restrictions on use. The auditor is happy with the findings and how the audit was conducted.

Chapter

3

IT Governance

THE OBJECTIVE OF THIS CHAPTER IS TO ACQUAINT THE READER WITH THE FOLLOWING CONCEPTS:

✓ Defining governance and IT governance

✓ Identifying who is responsible for implementing governance

✓ The fiduciary responsibility and security requirements that every organization must exercise to protect assets and information

✓ Defining the executive strategy, direction, and objectives

✓ Accepted management practices that are in use to optimize allocation of available resources

✓ How management establishes adequate internal controls for the IT organization

✓ What management needs to do to protect the critical dependencies of information systems in economic transactions

✓ How an organization demonstrates that it has exercised the best available management options to protect itself

✓ Using business process reengineering to fix missing and nonworking processes

Information technology (IT) governance specifies the level of integration and control an organization has over its information technology investment. Information technology is pervasive in business today. The intrinsic value of information technology must be fully incorporated into every aspect of the business, rather than separated into a distinct IT function. The level of IT integration will have a dramatic effect on how the organization defines its mission, achieves strategic goals, and communicates its vision of growth. The auditing of IT governance will include the highest levels of organizational management and will cross internal boundaries between divisions and departments.

Strategy Planning for Organizational Control

To be successful, management must define a strategy and provide for effective corporate governance. _Strategy_ is defined as "an adaptation of behavior or structure with an elaborate and systematic plan of action." Another more specific definition of strategy is "to create a fundamental change in the way the organization conducts business." Obviously the second definition indicates that there are only a handful of people with that much authority. _Corporate governance_ is often defined as "ethical behavior of corporate executives toward shareholders and the stakeholders to maximize the return of a financial investment." To clarify who is responsible for corporate governance, we could use this definition: "to lead by position or authority."

Three high-level management objectives to be verified by the auditor are as follows:

- A strategic alignment between IT and the enterprise objectives (formal strategy). Proper planning is required to deploy resources in the right place for the right reason. Management is always responsible for getting it done (corporate governance, preventive controls).

- A process of monitoring assurance practices for executive management. The senior executives need to understand what is actually occurring in the organization (staying involved by using detective controls).

- An intervention as required to stop, modify, or fix failures as they occur (corrective action). Everyone has some kind of problem. Management should be working to resolve the issue immediately rather than covering it up by hiding the truth.

Each organization needs to develop their directional strategy. What direction should the business take to fulfill its goals? The strategy selected progresses to focus on client needs and see pgs 261, 461

how to fulfill that market. <u>Critical success factors</u> are selected. Marketing initiatives are designed to generate revenue with plans for fulfillment to the buyer. Figure 3.1 demonstrates the path of organizational requirements in conjunction with the IT requirements.

The revenue process entails a significant amount of administrative overhead and record keeping. The expectation in every business is to make money and not be hampered by a particular technology nor tied to a particular vendor.

The IT department is looking for a clearly stated purpose that IT is expected to fulfill. The department looks at the demands and requirements necessary to be successful. A structured service-level agreement can be generated with this data, complete with staffing and technology growth plans.

Technology plans have to fulfill a business objective. For instance, take Amazon.com. This very successful bookseller isn't necessarily hung up on using Microsoft Windows, Macintosh, or Unix. What the executives want to know is that all the money is processed and the product arrives on time to fulfill their customers' expectations. Systems management and auditing on the back end will verify that all their bookkeeping and internal controls are functioning effectively. In an industry leading move, Amazon added same-day shipping as a $5 option on select stock for customers geographically located in vicinity of the Amazon warehouses. The bookseller downloaded the daily courier route schedules, and then compares the pickup and delivery schedule to the buyer's address. Orders placed in the morning can arrive the same afternoon in select major cities. A same day delivery option is automatically added to the shopping cart for eligible purchases. Amazon demonstrates excellent integration of the business and IT strategy.

FIGURE 3.1   IT alignment with organizational objectives

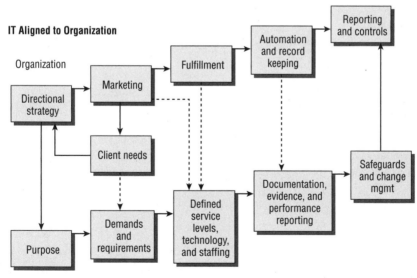

The top side of this diagram is motivated by gains in revenue. Executives take calculated risks to exploit new opportunities for their business to make more money. Conversely, IT is expected to prevent service failures that hurt revenue. IT may also be expected to focus on activities that enable revenue and concurrent activities to prevent loss based on risk management planning. This can make it difficult to determine which problem or goal is the priority. Auditors can gain insight by looking into the IT reporting structure. IT functions reporting to the chief operating officer (COO) are services that generate revenue. IT functions reporting to the chief financial officer (CFO) are internal functions of reporting and processing controls. Refer to Figure 3.2.

FIGURE 3.2 Reporting structure demonstrates IT's purpose

The principal mechanism for ensuring IT alignment is to implement an IT steering committee.

Overview of the IT Steering Committee

Most organizations use an IT strategy committee or IT steering committee. An *IT steering committee* is used to convey the current business requirements from business executives to the *others* IT executive. The name of the committee is not as important as the function that it performs; a committee may perform more than one function. An IT steering committee may possibly be the same committee used for the purpose of a business continuity steering committee, but with a slightly different charter (focus). What's important is that the job of steering operations to business requirements is occurring.

Steering committees should have a formal charter designating the participation of each member. This charter grants responsibility and authority in a concept similar to an audit charter. An absence of a steering committee charter would indicate a lack of formal controls—a condition warranting management oversight review.

The steering committee is also discussed in Chapter 5, "Life Cycle Management."

 The steering (or strategy) committee is made up of quite a few individuals. Each individual is required to have the authority to act on behalf of their department. These members are vice president–level or higher in the organization so they can help align the IT efforts to specific business requirements. Figure 3.3 shows the basic organizational structure of the steering committee.

Purpose of steering Committee - btm of pg 122 + here, Fig 3.2 ensuring IT alignment w/ business strategy

FIGURE 3.3   Organizational structure of a steering committee

The committee is managed by an executive chairperson. The CEO is expected to provide directional guidance in person or via a representative, such as the COO, to identify targeted sources of revenue. Each member of the committee is expected to participate in focus discussions concerning business issues. On occasion, the committee may invite trusted observers or presenters to the meeting to increase awareness of a particular area.

After the business objectives are identified, the next step is to determine the business objectives for IT to fulfill. The steering committee sticks to high-level objectives rather than dictating technical detail.

Let's look at the representation necessary on the steering committee:

Marketing   Marketing should be represented on the steering committee. The purpose of all marketing is to attract buyers for the organization's product or service. Even if the organization builds the world's finest product, it will not matter unless a steady stream of buyers make a purchase.

Manufacturing/Software Development   The input from manufacturing or software development is required to align production efforts to sales efforts.

Sales   The sales function is to convert interested prospects from marketing campaigns into closed sales. Sales executives are interested in using technology to facilitate more sales. The cooperation of manufacturing and technology is necessary to assist the sales effort.

Finance   Financial guidance and budgeting skills are essential to optimize the organization's investment. Obtaining funding approval for projects would be difficult without the cooperation of the finance comptroller.

Legal   The executive from the legal department should ensure compliance to the law. Qualified legal counsel advises management in areas of uncertainty. Expert legal counsel should help protect the company from excessive liability or undue risk as a result of a control failure.

Quality Control   The quality process provides consistency in operations, manufacturing, and risk mitigation. A well-run quality process is a major contributor to the organization's survival. Failures in quality control can damage market image or lead to liability problems.

Use the composition and performance of the steering committee for clues & evidence for the audit. ~ Pg 139

Research and Development (R&D)   The Research and Development staff is constantly working on creating new products and improving existing products. The R&D effort is focused on developing products that will generate revenue six months to two years in the future.

 Depending on the organization, R&D may be suspended during times of financial shortfall. The planned R&D budget would be applied to projects with a faster return or to pay past-due obligations.

Project and Program Management   The head of the Project Management Office, if one exists, should be on the committee to advise members on current and proposed projects. Ideas presented by customers may require changes, causing the need for new projects to modify existing programs. Change is required to be successful in business. Remember that projects are temporary, while programs are ongoing for multiple years or even perpetual.

Business Continuity   The head of business continuity planning should always be in attendance. This person may possess the title of continuity manager or program manager and have the authority of a vice president or major director. This person's job is to assess impact or help exploit opportunities presented in support of the organizational strategy. It's important not to sacrifice continuity in favor of shortsighted decisions.

Information Technology   The chief information officer (CIO) or vice president of IT listens to business ideas and objectives raised by committee members. This person acts as a liaison to facilitate the involvement of IT. The IT member may delegate planning and research activities to members of the IT organization.

Human Resources   The management of personnel grows more complex each week. Compliance with federal labor standards is mandatory. International organizations require special assistance that is beyond the expertise of most non-HR executives. Noncompliance can carry stiff penalties.

Labor Management   An executive representative from any labor organization, such as a labor union, may need to be involved in decisions concerning labor. This can be a touchy subject depending on the organization.

Administration   Office administration functions include bookkeeping, record keeping, and the processing of paperwork. Every executive would be handicapped without an administrative assistant.

The steering committee reviews ideas and opportunities to make recommendations. Those recommendations go to the board of directors for review. If the idea receives preliminary approval, resources are allocated for project planning. The steering committee executives perform a final review of comparing the total cost and benefit to determine whether the project is a "go" or "no-go."

If a go decision is reached, the organization specifies details, charters the project, allocates funds, commits resources, and moves the plan into execution. If the project is scheduled to be a repeating event, the project is assigned to program status. Otherwise, it is managed as a project with fixed time duration, and the assigned project team members will disband after project completion.

Figure 3.4 is a flowchart of the IT steering process.

FIGURE 3.4   The IT steering committee process

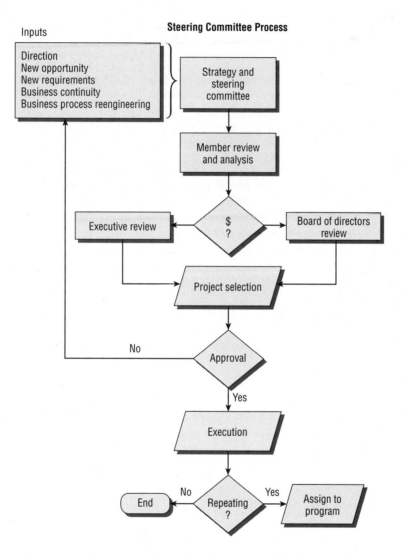

In strategic planning, plans generally run in a time frame of three to five years. A tactical plan is going to be carried out over six months to a year and it may go into two years. Daily plans are no more than steps in the tactical plan. When an organization projects three to five years, it is really developing a strategy. This strategy can be to run a streamlined low-cost airline operation

Executives dictate — Strategic Plan — 3 to 5 yrs

Steering committee oversees } Tactical Plan — 6 mths to 2yrs

Daily Plan — daily/weekly/monthly tactical plan details

🌐 Real World Scenario

How Many Hamburgers Do You Want to Sell?

One of our famous awareness questions is to help people understand the issues of strategy and focus: If someone wanted to be in the hamburger business, *what is the number one critical success factor that would be necessary for the hamburger business to be successful?* Interestingly enough, we have heard a lot of answers, and none of them were correct.

Claude Hopkins, the original master of marketing, would tell you that the answer would not be menu, nor would it be location, nor would it be staffing, nor secret recipe. Although each of those points may offer support, the real answer is hungry customers. If we could establish where the hungry customers are, we could make money reselling cold cheeseburgers out of the back of a station wagon.

In that regard, it is important to ask how IT is aligned to the organization. Does IT seek to satisfy the hungry customers, or is there an expectation for the customer to wander over on their own? Does IT provide repair-level support or is it truly strategic, carrying the company to their most noble objective? The reality is that when you build the world's best mousetrap, customers don't naturally come knocking at the door. The reality is that someone will need to find the customer and what the customer wants. Value is simply a perception of benefit and desire.

---

like Southwest Airlines, offer the best market reach like eBay, provide competitive rate marketing like Progressive insurance, or use the shipping model of FedEx to assure your package is absolutely positively delivered overnight.

Table 3.1 compares strategic plans, long-term plans, and operational plans.

TABLE 3.1   Differences between Strategic, Long-Term, and Operational Plans

Item	Strategic Planning	Long-Term Planning	Operational Planning
Time frame	3 years +	1–3 years	1 year or less
Question	What business are we in? Should we expand or contract?	What are the major business components? What should we concentrate on now? What products and services are planned?	What specific tasks must be done to meet the long-term plan?

TABLE 3.1   Differences between Strategic, Long-Term, and Operational Plans *(continued)*

Item	Strategic Planning	Long-Term Planning	Operational Planning
Output	General broad statement of what business the company is in	Financial goals Market opportunities Management organization Next review period	Assumptions for the period Changes needing to be made Production times Responsibilities Budget

Now that we have discussed the definition of strategic planning, it is time to get specific about the content of the executive strategy.

Using the Balanced Scorecard

To set forth a strategic goal without proper planning and meaningful definitions would be both negligent and reckless. One of the most powerful executive planning tools available is the *balanced scorecard (BSC)*. The BSC is a strategic methodology designed for senior executives.

Originally, the balanced scorecard was designed in a university environment to be used by business executives for reporting metrics. A very smart person once said, "the product's actual use will be invented at the customer site," meaning you can build what you want, but the customer will determine how it's used to solve their problem. It turns out that the most successful executives are using the BSC to define internal cause-effect relationships of smaller plans that run their business, not just to report metrics as originally conceived.

The scorecard approach converts organizational objectives of customer perception, business processes, employee growth and learning, and financial goals into a series of defined actions. We typically call these actions either *projects* or *programs*, but the BSC doesn't care. The BSC refers to projects and programs as *initiatives* (what you are doing).

Three years ago, after a less-than-successful board meeting, I set a personal goal to learn how to apply the BSC tool. I searched all websites in the first 200 Google results and read every book available from Barnes & Noble. Plenty of people claimed knowledge of the BSC, yet consistently failed to demonstrate how the inner details actually worked. Frankly, none provided enough direction to make it work. I fell into the same trap as everyone else. It takes special training with firsthand experience to receive the benefits that this type of advanced planning tool offers. ISACA just wants you to know it exists. I teach my students in our seminars how to use it, exceeding the exam study requirement. So this section is my short brochure-level introduction on how it works. I use BSC constantly each week and stand behind all my statements with supporting evidence.

When properly implemented, <u>the scorecard</u> concept enforces better alignment by <u>defining details of strategic business objectives.</u> Overused terms such as *world class* and *customer driven* are <u>broken down into low-level definitions that the staff can actually implement,</u> Using the scorecard should eliminate activities of little or no strategic value.

The scorecard methodology is common outside the IT environment. Information technology can benefit from using the balanced scorecard if it is implemented by the CEO or CFO. To be effective, the scorecard must be driven from the top down.

Table 3.2 illustrates the four scorecard perspectives and matching emphasis area of the BSC methodology. For example, the finance perspective will place emphasis on cost control and company profits.

TABLE 3.2   Balanced Scorecard Methodology

Perspective	Emphasis
Customer	What is our market image? What makes us different? How should the organization appear to the customer? Why would a client want to do business with us?
Business process	What is our mission? How can we create a genuine competitive advantage? What are our critical success factors? What are the key performance indicators?
Financial	What are the financial goals? What are the shareholder goals? Are we a cash cow or a pioneer?
Growth and learning	What information do we need to beat our competition? What are the organization's growth plans? How will we keep or obtain the knowledge and workers necessary to support the organization's plans?

A smaller number of organizations are successful at using the balanced scorecard approach, while many fail. Upon investigation, several of the failing executives referred to BSC as old news. It did not take long to discover that these executives had a lack of BSC training, misunderstood the objective, and possessed little BSC experience. Let's investigate why this occurs.

The advantages and disadvantages of using the scorecard methodology are as follows:

Scorecard advantages   It promotes a focus on the specific if-then linkage between different objectives and their budgets. The goal is direct support of organizational objectives. If you change funding or strategy on a linked initiative (project or program), the effect can be seen rippling through the scorecard. We are actually using the BSC to create well-defined articulated strategies.

All the initiatives (project or programs) are linked into a complete process flow that ignores departments and traditional boundaries. Never again will strategy be determined in one meeting and budget determined somewhere else.

When fully implemented, none of the departments will have their own budget to spend. The result is project-based, program-based staffing. It does not matter whether the department function is internal or external.

Each department pledges its level of support to a defined strategy initiative. The corresponding budget money is issued to the department, provided it is meeting its delivery goals. No support of the linked project means no money, no people, and no job. This blocks waste and personal agendas.

Each employee works from a personal scorecard created by cascading the BSC down into specific execution tasks. The combined effect of the personal scorecards will achieve their department's objective. Achievement of the departmental objectives will help fulfill the organizational objectives.

Scorecard disadvantages   The scorecard requires a careful selection of initiatives by the CEO or CFO. It is reported in executive trade journals that metrics derived from a committee will consistently fail. Interestingly, observations indicate that executives unwilling to adapt to the scorecard methodology may lack a genuine interest in being a team player or may possess more interest in building their own empire within the organization. Politics can kill the BSC unless the sponsor eliminates the people creating political conflict. *— It'll never work at BAH, then!*

The balanced scorecard can contain whatever you need to define. It is flexible in having three, four, or five perspectives depending on what your executives decide is needed. The typical approach of four perspectives is shown in Figure 3.5. Notice how the different initiatives are linked into a complete process.

FIGURE 3.5   Balanced scorecard with four perspectives

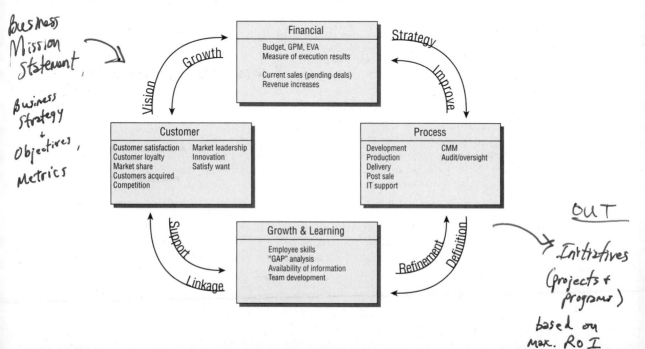

There are several secrets involved in making the scorecard generate true results. Using a BSC will most likely take beginners at least 20–30 failed attempts, which end in frustration, before it begins to show a glimmer of success. Keep trying; the benefits will far outweigh the effort. Each failed attempt is simply an indicator of an existing relationship problem or definition problem. Problems need to be fixed one by one before you can build an effective linkage. Often this includes retreating a few steps to adapt for changes as they are discovered. That's part of the magic in using BSC. The strategy becomes more defined with each pass, forcing each problem to be fixed before it can effectively function inside the overall strategy plan.

Every planning exercise brings more clarity as you roll the linkages forward and backward to fine-tune the details. It's like using algebra to solve a problem and then using calculus to prove you actually did solve the problem by returning to zero. Now the strategy works forward and backward, with excellent definitions exploding all the details into specific action items. Initiatives (projects or programs) are now selected, scoped, and funded based on which ones generate the highest return on investment (ROI).

What if your project or program doesn't generate revenue? Simply put, it would be linked with a function that is generating revenue and used to calculate the combined operating costs. For example, security costs in a bank are coupled with the profits the bank generates. The final ROI estimate is used to decide whether that area of the business is expanded or shut down. What if you make more money from brokering mortgages? You may switch from being a full-service bank into focusing on mortgages. The final goal is to find the highest-earning ROI and quit wasting resources on marginal or losing activities.

Executives at AMR operate American Airlines and Sabre reservations as two separate companies. One reporter asked which one they would sell if necessary. The response was that American Airlines' business need created Sabre, yet they would keep Sabre, selling the airline if that day ever came. Sabre's reservation system is a better ROI.

The balanced scorecard fundamentally changes how employees prioritize and report their work. Activities and projects are selected on the basis of the value created under established metrics. This also results in a change in how the employee is evaluated. It is essential that management and staff receive proper training prior to implementation. Just remember, without full buy-in at all levels, the balanced scorecard is likely to fail.

IT Subset of the BSC

The IT balanced scorecard should be a subset of the organization's overall balanced scorecard. When properly implemented, the scorecard methodology supports the highest-level business objectives.

As a CISA, you need to understand how the balanced scorecard can be applied specifically to information technology. ISACA describes the scorecard by using three layers that incorporate the more common four perspectives (customer, business process, financial, and growth and learning). The three layers for IT scoring according to ISACA are as follows:

Mission   Develop opportunities for future needs. Become the preferred supplier of IT systems to the organization. Obtain funding from the business for IT investments. Deliver effective and cost-efficient IT services. Often the mission statement sounds like an advertising slogan. In reality, the mission statement should be less of a political statement and more specific in definition. Therefore, each mission statement needs supporting details contained in the strategy definition. The goal of the BSC is to convert vague mission statements into clear-cut action items that the staff can understand and then implement.

Strategy   Attain IT control objectives. Obtain control over IT expenses. Deliver business value through IT projects. Provide ongoing IT training and education. Support R&D to develop superior IT applications. All these sound great, but they need significantly more detail before they can be implemented. Using the BSC can help define the lower-level initiatives necessary to make the mission functional. Far too many executives fail to provide a well-defined, articulate strategy. A definition is needed that maps detailed cross-coordination rolling across departmental boundaries.

Metrics   Develop and implement meaningful IT metrics based on critical success factors and key performance indicators. We'll cover more in metrics in Chapter 6, "IT Service Delivery."

The balanced scorecard method is a wonderful tool for the auditor to gain invaluable insight into the organization. A simple BSC exercise will uncover the organization's critical path while illuminating its ROI dependencies.

Selecting an IT Strategy

Executive management selects an IT strategy to fulfill their business objectives. The strategy should be approved from the top down. The strategy is then formalized into a policy and communicated throughout the organization. Figure 3.6 shows the executives involved at the strategy level (in policy making).

FIGURE 3.6   Executives involved at the IT strategy level

You should assume that the executives have already gone through the process of gathering requirements. Their strategy may be to insource or to outsource. However, one of their most important questions is to determine how the strategy will be funded. Each of the following methods of funding bears unique advantages and disadvantages:

Shared cost   It is common for the bulk of IT costs to be allocated as a shared cost across all members of the organization. This method is relatively easy for the finance department to implement. Unfortunately, it may lead to user dissatisfaction. Some users and their managers may feel that they are paying for a service that is not received.

Charge-back   Individual departments receive a direct charge for system use. This is designed to be a pay-as-you-go style of accounting for IT expenses. Charge-back schemes are quite effective if properly implemented. Mainframe charge-back schemes are particularly effective for usage billing.

Sponsor pays   This last type can present a significant challenge to IT governance. The project sponsor pays all the bills. In exchange, the sponsor may demand more authority over decisions. This method is notorious for creating shadow support organizations. Shadow organizations indicate willful distrust between executives. Usually the basis of shadow groups is a self-centered agenda that creates a design contributing toward a functional failure. Additional conflicts usually occur with IT management in disputes over budget responsibilities, not implementing all the proper controls, lack of effective monitoring, and improper reporting of failures. The best way to solve the conflict is by fully enforcing separation of duties.

Specifying a Policy

Executive management has the responsibility of setting goals. Each goal should be supported with a defined set of objectives. A strategy should be in place to achieve those objectives. The next step is to specify a policy to communicate management's desires to the subordinates.

Every policy should be designed to define a high-level course of action. The purpose of the policy is to inform interested parties of a chosen solution. A well-designed policy is based on a statement by management of the policy's importance. The statement explains how this particular policy supports a business objective. The policy is signed by the most senior person available to prove authorization.

We discussed the role of policies, standards, and procedures in Chapter 1, "Secrets of a Successful IS Auditor." Table 3.3 should serve as a memory refresher concerning the role of policies, standards, and procedures.

TABLE 3.3   Strategic Role of a Policy

	Strategic	Tactical	Operational
Goal objective	X		
Policy	X		

TABLE 3.3   Strategic Role of a Policy *(continued)*

	Strategic	**Tactical**	**Operational**
Standard		X	
Procedure			X

Successful policies are issued from the top down to all subordinates. The policy may designate a department director to create a standard in support of the policy. The final procedures are generated from the workers at the bottom of the hierarchy. Common procedures are intended to be implemented from the bottom up. The procedure is a lower-level person's response in support of the executive's policy.

Types of Policies

Policies are designed to inform interested parties about a particular situation. The policy may be advisory, regulatory, or informational:

Advisory policy   An advisory policy explains the condition to be prevented by the policy and provides notice as to the consequences of failure. The interested party may be an employee. The subject could be acceptable use of the Internet. In the Internet example, the advisory mandate is to either comply or be fired.

Regulatory policy   The term *regulatory* indicates that this policy is mandated by some type of law. All organizations under the jurisdiction of the regulation are expected to comply. Failure to comply will result in criminal liability.

Informational policy   Informational policies inform the public of the organization's operating policies. Examples include the customer privacy policy, the customer refund policy, and the customer exchange policy.

 NOTE   IS auditors should be aware that undefined policies indicate a lack of control.

After the strategy is selected and the goals are set and the policy is created, it's time to begin the planning process. In planning, the strategy is broken down into useable definitions to move it closer to reality.

Implementation Planning of the IT Strategy

IT strategy plans must be created to aid the organization in the fulfillment of long- and short-term business objectives. Each IT plan should correlate to a specific organizational goal. The business goal may be to improve customer contact management, expand e-commerce services,

Strategy
Goals/objectives
Policies
Plans of execution

or improve operating speed with better software integration. The supporting IT plan could define implementation and support for a new Customer Relationship Management (CRM) system. IT's role is that of a requirements facilitator and custodian. The true strategic value will be determined in the minds of the business executives. There should be a concern if IT's influence is overriding other non-IT business objectives. The IT strategy will be composed of plans for data, software applications, technology, personnel, and facilities.

Data Plans

IT data plans are created in support of the organization's intended use of the data. An example is the creation of a new customer survey system, database marketing system, or financial record-keeping system. The key is to determine what data you really need and how you will protect it. This is accomplished by implementing an information classification program with administrative policies and procedures. Well-run businesses and governments have been doing this for hundreds of years to explain how each piece of data should be handled. After the intended use of the data is recognized, the next step is to define the application to manipulate the data.

Application Management Plan

Computer software applications are actually methods of accomplishing work. Therefore, a software management plan is necessary to define the type of work to be performed. A consumer bank may be in the same industry as a debt collection company, for example. However, both organizations use different software applications. Computer software applications need to be tailored to fit the client's needs.

Computer software is not an advantage if the competitor uses the same software, unless the implementation is unique and highly customized.

It is possible to gain a competitive advantage by using a different product than the competitor uses. The advantage is attaining a higher level of business integration and/or lower operating costs. The cost argument is the very reason why some software applications use open source MySQL for the database rather than Oracle. Both are fine products. The cost difference may allow for a significant investment in specialized customization by a guru to build highly integrated software, which can create a competitive advantage with a lower overall operating cost. The resulting integrated software may perform a unique function that the competitor will have difficulty obtaining because of required knowledge, lead time needed, or additional capital investment. Cost avoidance can be a competitive advantage. The application risk is that the integration does not occur or the intended application usage is flawed.

Computer application software represents a substantial investment in capital. Computer software creates business risks that must be managed. The risks include process failure, increased operating risk, ineffective results, waste of capital resources, lost time, and increased operating cost for the same effective output.

Technology Plan

Technology plans address an organization's technical environment by indicating the types of hardware and software that will be used. Unfortunately, some organizations start with the hardware technology first and attempt to force the data and application requirements into their desired technology. Putting the technology plans first may hinder the results.

Organizational Plan

The IT organizational structure needs to be designed to support the business strategy. Information technology is usually regarded as a function of internal administration. This would place IT under the head of internal controls (the CFO, VP of finance, or the comptroller). Figure 3.7 illustrates a typical IT organization. We will discuss the individual positions as we proceed through this chapter.

 Figure 3.7 can serve as a roadmap if you're unsure about the authority of positions we discuss in this chapter.

FIGURE 3.7   Typical IT organizational structure

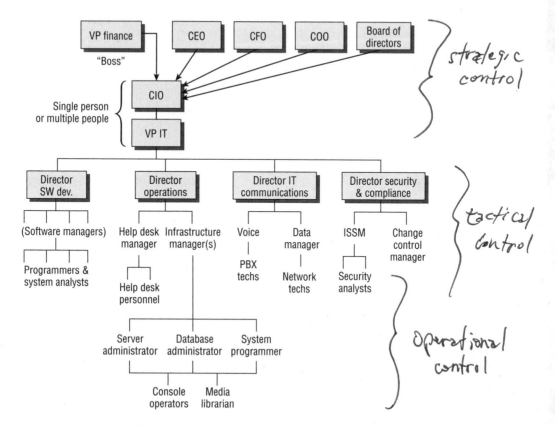

Facilities Plan

Finally, the strategy needs to incorporate a facilities plan. Where will the data applications and technology reside? Who will manage the environment? The final decision will be based on the desires of management. These desires can include increased control, insourcing, outsourcing, or a hybrid combination.

Using CObIT

Knowing what to do is a challenge for all auditors. Discussions were occurring on this subject long ago in the old Electronic Data Processing (EDP) audit association, before it was renamed ISACA. One of the goals of every association is to add value by improving the performance of its members. ISACA has definitely delivered on this goal. The definitive framework for IS auditing is called the Control Objectives for Information and related Technology, also known as CObIT.

This framework contains a complete set of strategies, processes, and procedures necessary for executives to lead the IT organization. CObIT is now in its fourth edition. Within the supporting manuals, you will find the guidance provided in their audit toolkit invaluable. CObIT is protected under copyright, so it's a good idea not to lose your CISA certification by doing something stupid like having a bootleg copy.

The audit guideline section contains more than enough questions necessary for a first-class audit. It covers the entire spectrum from executive strategy down to device settings. BSC properly combined with CObIT would make a phenomenal audit practice.

Now let's get back to the auditing plan. We have discussed strategy, so the next step is to figure out the work location.

Identifying Sourcing Locations

The next step is to identify sourcing locations. The sourcing decision may be based on the operating cost for particular geographic locations. Operating cost is a combined factor of facilities, labor, regulations, and available resources. Organizations may choose to perform functions *onsite*, in their facility. Alternatively, there may be an advantage to performing functions *offsite*, at other offices or with an outside vendor. This is a common practice for customer support, employee payroll, and manufacturing. Cheap labor may influence management's decision to move the location *offshore*, to another country.

 NOTE Three popular offshore locations include China, India, and Russia. The expected benefits include cheaper labor or lower standards for environmental compliance. The effective cost of steel, concrete, and materials to construct an office is approximately the same worldwide.

Performing functions offshore introduces both opportunities and burdens. The opportunities include a potentially lower production cost. There is also an advantage for an organization to operate 24 hours a day in order to lower turnaround times. Consider the effect when the day shift identifies a problem and the night shift in another country fixes it before the day shift returns in the morning.

Disadvantages include the potential loss of control or the disclosure of proprietary intellectual property. In some countries, the culture, language, or level of education presents unique challenges.

Cultural examples of potential conflicts include India's caste system and Africa's ongoing tribal wars. Another example is the attitudes in some societies toward a woman in an authoritative role.

🌐 Real World Scenario

The "Follow the Sun" Concept

Executive management may choose to service its customers by using a *follow the sun* concept, which in simple terms means that the organization moves daily support functions to an *offsite* location 8 to 12 hours away. The second (or third) office is starting their morning when the current office is closing at the end of the day. Each day, as one office closes, another office located in a different time zone takes over support (each time traveling to the west with the new day). Customers could always have a full staff available to help, regardless of the time of day.

A company might instead choose to schedule multiple shifts within the same office. As an auditor, you should inquire how the client retains full control with multiple shifts of personnel. What management controls are in place? Frequently the late-night staff has less supervision or greater access to shared work areas without detection.

Sourcing Practices

The world is growing smaller as transportation and communication services improve. Many of the old cultural barriers have been reduced by the global economy. This global economy also has increased the number of competitors in the fierce battle for revenue. An organization at one time worried only about servicing clients in a small number of local time zones. Now customers depend on businesses 24 hours a day, worldwide.

Most administrative and technical support functions can be performed from alternate locations. Some of the services that could be fulfilled from remote locations include the following:

- Accounting and bookkeeping
- Accounts payable (AP) and accounts receivable (AR)
- Data entry and transcription
- Live telephone support (including IT, customer service, order taking)
- Legal and medical records management and processing
- Human resources and benefits administration
- Creative advertising production
- Printing
- Software development
- Systems administration

In the following section, you will look at the various types of sourcing methods, what factors go into choosing a sourcing method, and why it is important for you as an IS auditor to be familiar with them.

Sourcing Methods

The decision of location is usually based on the cost of operation, market pressures, or a centralization versus decentralization strategy. Management may choose to hire personnel by using a combination of insourcing and outsourcing. Services provided by internal staff are referred to as *in-house (insourced)*. Services provided by an external vendor are referred to as *outsourced*. The insourced versus outsourced decision may be based on a case-by-case or project-by-project requirement.

On occasion, an opportunity may present itself that exceeds the capability of the existing service provider. *Hybrid sourcing models* may be effective under a joint venture or to provide additional capability. The hybrid model combines insourcing and outsourcing on a function-by-function basis.

The advantage of outsourcing is that someone else may be able to perform the work better or cheaper, or frankly may know how to do something others don't. Insourcing provides more control. The hybrid method retains control in selected areas and uses the outsource contractor for collateral work. Outsourcing may allow the client to focus on what they do best, their core revenue generator. A potential disadvantage is losing control under the contract. Maybe the methods used by a subcontractor will cost less because they are cutting corners that, if known, a company might find unacceptable.

The basic decision may result from an executive thinking about the following:

- Is this something that the organization wants to do in-house?
- Is this something the company should outsource?
- Is there an advantage to sending this offshore?
- Is the organization bringing it back from offshore?
- Will local processing be a competitive advantage?
- Is the location here, in this building, or is it in another building?

Globalization Issues

Businesses may encounter a variety of globalization issues, including international regulation, local laws, tribal rivalries, or cultural class or caste systems. As an organization begins to look at opportunities for global outsourcing, they have to keep in mind the controls and the total costs related to that decision.

A business looks for inexpensive operating facilities with a high-quality labor pool willing to work for lower wages. If the business is going to decide whether to outsource, it needs to look at all the practices and strategies that are in place.

A business can run into problems over the differences in legal regulations between governments. Additional concerns can arise in different currency exchange rates and government taxation methods. Some of these requirements may indicate that foreign outsourcing would not provide any advantage.

Competitive advantage should be a factor in the sourcing decision. For example, American Apparel manufactures clothing exclusively inside the United States and pays better-than-average wages for their industry. Their advantage is a shorter cycle time from market idea to delivery and sale in their stores. American Apparel touts a one-day turnaround from a finished idea. Their competition has to contend with manufacturing and shipping delays measured in months.

In the last few years, Russia and the Baltic states have benefited from increased popularity, as companies reconsider India or choose to outsource for the first time. Increasing operating costs and U.S. consumer rejection are troublesome to companies outsourcing to India. The cost of real estate in India is skyrocketing. China is reeling backward after a virtual tidal wave of product recalls. Additional reasons cited for Russian sourcing include a more convenient proximity to Western Europe, more positive consumer attitudes of acceptance, a well-educated population, financial savings in real estate prices, and the competitive low cost of labor.

Legal Compliance Issues

When dealing with outsourcing issues, companies need to be aware that what might be legal in one country might not be legal in another. Examples include the European Union (EU) privacy laws, which are much stricter than those of the United States, or the shortfall of intellectual-property laws in China, which frankly don't exist. In China the attitude is that if someone has a copy, they own it. This is where business management needs to understand: How does that country or culture see it?

As a primitive example, just compare the religious holidays and lifestyles that different countries observe. For example, the flow of harmony in the office is considered upset in Japan if everyone does not go to lunch at the exact same time, and return within a couple of minutes of one another. In Mexico, the lunch hour is two hours and often includes drinking alcohol followed by a siesta (nap). It is not uncommon for employees to drink alcohol during the office lunch hour in the United Kingdom (referred to as having a few pints or getting pissed over a few drinks).

While management plans their labor strategy, there should be a provision ensuring continuity of operations for both in-house and outsourced activities.

Subcontractor Liability Trap   — *You picked them, you're liable for them.*

The biggest downside of outsourcing is liability. Outsourcing permits an organization to reassign the tasks to be performed but not the liability. It's not possible to transfer the actual liability for failure. Insurance may help cover some of the expenses but not the damage to your reputation, the cancelled sales, or the costs of defending a lawsuit.

Consider the situation of Value Jet airlines. A subcontractor violated cargo-loading procedures when it placed a hazardous container in the cargo bay. The container exploded, causing the airplane to crash. A massive media circus was spawned by the event. Value Jet held their subcontractor liable. The public held Value Jet responsible. The public didn't pick the subcontractor; Value Jet did. Value Jet was expected to spend extra time and money to supervise the subcontractor. The airline folded.

Let's consider the long-term effects of the following well-publicized examples of food contamination:

- Recently, problems surfaced in many well-known brands of canned pet food. A supplier of ingredients shipped tainted flour, which led to the death of many beloved family pets. Other pet owners reported paying expensive medical bills for emergency care by veterinarians. Retailers trashed their entire inventories of canned pet food and asked for refunds to cover the losses. Pet owners are pursuing lawsuits against the brand for the harm to their pets and their own emotional strain.

- ConAgra is involved in legal battles over a bad batch of ingredients used in Peter Pan peanut butter. One lawyer is advertising on television to "keep the jar and call attorney Loncar," thus promoting possible monetary awards for the consumer to sue ConAgra. Wal-Mart sold the same ConAgra peanut butter under its own house brand.

- Several products manufactured in China are now banned from the United States and other countries because of unacceptable chemicals in foods or illegal hormones used to grow vegetables and fish.

- Outsourcing does not relieve the company's responsibility to test products or services for compliance. In fact, the outsourcer should be trusted less and tested more. The auditor is always interested in how the process of governing all outsourced services is handled.

In-House Operations Return

It's interesting how some vendors can perform the task cheaper than in-house. Unfortunately, the cost and benefit structure might not be telling the whole story. Outsourcing is frequently an option when the organization

- Is unable to get the right result
- Considers the process is too much work
- Fails to define their actual needs

As time goes by, it may be discovered that the outsource provider is taking unacceptable shortcuts or charging higher prices than expected. Additional issues to consider include turnaround time plus increased costs of supervision necessary to maintain the desired results.

Heartland Payment Systems moved their processing back in-house after years of outsourcing. Their service provider was identified as the bottleneck slowing responses for customers and creating other delays in distributing information within Heartland. Management realized that the service provider was limiting their ability to compete in their market. Bringing their processing back in-house saved $3 million and enabled them to deliver next-day funding. Heartland is now able to respond faster to customers, thus winning new business. —Source: *Information Week*, "20 Great Ideas"

We have discussed strategy and sourcing. Next, we'll discuss the performance of the executives in delivering results.

Conducting an Executive Performance Review

The executive staff is subject to review by the audit committee. As you recall, it is this committee's job to challenge the assumptions and assurances in the organization. The audit committee is expected to provide management oversight and allow executives the opportunity to discuss confidential issues about the business. An effective audit committee will advise individual executives with an opinion for possible solutions to internal problems.

Independent auditors are hired by the audit committee to provide an impartial (independent) opinion as to the status of internal controls. Audit committees are frequently the client of external audit engagements.

Understanding the Auditor's Interest in the Strategy

As an IS auditor, you need to find evidence of management governing IT and the enterprise. The composition and performance of the steering committee could be a powerful source of evidence. You may be able to review the plans and meeting minutes from the committee. The auditor's goal is to assess the performance of the CEO and executive management in developing and leading a successful strategy based on business objectives.

Overview of Tactical Management

By using tactical management, an organization selects a maneuver or technique that will render a better result. The goal of tactical management is to manage the return on investment for information systems. The successful manager will need to establish a requirement for the collection of performance metrics. The performance metrics are used to determine whether the results are improving or deteriorating against a baseline. The same metrics are used to demonstrate management success to the executives and stakeholders.

Figure 3.8 illustrates the tactical level in the organizational chart.

FIGURE 3.8   Tactical level in the organization

Individuals at the tactical level should be providing support to the strategic objectives. The majority of planning work accomplished at the director level is tactical in nature. Strategic plans are handed down from top management. The director level is expected to fulfill the strategic goals by providing solutions without the authority to make changes in other areas of the organizational structure. A director's authority outside of their own department is limited to requesting and negotiating.

Planning and Performance

Every IS organization has a number of functions that it should implement to fulfill its strategic plan, its tactical plan, and its daily plan. An auditor looks at any industry-standard benchmarks for performance optimization that have been adopted. Several are available, including the National Institute of Standards and Technology's controls matrix and the Federal Information Security Management Act (FISMA). In addition, the organization may use an organizational planning maturity model such as the Organizational Project Management Maturity Model (OPM3) by the Project Management Institute.

It is possible that the organization benchmarks its business continuity plans and disaster plans after the public domain version of the Business Continuity Maturity Model (BCMM). The organization may have an information assurance program and be using the ISO 27002 or Capability Maturity Model (CMM).

The value of benchmarking is to determine the organization's position and progress as compared to a recognized reference. There are several competitive advantages to benchmarking, the first of which is the ability to attract respect and more-favorable terms from stakeholders. Every IS organization has an issue regarding financial management.

The question comes up, what does IS pay for?

What does the department pay for?

What does the project pay for?

Individual departments may be operating a shadow IT group funded by department budgets. This condition usually indicates some type of failure to align to the business objectives in the strategic plan.

Management Control Methods

All levels of management are responsible for providing leadership. Good leaders generate better performance from individual employees. To manage is to create an unnatural result. If the same result would naturally occur by itself, then you are not managing it. The objective of management is to get a better result. Every organization needs to plan for how to collect continuous evidence of performance. The minimum requirements of good management include the following:

- Performance reporting
- General record keeping
- Safeguards and implementation details of controls

The auditor needs to review a variety of documents, including the organization's strategic plan, policies, IT plans, and operating procedures. These include plans for training, system mitigation, system certification, disaster recovery, continuity, and the inevitability of change. As an auditor, you will need input from people besides IT management to ensure alignment with the enterprise objectives.

Performance Review

Performance review refers to the identification of a target to be monitored, tracked, and assigned to a responsible party, and the resolution of any open issues.

Existing systems require a regular review to determine the ongoing level of compliance to internal controls and the next steps to take.

The Capability Maturity Model (CMM) is a method for evaluating and measuring the maturity of processes in organizations. A rating scale from 0 to 5 is used. A score of zero indicates that nothing is occurring. Level 1 maturity indicates that the initial activity was successful and may later progress up to level 5, when the activity is statistically controlled for continuous improvement. The see pg 97 CMM rating scale was developed by the Software Engineering Institute at Carnegie Mellon University and has been widely used for rating business process capabilities.

 The Capability Maturity Model is also discussed in Chapter 5.

Levels of the CMM are as follows:

Level 0 = Nothing yet   The level of zero is implied in the CMM but may not be noticed. This is important when evaluating process maturity. Missing processes and controls without evidence will be rated as zero. Many individuals assume that all controls are present when, in fact, some may be missing. A process or control must have occurred in order to reach a level of maturity (1–5).

Level 1 = Initial   Processes are unique and chaotic. The organization does not have a stable environment. Success is based on individual competencies and heroics. This level often produces products and services that work. However, output may exceed the available resources or be dependent on specific individuals. At level 1, people have the most freedom and flexibility to make their own decisions.

Level 2 = Repeatable   Processes are repeatable. The organization uses project management to track projects. The project status is communicated by using milestones with a defined work breakdown structure. The basic standards, processes, descriptions, and procedures are documented.

Level 3 = Defined   Processes are well documented and understood. Level 3 is more mature and better defined than level 2. Processes have objectives, measurements, improvement procedures, and standards. The results in level 3 are predictable by qualitative measure.

Level 4 = Managed   Management can use precise measurement criteria to control the processes and identify ways to adjust the results. Processes at level 4 are predictable by quantitative measure. see pg 149

Level 5 = Optimized   This is the highest level, with continuous improvement of processes. Objectives for improvement are defined and continually revised to reflect business needs and objectives. Products at CMM level 5 have been so well defined that they are effectively converted into a commodity.

Level 5 is the ideal maturity for the maximum level of control in outsourcing. It allows the company to switch to using less-skilled people who are told what to do, pay less, and demand unquestionable authority. People have the least authority with the fewest decisions at level 5.

CObIT version 4.1 uses the CMM approach to rate auditee performance by the maturity of their control environment.

Figure 3.9 shows the five maturity levels of the CMM in a lateral view.

FIGURE 3.9   Capability Maturity Model

Frankly, attaining higher levels in the maturity model increases the likelihood that internal controls are successful. A higher CMM grade indicates a definition of maturity with a higher degree of control.

Consider the typical hooks in an outsource contract. The buyer is hooked to it, and so the following questions should be asked:

- Did the client give away resources, intellectual-property knowledge, or procedures of value that will not be recoverable?

- Has the client given away highly qualified personnel who will no longer be in-house?

- What will a contract change cost, if desired?

- Can the contract be cancelled?

- If a decision is made to cancel, what will it take to get the replacement function online?

This should be enough information for the prospective CISA. Let's take a look at two other sources of governance models. The first is the U.S. National Institute of Standards and Technology.

National Institute of Standards and Technology

The U.S. government has set forth standards for engineering, weights and measures, and even computer processing. Management of the standards is assigned to the *National Institute of Standards and Technology (NIST)*. The NIST standards for information technology management are mandatory for government agencies and optional for nongovernmental organizations. Many of the IT best practices were derived from NIST.

The U.S. government passed new internal control regulations under FISMA to unify the former Federal Information Processing Standards (FIPS). The U.S. internal control rating requirements for compliance are posted on the NIST website under the heading for special reports (`http://csrc.nist.gov`). NIST is an excellent resource with governance models that implement the CMM. Now let's look at an international standard.

International Standards

Not to be outdone by the United States, the British government enacted their own security standard for government systems in 1995. The standard for British information security is British Standard 7799-1 (BS-7799 part 1). This uses similar internal controls for governance of IS systems. The ISO ratified the BS-7799-1 framework as ISO standard 17799. It then renamed 17799 as ISO standard 27002. ISO 27002 contains numerous points that are identical to the U.S. standards and work in concert. The ISO 27002 is actually functioning quite well as the executive summary for implementing the U.S. NIST 800-53 standard.

Just a reminder: ISO standards are protected by international copyright. Each country sells a single-user copy for the equivalent of $1 U.S. per page. That's how ISO gets funding. CISAs should not have bootleg copies under any condition. Besides the illegal issues, it violates your certification. Remember, the person who turns you in will usually get amnesty.

With so much attention on internal controls, the most important step an organization can take is the first—to implement controls. Any one of these best practices models should already be implemented.

Quality Management

We have already discussed the basics of quality management in Chapter 2, "Audit Process." Every organization should have processes in place to ensure that people are taking steps to do the right job at the right time. Quality management is a pervasive requirement.

We will discuss quality further in Chapter 5.

Project Management

In Chapter 1, we discussed a few basics of project management and the defined project management processes. Every organization should be following a well-defined project management methodology. Larger organizations will implement a Project Management Office (PMO). The PMO is composed of project managers for the organization. Their function is to manage the larger or more-critical projects.

As a CISA, you should recall that each project will have at least four distinct phases. Recall that the Project Management Institute defines five phases of project management: Initiating, Planning, Executing, Monitoring and Controlling, and Closing. However, PMI considers the process of getting a sponsor as the phase of project initiation. Most employees will never be involved in the Initiating phase. Therefore, ISACA wants the IS auditor to understand the four common phases of Planning, Executing (scheduling), Monitoring and Controlling, and Closing.

Now let's look at risk management in IT governance.

[handwritten top margin: 1. Analyze. 2. Identify risks. 3. Manage risks. {audits and assessments are used for risk evaluation and control - pgs 69 - 73]

Risk Management

Risks occur at all levels. There are strategic risks, tactical risks, operational risks, and inherent risks. We have discussed these definitions in Chapters 1 and 2. Now let's look at one of the more common risk management formulas.

The first step in risk management is to calculate how much a single loss event would cost. This formula multiplies an asset value (expressed in dollars) by the percentage of loss for a particular event. For example, the percentage of loss of a stolen purse is likely to be 100 percent. In that example, the loss would be 100 percent of purse value. The loss due to data-entry errors may be equal to .007 percent of labor cost. This first formula is expressed as follows:

$$x \frac{\text{Asset value (AV) \$}}{\substack{\text{exposure factor (EF) \%}}} = \text{single loss expectancy (SLE)}$$

[handwritten left margin: ex: # of bugs in a progn? or using WebSphere instead of Spring + open source | EJBs]

[handwritten right: ← how to determine this? ex: How many foreigners you've hired to do government work]

The single loss expectancy can be multiplied by the number of related events that are likely to occur for the year. The final result would be the estimated annual loss, as shown in the following formula:

$$x \frac{\substack{\text{Single loss expectancy (SLE)}}}{\substack{\text{annual rate of occurrence (ARO)}}} = \text{annual loss expectancy (ALE)}$$

[handwritten left margin: See pgs 5, 570]

Threat + Vulnerability = WHAM! } X Estimated frequency = AR

Negative action or event | Path that threat could take | Loss | Single or annual rate of occurrence | Annualized risk

[handwritten near diagram: any negative event | path that allows threat to occur | ← filter = exposure factor? controls not really | The answer is to what extent are you using the controls to avoid the threat]

Risk management should be pervasive in all areas of business, including the IT department. As you might recall, we covered risk management previously in Chapter 2. The choices are to avoid, mitigate, transfer, accept, or eliminate the risk, and the goal is to reduce the level of risk.

When developing a risk management program, the auditor wants to find evidence that the risk management function has been implemented with an established purpose—in other words, that someone has been assigned responsibility, and risk management is a formal ongoing process, not just a review by lawyers.

Risks can involve many areas of the business. Impacts can be direct or indirect, but in either case can damage the organization's position, capital, or future opportunities. Typical assets include the organization's customer list, general information (which could be information about marketing or development), data, files, hardware, and software. Assets could also include the facility, a particular document, or services rendered. The risks, or threats, could be terror acts, malicious fraud, executing the wrong procedure, theft, or failure of controls.

It's interesting that criminals do not look at vulnerabilities the same way as an upstanding individual. To a criminal mind, a window becomes an entry or exit point to a building with the aid of a brick.

[handwritten bottom margin: see pg 95 for strong controls vs. weak controls]

Risk management operates at a variety of levels: Management at the strategic level focuses on whether going forward with a particular strategy over a period of years is a good idea. Management could be at a project level—is the project on track? Or it could be at a daily or hourly or by-the-minute operational level to ensure that personnel are doing what they are supposed to do. Frankly, most major disasters are caused by a domino effect of a tiny failure multiplying into multiple failures that become catastrophic.   *Ex: Space Shuttle disasters - 2 + counting!*

Overall, situations of high risk—where high loss, high consequence, or high impact is possible—require a method to ensure that the problem receives adequate consideration and the appropriate level of effort to prevent an unfortunate outcome. It is extremely common for IT staff to execute poor change control when dealing with interruptions, failures, theft, fraud, or just general risk while under pressure.

Personnel Risk

Determining the requirements related to hiring or terminating outsourced personnel can be challenging. Several companies have discovered way too late that certain organizations in the European Union have some rather stout requirements for expatriation and repatriation. The company may be liable for future employee benefits and the individual's cost of relocation. The requirements could also include severance plans that provide advance pay of up to about a year, the company's purchase of the former employee's home because that person did not have time to sell it, and payment of medical expenses for six months to a year. These requirements can make a huge difference if a company is planning changes such as layoffs or is trying to determine whether hiring a contractor is a good idea.

Information Security Risk

Every organization communicates sensitive data over delicate communication lines, which are not necessarily secure. In fact, every government has mandates to conduct surveillance for foreign intelligence in order to provide trade advantages for their citizens. News articles indicate that government organizations from competing countries are attempting to bring foreign technology to domestic organizations. It's the old game of economic espionage and political advantage. Data security is the number one concern when planning for communication crossing the border. We refer to this as *transborder communication*. One of the challenges is determining whether the data is legal or regulated across the border. The next concern may be that infrastructure issues impede delivery or quality of service from a geographically remote location.

NOTE   France was the first country to implement an organized system of spying on foreign nationals, beginning in the fourteenth century. The United States was one of the later countries to follow this initiative. Surveillance is mandated in the United States under the Foreign Intelligence Surveillance Act of 1978 (USC Title 50 Chapter 36, FISA).   ✗

Risk reduction efforts plus insurance comprise a minimum risk mgmt strategy

Implementing Standards

IT governance is founded on the implementation of formal policies and standards. Each standard is supported by a matching procedure. The purpose of IT governance is to ensure that the risks are properly managed by mitigation, avoidance, or transfer. Let's review a short list of the policies required to address issues faced by IT governance:

Intellectual property   The term *intellectual property* refers to data and knowledge that is not commonly known. This information possesses a commercial value. The IS auditor should understand how the organization is attempting to protect its intellectual property. There is no method for registering a trade secret. The owner has to undertake all control measures necessary to keep it secret. The rights of intellectual property can be destroyed by a failure of the organization to take preemptive action.   *- nondisclosure or non-compete agreements -pg 197*

Data integrity   What mechanisms have been put in place to ensure data integrity? Does the organization have input controls? How is the data validated for accuracy? Are the systems formally reviewed in a certification and accreditation process? What level of security management and access controls are present? Internal controls for data integrity are required by most industries and government regulation. The goal of data integrity is to ensure that data is accurate and safely stored.

> **Backup and restoration**   What are the plans and procedures for data backup and restoration? The number one issue in IT is loss of data due to faulty backup. The failures can be procedural or technical.

> **Security management**   Without security controls, ensuring data integrity is impossible. Internal controls prevent unauthorized modifications. SOX and FISMA mandate strong security controls.

Mandatory versus discretionary controls   Every control is based on the human implementation. The organization needs to clearly identify its management directives for implementation of controls. Every control will be one of two fundamental types:

> **Mandatory control**   This is the strongest type of control. The implementation may be administrative or technical. A mandatory control is designed to force compliance without exception. Mandatory controls are managed from a centralized authority.

> **Discretionary control**   The weakest type of control is discretionary. In a discretionary control, the user or delegated person of authority determines what is acceptable.

Monitoring   The IT systems should be monitored throughout the entire life cycle and in daily operations. The monitoring process provides valuable metrics necessary to compare alignment to business objectives. The purpose of governance is to lead. It would be impossible to lead without understanding ongoing conditions. Monitoring may prove that the organization is well run or a ticking time bomb. Without monitoring, determining whether an incident needs attention would be impossible.

Incident response   A response is required for skilled individuals to deal with technical problems or the failure of internal controls. An incident may be major or minor depending on the circumstances. It is necessary to have an established policy, standard, and procedure for handling the incident response. At the beginning of an incident, it is impossible to accurately foretell the full impact of possible consequences. An incident response team should be in place to investigate suspicious situations. Care and diligence is necessary because it may later be determined that the initial response area is a crime scene. The mishandling of evidence could lead to forfeiture of the organization's damage claims. Unproven allegations against an individual or organization will frequently result in financial liability by the accuser.

Ex: was the fire accidental or arson?

We discuss the details of monitoring and incident response in Chapter 6.

Human Resources

IT governance is conjoined with requirements to properly manage people. Good management is founded on human resource management that is well defined, fair, and consistent. Let's take a look at a few of the HR-related policies that affect IT management:

Hiring   What are the organization's policies for selecting the best candidate? How should the interview process be handled? Quality management is required during the hiring process to ensure that the organization is in compliance with equal opportunity standards.

Termination   Personnel may be terminated via either friendly or unfriendly procedures. The requirements for layoffs are relatively clear. What are the procedures for terminating personnel over extended periods of time? A special procedure may be necessary in the case of an upcoming personal retirement. A different procedure may apply to an employee who will be returning as a contractor on the same project. A hostile termination could stem from workplace violence, a criminal act, fraud, or a dispute with other personnel.

Employee contracts   Many organizations use employee contracts to specify terms of employment. This technique is typically in effect in states with a Right to Work law. Right to Work laws are primarily about *union versus nonunion employment*—that people have a right to decide whether they want to be part of a union, that union membership can't be a condition of employment. The use of employment contracts is invaluable for identifying the ownership of new discoveries. The employment contract details that the individual is performing work for hire, to the benefit of the employer organization.

Confidentiality agreement   A standard practice is for employees and contractors to sign a confidentiality agreement. The purpose is to ensure that strategic, tactical, and operational details are not divulged outside the organization. Operating without a confidentiality agreement is usually a significant risk.

Noncompetition agreement   The employer may implement a noncompete agreement to prevent the employee from working for a competitor until after a specific period of time. The terms of this type of agreement may be successful as long as they are not overly restrictive for the amount of money paid to the employee.

Ethics statements   The organization should provide a statement of what is acceptable and unacceptable behavior. The best method for preventing a problem is to explain to an individual what actions are acceptable. Unacceptable behavior includes any activities for personal gain at the expense of the organization.

Performance evaluation   A standardized process should be in place for reviewing an employee's performance. Each employee in the same basic role should be judged by their manager on defined criteria, pertinent to their organizational role. A quarterly or annual review is customary. More-progressive organizations may conduct reviews on a weekly or monthly basis. The morale of hard-working employees is damaged if the boss fails to notice their good work. The results of each review fall under HR record retention requirements for several years.

Promotion policy   What is the organization's promotion policy? Is it based on job performance, education, or something else? The organization is required to demonstrate a fair and objective promotion policy in order to meet equal opportunity compliance.

Work schedule   Work schedules and vacation schedules should be clearly defined. In some financial organizations, the vacation schedule is implemented as a detective control. An individual is forced to take vacations in one- or two-week increments. During their absence, another individual performs that job, and a discovery audit may take place to ensure that no irregular or illegal acts have been committed by the employee.

Corrective counseling   What are the organization's policies for corrective counseling after poor performance from the employee? Care must be taken to prevent discrimination. An improper termination can create a financial liability. An employee may collect monetary damages if able to prove wrongful termination.

These are just a few of the many policies and procedures necessary to manage human resources. The IS auditor should be concerned about activities that increase the organization's level of risk. This includes Human Resources activities.

System Life-Cycle Management

All computer systems need to be managed through their entire life cycle. Each system will go through a series of phases starting with a feasibility study. Next, requirements are generated and followed by system design. Systems are tested for integrity, and their fitness of use is determined. The life cycle continues into system implementation. After successful implementation, the system can migrate into production use. Each year of production, the system should undergo a review. The annual post implementation review focuses on the system's present condition compared to the more current requirements. A system may be upgraded to the new requirements or retired. This is just a summary.

The CISA is interested in understanding how the organization manages each phase of this process. Evidence should be obtained to support the auditor's conclusions.

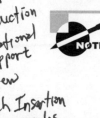

We cover the system life cycle in more depth in Chapter 5.

Continuity Planning

Information technology systems are so pervasive today that most organizations would cease to operate if their computers were unavailable. IT governance requires continuity planning for systems and data. Any disruption to operations could have far-reaching effects. Members of the media can be merciless in their quest to report an interesting story. The damage to an organization's reputation and brand can be fatal. ISACA wants every CISA to be aware of the need for continuity planning. We have expanded coverage of business continuity in Chapter 8, "Business Continuity and Disaster Recovery."

Insurance

Adequate insurance is the minimum response for asset protection. This is a corrective administrative control. There are issues concerning insurance including the cost versus actual benefits received. Insurance does not replace lost market share, nor damage from unauthorized disclosure of confidential information. Acts of god, war, and terrorism are exempt from coverage in most insurance policies. Proper risk management reduces the organization's exposure. Risk reduction efforts, combined with insurance, are a good practice.

 NOTE Normally, the term *self-insurance* implies a level of protection that does not exist. Self-insurance means the organization is accepting the risk with full liability for any consequences.   *see pg 71*

The CISA should be aware that there is a difference between real insurance and self-insurance.

Performance Management

Performance management serves to inform executives and stakeholders as to the progress of current activities. A fair and objective scoring system should be used. Scores may be based on a current service-level agreement. Another method is to use key performance indicators (KPIs), which tend to represent a historical average of monitored events. Unfortunately, a key performance indicator may indicate a failing score too late to implement a change. A perfect example of a KPI is the high-school report card. By the time the score is reported, the target child may not be eligible to graduate.

A process should exist to report the performance of IT budgets and noncompliant activities. Executive management should encourage the reporting of issues without punishing the messenger. Some effort is necessary to ensure the accurate and timely flow of information upward to the executives. False information can be very damaging.

Instead of just having a qualitative assessment of good or bad, or high, medium, or low, this should be an accounting exercise using a quantitative measure. It could be semi quantitative, using a ranking scale similar to scoring in a school: 70 to 79 is a C, 80 to 89 is a B, 90 to 100 represents an A, and then percentages such as A– or A+. This technique will convert a subjective decision into a more objective review. The Capability Maturity Model is very effective for communicating performance metrics.

Figure 3.10 shows a brief glimpse of the CMM used to report metrics.

FIGURE 3.10   Excerpt of CMM to report metrics

Metric	CMM process maturity	Change	% Compliance
Help desk support	0 — 3.9 — 5	▲	100%
Laptop security plan	0 — 2.9 — 5	▲	73%
Laptop data encryption	0 — 3.4 — 5	●	67%
New user security training	0 — 3.4 — 5	▲	58%
Existing user security training	0 — 1.5 — 5	▼	19%
Vulnerability scan users	0 — 1 — 5	▲	8%

Managing Outsourcing

When an organization decides to consider outsourcing, one of the concerns is that the organization may lose the visibility necessary to effectively operate the processes. The outsource contract should require a *right to audit* the service provider. Occasionally the response is that they cannot be audited by everyone because they do not have the time or the money, but will give you a copy of the SAS-70 service provider's audit report, which is a standard audit format.

Unfortunately, the report may be insufficient to management needs, because the report is probably vetted and groomed to ensure it states the level of information the service provider wants to convey, not necessarily what may be observed during your own audit.

Our suggestion is that if a company is considering outsourcing, the auditor could ask, "Why not run a controls audit and an SLA audit using the client's auditor, or a full audit before signing the contract?" The goal is to determine whether the service provider is fulfilling their entire obligation before signing a contract. Why risk the time and money to sign a contract while silently hoping and praying that the requirements are met?

An excellent idea is to implement a business process review before outsourcing.

Overview of Business Process Reengineering

One of the principles in business that remains constant is the need to improve your processes and procedures. Most trade magazines today contain discussions of the detailed planning necessary for implementing change in an organization. The concept of change must be accepted as a fundamental principle. Terms such as *business evolution* and *continuous improvement*

See pgs 74, 103

ricochet around the room in business meetings. It's a fact that organizations which fail to change are destined to perish.

As a CISA, you must be prepared to investigate whether process changes within the organization are accounted for with proper documentation. All internal control frameworks require that management be held responsible for safeguarding all the assets belonging to their organization. Management is also responsible for increasing revenue. Let's discuss why business process reengineering (BPR) review is important.

> Every IS auditor is required to choose sides. An IS auditor's independence would be compromised by participating in a nonaudit role on the BPR project. You can't audit your own work. If an IS auditor has participated in the design of systems, processes, or procedures as part of the BPR team, that auditor is required to refuse the audit of those functional areas. Therefore, it's common to have two sets of auditors during BPR projects. One set works on the BPR team to help steer the project, and auditors from a second firm perform verification audits. *Cha-ching!*

Why Use Business Process Reengineering

Times change. People change. Needs change. It is said that change is the only constant in life. BPR is used to improve process performance by removing, combining, or replacing steps that are no longer important.

BPR is concerned with reducing costs of the existing process while increasing performance. BPR includes three major areas for improvement:

Business efficiency   Efficiency will increase as the proficiency of workers increases as they gain experience. In the very beginning, work is slow with multiple test inspections to ensure that results will be acceptable. Workers will progress through the *learning curve*. With more experience, the workers' technique will become more refined. Eventually, the number of inspections may be reduced after the quality becomes consistent.

Improved techniques   New improvements in the existing techniques will be discovered with more experience. An updated technique may eliminate previous steps that become unnecessary because of higher consistency. Improved methods and advances in technology can change how a process is performed. Several steps may be combined into a single step; eliminating the unnecessary steps increases efficiency. It may be necessary to add extra steps in the process if quality begins to decline.

New requirements   New requirements may be added in response to a regulation, business need, or customer. The existing business process will be reworked to comply with the updated requirements.

BPR activities are performed as a unique project. The BPR project will design a new process or improve existing processes to replace the outdated, inefficient processes.

You may want to refer to Chapter 1 for a quick refresher on project management.

BPR Methodology

Every good methodology specifies a basic vision to illustrate its strategy, and recommends standards to follow and procedures to use. There is more than one version of the BPR methodology available for businesses. For clarity, we are going to focus on the views representative of ISACA and the COBIT framework of management guidelines. These are considered an excellent resource in the industry.

The key to governance is for management to take responsibility as the leader for implementing change, while establishing an adequate system of internal control. This would include implementing a culture of continuous monitoring to fuel continuous improvement. There is a saying: "You can't fix what you can't prove." It would be ridiculous to charge off on a whim under the guise of BPR without supporting evidence. Yet some companies do it all the time. BPR is often coupled with an enterprise resource planning (ERP) implementation. It would be a reckless misuse of company resources to switch to a particular ERP system just because it sounds cool, makes you look important, or aids your political agenda because it's the same system used at a former employer.

Consider for a moment that many of us are members of the general public. Stock-holding investors are on the outside of the business without full knowledge of the internal processes. We expect you as the auditor to investigate the supporting evidence and tell us whether management is making good, solid decisions based on intelligent facts. We hold you, the auditor, responsible for telling the truth. Please keep this fiduciary responsibility in mind when working on BPR-related projects.

Genius or Insanity?

It is a commonly held belief that there is a fine line between genius and insanity. The secret is to know which side of the line you're on. The latter is beyond the scope of this book, so let's focus on the genius side. True genius is grounded in a logical progression of intelligent thought.

History is loaded with the names of famous people regarded as the inspired genius in their fields. One characteristic is pervasive: Every great accomplishment was based on lessons learned from careful observations. These observations provided the facts necessary to fuel a progression of ideas into an intelligent hypothesis. The next step was to determine an objective method for testing the hypothesis. Useful metrics were created to help measure results. If the hypothesis failed, it was back to the drawing board to check their work and revise their ideas. Each test simulation yielded additional data to steer their thoughts.

Even Leonardo da Vinci's ideas were considered wild hallucinations until it was realized he had collected evidence indicating a crystal-clear thought process involving observation, hypothesis, and testing.

Goal of BPR

— Strategic Plans are for 3-5 yrs into future.

All BPR projects are intended to be strategic in nature. We are going to change the way the business operates. Service organizations and manufacturers need a mechanism to support their evolution. Continuous improvement is necessary to survive the challenges of increasing competition with the constant pressure of rising costs. Any change to a running business introduces new magnitudes of risk. Thin profit margins leave little tolerance for bad ideas or inadequate implementation. Proper reengineering will involve comprehensive changes affecting the design structure of management, people in support roles, information systems, and operating policies.

One of the auditor's duties is to impress upon management that controls are necessary. You may need to correct their view that controls appear to slow the process by explaining how controls are necessary to offset the risks that would be difficult to manage or to measure. The most damaging risks are those whose likelihood or effect you cannot calculate. Repeated answers of "I don't know" may indicate that you're on the wrong side of the genius-insanity line.

Guiding Principles for BPR

Let's instill a few guiding principles for your BPR activities. The purpose is to lend a structure to support the innovative thinking necessary for you to be successful. Reengineering projects are founded on specific situations and require creative ideas to generate the appropriate solution. Let's look at three possible approaches:

Think big   This is an unconstrained top-down approach. The focus is on determining how the organization's strategy can be implemented without being restrained by existing processes. Many of the details in the current processes are ignored. All emphasis is placed on the future process to be (end state). Ideas are generated to answer the question, what will it ultimately be? This is consistent with the step change philosophy presented by authors Michael Hammer and James Champy in *Reengineering the Corporation* (Collins, 2006). Donald Trump is famous for using this approach because people naturally want to be involved in big projects. Tom Peters illustrates the power of thinking big in his fabulous book *Re-imagine!* (Dorling Kindersley, 2006). The risk is bigger and so are the rewards.

Incremental   This is a bottom-up approach that models existing processes to gain deeper understanding. Metrics are created and compared to identify what can be changed to streamline the process. The focus is on making incremental changes to the current process by identifying opportunities for improvement. The downside of the bottom-up approach is the tendency for BPR teams to spend too much time documenting the current process. By focusing so hard on the current process, their innovative thoughts and ideas are stifled. Overall gains are small because creative genius is lost. This tends to fit the stereotype of detail-oriented accountants spending too much time counting the beans while ignoring the potential that could be realized by exploiting a broader strategy.

Hybrid approach   The most practical application is a mixed approach. Planning begins with a top-down view of the big-picture strategy. Bottom-up research is performed to understand the current functionality and define the processes in use. The process starts by grading what you have as good, average and poor (GAP). Then comparing it to what you want. This GAP analysis is used to identify the differences between what is getting done and what needs to occur. The GAP will provide valuable insight for determining the best transition path. This will result in an initial recommendation that may require relatively small changes to remove bottlenecks. Alternatively, it could yield a series of more-complex projects, thus charting a course that places the organization ahead of its competitors. This is a noble route that the auditor is advised to undertake.

Knowledge Requirements for BPR

To be competent in BPR requires a working knowledge of auditing standards and the control frameworks such as CObIT. The competent auditor must possess the following skills before undertaking a BPR project:

- Up-to-date information systems auditing skills
- Specialized CISA audit standard knowledge
- Specialized knowledge of the company processes and procedures
- Specialized knowledge of the functional area being audited
- General management knowledge and skills
- Interpersonal "people" skills

The IS auditor can make an important contribution to their knowledge of internal controls and systems. Frequently the auditor will have to reengineer their own skills and audit approach to deal with the radical changes created by BPR. When auditing BPR, the CISA complements the other auditors on the BPR team who will be representing the special needs of finance and regulatory compliance.

BPR Techniques

ISACA expects every CISA to understand the operating techniques used in BPR projects. There are some conflicting viewpoints by different BPR experts; however, most of the suggested techniques include the following:

- Revising the logical order of individual processes to simplify the process of improving overall quality
- Reviewing a logical diagram of an existing process to determine whether multiple jobs can be combined into fewer steps
- Giving workers additional authority to make operational decisions while maintaining an acceptable level of control
- Eliminating superfluous or overlapping processes
- Standardizing processes, procedures, methods, products, and tools across the organization
- Using the most effective controls to ensure governance
- Converting manual processes into automated methods
- Establishing parallel processes for business continuity

BPR projects should be undertaken only when the business value can be demonstrated. Three simple methods to demonstrate business value are to increase capability, to reduce operating cost, or to obtain compliance with a new requirement. The BPR project may commence after the steering committee has reviewed the ROI evidence, agreed with the scope, and granted formal approval to proceed.

BPR Application Steps

ISACA cites six basic steps in their general approach to BPR. These six steps are simply an extension of Shewhart's Plan-Do-Check-Act model for managing projects:

Envision   Visualize a need (envision). Develop an estimate of the ROI created by the proposed change. Elaborate on the benefit with a preliminary project plan to gain sponsorship from the organization. The plan should define the areas to be reviewed and clarify the desired result at the end of the project (aka *end state objective*). The deliverables of the envision phase include the following:

- Project champion working with the steering committee to gain top management approval
- Brief description of project scope, goals, and objectives
- Description of the specific deliverables from this project

With a preliminary charter to evidence management's approval, the project may proceed into the initiation phase.

Initiate   This phase involves setting BPR goals with the sponsor. Focus on planning the collection of detailed evidence necessary to build the subsequent BPR plan for redesigning the process. Deliverables in the initiation phase include the following:

- Identifying internal and external requirements (project specifications)
- Business case explaining why this project makes sense (justification) and the estimated return on investment compared to the total cost (net ROI)
- Formal project plan with budget, schedule, staffing plan, procurement plan, deliverables, and project risk analysis   *— see pg 72*
- Level of authority the BPR project manager will hold and the composition of any support committee or task force that will be required
- From the profit and loss (P&L) statement, identify the item line number that money will be debited from to pay for this project and identify the specific P&L line number that the financial return will later appear under (to provide strict monitoring of the ROI performance)
- Formal project charter signed by the sponsors

It's important to realize that some BPR projects will proceed to their planned conclusion and others may be halted because of insufficient evidence. After a plan is formally approved, the BPR project may proceed to the diagnostic phase.

Diagnose   Document existing processes. Now it's time to see what is working and identify the source of each requirement. Each process step is reviewed to calculate the value it creates. The goal of the diagnostic phase is to gain a better understanding of existing processes. The data collected in the diagnostic phase forms the basis of all planning decisions:

- Detailed documentation of the existing process   — *see Business Impact Analysis pg 160*
- Performance measurement of individual steps in the process
- Evidence of specific process steps that add customer value
- Identification of process steps that don't add value
- Definition of attributes that create value and quality

Put in the extra effort to do a good job of collecting and analyzing the evidence. All future assumptions will be based on evidence from the diagnostic phase.

Redesign   Using the evidence from the diagnostic phase, it's time to develop the new process. This will take several planning iterations to ensure that the strategic objectives are met. The formal redesign plans will be reviewed by sponsors and stakeholders. A final plan will be presented to the steering committee for approval. Here's an example of deliverables from the redesign phase.

- Comparison of the envisioned objective to actual specifications
- Analysis of alternatives (AoA)
- Prototyping and testing of the redesigned process
- Formal documentation of the final design

The project will need formal approval to proceed into the reconstruction phase. Otherwise, the redesign is halted pending further scrutiny while comparing the proposed design with available evidence. Insufficient evidence warrants halting the project.

Reconstruct   With formal approval received, it's time to begin the implementation phase. The current processes are deconstructed and reassembled according to the plan. Reconstruction may be in the form of a parallel process, modular changes, or complete transition. Each method presents a unique risk and reward opportunity. Deliverables from this phase include the following:

- Conversion plan with dependencies in time sequence
- Change control management
- Execution of conversion plan with progress monitoring
- Training of users and support personnel
- Pilot implementation to ensure a smooth migration
- Formal approval by the sponsor.

The reconstructed process must be formally approved by management to witness their consent for fitness of use. IT governance dictates that executive management shall be held responsible for any failures and receive recognition for exceptional results. System performance will be evaluated again after entering production use.

Evaluate (post evaluation)   The reconstructed process is monitored to ensure that it works and is producing the strategic value as forecast in the original justification.

- Comparison of original forecast to actual performance
- Identification of lessons learned
- Total quality management plan to maintain the new process

A method of continuous improvement is implemented to track the original goals against actual process performance. Annual reevaluation is needed to adapt new requirements or new opportunities.

These steps are easier to practice if you can relate them to something meaningful. Let's compare the BPR process steps with similar objectives in PMI project management and System Development Life Cycle (SDLC). An excellent way to get buy-in is to communicate by relating BPR steps to other methodologies already in use. Table 3.4 provides an illustration of the objectives in common.

TABLE 3.4   Comparison of Common Objectives

BPR Process Areas	PMI Project Management Phases	System Development Life Cycle (SDLC)	Objectives in Common
Envision	Initiating	Feasibility	Determine scope, get a strong sponsor, target a process, set goals
Initiate		Requirements definition	Obtain stakeholder buy-in, Identify external customer needs
Diagnose	Planning		Identify process attributes, possible benchmarks, activities, resources, roles, cost estimates, and communication needs
Redesign		System design	Devise solutions and alternatives through brainstorming and creative techniques
	Executing	Development	Build prototypes to test the new design
Reconstruct		Implementation	Install IT systems, train users and support staff, begin transition

TABLE 3.4 Comparison of Common Objectives *(continued)*

BPR Process Areas	PMI Project Management Phases	System Development Life Cycle (SDLC)	Objectives in Common
Evaluate	Managing and Controlling	Post implementation	Monitor and review the new process to see whether goals were attained
	Closing		Document lessons learned, archive files, assign the process to a quality program (TQM).

Now we need to clarify the role of information systems in the BPR effort. Just how does IS help make this project successful?

Role of IS in BPR

ISACA has identified four distinct roles to be delivered by information systems within the BPR projects. IT is a key supplier of tools necessary for the business to be successful. The four roles of IS are as follows:

- Enable the new processes by improving automation.

- Provide IT project management tools to help analyze the process and defined requirements.

- Provide IT support for collaboration tools, teleconferencing, and specialized software supporting the business users.

- Help business unit managers to integrate their business process with ERP systems. This may include integrating business partners through online transaction processing.

Business Process Documentation

When looking at changes to business processes or when implementing these changes, the CISA should consider the use of the following tools to help define and document the processes being changed:

Process maps   Diagram business processes by using flowcharts, influence diagrams, and fish-bone diagrams to assist in the definition and documentation of the process.

Risk assessment   Look at the process by using the preceding risk categories as well as other categories. External risk and organizational risk should be assessed. Tools for risk identification, such as interviewing experts, brainstorming, holding risk identification roundtable sessions, and using the Delphi technique, should be considered. The Delphi technique uses a blind interaction of ideas between members of a group. Each member provides suggestions without knowledge of the suggestions by other participants. The exercise continues until a consensus is reached. We covered some of the other methods of performing a risk assessment in Chapter 2.

Pg 72

Benchmarking   Compare your process to another process that is the same or similar.

Roles and responsibilities   Define and document who is responsible for what process or what portions of the process. Many times the auditor will discover through interviews that several people know a portion of the process but no one knows the whole process.

Tasks and activities   Define tasks and activities in conjunction with defining roles and responsibilities. The purpose is to define who performs what work and how it affects the over-all process. The results may be documented in a work breakdown structure (WBS). All the tasks in the project are grouped into related work packages. Each task is assigned with its pre-decessor and successor dependencies identified. The list of tasks is referred to as the WBS.

Process controls and data process restrictions   Document the current process with clearly defined checkpoints and/or checklists to ensure that the entire process is being performed. Define the data available for the process. This includes defining contributory sources and defining all data available from the process being considered for review.

Now it's time to discuss the types of planning tools available for BPR projects.

BPR Tools and Techniques

High-quality data can be assembled into information that will create significant power. Several planning tools and techniques have been developed to capture the data. We need good tools to combine this data into meaningful information. Let's look at a few of the available options:

- Traditional project management such as PMI
- Analysis tools such as Critical Path Method (CPM) or PERT charting   — *19 47*
- Presentation using graphical flowcharts (process flow diagrams) with decision trees
- Manual process of setting goals, and performing root cause analysis and risk analysis

The right tools will harness the power necessary for your BPR project to be successful. Let's start with the manual process of setting goals through benchmarking. Later we will discuss the manual process of risk analysis in the BIA project.

Benchmarking as a BPR Tool

Benchmarking is the process of comparing performance data (aka *metrics*). It can be used to evaluate business processes that are under consideration for reengineering. Performance data may be obtained by using a self-assessment or by auditing for compliance against a standard (reference standard). Evidence captured during the diagnostic phase is considered the key to identifying areas for performance improvement and documenting obstacles. ISACA offers the following general guidelines for performing benchmarks:

Plan   Identify the critical processes and create measurement techniques to grade the processes.

Research   Use information about the process and collect regular data (samples) to build a baseline for comparison. Consider input from your customers and use analogous data from other industries.

Observe   Gather internal data and external data from a benchmark partner to aid the comparison results. Benchmark data can also be compared against published standards.

Analyze   Look for root cause-effect relationships and other dependencies in the process. Use predefined tools and procedures to collate the data collected from all available sources.

Adapt   Translate the findings into hypotheses of how these findings will help or hurt strategic business goals. Design a pilot test to prove or disprove the hypotheses.

Improve   Implement a prototype of the new processes. Study the impact and note any unexpected results. Revise the process by using controlled change management. Measure the process results again. Use preestablished procedures such as total quality management for continuous improvement.

The benchmarking process is a valuable first step toward self-improvement. Figure 3.11 illustrates the benchmarking process.

FIGURE 3.11   Benchmarking process

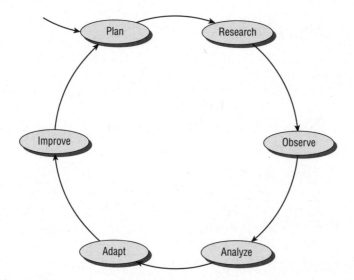

Another excellent tool is the Business Impact Analysis (BIA). This would be more involved than benchmarking, yet a properly executed BIA will yield extremely valuable information.

Using a Business Impact Analysis   — see also similar section in Ch 8 pg 467

The *Business Impact Analysis (BIA)* is a discovery process. Its purpose is to uncover the inner workings of any process. The BIA will answer questions about actual procedures, shortcuts, workarounds, and the types of failure that may occur. Armed with this knowledge, it is possible to assess priorities.

Part of the BIA is to determine what the process does, who performs the process, and what the output is. The BIA also determines the value of the process output to the organization. The BIA interviewer will ask key managers and key workers a series of questions to discover the low-level details of current processes. Some sample BIA questions that might be asked of key personnel in a BPR process review include the following:

1. What processes do you perform?
2. Who do you perform these actions for?
3. What tools, equipment, and systems do you use?
4. What request, event, or system provides an indication for you to start work on the subject (input)?
5. Get/show examples of the work the person performs (processes). Do multiple processes exist? If so, be sure to document each process for later review.
6. Who is the key vendor and the alternate vendor?
7. What is the time sensitivity of the process?
8. What is the basic priority of the process?
9. Where do you record your work (output)?
10. Who uses the output of your process next, and who depends on your output?
11. What happens if the process is
    - not used?
    - not available?
    - not performed?
    - not accepted?
12. What other methods could you use to accomplish the process? Are there workarounds or alternate processes that might already exist?
13. Would the alternate procedure really work?
14. How can you test it, or has it already been tested?
15. Who else knows this process and could do this in a crisis?
16. Who is the ultimate customer for this process?
17. How much revenue does this process create or support?
18. Is documentation on this process readily available?
19. Is documentation on the technical requirements for the process readily available?
20. Are there previous audit reports about this process that can be examined?
21. What is the projected lifetime of this process? Will the process continue to be used, or is this process being made obsolete by a future process or projected change in business?

Questions 17 and 21 provide key information for determining the true value of the process. Determining how much revenue the process creates or supports helps define its true value to the enterprise. Another measurement for value is to determine how long the process will remain in use.

For example, an organization can afford to spend $50,000 to reengineer a shipping process if they intend to use the process in perpetuity. The cost savings or cost avoidance saved each year will be used to pay for this effort. Processes expected to end within one year will need to be carefully evaluated to determine whether the payback is worth the effort. Practical advice suggests that processes selected for reengineering should have a lifetime in excess of one year, or be nonworking processes, to provide enough return value for the time and effort expended to reengineer them.

Real World Scenario

BIA Improves Awareness

Consider the example of a multinational company that owns a division manufacturing radios. During the BIA process, it was determined that 31 percent of the overall net retained revenue for this organization was generated by the small group manufacturing radios in the United States. Their number one customer is the U.S. military, which favors products made in the United States. This tiny little division represents only 7 percent of the multinational company. It brings up an interesting question regarding the net performance from the other 93 percent of the company. The radio division is definitely a top asset. A smart person would wonder whether the executives should implement a BPR project to reproduce the similar results in the other 93 percent of their business or sell off less-profitable divisions. To outsource manufacturing overseas would compromise their advantage of supplying U.S.-made products. Overall, internal awareness was improved by spotlighting how profitable this division is. Additionally, it sparked conversations that overseas manufacturing would remove their market advantage by throwing their product into an import price war.

Proper planning of the process reengineering project requires documentation of the process to be modified. If the process has been correctly documented with all outputs and all interrelated activities, the chances of having "leftover parts" is minimized.

BPR Project Risk Assessment

Radical improvements are not possible without increased risk. BPR projects are known to have a high rate of failure. Risks associated with changing an existing process must be identified. The *ISACA Audit Standards, Guidelines, and Procedures* identify several risk areas to consider when planning a BPR project. The risks can be broken down into three broad areas of design risks, implementation risks, and operational risks:

Design risks   A good design can improve profitability while satisfying customers. Conversely, a design failure would spell doom to any BPR project. It would be reckless to undertake new projects without dedicated resources capable of committing the time and attention necessary to develop a quality solution. Often this type of detailed planning may consume more money and time than is available from key personnel. ISACA wants all CISA candidates to recognize the risks that may occur in the BPR design:

Sponsorship risks   C-level management is not supportive of the effort. Insufficient commitment from the top is just as bad as having the wrong person leading the project. Poor communication is also a major problem.   *corporate*

Scope risks   The BPR project must be related to the vision and the specifications of the strategic plan. Serious problems will arise if the scope is improperly defined. It's a design failure if politically sacred processes and existing jobs are excluded from the scope of change.

Skill risks   Absence of radical "out of the box" thinking will create a failure by dismissing new ideas that should have been explored. Thinking big is the most effective way to achieve the highest return on investment. Participants without broad spatial skills will experience serious difficulty because the project vision is beyond their ability to define an effective action plan.

Political risk   Sabotage is always possible from people fearing a loss of power or resistance to change. Uncontrolled rumors lead to fear and subversion of the concept. People will resist change unless the benefits are well understood and accepted.

2) **Implementation risks**   The implementation risks represent another source of potential failures that could occur during the BPR project. The most common implementation risks include the following:

Leadership risks   C-level executives may fail to provide enough support for the project to be successful. Leadership failures include disputes over ownership and project scope. Management changes during the BPR project may signal wavering needs that may cause the loss of momentum. Strong sponsors will provide money, time, and resources while serving as project champions with their political support.

Technical risks   Complexity may overtake the definition of scope. The required capability may be beyond that of prepackaged software. Custom functions and design may exceed IT's creative capability or available time. Delays in implementation could signal that the complexity of scope was underestimated. If the key issues are not fully identified, disputes will arise about the definitions of deliverables, which leads to scope changes during implementation.   *} sevis I*

Transition risks   The loss of key personnel may create a loss of focus during implementation. Personnel may feel burned out because of workload or their perception that the project is not worth the effort. Reward and recognition are necessary during transition to prevent the project from losing momentum.

Scope risks   Improperly defined project scope will produce excessive costs with schedule overruns (variance from schedule). Poor planning may neglect the human resource requirements, which will lead team members to feel that the magnitude of effort is overwhelming. The reaction will cause a narrowing of the scope during implementation, which usually leads to a failure of the original BPR objectives.

3) **Operation/rollout risks**   It's still possible for the BPR project to fail after careful planning. Common failures during production implementation include negative attitudes and technical flaws. These problems manifest in the form of management risks, technical risks, and cultural risks:

> **Management risks**   Strong respected leadership is required to resolve power struggles over ownership. Communication problems must be cured to prevent resistance and sabotage. Executive sponsors need to provide sufficient training to prevent an unsuccessful implementation.

> **Technical risks**   Nothing kills a rollout faster than insufficient support. Inadequate testing leads to operational problems caused by software problems. Data integrity problems represent a root problem capable of escalating into user dissatisfaction. Perceptions of a flawed system will undermine everyone's confidence.

> **Cultural risks**   Resistance in the organization is a result of failing to achieve user buy-in. Resistance will increase to erode the benefits. Effective training is often successful in solving user problems. Dysfunctional behavior will increase unless the new benefits are well understood and achieved.

Practical Application of BPR

BPR projects require the use all the principles found in project management. It is advisable to consider project management as the framework for your BPR project. Many of the PMI processes, mentioned in Chapter 1 will be utilized to manage the project inputs, tools (techniques), and outputs necessary for the project to be successful. By following a recognized standard, the project manager can prevent most of the errors and common omissions inherent in almost any project.

Let's discuss some practical ground rules for BPR projects:

- Don't fix an existing process unless it's broken.
- Calculate the ROI before investing any resources.
- Make sure you fully understand the process before you try to fix it.
- Make sure you don't have any "leftovers" after reengineering the process. All the original components should be reused, modified, or formally retired.

The following points illustrate how each of these ground rules applies to planning a BPR project.

Don't Fix an Existing Process Unless It's Broken

The return on investment is usually very small unless the existing process is already broken. Small improvements can be gained at lower cost by using the normal change control process. There is no need to implement a BPR project unless dramatic changes are required. The highest return on your investment will be realized by collective brainstorming to fix a missing or broken process.

Calculate the Return on Investment (ROI) Before Investing Any Resources

There is never enough money for all the proposed projects. Opportunity is synonymous with the availability of resources. Businesses must change and evolve to remain competitive. It would be both reckless and negligent to charge off on a new project without having first calculated the potential return on your investment. So ask, "What will we actually get back for our money?" Resources should be spent using the principles of *highest and best use*, also known as *portfolio management*.

If you only had $10,000, what is the best use of that money? Where should you invest your thoughts and time? You may consider only those ideas that have a profound or life-changing effect rather than just prepaying some outstanding bills. For example, is the money best spent on a minor system upgrade or by investing in additional staff training? Choose the solution that best improves your bottom-line profits. Don't waste money on something with no return or a low return.

Make Sure You Fully Understand the Process Before You Try to Fix It

Even if the process is suspected to be faulty, it's important to have proper evidence before making any changes. The fastest way to failure is to start making changes based on incorrect assumptions. *B/A = Business Impact Analysis - 63/60*

The BIA is an efficient method for collecting high-quality data. The BIA process involves interviewing subject matter experts to determine what the process does and tracing the root sources of process specifications. A well-run BIA will uncover a complete blueprint of the entire process flow in sequence with influential dependencies and some of the known alternative methods to accomplish the desired results. BIAs are frequently used in organizational acquisitions, divestitures, business continuity planning, and business process reengineering. The value of the BIA is the ability to make decisions factoring in all of the low-level details indicating over reliance, untapped capacity, and alternative sources with the potential to increase net revenue.

Make Sure You Don't Have Any "Leftovers" After Reengineering the Process

Everything in the current process exists for a reason. This is why it's necessary to discover the specifications for inputs, actions, and outputs of the process before making any changes. Some specifications will be new, whereas others may be eligible for retirement. Each specification needs to be thoroughly investigated, no matter how small. The purpose and relationship of every specification needs to be considered before you can determine its disposition.

At one particular organization, the inventory manager misunderstood the reason why the factory needed to warehouse more than 100,000 product labels. It turned out that the label was a custom-made warning label that cost almost nothing if ordered in very large quantities. The labels had a moderate delay from ordering until shipping to the factory. It turned out to be an extremely serious violation of government law if the product shipped without the required warning label. In fact, it was better to halt production than to ship without the mandated warning label.

Real World Scenario

Example: USAA Insurance converts to 100% digital imaging

The United Services Automobile Association (USAA) offers insurance and banking services to military and former military personnel. The insurance side of the business needed to fix the problem of files being misplaced. A suggestion was made to switch to document imaging. This would require a complete change in the way the business operates. After careful study, it was determined that USAA could reduce the number of administrative steps in processing claims from 36 to just 6 steps. To accomplish this, their mailroom needed to scan every piece of paper arriving from customers. The benefit was that incomplete claims could be processed through the system while the company simply waited for a final signature or missing evidence to finish the process. The new system went live in 1990 and has been successful. Subsequent BPR projects have expanded the scope to include USAA's other financial services.

Every hour spent in research and planning should be focused on tracing the most current specifications. Each specification will either be reused, modified, or formally retired.

Practical Selection Methods for BPR

The BPR selection process looks for areas with the greatest return on investment. The needs of each organization are unique. Executive governance dictates that the executives must define unique selection criteria and a selection process. Each process under consideration for reengineering must be evaluated and generally fits into one of the following categories:

- Nonworking process
- Marginal process
- Working process
- Excluded process

In addition to these categories, the overall value needs to be considered in the equation. Is there a reasonable ROI for reengineering each process under consideration? Using a report in the format of Table 3.5 is helpful for organizing the discussion of investment, return, and priority.

TABLE 3.5 BPR Return on Investment and Priority

Category	No ROI Anticipated (Probably Not Selected for BPR)	ROI Anticipated	Priority for BPR
Nonworking process	*Insert your process names without ROI*	*Insert your process name having ROI*	1
Marginal process	"	"	2

TABLE 3.5   BPR Return on Investment and Priority *(continued)*

Category	No ROI Anticipated (Probably Not Selected for BPR)	ROI Anticipated	Priority for BPR
Working process	"	"	3
Excluded process	"	"	4

 You should remember that your goal during BPR is to ensure that the organization is properly managing the entire process.

Let's summarize each of these categories with a little more detail:

Nonworking process   Some elements of the process are simply not working. It may be a manual or an automated process that can't deliver to the expectations of the user. This is an ideal target for process reengineering. Nonworking processes are usually the highest priority if their business value can be justified. Priority will be based on the anticipated financial return that the process can generate.

Marginal process   This type of process seems to work yet fails to generate any tangible benefit. Something about the design may be preventing it from generating its full potential. It may be a control issue or design failing to deliver to a specific need. The output of the process needs to be closely reviewed to determine what need it was intended to solve and whether there is any value created by reengineering it. Otherwise, the process might be discontinued.

Working process   This process is currently in use and generating some type of meaningful benefit. It should have existing documentation of how the process works and its related specifications. Working processes are expected to have a support staff and the necessary controls to achieve compliance with their business objective.

Excluded process   An excluded process might be exempt from BPR because of its special nature or limited frequency of use. Politics is never a valid reason for exclusion. A process nearing retirement may be excluded because BPR would not generate any increase in value.

Troubleshooting BPR Problems

Without excellent leadership, the BPR project can become a convoluted mess. Even the simplest of objectives may wander aimlessly into failure. We want to take a few minutes to diagnose some of the more common BPR problems you may encounter as an auditor:

Problem: Reengineered process resembles the existing process   Compare the process to its current objectives and specifications. It will not be identical unless the initiation and diagnostic phases were compromised. If the diagnostic phase was objective, the best solution is to rethink the redesign by using a higher-level approach. Too much emphasis was placed on duplicating the attributes of the old process if the redesign occurred at too low a level or protected a politically sacred area. Approach it again with a "think big" philosophy.

Problem: Business process does not fit all the customers   Unserved customers may be outside the target market. Analyze the intended audience to determine whether it represents your most profitable clients. If so, there is no problem in the BPR design. Use the Pareto principle (aka 80/20 rule) to evaluate the net revenue created by the unserved customers. Stick to those clients who generate the highest return in net profits. Times change; everyone else may not be your target customer.

Problem: Implementation of the new process is stalled or slowing   Failure to implement indicates problems in reconstruction or political blocking. Implementing a smaller pilot project may work to smoke out the problem. Extra effort may be needed to resell the concept and to train the users. A strong leader is usually willing to remove political obstacles (or the person obstructing progress) as long as the effectiveness of the new process has been proven.

Problem: New process is not performing as expected or generates hidden incompatibilities
Business processes have informal relationships that may have been missed during BPR planning. Perform a stakeholder analysis to identify missing stakeholders or underrepresented dependencies. The problem can be rooted in leadership failure during initiation, inadequate diagnosis, missed material specifications, or poor planning during reconstruction. This is a frequent problem found in outsourcing arrangements after the impact of total costs are calculated. It may occur during initial implementation or post evaluation.

NOTE   Additional information on business process reengineering can be found under the BPR guideline G-26 in the ISACA *Audit Standards, Guidelines, and Procedures.*

Understanding the Auditor's Interest in Tactical Management

pg 139

Tactical management involves the departmental director and manager. Tactical performance reporting should occur during weekly and monthly status meetings with senior-level executives. Tactical performance is frequently included during a regular audit.

As an IS auditor, you will be interested in learning the scope and extent of project management methodologies in use. Your interest will include gaining an understanding of the management tools in use and application of management controls. Tactical management should be using a change control process that exercises advance planning, risk management, and due diligence. The auditor should seek materially relevant evidence demonstrating management's efforts in support of the strategic objectives. The auditor's opinion should include a determination of the effective level of IT integration with various stages of project management. Is tactical management well integrated with measurable performance?

Operations Management

We start the discussion of operations management with a simple definition. An _operation_ is a procedure to set forth or produce a desired result.

The objective of operations management is to promote consistency with an effective response to the user requests. Operations management represents support for issues faced in day-to-day business. The operations support is sometimes referred to as _firefighting_ or _user support_. This section briefly covers the IT goals and operations management.

Sustaining Operations

Every organization faces the challenges of sustaining operations. You will investigate whether the IT staff has the capability to sustain current operations. Three areas of interest are immediately identifiable. The auditor should seek evidence to discover whether the following three sustaining factors are met:

- Adequate staffing
- Written procedures
- Level of staff integration

It would be practically impossible to sustain regular operations without documented procedures executed by an adequate number of well-trained IT staff members. The staff members must be able to interact and communicate effectively inside the IT organization and with the business organization. To ensure these objectives, each member of the IT team will need to have specified roles and responsibilities.

Tracking Performance

Performance of all operations should be tracked and reported by using metrics developed for the user's needs. These metrics should be based on best practices of NIST, COSO, ISACA's CObIT, and other industry standards. It is the responsibility of tactical management to develop the metrics. Operations management is required to report the detail necessary to generate a score.

NOTE   Chapter 6 covers operations and metrics in more detail.

Controlling Change

Change control is an organized process for making sure that the best possible decision is reached. The reality is that any change introduces new variables. A person can execute a minor change that

To minimize the "Whenever you fix somethin', you've gotta fix somethin' else!" effect.

does what it intended, but then also has unintended consequences such as disabling or invalidating a previous control setting or a processing method. So change control must be a methodical process.

The change process should be evidenced by supporting policies and procedures. One employer, for example, had a policy that changes would occur only on Tuesdays and Thursdays in the evening. Users were required to provide their work-acceptance test procedures along with a competent user from their department. The user would run their own tests to prove whether the evening change had an impact. Positive impacts were desired. Negative impacts signaled the need to rerun the intended change procedure or restore the system to its earlier condition. Management allowed changes over the weekend if the requirement was so broad as to exceed an 8-hour window. Their preference was to avoid scheduling changes that would result in the next workday being on Monday. Problems occurring on Monday tend to set a negative tone for the entire week.

Internal auditors should be involved in change control meetings. The visibility and experience of the internal auditor present a valuable opportunity for the client. An internal audit should review requested changes to ensure that each change complies with the best practices of change management. You can bet that the staff will become more alert when they realize that the internal auditors are watching.

Understanding the Auditor's Interest in Operational Delivery

The auditor will need to evaluate whether the organization has provided effective daily support in accordance with the IS strategy. What is IT expected to deliver? Taking that into consideration, what are the issues considering fulfillment and capacity to supply this need? There should be a systematic decomposition of how each business objective is translated down into specific needs, which are fulfilled by specific tasks. If there is no stated requirement in a business objective, there should be no specific need, only a request. The IT alignment concept is to dedicate all efforts toward bona fide goals identified in the business strategy, not requests.

The auditor's job is to ensure that proper controls are in place and are appropriate to the unique risks of each source and location.

Summary

In this chapter, we have reviewed the authority levels in the organization and controls used for IT governance. A short definition of *IT governance* is to effectively lead and monitor performance of the information technology investment. IT governance exists at three levels: strategic, tactical, and operational management. Top executives are responsible for providing the strategic guidance with policies and decisions to define objectives; department directors provide tactical management with standards and plans for their subordinates. The operational functions and procedures are controlled by the managers with execution by staff workers.

Exam Essentials

Know how to evaluate the performance and effectiveness of the IT governance structure.   Does IT support the organizational objectives? You will investigate how the IT management decisions are made. After a decision is reached, it is important to understand how the directions are communicated to ensure that the decision supports the desired outcome. Does evidence indicate that management is leading the activities necessary to fulfill the business strategy?

Understand that the organizational structure must be designed to support the business strategy and objectives.   Does the client have a well-documented organizational chart with accurate job descriptions? How does the client handle problem reports, user complaints, and staff member concerns? Is there a mechanism for management oversight?

Be aware that the IT policy, standards, and procedures must be developed under the supervision of management.   A formal process should exist to ensure that each policy is in support of legal requirements and fulfills a business objective. You need to understand how the client determines policies and standards. Who approves the adoption and implementation? Do the policies and standards directly support the business strategy? Do the standards and procedures support the resulting IT strategy?

Know that management is responsible for ensuring compliance with policies and standards.   Operating procedures must be developed to promote compliance and consistency. Have policies, standards, and procedures been formally implemented? How does management monitor compliance? How are violations detected, corrected, and prevented?

Understand that risk management practices should be in use at all times.   Risk management applies to decisions concerning vendors, operational support, and projects. Is an effective risk management practice in use? Does the evidence show that risks are properly managed?

Know that quality management requires the use of generally accepted IT standards.   A benchmarking process should be in use, with a control framework such as CObIT, ISO 17799, COSO control framework, and the OECD security guidelines. A maturity model such as CMM should be in use to show progress or regression in regard to internal controls.

Understand that IT performance and IT vendors should be tracked by using key performance indicators.   The goal of IT governance is to align IT resources to support the business strategy. The role of IT is to solve support problems faced by business users. The IT steering committee is designed to identify business support issues to be resolved by IT. Key performance indicators are based on business needs and used to determine the IT return on investment.

Review Questions

1. Which of the following would be included in an IS strategic plan? *(3 – 5 yrs)*

    A. Brochures for future hardware purchases

    B. At least a six-month list of goals from the IT manager

    C. Target dates for development projects

    D. Plans and directives from senior non-IT managers

2. What is the primary purpose of the IT steering committee?

    A. Make technical recommendations

    B. Identify business issues and objectives

    C. Review vendor contracts

    D. Specify the IT organizational structure

3. Which of the following functions should be separated from the others if segregation of duties cannot be achieved in an automated system?

    A. Origination

    B. Authorization

    C. Correction

    D. Reprocessing

4. The Software Engineering Institute's Capability Maturity Model (CMM) is best described by which of the following statements?

    A. Measurement of resources necessary to ensure a reduction in coding defects

    B. Documentation of accomplishments achieved during program development

    C. Relationship of application performance to the user's stated requirement

    D. Baseline of the current progress or regression

5. What would be the area of greatest interest during an audit of a business process reengineering (BPR) project?

    A. The steering committee approves sufficient controls for fraud detection.

    B. Planning methods include Program Evaluation Review Technique (PERT).

    C. Risk management planning with alignment of the project to business objectives.

    D. Vendor participation including documentation, installation assistance, and training.

6. If separation of duties cannot be achieved, which of the following is an acceptable alternative?

    A. Compensating controls.

    B. Mandatory hiring of additional personnel.

    C. Change control review board.

    D. Separation of duties is required.

7. What is the correct sequence for benchmark processes in business process reengineering (BPR) projects?

    A. Plan, research, observe, analyze, adapt, improve

    B. Research, test, plan, adapt, analyze, improve

    C. Plan, observe, analyze, improve, test

    D. Observe, research, analyze, adapt, plan, implement

8. Which of the following statements is true concerning the steering committee?

    A. Steering committee membership is composed of directors from each department.

    B. The steering committee focuses the agenda on IT issues.

    C. Absence of a formal charter indicates a lack of controls.

    D. The steering committee conducts formal management oversight reviews.

9. What is the primary purpose for running a lights-out data center?

    A. Save electricity

    B. Reduce risk

    C. Improve security

    D. Reduce personnel expense

10. The Capability Maturity Model (CMM) contains five levels of achievement. Which of the following answers contains three of the levels in proper sequence?

    A. Initial, Managed, Repeatable

    B. Initial, Managed, Defined

    C. Defined, Managed, Optimized

    D. Managed, Defined, Repeatable

11. Segregation of duties may not be practical in a small environment. A single employee may be performing the combined functions of server operator and application programmer. The IS auditor should recommend controls for which of the following?

    A. Automated logging of changes made to development libraries

    B. Hiring additional technical staff to force segregation of duties

    C. Procedures to verify that only approved program changes are implemented

    D. Automated controls to prevent the operator logon ID from making program modifications

12. Which of the following is the best example of mandatory controls?

    A. User account permissions

    B. Corporate guidelines

    C. Acceptable use policy   *According to pg 6, policies are mandatory*

    D. Government regulation

13. What is the objective of incident response?

    A. Ensure that the problem is reviewed by appropriate personnel using an established procedure to protect evidence.

    B. Reduce the impact of a virus outbreak without inconveniencing users.

    C. Provide an immediate estimate as to the consequence or impact of the damage.

    D. Fix the user's problem as quickly as possible. The final resolution should be reported to the help desk.

14. An IS auditor is auditing the controls related to employee termination. Which of the following is the *most* important aspect to be reviewed?

    A. Company staff members are notified about the termination.

    B. All login accounts of the employee are terminated.

    C. The details of the employee have been removed from active payroll files.

    D. Company property provided to the employee has been returned.

15. Which of the following is *not* true concerning the process of terminating personnel?

    A. The company must follow HR termination procedures.

    B. Any company property in possession of the employee must be returned.

    C. The employee must be allowed to copy any personal files from their computer.

    D. The employee's recent history of login account activity should be reviewed in the audit log.

16. Which of the following represents the best explanation of the balanced scorecard?

    A. Provides IT benchmarking against standards

    B. Ensures that the IT strategy supports the business strategy

    C. Measures IT help desk performance

    D. Specifies procedures for equal opportunity employment

17. What is the primary business purpose behind business process reengineering (BPR)?

    A. Eliminate jobs

    B. Reduce steps to improve business efficiency

    C. Change management direction

    D. Increase stockholder value

18. Which of the following business process reengineering (BPR) risks are likely to occur during the design phase?

    A. Transition risk, skill risk, financial risk

    B. Management risk, technical risk, HR risk

    C. Technical risk, detection risk, audit risk

    D. Scope risk, skill risk, political risk

19. Which of the following answers contains the steps for business process reengineering (BPR) in proper sequence?

    A. Diagnose, envision, redesign, reconstruct

    B. Evaluate, envision, redesign, reconstruct, review

    C. Envision, initiate, diagnose, redesign, reconstruct, evaluate

    D. Initiate, evaluate, diagnose, reconstruct, review

20. What is the purpose of job descriptions and the change control review board?

    A. Provide optimum allocation of IT resources

    B. Eliminate disputes over who has the authority

    C. Identify the hierarchy of personnel seniority

    D. Provide guidance to the IT steering committee

21. What is the primary purpose of employee contracts?

    A. Define the relationship as work for hire

    B. Prevent individuals from ever working for competitors

    C. Enforce the requirement to join a union

    D. Specify the terms of employee benefits

22. What is the simple definition of *strategy*?

    A. Ethical behavior of the executive management team to follow an iterative process of development

    B. Using best practices in a uniform application

    C. Implementing standards and procedures in a multilayered approach to accomplish the business requirements

    D. Fundamental change in the way we do business

23. Which of the following is a governance problem that may occur when projects are funded under the "sponsor pays" method?

    A. Deliverables are determined by the sponsor.

    B. The definition of quality may be insufficient.

    C. The sponsor may not implement the proper controls.

    D. The sponsor may not have enough funding.

24. Which of the following is not a reason cited in the text that the balanced scorecard (BSC) could fail?

    A. Politics of losing the department budget

    B. Top management provides full support

    C. Lack of BSC training and awareness

    D. Empire building by the department head

25. Which of the following is *not* true concerning mandatory access controls?

   A. Someone in authority determines what is acceptable.

   B. The controls are implemented by using technical methods.

   C. They are administrative controls.

   D. They are administered from a central authority.

26. Which of these strategies is used in business process reengineering with an incremental approach?

   A. Bottom-up

   B. End-state

   C. Unconstrained

   D. Top-down

27. *Shadow organization* refers to two groups performing similar functions under different departments. What does the presence of a shadow organization indicate?

   A. Twice the support coverage

   B. A relationship of trust and proper delegation of authority

   C. Executive distrust or failure to integrate

   D. A sponsor who is cooperating as a team player with separation of duties

28. Which type of charge-back scheme is notorious for violating separation of duties or for attempting to exceed authority?

   A. Sponsor pays

   B. Actual usage billing

   C. Charge-back

   D. Budgeted cost

29. What is the advantage of using PERT analysis during projects for business process reengineering (BPR)?

   A. It charts a detailed sequence of individual activities.

   B. It is a critical path methodology.

   C. It is used to perform root cause analysis

   D. It enables the use of decision tree reporting

30. Which one of these is not a good reason for an organization to decide to reverse its outsourcing decision and bring the work back to be performed in-house?

   A. Realizing a loss of control

   B. Recognizing added delays in the overall delivery of service to their customers

   C. Recognizing added expense after considering the total cost of long-distance supervision and price to make changes

   D. Wanting to copy a competitor without doing the hard research

31. Which statement about the Capability Maturity Model is *not* true?

    A. Level 3 provides quantitative measurement of the process output.

    B. Level 3 processes have published objectives, measurements, and standards that are in effect across departmental boundaries.

    C. Level 5 provides maximum control in outsourcing because the definition of requirements is very specific.

    D. Level 5 maturity converts a product into a commodity and allows a company to pay less and demand unquestionable adherence to management's authority.

32. Which of the following statements has the best correlation to the definition of *strategy*?

    A. Defines the supporting techniques to be used in support of the business objective

    B. Defines the necessary procedures to accomplish the goal

    C. Defines guidelines to follow in a recipe for success

    D. Defines what business we are in for the next three years

33. Why is change control considered a governance issue?

    A. It forces separation of duties to ensure that at least two people agree with the decision.

    B. Change control increases the number of people employed and therefore provides a valuable economic advantage.

    C. It allows management to hire less-skilled personnel and still get the same results.

    D. Proper implementation of governance saves money by reducing the need for change control.

34. Which of the following is *not* considered a control failure?

    A. Using a policy which lacks a detective mechanism to identify violations

    B. Modifying an ineffective procedure outside of change control

    C. Testing to discover how many policy violations have occurred

    D. Implementing a policy or standard without consequences of failure

35. Which of the following is likely to be the most common method of IT control used in business?

    A. Mandatory

    B. Discretionary

    C. Executive order

    D. Preventive

Answers to Review Questions

1. D. The IS strategy must support business objectives from senior managers in other departments of the business. The IT plans should be designed to support the strategic business plans of the organization.

2. B. The purpose of the steering committee is to bring the awareness of business issues and objectives to IT management. An effective steering committee will focus on the service level necessary to support the business strategy.

3. B. Authorization should be separate from all other activities. A second person should review changes before implementation. Authorization will be granted if the change is warranted and the level of risk is acceptable.

4. D. The Capability Maturity Model provides a baseline measurement of process maturity. The CMM begins with no process defined and progresses through five phases of documentation and controls. The fifth phase represents the highest level of maturity.

5. C. The steering committee provides guidance to IT concerning business objectives. A risk management plan must be in use for every BPR project. The purpose of risk management is to determine whether the project can actually fulfill a business objective. The second part of risk management is to determine whether the organization will be able to complete the project and generate the desired results.

6. A. Compensating controls may be used when separation of duties cannot be achieved. Compensating controls include supervisory review, audit trails, exception reporting, and job rotation. An auditor would recognize that the lack of separation of duties is a control failure unless compensating controls are in place. Lack of compensating controls is also control failure.

7. A. The business process reengineering sequence is to plan for change, research possible implications, observe the current process, analyze potential opportunities for improvement and verify key performance indicators, adapt to the new/updated process, and work to improve the results.

8. C. The steering committee should be authorized by a formal charter. The lack of a steering committee indicates that IT is not governed by formal alignment to business objectives. The technology investment is not properly managed as an investment portfolio should be managed. The purpose of the steering committee is to convey business issues that IT should consider and objectives to fulfill. Membership of individuals on the steering committee should be formally designated.

9. B. The primary purpose of a lights-out operation is to reduce the personnel risk and environmental risk. Errors can be eliminated by separating equipment from the support IT personnel. Environmental risk is reduced by eliminating contamination from liquids, food particles, and debris. Maintenance and support personnel enter the lights-out operation for a short duration to perform any required functions.

10. C. The five levels of achievement in the Capability Maturity Model (CMM) are level 1 Initial, level 2 Repeatable, level 3 Defined, level 4 Managed, and level 5 Optimized.

11. C. Procedures should be implemented to ensure that only approved program changes are implemented. The purpose of separation of duties is to prevent intentional or unintentional errors. A logical separation of duties may exist if a single person performs two job roles. The ultimate objective is to ensure that a second person has reviewed and approved a change before it is implemented.

12. D. A government regulation is a mandatory control that forces compliance. Mandatory controls are the strongest type of control. Permission is explicit or it must be denied.

13. A. Incident response is intended to ensure that the problem is reviewed by appropriate personnel. Personnel should be properly trained and should execute an established procedure to document the condition, protect evidence, and resolve the problem. During the incident response, the problem will be analyzed to determine whether it was malicious or unintentional.

14. B. The former employee's access to information systems should be terminated immediately. The accepted practice is to terminate access while the employee is being informed of the termination in the HR department.

15. C. Employee access should be disabled upon termination from the organization. All of the other statements are true.

16. B. The balanced scorecard is used in management to ensure that all projects and activities are in direct support of the organization's strategy and objectives. The IT balanced scorecard is a subset of the organization's overall scorecard.

17. B. The purpose of BPR is to improve efficiency by reducing unnecessary steps or to implement improved techniques. Business process reengineering may be implemented to reduce operating costs or to achieve compliance with requirements.

18. D. The primary risks during the BPR design phase are improper scope, lack of necessary skills, political resistance, and a failure by management to support the project.

19. C. According to ISACA, the general steps in business process reengineering are to envision the need, initiate the project, diagnose the existing process, redesign the process, use change management to reconstruct the organization in transition, and evaluate the results.

20. A. Job descriptions specify the roles of each individual to ensure proper allocation of personnel. The change control review board ensures that changes and related activities are properly managed.

21. A. Employee contracts provide evidence of the work relationship: that the employee is providing "work for hire" to the company. All of the employee's discoveries and development become the intellectual property of the employer.

22. D. Strategy is best defined as a fundamental change in the way we do business. Strategy is the highest level of management and frequently a noble goal or idea. Standards provide a reference point for mid-level objectives. Procedures (aka best practices) are a low-level cookbook recipe for achieving a standard with repeatable performance.

23. Answer: C. The auditor needs to recognize that the sponsor may attempt to exceed their authority or fail to implement proper controls. Project scope should be controlled and verified to include separation of duties with preventative, detective, and corrective controls. It would be a failure in governance to allow a project to occur otherwise.

24. B. Using the balanced scorecard helps executives create a linked strategy to unite the activities of each department. Department budgets no longer exist. Funding and people are allocated in a strong-matrix style of project management. Departments get funding based on their share of the work supported in each project. Employees work from a personal scorecard, which has been created out of the project's work breakdown structure (WBS). This eliminates empire building and ensures that only the most valuable tasks receive any resources. Employees are graded on how many of the tasks are performed properly. Full support of top management is required for the balanced scorecard to work.

25. A. Mandatory controls are the strongest type of controls. They can be implemented by using both administrative and technical methods. Mandatory controls are centrally managed. There is no way to increase access except by formal promotion of access by the central authority. With discretionary controls, we allow someone to decide.

26. A. The incremental approach uses bottom-up modeling of the existing process. Overall gains tend to be small because this method focuses so hard on current processes. All the other choices represent a think-big (top down) approach without limitations. Top-down looks at what it could be, not what it is (end-state).

27. C. Shadow organizations indicate an integration failure caused by executive distrust or similar conflict. This creates additional conflict with inefficiencies of scale. Problems include conflicting strategies, and the sponsor violating separation of duties or exceeding their normal authority. Shadow organizations are known for duplication of effort, creating a high combined cost to the organization.

28. A. Sponsor pays is notorious for problems of exceeding authority, violating separation of duties, and failing to implement all the governance controls. Sponsors tend to pay for only what they want. Exceptionally good sponsors consider everyone's need ahead of their own agenda.

29. B. PERT analysis shows the critical path to illustrate the minimum specific tasks necessary to complete the project's objective. The CPM technique is a valuable tool for demonstrating what must be accomplished versus what was requested. High-dependency tasks get performed, while low-dependency tasks may be cancelled from the project.

30. D. Poor leaders may be playing the copycat game of making decisions without sufficient formal research (not using BPR). Decisions shall be made using supporting evidence, including total cost analysis of the combined overall impact, not just the function under consideration. Several organizations have realized that outsourcing was a poor choice after learning that it slowed their ability to deliver to the customer. Unique customer service, efficiency with better integration, and total delivery time to the customer are competitive advantages.

31. A. Qualitative measurement occurs at level 3, and quantitative measurement is at level 4. Level 5 effectively converts the product into a commodity with the intent to squeeze out every last percentile of improvement. All workers are expected to just do what they are told and have no authority. At level 5, the company has the most control and may decide to outsource with lower-paid workers.

32. D. Strategy defines the primary business we are in for the next three to five years. Using this information, the business can develop or adopt supporting standards and then create low-level procedures to accomplish the strategic objective.

33. A. Change control is a foundation of good governance. The purpose is to reduce questionable decisions. Benefits of change control include no longer wasting resources on low-profit tasks and preventing failure by reducing the risk (risk mitigation).

34. C. All of the available options except testing indicate that a control failure was present. The minimum effective control must include a preventative, detective, and corrective action.

35. B. Discretionary control is usually the choice in business. Its weakness is that someone decides rather than uses a formal centralized authority. Auditors should investigate how decisions are made and who makes each decision. This is usually a good place to look for control failures.

Chapter

4

Networking Technology

THE OBJECTIVE OF THIS CHAPTER IS TO ACQUAINT THE READER WITH THE FOLLOWING CONCEPTS:

✓ Computer hardware terms, and advantages of different types of system architecture

✓ Functional introduction to the OSI model and its relationship with TCP/IP

✓ Methods of creating different types of area networks (LAN, WAN, PAN, WLAN)

✓ Network addressing and methods for routing data communications

✓ Different types of networking equipment and their purposes

✓ Network services including DHCP, Domain Name System, and firewalls

✓ An introduction to network management

In this chapter, you will study networking technology equipment and concepts. ISACA expects every auditor to understand the functionality of the IT infrastructure. The infrastructure comprises a unique architecture of computer hardware and special-purpose software. You will study the advantages of implementing different types of system architecture. Technology-savvy IT professionals need to study this entire chapter just as much as everyone else. The objective is to understand how ISACA views the use of networking technology rather than how your favorite vendor views it.

A functional introduction of the OSI model will be presented with its relationship to the TCP/IP model used in the real world. Using the OSI model as the backdrop, we will discuss the functions of different types of network equipment. It is important for CISAs to understand the purpose and capabilities presented by the operating systems, routers, switches, firewalls, and other peripherals. The goal of this chapter is to provide a general understanding of how the infrastructure could be assembled in a manner that fulfills most of the internal control requirements.

We'll wrap up the chapter with a discussion on network management because auditors are expected to understand network analyzers, capacity planning, and monitoring techniques. Several of the points regarding network security are covered again in Chapter 7, "Information Asset Protection." The purpose of this chapter is to provide you a firm foundation in networking technology.

Understanding the Differences in Computer Architecture

All computers are not created equal. The differences in architecture have a substantial impact on performance and system security. However, every computer has three basic types of components:

Central processing unit   The first component group centers around the central processing unit, also known as the *CPU*. The CPU performs mathematical calculations with the assistance of an internal arithmetic logic unit, a high-speed memory cache, and working memory space known as random access memory (RAM). Data stored in random access memory is erased when power is turned off.

Input/output   The second component group provides input and output to peripheral devices such as keyboards, monitors, and disk drives. This input and output channel is used to transmit data to and from the CPU for processing. Computers with a simple architecture may use a common channel for all communication with the CPU. This channel may be an individual connector or a shared data bus of several devices.

Data storage   The third component group is data storage. Every computer requires additional storage space, such as a hard disk. Data storage may be fixed in a semipermanent location or removable. When a computer is turned on, the initial startup process is executed from internal programmable chips and data storage disks. This startup function is called *boot strapping (boot)* or *initial program load (IPL)*. The operating system is loaded from data storage, along with device driver information for the Basic Input/Output System (BIOS). The system is available for use after completion of the boot, or IPL, process.

Figure 4.1 is a general diagram illustrating the architecture of a computer. Notice the CPU on the upper left. The CPU is the brains of the system and is attached to all of the other components with a string of electrical conductors. This string of conductors is called the system *data bus*, which is represented as the lines drawn across the middle of the diagram. *Bus* is an electrical term that means a shared electrical path. The CPU could not run effectively without the support of solid-state memory, known as *random access memory (RAM)*. Random access memory is not as fast as the CPU. A special type of superfast memory is used to buffer between the CPU and RAM to help the CPU run at maximum speed. This high-speed CPU buffer memory is known as *cache*. The heart of computer processing occurs between the CPU, cache, and RAM. Other devices are attached to the data bus through computer expansion slots and interfaces. The disk drives and network each have their own electronic interface or add-in card connected to the data bus. This is how the information flows to and from the electronic components.

FIGURE 4.1   Computer hardware architecture

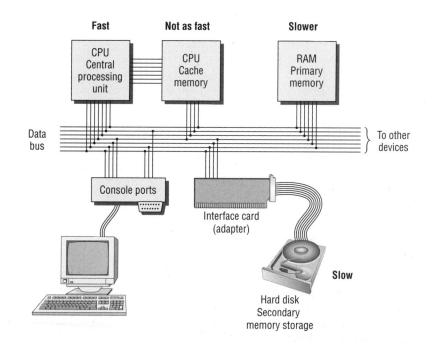

Integrated circuits of the CPU can perform mathematical calculations faster than we can think or act. In fact, a computer with a single CPU will spend a great deal of time waiting for human input. The CPU can therefore support light processing for several users at one time with little delay. The process of CPU sharing for multiple users is called *time-sharing* (see Figure 4.2). Each user or system process receives a tiny segment of time for processing their request. Only one request is processed at a time. All other processing requests are parked in memory, awaiting their turn. Each processing request is serviced by generating a system interrupt. The CPU halts on interrupt and swaps processing with the task stored in memory. This process is similar to how you handle interruptions when the telephone rings. The computer is presumed to be running so fast that the other users do not notice any significant delay.

FIGURE 4.2   Single-CPU system with multiple users (time-sharing)

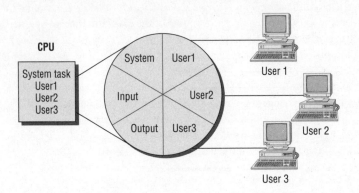

Computers with single processors have two major drawbacks. The first issue is related to systems security. Each system interrupt halts any security software that is running and allows the task to be processed before restarting the security software. The second drawback is the CPU bottleneck created by processor-intensive activities of database and graphics-rendering software.

Multiprocessor computers and computers based on multicore CPUs are designed to deal with the demands of process-intensive applications. Multiprocessor systems are ideal for high-security environments since the security software will be able to run without any interruption. The processor may still perform time-sharing functions for multiple users; however, the load is allocated across multiple CPUs. Figure 4.3 shows a typical multiprocessor architecture.

Security software on a computer with a single CPU is halted during each system interrupt request to allow the next task to be processed. The security software is then restarted and halted again between each request by another program to run on the single CPU chip. Computer interrupts occur in normal operation hundreds or thousands of times per second.

When the multiprocessor system is booted, the first processor accepts the responsibility of running system functions for control, input, and output. The first CPU schedules processing tasks across the other CPUs. These tasks include the dedicated servicing of requests from programs such as an SQL database on CPU 2, running dedicated monitoring software without any interruptions on CPU 3, and off-loading miscellaneous user requests to CPU 4.

FIGURE 4.3   Multiple-processor architecture

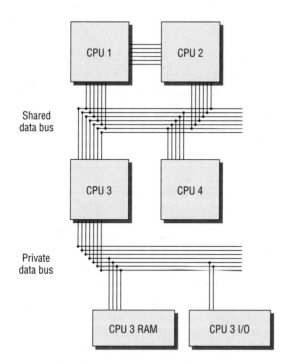

The operating system becomes a resident on CPU 1 and performs hardware checks for input and output. The second processor loads as a task processor only. Each additional processor does the same. This allows the first CPU to have uninterrupted control of the system operations, including security, while the other CPUs perform problem-solving tasks in response to user requests.

Figure 4.4 shows how the workload is stacked and processed through the CPUs. Notice that each CPU has a small stack of tasks that are each in different phases of processing. This stacking of tasks is referred to as *pipelining*. Think of it as a pipeline full of people standing at your door and wanting you to do work for them.

A single CPU would be maxed out with a small pipeline. The multiprocessor system, on the other hand, designates one CPU to be the equivalent of a manager, while the other CPUs each process their own pipeline full of requests. In the real world, this could look like a room full of people talking on the phone, smoking cigarettes, drinking coffee, and answering email all at the same time. As you're aware, a group of people can smoke a lot more cigarettes and process a lot more email than one person. The same can be said about computers with multiple processors.

Multiprocessor systems can perform high-security processing with a separation of duties. Individual processors could be dedicated to perform security functions without interruption. The CPU can be programmed to ignore interrupt requests. Ignoring a processing request is referred to as *interrupt masking*. Interrupt masking is useful for ensuring that high-priority tasks are not interrupted.

FIGURE 4.4   Multitasking systems (single-processor and multiprocessor workload)

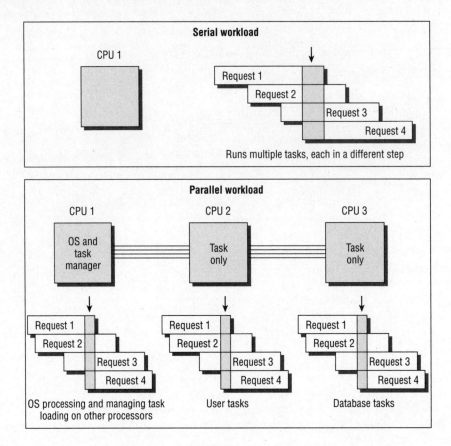

Selecting the Best System

In this section, you will look at various computer operating systems, as well as how to determine the best computer for you. In addition, you will compare some of their capabilities and look at supervisory versus problem states. Finally, you will look at data storage and port controls more closely.

Identifying Various Operating Systems

Every computer uses some sort of operating system (OS) to control the hardware. Each make and model of computer hardware is slightly different. For example, the processor type might be different, or the computer might use a specialized disk drive subsystem.

Computer programs of the 1950s and 1960s were not as portable as they are today. The old computers required the programmer to write a unique program for each model of system. As time progressed, computer software evolved with the development of new programming languages and then new operating systems.

Rocket to the Moon

The Unix operating system was created by Ken Thompson to run a computer program called Space Travel. The more advanced operating system used in the 1960s was the Multiplexed Information and Computing Service (Multics). This is why you may encounter references to Multics in older Unix documentation. Thompson noticed two problems while trying to run the space travel program.

First, the time-sharing design of running Multics on the available hardware did not give Thompson's program the dedicated speed necessary for it to run fast enough. So Thompson decided to delete the Multics time-sharing functions. The revamped single-user operating system was named the Uniplexed Operating and Computing System (Unics). It was later renamed Unix after some multiuser capabilities were re-added.

The second problem was software portability across hardware. Each time Thompson attempted to move the space travel program from one computer to another, it was necessary to rewrite the program to accommodate differences in hardware. Dennis Ritchie joined Thompson to work on projects for software portability across different hardware. They created a series of programming languages known as B, and then C. This is the same C programming language that you hear about today. All later additions to the original C programming language bear the designators C+, C++, and C# (also known as C Sharp). Chapter 5, "Life Cycle Management," covers more details on programming.

Portable Software Systems

Modern computers use a more refined operating system. You will typically use an operating system designed for the type of hardware you intend to use. IBM's OS MVS is common in the IBM mainframe world, whereas Unix is run on a variety of systems. Microsoft Windows is popular for its relatively low initial cost and widespread availability. The Apple Mac OS has a smaller, yet growing, market share with a devoutly dedicated following in the graphics and motion picture industry.

Each of these operating systems shares common traits. The operating system vendor works with the hardware manufacturer to create specialized hardware support within the operating system. The application programmer simply compiles their program for a particular operating system. All the user needs to do is to match their desired application software to the operating system, and then match the operating system to the available hardware.

Figure 4.5 shows what a common computer operating system looks like.

Every commercial-grade computer OS provides at least the following functions:

- Provides a user interface to the computer. The interface is often called a *shell*. This is the command line or graphical interface supporting the directions to the computer.

- Manages security and event logging during the interaction between a user and the computer hardware.

FIGURE 4.5 Computer operating system

- Provides a common software platform to run application programs. Computer programs run on top of the operating system. The operating system acts as a translator between the program and the hardware. Application programs no longer need to be rewritten for hardware changes if using the same OS.

- Provides an organized file system to store and retrieve data.

- Provides a method of input and output to various devices, including disk drives, network connections, printers, and video displays.

- Coordinates internal communications between programs and processing of tasks by the CPU.

- May provide no security, primitive login security, or advanced security to protect the data and programs from harm.

Operating systems can be designed to support a single user or multiple users. You can run software slowly in a batch of requests (set of requests, also known as batch mode) or in smaller and faster batches to simulate real-time transactions.

Computers can function in an ever-increasing variety of roles. Some computers are designed for special-purpose functions, for example, the Palm handhelds or new 3G integrated wireless phones. Many computers are designed for general-purpose use as a desktop or laptop computer. Table 4.1 lists some of the typical functional roles that computers fulfill.

TABLE 4.1   Typical Computer Roles

Role	Function	Examples
User workstation	Runs applications to solve problems and can access data on network servers	Microsoft Office, personal spreadsheets, email client, web surfing. Usually desktop or laptop.
File server	Stores data files for shared user access	Microsoft and Novell shared network drives (usually labeled F: through Z:), Unix file mounts (/usr/home/~your_name), mainframe file share to PC using drive letters or links.
Website server	Performs the same function as the file server	www.certtest.com
DNS server	Converts server domain names into their matching IP addresses	Converts an easy-to-remember name such as www.certtest.com into its corresponding IP address. Domain Name System is a program to find the IP address matching the name you entered. DNS works like an automated phone book.
Database server	Stores raw data and organizes it in tables for authorized users to access	Accounting software, sales automation, and online shopping carts. Can exist on a file server, web server, or dedicated machine. May be internally developed or built using a commercial product such as Oracle SQL, MySQL, IBM Informix, or IBM DB2.
Appliance or special-purpose device	Performs dedicated processing	Web cache, proxy server, email server, network router, or gateway. *Appliance* refers to a preconfigured computer designed to support a single need. Built from a general-purpose computer or unique hardware and configured to run a special-service program. Your home satellite receiver for the Dish Network or DirecTV is a PC hardware appliance running Linux.

Determining the Best Computer Class

Computers come in a variety of sizes and prices, based on their processing power and throughput. (*Throughput* is a measure of how much information passes through the system in a specific period of time.) There are four major classes of computer systems: supercomputers, mainframe computers, minicomputers, and personal computers.

Supercomputers

Supercomputers are designed for intense scientific calculations. A supercomputer would be used to calculate the incredible details of a nuclear reaction and to trace the particles through their life cycle, for example. Supercomputers are not measured in size, but instead by the lightning speed at which transactions can occur. They tend to be specialized systems running large-scale simulation and analysis programs. The mission of supercomputers is to solve complex mathematical calculations. Supercomputers are not used for processing a business database or corporate financial records.

Mainframe Computers

Mainframe computers are large, scalable, general-purpose systems designed to support incredible volumes of data. These are the large boxes you would see in a traditional data center. A single mainframe computer could be as small as a filing cabinet or as large as a roomful of refrigerators, all depending on its configuration.

Mainframes have the advantage of being able to process massive amounts of data in parallel, with incredible throughput. These systems are capable of multithreading thousands of programs simultaneously. *Multithreading* allows programs to be executed in parallel to minimize idle time within the processors. Mainframe computers have provided the role model for other systems to follow.

Prices range from $50,000 to tens of millions of dollars. A mainframe offers several advantages to those who can afford one, including the following:

Rock-solid virtual machine that can partition resources into smaller environments. You can easily set up one mainframe to act as 300 to 5,000 PC servers, without the administrative headache.

Outstanding security. The internal system-partitioning controls have built-in segregation of duties with multiple layers of security. Internal system control reporting is excellent.

Lower software licensing costs. Software licenses are based on the physical machine or CPU. The mainframe software-licensing model provides a wonderful economy of scale with the added ability to share the license across multiple users inside the virtual machine (VM) feature. This can save hundreds of thousands of dollars.

Excellent financial-reporting controls. Most mainframes were designed to bill individual usage as a profit center. You can practically charge the user for each electron in the processing of their job across each device used.

Very high throughput with stability that is measured in years.

Mature 40-year arsenal of system support programs. Mainframes are highly respected for their vast libraries of programs designed for advanced internal control.

IBM is the dominant vendor in the mainframe market, with 90 percent of the market share. Sales of mainframe systems are increasing in response to issues of control and economies of scale. For large operations, the mainframe is proving again to be an economical choice. Its high-volume parallel throughput cannot be matched by smaller systems.

Midrange

Midrange computers, also referred to as *minicomputers*, are designed to be operated by individual departments or smaller organizations. The upper end includes the IBM AS/400 and newer z9 class which are designed to be either a mainframe or midrange computer, depending on the configuration selected by the buyer. PC style super servers with multiple processors from IBM, Dell, HP and Sun represent the most common midrange systems.

Unix is also popular as a midrange operating system. Unix lacks several of the partition and security controls of a mainframe environment, but it does have many of the important job-processing features at a lower overall operating cost. Microsoft's operating system is used by organizations operating without system programmers. The later customers let Microsoft control their system's design, security and overall cost structure.

Microcomputers

Microcomputers are small systems that can be implemented as a PC, notebook, or personal digital assistant (PDA). Most microcomputers are designed to service the needs of an individual user. The operating system may have multiuser capability if running on sufficient hardware to support the requirement.

Microcomputers can run a variety of general-purpose operating systems, including Unix, Microsoft Windows, and the Apple Mac OS X. Microcomputers were invented to meet users' demands for more control over their individual processing needs. At the time, mainframes were dedicated to large-volume batch processing and ignored many of the user requests for processing.

The explosion of microcomputers has created a growing awareness of all the internal security controls that are missing. The biggest problem with microcomputers is the lack of mainframe-grade controls.

As an IS auditor, you may hear the term *MIPS*. MIPS is an acronym for *millions of instructions per second*. It is often used as a numerical claim of system performance with little regard for the real-world environment. MIPS is actually a highly subjective number used to hype a particular computer. The true measure of performance is system throughput, measured in the total volume of transactions processed from end to end.

Comparing Computer Capabilities

It is your job as an auditor to determine whether the IT environment is aligned to the business requirements. Figure 4.6 is a simple graphical representation of the differences in capabilities among mainframes, minicomputers, and microcomputers.

The dominant criteria used for system selection is the desired throughput. Another area of interest is the level of internal control required by the user.

FIGURE 4.6   Comparing mainframes, minicomputers, and microcomputers

 Chapter 6, "IT Service Delivery," covers capacity and workload management issues.

Figure 4.7 demonstrates the simple hierarchy of the classes of computer systems and their market share.

At the top of the pyramid is a mainframe, which has the highest level of capability. Mainframes are not as numerous because of initial purchase cost. In the middle is the midrange computer for individual departments or a smaller organization. Midrange-processing computers are extremely popular for running databases such as Oracle Financials, SAP Manufacturing, or Oracle's PeopleSoft. At the bottom are the vast numbers of PC workstation users with a lower-end processing requirement.

Ensuring System Control

With all this computer processing, it is necessary to ensure adequate management controls.

FIGURE 4.7   Computer processing market share

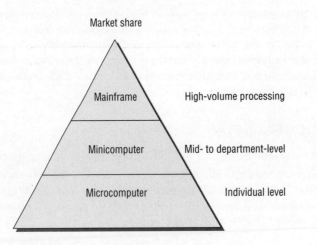

The first level of control in the computer is the privileged *supervisory user*. Every computer needs a special user account representing the highest level of authority, for the purpose of controlling change. This supervisory user is also known as the *superuser, root user*, or *administrator*. The names may be different, but the purpose is the same. This privileged user is responsible for configuration, maintenance, and all ongoing administrative tasks. The supervisory user is often exempt from the internal controls imposed on other users. This exemption gives the administrative user much more power and poses a unique challenge to system control.

The typical user spends their day trying to get the computer to solve problems. This common user has limited access and is subject to a variety of system controls. All office workers fall into this second category.

The technology world has created simple terminology to illustrate the differences between the supervisory user and everybody else. All computers operate in these three basic operating states:

Supervisory state   The system security front-end is not loaded. All processing requests are run at the highest level of authority without any security controls.

General user, or problem, state   Security is active, and the computer is supposed to be solving problems for the user.

Wait state   The computer is busy working to service other tasks and unable to respond to another user request.

The goal of a computer hacker is to gain problem state access (general user access) and convert it into supervisory state access (supervisor access). After the hacker gains access to the system, they will use a variety of attempts to break into supervisory control. The hacker may use invalid parameters to cause a supervisory-level program to fail. Some programs, such as password-change utilities or print queue management, may default to a supervisory-level command prompt upon failure. This allows the hacker to bypass the normal security front-end. An attacker or poorly written software program can trigger an overload of processing requests, which creates an extended series of wait states. When the computer is overloaded with requests, the condition is called a *denial of service*. The computer is too busy to help the user.

Software parameter control is important for multiple reasons. As stated, invalid software parameters may be used by a hacker. Another risk is valid software parameters that should be run only for a special administrative purpose. For example, the command `mysql-i` instructs the MySQL database manager to reinitialize the database tables, which would erase any current data. Access to the command line should be restricted. It is much safer to design menus or restricted user interfaces to ensure security.

Dealing with Data Storage

Adequate data storage is an important issue in a production environment. Controls need to be in place to ensure safe storage of data. The auditor is concerned with how many copies of the data exist and the controls that are in use. It is amazingly easy to lose control over electronic data. As an auditor, you would be concerned about both the integrity and security mechanisms in use by the client.

Tape management systems (TMSs) and disk management systems (DMSs) are used to help retain control over data files. These automated systems can provide label and tracking management. The security of the data is always an issue. Good media management practices include the ability to rapidly identify every version of data under the organization's control with the label, location, and status of each piece of media that data is stored on. This is the job function of a good tape or media librarian.

The following are some of the common types of data storage media:

Magnetic hard disk   These rigid, metal disks mounted inside a sealed disk drive are high-speed devices that are designed for permanent installation. Capacity can go from gigabytes to terabytes. Hard disks are the most common method of online data storage. By using special software, you can cluster drives into high-availability storage arrays. An example is RAID. Depending on who you ask, the definition is either *Redundant Array of Inexpensive Disks* or *Redundant Array of Independent Disks*. A vendor might use the latter to facilitate a higher sales price.

Let's talk about capacity planning for a RAID system. RAID level 0 (zero) offers no protection, but RAID level 1 provides full redundancy using total duplication. Full duplication is referred to as *disk mirroring*.

The initial issue for RAID-1 was cost and capacity sizing. If you had a total of 500 gigabytes of disk and installed RAID-1, the result was a maximum of 250 usable gigabytes. RAID 1 used twice the disk space for half the capacity. Next you had to subtract room for the 20 percent minimum free disk space needed to run the operating system, so now the RAID-1 usable capacity was only 200 gigabytes out of 500 gigabytes. Some customers liked the idea but others were confused. This led to creating other methods for RAID in an attempt to accomplish redundancy equivalent to RAID-1 at a lower cost. Lower cost meant using fewer disk drives.

RAID levels 2, 3, and 4 are considered operational failures. The time to rebuild damaged data took too long after a single disk failure. RAID uses multiple disks connected into *disk strings*. The failure of a single disk is not supposed to be a problem. Two or more disk failures in the same disk string would kill the RAID system.

RAID level 5 is considered a successful alternative. It uses fewer disks than RAID-1 with more usable space. Most drive arrays sold in the market feature a RAID-5 design.

RAID level 6 was another operational failure. The next design was more successful. RAID level 7 uses independent disks with a very high transfer rate. In RAID-7, it's possible to combine multiple disks into a single spanning partition operating at much higher speeds.

Hybrid RAID systems have also entered the market. These crown jewels implement two different RAID methods into one system:

Hybrid RAID 0+1 systems implement two sets of RAID-0 disks into two mirrored strings running under RAID-1.

Hybrid RAID 5+1 systems put two RAID-5 disk strings into a fully duplicated pair. The pair is extra redundant because two RAID-5 disk arrays are duplicated as two RAID-1 sets for a double redundant approach.

Depending on your system hardware capabilities, you can have single mirror, double mirror, or triple mirror disks:

Single mirror is two disks (or sets of disks, also known as disk arrays) holding two mirror image copies of the same data. The disks function independently if one fails. This is the typical RAID-1 implementation.

Double mirror has three disk sets holding three copies of the same data. Each disk set functions independently for extra redundancy.

Triple mirror uses four sets of disks offering quadruple copies of data. IBM has offered this feature for about two decades. The extra disk set can be unpaired to allow live backups during the peak usage time in your workday. System administrators refer to this type of backup process as *unmounting, breaking the mirror,* or *remounting* disk to tape. Triple mirror ensures that you never have fewer than three copies of live data online, and you have an incredibly low risk of disk failures. After backup is completed, the fourth set is remirrored to make the data current.

You are expected to understand a few basic differences between RAID levels. Table 4.2 covers these basic differences. You could copy and then cut out the table to be used as flash cards for memorization.

TABLE 4.2   Description of RAID Operating Levels

RAID Level	Operating Mode	DESCRIPTION
RAID-0	Striping across multiple disks	Not fault-tolerant. This design simply makes several small disks appear as one big disk.
RAID-1	Mirroring	Excellent way of creating two live copies of the data. Most expensive to implement; cuts disk space in half.
RAID-2	Hamming error-correcting code (ECC)	Interweaves data across multiple drives with error-correcting parity code. Too resource intensive.
RAID-5	Block-level distributed parity	This method is commonly used in disk arrays. The design uses less disk space than RAID-1 for the same amount of usable storage.
RAID-7	Optimized asynchronous	Uses independent, asynchronous transfer mode of very high transfer rates. Rather expensive.
RAID 0+1	High transfer rate	Combines two sets of RAID-0 disks with a RAID-1 mirroring design. The objective is to increase performance. Unfortunately, a two-drive failure can cause major data loss.

Figure 4.8 is a basic diagram of the different RAID systems. Notice that individual disks are attached to form *disk strings*.

FIGURE 4.8   Graphical diagram of RAID disk systems

Magnetic soft disk   This includes floppy, Zip, and Jaz drives. They are designed with a soft read-write disk inside a hard shell. This highly portable media is available in capacities from 1MB to more than 4GB.

Magnetic tape   Available in reel or cartridge design, magnetic tape is the most common method of long-term data storage. Its original use was in 2400bpi (bits per inch) tape mounted on a reel. Capacities have grown dramatically. With higher capacity came the cartridge version. Cartridge tapes can have an internal design similar to a reel-to-reel cassette or a single-reel design like the old 8-track tape. Examples include digital linear tape (DLT), 4mm–8mm Digital Data Storage (DDS), 9-track reel, 3480 and newer 3590 cartridge, VHS video, DVD video, and others. High-quality tapes can be expensive when you buy the hundreds of blanks necessary to properly stock a backup library. Different backup vendors require very particular hardware devices with special software for backups. Frequently, tape media is portable only to identical tape drives with identical software from the same manufacturer. A malfunctioning tape drive can permanently destroy the tape and all the data it contains.

Tapes offer the luxury of allowing the administrator to back up 100 percent of the operating system, its invaluable configuration data, complete programs, and user data in one process. Individual files or the whole system can be fully restored from tape to match a specific point in time from years ago.

Read-only memory   Programmable read-only memory (ROM) is used to permanently record software programs on integrated circuits (chips). The advantages are lightning-fast program loading and solid-state nonvolatile storage without moving parts. Programming is accomplished by using specialized equipment to burn or fuse microscopic links inside the semiconductor chip. Once programmed, the software becomes permanent and cannot be changed or erased. This can be either a product limitation or security advantage depending on the intended purpose. To upgrade, you must physically replace the ROM chip. These chips are not portable between devices.

Flash memory   A special type of electronically erasable programmable read-only memory (EEPROM) is used in computers for flash BIOS, video cameras, USB handheld removable memory sticks, and newer portable devices. These are designed to supplement or replace magnetic disks. Unfortunately, the flash devices are easily lost or stolen. The small size and high capacity can be a real security concern. Some of these devices are bootable and can bypass your security controls. They have limited portability but are improving daily.

Optical CD-ROM   Used to store read-only data or music, optical CD-ROMs have a typical capacity of 80 minutes of audio or 700MB of data. This is an excellent method for archiving files or data backup when using a CD disk burner. It is a highly portable media. Blank disks are inexpensive and may be referred to as WORM (write once, read many).

Optical CD-RW   A rewritable version of the old CD-ROM design, these disks can be erased and rewritten just like all other magnetic disk media. If you used the old WORM nomenclature, this would be called a WMRM disk (write many, read many). Today nobody calls them anything but CD-RW.

Optical DVD   This is a newer variation of the optical CD with higher capacity measured in gigabytes. The DVD is commonly used for video or data storage. This is a highly portable media.

Using Interfaces and Ports

Computers use interfaces to connect different types of hardware, also called accessories. According to the Institute of Electrical and Electronics Engineers (IEEE), an *interface* is a combination of physical design characteristics, voltages, electrical signals, and a protocol for communicating. The term *protocol* refers to a standard procedure or rule used to organize the communication process. Common computer slang may refer to the physical interface connector as a *computer port*. A common example is the USB hardware port.

Hospitals refer to standard procedures for treating a patient as the *protocol*. This definition is similar in meaning to the procedures a computer uses to process communication requests.

Protecting Hardware Port Controls and Port Access

Every security professional is acutely aware of how physical access can bypass logical security controls. Physical input/output (I/O) ports provide an avenue for an individual to gain a higher degree of system access. The simultaneous connection of a modem and network card creates an unregulated pass-through opportunity that can circumvent perimeter defenses. As an auditor, you would want to see what controls have been implemented regarding physical access to input/output ports.

Microcomputers are particularly susceptible to port access via the keyboard, USB, RS-232, or network connection.

 The ISACA CObIT contains a section covering physical security controls for servers, routers, and other high-value network devices.

Figure 4.9 shows the basic computer ports. Notice the PC ports for keyboard, video, printer, and serial attached devices. The mainframe has similar ports that are distributed between several large equipment chassis. No matter where they're located, all of the ports must be protected.

Computers communicate over these I/O ports to a variety of storage devices. Physical security controls are intended to protect the physical ports. Logical controls are used to protect data communications. A logical control is usually implemented as a software program control.

FIGURE 4.9 Hardware input and output ports

Software Ports

A second type of computer interface is the software operating system port. These are commonly referenced in discussions about data communication, programming, and networking. *Software ports* (or *sockets*) function similarly to hardware ports. The software port does not have any physical hardware. Instead, it exists as simply a reference location, or *buffer*, for software to send data during transmission. As data arrives at the designated software port, another program is waiting for it. The program detects new data and processes it by using whatever set of rules have been designated within its protocol. Different requests will be processed by using different rules as specified in their unique protocol.

Each software port has a designated function assigned to it by its programmer. To promote compatibility, IEEE designated the usage (protocol) for the first 1,023 software ports used in the TCP/IP protocol. Visualize these as post office mailboxes. Each mailbox represents a different destination. The protocol in business is for people to pay bills after an invoice arrives in their mailbox. The payment is sent back using a return address. A computer using the File Transfer Protocol (FTP) sends data on port 21, as per its protocol standard. Terminal login (telnet) uses port 23 for its communications. This port design provides an orderly method of flow control between programs.

Software ports have to be protected too. The most common methods involve making detailed settings in the software configuration. Unfortunately, it's common for a software vendor to set the factory default, which uses insecure promiscuous settings. The vendor's intention is to eliminate calls for installation assistance to their help desk. This is why vendors often compromise your safety by requiring new software to be installed with the unrestricted access privileges of the root user or system administrator. It ensures that their software installs while leaving the remaining security consequences for someone else to deal with.

WARNING Beware of default settings. Richard Feynman was a bright physicist who worked at the secretive Los Alamos research labs during the development of the first atomic bomb. Using his brilliant powers of observation, Feynman deduced how to discover portions of safe combinations by detecting the tumbler's position after the safe's lock was opened by someone else. One day, a locksmith opened a safe within minutes after everyone thought the combination was lost. Feynman set out to discover the locksmith's secret. He spent several weeks building rapport with the locksmith. Then one day he asked the big question, "How did you open the safe?" The locksmith replied, "I called the manufacturer and asked for the default combination used when the safe was originally shipped." You can read more fascinating stories in the book *Surely You're Joking, Mr. Feynman!* (W.W. Norton & Company, 1997). Computer software vendors publish their default settings in technical books and training manuals and on the Internet for the whole world to see.

A second level of protection is provided by blocking access to software ports via a firewall. Chapter 7 discusses firewalls.

One of the best methods of illustrating software communication is the Open Systems Interconnect (OSI) model. The model is intended to demonstrate the activities that occur by using a method of hierarchal layers.

Overview of the Open Systems Interconnect (OSI) Model

In the early 1980s, the International Organization for Standardization (ISO) was busy creating a new data communications model. Its intention was to build the next generation of communications protocols to replace both proprietary protocols and the de facto Transmission Control Protocol/Internet Protocol (TCP/IP). In the end, the cheaper TCP/IP protocols won the battle.

Many customers had no interest in paying for the cost of developing the Open Systems Interconnect (OSI) protocol. The OSI model is still used as a network training tool. This model stratifies data communication into seven distinct layers. Each layer provides a unique function in support of the layer above.

We are going to walk through the OSI model layer by layer and compare each function to the TCP/IP protocol model. The seven layers of the OSI model are as follows:

- Physical layer
- Data-Link layer
- Network layer
- Transport layer
- Session layer
- Presentation layer
- Application layer

Let's start with a simple memory trick to remember each of the OSI layers in proper order (see Figure 4.10). My favorite mnemonic is *Please Do Not Throw Sausage Pizza Away (PDNTSPA)*.

 We have been using this mnemonic for two decades. This mnemonic holds a unique association with a TCP/IP memory aid.

FIGURE 4.10   Mnemonic for seven layers of the OSI model

OSI memory aid

Away	= (Application)	Layer 7
Pizza	= (Presentation)	Layer 6
Sausage	= (Session)	Layer 5
Throw	= (Transport)	Layer 4
Not	= (Network)	Layer 3
Do	= (Data-link)	Layer 2
Please	= (Physical)	Layer 1

Each of the first letters relates to the first letter of an OSI layer, working your way up from the bottom. It is in your best interest to learn how to draw the OSI model and these layers from memory. You will find it helpful on your CISA exam. You will also find it helpful during discussions when you're trying to uncover the details about a particular product. It will impress clients.

The second, related mnemonic (see Figure 4.11) is *No Interest Having Anchovies (NIHA)*. Once again, each letter refers to a layer of the official DoD TCP/IP model, working up from the bottom.

FIGURE 4.11   Mnemonic for TCP/IP layers

OSI		TCP/IP memory aid	
Application	Layer 7		
Presentation	Layer 6		
Session	Layer 5	(Application)	Anchovies
Transport	Layer 4	(Transport)	Having
Network	Layer 3	(Internet)	Interest
Data-Link	Layer 2	(Data-Link)	
Physical	Layer 1	(Network)	No

Let's review the basic OSI process for handling data. The top layer is where your application is running. The lower layers process the request and prepare the data for transmission as it works its way down to the bottom. When it reaches the bottom of the OSI model, the data has been broken down into electrical signals.

These electrical signals will be received by the other computer. Upon receipt, the transmission headers are stripped off. The remaining data message is passed to the application software running on the other computer. Figure 4.12 shows how this looks.

FIGURE 4.12   OSI processing of headers and data

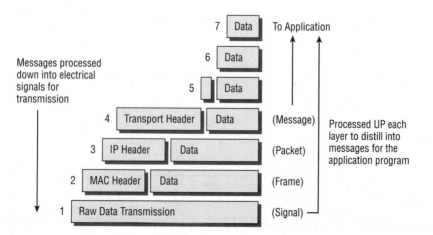

Now that you understand in general how data is transmitted when using the OSI and TCP/IP models, let's go inside the individual layers, one by one.

Layer 1: Physical Layer

The Physical layer defines physical requirements in the cables and voltages (see Figure 4.13). This layer specifies functional specifications for creating, maintaining, and deactivating an electrical link between systems. Wireless transmitters substitute radio signals for the physical cable connection. Similarly, lasers substitute flashes of light to simulate electrical signals over fiber-optic cable.

FIGURE 4.13   OSI Physical layer

Layer 2: Data-Link Layer

The Data-Link layer (see Figure 4.14) focuses on establishing data communications via hardware device drivers and their transmit/receive function. Layer 2 provides flow control, error notification, and the order sequence during transmission.

FIGURE 4.14   OSI Data-Link layer

Communication in layer 2 is established between each network card's Media Access Control (MAC) address. A *MAC address* is a burned-in serial number that is unique to every network card ever manufactured. The address is unique because it uses the manufacturer's ID and the board serial number. Each computer uses the MAC address for "to" and "from" communications within the same broadcast domain (layer 2). You can view the MAC address on your computer by using the following software commands:

For Microsoft Windows, type **ipconfig /all** at the command line in the DOS command box. In Unix, type **ifconfig -al** at the command-line prompt.

The computer will display something like what you see in Figure 4.15.

FIGURE 4.15   Viewing your MAC address

```
C:\> ipconfig /all

IP Configuration
      Host Name.............................: CertTest54
      Primary DNS Suffix....................:
      IP Routing Enabled....................: No
      WINS Proxy Enabled....................: No
      Appletalk Enabled.....................: No

Ethernet adapter Local Area Connection:
      Description...........................: Intel(R) PRO/100
      Physical Address......................: 00-80-3F-AA-D6-82 YOUR MAC ADDRESS
      DHCP enabled..........................: No
      IP Address............................: 209.43.221.35
      Subnet Mask...........................: 255.255.255.0
      Default Gateway.......................: 209.43.221.1
      DNS Servers...........................: 206.199.8.4
                                              101.2.253.11
```

Every device on every network is supposed to have a unique MAC address. Imagine in the office how two people with the exact same name or exact same email address would create a communication conflict. The same is true of MAC addresses. In OSI layer 2, the computers communicate by sending messages to each other's MAC address.

The combined group of MAC addresses on the same network is referred to as a *broadcast domain*. *Domain* refers to scope boundaries of items located under the same controlling influence. Domains indicate relationships within the same general space. Computers in the same broadcast domain will hear (or see) all the traffic of the other computers.

Broadcast domains are no more than a noisy shouting match between computers on the same subnet. Every computer in that segment will hear every conversation from all the computers. For example, Microsoft NetBIOS is a layer 2 protocol. Dynamic Host Configuration Protocol (DHCP) is also a layer 2 protocol.

FIGURE 4.16   Layer 2 communicates by MAC address

We talk about DHCP later in this chapter.

If too many computers were talking at the same time, we would have a congestion problem. This is referred to in Ethernet as a *collision*. Upon detecting a collision, the computers will stop to listen to the traffic, wait a few microseconds, and then attempt to transmit again. Too many collisions will render the data link unusable. Consider the analogy of two people talking over each other on a cell phone.

Ethernet networks can rarely sustain traffic loads over 45 percent. The rule of thumb for Ethernet is that you budget for network upgrades at 35 percent sustained utilization, and get out the boss's credit card to place an order for overnight delivery at 50 percent sustained bandwidth utilization. Ethernet will not run dependably over 50 percent. The 100 percent mark is both theoretical and unattainable.

Layer 3: Network Layer

The Network layer defines networking (see Figure 4.17). Computers are stupid. The computer simply follows the directions of the person who programmed its settings or loaded the detailed list of instructions (a program). Your network administrator uses a numeric grouping of addresses to identify systems within the network.

FIGURE 4.17   OSI Networking layer

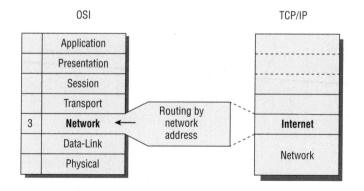

Networks can be administratively divided into logical groups, or segments. (Dividing services is also called *provisioning* in the telephone industry.) The purpose is to create a logical hierarchy to facilitate easier management. We refer to this grouping as IP *subnetworks (subnets)*.

Each subnetwork has its own individual network address that is unique on the network. Separating similar traffic into subnets provides better performance and promotes logical separation of duties for better security.   └ *less collissions*

The number one weakness of internal networks is a lack of separation. Simple traffic filters could be installed to prevent Finance department users from accessing computers in the research labs, for example. Would the Finance employees ever need to access the research computers, or better yet, would the Research employees ever need direct access to the company financial data? No, they would not in the normal course of business. Subnetworks support the concept of least privilege.

Every system requires its own unique IP address to prevent communication conflicts. IP addresses can be divided into smaller groups of addresses to create a smaller subnetwork. This is accomplished by using hexadecimal overlays to parse the address into smaller pieces—this is known as *netmasking.* Each time the IP address range is subdivided, the result must be of equal size. Subnetworks can turn one large network into two smaller networks that are equal in size— or into 4, 8, 16, 32, or even 64 tiny subnets.

Several of the usable IP numbers will be lost in the overhead of subdividing. This is because every subnet must have four specific addresses allocated to a certain function:

1. The **numeric name** (for example, 192.0.0.0) is used in the router to identify the network path to each system on the network.

2. The **starting IP address** is the first available IP address you can assign to a device on the network.

3. The **ending IP address** is the last available IP address you can assign to a device on the network. You can use every address in the range between the starting IP address and the ending IP address. The range of useable IP addresses in a network or subnet is called the *IP address space*.

4 The **broadcast IP address** is the default method used to send traffic to all the devices on the same subnet. Think of it as the computers' version of a public address system with loudspeakers paging information over the intercom. This layer 3 *broadcast domain* is composed of IP addresses. (Layer 2 uses MAC addresses for its broadcast domain.)

Every time an IP address is subdivided, these four IP addresses are consumed in overhead to create the subnet (numeric network name IP, starting IP, ending IP, and broadcast IP). The IP address reserved for the network name and the broadcast IP address cannot be assigned to any devices.

FIGURE 4.18   Dividing IP addresses into subnets

Big subnet 254 hosts

Divides into two subnets (halves)

Divides into four subnets (quarters)

Divides into eight subnets (eighths)

And keeps dividing down to subnets of four IP addresses

Your computer acquires an IP address from either a static configuration setting or a dynamic configuration by using DHCP/BOOTP. The computer ties the IP address to its layer 2 MAC address. We refer to this as *binding* an IP address. Routing decisions are based on the IP address.

The computers and routers implement the Address Resolution Protocol (ARP) to match the IP address with the correct MAC address. Each IP address and corresponding MAC address is stored on computers and routers in tables used during lookup, just like a telephone book. Figure 4.19 illustrates how ARP works.

FIGURE 4.19   Using IP address resolution to find a MAC address (ARP)

ARP
Layer 2
protocol

IP address table (ARP)
194.2.13.7
206.17.49.55 ————————————→ 0080AF31C093

MAC address
0091BE273ACC
0080AF31C093

2) Finds MAC address

1) Computer looks here automatically in software.

The system uses Reverse ARP (RARP) with a MAC address to find the corresponding IP address. Some systems can determine their own IP address by sending their own MAC address to a RARP server, as in the case of DHCP. For example, there are two kinds of telephone books: one is sorted by name order (like ARP), and the other is reverse sorted by street address. Figure 4.20 shows RARP using the MAC address to find the corresponding IP address. Later in this chapter, we discuss an additional method called Domain Name System (DNS) to assign human-friendly alphabetic names to IP addresses.

FIGURE 4.20   Using the Reverse Address Resolution Protocol (RARP) to find the IP address)

```
MAC address table (RARP)              IP address
0091BE273ACC                          194.2.13.7
0080AF31C093 ─────────────────────→   206.17.49.55
                2) Finds IP address

      ↑
1) Computer looks in RARP table
```

RARP
Layer 2
protocol

As you may you recall, the problem in layer 2 is that all the systems are transmitting so much that noise is created across the subnet. The issue is similar to noise in a school cafeteria. Some conversations are broadcast with everyone listening, while a few are discreet between a couple of users. With a layer 3 network address, it is possible to reduce traffic noise by unicast transmission to an individual address. *Unicasting* makes a point-to-point communication to only one device (a private call). So what if you need to send a message to more than one address, but not everyone? You could use *multicasting* to deliver the same data transmission to a group of addresses very efficiently. A multicast is similar to a conference call and is the basis of virtual networking and webcasts.

See Pg 215

Network switches are layer 1 + 2 devices

🌐 **Real World Scenario**

Technical Trivia

Internet Protocol (IP) uses a four-position numerical address. This IP address structure is similar to your postal mail routing address in reverse. If you used your mailing address in IP format, the result would look like State.City.Street.House number. IP version 4 uses addresses that are 4 bytes, or 32 bits, long. The new IP version 6 is designed for 8-byte, or 128-bit, addresses to give the expanding world more addresses. Computers use a method of grouping IP v4 addresses, starting with 000.000.000.000 through 255.255.255.254.

Comb. Switches/Routers use layers 1-3

Finding a Path across the Network

Network routing is the process of directing traffic to the intended destination. This can be accomplished by using static settings or by allowing the computer to follow instructions provided by a *routing protocol*. Routing protocols have been used for centuries to help ships navigate the globe,

Single-function Routers use layer 3 only

trains to switch tracks while heading to their destinations, and airplanes to safely navigate the clouds.

Static routing uses specific to-from mappings of IP addresses created by the network administrator. This is similar to following highway road signs. When driving to New York from Texas, for example, the driver gets on Interstate 20 and just follows the signs for turns and exits until they reach New York. The router's static mapping is quite similar. To-from settings are manually typed into the router and stored in the routing table of each router. The user's computer is set to use the router as their *default gateway* for every IP address located outside their subnet. Their default gateway is like an electronic on-ramp to the information superhighway. Each router on your journey points you to the next router (like a turn or exit ramp sign) until you reach your destination. Return traffic is routed back the same way. So both ends need to have their own set of directions to form a complete path for communications. These route settings will not change unless the network administrator manually changes them. Static routes are good for security and are used when the network traffic is both predictable and relatively simple. Figure 4.21 illustrates the analogy of the network routing protocol compared to a driver following highway road signs.

FIGURE 4.21   Static routing analogy to highway signs

The settings used in the routers act as sign posts guiding your path.

Larger or more-complex networks may have multiple paths to the same destination. The network might even have redundant connections for better fault tolerance. This could make static routing rather difficult to maintain. The routers get confused, just like people, if duplicate routes exist. Which route should we take? Routing tables contain a set of metrics such as cost, speed, and number of links to cross. The administrator can set these manually to help the computer use the best available route. An automatic *split-horizon* feature in the routing protocol blocks any loops that may occur by forcing travel in only one direction (path).

Dynamic routing uses a protocol algorithm to automatically adjust the path to the intended destination. This method uses special router information protocols to signal available paths (routes), dead routes (unroutable), and other changes. The routers will monitor routing updates

[handwritten margin note: Default Gateway is router for sending + receiving Network traffic outside your subnet]

and signal other routers to reconfigure their routing tables as changes occur. Dynamic routing is easy to enable. It removes the complexities of building an advanced configuration. To some individuals, this seems like the best answer; however, dynamic routing can be both beneficial and dangerous. Dynamic routing changes can be initiated by the following:

- Router equipment failure

- Addition of new networked devices

- Incorrect configuration of a network-attached device, including a common workstation

   Figure 4.22 shows how a false network route can be accidentally created through a user's PC. The user's computer software caused the problem by transmitting a route that should not exist.

FIGURE 4.22   False network route via user PC

New dynamic route
Bypass-intended design

   By default, all network devices will listen to route updates. This can create a nightmare if left to default settings. Poor administration of computers and routers can cause traffic to be misdirected into a dead-end route or bandwidth bottleneck. Common examples of the dynamic routing protocols include the following:

- Routing Information Protocol (RIP), which is a primitive method with few control safe-guards. RIP is enabled on computers by default. RIP updates generated from a user's computer can inadvertently change the route path for everyone on the network (see Figure 4.22).

- Open Shortest Path First (OSPF), which uses manually configured reference tables. OSPF is popular in larger networks.

- Interior Gateway Protocol (IGP), which routes traffic within the same organization.

- Border Gateway Protocol (BGP), which communicates between separate networks.

Proper design of the network usually includes implementing both static and dynamic routing. Static routes can provide a designated *router of last resort* if prior dynamic routes fail. Using a router of last resort is similar to saying, "Honey, I think we are lost; would you please pull over and ask this nice router for directions?"

For higher security, the routers should be configured to accept updates from only a trusted router—one the network administrator knows and indicates we can trust. The trusted router is authenticated by its MAC address, digital certificate, or access control list (ACL). Trust is established by forcing in depth testing using detailed challenges. Each test result provides a determination of the degree of trust. Trust is always temporary. Trust does not exist by a leap of faith, nor by legal contracts. Trust is measured per transaction. Constant unrelenting challenge-response continues trust until a single failure kills the trust. This helps prevent route corruption. Chapter 7 covers more details of security.

Layer 4: Transport Layer

The Transport layer specifies the transport delivery method (see Figure 4.23). There are two basic methods:

Confirmed delivery uses a TCP connection to the destination. This is similar to requesting a return receipt and sending certified mail from the post office. TCP is slower and provides error correction.

Unconfirmed delivery operates on a User Datagram Protocol (UDP) connectionless datagram, which is typically broadcast across the network like a shout in a dark room. UDP is faster with less overhead. Even if transmissions are unicast between two stations, the higher-level software application would have to confirm delivery, because UDP does not offer delivery confirmation. There is no guarantee of the data being received on the other end. It is the responsibility of the recipient program to detect errors.

Next comes the session layer, where we get a login screen or other type of access.

FIGURE 4.23 OSI Transport layer

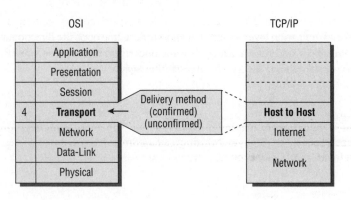

Layer 5: Session Layer

The Session layer governs session control between applications (see Figure 4.24). This is where you initiate communications to a system and establish, maintain, and terminate a communication session. Examples include Network File System (NFS), SQL*net database sessions, and Remote Procedure Call (RPC).

FIGURE 4.24 OSI Session layer

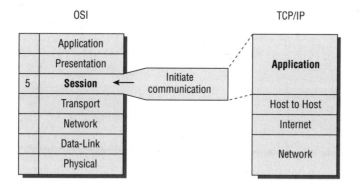

Layer 5 functions of session and error control are handled in TCP/IP by the user's application software. Under TCP/IP, it is the responsibility of the user's application to manage the functions of session, presentation, and application.

Layer 6: Presentation Layer

The Presentation layer defines the presentation format (see Figure 4.25). This is where you specify the format and data structure to be used for programs. Layer 6 will specify the differences between a PDA, VT100 terminal, or workstation with What-You-See-Is-What-You-Get (WYSIWYG) display capabilities.

Layer 6 converts data received from the Session layer into an electronic format that can be handled by the upper-level Application layer (layer 7). It also works in the opposite direction, receiving application data from layer 7 and reformatting it for the underlying layer 5. For TCP/IP, the presentation function is combined into the TCP/IP Application layer.

Layer 6 provides screen formatting. The purpose of encryption is to prevent layer 6 from displaying your secrets. The encryption-decryption process occurs in OSI layer 7 through a custom software application or inside a layer 7 gateway process.

FIGURE 4.25   OSI Presentation layer

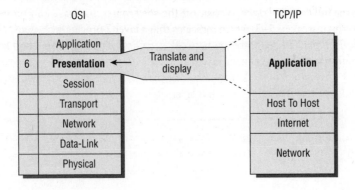

Layer 7: Application Layer

The Application layer is where the problem-solving calculations of the computer software program run (see Figure 4.26). Various types of computer application software execute in the Application layer, including the following:

- Systems Network Architecture (SNA) gateways, which convert the ASCII 7-bit data structure into an IBM Extended Binary Coded Decimal Interchange Code (EBCDIC) 8-bit data structure for the mainframe

- Domain Name System (DNS), which is the program that associates a domain name to the matching IP address (for layer 3)

- File, print, and web servers

- Databases and office automation software (such as OpenOffice.org and Microsoft Office)

- User's data encryption, such as Pretty Good Privacy (PGP) using variables (keys) to encrypt and decrypt the output. We explore encryption methods in Chapter 7.

FIGURE 4.26   OSI Application layer

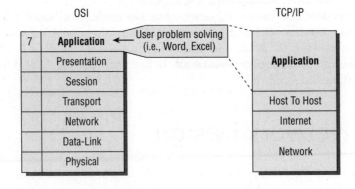

It's best to remember that Layer 7 is the problem solver of work automation. User programs and workflow automation occur here. To help alleviate confusion, the common practice is to refer to the seven layers as the full *protocol stack*. A basic off-the-shelf router may have only parts of the OSI protocol stack to run just layers 1–3, which indicates that a layer 7 process such as a SNA gateway is beyond the devices' capability. Common network switches have only layer 1 and layer 2 stacks, while combination switch-routers have layers 1, 2, and 3 implemented. All-in-one network appliances may have the full protocol stack implementing all seven layers with different degrees of capability. Servers and workstations have all seven layers in use.

It is important to remember that a gateway will run at the Application layer, which is the highest level of the OSI model.

Understanding How Computers Communicate

Now that we've covered all seven layers of the OSI model, let's take a finished look at the communication between two computers across the network using the OSI model. We will assume that a router is being used in the communication path.

First, the user makes a request in their application software on layer 7. That request is passed down through each layer on its way to the bottom. Along the way, each layer performs its function to ultimately transform the request into a series of electrical signals or light flashes for transmission on layer 1 (the physical layer of cable and voltages).

Next, the network hub (or network switch) on layer 1 passes the signal up to the layer 3 network router. The packet is routed through one or more routers directing the user's request to the intended destination computer. It helps to remember that network routing is similar to routing airline flights through particular cities, or railroad trains switching tracks as they travel across the country.

Finally, the request is received as a series of electrical signals (or light flashes) on layer 1 of the other computer. The request is passed up through each layer of the OSI model and processed accordingly. The request is then received in its Application layer, where it is executed. The response is packaged and sent back through the OSI model in reverse, until it reaches the application program on the other computer.

An example of how this looks is displayed in Figure 4.27.

Congratulations, you have now learned the secrets of the OSI model. You'll need to be sure to review its relationship with the TCP/IP model. The OSI model will be used as a discussion tool, while the TCP/IP model is the de facto standard of the real world.   — *Pg 203*

Now we will move into discussing the physical side of networking. We will begin with a simple illustration of physical networks.

Physical Network Design

The first computer networks were created by connecting serial ports between two or more computers. This primitive design used modem software to handle file transfer between systems.

FIGURE 4.27   OSI communication between systems

Networks evolved with the invention of token passing and broadcast transmissions. The invention of the hub, or shared media access unit, created the opportunity to connect multiple computers together on the same segment (again, referred to as a subnet). The concept of a network *bridge* was created to connect two subnets into the same, single subnet. A layer 2 bridge allows all traffic to pass from one side to the next. The bridge could be configured to allow broadcast across it or configured to filter broadcasts and reduce noise—it depended on the bridge manufacturer's design.

Later, it became apparent that it would be necessary to connect two separate networks together without merging them into a single subnet as a bridge would. Many people complained that too many systems were creating too much traffic when all the computers were located within one giant subnet.

Thus came the development of the *router*. Early routers were simply computers with two interface cards. Interface 1 serviced a connection to LAN 1, and interface 2 provided a connection to LAN 2. A software-routing program was then loaded to be run on the computer's CPU.

The routing program basically determines whether individual traffic requests need to cross to the other side. If so, the router passes the request through the other LAN interface to reach its destination. If the destination is within the same subnet (LAN 1 to LAN 1), the router ignores the traffic. This protects the other subnet from unnecessary data transmission noise (LAN 2). That is the basic function of a router. Routers forward data traffic when necessary and insulate users on other subnets.

Figure 4.28 shows what some of the networks would look like.

FIGURE 4.28 First computer networks

[handwritten annotations:] one large subnet   splits ntwk into mult. subnets

Hub

router

Two computers

LAN 1   LAN 1

Computers on hub   LAN router connecting networks

[handwritten annotations:] All computers see all ntwk traffic   Ntwk traffic is filtered by subnet

In modern networks, the routing function can be loaded onto a router card installed in the network switch chassis. Traditional routers are usually a dedicated device in their own chassis.

Overview of Network Topologies

As networks grew, creating a standardized topology for all the connections became necessary. Early networks were very proprietary. It was difficult to mix equipment from different vendors. Although this was good for the manufacturer, it drove computer users nuts. Over the years, three basic network cable topologies have become widely accepted: bus, star, and ring. Let's look at the design of these three topologies.

Identifying Bus Topologies

One of the first topologies to become accepted was the *bus topology* (see Figure 4.29). This presented a relatively inexpensive method for connecting multiple computers.

In a bus topology, each computer is daisy-chained to the next computer. A single coaxial cable passes through the connector on the back of each computer on the network. This cable runs through the office like a single rope, which ties all the systems together.

The design has one major drawback: A break in the bus cable would interrupt transmission for all the computers attached to that cable. Cabling a bus topology can also be cumbersome.

FIGURE 4.29 Bus topology

Daisy-chained connection

Identifying Star Topologies

The star topology is the most popular topology in use today (see Figure 4.30). In a *star topology*, each computer has a dedicated cable connection running to a network hub (or switch). This design offers the most flexibility for placement of workstations. It also offers the highest degree of cable redundancy. The cable redundancy ensures that other computers are not affected by a failure of another workstation's connection.

This is the design of most data networks. It is also used by the PBX telephone switch to connect individual telephone stations. The primary drawback to the star topology is the cost of all the additional cable required to make connections for each station.

FIGURE 4.30   Star topology

Figure 4.31 demonstrates the practical application of the star topology. Notice that each workstation has a connection to a nearby wiring closet. This design ensures that you do not exceed the maximum recommended cable length. The acceptable length of cable varies depending on the cabling type used. Normally it is 100 meters on unshielded twisted-pair (UTP). The star topology helps reduce the cabling cost by shortening the cable distance to reach each user. The hubs and switches are located in the wiring closet to connect users to the network.

Every cable is terminated at the wall plate near the user and at a patch panel in the wire closet. A patch cord connects the building cable from the patch panel to the ports of the hub/switch. A backbone connection is then run from the data center to the wiring closet to establish a complete path for network communication. Figure 4.31 shows the real-world implementation of a star topology, complete with wiring closet and backbone to the data center.

Identifying Ring Topologies

The most famous token-passing LAN protocol is IBM's ring topology, known as Token Ring (see Figure 4.32). Each LAN computer is connected to a media access unit (MAU). Each MAU is connected to both an upstream MAU and downstream MAU to form a backbone loop. Network traffic can be transmitted in either direction. This bidirectional loop is referred to as the *ring*.

A network ring topology has the advantage of built-in redundancy. If the ring breaks, all traffic will travel through the ring in the opposite direction, thereby avoiding the break point. The individual workstations are then connected into the ring by using a star topology.

FIGURE 4.31   Practical application of the star topology

FIGURE 4.32   Ring topology

The telecommunications companies use the ring technology in their fiber-optic networks. This design allows the redundant path necessary to create a fault-tolerant network.

Identifying Meshed Networks

The important network links can have alternate path connections to increase redundancy. The meshing of star networks is a common method of providing redundancy similar to the approach used by a ring topology. The principal difference is that a meshed network is a series of point-to-point connections between critical backbone connections. The router determines which link to use based on predefined routing criteria. A network administrator defines the best link and the alternate path link to use if the best link is down.

There are essentially two types of meshed networks:

Full mesh   A fully meshed network has alternate connections for every major backbone point on the network (see Figure 4.33). The primary obstacle to this design is the cost of implementation.

FIGURE 4.33   Full mesh network (N-1 design)

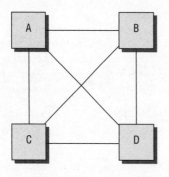

Partial mesh   When you cannot afford a full mesh network, you may decide to implement a partial mesh for the most critical links (see Figure 4.34). Occasionally, the critical link may not be determined by the overall value of traffic. The additional link may be determined by the ability of the sponsor to pay the additional cost. A partial mesh is better than no redundancy at all.

FIGURE 4.34   Partial mesh network

No redundant link between
C and D, and A and D

Network Cable Types

IS auditors are fortunate to have the guidance of industry cable standards provided by the IEEE and the Electronic Industries Alliance/Telecommunications Industry Association building wiring committee (also known as EIA/TIA). Several methods have been developed to use a variety of cables to create a network. Each type of cable has its own unique characteristics of construction or transmission capability. Some cables are better suited for voice, for example. Others are designed for the high demands of data.

> You are not expected to design the cabling system used in a network. That is the job of a Registered Communications Distribution Designer (RCDD), a certified expert in the layout of cable systems. Industry reports verify that 97 percent of network problems are related to the cabling design, cable quality, cable implementation, or connector failure. Design services of an RCDD are usually affordable when justified against cumulative cost of downtime. IEEE and EIA/TIA standards specify more than 100 details for operating stability, safety, and building-code compliance. Details of proper design will far exceed the capability of a Microsoft Certified Systems Engineer (MCSE) or Unix administrator for all but the smallest of networks.

Cable installations are commonly referred to as *cable plants.* The cabling system for data and voice can be complex, depending on the requirement. A CISA is required to have a basic understanding of the three most common cables used to build a network. You should understand the description and limitations of each type.

Coaxial Cable

Early networks used a form of *coaxial* (or *coax*) cable with mesh shielding to prevent electrical interference. The wire is similar to antenna cable or the cable for your television set. Coax has been replaced by unshielded twisted-pair (UTP) for most indoor environments. You can still use coaxial cable in areas prone to electrical interference or for outdoor connections. Figure 4.35 shows an illustration of coax cable.

FIGURE 4.35   Coaxial cable

Coaxial cable is an older and slower design than UTP. It contains two electrical conductors (copper center, metal outer shielding covered with PVC plastic sheathing). It is commonly used for Ethernet networks with a bus topology. It's often used in distances up to 185 meters, but can be extended by using a repeater.

Unshielded Twisted-Pair (UTP) Cable

Unshielded twisted-pair (UTP) cable is the most popular for connecting computers to a network. *Unshielded* means that the wire does not have any protection from electrical interference. The twisting creates an electrical cancellation to prevent the wire from broadcasting like an antenna. Untwisted wire will create magnetic fields of interference that can swing a compass needle, whereas twisted wire will be invisible to the same compass.

UTP is an inexpensive, twisted, four-pair wire used for 10/100Mb Ethernet. Pairs are twisted to reduce electromagnetic interference (EMI). Each wire is run directly to a hub/switch in the wiring closet. Figure 4.36 illustrates the twisted wire pair construction.

FIGURE 4.36   Twisted-pair wiring

Notice how each connector has two transmitting wires (send) and two receiving wires, which give UTP the ability to carry more data than coaxial cable. There are four common categories of UTP:

- CAT-3 (Category 3) for voice only
- CAT-5 (Category 5) for voice and data
- CAT-5e (enhanced) for 1GB, 100Mhz data
- Higher-rated CAT-6 and CAT-7 are also available for transmission up to 1,000Mhz.

Fire codes in commercial buildings specify that one type of jacket be used for twisted-pair cabling. The cheaper twisted-pair cabling uses PVC as the covering jacket. Unfortunately, PVC burns like a fuse when lit and produces toxic fumes. Fire codes call for plenum-grade Teflon jacketing to be used in plenum spaces to prevent the spread of fire.

UTP is used in distances less than 200 feet and is commonly used in star topologies. Special types of UTP are used for distances of up to 100 meters. Coaxial is used for longer runs or where some electrical interference may be an issue.

Fiber-Optic Cable

A fiber-optic cable is constructed of tiny strands of glass fiber. Lasers or light-emitting diodes (LEDs) are used to flash signals through the glass strands. Fiber-optic cable is commonly used for backbone connections and long-haul installations. You can send multiple streams of data concurrently through the same strand of glass by using different color wavelengths. The process is called *dense wave multiplexing*. The drawbacks are price and the fragile glass strands, which break easily when stressed.

Fiber-optic cable has an extremely wide bandwidth. It can support concurrent transmission of voice, video, and data traffic by using multiple lasers to transmit light. Each laser color is a separate channel, allowing 12, 24, and 64 lasers to share one fiber without degradation. Higher end equipment can have even more lasers sharing the same stand of glass fiber. Speed, based on equipment used, is between 1 gigabit (Gb) and 100 terabits (Tb). Fiber-optic cable is also difficult to tap. Figure 4.37 shows the basic concept of a fiber optic cable multiplexing light into separate streams of traffic.

It is important to understand when you would use copper twisted-pair and when you would use fiber-optic cable.

FIGURE 4.37   Fiber-optic cable

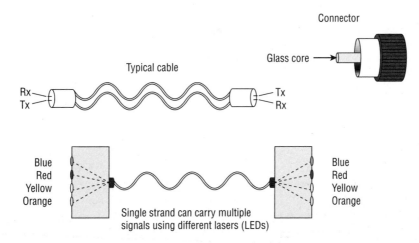

Network Devices

Now that you understand the OSI model and cabling, it is time to discuss the various devices necessary to build a network. Every CISA is expected to understand the purpose of common networking equipment.

Let's begin from the bottom up. The first thing you need is the customer requirements. What do they intend to connect to the network? The next question, what is their intended usage while on the network? We are constantly amazed at how many times the client expects a network to magically be all things to all people. Proper identification of requirements will go a long way toward aligning the network to the organizational objectives.

Hub (handwritten margin note)

We can start with the number of user connections. Each user will need to plug into a network hub or switch. A *network hub* is an electrical connection box that amplifies and retimes the electrical signals for transmission. A hub is similar to an electrical junction box. All traffic is shared across each port.

Switch (layer 2 devices) (handwritten margin note)

A *network switch* performs the functions of a hub and contains an intelligent processor capable of running logic programs. Switches separate traffic between ports to create the appearance of a private communications line. This is the same design that is in PBX telephone switches and in LAN switches.

The network architect may encounter a problem with the distance between network devices. The solution may be to use a special cable type for that run, or to add another device to compensate for the distance. A *network repeater* can amplify the tiny electrical signals to drive longer distances. Repeaters receive a signal and then repeat the transmission down the next link. We could also use fiber-optic cable from that particular leg of the run. Fiber-optic cables are popular for use in long runs across the building or across the globe.

Maybe the issue is that wires are not acceptable for your intended usage. For example, it would be difficult to use a wire-line connection for counting inventory in a warehouse. The users would be unhappy, and the heavy steel wheels of the forklift would not be kind as they ran over the fragile cable.

Wi-Fi radio is good for communication over short distances. This will work in a warehouse. It will also work within a building for connecting handheld devices such as a PDA. Another wireless method includes infrared (IR) light, which requires line-of-sight access. This is good for limiting communication to the immediate area, but still needs security.

Wireless security is always a major issue. Chapter 7 covers this topic.

There may be a need to divide a network into small sections because of the sheer number of systems. Maybe you want to divide the network to put each group into their own subnet. Subnetting could protect the Accounting department from the Research and Development traffic, for example. This is performed by segmenting the big network into smaller groups of subnetworks (subnets).

Router (layer 3 device) (handwritten margin note)

You can subnet by using a *router* to provide access across the subnets while eliminating unnecessary traffic on each subnet. As you will recall, a router will insulate subnets from traffic conversations that do not involve their systems. Just connect the router to the switch/hub for each subnet and set up the router configuration.   — *See pg 219*

You can also implement virtual subnets known as _virtual LANs (VLANs)_ to divide the users. A VLAN is like an automatic conference calling list configured on the network switch (layer 2). A VLAN will simulate one subnet for all the target computers (that's where the term *virtual* comes into the name). The VLAN methods vary depending on the comprehension of the installer and the capability of the manufacturer. The basic methods of creating a VLAN are to use specific ports, to associate MAC addresses into a VLAN, or to create policy rules if the switch hardware has that capability. Let's discuss each of these methods here:

Port-based VLAN (layer 1)   The administrator manually configures a specific port into a specific VLAN. Works well for uplinks, systems that don't move, and small networks.

MAC-based VLAN (layer 2)   Ties the MAC address into a VLAN by reading the network traffic and then automatically reconfiguring the network port on your switch.

Policy- or rule-based VLAN (layer 3 with layer 2 supporting)   A high-quality network switch reads the IP header in your traffic and executes an administrator's rule to join a VLAN based on protocol or by IP address. When correctly implemented, the process is automatic and does not require any software on the workstation. Switch ports will reconfigure automatically when the system is moved.

No matter what, every VLAN needs a router to access the other subnets. This router may be a physically separate device or a router CPU inside the same chassis. Now add the network servers and you will have a working computer network. Just be sure to include enough net-work-attached printers to make everyone happy.

Table 4.3 provides a summary of the various local area network devices that you will encounter.

TABLE 4.3   Local Area Network Equipment

LAN Equipment	Purpose
Router (layer 3)	Connects to separate subnetworks or adapts a connection to different transmission media. Routers decide whether the traffic needs to pass along another route or should just stay in the original subnetwork. This relieves traffic congestion across the network. Examples include LAN 1–to–LAN 2 and LAN-to-WAN circuits. Routers can also convert between Ethernet, Token Ring, and telephone company communication protocols.
Switch (layer 2)	Provides intelligent process of creating discreet communication on each port. Same function as the PBX telephone switch, which creates the illusion of private communication lines for each user. Network VLANs are similar to administrator-designated group conference calling. Requires a router (layer 3 router function) to communicate with a different subnetwork or between VLANs.

TABLE 4.3 Local Area Network Equipment *(continued)*

LAN Equipment	Purpose
Bridge (layer 2)	Connects two separate networks by using the same network addressing in one subnet. Intelligent bridge is the same as layer 2 switch.
Hub (layer 1)	Connects individual cables to share data between ports. Amplifies and retimes the tiny electrical signals. Similar to an electrical junction box for networking cables.
Repeater (layer 1)	Designed to boost the signal strength across a cable to overcome distance limitations.
Wi-Fi transmitter (layer 1)	Short-range wireless transmitter/receiver to connect laptops and PDA devices to the LAN. (May be integrated into an all-in-one router offering both layer 1 and layer 3 functions.)

To connect different networks, you need a router.

Routers provide intelligent decisions about routing traffic down particular links. The router is like a cop directing traffic in the direction it needs to travel. Routers come in a wide variety of shapes, sizes, and capabilities. An Internet router needs at least one Internet port and one LAN port. The type of router port depends on the type of circuit you need to connect.

We will also need a firewall to protect our network. We discuss firewalls in depth in Chapter 7.

Network Services

Several pages ago, we discussed the OSI model with examples of network services running on layer 7. In the example, we mentioned network servers with a few of the services they provide. Let's discuss two common network support services that relate to everyone using a network: DNS and DHCP.

Domain Name System   (Layer 7)

Computers like to use hexadecimal numbers, network administrators like to use IP addresses, and all of us who run computers like to refer to machines by name. Names are so much easier to remember. Even names can get confusing, so the Internet is designed to allow fully qualified domain names. A *fully qualified domain name* (FQDN) is what you see on the left side in the URL portion of the browser as you surf the Internet. Have you ever wondered how the web browser finds the website you typed? The answer is by using the Domain Name System (DNS).

Routers have tables of IP addresses, along with the routes to take to reach those addresses. DNS servers are a layer 7 software application that contains a list of alias names and their associated IP addresses. DNS is how you end up reaching a website without knowing its IP address.

DNS offers additional flexibility. You can change the IP address without having to tell everyone about the address change. Just keep the DNS server updated with your new IP address. If DNS fails, you will not be able to access the target or you will resort to typing the IP address (if known).

Figure 4.38 shows the process of DNS looking at the company name and responding to your request.

FIGURE 4.38   DNS name service (address lookup)

A major problem with traditional DNS is the lack of security. Network productivity is essentially shut down if the DNS server is lost or attacked. Attackers can poison DNS by using fake servers or injecting fake DNS updates. This is the same problem discussed with layer 3 routing-table updates. The preferred method is to implement Secure DNS (S-DNS) by using ACLs and digital certificates. Name-lookup services and DNS updates would be accepted only from DNS servers able to continually verify their identity. Trust is destroyed upon the first failure in an ongoing challenge-response process.

Dynamic Host Configuration Protocol

For years, the job of a network administrator entailed the tedious task of configuring IP addresses on each computer. Manual settings are still the best choice for network servers; however, the user workstation is another matter.

Dynamic Host Configuration Protocol (DHCP) can automatically configure the IP address, subnet mask, and DNS settings on a computer. DHCP is an improved version of the original BOOTP using RARP. Both DHCP and BOOTP have the same operational design.

The theory of operation is simple. Figure 4.39 shows how DHCP works. Here are the steps:

1. A computer on your network is set up as the DHCP server. For remote dial-up, the better access servers will have this ability built in to support the modems. The DHCP server will be configured by your network administrator with a pool of IP addresses eligible for dynamic allocation.

2. The DHCP server listens on the network for an IP packet containing a type 67 code in the header. (Don't worry, that level of detail is not on your exam.)

3. A computer is booted on your network without an IP address. During the boot process, the computer recognizes that an IP is needed. The computer sends out a type 67 request asking for any DHCP server to assign it an IP address. The request contains the MAC address of the computer asking for an IP.

4. The requesting computer waits several seconds for a response.

5. Your DHCP server recognizes the type 67 request and responds with a type 68 reply addressed to the MAC address of the sender.

6. If the reply is received in time, the computer will accept the IP address and configuration settings. Then it will finish bootup and begin talking on the network.

FIGURE 4.39   How DCHP works

Every idea in the world has its Achilles heel. DHCP is no different. DHCP is implemented on OSI layer 2. This means that the DHCP mechanism is dependent on making a broadcast with its MAC address. Routers will not pass broadcasts because the resulting traffic is undesired on all other occasions. Remember, the router has two jobs: one is routing, and the second is providing insulation from unnecessary traffic. The DHCP server needs to be located on the same subnet to hear the computer making a DHCP request. Figure 4.40 shows how DHCP is blocked by the router.

Either ' or

FIGURE 4.40   DHCP and the router issue

The DHCP Router Solution

Rather than building a bunch of DHCP servers, you can make a simple change to the router configuration. The router will still perform its normal functions; however, it can be set to forward DHCP requests to another subnet. The router command setting is called a bootup-helper-address or DHCP-helper-address.

This helper address setting will forward both the initial request and the associated DHCP server reply. The process is simple, as shown in Figure 4.41.

> Dynamic IP addressing under DHCP is quite convenient for users. However, unsecured implementations of DHCP could grant an intruder easier access into the network. We discuss this security issue further in Chapter 7.

FIGURE 4.41   Router with DHCP helper address

Expanding the Network

Modern routers can connect high-speed LANs to remote places for the purpose of creating a wide area network (WAN). Figure 4.42 shows what a WAN might look like.

or fiber Remote access is a popular feature. WANs are similar to a LAN; however, the implementation is different. Special equipment is necessary to adapt the transmission signal to telephone and radio equipment. Figure 4.42 shows the basics of expanding a network.

Setting up a WAN requires planning. Let's start with the most important component, which is information. The first thing you need is the customer requirements. What do they intend to connect to the network? Questions should be asked about who will be connecting to the network. Will the users be employees, business partners, or clients? Once again, you ask questions about their intended usage while on the network. What controls are planned? Hopefully, the client will be able to impress the auditor with answers that are well thought out.

FIGURE 4.42 Expanding the network

Your client might want to have dial-in access to the network for their users. This can be accomplished in two ways:

Individual modems An individual modem can be connected to a computer on the network. This is a simple method that is adored by every hacker in the world. Individual modem connections bypass the majority of network security controls. Your monitoring tools may think this is just an ordinary internal computer with free rein over the attached subnet—or worse, the whole network. A hacker can easily find modems by using automated dialing tools or checking a list of known modems posted at hacker sites. Insecure modems are still a threat to security. A sharp auditor will investigate the compliance of dial-in modems to their security policy.

Network access server   An access server can be used with a modem pool. It can be a slick product from Cisco or a PC configured with special software such as Microsoft Remote Access Service (RAS). The access server should have special monitoring and security controls.

It is safe to assume that the remote connection will be attached to one of the routers. You should encourage the practice of separating remote connections into their own subnet. This promotes separation of duties with the benefit of simplifying the implementation of security controls. Remote router connections will probably need a firewall if the connection is wireless or could involve someone besides the organization's employees.

Using Telephone Circuits

High-speed telephone circuits such as T1 (1.54Mbps) and T3 (44.5Mbps) use a channel service unit (CSU) instead of a regular modem. The CSU is a special device used by the telephone company and designed for connection to their equipment. Telephone circuits like this can be divided or combined by using a multiplexor. A *multiplexor* converts one high-speed telephone port into many lower-speed ports, or combines several lower-speed lines to appear as one high-speed line. Multiplexors are invisible to the user.

Table 4.4 summarizes the various types of equipment you might use when connecting to a WAN.

TABLE 4.4   Networking Equipment

Device	Purpose
Router with WAN port	Connect LAN to remote WAN via telephone circuits.
Modem	Low-speed telephone dial-up connection to the access server for users, or attached to the router for remote administration.
Channel service unit (CSU)	Similar to a very special modem. Designed to connect a router port to a high-speed telephone company circuit. Fast transmission speeds from 1MB to 44MB per line. Common in WANs.
Multiplexor	Combines multiple lower-speed telephone circuits to appear as a single fast circuit, or splits a fast circuit into multiple lower-speed connections. It has a function similar to that of any splitter or combiner.

The telephone company will provide whatever service the client is able to afford. In some areas, the services may be limited. High-speed services such as Digital Subscriber Line (DSL) are available in only limited areas. The limitation is based on cost: Your telephone company will invest in areas that have enough demand to warrant the business cost. In rural areas, people have few choices. These are known as last-mile service areas, where the phone company will lose money.

[handwritten in margin: DWM Pg 223]

The world of telephone circuits is based on several generations of telephone company equipment. The older generation is based on the <u>Integrated Services Digital Network (ISDN)</u>. The newest generation is built by using <u>Dense Wave Multiplexing (DWM)</u> with multiple lasers over fiber optics with <u>Asynchronous Transfer Mode (ATM)</u>. Each generation of technology has intrinsic advantages and disadvantages. Let's run down the list. We suggest you pay attention because these details may be of value.

The following are various ways you can connect to your network via a wired route.

Dedicated Telephone Circuits

Dedicated telephone circuits are billed by location with actual usage billed by distance. The user is charged a monthly fee plus any long-distance charges.

Plain old telephone service (POTS)   POTS is available almost everywhere. This is the regular telephone line capable of data transmission up to 56Kbs. POTS is based on using half of an ISDN circuit. POTS is the only circuit that is considered to be "off" when not in use. Transmission is halted when you hang up the phone. All the other telephone circuits we discuss are always live and transmitting.

Integrated Services Digital Network (ISDN)   ISDN is the foundation of POTS. Therefore, you should be able to get ISDN almost anywhere. The basic rate interface (BRI) bandwidth starts at 128K per line. It can be used as one 128 K/bps channel or divided into two 56 K/bps circuits. Optional ISDN speeds on a primary rate interface (PRI) can go up to 1.544 Mbps. You can run up to 23 channels of data, voice, and video over ISDN. In Europe and Australia, the PRI speeds are 2.048 Mbps, equal to 30 channels. Most video conference sets use ISDN. The ISDN circuit is always on and live.

Primary trunk line (T1)   T1 is a dedicated trunk line equal to 28 POTS circuits. *[handwritten: or 14 ISDN circuits]* The user is charged by the mile for basic T1 service. Telephone PBX systems are usually connected by one or more T1 trunks running back to the telephone company's central office. The administrator can provision (divide) the trunk into whatever variety of factional service they desire for voice, video, or data. T1 lines never shut down. In North America, T1 speeds are 1.544Mbps each, and 2.048Mbps in Europe.

Digital Subscriber Line (DSL)   DSL is usually the least-expensive high-speed circuit using a higher frequency over a standard telephone line. This allows your standard voice telephone line to simultaneously carry DSL higher-speed traffic without conflict. DSL is substantially limited by distance. It is available only in high-density areas where the phone company can make a profit. Speeds range from 368Kpbs to 1.544Mbps. The DSL circuit is always on and live. If you turn off DSL equipment, the phone company disables your circuit.

Each of the circuits listed above represent a dedicated connection which is either: 1) between the telephone company and the buyer's office, or 2) installed as a private line between the buyer's offices. Figure 4.43 shows the relationship of the different telephone circuits.

FIGURE 4.43   Usage of the different telephone circuits

Packet-Switched Circuits

Packet switching evolved to eliminate the need for everyone to set up expensive dedicated lines. The Internet is a packet-switched network. Transmissions can route anywhere without regard to distance. This means that the path from Los Angeles, California, to Mexico City, Mexico, might pass through Atlanta, Georgia, depending on the carrier and the time of day. Similarly, using a special diagnostic tool, we noticed our downloads from Dell were routed from Grapevine, Texas (near Dallas), to Parsippany, New Jersey, and then to Austin, Texas (a journey of more than 2,700 miles). Interesting, because our Grapevine office is only 229 miles from Dell in Austin, Texas. In packet switching, the source and destination are known, but the path automatically changes (it is variable).

International telecommunication standard X.25 (X.25)   X.25 was an early 1970s digital packet-switching protocol designed to create WANs over public data networks run by the telephone company. It's considered the foundation of modern switched networks. X.25 contained three major advances:

- A field for handling special transmission parameters called the facility code. This allowed you to specify a quality of service.

- Ability to create permanent virtual circuits (PVCs). This administrative configuration setting allowed the administrator to specify a fixed path for all communication. PVCs were created to replace the leasing of dedicated telephone lines.

- Ability to create switched virtual circuits (SVCs). The source and destination were specified, but the path was temporary, dynamic, and constantly changing. SVCs were not dedicated.

X.25 is now used primarily as a reference model, except for a few old die-hard customers. The lessons learned in X.25 created new technology for communications.

Frame relay   Frame relay (FR) is an inexpensive packet-switching system using the same type of interface protocol as X.25 with PVC and SVC capability. Frame relay is different from X.25 in format and functionality. The FR data packets may arrive out of sequence. Therefore, it is important to have equipment capable of caching enough data in memory for reassembly sequencing before use by the user. Frame relay works great for data/voice applications, but some video transmissions may appear choppy to the viewer unless adequate memory caching is used. End connection points are specified by using data link connection identifiers (DLCI numbers). The DLCI specifies the destination, similar to a phone number. Frame-relay speeds range from less than 1.544Mbps up to 44.5Mbps. The frame-relay circuits are always on and live unless you want the telephone company to disable your circuit for several days.

Asynchronous Transfer Mode (ATM)   ATM is the new backbone of the telecommunications industry. The transmission speeds are very high, from 155Mbps to more than 1GBps. That is more bandwidth than most companies could ever use in this decade. The ATM design implements cell switching and multiplexing to ensure solid delivery. Data is sent down multiple concurrent paths to the same destination. The first data cell to arrive will be used, while later duplicates will be discarded. ATM can use 132 switched paths (SVCs) during transmission. It is very reliable. The ATM circuit is always on and live unless you want the telephone company to shut down your circuit for several days.

Switched Multimegabit Data Services (SMDS)   This is a very high-speed data communications service. I doubt it would ever be mentioned on your exam. It's included to demonstrate where public data networks are going. The first ATM services offered speeds of only 1.5Mbps, and SMDS was 3.4Mbps. Advances in technology raised the speeds 100 times. SMDS is available on a limited basis at 340Mbps to 3.4Gbps (3,400Mbps). It's designed for transmitting over a dual bus in metropolitan networks. The SMDS payload is big enough to encapsulate (carry) entire LAN traffic (Ethernet 802.3, 802.4, and Token Ring/FDDI 802.5).

SMDS has two interesting features: security and group addressing. Source addresses are verified by the network to ensure that the assigned interface is legitimate. The user is protected from *address spoofing* (fraudulent devices). Source and destination addresses can be screened to prevent delivery of unwanted traffic. Group addressing allows multicasting of a single transmission to a specific group of addresses without sending to anyone else. The private virtual network features add additional security and efficiency.

We have discussed several communication circuits that are always on and live. This can allow a hacker to attack you 24 hours a day, every day. High-speed circuits can support high-speed attacks or high-speed theft of your data. Think firewalls!

Wireless Access Solutions

The basic network concepts are identical for developing a network solution sans wire. Wireless is used when the wiring costs are prohibitive or the wires would defeat the intended purpose.

Each wireless system requires a minimum of two antenna systems. The antenna stations have both transmitting and receiving capabilities.

The following are various ways you can connect to your network via wireless access:

Wi-Fi radio   This is the most common type of wireless access. The design uses a layer 1 transmitter/receiver to support a signal range of up to 1,500 feet. It uses digital spread spectrum or frequency hopping over a private radio channel. It is commonly used by the military and private companies operating mobile fleets. Large-scale Wi-Fi may use cellular service. Smaller-scale use includes Wi-Fi hot spots.

It's relatively simple to construct a wireless LAN. Several vendors offer low-cost wireless access points (APs), which are similar to a wireless hub or router. The AP is connected to a wired network and broadcasts connectivity to handheld devices. Usually the range of an AP is 300 feet, equivalent to 100 meters. Users can move freely within the 300-foot broadcast range without losing any connectivity. The individual broadcast area (range) is also known as a *cell*. This is comparable to the design of cellular telephone networks. The effective range can be increased by combining APs and their multiple cells (service range). Wireless LANs (WLANs) are based on the IEEE 802.11 standard.

Station (STA)   The station, or Independent Basic Service Set (IBSS), is a wireless device on the end of the network, such as PDA, laptop, or mobile phone.

Access point (AP)   This is a wireless transmitter/receiver that provides basic network services, usually within 300 feet, equivalent to 100 meters. Higher-power transmitters with longer ranges are entering the marketplace. The AP and STA compose a basic WLAN.

Cell   The individual AP broadcast range is known as the cell, or span of coverage. Multiple AP cells are linked together to increase the range and allow roaming within the building or between buildings. The relationship is shown in Figure 4.44.

A group of wireless devices uses an ad hoc arrangement when communicating directly with each other in a peer-to-peer relationship without an AP. The terminology *ad hoc* is based on the dynamic master-slave relationship between devices. Ad hoc networks have a short broadcast range, which is also referred to as the piconet, or personal area network (PAN). Bluetooth is the most common ad hoc network for providing connectivity between a cell phone and a wireless headset.

FIGURE 4.44   Basic wireless network

Pico means one trillionth or very small. Bluetooth technology creates an ad hoc network of one master and one to seven slaves, up to a total of eight devices. This teeny network provides short-range direct-link interconnectivity.

> **WARNING** The lack of effective security is an enormous drawback in wireless networking. IEEE's original design of Wired Equivalent Privacy (WEP) proved to be practically worthless. As of 2005, wireless networks using 802.11a, 802.11b, 802.11g, and 802.11n have been officially deemed unsafe. Those unsafe implementations represent the majority of wireless LAN equipment installed worldwide. In response, IEEE issued a revised wireless standard in 2005 called 802.11i Robust Security Networks (RSNs). A third-party security VPN must be used when RSN is not available. We discuss RSN in Chapter 7.

Satellite radio   This is the next most common method. The signal is bounced off a low-orbit satellite in space. Obviously, the service area is huge. Very popular for remote communications or linking to numerous field locations, satellite is heavily used in trucking fleets, ships, and retail chain operations. The transmission speeds are lower, and cost is an issue unless you buy a large volume of air time. Private uplinks are available for telephone, data, fax, and video applications. Satellite data-phones are common for emergency response. Transmission speeds are 9.6bps to 4MBps, with specialized hardware required. Satellite communication has a 2- to 5-second transmission delay due to signal propagation delay. For example, the Iridium satellites are less than 500 miles up compared to 23,000 miles for geosynchronous satellites.

Microwave   Microwaves are used in short-distance runs—1 to 30 miles— across cities and over mountain ranges. Microwave service has been around for 50 years. The only drawbacks are the clear line of sight required for transmission and the construction cost. Connection speeds range from 1MBps to 100MBps. The primary advantage is no recurring transmission costs aside from equipment purchase and regular maintenance. Severe weather and fog can disrupt signals.

Laser   Lasers are being used as an alternative to microwaves. Lasers also work to connect two offices by using the unobstructed aerial space to cross above public roads. It is similar to fiber optics without the fiber cable. Transmission speeds from are from 1MBps to 100MBps. Severe weather and fog can disrupt signals.

> **WARNING** It is strongly recommended that every land-based wireless connection have a firewall installed between the wired network and the wireless equipment. Many implementations of wireless encryption still contain holes in security. Motivated hackers can access radio connections by using technology available in the amateur radio community. Laser access may be more difficult, but hackers have proven it is possible.

It is important that we address the subject of short-range wireless networking for use with radio frequency identification tags. This is an area that will increase as more organizations attempt to implement automated tracking.

Wireless RFID Systems

Radio frequency identification (RFID) is a hot topic. RFID uses a tiny tag, which contains silicon chips and antennas that enable the tag to be detected by scanners. The original purpose was to protect inventory from department store shoplifters. Later RFID was expanded to include planting tags in boxes for better warehouse control.

The security and privacy issues regarding RFID are increasing every day. As an IS auditor, you are expected to have a basic understanding of RFID. You will encounter an increasing number of issues regarding RFID implementations. Citizens are growing more concerned about their privacy.

Passive RFID tags are regularly used in inventory control and for implant in live animals. These tags may be covertly read at a distance. Newer tags are built into the product and are not detectable. The user could be scanned as they walk through a building. RFID tags in adult products or medical prescription packages could lead to interesting conversations about privacy.

Under President Bill Clinton's administration, the U.S. Food and Drug Administration and other government agencies have approved the use of RFID tags for human implant. There are multiple human implant vendors on the market today. The ads for human implant claim RFID tags are safe and nonremovable. One vendor claims that the intended purpose is to protect newborn infants by tracking your baby in the hospital. Other advertised uses include prisoner identification or the identification of elderly individuals unable to provide information for themselves. This new RFID situation poses an increasing variety of privacy concerns.

Another type of RFID uses a transponder to transmit a signal. The RFID transponder uses an internal power source to respond to queries by an antenna in the area. A common example is the toll tag used by a toll road authority for the electronic collection of usage fees. A variety of organizations including law enforcement collect surveillance data on common citizens by using active RFID toll tags along with automobile satellite services and cell phone records.

Government researchers have determined RFID tags can be easily cloned without the user's or recipient's knowledge. Any RFID signal you can read can be duplicated. The implications may be either good or evil depending on the desire of individuals. You can expect more controversy as the issues develop.

Summarizing the Various Area Networks

The IT management may choose to maintain a network administration staff at each site or use remote access. Either choice has its advantages and disadvantages.

Routers can use a modem for individual low-speed telephone connections of 56K. This would be intended for remote support of the router itself. (Turn off the modem when not in use to keep out the hackers.)

We have discussed both LAN and WAN networks. The discussion would not be complete without mentioning the multitude of variations. In the beginning, the LAN was the focus. Then the need arose to connect to remote users. Supporting remote connections became rather involved, and the whole idea was termed a WAN. Since that time, the world has continued to generate new products with a combination of need, politics, and marketing. The LAN-WAN naming convention has brought us new terminology for other types of area networks, including personal area networks

(PANs), campus area networks (CANs), metropolitan area networks (MANs), and storage area networks (SANs).

Table 4.5 introduces you to the types of area networks that the CISA is expected to encounter. You need to know the descriptive features of each one.

TABLE 4.5   Common Networking Acronyms

Network Acronyms	Description
Local area network (LAN)	Connecting computers within the building by using hubs, switches, and routers. Usually very fast connection speed of 100/1,000MB.
Virtual local area network (VLAN)	Artificial grouping of disparate workstation ports across various LAN switches to appear as if all were connected to a common subnet. Similar to a PBX conference-calling group. Primitive VLANs use fixed ports. Advanced VLANs use dynamic rules to automatically assign ports without user/administrator intervention. The user can plug in anywhere, and the switch reconfigures the port within fractions of a second. Moves are automatic using IP address rule, protocol rule, or MAC address rule.
Storage area network (SAN)	A cluster solution for interconnecting different kinds of file storage for server farms. Often use Ethernet, SCSI, ATM, or fiber-optic connections.
Personal area network (PAN)	Coverage is within 10 feet of the immediate area. Used for connecting PDA and handheld personal devices to synchronize with your computer. Also known as a Piconet.
Campus area network (CAN)	Connecting computers between buildings in a school or corporate campus by using cable, fiber optics, or wireless transmitters.
Metropolitan area network (MAN)	Connecting computers between different buildings located in the same city.
Wide area network (WAN)	Multi-city connection over longer distances. Connection speeds range from under 1MB on cheap telephone circuits to over 1GB on optical carrier circuits (OCx).

Political battles over authority will exist regarding the control over most networks. The basic operation of local and wide area networks is quite similar. The principal difference is the area of coverage and who is in charge of that area.

Managing Your Network

Networks are constantly increasing in complexity. A network outage can cause significant impact to an organization's business activities. It would be naive to assume that the systems could run without supervision. The network administrator holds the duty of monitoring network performance and is the first line of defense for detecting security violations. This is possible only with specialized tools designed to manage network assets. Let's take a look at the basic tools used to manage the network.

Syslog

Today almost all computers and network devices have the capability for centralized system logging, known as *Syslog*. The design sends audit log messages to a centralized server for aggregation of event logs and alerts. Syslog is a common and simple utility that requires little processing power.

It is an excellent tool to aid the monitoring efforts of system administrators. This form of centralized logging is excellent for security monitoring and audit log retention. Syslog can be enabled on an individual system within a few minutes.

Syslog has some disadvantages. Unfortunately, it does not contain message authentication. There is still no mechanism for providing message integrity. The Syslog design also lacks the mechanism to verify delivery of a message.

The principal advantage of Syslog is that audit logs can be automatically transmitted to another server for safe storage. This assists in providing evidence for the auditor. It can also be a compensating control in environments where the logs may be deleted.

Automated Cable Tester

Cable industry studies report that 97 percent of all network problems are related to faults in the physical cable plant (layer 1). Advanced handheld cable testers are used to certify the quality of network wire runs. These handheld scanners test individual data cables by automatically running a series of electrical tests and transmission tests. The tests check a variety of conditions, including compliance to recommended length, signal strength, transmission cross talk, electrical noise interference, and electrical pin connections. Cables that pass these tests are certified as compliant. Once certified, the cable is ready for production use.

Protocol Analyzer

A computer can be configured with special software designed to record and analyze network transmissions. This software is often referred to as a *packet sniffer.* Network administrators use this as a tool for troubleshooting network performance problems. The sniffer operates in promiscuous mode and records transmissions of every packet transversing the segment. The sniffer can see only traffic within the segment to which it is attached. It cannot see traffic across the routers or switches unless the traffic is passing down the segment where the computer is attached. The sniffer will show you communication between systems and the passwords used.

Hackers can use a sniffer to capture user IDs, passwords in clear text, and map the network. This is why sniffers are considered a tremendous threat in the wrong hands.

Simple Network Management Protocol

Networks can be monitored and controlled by using the Simple Network Management Protocol (SNMP). The network administrator usually runs an SNMP network management program such as HP OpenView to monitor servers and routers. A Network Management System (NMS) gives you the capability to check the up/down status of individual network devices.

You can use SNMP to monitor almost any network device, including servers, routers, gateways, hubs, and workstations. By default, SNMP provides the capability to do the following:

- Read: Monitor a device with notification of possible error conditions

- Write: Reconfigure limited system parameters

- Use SNMP to reboot or shut down the network device

The SNMP security mechanism is extremely weak and relies on simple passwords transmitted in clear text that are easy to read. As an auditor, you should be concerned about SNMP being allowed to travel unregulated across the network. All SNMP-managed devices need to use unique passwords rather than the default passwords *public* and *private*.

Vendor documentation will refer to the passwords of *public* and *private* by using the term *community strings*. A community string is actually a simple password used to gain control of the target system. All that is needed is the target system IP address and matching SNMP password (community string). Many organizations are not properly educated about the *public* and *private* password risk. It is the network administrator's job to define SNMP access control lists and to manage the implementation of unique SNMP passwords for each device. Failure to do so would grant anyone control of any system using the same SNMP password (community string). Otherwise, SNMP is a good internal monitoring tool.

Remote Monitoring Protocol Version 2

The Remote Monitoring Protocol version 2 (RMON2) is a major improvement over version 1, offering data beyond basic network health via up/down status. RMON2 gives you the ability to monitor all seven layers of the OSI model, including application performance. You can view the performance of a single application running across the network or select a stratified view of the combined bandwidth allocation.

Twenty-one layers of RMON performance data are available. By comparison, a network packet sniffer can record only a snapshot containing a few minutes or hours of layer 1, 2, and 3 data. RMON2 can provide a broader range of nonstop performance while recording tremendous levels of detail covering a time span of hours, days, months, and even years. Most RMON2 implementations write the records to an SQL database for reporting and long-term retention. This is a true enterprise-class monitoring system.

NOTE   It is important to remember that useful administration tools also make good hacker tools. Every administrative tool needs to be governed by the organization's internal controls.

Summary

The information systems auditor is expected to understand common networking technology. You should know the name of each piece of equipment and its role in the computer network. Occasionally, you may encounter systems that are filling an all-in-one role. In that event, you should remember computer architecture limitations: It is not possible for single-processor systems to perform all functions without a momentary interruption of the security software. Both single-user systems and multiuser systems have design vulnerabilities that can be exploited.

It is the job of the CISA to evaluate the auditee's technology implementation. Despite advancements in technology, common problems will usually be rooted in fundamental errors of design or implementation. Security is best implemented in multiple layers to provide compensating control for design vulnerabilities. The purpose of this chapter has been to familiarize you with the basic concepts. The world depends on the CISA to review the client's design for the purpose of identifying vulnerabilities or failure points. You should always ask yourself whether the technology truly fulfills the objectives of the business and the objectives of security controls. If not, it might just be a superfluous investment in way-cool technical junk. Technology without proper internal controls is a bomb waiting to explode.

Exam Essentials

Understand the basics of computer architecture.   Computer architecture comprises a central processor unit with high-speed cache memory and solid-state RAM memory. All the computer's components communicate by using a shared data bus, constructed of electrical wires. Interfaces connect the data bus to the electronic components such as the video display or the hard disk drive. There are different classes of computers based on size and capability, including the personal computer, midrange computer (mini), mainframe, and supercomputer.

Remember that computers may use single CPUs or multiple CPUs.   In either case, the system can be running in time-sharing mode to support multiple users (multiuser mode). With multiple CPUs, it is possible to assign each processor to a particular task. Multiple-CPU architecture provides a way for security software to run completely uninterrupted. Otherwise, the computer security software will be interrupted in the normal course of servicing processing requests.

Know that the computer operating system manages communications between the hardware and user programs.   The operating system provides services for scheduling, dispatching, security, and input and output functions. All operating systems are not equal in their implementation of internal controls. The mainframe represents a role model for the highest level of system controls. Security controls are lacking while the system is in supervisory state during maintenance or initial program load (IPL).

Understand that system ports must be protected from physical access and logical access. Examples of system ports include interface ports, the console or master terminal, and all network communication ports.

Know that computer networking is accomplished by using a variety of devices. Network cables are joined together by hubs or network switches to form a network. Smaller networks are known as subnets. Multiple subnets can be joined together by using a router. The purpose of the router is to direct traffic between different networks. A firewall is a specially configured device that selectively routes traffic between two networks. The firewall's method depends on its internal architecture. A proxy firewall prevents direct access into the network. Traffic still goes through the holes in the firewall, but the proxies relay the request on behalf of the user.

Remember that wide area networks are created by using wired telephone circuits or wireless transmitters to connect LANs. Network security at external access points is always a concern. Every network access point presents an opportunity to motivated hackers. High-speed communications circuits allow for high-speed attacks. Modern telephone circuits, except for POTS, are always on and present a 24-hour attack opportunity. The first wide area networks were created by using circuit-switched telephone lines that were billed by distance traveled. Newer packet-switching technology charges for the data sent, not the distance traveled.

Understand that the OSI model provides a simple reference for explaining the functions occurring in computer networking. Nobody actually runs the OSI protocol; in the real world, most communication is performed over the Internet Protocol (IP). A CISA must demonstrate an understanding of how OSI relates to IP.

Remember that computer networks can be complex and require constant monitoring. Typical monitoring tools include the packet sniffer to analyze communications, Syslog to transmit system logs to a safe location for review, and Simple Network Management Protocol (SNMP) to alert administrators about conditions impacting network operations. SNMP can feed a network management system, such as HP OpenView or Remote Monitoring Protocol (RMON2).

Review Questions

1. Which RAID level does not improve fault tolerance?

    A. RAID level 0

    B. RAID level 1

    C. RAID level 2

    D. RAID level 5

2. Which type of network device directs packets through the Internet?

    A. Hubs

    B. Routers

    C. Repeaters

    D. Modems

3. This type of data transmission is often used to transmit video signals across the network.

    A. Unicasting

    B. Broadcasting

    C. Multicasting

    D. Pinging

4. This address is manufactured or burned into network equipment and is totally unique.

    A. Domain name

    B. IP

    C. Media Access Control

    D. Street address

5. This network is often used to provide vendors and customers limited access to corporate network services.

    A. Internet

    B. Extranet

    C. Intranet

    D. Access net

6. Which of the following is a list of OSI model levels from the top down?

    A. Application, Physical, Session, Transport, Network, Data-Link, Presentation

    B. Presentation, Data-Link, Network, Transport, Session, Physical, Application

    C. Application, Presentation, Session, Transport, Network, Data-Link, Physical

    D. Presentation, Data-Link, Network, Transport, Session, Physical, Application

7. Which of the following is the most popular media for connecting workstations in a corporate environment?

    A. Coaxial

    B. Shielded twisted-pair

    C. Unshielded twisted-pair

    D. Fiber optics

8. This protocol is layer 3 routable and is the backbone of the Internet.

    A. IP

    B. OSI

    C. TCP

    D. NetBIOS

9. What type of network firewall is often the simplest to implement but has the worst logging capabilities?

    A. Proxy

    B. Application

    C. Packet-filtering

    D. Adaptive

10. What does the third layer of the OSI model equate to in the TCP/IP model?

    A. Network

    B. Data-Link

    C. Transport

    D. Internet

11. At which layer of the OSI model does a gateway operate?

    A. Layer 3

    B. Layer 5

    C. Layer 6

    D. Layer 7

12. Which of the following network topologies provides a redundant path for communication?

    A. Fiber-optic

    B. Star

    C. Ring

    D. Bus

13. What is the purpose of the Address Resolution Protocol (ARP)?

    A. Find the IP address

    B. Find the mailing address

    C. Find the MAC address

    D. Find the domain name

14. What is the security issue regarding packet analyzers?

    A. Viewing passwords

    B. Special training

    C. Purchase cost

    D. Only for auditor's use

15. Which of the following is an implementation of the demilitarized zone concept?

    A. Dedicated processor and a multiprocessor system

    B. Screened subnet

    C. Bastion host on the network

    D. Dedicated subnet for internal users

16. Which of the following protocols is likely to be used for monitoring the health of the network?

    A. OSI

    B. SNMP

    C. SMTP

    D. RIP

17. What does the designation of N-1 best represent?

    A. Need for additional equipment

    B. Number of routers

    C. Meshed network

    D. Number of links

18. What is the difference between a router and a switch?

    A. Both operate at layer 2; the router routes traffic, and the switch connects various users to the network.

    B. Both operate at layer 3; the router routes traffic, and the switch connects various users to the network.

    C. They operate at OSI layer 3 and layer 2, respectively.

    D. They operate at OSI layer 2 and layer 3, respectively.

19. Which type of network cabling is relatively immune to interference, difficult to tap, and can run extended distances?

    A. Coaxial

    B. Shielded twisted-pair

    C. Unshielded twisted-pair

    D. Fiber-optic

20. Which type of memory is used to permanently record programs on solid-state chips and retains the data even after power is turned off?

    A. Random access memory

    B. Read-only memory

    C. Flash memory

    D. Optical memory

21. What is the auditor's interest concerning SNMP community information?

    A. Community strings are actually passwords, and the *private* password can write changes to the device configuration or force a reboot.

    B. Network-attached devices should be configured into individual communities for separation of duties.

    C. Security is nonexistent in the first two versions of the SNMP protocol.

    D. Operations staff should use SNMP to monitor the network and to provide early notification of problems or of information indicating that incident response is needed.

22. The _____ network topology provides a redundant path to transmit data.

    A. Bus

    B. Star

    C. Chain

    D. Ring

23. Which of the following statements is false concerning the communication circuits used in wide area networking?

    A. Switched virtual circuits (SVCs) may use different routes to reach the destination.

    B. Digital circuit-switched lines are dedicated between locations.

    C. Packet-switched circuits are charged according to distance.

    D. Circuit-switched lines allow the user to transmit any amount of data.

24. The architecture of a computer with a single central processing unit (CPU) contains which of the following points that represents the biggest area of interest to the auditor?

    A. Time-sharing is used to service the different processing tasks one at a time.

    B. An upgrade to a multiprocessor system should be justified to improve response times.

    C. System control software is halted between processing tasks.

    D. A pipeline design should be implemented to minimize system idle time.

25. Which of the following RAID implementations is designed for the disk array to be configured into one large virtual disk partition using high-speed asynchronous data transfer?

    A. RAID-1

    B. RAID-7

    C. RAID-5

    D. RAID-6

26. Even with advanced security software running on the network, which of the following OSI layers represents the vulnerability to subversion created by hardware port access?

    A. OSI layer 1

    B. OSI layer 2

    C. OSI layer 3

    D. OSI layer 7

27. In network communications, the _____ transmission sends a single data packet to multiple addresses for applications such as Internet-based television.

    A. Broadcast

    B. Multicast

    C. Visicast

    D. Unicast

28. Which of the following network protocols uses the MAC address to find a computer's IP address?

    A. Domain Name System (DNS) protocol

    B. Reverse Domain Name System (RDNS) protocol

    C. Reverse Address Resolution Protocol (RARP)

    D. Address Resolution Protocol (ARP)

29. The Internet Protocol (IP) contains a special feature for separating different types of communication between network addresses. What is this feature called?

    A. Software port

    B. Hardware port

    C. Dynamic Host Configuration Protocol

    D. Virtual Communication Protocol

30. Default settings are used by vendors to help users get the system up and running. What is the auditor's primary area of interest regarding default settings?

    A. Saves time and money for the user

    B. Represents the manufacturer's recommended settings

    C. Well-known settings published by the vendor

    D. Reduces support headaches, which increases operational uptime

31. At which OSI layer does software encryption and decryption occur?

    A. OSI layer 7

    B. OSI layer 6

    C. OSI layer 5

    D. OSI layer 4

32. The _____ can be poisoned by a hacker to prevent the computer from converting computer names into network addresses.

    A. Address Resolution Protocol (ARP)

    B. Reverse Address Resolution Protocol (RARP)

    C. Border Gateway Protocol (BGP)

    D. Domain Name System (DNS)

33. Which of the following best describes ad hoc networks?

    A. Dynamic connection of remote devices

    B. Fixed connection of devices

    C. Active Device HOst Communication

    D. Wireless connection using a static configuration

34. Except for the older plain old telephone service (POTS) lines, what is the primary issue of remote access over telephone company circuits?

    A. The cost of service may be expensive.

    B. The available bandwidth may be too slow.

    C. A remote-access circuit is always active to accept communication.

    D. Remote access servers (RASs) may be used to create a dial-up modem pool.

35. Why are firewalls used with OSI layer 7 (Application layer) proxies?

    A. Firewalls operate at the network layer by using filters based on to-from addressing.

    B. Proxies perform the request on the user's behalf without granting direct access.

    C. Firewalls close communication ports to prevent access.

    D. Proxies grant direct Internet access without the need of a firewall.

Answers to Review Questions

1. A. RAID level 0 improves performance and can provide large logical drives but it does not increase redundancy. It is often used in combination with other levels to improve performance and redundancy. The purpose of RAID-0 is to combine multiple disks into one giant virtual disk.

2. B. The function of network routers is to route IP packets throughout the network or the Internet. The router does not know the entire route to the destination. The router holds a routing table that simply provides the address of the next point down the path to the destination. Network routing is like a game of connect-the-dots. The data must travel sequentially from one router to the next router until it reaches the intended destination.

3. C. Multicasting is used to transmit packets to multiple systems simultaneously but does not transmit to all systems. It is often used to transmit video across the network. Broadcasting is used when transmitting to all systems. Unicasting is transmitting packets to a single-destination system only.

4. C. The 48-bit MAC address is manufactured into network equipment. Often, it is possible to override by using configuration tools. In a local area network, a 32-bit IP address is used for routing.

5. B. An extranet allows certain people limited access to corporate network services. An intranet is an internal corporate network. *Access net* is made up.

6. C. It helps to remember the memory tool *Please Do Not Throw Sausage Pizza Away*.

7. C. The most popular media is UTP, or unshielded twisted-pair. STP, or shielded twisted-pair, is more resistant to electronic noise and may be used in a shop environment. Coaxial cable is no longer used for connecting workstations. Fiber-optic cable is often used for interconnecting servers.

8. A. Internet Protocol (IP) is the major routable protocol. Transmission Control Protocol (TCP) is used on top of IP to provide reliable sessions. User Datagram Protocol (UDP) is connectionless without delivery confirmation. NetBIOS is not a routable protocol. The OSI model is used to explain network communications.

9. C. A router can be configured as a simple packet-filtering firewall by using an access control list. Packets are filtered based on the source address, destination address, and type of service. The problem is that packet filters have poor logging and the filter rules may be too broad to be effective. Packet filters do not support complex rules using `if-then` statements.

10. D. The third layer of the OSI model is the Network layer. Use the memory tool of *Nor Do I Throw Apples* to remember the layers of the TCP/IP model. The third layer of the TCP/IP model is the Internet layer.

11. D. According to ISACA, the gateway operates at application layer 7 in the OSI model. The function of the gateway is to convert data contained in one protocol into data used by a different protocol. An example is an SNA PC-to-mainframe gateway converting ASCII to mainframe Extended Binary Coded Decimal Interchange Code (EBCDIC).

12. C. The ring topology provides two paths for communication. If the ring is damaged, the data can be transmitted in the other direction through the undamaged segment. The most common implementation of a ring topology is IBM Token Ring and looped fiber-optic rings used by the telephone company to connect the central office wiring centers.

13. C. The Address Resolution Protocol (ARP) is used when you have an IP address and need to find the MAC address. Reverse ARP (RARP) is used going in the other direction, when you have a MAC address that needs the IP address.

14. A. Network protocol analyzers, also known as sniffers, can view clear-text passwords being transmitted across the network. The sniffer can decode packets being transmitted and is useful for troubleshooting network protocol problems.

15. B. The screened subnet off of a firewall is also known as the demilitarized zone (DMZ). The DMZ concept is based on a military concept of providing a semiprotected transfer area. Data is relayed from the DMZ to external users. Data is also transferred from the DMZ to internal users by some method to ensure data integrity.

16. B. The Simple Network Management Protocol (SNMP) is frequently used to monitor the health of the network in conjunction with a Network Management System (NMS) such as HP Open-View. The security of the SNMP configuration on each device can be a concern for the auditor. SNMP can be used in a malicious fashion to paint a picture of the network's design.

17. C. The N-1 designation is frequently used to represent a fully meshed network.

18. C. The network router operates at layer 3 for the purpose of directing traffic across the network to other subnets. The network switch operates at layer 2 to provide Data-Link services between the computers in the same subnet. A router connects different subnets.

19. D. Fiber-optic cable can transmit signals for several miles. The primary issue regarding fiber optics is the cost and special handling to prevent damage. Fiber-optic cable can be tapped by using special tools and skills; however, the process is relatively difficult for most individuals.

20. B. Solid-state integrated circuits implementing read-only memory (ROM) will provide permanent storage of data, regardless of electrical power. ROM is programmed by burning electrical connections inside the integrated circuit (IC) chip. Optical memory is not a solid-state process. Flash memory can be erased and reprogrammed. Random access memory (RAM) is volatile and will be erased when power is turned off.

21. A. SNMP community strings are actually passwords. The word *public* in the community string allows any network device running SNMP with a matching password such as the word *public* to read configuration settings off the other device. The *private* community string also uses a simple match to allow any device with the password (word) *private* to write configuration changes to the device or force it to reboot.

22. D. The ring topology provides a redundant path for communications. Common examples include the older IBM Token Ring and the modern fiber-optic rings (SONET) used to connect central offices (local exchanges) for the telephone company. The ring topology is extremely popular in fiber-optic networks, where traffic is simultaneously transmitted to different directions (counterrotating transmission) around the same ring for maximum reliability.

23. C. Circuit-based communication lines such as T1 and T3 are billed according to distance traveled. Almost all high-speed lines in use today are digital. Circuit-switched lines are dedicated connections between locations, with billing based on the distance between the locations. Circuit switching is more expensive but has some security advantages. Conversely, packet-based lines such as frame-relay are billed according to the amount of data sent, without regard to the distance traveled. The Internet uses packet switching to span the globe.

24. C. The computer's central processing unit (CPU) operates in time-sharing mode by using interrupts to start and stop the processing of requests (tasks). In computers with a single CPU, internal system controls such as security software are constantly started and stopped as the CPU switches back and forth between different tasks. A multiprocessor system allows the security software to be run in dedicated mode on a dedicated CPU without any interruptions, which improves overall system security.

25. B. RAID level 7 is designed to allow several high-speed disks (disk array) to be configured as one large virtual drive partition using asynchronous transfer mode.

26. A. The OSI model can be used to help identify and map areas of strength and weakness in the network controls. Network security software runs in the layers above the physical network, at OSI layer 1. Physical access can subvert network security. This is why physical controls are required. Proper controls will include a combination of administrative, physical, and technical safeguards.

27. B. Multicasting is used to efficiently send a single transmission to multiple addresses.

28. C. Address Resolution Protocol (ARP) is used when the IP address is known, to find the computer's MAC address. ARP is used just like a telephone directory to use a name to find a street address. A different protocol, called Reverse Address Resolution Protocol (RARP), is used when you know the MAC address and need to find the corresponding IP address. RARP works like a pay-telephone directory listing street addresses and enabling you to look up the name of a resident (person).

29. A. Software ports, also known as sockets or buffers, are used to create an orderly communications flow between programs. These software ports are analogous to individual post office mailboxes; each box has a special destination and purpose.

30. C. Beware of default settings on computers and network devices. Default settings are published on the Internet and in service manuals. The default settings benefit a vendor by reducing customer support and presenting the image that the vendor's product is easy to use. Unfortunately, the use of default settings creates a security nightmare. This information is frequently used by hackers to compromise a system. The most cost-effective technique for providing security is to change the default settings to use a unique setting at every opportunity.

31. A. Software encryption and decryption occur in OSI layer 7, the problem-solving Application layer. Encryption in layer 7 prevents the Presentation layer (layer 6) from exposing the secrets. The new IP security (IPsec) uses layer 7 application gateways to perform the encryption and decryption prior to transmitting the packets on the OSI Network layer (layer 3). Auditors use the OSI model to help decode confusing and overlapping concepts in the network design.

32. D. The Domain Name System (DNS) protocol is used to associate computer names such as *magic*, *development2*, and `www.certtest.com` to their corresponding IP addresses. The original design of DNS did not include any real provisions for security. Secure DNS (S-DNS) uses access lists and two-factor authentication with digital certificates to help thwart hackers' attempts to poison the DNS server, or substitutes a fake DNS server that points to the wrong computers.

33. A. Ad hoc networks are a dynamic grouping of devices in ever-changing configurations. Imagine the wireless devices connecting via Bluetooth when you enter a coffee shop, client's office, or your own automobile. As you move though your activities each day, the configuration of this overall network is changing. *Ad hoc* means unstructured and ever changing.

34. C. Digital high-speed circuits (for example, ISDN, T1, T3, frame relay, ATM, and DSL) are always on (live) by design. If you attempt to turn off (or disable) a high-speed digital circuit, the telephone company will disable the circuit for several days. The original plain old telephone service (POTS) disconnected your equipment from the hacker's reach when you hung up the phone line. Digital circuits never allow the user to "hang up the receiver" and therefore are never disconnected. Firewalls are required on digital high-speed circuits because the hacker could attack 24 hours a day.

35. B. Proxies are used to perform the request on a user's behalf without granting direct access. User requests may be from a live user or from another software program. The proxy may check the formatting and nature of the request to determine whether it is acceptable for processing. Requests that are uncharacteristic or outside the normal behavior are discarded as hacker attacks. The proxy protects the target application from harm.

Chapter

5

Life Cycle Management

THE OBJECTIVE OF THIS CHAPTER IS TO ACQUAINT THE READER WITH THE FOLLOWING CONCEPTS:

- ✓ Implementing all seven phases of the System Development Life Cycle

- ✓ Understanding how to evaluate the business case for proposed system and feasibility to ensure alignment to business strategy

- ✓ Impact of international standards relating to software development

- ✓ Understanding the process of conducting the system design analysis

- ✓ Understanding the process for developing systems and infrastructure requirements, acquisition, and development and testing to ensure it meets business objectives

- ✓ Understanding how to evaluate the readiness of systems for production use

- ✓ Knowledge of management's responsibility for accepting and maintaining the system

- ✓ Understanding the purpose of postimplementation system reviews relating to anticipated return on investment and proper implementation of controls

- ✓ Evaluating system retirement and disposal methods to ensure compliance with legal policies and procedures

- ✓ Basic introduction to the different methodologies used in software development.

In this chapter, you will study the methodology of best practices for software development. You will learn an overview of the preferred management techniques for designing, building, and maintaining custom computer software. This is referred to as the *System Development Life Cycle.*

When auditing software development, you will assess whether the prescribed project management, System Development Life Cycle, and change-management processes were followed. You are expected to evaluate the processes used in developing or acquiring software to ensure that the program deliverables meet organizational objectives.

We will discuss software design concepts and terminology that every CISA is expected to know for the CISA exam.

Governance in Software Development

Every organization strives to balance expenditures against revenue. The objective is to increase revenue and reduce operating costs. One of the most effective methods for reducing operating costs is to improve software automation.

Computer programs may be custom-built or purchased in an effort to improve automation. All business applications undergo a common process of needs analysis, functional design, software development, implementation, production use, and ongoing maintenance. In the end, every program will be replaced by a newer version, and the old version will be retired. This is what is referred to as the *life cycle*.

It is said that 80 percent of a business's functions are related to common clerical office administration tasks. The clerical functions are usually automated with commercial off-the-shelf software. Each organization does not need to custom-write software for word processing and spreadsheets, for example. These basic functions can be addressed through traditional software that is easily purchased on the open market. This type of commodity software requires little customization. The overall financial advantages will be small but useful. When purchasing prewritten software, an organization follows a slightly different model that focuses on selection rather than software design and development. Prewritten software follows a life cycle of needs analysis and selection, followed by implementation, which leads to production use and ongoing maintenance.

The remaining 20 percent of the business functions may be unique or require highly customized computer programs. This is the area of need addressed by custom-written computer software. The challenge is to ensure that the software actually fulfills the organization's strategic objectives.

Let's make sure that you understand the difference between a strategic system and a traditional system.

A *strategic system* fundamentally changes the way the organization conducts business or competes in the marketplace. A strategic system significantly improves overall business performance with results that can be measured by multiple indicators. These multiple indicators include measured performance increases and noticeable improvement on the organization's financial statement. An organization might, for example, successfully attain a dramatic increase in sales volume as a direct result of implementing a strategic system. The strategic system may create an entirely new sales channel to reach customers.

Auction software implemented and marketed by eBay is an example of a strategic system. The strategic software fundamentally changes the way an organization will be run. For a strategic system to be successfully implemented, management and users must be fully involved. Anything less than significant fundamental change with dramatic, measurable results would indicate that the software is a traditional system.

> You should be aware that some software vendors will use claims of strategic value with obscure results to try to sell lesser products at higher profit margins. Your job is to determine whether the organizational objectives have been properly identified and met. Claims of improvement should be verifiable.

Traditional systems provide support functions aligned to fulfill the needs of an individual or department. Examples of traditional systems include general office productivity and departmental databases. The traditional system might provide 18 percent return on investment, whereas a strategic system might have a return of more than 10 times the investment.

Managing Software Quality

Controlling quality is an ongoing process of improving the yield of any effort. True quality is designed into a system from the beginning. In contrast, inspected quality is no more than a test after the fact. This section covers models designed to promote software quality:

- Capability Maturity Model (CMM)
- ISO Software Process Improvement and Capability dEtermination (SPICE)

Let's review the Capability Maturity Model and introduce the related international standards.

Capability Maturity Model

As you may recall from Chapter 3, "IT Governance," the Software Engineering Institute's Capability Maturity Model (CMM) was developed to provide a strategy for determining the maturity of current processes and to identify the next steps required for improvement. The CMM roots are based in lessons learned from assembly-line automation during the U.S. industrial age of the early 1900s. Several analogies exist between CMM and the manufacturing process quality concepts of Walter Shewhart, W.W. Royce, W. Edwards Deming, Joseph Duran, and Philip Crosby. Most of the people who understood the analogy relating manufacturing processes to business processes have long since retired. This promotes a false impression that CMM is new, when it's just new to them. Let's take a quick overview of the levels contained in the CMM model:

Level 0   This level is implied but not always recognized. Zero indicates that nothing is getting done.

Level 1 = Initial   Processes at this level are ad hoc and performed by individuals. Typical characteristics are ad hoc activities, firefighting, unpredictable results, and management activities that vary without consistency.

Level 2 = Repeatable   These processes are documented and can be repeated. Characteristics are more semiformal methods, tension problems between project managers and line managers, inspected quality rather than built in, and no formal priority system.

Level 3 = Defined   These are lessons learned and integrated into institutional processes. Standardization begins to take place between departments with qualitative measurement (opinion of quality). Formal criteria is developed for use in selection processes.

Level 4 = Managed   This level equates to quantitative measurement (numeric measurement of quality). Portfolio management is engrained into all decisions. A formal project priority system is practiced with a Project Management Office (PMO) governing projects.

Level 5 = Optimized   This is the highest level of control with continuous improvement using statistical process control. A culture of constant improvement is pervasive with a desire to fine-tune the last available percentages to squeak out every remaining penny of profit.

The Software Engineering Institute (SEI) estimates that it may take 13 to 25 months to move up to each successive level. It's just not possible to leapfrog over to the next level because of the magnitude of change required to convert the organization's attitude, experiences, and culture. SEI was one of the first organizations to define the evolution of software maturity. The CMM model has been expanded to cover all types of processes used to run a business or a government office.

International Organization for Standardization

A significant number of the best practices for quality in American manufacturing have been adopted by the International Organization for Standardization (ISO). ISO is a worldwide federation of government standard bodies operating under a charter to create international standards in order to promote commerce and reduce misrepresentation. One of the functions of the ISO is to identify regional best practices and promote acceptance worldwide. The original work of Shewhart and derivative works of Crosby, Deming, and Duran focused on reducing manufacturing defects. Their original concepts have been expanded over the last 50 years to include almost all business processes. The CMM represents the best-practice method of measuring process maturity. It makes no difference whether the process is administrative, manufacturing, or software development. ISO has modified the descriptive words used in the levels of the CMM for international acceptance.

As a CISA, you should be interested in three of the ISO standards relating to development and maturity.

ISO 15504: Variation of CMM

The ISO 15504 standard is a modified version of the CMM. These changes were intended to clarify the different maturity levels across different languages and cultures. Notice that level 0 is relabeled as *incomplete*. Level 1 is renamed to indicate that the process has been successfully performed. Level 2 indicates that the process is managed. Level 3 shows that the process is well established in the organization. Level 4 indicates that the process output will be very predictable. Level 5 shows that the process is under a continuous improvement program using statistical process control. Table 5.1 illustrates the minor variations between the CMM and the ISO 15504 standard, also known as SPICE.

TABLE 5.1   CMM Compared to ISO 15504 (SPICE)

CMM Levels	ISO 15504 Levels
0 = process did not occur yet	ISO level 0 = Incomplete
CMM level 1 = Initial	ISO level 1 = *Performed*
CMM level 2 = Repeatable	ISO level 2 = *Managed*
CMM level 3 = Defined	ISO level 3 = *Established*
CMM level 4 = Managed	ISO level 4 = *Predictable*
CMM level 5 = Optimized	ISO level 5 = Optimized

The purpose of ISO 15504 is identical to the CMM. Variations in language forced the ISO version to use slightly different terminology to express their objectives. Let's move on to a quick overview of two ISO quality-management standards.

ISO 9001: Quality Management

The ISO has promoted a series of quality practices that were previously known as ISO 9000, 9001, and 9002 for design, manufacturing, and service, respectively. These have now been combined into the single ISO 9001 reference. Many organizations have adopted this ISO standard to facilitate worldwide acceptance of their products in the marketplace. ISO compliance also brings the benefits of a better perception by investors. Compliance does not guarantee a better product, but it does provide additional assurances that an organization should be able to deliver a better product.

Within the ISO 9001 reference, you will find that a formally adopted quality manual is required by the ISO 9001:2000. The ISO 9001:2000 quality manual specifies detailed procedures for quality management by an organization. The same quality manual provides procedures for strong internal controls when working with vendors, including a formal vendor evaluation and selection process. To ensure quality, the ISO 9001:2000 mandates that personnel performing work shall be properly trained and managed to improve competency. Because an organization claiming ISO compliance is required to have a thoroughly written quality manual in place, an IS audit may request evidence demonstrating that the quality processes are actively used.

 It's important to understand the naming convention of ISO standards. Names of ISO standards begin with the letters *ISO*, which are then followed by the standard's numeric number, a colon (:), and the year of implementation. You would read ISO 9001:2000 as ISO standard 9001 adopted in year 2000 (or updated in year 2000).

ISO 9126: Software Quality

ISO 9126 is a variation of ISO 9001. The ISO standard 9126-2:2003 explains how to apply international software-quality metrics. This standard also defines requirements for evaluating software products and measuring specific quality aspects.

The six quality attributes are as follows:

- Functionality of the software processes
- Ease of use
- Reliability with consistent performance
- Efficiency of resources
- Portability between environments
- Maintainability with regard to making modifications

 You need to know the six major attributes contained in the ISO 9126 standard.

Once again, organizations claiming ISO compliance should be able to demonstrate active use of software metrics and supporting evidence for ISO 9126-2 compliance. You need to remember that no evidence equals no credit.

As a CISA, you should be prepared to identify the terminology used by the CMM and various ISO quality standards. Now that we've reviewed these maturity standards, it is time to mention the matching ISO document-control requirements.

ISO 15489: Records Management

ISO records retention standard 15489:2001 was designed to ensure that adequate records are created, captured, and managed. This standard applies to managing all forms of records and record-keeping policies. It does not matter whether the record format is electronic, printed, or voice. It makes no difference whether the records are used by a public or private organization. The 15489 standard provides the guidance necessary for minimum compliance with ISO 9001 quality standards and records management under ISO 14001. Therefore, an organization must be 15489 compliant to be ISO 9001 or ISO 14001 compliant.

Does it apply to anyone else? The answer is definitely yes. Records management governs the record-keeping practices of any person who creates or uses records in the course of their business activities. It also applies to those activities in which a record is expected to exist. Examples include the following:

- Financial bookkeeping records
- Contracts and business transactions
- Government filings
- Setting policies and operating standards
- Payroll and HR records
- Establishing procedures and guidelines
- Keeping records in the normal course of business

All organizations need to identify the regulations that have bearing on their activities. Record keeping is necessary to document their actions in order to provide adequate evidence of compliance. Remember that no evidence equals no proof, which demonstrates noncompliance. Business activities are defined broadly by ISO to include public administration, nonprofit activities, commercial use, and other activities expected to keep records. All fundraising campaigns fall under the ISO 15489 standard.

A record is expected to reflect the truth of the communications between the parties, the action taken, and the evidence of the event. Records are expected to be authentic with reliable information of high integrity. Auditors need to be aware of the legal challenges whenever records are introduced as evidence in a court of law. Every good defense lawyer will attempt to dispute the authenticity or integrity of each record by allegations of tampering, mishandling, incompetence, or computer system compromise. Without excellent record keeping, the value of the record as evidence may be diminished or completely lost. This is why the chain of custody actually starts with how records are created in the first place.

ISO 15489 is used by court judges and lawyers as the international standard for determining liability in addition to sentencing during prosecution. All organizations, including yours, should have already adopted a records classification scheme (data classification). The purpose is to convey to the staff how to properly protect assorted records. Consider the different requirements for each of the following types of records:

- Trade secrets
- Unfiled patent applications
- Personal information and privacy data such as HIPAA or bank account numbers
- Intellectual property rights
- Commercial contracts (possibly a confidential record) versus government contracts (a public record)

- Financial data
- Internal operating reports
- Privileged information, including consultation with lawyers
- Customer lists and transaction records (including professional certification)
- Retirement and destruction of obsolete information

Record retention systems should be regularly reassessed to ensure compliance. The corresponding reports also need to be protected because they serve as evidence in support of compliance activities. Most of the fraud mentioned in the beginning of this book was discovered and prosecuted under ISO 15489 standards.

> CISA certification is recognized under the ISO 17024 requirements for all bodies issuing professional certification. ISACA complies with the ISO 15489 records management and ISO 17024 professional requirements governing all professional certifications. CISA certification simply meets the minimum standard under ISO 15489 and ISO 17024 for compliance. CISA is not an ISO standard, just ISO standards compliant.

Let's move on now. It is time to discuss the leadership role of management. We will begin with an overview of the steering committee.

Overview of the Steering Committee

The steering committee should be involved in software decisions to provide guidance toward fulfillment of the organizational objectives. We have already discussed the basic design of a steering committee in Chapter 3.

As you may recall, the *steering committee* comprises executives and business unit managers. Their goal is to provide direction for aligning IT functions with current business objectives. Steering committees provide the advantage of increasing the attention of top management on IT. The most effective committees hold regular meetings focusing on agenda items from the business objectives rather than IT objectives. Most effective decisions are obtained by mutual agreement of the committee rather than by directive. The steering committee increases awareness of IT functions, while providing an avenue for users to become more involved. In this chapter, we are focusing on the identification of business requirements as they relate to the choices made for computer software.

As a CISA, you should understand how the steering committee has developed the vision for software to fulfill the organization's business objectives. What was the thought process that led the steering committee to its decision? Two common methods are the use of critical success factors (CSFs) and a scenario approach to planning.

Identifying Critical Success Factors

A *critical success factor (CSF)* is something that must go right every time. To fail a CSF would be a showstopper. The process for identifying CSFs begins with each manager focusing on their current information needs. This thought process by the managers will help develop a current list of CSFs.

Some of the factors may be found in the specific industry or chosen business market. External influences—such as customer perception, current economy, pressure on profit margin, and posturing of competitors—could be another source of factors. The organization's internal challenges can provide yet another useful source. These can include internal activities that require attention or are currently unacceptable.

As an IS auditor, you should remain aware that critical success factors are highly dependent on timing. Each CSF should be reexamined on a regular basis to determine whether it is still applicable or has changed.

Using the Scenario Approach

The *scenario approach* is driven by a series of "what if" questions. This technique challenges the planning assumptions by creating scenarios that combine events, trends, operational relationships, and environmental factors. A series of scenarios are created and discussed by the steering committee. The most likely scenario is selected for a planning exercise.

The major benefit of this approach is the discovery of assumptions that are no longer relevant. Rules based on old assumptions and past situations may no longer apply. The scenario approach also provides an opportunity to uncover the mindset of key decision-makers.

The role of the scenario is to identify the most important business objectives and CSFs. After some discussion, the scenario should reveal valuable information to be used in long-term plans. Remember, the goal is to align computer software with the strategic objectives of the organization, which we will look at next.

Aligning Software to Business Needs

As a CISA, you should understand the alignment of computer software to business needs. Information systems provide benefits by alignment and by impact. *Alignment* is the support of ongoing business operations. Changes created in the work methods and cost structure are referred to as *impact*.

Each organizational project will undergo a justification planning exercise. Management will need to determine whether the project will generate a measurable return on investment. The purpose of this exercise is to ensure that the time, money, and resources are well spent. The basic business justification entails the following four items:

Establish the need   Business needs can be determined from internal and external sources. Internal needs can be developed by the steering committee and by interviewing division managers. Internal performance metrics are an excellent source of information. External sources include regulations, business contracts, and competitors.

Identify the work effort   The next step is to identify the people who can provide the desired results. Management's needs are explained to the different levels of personnel who perform the work. The end-to-end work process is diagrammed in a flowchart. Critical success factors are identified in the process flow. A project plan is created that estimates the scope of the work. This may use traditional project management techniques in combination with the System Development Life Cycle.

see pg
149

Summarize the impact   The anticipated business impact can be presented by using quantitative and qualitative methods. It is more effective to convert qualitative statements into semiquantitative measurements. Semiquantitative measurements can be converted into a range scale of increased revenue by implementing the system or by cost savings. The CISA candidate should recall the discussion in Chapter 2, "Audit Process," regarding the use of semiquantitative measurement with a range scale similar to A, B, C, and F school report card grades.

Present the benefits   Management will need to be sold on the value of the system. The benefits will typically entail promises of eliminating an existing problem, improving competitive position, reducing turnaround time, or improving customer relations.

In this chapter, we are focusing our discussions on computer software. The steering committee should be involved in decisions concerning software priorities and necessary functions. Each software objective should be tied to a specific business goal. The combined input will help facilitate a *buy* versus *build* decision about computer software. Should the organization buy commercial software or have a custom program written? Let's consider the questions to ask in regard to making this decision. The list presented here is for illustration purposes; however, it is similar to the standard line of questions an auditor will ask:

- What are the specific business objectives to be attained by the software? Does a printed report exist?

- Is there a defined list of objectives?

- What are the quantitative and qualitative measurements to prove that the software actually fulfills the stated objectives?

- What internal controls will be necessary in the software?

- Is commercial software available to perform the desired function?

- What level of customization would be required?

- What mechanisms will be used to ensure the accuracy, confidentiality, timely processing, and proper authorization for transactions?

- What is the time frame for implementation?

- Should building the software be considered because of a high level of customization needed or the lack of available software?

- Are the resources available to build custom software?

- How will funding be obtained to pay for the proposed cost?

The steering committee should be prepared to answer each of these questions and use the information to select the best available option. Effective committees will participate in brainstorming workshops with representation from their respective functional areas. The goal is to solicit enough information to reach an intelligent decision. The final decision may be to buy software, build software, or create a hybrid of both.

Organizations may use the answers from the questions asked in conjunction with a written request to solicit offers from vendors. The process of inviting offers incorporates a statement of the current situation with a request for proposal (RFP). The term *RFP* is also related to an invitation to tender (ITT) or request for information (RFI).

RFI/RFP Process

The steering committee charters a project team to perform the administrative tasks necessary for an information request (RFI) or proposal request (RFP). The request is sent to a small number of prospective vendors or posted to the public, depending on the client's administrative operating procedure. An internal software development staff may provide their own proposal in accordance with the RFP or participate on the review team. A typical RFP will contain at least the following elements:

- Cover letter explaining the specific interest and instructions for responding to the RFP
- Overview of the objectives and time line for the review process
- Background information about the organization
- Detailed list of requirements, including the organization's desired service level
- Questions to the vendor about their organization, expertise of specific individuals documented in a *skills matrix*, support services, implementation services, training, and current clients
- Request of a cost estimate for the proposed configuration with details about the initial cost and all ongoing costs
- Request for a schedule of demonstrations and visit to the installation site of existing customers

NOTE All government agencies and many commercial organizations require separation of duties during the bid review process. A professional purchasing manager will become the vendor's contact point to prevent the vendor from having any direct contact with the buyer. The intention is to eliminate any claims of bias or inappropriate influence over the final decision to purchase.

The RFP project team works with the steering committee to formulate a fair and objective review process. The organization may consult ISO 9001:2000 and ISO 9126-2:2003 standards for guidance. The proposed software could be evaluated by using the CMM. In addition, ISACA's Control Objectives for Information and related Technology (CObIT) provides valuable information to be considered when reviewing a vendor and their products.

As an IS auditor, you should remember that your goal is to be thorough, fair, and objective. Care should be given to ensure that the requirements and review do not grant favor toward a particular vendor. The reviews are actually a form of audit and should include the services of an internal or external IS auditor. It is essential that vendor claims are investigated to ensure that the software will fulfill the desired business objectives.

Reviewing Vendor Proposals

The systematic process of reviewing vendor proposals is a project unto itself. Each proposal has to be scrutinized to ensure compliance requirements identified in the original RFP documents provided to the vendor. You need to ask the following questions:

- Does the proposed system meet the organization's defined business requirements?

- Does the proposed system provide an advantage that our competitors will not have, or does the proposed system provide a commodity function similar to that of our competitors?

- What is the estimated implementation cost measured in total time and total resources?

- How can the proposed benefits be financially calculated? The cost of the system and the revenue it generates should be noticeable in the organization's financial statement. To calculate return on investment, the total cost of the system including manpower is divided by the cost savings (or revenue generated) and identified as a line item in the profit and loss statement.

[handwritten margin note: ROI = total cost × cost savings or total cost revenue generated]

- What enhancements are required to meet the organization's objectives? Will major modifications be required?

- What is the level of support available from the vendor? Support includes implementation assistance, training, software update, system upgrade, emergency support, and maintenance support.

- Has a risk analysis been performed with consideration of the ability of the organization and/or vendor to achieve the intended goal?

- Can the vendor provide evidence of financial stability?

- Will the organization be able to obtain rights to the program source code if the vendor goes out of business? *Software Escrow* refers to placing original software programs and design documentation into the trust of a third party (similar to financial escrow). The original software is expected to remain in confidential storage. If the vendor ceases operation, the client may obtain full rights to the software and receive it from the escrow agent. A small number of vendors may agree to escrow the source code, whereas most would regard the original programs as an intellectual asset that can be resold to another vendor.

> Modern software licenses provide only for the right to benefit from the software's use, not software ownership.

One of the major problems in reviewing a vendor is the inability to get a firm commitment in writing for all issues that have been raised. There are major vendors that will respond to the RFP with a lowball offer that undercuts the minimum requirements. Their motive is to win by low bid and then overcharge the customer with expensive change orders to bring the implementation up to the customer's stated objective.

A CISA reviews the documentation of business needs and that of the proposed system. The objective is to ensure that the system is properly aligned to business requirements and contains the necessary internal controls.

Change Management

The accepted method of controlling changes to software is to use a change control board (CCB). Members of the change control board include IT managers, quality control, user liaisons from the business units, and internal auditors. A vice president, director, or senior manager presides as the chairperson. The purpose of the board is to review all change requests before determining whether authorization should be granted. This fulfills the desired separation of duties. Change control review must include input from business users. Every request should be weighed to determine business need, required scope, level of risk, and preparations necessary to prevent failure.

You can refer to the client organization's policies concerning change control. You should be able to determine whether separation of duties is properly enforced. Every meeting should include a complete tracking of current activities and the minutes of the meetings. Approval should be a formal process. The ultimate goal is to prevent business interruption. This is performed by following the principles of version control, configuration management, and testing. We discuss separation of duties with additional detail in Chapter 6, "IT Service Delivery."

Managing the Software Project

Let's move on to a discussion of the challenges in managing a software development project. In this section, you'll learn about the two main viewpoints for managing software development. You'll then take a closer look at the role of traditional project management in software development.

Choosing an Approach

There are two opposing viewpoints on managing software development: evolutionary and revolutionary.

The traditional viewpoint promotes *evolutionary development*. The evolutionary view is that the effort for writing software code and creating prototypes is only a small portion of software development. The most significant work effort occurs during the planning and design phase. The evolutionary approach works on the premise that the number one source of failures is a result of errors in planning and design. Evolutionary software may be released in *incremental stages* beginning with a selected module used in the architecture of the first release. Subsequent modules will be added to expand features and improve functionality. The program is not finished until all the increments are completed and assembled. The evolutionary development approach is designed to be integrated into traditional software life cycle management.

🌐 **Real World Scenario**

An Example of Evolutionary Development

The creation of this Study Guide began with the evolution of study objectives. A prototype outline was created. The outline was refined and later divided into chapters. Each chapter was written as a separate increment. Our technical editor and developmental editor provided independent review of every page. The results of the review were compared to the objectives. Deficiencies were identified for correction and then rechecked. Finally, the finished chapters were assembled to create a working draft. The draft was edited in two more iterations until the final edition was obtained. Each version of this Study Guide will be updated following a similar process until retirement.

The opposing view is that a revolution is required for software development. The invention of advanced fourth-generation programming languages (4GL) empowers business users to develop their own software without the aid of a trained programmer. This approach is in stark contrast to the traditional view of developing specific requirements with detailed specifications before writing software. The *revolutionary development* approach is based on the premise that business users should be allowed to experiment in an effort to generate software programs for their specific needs. The end user holds all the power of success or failure under this approach. The right person might produce useful results; however, the level of risk is substantially greater. The revolutionary approach is difficult to manage because it does not fit into traditional management techniques. Lack of internal controls and failure to obtain objectives are major concerns in the revolutionary development approach.

> **NOTE** The analogy to revolutionary development would be to tell a person to go write their own software. A tiny number of individuals would have the competence necessary to be successful.

Using Traditional Project Management

Evolutionary software development is managed through a combination of the System Development Life Cycle (SDLC) and traditional project management. We covered the basics of project management using the Project Management Institute (PMI) methodology in Chapter 1, "Secrets of a Successful IS Auditor." The SDLC methodology—which is discussed in detail in the following section—addresses the specific needs of software development, but still requires project management for the nondevelopment business management functions.

When using traditional project management, the advantages include Program Evaluation Review Technique (PERT) with a Critical Path Methodology (CPM). You will need to be aware of the two most common models used to illustrate a software development life cycle: the waterfall model and the spiral model.

Waterfall Model

Evolutionary software development is an iterative process of requirements, prototypes, and improvement. In the 1970s, Barry Boehm used W.W. Royce's famous waterfall diagram to illustrate the software development life cycle. A simplified version of the *waterfall model* used by ISACA is shown in Figure 5.1.

FIGURE 5.1   Simplified waterfall model (W.W. Royce)

— *mgmt of* Implies one version of software – from start to finish

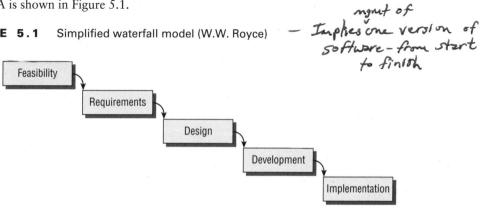

Based on the SDLC phases, this simplified model assumes that development in each phase will be completed before moving into the next phase. That assumption is not very realistic in the real world. Changes are discovered that regularly require portions of software to undergo redevelopment.

Boehm's version of the software life cycle model contained seven phases of development. Each of the original phases included validation testing with a backward loop returning to the previous phase. The backward loop provides for changes in requirements during development. Changes are cycled back to the appropriate phase and then regression-tested to ensure that the changes do not produce a negative consequence. Figure 5.2 shows Boehm's model as it appeared in 1975 from the Institute of Electrical and Electronics Engineers (IEEE).

Spiral Model

About 12 years later, Boehm developed the *spiral model* to demonstrate the software life cycle including evolutionary versions of software. The original waterfall model implied management of one version of software from start to finish. This new spiral model provided a simple illustration of the life cycle that software will take in the development of subsequent versions. Each version of software will repeat the cycle of the previous version while adding enhancements. Figure 5.3 shows the cycle of software versions in the spiral model.

FIGURE 5.2   Boehm's modified waterfall model

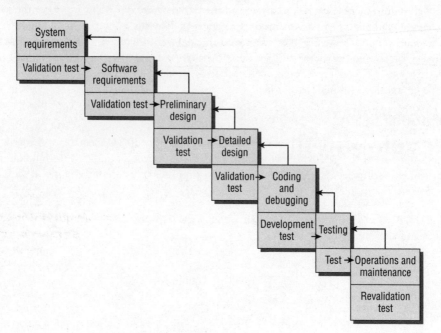

FIGURE 5.3   Spiral model for software life cycle

RA - Risk Analysis

Notice how the first version starts in the planning quadrant of the lower left and proceeds through requirements into risk analysis and then to software development. After the software is written, we have our first version of the program. The planning cycle then commences for the second version, following the same path through requirements, risk analysis, and development. The circular process will continue for as long as the program is maintained.

Overview of the System Development Life Cycle

All computer software programs undergo a life cycle of transformation during the journey from inception to retirement. The System Development Life Cycle (SDLC) used by ISACA is designed as a general blueprint for the entire life cycle. A client organization may insert additional steps in their methodology. This international SDLC model comprises seven unique phases with a formal review between each phase (see Figure 5.4).

Auditors will encounter SDLC models with only five or six phases. Upon investigation, it becomes obvious that someone took an inappropriate short-cut, skipping one of the seven phases. A smart auditor will pick up on this lack of understanding to investigate the organization further and discover any additional weakness created by this mistake. Failure to implement all seven phases indicates that a major control failure is present.

Let's start with a simple overview of SDLC:

Phase 1: Feasibility Study   This phase focuses on determining the strategic benefits that the new system would generate. Benefits can be financial or operational. A cost estimate is compared to the anticipated payback schedule. Maturity of the business process and personnel capabilities should be factored into the decision. Three primary goals in phase 1 are as follows:

- Define the objectives with supporting evidence. New policies might be created to demonstrate support for the stated objectives.
- Perform preliminary risk assessment.
- Agree upon an initial budget and expected return on investment (ROI).

Phase 2: Requirements Definition   The steering committee creates a detailed definition of needs. We discussed this topic a few pages ago. The objective is to define inputs, outputs, current environment, and proposed interaction. The system user should participate in the discussion of requirements. In phase 2 the goals include the following:

- Collect specifications and supporting evidence.
- Identify which standards will be implemented in the specifications.
- Create a quality control plan to ensure that the design remains compliant to the specifications.

- ERD
- Flowcharts   ~ see pg 279
- Security controls   • user acct ctrls

FIGURE 5.4 Seven phases of SDLC

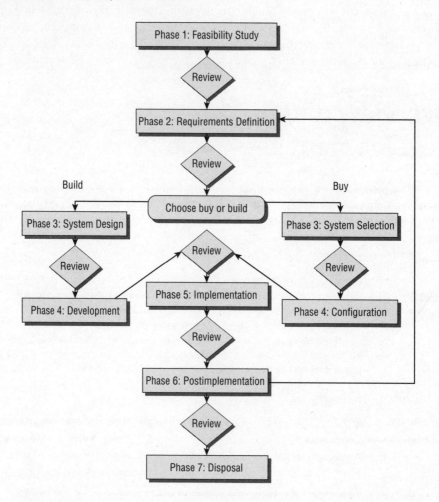

Phase 3: System Design or Selection In phase 3, the objective is to plan a solution (strategy) using the objectives from phase 1 and specifications from phase 2. The decision to buy available software or build custom software is based on management's determination regarding fitness of use. The client moves in one of two possible directions based on whether the decision is to build or to buy:

Build (Design) It was decided that the best option is to build a custom software program. This decision is usually reached when a high degree of customization is required. Efforts focus on creating detailed specifications of internal system design. Program interfaces are identified. Database specifications are created by using entity-relationship diagrams (ERDs). Flowcharts are developed to document the business logic portion of design.

[handwritten margin note: Market Research or trade study or Assessment of Alternatives]

Buy (Selection)   The decision is to buy a commercial software program. The RFP process is used to select the best vendor and product available based on the specification created in phase 2.

Phase 4: Development or Configuration   The client continues down one of two possible directions based on the earlier decision of build versus buy:

Build (Development)   The design specifications, ERD, and flowcharts from phase 3 will become the master plan for writing the software. Programmers are busy writing the individual lines of program code. Prototypes are built for functional testing. Software undergoes *certification testing* to ensure that everything will work as intended without any surprises or material defects. Component modules of software will be written, tested, and submitted for user approval. The first stages of *user acceptance testing* occur during this phase.

Buy (Configuration)   Customization is typically limited to program configuration settings with a limited number of customized reports. The selection process for customization choices should be a formal project.

Phase 5: Implementation   This phase is common to both buy and build decisions. The new software is installed using the proposed production configuration. Everyone from the support staff to the user is trained in the new system. Final user acceptance testing begins. The system undergoes a process of final certification and management accreditation prior to approval for production use:

- Certification is a technical process of testing the finished design and the integrity of the chosen configuration.   *[handwritten: — pg 294]*

- Accreditation represents management's formal acceptance of the complete system as implemented.   *[handwritten: executive   — pg 297]*

Accreditation includes the environment, personnel, support documentation, configuration, and technology. With formal management accreditation, the approved implementation may now begin production use (go live).

Phase 6: Postimplementation   After the system has been in production use, it is reviewed for its effectiveness to fulfill the original objectives. The implementation of internal controls is also reviewed. System deficiencies are identified. Goals in phase 6 include the following:

- Compare performance metrics to the original objectives.

- Analyze lessons learned.

- Re-review the specifications and requirements annually.

- Implement requests for new requirements, updates, or disposal.

The last step in phase 6 is to perform an ROI calculation comparing cost to the actual benefits received. Over time, the operating requirements will always change.

Phase 7: Disposal   The final phase is the proper disposal of equipment and purging of data. Assets must undergo a formal review process to determine when the system can be shut down for dismantling. Legal requirements may prohibit the system from being completely shut down. In phase 7, the goals include the following:

- Archive old data.

- Mark retention requirements and specify destruction date (if any). Be aware that certain types of records may need to be retained forever.

- Management signs a formal authorization for the disposal and formally accepts any resulting liability.

If approved for disposal, the system data must be archived, remnants purged from the hardware, and equipment assets disposed of in an acceptable manner. Nobody within the organization should profit from the system disposal.

Be careful not to confuse the SDLC with the Capability Maturity Model (CMM). A system life cycle covers the aspects of selecting requirements, designing software, installation, operation, maintenance, and disposal. The CMM focuses on metrics of maturity. CMM can be used to describe the maturity of IT governance controls.

Now that you have a general understanding of the SDLC model, we will discuss the specific methods used in each phase. These methods are designed to accomplish the stated SDLC objectives.

Phase 1: Feasibility Study

The *Feasibility Study phase* begins with the initial concept of engineering. In this phase, an attempt is made to determine a clearly defined need and the strategic benefits of the proposed system. A business case is developed based on initial estimates of time, cost, and resources. To be successful, the feasibility study will combine traditional project management with software development cost estimates.

Let's start with the business side of feasibility. The following points should be discussed and debated, and the outcome agreed upon with appropriate documentation:

- Perception of need. Describe the present situation while defining a specific need to be met.

- Link the need to a specific mission objective within the long-term strategy.

- State the desired outcome.

- Identify specific indicators of success and indicators of failure.

- Perform a preliminary risk assessment. The outcome should include a statement of the security classification necessary if the decision is to proceed. Will it be common knowledge, or will it involve business secrets, classified data, or the need for other special handling?

- Make an assessment of alternatives (AoA). Determine formal and informal criteria in support of the decision for whichever option is selected as the best choice. Document all the answers.

- Prepare a preliminary budget for investment review. Traditional techniques need to be combined with an expert estimation of software development costs.

The most common model for estimating software development cost is the constructive cost model, which uses an estimated count of lines of program code and Function Point Analysis. Let's begin with the Constructive Cost Model.

Software Cost Estimation

The *Constructive Cost Model (COCOMO)* was developed by Boehm in 1981. This forecasting model provides a method for estimating the effort, schedule, and cost of developing a new software application. The original version is obsolete because of evolution changes in software development. COCOMO was replaced with COCOMO II in 1995.

The COCOMO II model provides a solid method for performing "what if" calculations that will show the effect of changes on the resources, schedule, staffing, and predicted cost. The COCOMO II model deals specifically with software programming activities but does not provide a definition of requirements. You must compile your requirements before you can use either COCOMO model. COCOMO II templates are available on the Internet to run in Microsoft Office Excel.

The COCOMO II model permits the use of three internal submodels for the estimations: Application Composition, Early Design, or Post Architecture. Within the three internal submodels, the estimator can base their forecast on a count of source lines of code or Function Point Analysis.

Source Lines Of Code (SLOC) forecasts estimates by counting the individual lines of program source code regardless of the embedded design quality. This method has been widely used for more than 40 years and is still used despite advances with 4GL programming tools. It is important for you to understand that counting lines of code will not measure efficiency. The most efficient program could have fewer lines of code, and less-efficient software could have more lines. Having a program with few lines of program code typically indicates that the finished software will run faster. Smaller programs also have the advantage of being easier to debug.

Function Point Analysis (FPA) is a structured method for classifying the required components of a software program. FPA was designed to overcome shortfalls in the SLOC method of counting lines in programs. The FPA method (see Figure 5.5) divides all program functions into five classes:

- External input data from users and other applications
- External output to users, reports, and other applications
- External inquiries from users and other applications
- Internal file structure defining where data is stored inside the database
- External interface files defining how and where data can be logically accessed

The five classes of data are assigned a complexity ranking of low, average, or high. The ranking is multiplied by a numerical factor and tallied to achieve an estimate of work required (see Figure 5.6).

FIGURE 5.5   Concept overview of Function Point Analysis

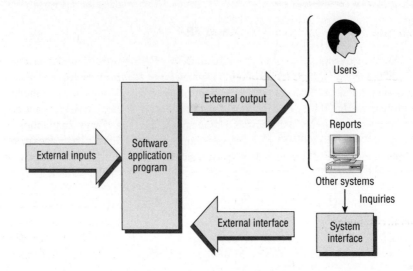

FIGURE 5.6   Calculating function points

Function Class	Complexity Ranking							
	LOW		**MEDIUM**		**HIGH**		Adjusted Weight
Counts per	Count	Multiplier	Count	Multiplier	Count	Multiplier	
External inputs	____	X 3 =____	____	X 4 =____	____	X 5 =____	
External outputs	____	X 4 =____	____	X 5 =____	____	X 6 =____	
External inquiries	____	X 3 =____	____	X 4 =____	____	X 5 =____	
Internal files	____	X 7 =____	____	X 9 =____	____	X 12 =____	
External interfaces	____	X 5 =____	____	X 7 =____	____	X 9 =____	
					Total Adjusted Value =		

FPA is designed for an experienced and well-educated person who possesses a strong understanding of functional perspectives. Typically this is a senior-level programmer. An inexperienced person will get a false estimate. This model is intended for counting features that are specified in the early design. It will not create the initial definition of requirements. Progress can be monitored against the function point estimate to assess the level of completion. Changes can be recorded to monitor scope creep. _Scope creep_ refers to the constant changes and additions that can occur during the project. Scope creep may indicate a lack of focus, poor communication, lack of discipline, or an attempt to distract the user from the project team's inability to deliver to the original project requirements.

You should acquire formal training and consult a Functional Point Analysis training manual if you are ever asked to perform FPA.

Real World Scenario

Getting a Fair Estimate with SLOC and FPA

Estimation of software projects by using either the SLOC or FPA method will render an incorrect estimate if you are using multiple levels of programming languages such as 3GL and 4GL. It is important to mention that programmers refer to each programming language generation as a unique level (third generation equals third level, fourth generation equals fourth level, and so on). We discuss the different levels of programming languages later in this chapter, in the subsection "Writing Program Code." As an auditor, you should simply be aware that the issue does exist and will have a negative effect on the accuracy of an estimate. Each generation level of programming language used will have to be estimated separately to achieve reasonable accuracy.

The overall cost budget should include an analysis of the estimated personnel hours by function. The functions include clerical duties, administrative processes, analysis time, software development, equipment, testing, data conversion, training, implementation, and ongoing support.

Phase 1 Review and Approval

Best practices in software development require a review meeting at the end of each phase to determine whether the project should continue to the next phase. The review is attended by an executive chairperson, project sponsor, project manager, and the suppliers of key deliverables.

The meeting is opened by the chairperson. The project manager provides an overview of the business case and presents the initial assessment reports. Presentations are made to convey the results of risk management analysis for the project. Project plans and the initial budget are presented for approval. Meeting attendees review the phase 1 plans to ensure that the skills and resource requirements are clearly understood.

At the end of the phase review meeting, the chairperson determines whether the review has passed or failed based on the evidence presented. In the real world, a third option may exist: deciding that the project should be placed on temporary hold and reassessed at a future date. All outstanding issues must be resolved before granting approval to pass the phase review.

Formal approval is evidenced by a signed project charter accompanied by a preliminary statement of work (SOW). The project manager is responsible for preparing the project plan documentation. The sponsor grants formal authority by physically signing the documents. Without either of these documents, chances are a dispute will evolve into a conflict that compromises the project. A signed charter and SOW are frequently used to force cooperation by other departments or to prevent interruptions by politically motivated outsiders.

Auditor Interests in the Feasibility Study Phase

In the Feasibility Study phase, you should review the documentation related to the initial needs analysis. As an auditor, you review the risk mitigation strategy. You ask whether an existing system could have provided an alternative solution. The organization's business case and cost justifications are verified to determine whether their chosen solution was a reasonable decision. You also verify that the project received formal management approval before proceeding into the next phase.

Phase 2: Requirements Definition

The *Requirements Definition phase* is a documentation process focused on discovering the proposed system's business requirements. Defining the requirements requires a broader approach than the initial feasibility study. It is necessary to develop a list of specific conditions in which the system is expected to operate. Criteria need to be developed to specify the input and output requirements along with the system boundaries. Let's review the basic steps that can help define the requirements:

- Functional statement of need as described in phase 1.

- Competitive market research. Has the auditee defined what the customer wants? What does the competition offer?

- Identification of legal requirements for data security. Somebody needs to download each regulation and create a list of specific *shall* points referenced by page, paragraph, and line number. This will eliminate scope creep and quell attempts to subvert the project scope. Look at this tiny example relating to compliance under the Payment Card Industry (PCI) laws.

PCI Compliance Mapping Report

Item	Requirement/Specification	Action
6.1	Patch management tracking	Create formal log and pretes
8.3	Implement two-factor authentication	Install digital certificates with
10.2	Develop configuration standards for all components, firewalls, wireless	Implement form configuration m
10.7	Retain audit history for at least one year	Back up and archive Syslog
11.2	Quarterly testing of system	
11.5	Implement file integrity monitoring	

- Identification of the type of reports required for legal filings, both government and customer.

- Formal selection of security controls. Ignorance of the law is a wonderful way to assure a speedy conviction. The same concept applies to apathy.

- Software conversion study. How will the data be migrated to the new system? When will the switch to production occur?

Data Migration Plan

- Cost benefit analysis to justify selection of features or functionality. It's doubtful that the first version will have all the features that everyone imagined. However, security and controls should never be compromised.

- Risk management plan. A trade-off always occurs in relation to cost, time, scope, and features. An example is to limit internal use to a physical area rather than to violate security by allowing remote access. Later versions may include the additional security controls necessary for safe remote access. The number of uses may be initially restricted. Technical risks must be managed.

- Analysis of impact with business cycles. How could the software be developed, tested, and later deployed without conflicting with the business cycle? Traditional project management plans are created to control the tasks.

In this phase of gathering detailed requirements, the entity-relationship diagram (ERD) technique is often used. The ERD helps define high-level relationships corresponding to a person, data element, or concept that the organization is interested in implementing. ERDs contain two basic components: the entity and the relationship between entities.

An *entity* can be visualized as a database comprising reports, index cards, or anything that contains the data to be used in the design. Each entity has specific attributes that relate to another entity. Figure 5.7 shows the basic design of an ERD.

FIGURE 5.7   Entity-relationship diagram

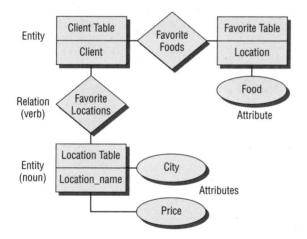

It is a common practice to focus first on defining the data that will be used in the program. This is because the data requirement is relatively stable. The purpose of the ERD exercise is to design the data dictionary. The *data dictionary* provides a standardized term of reference for each piece of data in the database. After the data dictionary is developed, it will be possible to design a database schema. The *database schema* represents an orderly structure of all data stored in the database.

After the ERD is complete, it is time to begin construction of transformation procedures used to manipulate the data. The transformation procedures detail how data will be acquired and logically transformed by the application into usable information. Transformation procedures exceed the capability of fourth-generation (4GL) programming tools. It takes old-fashioned knowledge of the business process and the aid of a skilled software engineer (programmer) to refine an idea into usable logic. Business objectives should always win over the programmer's desire to show off the latest tools, or worse, to subvert a good idea that requires more effort.

High-level flowcharts define portions of the required business logic. A low-level flowchart illustrates the details of the transformation process from beginning to end. The flowchart concept will map each program process, decision choice, and handling of the desired result. The flowchart is a true blueprint of the business logic used in the program. Figure 5.8 shows a simple program flowchart.

FIGURE 5.8   Program flowchart

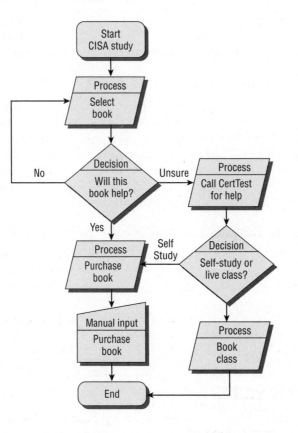

The ERD and flowcharts from phase 2 provide the foundation for the system design in SDLC phase 3. Security controls are added into the design requirement during phase 2. You should understand that internal controls are necessary in all software designs.

Internal Controls

The internal controls for user account management functions are included in this phase to provide for separation of duties:

Preventative controls such as data encryption and unique user logins are specified.

Detective controls for audit trails and embedded audit modules are added.

Corrective controls for data integrity are included. Features that are not listed in the requirements phase will most likely be left out of the design.

It is important that the requirements are properly verified and supported by a genuine need. Each requirement should be traced back to a source document detailing the actions necessary for performance of work or legal compliance.

A gap analysis is used to determine the difference between the current environment and the proposed system. Plans need to be created to address the deficiencies that are identified in the gap analysis. The deficiencies may include personnel, resources, equipment, or training.

Phase 2 Review and Approval

At the end of phase 2, a phase 2 review meeting is held. This meeting is similar in purpose to the previous phase 1 review. This time, the review focuses on success criteria in the definition of software deliverables and includes a timeline forecast with date commitments. The proposed system users need to submit their final feedback assessment and comments before approval is granted to proceed into phase 3. The purpose of the phase 2 review meeting is to gain the authority to proceed with preliminary software design (phase 3). Once again, all outstanding issues need to be resolved before approval can be granted to proceed to the next phase.

Auditor Interests in the Requirements Definition Phase

You should obtain a list of detailed requirements. The accuracy of the requirements can be verified by a combination of desktop review of documentation and interviews with appropriate personnel. Conceptual ERD and flowchart diagrams should be reviewed to ensure that they address the needs of the user.

The Requirements Definition phase creates an output of detailed success factors to be incorporated into the acceptance test specifications. As an auditor, you will verify that the project plans and estimated costs have received proper management approval.

Phase 3: System Design

The System Design phase expands on the ERD and initial concept flowcharts. Users of the system provided a great deal of input during phase 2, which is then used in this phase for in-depth flowcharting of the logic for the entire system. The general system blueprint is decompiled into smaller program modules.

pg 279>

Internal software controls are included in the design to ensure a separation of duties within the application. The work breakdown structure is created for effective allocation of resources during development. Design and resource planning may be one of the longest phases in the planning cycle. Quality is designed into a system rather than inspected after the fact.

see pg 34

The 1-10-100 rule provides an excellent illustration of the costs of quality-related problems. Figure 5.9 shows that for every dollar spent preventing a design flaw in planning, design, and testing, the organization can avoid the additional cost of noncompliance failures:

- $100 to correct a problem reaching the customer
- $10 to correct a problem or mistake during production
- $1 to prevent a problem

FIGURE 5.9   1-10-100 rule of quality

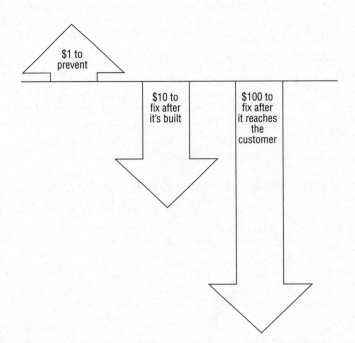

According to quality guru Philip Crosby, there are two primary components of quality—the extra expenses known as the price of nonconformance, and the savings in the price of conformance:

Price of nonconformance (PONC)   This represents the added costs of not doing it right the first time. Think of this as the extra time and cost of rework or uncompensated warranty repair. It's not uncommon for the overall cost of the rework to exceed your original profits.

Price of conformance (POC)   Avoiding the headache by doing it right the first time is known as the price of conformance (POC). Employee training and user training is a POC expense that conserves time and money by avoiding the added cost of nonconformance (PONC).

Quality failures will occur because of variation. Poor planning, flawed design, and poor management are the most frequent sources of failure. We can categorize quality failures as common or specific in nature:

Common quality failures   Common failures are the result of inherent variations inside the process, which are difficult to control. Let's consider writing the software programs for a robotic assembly line. Extreme heat affects the finish or adhesion of drying paint. New people may have been hired during production without enough training or experience. This type of common failure is inside the production process, which can affect the quality of a paint job. Management would be held responsible for fixing the problem because it was inside the process. It's management's responsibility to design a solution to prevent the problem.

Special quality failures   Special failures occur when something changes outside the normal process. What if the weather was fine, but the paint finish came out wrong? Upon investigation, it was discovered that the problem resulted from using the wrong type of paint or an unapproved substitution. This special failure is something that the workers should be able to fix with their purchasing agent by working with their vendor. It's more of a supply issue than a process problem. Improvements in employee discipline to follow change control for substitution would prevent the defect.

Customer Satisfaction

The best way to create loyal customers is to exceed their expectations. It's important to deliver within the original scope to satisfy customer needs. Failing project managers may make the dangerous mistake of attempting to switch the deliverables by using a bait-and-switch technique referred to as *gold plating*. If you gold-plate doggy poop, it's nice and shiny, but still just fancy poop.

We discussed Deming's planning cycle in Chapter 2 as it related to audit planning. Figure 5.10 shows that the Plan-Do-Check-Act cycle also applies to software design.

FIGURE 5.10   Planning for quality during design (Plan, Do, Check, Act)

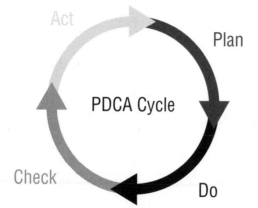

Phase 3 is the best time for the software developer to work directly with the user. Most professional programmers encourage the progression of meetings necessary to refine the design before a single line of program code is written. A series of meetings are necessary to help convert user ideas and whims into a structured set of deliverables. Time should be spent on creating screen layouts, designing formats, and matching their desired workflow. Initial plans for developing a prototype in phase 4 are created during this System Design phase.

A significant output during the design phase is to identify how each of the software functions can be tested. Data derived during design provides the base criteria for behavior testing and inspection during phase 4 development testing. Data from user meetings provides a solid basis for user acceptance testing. The documentation created during the design phase initially serves as the road map for programmers during development. Later the phase 3 design documentation will provide a foundation for support manuals and training.

Reverse Engineering and Reengineering

In certain situations, *reverse engineering* may be used to accelerate the creation of a working system design.

The 2003 movie *Paycheck* starring Ben Affleck was themed around reverse engineering a competitor's product to jumpstart product development for Affleck's employer.

Reverse engineering is a touchy subject. A software decompiler will convert programs from machine language to a human-readable format. The majority of software license agreements prohibit the decompiling of software in an effort to protect the vendor's intellectual design secrets.

An existing system may loop back into phase 3 for the purpose of *reengineering*. The intention would be to update the software by reusing as many of the components as is feasible. Depending on the situation, reengineering may support major changes to upgrade the software for newer requirements.

Software Design Baseline

At the end of the System Design phase, a *software baseline* is created from the design documents. The baseline incorporates all the agreed-upon features that will be implemented in the initial version of software (or next version in the case of reengineering). This baseline is used to gain approval for a design freeze. The design freeze is intended to lock out any additional changes that could lead to scope creep.

Phase 3 Review and Approval *of System Design*

The phase 3 review meeting starts with a review of the detailed design for the proposed system. Engineering plans and project management plans are reviewed. Cost estimates are compared to the assumptions made in the business case. A comparison is made between the intended features and final design. Final system specifications, user interface, operational support plan, and test and verification plans are checked for completeness. Data from the risk analysis undergoes a review based on evidence. Approval is requested to proceed to the next phase. Once again, all outstanding issues must be resolved before proceeding to the next phase. Each of the stakeholders and sponsors should physically sign a formal approval of the design before allowing it to proceed into development. This administrative control enforces accountability for the final outcome.

Auditor Interests in the System Design Phase

You need to review the software baseline and design flowcharts. The design integrity of each data transaction should be verified. During the design review, you verify that processing and output controls are incorporated into the system. Input from the system's intended power users may provide insight into the effectiveness of the design.

It is important that the needs of the power users are implemented during the design phase. This may include special functions, screen layout, and report layout. You should have a particular interest in the logging of system transactions for traceability to a particular user. You look for evidence that a quality control process is in use during the software design activities. It is important to verify that formal management approval was granted to proceed to the next phase.

WARNING   A smart auditor is wary of systems being allowed to proceed into development without formal approval. The purpose of IT governance is to enforce accountability and responsibility. Even the smallest, most insignificant system represents an investment of time, resources, and capital. None of these should be wasted, squandered, or misused.

Phase 4: Development

Now the time has come to start writing actual software in the *Development phase*. This process is commonly referred to as *coding* a program. Design planning from previous phases serves as the blueprint for software coding. The systems analysts support programmers with ideas and observations. The bulk of the work is the responsibility of the programmer who is tasked with writing software code.

Implementing Programming Standards and Quality Control

Standards and quality control are extremely important during the Development phase. A talented programmer can resolve minor discrepancies in the naming conventions, data dictionary, and program logic. Computer software programs will become highly convoluted unless the programmer imposes a well-organized structure during code writing. Unstructured software coding is referred to as *spaghetti bowl programming*, making reference to a disorganized tangle of instructions.

The preferred method of organizing software is to implement a top-down structure. *Top-down structured programming* divides the software design into distinct modules. If top-down program structures were diagrammed, the result would look like an inverted tree. Within the tree, individual program modules (or subroutines) perform a unique function. Modules are logically chained together to form the finished software program. The modular design exponentially improves maintainability of the finished program. Individual modules can be updated and replaced with

783-7292

Also, easier to debug - pg 291

relative ease. By comparison, an unstructured spaghetti bowl program would be a nightmare to modify. Modular design also permits the delegation of modules to different teams of programmers. Each module can be individually tested prior to final assembly of the finished program.

Adhering to the Development Schedule

The software project needs to be managed to ensure adherence to the planned schedule. Scope creep with unforeseen changes can have a devastating impact on any project. It is common practice to allow up to a 10 percent variance in project cost and time estimates. In government projects, the variance is only 8 percent.

The development project will be required to undergo *management oversight review* if major changes occur in assumptions, requirements, or methodology. Management oversight review would also be warranted if the total program benefits or cost are anticipated to deviate by more than 8 percent for government or 10 percent in industry. The project schedule needs to be tightly managed to be successful. The change control process should be implemented to ensure that necessary changes are properly incorporated into the software development phase.

A *version control* system is required to track progress with all of the minor changes that naturally occur daily during development.

Writing Program Code

The effort to write program code depends on the programming language and development tool selected. Examples of languages include Common Business Oriented Language (COBOL), C language, Java, the Beginner's All-purpose Symbolic Instruction Code (BASIC), and Visual Basic. The choice of programming languages is often predetermined by the organization. If the last 20 years' worth of software was developed using COBOL, it might make sense to continue using COBOL.

Understanding Generations of Programming Languages

Computer programming languages have evolved dramatically over the past 50 years. The early programming languages were cryptic and cumbersome to write. This is where the term *software coding* originated. Each generation of software became easier for a human being to use. Let's walk through a quick overview of the five generations of computer programming languages:

First-generation programming language   The first-generation computer programming language is machine language. *Machine language* is written as hardware instructions that are easily read by a computer but illegible to most human beings. First-generation programming is very time-consuming but was useful enough to give the computer industry a starting point. The first generation is also known as 1GL. In the early 1950s, 1GL programming was the standard.

Second-generation programming language   The second generation of computer programming is known as *assembly language*, or 2GL. Programming in assembly language can be tedious but is a dramatic improvement over 1GL programming. In the late 1950s, 2GL programming was the standard.

Third-generation programming language   During the 1960s, the third generation (3GL) of programming languages began to make an impact. The third generation uses English-like statements as commands within the program, for example, if-then and goto. Examples of third-generation program languages include COBOL, Fortran, BASIC, and Visual Basic. Another example is the C programming language written by Ken Thompson and Dennis Ritchie. Most 3GL programs were used with manually written databases.

Fourth-generation programming language   During the late 1970s, the fourth-generation programming languages (4GL) began to emerge. These include prewritten database utilities. This advancement allowed for rapid development due to an embedded database or database interface. The fourth-generation design is a true revolution in computer programming. The programmer creates a template of the software desired by selecting program actions within the development tool. This is referred to as *pseudocoding* or *bytecoding*. Their development tool will convert bytecode into actual program code. An untrained user could write a program that merely formats reports on a screen and allows a software-generation utility to write the software automatically. Figure 5.11 illustrates the general concept of pseudocoding inside a 4GL development tool.

FIGURE 5.11   Pseudocoding inside a 4GL development tool

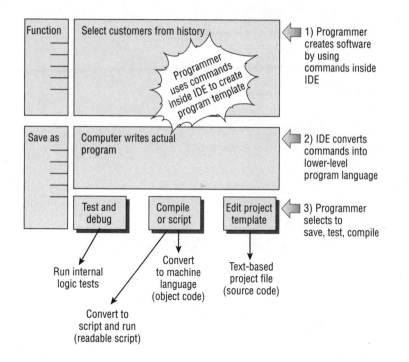

A 4GL is designed to automate reports and the storage of data in a database. Unfortunately, it will not create the necessary business logic without the aid of a skilled programmer. An amateur using a 4GL can generate nice-looking form screens and databases. But the amateur's program will be no more than a series of buckets holding data files. The skilled programmer will be required to write transformation procedures (program logic) that turn those buckets of data into useful information. Examples of commercial 4GL development tools include Sybase's PowerBuilder, computer-aided software engineering (CASE) tools, and YesSoftware's Code Charge Studio. 4GL is the current standard for software development.

Fifth-generation programming language   The fifth-generation programming languages (5GLs) are designed for artificial-intelligence applications. The 5GL is characterized as a learning system that uses fuzzy logic or neural weighing algorithms to render a decision based on likelihood. Google searches on the Internet use a similar design to assess the relevance of search results.

Figure 5.12 shows the hierarchy of the different generations of programming languages.

FIGURE 5.12   Generation levels of programming languages

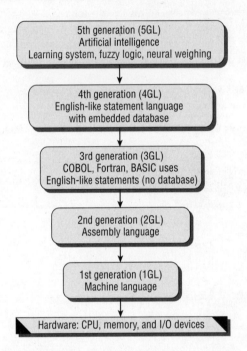

5th generation (5GL)
Artificial intelligence
Learning system, fuzzy logic, neural weighing

4th generation (4GL)
English-like statement language
with embedded database

3rd generation (3GL)
COBOL, Fortran, BASIC uses
English-like statements (no database)

2nd generation (2GL)
Assembly language

1st generation (1GL)
Machine language

Hardware: CPU, memory, and I/O devices

Using Integrated Development Environment Tools

After the programming language has been selected, the next step is to choose the development tool. There are still some programmers able to sit down and write code manually by using the knowledge contained in their head. This type of old-school approach usually creates very efficient programs with the smallest number of program lines.

The majority of programmers use an advanced fourth-generation software code program to write the actual program instructions. This advanced software enables the programmer to focus on drawing higher-level logic while the computer program creates the lower-level set of instructions similar to what a manual programmer would have done. Simply put, a computer program writes the computer program.

The better development tools provide an integrated environment of design, code creation, and debugging. This type of development tool is referred to as an *integrated development environment (IDE)*.

One of the best examples of an IDE is the commercial CASE tool software. You need to understand the basic principles behind CASE tools. CASE tools are divided into three functional categories that support the SDLC phases of 2, 3, and 4, respectively: – *see pg 270*

Upper CASE tools   Business and application requirements can be documented by using upper CASE tools. This provides support for the SDLC phase 2 requirements definition. Upper CASE tools permit the creation of ERD relationships and logical flowcharts.

Middle CASE tools   The middle CASE tools support detailed design from the SDLC phase 3. *= System Design or Selection* These tools aid the programmer in designing data objects, logical process flows, database structure, and screen and report layouts.

Lower CASE tools   The lower CASE tools are software code generators that use information from upper and middle CASE to write the actual program code.

You can see the relationship of CASE tools to the SDLC phases in the following diagram.

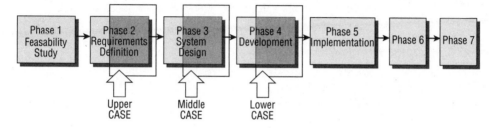

Using Alternative Development Techniques

As a CISA, you should be aware of two alternative software development methods: Agile and Rapid Application Development (RAD). Each offers the opportunity to accelerate software creation during the Development phase. The client may want to use either of these methods in place of more-traditional development. Both offer distinct advantages for particular situations. Both also contain drawbacks that should be considered.

Agile Development Method

Agile uses a fourth-generation development environment to quickly develop prototypes within a specific time window. The Agile method uses time-box management techniques to force individual iterations of a prototype within a very short time span. Agile allows the programmer to just start writing a program without spending much time on preplanning documentation. The drawback of Agile is that it does not promote management of the requirements baseline. Agile does not enforce preplanning. Some programmers prefer Agile simply because they do not want to be involved in tedious planning exercises.

When properly combined with traditional planning techniques, Agile development can accelerate software creation. Agile is designed exclusively for use by small teams of talented programmers. Larger groups of programmers can be broken into smaller teams dedicated to individual program modules.

Agile
to develop
prototype

 The primary concept in Agile programming is to place greater reliance on the undocumented knowledge contained in a person's head. This is in direct opposition to capturing knowledge through project documentation.

Rapid Application Development Method

A newer integrated software development methodology is *Rapid Application Development (RAD)*, which uses a fourth-generation programming language. RAD has been in existence for almost 20 years. It automates major portions of the software programmer's responsibilities within the SDLC.

RAD supports the analysis portion of SDLC phase 2, phase 3, phase 4, and phase 5. Unfortunately, RAD does not support aspects of phase 1 or phase 2 that are necessary for the needs of a major enterprise business application. RAD is a powerful development tool when coupled with traditional project management in the SDLC.

RAD supports
development and portions
of analysis

Building Prototypes

During the Development phase, it is customary to create system prototypes. A *prototype* is a small-scale working system used to test assumptions. These assumptions may be about user requirements, program design, or the internal logic used in critical functions. Prototypes usually are inexpensive to build and are created over a few days or weeks. The principal advantage of a prototype is that it permits change to occur before the major development effort begins.

Prototypes seldom have any internal control mechanisms. Each prototype is created as an iterative process, and the lessons learned are used for the next version. A successful prototype will fulfill its mission objective and validate the program logic. All development efforts will focus on the production version of the program after the prototype has proven successful.

WARNING There is always a serious concern that a working prototype may be rushed into production before it is ready for a production environment. Internal controls are typically absent from prototypes or insufficient for production use.

Compiling Software Programs *(interpreted)*

A computer program can be written as either a program script or a compiled program. *Program scripts* are written like movie scripts and contain instructions for the computer to follow. The programmer uses a scripting language such as Perl, JavaScript, or Visual Basic. The advantage of scripts is that they are easy to maintain. The program script is stored in human-readable form. The disadvantage is that program scripts are run by using a script interpreter. The script interpreter is slow to execute. A script interpreter compiles a temporary version of the scripted program as it is running on the computer. The scripted program is considered a crystal box, or white box, because a trained human being could read the program script and decipher the structural design of the program. *source code to object code*

Compiling programs is a process of converting human-readable instructions into machine-language instructions for execution. The human-readable version of software is referred to as *source code*. A computer programmer will compile programs to increase the execution speed of the software. A simple way to remember the definition is that source code is what the compiler started with. The compiled program is unreadable to humans. This unreadable version of the program is referred to as the *object code*.

Think of object code as the output object created by the compiler. Compiling software provides rudimentary protection of the program's internal logic from inquisitive people. The disadvantage of compiled programs is that reviewing the internal structural design would be practically impossible. The compiled program is essentially a black box. Figure 5.13 shows the different creation paths for compiled programs and program scripts.

Computer programmers will usually compile multiple versions of a program during development and debug testing. Without proper management, this scenario could become a nightmare. How do you ensure that the latest copy is in use? It is the job of configuration and version management to provide a traceable history of multiple versions of computer software.

Implementing Configuration and Version Management

Managing a changing environment is a significant challenge. Constant changes make it difficult to remain organized and coordinated, no matter what you're trying to accomplish. But suppose, for example, that a company wants to release a new software product. During software development, multiple programmers may be working on different modules of the same program. For this example, let's name the program *Report Whiz*. The programming used in the individual modules for Report Whiz may have different levels of maturity to consider. For example, the screen-printing utility might be in version 1.1, while the report-writer module may be in version 6.0. By combining these two modules into Report Whiz, the result will become our finished configuration for Report Whiz version 1.0. Does it sound like this could get confusing?

FIGURE 5.13   Compiled programs versus scripts

Well, it can. That is the challenge. How will the company manage and track all these different components with the correct versions?

Version control is the tracking of all the tiny details inside both major and minor version changes. By tracking these tiny details, we can understand the internal construction of our finished software configuration. Detailed version control is the foundation of configuration. With version control, we have a detailed configuration that is ready to be managed.

Configuration management is focused on management exercising control over the finished software version. The primary elements of configuration management are control, accounting and reporting.

Configuration Control   The control of all the design documentation, design changes, all specifications, parts and assemblies and manufacturing processes. Specifications include the informal notes, observations and advice written on the documentation.

Configuration Accounting   Timely reporting of any modifications to the originally agreed design documentation which occurs after the initial design release review. It's possible for engineering to design a product the organization is unable to build. CM accounting tracks the compromises and modifications necessary to produce a working product.

Configuration Reporting   This encompasses all the elements of control and accounting, going further to report the configuration as-built and delivered to the customer including any change or maintenance to the product after delivery. It becomes the life history of the product from conception through the useful service life until disposal.

The auditor needs to investigate how the client manages and records changes to a configuration. After obtaining this understanding, you need to ask who authorizes the changes. Finally, you need to ask how the changes are tested and accepted for production use.

Fortunately, there are software tools to assist software developers in managing version control. One of the most common commercial applications for tracking version changes is known as a Poly Version Control System (PVCS). PVCS software contains a database that manages the tracking of programming changes and revisions of software code. In industry slang, we may refer to the PVCS function as a _Top Copy_ or _Latest Copy_ system.

The purpose of PVCS is to ensure that each programmer is working with the latest version of the software program code. During the day, the programmer checks out the latest copy of the program code from the PVCS database. The checkout process is similar to the checkout of books from your local library. The PVCS database is designed to synchronize the work of every programmer. A programmer checks out the latest software version and then uses that version to start writing program code. Each day the programmer returns their finished work to the PVCS-controlled library by using a check-in process. During check-in, the PVCS database informs the programmer with a list of any related changes made by the other programmers. This provides coordination for the team of programmers.

🌐 Real World Scenario

Automated Version Control Tools

Version control software is available from multiple vendors. In addition to the commercial PVCS, other common software options include the Source Code Control System (SCCS), the Concurrent Version System (CVS), and the Revision Control System (RCS). There are license versions that are free for noncommercial use. Version control software was written to track revision changes in lines of programming code. The usage has grown to include tracking changes in server configuration, web pages, legal contracts, and complex printed documents.

Debugging Software

A vast assortment of errors occur naturally during the development process. These errors may include syntax errors, inconsistent naming structures, logic errors, and other common mistakes. Most online development tools will assist the programmer by debugging some of the errors. Using top-down structured programming techniques makes it easier to troubleshoot problems.

pg 283

Testing the Software

During the Development phase, it is imperative that tests and verification plans are created to debug the software programs. Tests should be performed to validate processing accuracy. Test plans are created to uncover program flaws, manage defects, and search for unintended results. A *logic path monitor* can be used to provide programmers with information about errors in program logic.

During development, software testing occurs at multiple levels. Any deficiencies or errors need to be discovered before the finished program is implemented. There are four basic types of test methods:

1) **White-box testing (for uncompiled programs)**   Also known as *crystal-box testing* because it allows the programmer to view and to test the logic of procedures and data calculations. The intention is to verify each transformation process as data passes through the system. This can be an expensive and time-consuming process. This testing is commonly used for unit and integrity testing of self-developed software. Legal obstacles concerning ownership and proprietary rights may be encountered when attempting to use this type of testing on commercial software. Script-based software is human readable and therefore can be crystal-box tested.

2) **Black-box testing (for compiled programs)**   Intended to test the basic integrity of system processing. This is the most common type of test. The process is to put data through the system to see whether the results came out as expected. You do not get to see the internal logic structures; all you get is the output. Commercial software is compiled into a form that is nonreadable by humans. Black-box testing is the standard test process to run when you buy commercial software. Black-box testing is often used for user acceptance tests.

3) **Functional, or validation, testing (for all programs)**   Compares the system against the desired functional requirements. We want to see whether the product has met our objectives for its intended use.

4) **Regression testing**   Tests changes against all the existing software models to detect any conflicts. The purpose of regression testing is to ensure that modifications do not damage existing processes. During regression testing, internal controls are retested for integrity.

All tests should follow a formal procedure in a separate testing environment. The following types of structured technical tests occur during the Development phase:

- Program module tests (unit test)
- Program interface tests (integration test)
- Internal security control tests
- Processing volume tests (stress test of maximum workload)
- Performance tests
- Integrity tests (processing accuracy)
- Recovery tests (to verify data integrity after failures)
- Sociability tests (to determine whether the program will have conflicts with another program on the system)
- Preliminary user acceptance testing (to approve the system functionality as delivered)

The test plan and results of each test need to be carefully documented. In environments where strong controls are desired, archiving test records for future reference is necessary. After all the technical tests have been completed to satisfaction, it is time for the most important test of all. The last test in the Development phase is <u>user acceptance testing.</u> This is when the project sponsor determines whether to accept the system. If accepted, the system moves into the Implementation phase. *— production environment, final user acceptance testing, certification + accreditation, training*

Software certification testing in phase 4 development measures the coded software against phase 2 specifications, phase 3 design, effective implementation of internal controls, and fitness of use for production.

↳ pg 279

Phase 4 Review and Approval

Once again, a phase review meeting is held. The phase 4 review focuses on the software being delivered by the programmers for the users. The Development phase has now concluded. The finished software is compared for compliance against the original objectives, requirements list, and design specifications. Evidence is presented from test results, which should indicate that the software is performing as expected. Plans for ongoing operation are compared to the previous gap analysis to uncover any remaining deficiencies. After all outstanding issues have been resolved, the plan is put before the chairperson for approval to proceed to the Implementation phase.

Auditor Interests in the Development Phase

As an auditor, your prime interest in the Development phase is to verify that a quality control process has been utilized to develop an effective computer program. All internal control mechanisms should be present in the finished program. The programs have undergone debugging with formal testing. Evidence from test results is expected to provide assurance of system integrity. Support documentation has been created in conjunction with <u>an operational support plan for production use.</u> The finished software capabilities have been verified for compliance to the original objectives. The user has accepted the finished computer program. And finally, management has granted formal approval for the software to be implemented.

— pg 279

Phase 5: Implementation *(production)*

The computer program is fully functional by the time it reaches phase 5. This phase focuses on final preparations for actual production use. Version control is a formal requirement to ensure that the right version of software is running for production.

Software Release and Patch Management

Computer software is authorized for distribution via a release process. Software is released from development and authorized to be installed for production use. Each vendor has their own release schedule.

Computer software releases fit one of the following profiles:

Major release   A significant change in the design or generation of software is known as a *major release*. Major releases tend to occur in the interval of 12 to 24 months.

Minor release or update   *Updates* are also known as *minor releases*. Their purpose is to correct small problems after the major release has been issued.

Emergency software fixes   These are known as *program patches*, or *hot fixes*. Emergency fixes should be tested prior to implementation. Every fix should undergo a pretest, even if the test is informal. Emergency software fixes may introduce new problems that are unexpected. Every emergency fix must undergo change control review to determine the following:

- What to remediate
- Whether the change should remain in use

The computer program is now a finished version ready for final acceptance testing and user training. The next step for implementation is to load the client's current data.

Data Conversion   + Data Migration Plan

A data conversion plan is developed to migrate existing data into the new system. Great care needs be taken to prevent loading garbage data into the new system. A successful technique to prevent loading garbage is to reload selected portions of shared data directly from the latest source file. An example is reloading a manufacturing kit list directly from the latest engineering design. This would eliminate the migration of outdated information into the new system.

A list of data files eligible for migration is developed. Each file is verified against the system design requirements. If the file is required, procedures would be created to scrub (remove) outdated entries from each file. It is a common practice to hire a data entry service to assist in data conversion. Sometimes it is easier to re-create a file with minimal data, as opposed to the tedious job of grooming existing files. The programmers may write a data conversion utility to reformat existing files, such as a customer list, into the new system. A comprehensive data conversion plan is always required.

System Certification

Certification is a technical process of testing against a known reference. The system is tested to ensure that all internal controls are present and functioning correctly. The system certification is based on measuring compliance to a particular requirement. Systems used in the government are required to undergo a certification process before being placed in production use.

Common Criteria (ISO 15408)

The original U.S. computer controls (Trusted Computer System Evaluation Criteria, or TCSEC) have been merged with developments from the European IT security countries (Information Technology Security Evaluation Criteria, or ITSEC) to form an international common criteria for evaluating computer security. This common criteria has been adopted by ISO as Common Criteria standard 15408. CC is the nickname for the complete set of common criteria. Several countries have adopted the CC, including Canada, France, Germany, the Netherlands, the United Kingdom, and the United States. All the ISO member countries are expected to use 15408.

The CC brings the benefits of accumulated wisdom with a flexible approach to standardization and evaluation assurance. Flexibility is provided in this specification of secure products by using seven standardized <u>evaluation assurance levels (EALs)</u>. Official testing is provided by an independent lab certified under the ISO 17025 standard for laboratories and testing facilities.

Within the CC is a well-defined set of IT security requirements for perspective products and systems. Here's how it works:

A system to be evaluated is referred to as the *target of evaluation* (TOE). Each TOE has security threats, objectives, requirements, and a summary of functions to be measured. Every TOE contains <u>security functions (TSF)</u> to be relied upon in the enforcement of the TOE's desired <u>security policy (TSP)</u>.

The grouping of evaluation test objectives is defined as the *protection profile* (PP). A variety of protection profiles have already been created for systems used as workstations, firewalls, network servers, secure databases, and so forth. A PP is intended to be reusable and effective in defining the security requirements for the system.

The party requesting evaluation simply picks a PP (protection desired), identifies the TOE (system to test), and pays for the tests to be performed to the appropriate EAL (assurance level 1 through 7). The goal is to make it easier for a vendor to advertise systems appropriate to the client needs. Let's take a brief overview of the elements to be tested.

TOE security functionality   The following is a sample list of the components used for security functionality. Each component represents a family of subcomponents required to obtain the EAL:

- Security management features
- Identification and authentication
- User data protection
- Communications with nonrepudiation
- Cryptographic support
- Audit
- Privacy

- Resource utilization
- TOE access (sessions and access parameters)
- Trusted paths/channels
- Protection of TOE security functions

Evaluation of protection profiles and security targets   All PPs and their associated security target (ST) evaluations contain the following criteria, each with underlying subcomponents of security that must be evaluated. The following list is a quick summary:

- Evaluation assurance
- Configuration management to verify the TOE's current configuration at the time of testing. Changes would require retesting to maintain the EAL.
- Secure system delivery installation and setup measures to ensure that the system is not compromised during these events.
- Assurance maintenance
- PP evaluation to demonstrate that requirements are consistent and technically sound.
- Development of the target's security functionality (TSF).
- Guidance documents for use by the users and system administrators.
- Life cycle support for the remediation of flaws found by TOE users.
- Security target evaluation to demonstrate that requirements are consistent and technically sound. This includes the TOE description, security environment, security objectives, and PP claims, the TOE security requirements, and the TOE summary security specification.
- Formal vulnerability assessment to identify vulnerabilities through covert channel analysis, configuration analysis, and examination of the strength of security mechanisms with the identification of flaws introduced during the development of the TOE.
- Tests demonstrating the coverage and depth of developer testing with requirements for independent testing.

Internal control standards require business systems to undergo a certification process. It may be an internal review or a formal review such as the Common Criteria. Every computer system and application should undergo a certification process prior to use in a production environment.

> You can find more information on system certification procedures in the U.S. Federal Information Security Management Act (FISMA) guide available through http://csrc.nist.gov and in the ISACA CObIT. Also visit www.commoncriteriaportal.org for information on system certification under the ISO 15408 Common Criteria. System certification is required by most regulations.

As a CISA, you will be required to undergo update and renewal training to keep your certification current. Existing information systems should also go through a recertification process to remain up-to-date. You should be concerned about systems that the customer has not certified for production, or systems for which the certification was not maintained and is now out-of-date.

System Accreditation

The next step after certification is *accreditation.* After passing the certification test, management determines how or where the system may be used. Accreditation is an administrative process based on management's comfort level with demonstrated performance or fitness of use (management acceptance). Management is responsible for accreditation of systems during the system's useful life cycle. The designated accreditation authority is a senior executive who will accept full responsibility for the consequences of operating the overall system (often the CIO or agency head). Accreditation is by site, type of use, or system.

Accreditation may be in the form of approval to operate in limited use for 90–180 days or (full) annual accreditation. The approved implementation may begin production use. Systems must be recertified and reaccredited annually.

User Training

— regular users
— admins, power users

Now it is time to train the users and system operators. Hopefully, the organization had some of its power users actively involved in prior phases. The new system's power users were usually involved in the phase 2 design. If so, these power users can serve as instructors and mentors to the new system users. A user training plan is necessary to ensure that everyone receives appropriate training for their role. During the training process, each user should receive specific instructions on the new functions of the system. Care should be taken to explain which of the old procedures will no longer be used. The training plan needs to provide for ongoing training of new users.

Special training is required for the system custodians (system administrator, database administrator, and computer console operator). The custodians need to be trained for normal operations and emergency procedures unique to the system. After the people are trained, it is time to move the system into production use.

Go Live and Changeover

The new system has been running separately from production up to this point. A plan is necessary for switching production processing from the old system to the new system. This process is commonly described by the term *changeover, cut over,* or *go live.* The changeover can be a substantial challenge depending on the complexity of the environment. A comprehensive migration plan is required in order to be successful. It is imperative that risk management is used to select and sequence changeover plans.

migrated + read-only data vs. new r/w data

(pg 71, 72,)
(144, 158, 162)

You need to be aware of the following changeover techniques:

Parallel operation   The old and new systems are run in parallel, usually for an extended period of time. Dual operation allows time to compare the operational differences between the two systems. During parallel operation, software developers can fine-tune any software discrepancies. The primary advantage of parallel operation is the ability to validate the results obtained from the new system against the accuracy of the old system. With parallel operation comes the added burden of simultaneously supporting two major systems. At a future date, the old system will be brought to an idle state while the new system takes over all production processing. Depending on data retention requirements, the field system may still need to be operational for a number of years. The switch from parallel operation to single operation may be performed by using a phase changeover or hard changeover.

Overall, parallel operation is an excellent technique with the lowest level of risk. Making changes in small doses is always advisable. Major failures during changeover can be a real career killer.

Phased changeover   In larger systems, converting to the new system in small steps or phases may be possible. This may take an extended period of time. The concept is best suited to either an upgrade of an existing system, or to the conversion of one department at a time. The phased approach creates a support burden similar to that of parallel operation. A well-managed phased changeover presents a moderate level of risk.

Hard changeover   In certain environments, executing an abrupt change to the new system may be necessary. This is known as a hard changeover, a full change occurring at a particular cutoff date and time. The purpose is to force migration of all the users at once. A hard changeover may be used after successful parallel operation or in times of emergency. One of the biggest concerns about a hard changeover is that it can cause major disruption of normal operations. For this reason, the hard changeover presents the highest level of risk. Risk mitigation activities are of the highest priority whenever the hard changeover technique is chosen. pgs 71, 144-162

Phase 5 Review and Approval

This is the last review meeting, and it is concerned with the implementation of a new system. The chairperson opens the meeting with the project sponsor present. The project manager makes a presentation of project updates and achievements. Progress is reported against the plan objectives. Attention then focuses on a review of outstanding engineering issues, system performance as realized in production use, and ongoing service and support plans. The final risk analysis is presented for management approval. After approval is obtained, the system is authorized for production use.

The 2006 movie *Man of the Year*, starring Robin Williams with Christopher Walken and Laura Linney, is based on a fictional electronic election. During testing of a new electronic voting machine, a software flaw is discovered in the tally of votes.

The development manager ignores the programmer's warning and allows the system to be used in full production. A hidden system flaw results in an unlikely candidate winning the popular vote in error. Ultimately, the truth is discovered, and the voting machine company is ruined and publicly disgraced. Proper certification testing was not performed before the system was placed into production. This fictional story bears striking resemblance to news stories about actual flaws detected in electronic voting machines.

Auditor Interests in the Implementation Phase

The system should be installed and fully operational by the Implementation phase. Support documentation must be in place prior to the system entering production use. All of the appropriate personnel will have been trained to fulfill their roles. The system has completed a final user acceptance test. A production operating schedule should now be in use. The completed system will have undergone a technical certification process. Management reviews the system's fitness of use for a particular task or environment. Management accredits the system for a specified use, based on fitness of use for a particular task or by site location.

You need to verify that appropriate quality control procedures have been executed in support of these objectives. You also need to verify that formal management approval was obtained before the system entered production use. Any deficiencies in management approval should be reported to the audit committee or project oversight.

Phase 6: Postimplementation

The sixth SDLC phase deals with project closure and the administrative process of verifying that the system meets the organizational objectives. A complete project management review is performed. Evidence is checked to verify that the system was implemented as originally designed, with all necessary internal controls present. The results of actual use are compared to the anticipated benefits originally cited in phase 1. The objective is to ensure that these benefits were actually realized by the finished system implementation. Performance measurements are reviewed. A celebration may be in order if the performance exceeded original expectations. Otherwise, a remediation plan may be created to improve current performance.

Additional phase 6 activities will include the following:

- Continuous monitoring to ensure that the controls are still effective. Periodic testing and reporting are necessary.

- Annual review of new requirements. This includes changes in legal regulations, system connections, and patterns of use. Consider the impact of HIPAA requirements mandating increased confidentiality for protecting access to data by unauthorized internal users. The PCI regulations force truncation of account numbers and mandate use of encryption. It's interesting how Amazon.com changed its software to be compliant, yet most hotels violate PCI regulations by retaining card numbers on file and improperly handling paper records by retaining the full account number plus card identification code (three-digit CID number). The associated hotel operating procedures instruct staff to continue violating PCI in spite of the enormous consequences of the law. Just because it used to be done that way does not mean it continues to be done that way.

- Application system review. This includes investigating risks related to system availability (uptime, downtime) and to integrity issues such as incomplete or unauthorized transactions. This is a major area of interest for the auditor. Integrity and security are temporary because of the constant changes made by the IT staff and by vendor updates. Whether *when you fix something, you always gotta fix something else!*

small or large, a change will always introduce another set of issues. This is referred to as *the law of unintended consequences.*

- System update. Will the newer version of software be installed? Changing versions of the operating system or the application may be a significant project. The updates need to undergo a full certification (recertification) and accreditation process prior to production implementation. Smart CIOs and IT managers have already implemented separate systems for testing and production. The costs were easily justified by comparing the cost of downtime against doing it right the first time.

- Environment changes. Changes in physical controls and personnel can have a major impact on overall control. Administrative policies may need to be added or refined to accommodate changes to the physical area. This could include overtaxing the generator capacity, testing aging batteries on the UPS, or other repairs that have not been performed. More training may be needed to keep the staff up-to-date. Staff rotation is just one manner in which special skills may become stale or lost.

- Replacement or migration to new systems.

Phase 6 Review Meetings

Periodic reviews are necessary to verify that the system is maintained in a manner that supports the original objectives and controls. The review should occur at least annually or following a significant change in the business, regulatory climate, or application itself. You may need to utilize the services of a professional expert to conduct the postimplementation review.

You need to remain aware of the conditions necessary to safely rely on using the work of others. The client will frequently request the auditor to use reports from internal staff in order to reduce audit costs. We discussed this issue in Chapters 1 and 2.

Auditor Interests in the Postimplementation Phase

As an auditor, you review evidence indicating that the system objective and requirements were achieved. You should pay attention to users' overall satisfaction with the system. You should review evidence indicating that a diligent process of support and maintenance is in use. In this phase, you review system audit logs and compare them to operational reports.

Auditors want to know whether support personnel are actively monitoring for error conditions. A process of incident response and change control should be in use. Management must demonstrate that they are aware of system limitations with regard to the changing requirements of the organization. Management needs to be cognizant of any deficiencies requiring remediation.

In addition, management and the audit committee should remain aware of any external issues that may dictate system modification or removing the application from service. Examples include changes in regulatory law governing minimum acceptable internal controls. A perfect example is the current trend for strong data encryption to be implemented to protect the privacy of individuals. Previously the concerns were focused on using encryption during external data transmission. The latest requirement is for data in databases and on backup tapes to be stored in encrypted form. The loss of unencrypted data will soon carry harsh penalties.

Phase 7: Disposal

This is the last phase of the SDLC life cycle. After the system has been designated to be removed from service, the security manager needs to perform an audit of the system components and remaining data. The goals of this final stage are to prevent accidental loss. Objectives include the following points:

- Information preservation. All data and programs need to be archived for long-term storage.

- Media sanitation. After the standing data has been removed, the system is decommissioned with the intention of shutdown.

- Hardware and software disposal. Policies and procedures need to exist for the assurance that every disposal is properly managed. No one should profit from the disposal of assets. It's important that the system shutdown does not violate document retention requirements.

A formal authorization from the system owner is required before initiating the disposal phase. Accounting will need to transfer the assets out of inventory. The system owner, accreditation manager, and custodian are to sign the official order moving the system from service. This is the evidence that each has performed their appropriate duties.

Auditor Interests in the Disposal Phase

Evidence should exist to document the disposal process and the records available about prior disposals. The objective is to determine whether the process was correctly followed. A quick check of the asset tags and financial records will help determine the truth. Look to see whether the disposed asset is still shown to hold value in the accounting records. Is it still on the books? Check their plans to preserve the old data. Did the auditee do a good job? Last of all, the auditor looks for evidence that the media was properly sanitized before disposal.

Overview of Data Architecture

A chapter on software development would not be complete without a discussion of the different types of data architecture. The selection of data architecture depends on multiple influences, often including the desires and objectives of the system designer. This section focuses on the fundamentals of data architecture.

Databases

A *database* is simply an organized method for storing information. Early databases were composed of index cards. Some of you may recall using the manual card catalog at the local library to look up the location of a particular book. Later, the library's manual card catalog system was automated with a computer database. Data may be organized into a table rows and columns similar to an Excel spreadsheet.

Databases are designed by using one of two common architectures:

DODB   A data-oriented database (DODB) contains data entries of a fixed length and format. The information entered into a data-oriented database is predictable.

OODB   An object-oriented database (OODB) does not require a fixed length, nor a fixed format. In fact, the object-oriented database was designed for data of an unpredictable nature.

> You may find that some people refer to the two common database architectures as a data-oriented structured database (DOSD) and an object-oriented structured database (OOSD).

Let's start the discussion with an overview of the data-oriented database.

Data-Oriented Database

The first type of database is designed around data in a predefined format, that is, numbers or characters of a particular length. A perfect example is the typical web form or Excel spreadsheet. This DODB the simplest type of database to create.

For this example, we would like to start with a simple database for client entertainment. Say that you have a few key clients to entertain. Your firm wants to ensure that you build rapport by inviting the client to join you in their favorite activities whenever possible.

The first step is to define the data to be recorded in the database. In the SDLC model, this would be part of phase 2, the Requirements Definition phase. Follow along by using Figure 5.14 as we explain the key points.

Let's start by defining a database table of rows and columns to hold the clients' contact information. The first table is named `client_table`. This will hold the name, address, phone number, and email address of every client.

Next, build a table for each location where you may take the client to be entertained. This is called `locations_table`. We have added a space to record the average price for this location and a space to record the specialty of the house.

A third table is created to keep track of all of the favorites: `favorites_table` could be used to record favorite food, a game such as billiards, sporting events, and so forth. One of the objectives in the DODB is to divide information into multiple tables that are relatively static. This allows the system to perform a basic search very fast and not have to process all the data at once. The standardization and removal of duplicates is referred to as *database normalization.*

Now you have your tables ready to store information. The next step is to link tables together with a referential link or relation. This is where the term *relational* enters into the description of the database: An item of data in one table relates to data contained in a separate table. Every entry in the database must have at least one required item to show that the entry actually exists. For example, an account number or a person's name would be required for each entry in the database, even if you don't have all the information. This single required entry is referred to as the *primary key.* Data items used to link to tables are referred to as *foreign keys.* The idea is that other data is foreign to the first table. Data that you can search is called a *candidate key* to the search. The purpose of using the term *key* is to illustrate that it would be impossible to unlock the information unless we know what to use as the key.

To be usable, a database must also have *referential integrity.* This means that data is valid across the linked entries (keys) in two tables. Take a look at Figure 5.15, and you will notice the reference lines drawn between client ID and location ID. This diagram is a primitive ERD.

FIGURE 5.14   Example of client entertainment database

Entity - Relationship Diagram

Name: Client Entertainment

Data elements hold a relationship to more data

FIGURE 5.15   Example database showing data relationships

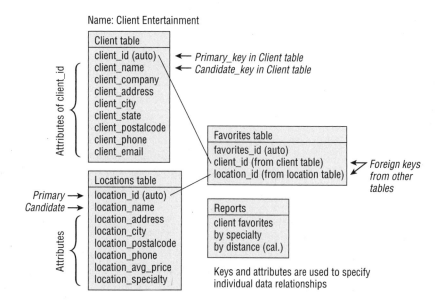

Keys and attributes are used to specify individual data relationships

Another way to view the database is to consider a box of index cards. Each entry is the equivalent of a separate index card. The box of index cards is referred to as the table. A table is made up of rows and columns, like an Excel spreadsheet. Computer programmers may use the term *tuple* in place of the word *row*. Figure 5.16 shows the database row, or tuple, as it would appear on index cards.

FIGURE 5.16 Database row, also known as a tuple

Tuples are the same as rows in a database.

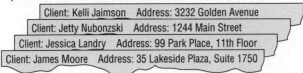

Client: Kelli Jaimson   Address: 3232 Golden Avenue
Client: Jetty Nubonzski   Address: 1244 Main Street
Client: Jessica Landry   Address: 99 Park Place, 11th Floor
Client: James Moore   Address: 35 Lakeside Plaza, Suite 1750

The actual database displays its contents as rows and columns. It is also common to hear the term *attribute* as a synonym for a database column. Figure 5.17 shows the columns, or attributes, as they would appear on the computer screen.

FIGURE 5.17 Database columns, also known as attributes

Database columns are also known as attributes.

ID	Name	Address	City	State
003691	CertTest Training Center	1701 W. Northwest Hwy	Grapevine	TX
014753	CertTest Training Center	320 E. Warm Springs	Las Vegas	NV
062291	CertTest Training Center	1616 King Street	Alexandria	VA
073441	CertTest Training Center	41st St	Miami	FL

Unique identifier

Attributes of primary key

In the illustration, you can see that the ID number is used as a unique identifier (primary key) for each entry. Using a unique ID number allows duplicate names to appear within the database. This is valuable if you have the same company listed with multiple shipping addresses. The unique ID number also permits a name to be updated without any headaches. A common example is to change a maiden name to a married name, or vice versa as the case may be.

In summary, the DODB is designed to be used when the structure and format of your data is well known and predictable. What about data whose structure and format is unpredictable?

What about a database that stores documents, graphics, and music files simultaneously? Well, that is the very challenge that led programmers to develop the object-oriented database.

Object-Oriented Database

In a data-oriented database, the program procedures and data are separate. An object-oriented database (OODB) is the opposite. In an OODB, the data and program method are combined into an object. Think of programmed objects as tiny little people or animals with their own way of doing things. Each programmed object has its own data for reference and its own method of accomplishing a required task. Figure 5.18 shows the basic internal design of program objects.

FIGURE 5.18   Concept overview of program objects

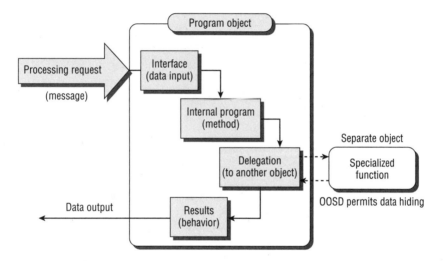

The number one advantage of using programmed objects is that you can delegate work to another object without having to know the specific procedure or characteristics in advance. An example is the computer display settings in the Microsoft operating system. Microsoft XP and Office are examples of object-oriented programs. When Microsoft Word was written, for example, the program did not need to know the details of the display screen. The Word program would simply delegate screen output to an object specified by the screen display setting. A configuration file would exist that contains the setting SET DISPLAY=*vendors_device_driver*. The hardware manufacturer for the display would write an object or driver to paint the image on the screen. The whole object-oriented design lends a great deal of flexibility for modular change.

Object-oriented programming is extremely powerful, and the functional design can be confusing to a novice. Objects are grouped together in an *object class*. An object class is quite similar to a particular class of economy automobiles or class of luxury automobiles, for example. The reference to class indicates the object's position in the hierarchy of the universe. Figure 5.19 shows an example of object classes.

FIGURE 5.19   Example of object classes

Examples of OOSD classes

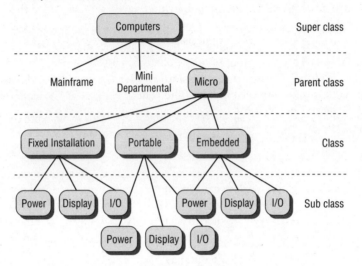

Database Transaction Integrity

Transaction management refers to the computer program's capability to deal with any failure in the logical data update operations used for a particular transaction. Integrity could be damaged if an incomplete transaction was permanently recorded into the database. This is commonly referred to as the ACID model for database integrity. *ACID* stands for atomicity, consistency, isolation, and durability.

- *Atomicity refers to the transaction being "all or nothing."* On the failure of a transaction, the change is backed out of the database, and the data is restored to its original state of consistency.

- Isolation means that each transaction operates independently of all others. A transaction must finish before another transaction can modify the same data.

- After a transaction is completed, the data must remain. This is referred to as durability.

This capability is based on a transaction log used with a *before-image* journal and *after-image* journal. The journals act as a temporary record of work in progress. A version of the database entry before the update is recorded is the before-image. Changes made are held in the after-image. The transaction can be reversed (undone) until the transaction is actually committed (written) to the master file. Once committed, the transaction is then deleted from the journals. A real-world example can be found in the redo and back-out capabilities of the MySQL Max database. Many databases use a *transaction processing monitor (TP monitor)* to ensure that database activity does not overload the processing capacity of the available hardware.

not always (handwritten annotation)

Decision Support Systems

see AHP
Analytic Hierarchy Process

Advancements in computer programming technology and databases have led to the creation of decision support systems. A *decision support system (DSS)* is a database that can render timely information to aid the user in making a decision. There are three basic types of decision support systems: *see definition of decision trees – pg 478*

Reference by context   This type of primitive decision support system supplies the user with answers based on an estimated level of relevance. The overall value is low to moderate.

Colleague, or associate, level   The colleague level provides support for the more tedious calculations but leaves the real decisions to the user.

Expert level   It has been reported in graduate studies that the mind of an average expert contains more than 50,000 points of data. By comparison, a colleague or associate might possess only 10,000 points of data. The expert system is usually written by capturing specialized data from a person who has been performing the desired work for 20 or 30 years. This type of information would take a human a significant amount of time to acquire. It is also possible that the events are so far apart that it would be difficult to obtain proficiency without the aid of a computer.

Every decision support system is built on a database. The data in the database is retrieved for use by the program rules, also known as heuristics, to sort through the knowledge base in search of possible answers. The heuristic program rules may be based on a fuzzy logic using estimation, means, and averages to calculate a likely outcome. The programmers refer to the process as *fuzzification* and *defuzzification* depending on whether we are sharpening the average with a stratified mean or derating the average. The meaning of information in the knowledge base can be recorded into a linkage of objects and symbols known as semantic networks. Another technique is to use weight averages in program logic designed to simulate the path of synapses in the human brain.

Let's look at the common terminology used with decision support systems:

Data mining   After the database and rules are created, the next step in the operation of a decision support system is to drill down through the data for correlations that may represent answers. The drilling for correlations is referred to as *data mining*. To be successful, it would be necessary to mine data from multiple areas of the organization.

Data warehouse   It is the job of the *data warehouse* to accomplish the feat of combining data from different systems. Data is captured from multiple databases by using image snapshots triggered by a timer. The timer may be set to capture data daily, weekly, or monthly depending on the needs of the system architect.

Data mart   The *data mart* is a repository of the results from data mining the warehouse. You can consider a data mart the equivalent of a convenience store. All of the most common requests are ready for the user to grab. A decision support system retrieves prepackaged results of data mining and displays them for the user in a presentation program, typically a graphical user interface (GUI).

Figure 5.20 shows the basic hierarchy of the databases loading the data warehouse, which is mined to create a data mart.

FIGURE 5.20 Design of data warehouse and data mart

Presenting Decision Support Data

The information presented from the data mart could indicate correlations of significance for the system user. Senior executives may find this information extremely useful in detecting upcoming trends or areas of concern throughout the organization. Keep in mind, the primary purpose of the decision support system is to give the senior-level manager timely information that will aid in making effective decisions.

The next step up from decision support systems is artificial intelligence.

Using Artificial Intelligence

Artificial intelligence (AI) is the subject of many technology dreams and some horror movies. The concept is that the computer has evolved to the level of being able to render its own decisions. Depending on your point of view, this may be good or bad. Artificial intelligence is useful for machines in a hostile environment. The Mars planetary rover requires a degree of artificial intelligence to ensure that it could respond to a hazard, without waiting for a human to issue instructions.

Now that the database has been developed, the next concern is to ensure that the transactions are processed correctly. Let's move along into a discussion of program architecture.

Program Architecture

Computer programs may be written with an open architecture or proprietary, also known as closed, design. The software architect makes this decision.

The *open system architecture* is founded on well-known standards and definitions. The primary advantage of open architecture is flexibility. Computer software can be updated and modified by using components from multiple sources. Fortunately, the design promotes the ability to use best-of-breed programs. The disadvantages include having a potential hodgepodge of unstructured programs. For a client, the open system architecture reduces dependence on a particular vendor.

A *closed system architecture* contains methods and proprietary programming that remain the property of the software creator. Most of the program logic is hidden from view or stored in encrypted format to prevent the user from deciphering internal mechanisms. Most commercial software products are a closed, proprietary system with industry standardized program interfaces for data sharing with other programs—in essence, closed architecture with open architecture interfaces. The advantage is that the user can still share data between programs. Another advantage is that the vendor can lock in the customer to their product. The disadvantage is that the customer may be locked in to the vendor's product.

Centralization versus Decentralization

Every organization will face the challenge of determining whether to use a centralized database or a distributed database application. The centralized database is easier to manage than a distributed system. However, the distributed system offers more flexibility and redundancy. The additional flexibility and redundancy of a distributed system carries higher implementation and support costs.

The decision of centralization versus decentralization would have been addressed by the steering committee and requirements gathered in the SDLC Requirements Definition phase (phase 1). Let's consider the requirements for electronic commerce.

Electronic Commerce

Electronic commerce is also known worldwide as *e-commerce*, which is the conducting of business and financial transactions electronically across the globe. This concept introduces the challenges of maintaining confidentiality, integrity, and availability for every second of the entire year. An additional challenge is to ensure regulatory compliance for each type of transaction that may occur over the e-commerce system.

Let's look at a few transactions, for example:

Business-to-business (B-to-B)   Regular transactions between a business and its vendors. This could include purchasing, accounts payable, payroll, and outsourcing services. This type of transaction is governed by business contracts in accordance with federal law.

Business-to-government (B-to-G)   The online filing of legal documents and reports. In addition, this includes purchasing and vendor management for the products and services used by the government. This type of transaction is governed by a variety of government regulations. An example is the U.S. Central Contractor Registration system (CCR). Vendors doing business with the U.S. government are required to maintain their company profiles in the CCR database.

Business-to-consumer (B-to-C)   Direct sales of products and services to a consumer. B-to-C also includes providing customer support and product information to the consumer. The payment transaction in this type of environment may be governed by banking, privacy, and credit authorization laws. Business-to-consumer applications require additional logging because the normal paper trail does not exist. The auditor will be interested in how the transactions are monitored and reviewed. Authorizations for processing online payments will require special security measures.

Business-to-employee (B-to-E)   The online administration of employee services, including payroll and job benefits. This type of transaction is governed by federal employment regulations and privacy regulations.

Figure 5.21 shows the common e-commerce avenues in use today. Each of these should be the subject of an IS audit.

E-commerce poses a number of challenges to security. Because of the level of risk, security should weigh heavily in any considerations of reducing protection for convenience. Strong internal controls are mandatory for e-commerce systems.

pg 279

> **NOTE**   We discuss data security in Chapter 7, "Information Asset Protection."

FIGURE 5.21   E-commerce programs

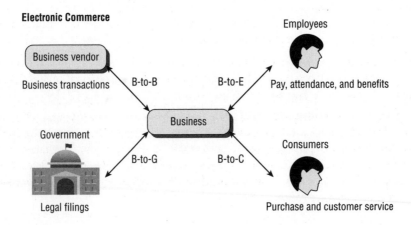

Summary

This chapter covered IT governance in the System Development Life Cycle. The primary objective of this governance is to ensure that systems are developed via a methodical process that aligns business requirements to business objectives. During this chapter, we touched on standards used in the development of computer software. This chapter included an introduction to the design of databases, program architecture, and e-commerce.

Throughout the entire System Development Life Cycle are a series of processes to ensure control and promote quality. It is the IS auditor's job to determine whether the organization has fulfilled its duties of leadership and control. The purpose of this chapter is to provide you with a basic understanding of the concepts and terminology used in software development.

Exam Essentials

Evaluate the business case for new systems.   You need to evaluate the requirements for a new system to ensure that it will meet the organization's business goals. You should understand how critical success factors are developed and risks are identified.

Evaluate risk management and project management practices.   You need to review the evidence of the organization's project management practices and risk mitigation practices. The objective is to determine whether the solution was cost-effective and achieved the stated business objectives. A formal selection process should be in use and clearly documented.

Conduct regular performance reviews.   Each project should undergo a regular performance review to verify that it is conforming to planned expectations. The review process should be supported by formal documentation and accurate status reporting. Management oversight review should be in use when plans deviate, assumptions change, or the scope of the project substantially changes.

Understand the practices used to gather and verify requirements.   The organization may use a steering committee with the assistance of various managers to identify critical success factors. Scenario exercises can be used to assist in developing requirements for planning. Additional requirements may be obtained from the business internal operation, specific business market, customer commitments, and other sources of information.

Know the system development methodology being used.   You need to review the thoroughness and maturity of processes by which all systems (including infrastructure) are developed or acquired.

Know the system development tools, including their strengths and weaknesses.   You need to understand the advantages and disadvantages of traditional programming, Agile, and RAD methodologies. You are expected to understand that 4GL programming languages do not build the necessary business logic without the involvement of a skilled programmer. You are expected to have a basic understanding of the differences between data-oriented programming and object-oriented programming.

Understand quality control and the development of a test plan. A quality control process should be in use throughout the entire project and system life cycle. Formal testing should occur in accordance with a structured test plan designed to verify software logic, defects, transaction integrity, efficiency, controls, and validation against requirements.

Be familiar with the internal control mechanisms in place and working. All systems are required to have functioning internal control mechanisms. You need to evaluate the effectiveness of the selected safeguards. Evidence should exist that each control was planned during the system specification phase and that the controls were implemented during development and tested for effectiveness.

Understand the difference between certification and accreditation. Every system should undergo acceptance testing, followed by formal technical certification testing for production use. After completing technical certification, the system should be reviewed by management for accreditation based on fitness of use. Systems should be recertified on a regular basis to ensure that they meet new demands of evolving requirements.

Be familiar with ongoing maintenance and support plans in use. You need to evaluate the process of ongoing support and maintenance plans. The intention is to ensure that the plans fulfill the organizational objectives. You verify that the internal control process is in use for authorizing and implementing changes. System changes should undergo a regression test to ensure that no negative effects were created as a result of the change.

Know how to conduct postimplementation reviews. Every system should undergo a postimplementation review. The purpose is to compare actual deliverables against the original objectives, and to compare performance to the project plan. Regular reviews should occur throughout the system's usable life cycle, preferably on an annual basis.

Know the various programming terms and concepts. You need to have a working knowledge of the terminology and concepts used in the development of computer software.

Review Questions

1.   The advantages of using 4GL software applications include which of the following?

   A. Automatically generates the application screens and business logic

   B. Includes artificial intelligence using fuzzy logic

   C. Reduces application planning time and coding effort

   D. Reduces development effort for primitive functions but does not provide business logic

2.   The best definition of database normalization is to

   A. Increase system performance by creating duplicate copies of the most accessed data, allowing faster caching

   B. Increase the amount (capacity) of valuable data

   C. Minimize duplication of data and reduce the size of data tables

   D. Minimize response time through faster processing of information

3.   Which of the following statements is true concerning the inference engine used in expert systems?

   A. Makes decisions using heuristics

   B. Contains nodes linked via an arc

   C. Used when a knowledge base is unavailable

   D. Records objects in a climactic network

4.   An IT steering committee would most likely perform which of the following functions?

   A. Explain to the users how IT is steering the business objectives

   B. Issue directives for regulatory compliance and provide authorization for ongoing IT audits

   C. Facilitate cooperation between the users and IT to ensure that business objectives are met

   D. Ensure that the business is aligned to fulfill the IT objectives

5.   The Software Engineering Institute's Capability Maturity Model (CMM) would best relate to which of the following statements?

   A. Measurement of resources necessary to ensure a reduction in coding defects

   B. Documentation of accomplishments achieved during program development

   C. Relationship of application performance to the user's stated requirement

   D. Baseline of the current progress or regression

6.   Which of the following best describes a data mart?

   A. Contains raw data to be processed

   B. Used in place of a data warehouse

   C. Provides a graphical GUI presentation

   D. Stores results from data mining

7. Object-oriented databases (OODBs) are designed for data that is _____.

    A. Predictable

    B. Consistent in structure

    C. Variable

    D. Fixed-length

8. What does the term *referential integrity* mean?

    A. Transactions are recorded in before-images and after-images.

    B. It's a valid link between a data entry contained in two tables.

    C. It's a completed tuple in the database.

    D. Candidate keys are used to perform a search.

9. Which of the following statements best explains a program object in object-oriented programming?

    A. It contains methods and data.

    B. Methods are stored separate from data.

    C. It contains 100 percent of all methods necessary for every task.

    D. It does not provide methods.

10. What is the primary objective of postimplementation review?

    A. Recognition for forcing an installation to be successful

    B. Authorize vendor's final payment from escrow

    C. Conduct remedial actions

    D. Determine that its organizational objectives have been fulfilled

11. What is the most important concern regarding the RFP process?

    A. Vendor proposals undergo an objective review to determine alignment with organizational objectives.

    B. The vendor must agree to escrow the program code to protect the buyer in case the vendor organization ceases operation.

    C. The RFP process requires a substantial commitment as opposed to a request for information (RFI).

    D. The RFP planning process is not necessary for organizations with internal programming capability.

12. Which SDLC phase uses Function Point Analysis (FPA)?

    A. SDLC phase 3: System Design

    B. SDLC phase 4: Development

    C. SDLC phase 1: Feasibility Study

    D. SDLC phase 5: Implementation

13. Which of the following statements is true concerning regression testing?

    A. Used to observe internal program logic

    B. Verifies that a change did not create a new problem

    C. Provides testing of black-box functions

    D. Compares test results against a knowledge base

14. Which of the following migration methods provides the lowest risk to the organization?

    A. Phased

    B. Hard

    C. Parallel

    D. Date specified

15. When is management oversight of a project required?

    A. If time, scope, or cost vary more than 5 percent from the estimate

    B. When the feasibility study is inconclusive

    C. To verify that total program benefits met anticipated projection

    D. When major changes occur in assumptions, requirements, or methodology

16. What are the advantages of the integrated development environment (IDE)?

    A. Generates and debugs program code

    B. Eliminates the majority of processes in SDLC phase 2

    C. Prevents design errors in SDLC phase 3

    D. Eliminates the testing requirement in SDLC phase 4

17. What is the difference between certification and accreditation?

    A. Certification is a management process, and accreditation is a technical process.

    B. No difference; both include technical testing.

    C. Certification is a technical test, and accreditation is management's view of fitness for use.

    D. Certification is about fitness of use, and accreditation is a technical testing process.

18. Which of the following development methodologies is based on knowledge in someone's head, as opposed to traditional documentation of requirements?

    A. System Development Life Cycle (SDLC)

    B. Program Evaluation Review Technique (PERT)

    C. Rapid Application Development (RAD)

    D. Agile

19. What is the IS auditor's primary purpose in regard to life cycle management?

    A. To verify that evidence supports the organizational objective and that each decision is properly authorized by management

    B. To verify that all business contracts are properly signed and executed by management

    C. To verify that internal controls are tested prior to implementation by a third-party review laboratory

    D. To verify that a sufficient budget was allocated to pay for software development within the allotted time period

20. Which of the following design techniques will document internal logic functions used for data transformation?

    A. Entity-relationship diagram

    B. Flowchart

    C. Database schema

    D. Function Point Analysis

21. Which of the following principles includes the concept of all or nothing?

    A. Transaction processing monitor

    B. Atomicity, consistency, isolation, and durability

    C. Runtime processing

    D. Referential integrity

22. Software development uses several types of testing to ensure proper functionality. Which of the following types of testing is used to test functionality on commercially compiled software?

    A. White-box

    B. Code review

    C. Black-box

    D. Crystal-box

23. Programming software modules by using a time-box style of management is also referred to as the _____ method. The purpose is to force rapid iterations of software prototypes by small teams of talented programmers.

    A. Agile

    B. Lower CASE

    C. Rapid Application Development (RAD)

    D. Fourth-generation (4GL)

24. How long does full system accreditation last?

    A. Six months

    B. One year

    C. Nine months

    D. As long as the system is used

25. During the SDLC, several risks can become real problems. Which of the following is the greatest concern to the auditor?

   A. User acceptance testing lasted only 1 hour.

   B. The depth and breadth of user operation manuals is not sufficient.

   C. The project exceeded a 14 percent cost overrun from the original budget.

   D. User requirements and objectives were not met.

26. What is the terminology that describes the coding of a program by using a template inside of an integrated software development environment?

   A. Pseudocoding

   B. Macro-coding

   C. Compiled coding

   D. Object coding

27. What is the real issue regarding software escrow?

   A. The vendor must use a subcontractor for safe storage of the original development software.

   B. The software contains intellectual value that is conveyed to the client.

   C. The client is entitled to the benefit of only using the software and not owning it, unless they pay more money.

   D. Commercial software is kept in escrow in case the vendor sells the rights to another vendor.

28. How can the price of designing and managing a quality program be justified?

   A. Price of failure

   B. Product profit margin

   C. Preventing regulatory changes and fines

   D. Using the 100-point rule

29. Which of the following is the best method of reviewing the logic used in software written in programming script?

   A. Black-box test

   B. Regression test

   C. Crystal-box test

   D. User acceptance test

30. Which of the software development methods includes planning activities in phase 1 of the SDLC model?

   A. Agile

   B. Rapid Application Development (RAD)

   C. Upper CASE tools

   D. Project management

31. What is the primary purpose of the reviews at the end of each phase in the SLDC?

   A. Approval for the funding to continue development

   B. Approval by management to proceed to the next phase or possibly kill the project

   C. Approval of the final design

   D. Provide the auditor with information about management's decision for regulatory compliance

32. What is the principle issue concerning users programming with a fourth-generation language (4GL)?

   A. Creates nice-looking screens and data buckets without logical data transformation procedures needed in business applications

   B. Provides an advantage with embedded database hooks to minimize the cost of hiring a professional software developer

   C. Provides the user with drag-and-drop functionality to build their own programs

   D. Uses the revolutionary development approach to reduce the cost and time of traditional development

33. What should be the basis for management's decision to buy available software or to build a custom software application?

   A. Cost savings by switching to a recognized best-in-class application used by others in the industry

   B. Converting from internal custom processes to how the new software operates in order to save money by avoiding the cost of customization

   C. Competitive advantage of using the same software as everyone else

   D. Data from the feasibility study and business specifications

34. When does software certification testing actually occur in the SDLC model?

   A. Phase 3 (System Design)

   B. Phase 3 (System Design) and phase 4 (Development)

   C. Phase 4 (Development) and phase 5 (Implementation)

   D. Phase 5 (Implementation)

35. What is the purpose of using international standards such as ISO 15489 and ISO 9126:2003 with the SDLC?

   A. Input as starting specifications for phase 2 requirements

   B. International reference for starting a quality assurance program

   C. Provides guidance for use in phase 4 development

   D. Lowers the initial cost of software development

Answers to Review Questions

1. D. The 4GL provides screen-authoring and report-writing utilities that automate database access. The 4GL tools do not create the business logic necessary for data transformation.

2. C. Database normalization minimizes duplication of data through standardization of the database table layout. Increased speed is obtained by reducing the size of individual tables to allow a faster search.

3. A. The interference engine uses rules, also known as heuristics, to sort through the knowledge base in search of possible answers. The meaning of information in the knowledge base can be recorded in objects and symbols known as semantic networks.

4. C. The IT steering committee provides open communication of business objectives for IT to support. The steering committee builds awareness and facilitates user cooperation. Focus is placed on fulfillment of the business objectives.

5. D. The Capability Maturity Model creates a baseline reference to chart current progress or regression. It provides a guideline for developing the maturity of systems and management procedures.

6. D. Data mining uses rules to drill down through the data in the data warehouse for correlations. The results of data mining are stored in the data mart. The DSS presentation program may display data from the data mart in a graphical format.

7. C. Data-oriented databases (DODBs) are designed for predictable data that has a consistent structure and a known or fixed length. Object-oriented databases (OODBs) are designed for data that has a variety of possible data formats.

8. B. Referential integrity means a valid link exists between data in different tables. When you follow the link from one table for "first_name" it matches the data we expect to find in the next table like "Samantha" rather than "1109 Mian Ave." An error indicates a lack of integrity.

9. A. Objects contain both methods and data to perform a desired task. The object can delegate to another object.

10. D. Postimplementation review collects evidence to determine whether the organizational objectives have been fulfilled. The review would include verification that internal controls are present and in use.

11. A. Each proposal must undergo an objective review to determine whether the offer is properly aligned with organizational objectives. RFP review is a formal process that should be managed as a project.

12. C. Function Point Analysis (FPA) is used to estimate the effort required to develop software. FPA is used during SDLC phase 1, the Feasibility Study phase, to create estimates by multiplying the number of inputs and outputs against a mathematical factor.

13. B. The purpose of regression testing is to ensure that a change does not create a new problem with other functions in the program. After a change is made, all of the validation tests are run from beginning to end to discover any conflicts or failures. Regression testing is part of the quality control process.

14. C. Parallel migration increases support requirements but lowers the overall risk. The old and new systems are run in parallel to verify integrity while building user familiarity with the new system.

15. D. Management oversight review is necessary when it is anticipated that the estimates are incorrect by more than 10 percent. Management oversight is also necessary if major changes occur in assumptions, requirements, or methodology used.

16. A. The integrated development environment automates program code generation and provides online debugging for certain types of errors. It does not replace the traditional planning process. IDE does not alter the testing requirements in SDLC phase 4. Full testing must still occur.

17. C. Certification is a technical testing process. Accreditation is a management process of granting approval based on fitness of use.

18. D. The Agile method places greater reliance on the undocumented knowledge contained in a person's head. Agile is the direct opposite of capturing knowledge through project documentation.

19. A. Evidence must support the stated objectives of the organization. Software that is built or purchased should be carefully researched to ensure that it fulfills the organization's objectives. Each phase of the life cycle should be reviewed and approved by management before progressing to the next phase.

20. B. A flowchart is used to document internal program logic. An entity-relationship diagram (ERD) is used to help define the database schema. Function Point Analysis is used for estimation of work during the feasibility study.

21. B. The ACID principle of database transaction refers to atomicity (all or nothing), consistency, isolation (transactions operate independently), and durability (data is maintained).

22. C. Compiled software is unreadable by humans. Black-box testing is used to run a sample transaction through the system. The original input is then compared to verify that the output is correct and that it represents what the customer wanted from the system.

23. A. Agile uses time-box management for rapid iterations of software prototypes by small teams of talented programmers. Agile does not force preplanning of requirements and relies on undocumented knowledge contained in someone's head, without complete documentation.

24. B. Full accreditation lasts up to one year. Annual renewal is required. Management must reaccredit systems every year. Temporary or restricted accreditation is for only 90 or 180 days.

25. D. The biggest concern would be a failure to meet the user requirements or user objectives. Cost overruns can occur. By comparison, the auditor's interest in why the overrun occurred would be less important.

26. A. Software developers use pseudocoding to write programs into a project template within the integrated development environment (IDE). The IDE tool converts the template's pseudocode information into actual program code for almost any language, including C#, Java, Perl, and the Microsoft .NET framework.

27. C. The client is entitled to the benefit of only using the software, not the right of ownership. Software escrow may be requested by the client to gain full rights to the software if the vendor goes out of business. This would damage the vendor's right to resell intellectual property rights to another vendor. Clients may gain ownership rights to software by paying the vendor for the total cost of development, not just the right to use it. Clients usually decline to pay development costs and will accept the risk of using someone else's software. For example, what would Microsoft charge for the full rights of ownership for Windows Vista? No client would pay it; it's cheaper to accept the risk.

28. A. Quality is measured as conformance to specifications. Added costs for failing to meet the specification are known as the price of nonconformance, or the cost of failure. Costs of failure provide an excellent tool to justify funding of preventative controls.

29. C. Crystal-box, also known as white-box testing, is used to review the logic in software written using programming script. The script is still readable by humans until the script is compiled. Compiled programs would be tested using a black-box method.

30. D. Traditional project management is the only methodology that covers all seven phases of the SDLC. Agile is for phase 4 development. Rapid Application Development (RAD) and CASE tools apply only to portions of phase 2 requirements, phase 3 design, and phase 4 development. Everything else requires good old-fashioned project management.

31. B. The review at the end of every SDLC phase is intended to prevent the project from proceeding unless it receives management's approval. The project can be approved, forced to fix existing problems, or killed. In each review, the decision is whether all specifications and objectives are being met or if the project should be cancelled.

32. A. Fourth-generation (4GL) development tools create nice-looking screens and data buckets without the logical data transformation procedures needed in business applications. Skilled software developers are still needed to write the business logic into the program. Nearly 100 percent of the user-developed applications lack the necessary internal controls. In addition, the concept of users developing their own software creates excessive risk. It also violates separation of duties. Maybe the user wanting to use a 4GL should switch professions to become a professional programmer instead of the job they were hired to perform.

33. D. All the decisions regarding purchasing existing software or building a custom application should be made by using data from the feasibility study and business specifications. More customization or the desire for competitive advantage indicate the need to build a custom application. Using the same software as your competitor converts your organization into a commodity pricing war and damages the business advantage of being different.

34. C. Software certification testing begins during phase 4 development and continues into phase 5 implementation testing. Initial certification tests are run for the individual models and internal controls as the program is developed. Phase 5 certification testing is expended to cover the operation of the entire software application prior to entering production use.

35. A. International standards such as ISO 15489 (record management), ISO 15504 (CMM/SPICE), and ISO 9126:2003 (quality management) are best used as inputs for starting specifications in phase 2 requirements. These standards aid in planning the secondary software specifications. Primary specifications are obtained by collecting information from the user to define their main objectives for the software, detailing the steps in its intended mission.

Chapter

6

IT Service Delivery

THE OBJECTIVE OF THIS CHAPTER IS TO ACQUAINT THE READER WITH THE FOLLOWING CONCEPTS:

- ✓ Knowledge of service-level management practices including operations workload, scheduling, services management, and preventative maintenance
- ✓ Knowledge of the Information Technology Infrastructure Library
- ✓ Knowledge of control functionality in the IT infrastructure
- ✓ Understanding specific personnel roles and responsibilities
- ✓ Data administration for integrity and optimization databases
- ✓ Issues facing the use of mobile code, Java, and ActiveX
- ✓ IT performance monitoring using analyzers, system utilization, and log management
- ✓ Understanding of change management, configuration release management, and emergency changes
- ✓ Knowledge of techniques for problem reporting and incident management
- ✓ Understanding digital forensic techniques

In this chapter, you will focus on the management of information technology (IT) operations designed to support the organization. You will learn about the recommended practices for monitoring service levels and controlling change in the organization. The best practices of incident management and problem resolution will also be discussed.

ISACA expects every IS auditor to understand how to evaluate the techniques and best practices used in IT support.

Nature of IT Services

Every time information technology is mentioned, the conversation turns toward operations. IT suffers from the same perceived fate as facilities management, the plumber, or the electrician. People in each of these fields feel that their contribution is invaluable. Yet the truth is that few possess a mastery of the intricate knowledge of how each business unit operates. This common drawback is the principal reason why IT outsourcing is a popular topic with users. Smart IT executives recognize that a fundamental change is necessary. The key to success is conveying how IT operations is a functional servant to its masters in the business unit.

Everyone in the organization is aware of IT operational problems. They may appear as slow response times, systems being unavailable for any reason, problems with data, and ongoing arguments between people who are trying to accomplish their jobs. So how can we improve operations? Let's start with the two most common statements:

✗ **Buy more**   New product advertisements and dropping prices make it appear as though the solution is to continually buy more until you run out of room, people to implement the product, or money.

✗ **Rearrange priorities**   Many organizations continuously fight fires and rearrange the priorities rather than fix the root problem. Changing priorities is more of a workaround to circumvent the problem. The result is lots of work without any real progress.

✔   A third choice gets us closer to the real solution. IT leadership will commit the resources necessary to document and measure the current situation. Time and effort will be expended to determine the root of the real problems. Let's investigate what needs to be accomplished to truly fix the problems:

- Policies will be added or amended.

- Standards will be adopted or modified.

- Job descriptions will be updated to reflect the actual jobs performed to ensure genuine assignment of responsibility and accountability.

- Better procedures will be created and updated.

- Change control will shift from the needs of IT toward the specific business objectives of the users in other departments.

The objective is to change the perception of IT from a bunch of blue-jeans-wearing introverts to organized professionals—sharp-looking individuals able to support the most critical aspects of the business. The vice president of information systems and chief information officer are responsible for creating a corporate culture that recognizes the valuable contributions of a diligent staff.

People strive for recognition. Nobody wants to take a thankless job, especially one that may have long hours. IT governance deals with executives recognizing their responsibility to take control. IT leadership, on the other hand, is focused on only two objectives:

Objective 1: Define IT's mission by using small, simple words, and then set out plans to accomplish it.

Objective 2: Provide the detailed directions and support necessary for your people to succeed.

Without good management, the nifty technical tools are useless. After leadership is in place and operating, the next step is moving to designing the service delivery operation. The majority of this chapter is dedicated to operational measures. Let's begin with a quick reference check of external versus internal measures:

External measures are the customer viewpoint.   Consider what the customer sees in regard to system availability, perception of the help desk, attitudes of the IT staff, response time, and backlog. All of these factors compose customer satisfaction. The user just wants it to work by calculating something or automating a business task.

Internal measures are of interest to systems people.   The good people in IT will gauge the impact of availability, disk storage capacity, service requests, and all the little technical details about how it will help or hurt their users get the job done. Some IT staff members may be overly concerned with technology itself. That could be a detrimental situation. Technology is not intended as a safe haven for hiding from the hazards of interacting with other people or becoming involved in the challenges and worries of running a business. Internal measures worthy of IT's interest are the details that help or hurt the user in the performance of business duties.

Auditors can recognize good IT people by their speech patterns. Questions and statements will start with a specific mention of the user they regard as their customer and friend. This type of IT person is genuinely trying to help. Good people like this can be hard for employers to find. The auditor should take care to be respectful and supportive of this type of individual. Without question, the auditor should never make any sarcastic or diminutive comments because the result may be deemed an unforgivable insult.

IT Operations Management

IT provides a service to business users. Technology is so pervasive that no organization can exist without computers and telephones. IT service represents a commitment to manage technology as efficiently and effectively as possible within the organization. As business needs change, IT services should adapt accordingly. This constant adaptation can be a significant challenge. There's always the possibility of a gap occurring between the IT services delivered and user expectations.

Meeting IT Functional Objectives

In previous chapters, we discussed the requirement for IT services to be aligned with business objectives. Many of the topics we discussed are practically transparent to business users. IT service delivery is different. In this chapter, we discuss the daily activities necessary to support information technology.

Let's begin with a basic review of the functions in IT operations:

Management of the IT department   The Information Technology department contains managers and staff workers focused on system availability, system integrity, and data confidentiality.

Systems life cycle   All IT systems are to be maintained in a systems life cycle by using the concepts of the System Development Life Cycle (SDLC) and Capability Maturity Model (CMM).

IT policies   Executive management and IT management are responsible for developing and issuing policies that support agreed-upon information technology objectives. Examples include a corporate acceptable use policy (AUP), antivirus protection policy, and the designation of information technology as the official custodian for corporate data.

IT standards   Operating standards are developed by managers and approved by executive management. One such standard is the separation of duties. Other examples include the hours of system availability and system certification prior to production use.

IT procedures   Operating procedures are developed by staff workers with the assistance of their manager. Operating procedures include the handling of software licenses and escalation procedures for user-reported trouble tickets.

IT job descriptions and responsibilities   To support the operating procedures, the IT department must have job descriptions that reflect the current requirements and responsibilities for each position. Out-of-date or inaccurate job descriptions indicate that nobody is actually responsible for completing the work. It's a control failure because nobody has formal responsibility, formal authorization, or formal authority.

IT risk management process   Risk management is required in all areas of an organization. The IT department is subject to a high level of inherent risk. Failures that occur in information technology have wide-reaching impact. The IT department is required to exercise risk mitigation on a daily basis. The process of change control is one technique used to help mitigate risk.

IT asset management   Every Information Technology department maintains control over numerous capital assets, including data, software licenses, computing hardware, networking equipment, and facility space. We view data as a capital asset because of the capital investment necessary to create and maintain current data. Creating a customer list requires substantial investment of capital through marketing campaigns. A list of customers and hot prospects can easily be valued at five to ten times annual gross sales. The organization's total investment in technology, inclusive of all departments, is usually in excess of 4.5 percent of annual gross sales. This makes IT the second-largest custodian of capital assets, following facilities.

IT service to the user   Information technology exists to support business users. The number one representation of value is IT user satisfaction. Attaining high user satisfaction results from a significant effort in back-office systems coupled with a prompt, helpful, and friendly help desk. The typical business user is interested only in how IT solves their individual problem. Customer satisfaction is earned by individual problem-by-problem solutions.

🌐 Real World Scenario

Lights-Out Operations

Based on business requirements and risks, an organization may adopt a policy of running a *lights-out operation*. This term refers to an unmanned facility—although personnel may be in other areas of the building, the control room or data center remains unmanned. Operations are either fully automated or run by remote control. Removing personnel from the data center significantly reduces the risk of environmental contaminants (liquids, debris, food), malicious actions, and human error.

We visited one data center that had so many cables under the raised floor that the floor tiles were bulging under our feet. This was not only unsafe, but also led to communication failures as some brittle cables broke when people walked across the tiles. Fewer problems occur when the servers are physically separate from the workers (physical separation of duties). Service personnel would occupy the computer room only for maintenance.

Now let's look at a framework of compliance that is not a regulation but does represent the best practices in the management of IT services.

Using the IT Infrastructure Library

The number of IT models and frameworks can be confusing. A well-managed organization will implement multiple frameworks including CObIT for governance, CMM for maturity, SDLC for life cycle, ISO standards, and some type of standard for running their help desk. In reality, each framework or standard is designed as a specific tool for different challenges faced in the overall business. Each has its own audience, which must ultimately function as one team.

The Information Technology Infrastructure Library (ITIL) is a collection of management best practices to guide the delivery of information technology services. ITIL provides a comprehensive and integrated set of service management processes targeted at what it takes to run a successful help desk. The goal of ITIL is to control the delivery of services that will be high quality while remaining cost-effective. Each of the service management processes is technology neutral, scalable, and comprehensive.

ITIL's intended audience is as follows:

- IT service providers
- IT directors
- Managers
- CIOs

Adopting ITIL's guidance could provide such benefits as reduced costs, improved IT services through the use of published best practices, higher customer satisfaction from a more professional approach to service delivery, less wasted effort by following a standard, and improved management of third-party services. ITIL is designed to complement the other IT frameworks, not to replace them. The help desk is usually the front line for the user to report problems; therefore, ITIL has an interface to ISO 27002:2007 information security services. We can use ITIL as one of the triggers for incident response outside of the help desk.

Eleven popular processes are associated with ITIL core functions. These functions and associated processes are as follows:

Service support   Service desk, incident management, problem management

Configuration management, change management, release management

Interface to connect with ISO 27002 Information Security Management System (ISMS)

Service delivery   Service-level management

Capacity management

IT service continuity management

Availability management

Financial management for IT services

Functional planning and management   Implementation service management, infrastructure management

Application management, software asset management

Business perspective on delivering better IT services to the business user

Several of these points may appear to be overlapping. However, ITIL is complementary, not competing. IT needs to function as a cohesive team rather than as separate groups of people based on individual function. ITIL's framework helps everyone become involved, whether junior or senior, help desk operator or tenured administrator. Implementing this set of practices helps an organization focus their effort to deliver better customer service to people working in the business unit. Figure 6.1 shows the overview of ITIL.

FIGURE 6.1   Overview of ITIL's purpose

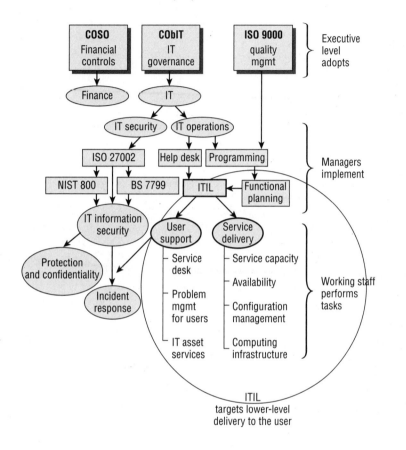

Supporting IT Goals

The goal of operations management is to sustain the business needs of their daily user. Strategy is defined by executive management, technical response is created by middle management, and actual hands-on work is performed by operations managers with their support staff. The work performed should be in direct support of the higher-level business objectives.

As a CISA, you should remain observant of the difference between personnel who are *busy* and those who are *effective*. The volume of work performed is not a single measure of success. IT personnel must be focused on specific business objectives and have the necessary skills to be effective.

Understanding Personnel Roles and Responsibilities

During any dispute over control, it can be challenging to determine who is actually in charge. The client's organizational chart can render a great deal of valuable information. The chart indicates who is in charge at each level, who each person reports to, and what the basic functions are for each job. It's not uncommon to walk into an organization and find that the organization does not have a current copy of their own organizational chart.

> You should recognize that the lack of a current organizational chart is a concern. All positions must have matching job descriptions that are accurate and reflect current responsibilities. Anything more than a small discrepancy in either of these documents indicates a lack of proper internal control. We included a sample organizational chart in Chapter 1, "Secrets of a Successful IS Auditor."

Let's take a quick look at several of the more common IT positions that should be of interest to you. Each of these roles has a unique degree of authority and influence in IT operations:

IT director   The IT director has the day-to-day responsibility of managing IS/IT managers and executing the executives' plan. He or she is an upper-level manager with the authority to make decisions for their group. IT operations managers receive orders directly from the IT director. The IT director role is similar to the role of a movie director.

IT operations managers   IT operations managers direct an IT staff working in software development, on the help desk, in server and network administration, and in information security. These managers are the first line of authority for the users. Each manager is responsible for the creation of effective procedures for their work area. IT operations managers are responsible for handling or delegating any issues that arise.

Systems architect   This individual reviews the data compiled from the systems analyst and determines the preferred design for new systems. A systems architect's role is to create the overall system layout, whereas the systems analyst works with the end user and creates the ideas of what the business users require to fulfill their job or to align IT to their ultimate objectives. The true objective is to create a system that facilitates the generation of revenue for the organization.

Information security manager (ISM)   The information security manager (ISM) should be an individual with training—such as a Certified Information Systems Security Professional (CISSP) from the International Information Systems Security Certification Consortium, an ISACA Certified Information Security Manager (CISM), or someone with an equivalent credential. The ISM specifies security standards to be implemented for all computer systems. The ISM reviews procedures for compliance to security policies. Security management requires special software and tools to perform effective tests and reviews. The ISM specifies control settings to be implemented by the server and network administrators. An ISM should be a very busy person working on security monitoring, security policy compliance, individual system security certification, and systems accreditation. The information security manager is supported by information system security analysts.

It is important to ensure that the ISM function is fulfilled by using a balanced set of security metrics such as NIST 800-53. The auditor likes to see that the organization is paying full attention to internal security controls (instead of management just saying yes and then turning a blind eye toward the implementation). The ISM function is impossible without full management support.

Information systems security analyst (ISSA) The information security manager leads a group of security professionals known as information system security professionals. This group may be large or small, while always in proportion to the size of the organization and its mission requirements. Security analysts work directly with the business users, IT administrators, and the help desk to improve their security posture. This may include investigating security requirements, conducting awareness training, or helping to test security settings. Security analysts work with every department and participate in key positions on the incident response team.

Change control manager This position is a quality assurance requirement. In small organizations, an individual may fill this role. Larger organizations may use a committee of managers to fill this function. The change control manager ensures that the staff is following proper procedures, controls, and approved plans.

Applications programmer Applications programmers write computer programs to solve problems for users. Their role is to create an automated solution for the business end-user. The applications programmer is supported by the systems analyst.

Systems programmer The systems programmer writes programs to change the behavior of the operating system or its design. Do not confuse this position with an enhanced operator. An enhanced operator selects settings, whereas a programmer writes software functions from scratch. The systems programmer role varies depending on the environment.

In a Microsoft Windows environment, the systems programmer is Microsoft Corporation unless the client hired a programmer to rewrite functions in the Microsoft operating system. Does the client have programmers to rewrite the internal functions of the XP or Vista operating systems? If not, the client organization is no more than a user, and their systems administrator is a glorified operator of enhanced authority who simply selects predefined options from menus.

In the Unix and mainframe environments, the systems programmer rewrites or modifies the operating system kernel, support utilities, and Job Control Language (JCL). In a nutshell, the systems programmer focuses on modifying or improving the operating system internal functions.

Network administrator This person is the network router technician who handles data communication between devices on the network. The duties include supporting system administrators, managing Internet Protocol (IP) addresses, and monitoring networked devices (usually via Simple Network Management Protocol, or SNMP). The network administrator may be delegated the daily maintenance responsibility of network security devices such as intrusion detection and prevention systems, vulnerability scanners, firewalls, and gateways. A network administrator's primary job is to keep data communications working across the network.

Server administrator The server administrator maintains the server hardware and software settings. In a Microsoft environment, the server administrator is an enhanced operator whose role is to select appropriate settings from a GUI interface or predefined menu. The Unix and mainframe administrator counterparts are usually skilled as script programmers or operating system programmers. The Unix or mainframe administrators frequently write their own support utilities or customize the program code of existing utilities to enhance system integration.

Database administrator   This is the custodian of data, who maintains the database systems. This is usually a role fulfilled by a person with prior experience as senior system administrator or systems programmer.

Computer operator   This is a junior server technician who assists the system administrator and database administrator. The computer operator functions include starting and stopping software, changing job prioritization, and identifying possible problems during normal processing. A computer operator acts as the eyes, ears, and hands under the direction of the administrator. Computer operators provide clerical assistance on issues of error and log reporting. Operators escalate problems to the attention of more-senior personnel.

Systems analyst   A systems analyst works with the business end-user to develop requirements. After the requirements are developed, the systems analyst works with the user to define screen layouts and report layouts. The systems analyst then communicates this information to the systems programmer. The systems analyst provides support for business methods to be implemented in technology.

Data entry staff   Data could be entered by a professional data entry staff for a large volume of data, or it could be entered by the end user. These days, with web forms and the online atmosphere of IT, data entry by the end user is quite common. If that has been the decision, we of course like to see compensating controls to ensure the integrity of that input.

Media librarian   A media librarian is a critical role even though it's a junior role. We will refer to this IT position by the short name of *librarian*. The librarian is responsible for keeping track of all media, no matter what type (tape, cartridge, CD, or even a Zip drive or a portable USB memory stick). The librarian is responsible for data storage and its tracking history, including creation date, current storage location, last time accessed, and what data is claimed to be contained on the media. The data may be referred to as a *data set*.

Backup media is sent to an offsite storage company for safe offsite storage. The librarian is required to track when the media was sent and when it arrived at the destination. Every tape and label must be accounted for at all times. Loss of backup media (tape) may constitute a breach of law or require mandatory public disclosure of loss, depending on contents.

The librarian assists with regular self-audits to verify that the property is still in safe storage with the offsite vendor. Media is recalled from storage by the librarian. Media containing old data is recycled by the librarian in accordance with the organization's reuse policy. The librarian is also responsible for proper disposal and destruction of old media.

Help desk   Every IS organization will have a help desk of some type to support computer hardware or particular software applications. This is where users initially call for first-level support; the caller is asking for IT assistance. The help desk person handles the most basic needs and then escalates problems to the appropriate personnel. The help desk follows the policies and procedures that are specified by management.

Staff on the help desk usually hold a junior role. This support role provides an interface with IT customers. Each help desk person should be trained to recognize problems that need to be referred to more-senior IT staff. The customer interface serves the business person—the end user. The business end-user's job is to make money, and the help desk is intended to help the business user work more effectively. The help desk must keep performance metrics for all requests, including metrics of escalation and problem delegation.

Each of the roles we discussed has a particular function that is necessary to sustain normal operations. It is important that each transaction is properly authorized before it is executed. A physical or logical separation of duties is necessary to provide proper authorization. With separation of duties, you look at who holds custody of the assets and what compensating controls are present.

Figure 6.2 illustrates separation of duties and authorization in the IT department.

FIGURE 6.2   Separation of duties

Job Role	Authorize Changes	Production Library Access	Development Library Access	Security Administration Configuration	Execute Production Changes
System user (end user)	Approve	Use	No	No	No
System administration (custodian)	Request	Monitor-Control	No	Implement	When approved
Security administration (custodian)	Approve	No	No	Specify control	No
Programming/ development	Request	No	Create software	No	No
Change testing	Test only	No (use isolated test)	No (use isolated test)	Test only	No
Change control	Approves	No	No	No	No

The purpose of separation of duties is to segregate authorization so that no individual can execute an action or have direct access to assets by bypassing control. Authorization is the most important element to separate from each job role. Every position should require authorization from another person before changes are made or before sensitive transactions are executed. The separation of duties is a control mechanism that separates the person doing the job from the person who renders authorization. The goal is to prevent stupid mistakes or possibly fraudulent activity.

Using Metrics

The performance of information technology is ultimately interpreted by three fundamental business-performance indicators: IT budget, user satisfaction, and technical indicators. Technical indicators could include a combination of automated and manual metrics. You can gain a reasonable understanding of IT performance by reviewing their chosen indicators and corresponding scores.

Using metrics to measure IT service is required. These service metrics are tools designed to demonstrate the effectiveness of IT operations. Many regulations require the use of IT metrics in general. Each metric should provide a quantifiable measurement corresponding to the organization's internal controls. The IT metrics aid in the evaluation of an organization's performance.

Metrics must be developed for each organization. Each metric should be developed by using the following four principles:

- Data for calculating metrics must be readily obtainable.

- Each process under consideration needs to be repeating and measurable. It must represent a value to the business.

- Each metric must demonstrate a level of performance by using quantifiable information in the form of a numeric total, average, or percentage.

- A metric can be derived by automated or manual means.

The success of IT metrics depends on finding useful measurements that are of value to the organization's stakeholders. Data can be obtained from automated system reports. Data can also be collected manually through self-assessment tools, questionnaires, and user surveys. The metrics may change as new processes and projects are developed in the organization. It is important that each metric selected is realistic and can be used for measuring performance improvement.

Understanding the Types of Metrics

The goal of every metric is to establish a performance target. Performance targets are combined to establish a baseline. Four basic types of metrics can be used to measure IT performance:

Implementation metric   An implementation metric provides a percentage or comparative count for the quantity of conforming installations—for example, the number of systems with antivirus software installed, or the number of users who have attended IT security orientation training.

Efficiency metric   The efficiency metric measures the timeliness of service delivery. Examples include resolution time from the help desk or elapsed time for response to an incident.

Effectiveness metric   This metric evaluates the quantifiable effectiveness of IT service activities. An example is the number of user-reported trouble tickets opened and closed by the help desk with a resolution that was satisfactory to the user. Another example is the number of systems currently maintained in a life cycle program by IT staff.

Impact metric   The impact metric provides a quantitative measure of incidents by their type—for example, the number of help desk tickets opened and closed for the month. Another example is the number of systems compromised by a virus attack. This metric can be presented as a numeric value, a percentage of the total population, or a dollar value.

Figure 6.3 illustrates the nature of the four basic types of measurement metrics.

(TP) Transaction Processing monitors - pg 344

FIGURE 6.3   Basic types of measurement metrics

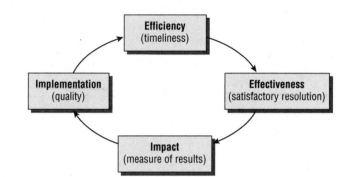

The IT department and each major stakeholder need to agree on which metrics to use. It is important to limit the number of metrics to a sustainable quantity. It is recommended that no more than five to ten metrics be collected for each major stakeholder. The metrics are not free; an organization must allocate resources to gather and create meaningful metrics. The data collection and subsequent reporting process must be standardized.

Developing and Selecting a Metric

Every metric developed will contain nine elements of information. ISACA does not expect you to recite each of these points in detail. The objective is to understand how a valid metric is created and managed. Let's look at the nine elements:

1. **Purpose**   Describe the overall functional value of this metric. Is this metric for customer measurement, compliance with a regulatory requirement, or internal performance?

2. **Performance goal**   State the desired results of implementation, or the question to be answered by this metric. For example, the goal may be orientation training for new hires or separation of duties on IT servers.

3. **Performance objective**   State the actions that are required to obtain the performance goal. This may be posed as one or multiple questions. For example, are participant-training materials in place for the orientation of new hires? What is the training schedule?

4. **Type of measurement**   Define the quantitative measurement to be used. The measurement is expressed as a percentage, average, number, or frequency—for example, the numeric count and percentage based on attendance.

5. **Data source**   Indicate where the data was captured from. List the specific tools, databases, and personnel that provided the data used in this metric—for example, a Human Resources (HR) employee count, and class attendance records signed upon entry and exit from training.

6. **Available evidence**   List the sources of proof that can document the success or failure represented by this particular metric—for example, an HR roster, invitation list, attendance sheet, or attendee exit examination.

7 **Frequency**   State the time period used for data collection. Is this information based on hours, days, weeks, months, or years? For example, data collection may be reported monthly.

4 **Formula used**   State the formula used in the calculation. One example is the number of incidents divided by the total number of systems. Another example is the formula (ratio) = (attendees ÷ total number of employees).

9 **Indicators**   Explain the goal of this metric and how it should be interpreted by the reader. For example, if the target for a metric on system certification is 100 percent, a low percentage would indicate a high risk exposure. A higher percentage would indicate a risk reduction by educating users about basic IS security safeguards and high-level notification procedures.

Evaluating the Help Desk

The purpose of a *help desk* is to provide ad hoc assistance to business users. The help desk is the point of origination for new support requests. A help desk may support specific applications or general computer needs. In service delivery, the objective is to provide high-quality and prompt service to the user during the appropriate work hours.

People may call in for help with a variety of computing problems. It is the help desk's responsibility to escalate trouble tickets in a timely manner. Some trouble tickets might be escalated to the system administrator or application support programmer. Other trouble tickets might be escalated to a third party. The help desk provides a single point of contact for the user. Each trouble ticket should be tracked by the help desk until closed or resolved to the user's satisfaction.

The help desk tracks call metrics so that trends can be analyzed. As an IS auditor, you should understand the help desk function. It would be beneficial to conduct a review of the staff on the help desk to determine their level of competency. An audit trail should exist, documenting the process for logging and tracking service requests. You should evaluate the level of documentation for help desk activities and troubleshooting procedures.

Performing Service-Level Management

A *service-level agreement (SLA)* represents an understanding between users and the service provider. The purpose of this agreement is to define performance criteria by specifying the quantity and quality of service desired by the customer.

Let's look at some of the components of the service-level agreement:

System availability   What are the scheduled hours of system uptime and system downtime for maintenance? How is the processing workload scheduled to prevent conflict? What is the nature and extent of continuity plans?

Service definition   What are the specific services expected by the user?

Personnel qualifications   What are the qualifications of the IT support personnel? Will these same personnel be supporting business users? Will the support personnel be trained in the unique requirements of the business?

Security requirements   What access controls will be implemented? How will physical and logical access controls be implemented? How will the program libraries be protected? How will the data be protected? Will separation of duties be fully implemented?

Data integrity   What are the data storage and retention requirements? What is the method and frequency of data backup? How will data be protected during transportation?

SLA performance reporting   Are all metrics reported against a quantifiable service level? What metrics will be reported? How will the content and format of the metrics be reported? Do the report metrics fulfill actual business objectives? What is the frequency of reporting?

Right to audit   What level of cooperation and access will a customer have to audit the service provider? Define any schedule or access restrictions in regard to auditing. This was discussed in Chapter 3, "IT Governance."

SLA change procedures   What is the process for making changes to the service? What is the cancellation process, and how much would it cost?

Cost of service   What is the cost of the service offered? How are the charges calculated? How will the service be billed? Are the charges realistic for the level of service provided?

This list is provided as an overview of the components in a service-level agreement. Every service-level agreement should be a formal contract between the vendor and customer. This contract should include the effective period of coverage and renewal options. It is understood that internal service-level agreements will take the form of an agreement of mutual understanding. Either type of agreement must be formally approved by appropriate management, representing both the provider's interests and the user's interests.

Outsourcing IT Functions

The subject of outsourcing can spark an emotional response. Selecting whether to outsource functions or keep them in-house is a decision that should be based on the facts in evidence. It is a common practice for individuals to outsource automobile repair, housecleaning, and lawn maintenance chores. A person purchasing a new home may choose to outsource interior decorating to a professional decorator. Take a look at the reasons why outsourcing may be considered:

- The scope of needs is unknown. Therefore, we need the help of someone more experienced who should know what to do.

- The current staff is not generating the expected results.

- Management decided it would be better to let someone else do it.

- The scope and requirements are extremely well defined—for example, CMM level 5. Now the objective is to reduce operating costs while delivering this well-defined level of service.

The auditor may want to investigate the maturity of the outsourced process, metrics, and user expectations. It is interesting how many times the decision to outsource is later reversed after the true scope is known, the actual requirements are identified, and the shock of the outsourcer's total invoice price is realized. Some processes may be outsourced with the long-term intention of remaining external.

At CertTest, we write two editions of our books, a special expanded edition for our class students plus a general version for Sybex. Both are commercially printed, professionally bound, and shipped by an outsource vendor. Writing the books is a core process we want to do. Printing and binding books internally would cost more money and therefore is not something to undertake. Executives will typically choose to outsource low-profit tasks in order to dedicate all available resources to processes with a high rate of return.

Blindly outsourcing is fraught with hazards. Every outsource agreement requires a contract as evidence of the details agreed upon by both parties. Let's take a moment to look at the minimum contents of a business contract according to ISACA:

Prior to negotiations   Identification of the parties to the contract, usually by company name and address

Legal name of entity providing service, and legal name of recipient entity (DBA, Inc., LLP, LLC)

Continuity of service assurances, or lack thereof

Delivery location and legal jurisdiction

Specific details   General description of services provided

Duration of the contract with applicable dates

Description of specific deliverables

Cost of service changes (fixed price, cost plus, or time and materials)

Performance during execution   Criteria of acceptance or rejection of deliverables

Anticipated service-level agreement with both qualitative and quantitative measurement

Security and confidentiality requirements (access levels, nondisclosure, and so forth)

Frequency of invoicing and payment for service

Roles of both parties during the contract, with specific points of contact

Reporting process, report content, distribution, and frequency

Right to audit

Dissolution process

Penalties for nonperformance

Changes and resolution of issues   Cost of changes in service (fixed price, cost plus, or time and materials)

Modification process to change terms, service, or price

Problem resolution process

Recourse

All contracts evidence a formal commitment to purchase and to pay for services or goods. The courts usually regard a contract as the sum total of the agreement between the parties. As a layperson, this means to me that services not specified in the contract should not be expected to occur. If the vendor made a special offer or promise, it should be prominently mentioned in the contract. IT contracts should always be negotiated with the assistance of a professional purchasing manager and legal counsel. A smart auditor allows the legal work to be performed by qualified lawyers. As a rule of thumb, the best lawyer keeps you out of court by preventing the disputes that lead to a lawsuit.

Monitoring the Status of Controls

Your job as a CISA is to evaluate an organization's internal controls. Internal controls are required during the normal processing at every computer terminal or computer workstation. Without proper controls, a minor error could become a major outage.

We have discussed a series of controls in this Study Guide. In Chapter 7, "Information Asset Protection," we discuss specific security controls for protecting information assets. Let's recap the controls that apply to IT service delivery:

- System monitoring
- Log management
- System access controls
- Data file controls
- Application processing controls
- Antivirus Software
- Active Content and Mobile Software Code
- Maintenance controls, including change management
- Separate Test Environment
- Administrative Management

System Monitoring

Technology systems require continuous monitoring to uncover operational inconsistencies, errors, and processing failures. Managing a system would be impossible if you did not know its present condition.

Let's discuss a few types of monitoring that should be implemented by IT:

Hardware Electronic hardware should be monitored for workload utilization, errors, and availability. Utilization and errors could indicate an upcoming condition that will affect system availability. The goal is for every system to be usable. The system administrator should always be aware of hardware conditions observed, problems reported, and alerts recorded in system logs.

Software Most computer software provides event logging. Event logs and audit logs should be enabled and configured to capture information of interest—for example, error conditions, successful logins, unsuccessful login attempts, and configuration changes.

Centralized system logging (Syslog)   It is a recommended practice for centralized system logging to be installed. This process forwards a copy of each system log to a centralized console for review. The configuration process is relatively simple. A log-reading tool is necessary to convert raw data into meaningful information. System logs contain a lot of duplicate entries. Without a log-reading tool, understanding the priorities would be difficult because of the volume of log entries.

Network device monitoring   Servers and routers on the network can be managed by using the SNMP discussed in Chapter 4, "Networking Technology." One of the most common SNMP platforms is HP OpenView, although less-expensive management platforms such as OpenNMS are also available. Network-management software provides insight into the overall condition of the networked environment. System alarms are generated before a user calls in to complain. The network-management system is useful only if someone is available to view the alert.

Uptime-downtime reporting   SNMP provides an excellent method of tracking uptime and downtime. Some people get very defensive about how this subject is reported. Let's clarify the point for everyone's benefit. There are only two categories, although additional descriptions may exist:

Uptime   The system is available for the user to process whatever they desire or need.

Downtime   The system is unavailable for any reason. This may be due to failure or a scheduled outage for service. The word *outage* indicates that the system is effectively down. *Down* means *down*. No matter what the user does, the system will not be available. If this is distasteful, the downtime statistics can be used to justify additional resources. Management may choose to accept the downtime in spite of IT's desire to have 99.999 percent uptime. IT is a humble servant to the business, not the other way around.

Downtime means the system is unavailable for any reason—including failure, maintenance, or while running the backup/restore operations. IT management may refer to downtime as planned maintenance or unplanned outage. Just consider this from the user's perspective. It's counted as downtime if the user is unable to use the system for any reason.

Log Management

Computer logs are an excellent source of information. The only drawback is that without the right tools, computer log files are difficult to read. Assuming you have the right tools, the next question is whether anyone is actually reading the logs. Software logs offer valuable insight into events occurring within systems and throughout the network. The *syslog* feature we discussed in Chapter 4 is one of the most powerful tools an organization could use.

Effective log management is based on six easy requirements:

1. Enable logging for security-related events.
2. Enable logging in application software.

3. Enable logging in the operating system.

4. Configure syslog to export logs from the device to be watched.

5. Configure a syslog server to receive the log files; this does not require any server license.

6. Read the log files. A simple log-reading utility is used to glean duplicate data.

The devices on the network continually generate log entries on an ongoing basis. Log files present valuable information for telling a story of what is actually occurring across the network. The benefit is obtained by reading the files as part of a regular monitoring procedure. Log files need to be continuously backed up and archived. The information discovered in the log file may be the best trigger for incident response.

System Access Controls

Access to computing resources needs to be controlled. It is imperative that the concept of *least privilege* be implemented with regard to user access of IT computing resources. No individual should be able to log in to the system by using a level of authority higher than their job requires. There are three types of login accounts you need to consider: user login, privileged administrator login, and maintenance login.

User Login and Account Management

New user login IDs are created after Human Resources notifies the IT department of an employee being hired. A similar process should exist when a contractor begins work. Some type of authorization mechanism must exist to control the creation of new accounts.

Each system user is required to have a unique login ID and password. The user login accounts should be given the minimum access rights necessary to perform their job (least privilege). Biometrics or electronic tokens may be implemented on systems with higher levels of security. Every user login should contain the following control attributes:

- A warning banner is displayed prior to login to inform the user that inappropriate access may result in prosecution.

- A minimum password length of six to eight characters is required. The password should be a mix of numbers and letters. The password should not be a printed word found in any dictionary, regardless of language. Automated password-cracking tools start the attack by trying common words and names obtained from dictionaries. (We discuss the details of this in Chapter 7.)

- Unique passwords are forced. The computer system will not allow a password to be reused.

- Passwords are required to be changed at a frequency of 30 to 60 days, depending on the organization's policy.

- A user login ID is suspended after three to five unsuccessful login attempts.

- Unauthorized attempts to access the system are recorded in audit logs.

- The date and time of the last successful login will be displayed to the user upon login. This is to inform the user of when their login ID was last used.

A user login account is suspended or disabled when a notice is received from HR that a particular user is no longer employed by the organization. The disabled account needs to undergo administrative review prior to deletion of the user ID. This review seeks to discover whether the user engaged in any attempts of unauthorized access. If not, the user's data files are archived and forwarded to the appropriate department manager.

Just setting account lockout at three to five failed attempts is not good enough to thwart an attacker. Most hackers will try only one or two login attempts and then wait until later. This type of under-the-radar attack is common. I bet it's already occurring somewhere on your systems. Nobody would be wise to the attack unless they are monitoring every failed login attempt. This type of attack may occur for months, until the hacker gets a successful login.

Privileged Login Accounts

Logical access to system administration functions needs to be protected by a separation of duties. Privileged login accounts should not be used for any function other than administration and maintenance. System administrators should possess two separate login accounts. The first login account should be used exclusively for system administration duties. The second login account should have no privileges other than the basic rights of the common user.

The system administrator should perform office administration functions while logged in as a regular user. This reduces the potential impact of errors. In addition, it improves security by reducing the time duration of privileged access. If the administrator walks down the hall to the restroom, the risk of another individual gaining physical access to the computer has been reduced. The logical separation of duties can be verified by reading system logs.

All privileged login accounts contain control attributes of a normal user plus the following additional controls:

- Passwords must be changed every 30 days.

- Retired passwords must be written down and stored with backup tapes. Those passwords may be necessary again when older files are restored. Both the tapes and the password lists shall be stored in a fireproof-rated media safe, and also in a secure controlled environment designed for offsite media storage.

- The current passwords should be written down and stored in a safe in case something unforeseen happens to the system administrator. Current passwords will be required for disaster recovery. A second copy of the passwords should be kept in a safe offsite location separate from the data files.

You may use CertTest's free password generator to help create unique passwords. We grant you limited permission, for nonhostile purposes, to link to our web page. Auditors should encourage the use of stronger passwords. Just visit www.certtest.com/passgen.

Maintenance Login Accounts

All computer systems have default user accounts for system setup and maintenance. The login IDs of these maintenance accounts are often well known and commercially published. Hackers love to use maintenance accounts that have been left open by careless administrators. Default login accounts should be disabled in a production system. Any valid maintenance accounts should utilize nontypical login names with strong passwords or station restrictions. A station restriction allows login to occur only from a particular system, based on the machine's serial number or address.

Data File Controls

Access to data files should be controlled to ensure that unauthorized access is effectively impossible. Data access can occur through a perimeter control, direct file access, and middleware. *Middleware* is software that handles data traveling from the user interface to its destination in the database. Each of these types of access requires special controls. It is naive to think that a perimeter control will be completely effective.

Four basic types of data protection controls are required:

Standing data controls   *Standing data* refers to information contained in a file or database table. The information should possess controls commensurate with the data value or regulatory requirement. Standing data can be found in file cabinets, on disk drives, and on tape backups. Standing data may require additional controls such as storage in encrypted format within the database.

A significant portion of credit-card-number theft on the Internet is due to unauthorized copying of standing data in shopping cart databases. The U.S. Fair and Accurate Credit Transactions Act of 2003 mandates increased security with truncation of account numbers on receipts and destruction of account numbers after the transaction is processed. The Payment Card Industry (PCI) has its own rules governing credit card data regardless of whether it's printed or electronic.

System control parameters   Data files should be protected from system control parameters that would change the way the files are processed. System control parameters are used to customize the configuration settings and software applications. These settings can alter performance, logging, or file security. Improper implementation can lead to the loss of data, unauthorized access, or undetected errors.

Logical access controls   All access to data files should be forced through authentication in a user rights management program (access control program). Direct access to data files through Open Database Connectivity (ODBC) should be prohibited unless controlled by a rights management program with user authentication. It is common for a user to request direct access to the database for the purpose of reading data from another program. This type of uncontrolled direct access should be discouraged.

Transaction processing controls All transactions involving data files should be controlled with authentication and validation checks. The data transformation procedure must be officially approved and managed as part of the system application life cycle. Transaction processing monitors (TP monitors) are frequently used to ensure that database activity does not overload the processing capacity of the available hardware.

Application Processing Controls

System security and integrity is assured through the use of *application processing controls*. Logical access controls require the user to log in with a unique ID and password. The user can begin processing after a successful login. Each application should provide at least three internal processing controls: input, authorization, and output.

Input Controls

An *input control* ensures that only valid and authorized information is entered into a transaction. Input controls operate by using a combination of user authorization rights, edit checking, and data entry validation. Sequence checks are used to ensure that each transaction is processed only once. For an excellent analogy, consider how checks and ATM transactions are authorized at a bank.

Input authorization controls include the following:

- Unique login and password
- Signatures on source documents
- Identification of client workstation or terminal

Processing Controls

The purpose of *processing controls* is to ensure that the data and transactions are valid. Production software programs reside in the production program library. Access to the production program library should be restricted to read-only. There is no reason for the computer programmer or the user to have write access into a production program library.

 Allowing a programmer to have write access to a production program library would be a violation of change control. The computer operator will move authorized software from the development library to the production library when instructed and authorized by the change control manager.

Most data processing occurs by using a batch processing mode. The data batch may be small or large. The frequency of processing may be seconds or hours. Regardless of the method, it is necessary to ensure data integrity by using data validation and edit procedures. Without operational processing controls, the database would be no more effective than a garbage can.

Processing controls include the following:

Batch totals To compare input against actual processing.

Total number of items To verify that each item was processed.

Transaction logs To record activity.

Run-to-run totals To provide verification of the data values during the different stages of processing. This helps ensure the completeness of all transactions.

Limit checks To prevent processing of any amount in excess of the expected average. Overly large transactions will not be processed. For example, no employee should receive a paycheck for $50,000. That amount would obviously be excessive.

Exception reporting To identify errors. The exception may hold the batch and suspension until the errors are corrected, or reject individual transactions containing errors, or reject the entire batch of transactions.

Job cost accounting The operating cost of computer processing may be billed to a particular department, project, or application. It is important to observe the effectiveness of job cost accounting when it is used.

Output Controls

Data generated by the system should be protected to ensure confidentiality until it is delivered to the designated user. *Output controls* are just as important for paychecks as confidentiality is for business plans or HR records.

Let's review a few basic output controls:

Report generation and distribution Confidential reports should be output on a printer with restricted access. The report title should indicate that the report is confidential. Exception reports should always generate a page to indicate the exceptions that occurred, or a page to indicate that no exceptions occurred.

Negotiable instruments Checks, bonds, and stock certificates are frequently printed on computers. These items should be protected by a combination of logical and physical controls.

Report retention Certain types of reports may be required to be controlled under a document retention policy. This applies to records used for regulatory or legal compliance.

Event logs Processing logs and audit trails should be protected for integrity and confidentiality at all times. These logs need to be placed under record retention controls.

Antivirus Software

Computers are constantly attacked by malicious software. The attack may be in an email or file attachment. Viruses work by attaching themselves to the end of a file. Antivirus (AV) software will search for the signature (attributes) of known viruses. Without the latest AV updates, the system will be susceptible to attack by new viruses. It's not uncommon for AV updates to cause a conflict with other software on the user's computer. The IT help desk may direct users to download updates from the vendor's website or instruct the users to download updates only from an internal IT server.

Auditors should inquire how the user is to acquire AV updates. Is it directly from the vendor or from IT? The auditor would be interested to see whether the IT staff is actually testing updates on a computer similar to the user. If so, what is the delay interval between a vendor releasing AV updates and the time to install this update on all the user computers?

Is JavaScript considered active content?

Active Content and Mobile Software Code

Every IS auditor needs to understand the concept of active code and how it affects system security. *Active content* is software that is readily available for download from the Internet. Downloading special drivers, templates, updates, and utilities is a useful function for many people. Anyone who has used FedEx Kinko's online print service would agree that their software utility makes it easy to get your print job formatted, printed, bound, and delivered without ever leaving your desk. The FedEx programmers did an excellent job of developing downloadable software that helps the user.

Web pages have evolved into multimedia portals capable of delivering live weather maps, streaming news reports, business intelligence, and online education for those without the resources to attend class. Active content provides a useful capability that cannot be ignored. Attackers can abuse the vulnerabilities of active content unless preventative, detective, and corrective controls are implemented:

- IT executives should develop a policy regarding the use of active content (preventative).

- Additional procedures need to be developed to help reduce the associated risk. These include making configuration settings, enabling virus detection, enabling intrusion detection on each system, and linking violations to an incident response mechanism (detective and corrective controls).

Web browser functions

When surfing the Internet, the web pages we see are composed of special formatting codes along with embedded function tags. Hypertext Markup Language (HTML) handles the screen formatting. Special function tags perform other actions such as retrieving images, playing a multimedia video, playing music, or linking into another program. Programs such as Java and ActiveX extend the browser functionality.

Multipurpose Internet Mail Extensions (MIME)

MIME was originally designed to be used for electronic mail, although it has evolved for use by all types of multimedia. These extensions include content for the following:

- Audio transmission.

- Video images.

- Embedding text, images, and other data into a file. This is how Portable Document Format (PDF) and email works.

- Support for plug-in applications.

The magic of the Internet is powered by MIME. Benefits of using the Internet are so great that IT has to deal with the situation and be prepared to clean up any mess that occurs. The alternative is to disable Internet access. This strategy of no access may work if the mission data is beyond valuation. Otherwise, the replacement IT staff will be called upon to provide a more palatable solution.

Mobile software *(Applets) also Flash, Javascript, VisualBasic, ActiveX*

It's easy to download new programs from the internet. Sometimes a web page will automatically download a program for the user to increase the functionality of the web page. This is referred to as Mobile software. It's also known as mobile code or applets. The two dominate leaders are Java and ActiveX. Let's explore the basic characteristics of each.

Java   Java is one of those wonderful programs that runs inside the browser with special security to protect the user's computer. Java uses the *Java Virtual Machine (JVM)* program inside your browser to provide an elaborate level of security. This helps prevent Java programs from damaging your computer. Java permissions can be set to allow digitally signed applications to be run from websites you trust. Unsigned applications can be rejected for security. Three of the most common implementations of Java include:

- Small Java programs that download to the user are called *applets*.

- Java programs that run on the server are known as *server-side includes (SSIs)*, or *servlets*.

- *JavaScript (JScript)* can be used in applets or servlets.

Java is object oriented, which provides the delegation capability for applets and servlets to offload work to another applet or servlet. Untrusted servlets can be executed in a secure JVM environment to protect users from undesirable behavior by the program. Java's security manager feature mediates all access to system resources. Java still poses a minor security issue because it does not prevent a program from creating a denial-of-service condition nor does it prevent the exportation of a user's identity.

Active Server Pages (ASP)   Microsoft's operating system is written using Beginners All-purpose Symbolic Instruction Code (BASIC) with C++ and C# (C Sharp). This software language for beginners has evolved to include additional functions. The latest version is called *Visual Basic* and *Visual Basic Scripting Edition* (VBScript). Windows XP and Vista share the same programming language used in ASP. This programming commonality with the operating system is the root issue of security problems. Let's look at the security problems created when using Active server pages.

- Visual Basic and VBScript create interactive web pages under the nickname ActiveX.

- In theory, Microsoft's programming language was supposed to provide isolation boundaries to create a relatively secure environment. Implementation flaws and increased integration of the browser to the operating system have violated the barrier concept.

- Well-written ASP programs of a malicious nature can subvert Microsoft security by executing commands throughout the entire Microsoft operating system.

ActiveX places no restrictions on what the programmer can do. ActiveX software is digitally signed by the author via a technology scheme called *authenticode*. The publisher certificate for authenticode requires the publisher to pledge that they will not knowingly distribute harmful code; it does not ensure that the program is well behaved. Poorly designed programs can still do damage. ActiveX and authenticode place responsibility for security upon the user. We can see a comparison of risks in Table 6.1.

TABLE 6.1   Comparing Security Risks of Mobile Code

Low Risk	Moderate Risk	High Risk
Portable Document Format (PDF)	Applets	ActiveX
Adobe Shockwave Flash (SWF)	PostScript (PS)	
JavaScript	Visual Basic (VB)	

Mobile Code Security Policy

The mobile code security risk can be managed by using one of four basic concepts. Each of these will be determined by the organization's mission, capability, and value of data. The business unit and IT need to agree on which of these basic choices will be used:

- Disallow functionality (no benefit, no risk)
- Allow functionality only from internal servers (lower risk)
- Allow functionality from trusted external servers (moderate risk)
- Let the user do whatever they want from any server (high risk)

Choices made can be supported by the addition of technical controls using automated filters, application settings, digital signatures, isolation tools, and software behavior controls. Administrative controls are required to provide security audit, version control, user awareness training, and incident handling.

 As an IS auditor, you will be interested in how the decision was reached regarding the use of mobile code. Particular areas of interest include available evidence supporting or challenging the decision, how problems are detected, and the implementation of corrective controls.

Maintenance Controls

Maintenance controls exist to ensure that hardware and software changes will have a minimum impact on processing schedules and system availability. All maintenance should be approved by the change control process before it occurs. It is not uncommon for an organization to issue blanket approval for small changes with low risk. Let's look at some of the issues that should be addressed prior to performing maintenance.

Backup and Recovery

System programs and data should be backed up before maintenance occurs. The backup tapes (or media) should be read/write verified. Verifying a backup ensures that the data copy matches the original. The backup provides a second copy of current data if something goes horribly wrong.

Project Management

Project management with a risk analysis should be performed prior to starting maintenance. Most maintenance is a mini project. As the scope of the maintenance increases, so should the project planning. Each project plan should include a provision for workarounds and fallback procedures. A fallback procedure will be executed if the change fails to deliver the desired result.

Change Control Review

This topic is so important that it deserves its own section. Let's talk about it with some additional detail right now.

Change Management

We discussed change management in Chapter 3 and Chapter 5, "Life Cycle Management." In terms of IT service delivery, change management concerns relate to hardware and software maintenance. The introduction of any change constitutes a risk to system integrity and availability. However, change is inevitable.

A flowchart of the change management process appears in Figure 6.4.   *Pg 350*

NOTE   ISACA wants every CISA to be aware of four concepts that apply to change management in IT service delivery.

Configuration Control

The configuration of production systems must be controlled. The method of configuration control is similar to the one we discussed in Chapter 5 concerning software development. Changes should not be made to a production system unless the change has undergone formal testing under the control of the change management process.

Change Authorization

No change should occur without management authorization, and any changes must remain within the authorized scope. It is unfortunate that some technicians will attempt to implement additional changes at the first opportunity. These changes have consistently proven to be the source of a related failure. The objective of change authorization is to ensure that nobody bypasses the life cycle management process.

Emergency Changes

At times, emergency changes are necessary to minimize system interruption. A senior individual should be consulted for review and approval prior to implementing an emergency change. If the emergency change works, it may remain in production. If it fails, the change should be withdrawn (backed out) immediately. After an emergency change is implemented, the standard change control process will be invoked after the fact. The change should undergo formal testing and analysis to determine whether it may have created additional problems.

FIGURE 6.4   Change management process

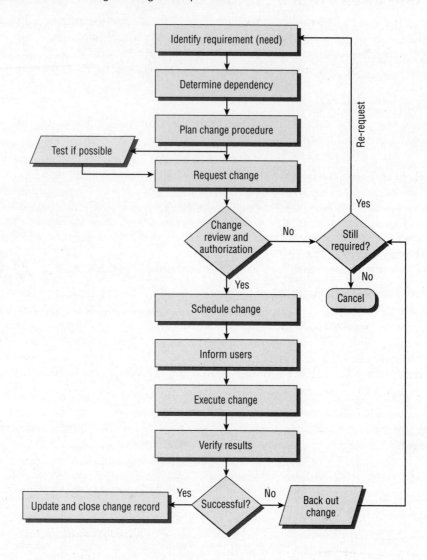

Separate Test Environment

The best way to prevent outages is through diligent testing. A separate test environment will save money by preventing outages that would otherwise occur. The price of nonconformance (failure) provides an excellent financial justification. Use the price of downtime to demonstrate the need (price of nonconformance). It will be more difficult if the auditee has misrepresented their actual downtime metrics. Remember system time is either counted as "up" for the user to operate at will, or it's counted as "down."

Administrative Management Controls

Administrative management controls are used to provide written policy and procedure guidance for people. These management controls help overcome shortfalls from the limited implementation of technical controls. You need to be aware of the common administrative controls used in IT service delivery. We will begin with software licensing.

Software Licensing

Software licenses are an asset of the corporation and need to be controlled and managed. All computer systems are required to have a valid, lawfully obtained software license for the operating system along with a license for each application and each utility installed. A violation of software copyright laws carries substantial penalties and the possibility of public embarrassment. You should observe the client's attitude toward software licenses. Most organizations purchase licenses by a per user count. There should be evidence to indicate that the licenses are managed for copyright compliance.

Asset and Media Tracking

Technology assets should be inventoried and tracked. Proper ownership labels or property tags should be in use. Tagging and labeling are preventative controls. The audit of inventory tags is a detective control. Media containing software and data should be managed under a physical asset program. This is required under several regulations, including Sarbanes-Oxley, Gramm-Leach-Bliley, HIPAA, Basel I & II, and the EU data protection act.

All media should be properly labeled. The media librarian is responsible for tracking the location of media. Evidence should exist to indicate that assets and media are properly controlled.

Canadian-based Absolute Software sells a special tracking service designed to recover stolen laptops. Their special utility installs on the laptop as a hidden software program. The laptop can be located by its unique beacon while on the Internet. Absolute's recovery desk notifies law enforcement and automatically provides all the paperwork necessary for search warrants. Absolute can remotely wipe the hard disk clean if necessary to prevent disclosure of the laptop data files. The company is run by former law enforcement officers and advertises a successful history of recovering three out of four laptops (75 percent).

Asset Disposal

A proper asset-disposal process contains procedures to ensure that data is purged (erased) from all equipment prior to disposal so that the data can never be recovered. Physical assets should be formally discharged from inventory. These assets can be destroyed, sold, or donated depending on the organization's desire. This is the seventh phase of the SDLC life cycle, as covered in Chapter 5.

All devices leaving the controlled environment must be purged of data by using disk-wiping utilities or degaussing methods. Disk reformatting is not an effective method because it will not destroy raw data that is accessible via special utilities that bypass the operating system. As an IS auditor, you need to determine whether the organization is following an acceptable asset-disposal process.

User Training

Proper training of system users can reduce the occurrence of problems. User training may include new hire orientation, security awareness training, software application training, and refresher programs for existing users. Well-educated users can provide valuable assistance to IT objectives. The educated user will understand when to bring potential concerns to the attention of IT management.

Procedures versus Actual Work

The procedures used in the operation of information technology systems should reflect the actual work performed. The purpose of a procedure is to ensure consistency with the desired result. Actual work that does not match the procedure would indicate a management control failure.

Ineffective and Inefficient Controls

A management review process should exist to deal with ineffective and inefficient controls. Failing controls should be reviewed for merit and potential impact. A compensating control may be implemented to overcome an ineffective control.

Using Compensating Controls

Compensating controls are used to reduce the impact of an error or omission. As you will recall from Chapter 2, "Audit Process," controls may be implemented by using a physical method (barrier), technical method (logical), or administrative method (policy and procedure). Compensating controls are used whenever there is a lack of segregation of duties. Examples of compensating controls include the following:

Job rotation   Rotating individuals between job functions reduces the potential of questionable activities. A person may be asked to take vacation in one- or two-week intervals. During that time, another person performs the job while looking to discover whether anything is out of the ordinary. This is a type of detective control. A collateral benefit is having more than one trained person capable of performing the function.

Audit   Auditing is an essential component of internal control. It is imperative that audit logs are functional and well preserved. The audits may be internal self-assessments or formal independent audits.

Reconciliation   Reconciliation is a type of audit in which records are compared to ensure that a balance exists. Reconciliation is used in financial reporting, project management, scope verification, computer processing batch verification, and other instances where an answer should be verified. Proper reconciliation increases the level of confidence.

Exception report   On occasion, an error or exception will exist in computer processing and audit logs. All jobs processed should print an automatic exception report to identify the jobs not processed correctly or print a report indicating that no exceptions existed. Exception reporting should be forwarded to the supervisor, escalating up each level until the problem is handled. The supervisor reviews evidence of the event and determines the action required. The goal is to ensure that exceptions are handled properly in accordance with the organizational goals, policies, and standards for internal control.

Transaction logs   Transaction logs provide audit trails that are designed to alert the user about a particular condition. The IS auditor needs to understand how the client reviews transaction logs, along with what action is taken. The absence of a transaction log would represent a major concern. A similar concern would exist if the transaction logs are not reviewed on a regular basis.

Supervisor review   The supervisor should review each of the compensating controls through observation and inquiry. Failure to do so may constitute negligence. The supervisory review is the last level of compensating control.

Capacity Management

Capacity management focuses on the monitoring of computing resources and planning for future availability. By using system-monitoring tools, the IT administrator should be able to reasonably estimate the system capacity needed. System utilization reports provide insight into the current processing workload. This workload can be prorated against the operating schedule to forecast future shortfalls.

External changes in the service-level agreements or number of users will have a direct impact on available capacity. During capacity management planning, it is important to assess single points of failure. There will always be a few single points of failure in a system because of the technology selected or the cost of redundancy.

Two Different Outcomes in Redundancy

When available, hardware redundancy may increase or decrease the normal operating capacity. For example, a duplicate disk drive system will never exceed 50 percent of combined total gross capacity. A 1,000 gigabyte (GB) drive array would split into two separate sets of disks with a total capacity of less than 500GB each. In fact, the usable capacity may be reduced to only 400GB each after allowing for the minimum free space. So only 400 would be usable from a total capacity of 1,000.

Duplicate firewalls, on the other hand, may double available capacity if they share the workload in parallel. The firewalls would provide two independent communication paths, thereby doubling normal capacity. We discuss this further in Chapter 7.

---

hmmm... interesting [handwritten annotation]

Problem Management

The IT operations staff should have a problem management process in place. Effective problem management provides a timely response by using predefined procedures that include a method for problem escalation.

Situations requiring problem management include the following:

Acceptable use policy (AUP) violation   Violation of the acceptable use policy could include the misuse of corporate resources or the presence of nonbusiness materials. The discovery of an AUP violation should trigger the incident-handling process and notification to Human Resources.

Job accounting   Computer processing is always subject to problems. Conditions of concern include abnormal job terminations and exception handling. Other problems can include jobs that run too fast or excessively slow for the volume of work. Jobs that end too fast may indicate that a portion of the processing was skipped. Consider, for example, a tape backup that appears to complete in record time. An investigation may find that the data written to tape is incomplete or nonexistent. Either condition would indicate a substantial problem.

Training   The training of users and staff is a good response to prevent the recurrence of a problem. Training plans should exist for new-hire orientation, basic user training, and additional awareness training. Test exercises for business continuity also serve to train individuals about their job role during a crisis.

All incidents, problems, and errors are to be recorded. Incidents reported to IT may be either accidental or malicious. An established procedure is required to ensure a thorough investigation.

Incident Handling

Certain events will need to be analyzed by a competent individual with the proper training. Every organization needs an incident response team (IRT) readily available. Whenever someone discovers or suspects that an incident has occurred, this team is quietly notified and called into action. One or more team members begin the investigation by analyzing available data to determine the possible impact. The objective is to limit the damage. A problem should be referred to the appropriate management to ensure that it receives the proper attention. All instances of problems are expected to be resolved in a timely manner. For example, computer security problems should be dealt with immediately. Network printer problems may be a lower priority.

Incident response teams are structured into one of three categories:

- Centralized team
- Distributed team reporting to a central authority
- Coordination team providing guidance and advice to individual responders

See pp 476 for emergency response planning & procedures and definition of "incident"

Members of the IRT should be formally designated via a written charter. This will help eliminate disputes over responding versus continuing to work on the tasks of their normal job. The staff of the IRT could be employees, outsourced, or a hybrid model. Team members may be needed 24/7, which creates a need for schedule planning. Each response will follow four phases of the incident response life cycle:

Phase 1: Preparation   The basic tasks include appointing team members, getting the team trained, and providing the necessary procedures with appropriate tools to perform the job. Preventative controls can save money by reducing the occurrence of problems. For example, properly maintained antivirus software eliminates many of the virus attacks. Dividing the network with predetermined disconnect points allows undamaged portions of the business to continue near-normal operation after infected areas have been isolated.

Phase 2: Detection and Analysis   System log reports and telephone calls to the help desk are excellent sources of detection. IT's constant monitoring should become the number one source of detection. The team is quietly activated after a problem is detected. In some instances, the incident may be a malicious attack. It is important not to signal the attacker that activity has been discovered. Certain events may require the assistance of outside experts, as in the case of forensic analysis. Test procedures and samples need to be documented. It is possible that the incident is a cyber crime scene containing evidence that must be protected.

Phase 3: Containment, Eradication, and Recovery   Incidents need to be contained as quickly as possible to prevent spreading more damage. Early containment helps keep the situation small enough to manage. Swift decisions are necessary to contain the problem. Acting too late will result in the situation overwhelming the available resources. This means that tough decisions should be preapproved with agreed-upon activation criteria. When the criteria are met, the predetermined action proceeds without any delay. Separate containment strategies should be developed for each major type of incident (fraud, theft, virus attack, server failure, and so forth).

Phase 4: Postincident Activity   After all the documentation is completed, the next step is to report the incident according to the requirements for your industry. Disclosure is becoming more common for legal compliance. One of the most valuable benefits from incident response is conducting a *lessons learned* meeting. The purpose is to analyze expected results and unexpected consequences in order to improve. Data and records collected from the event may need to be placed in longer-term evidence storage. (See the evidence life cycle in Chapter 2).

Now we need to finish the incident response section with a quick discussion about forensic computer investigations to dispel any misunderstanding.

Digital Forensics

Digital forensic investigations target computer data for laboratory analysis. This tiny section on the subject should not be construed as legal advice, because the scope of performing a digital forensic investigation exceeds the capability of this book. Our goal is to provide an introduction to the steps involved in conducting digital investigations related to criminal activity. New electronic discovery laws (e-discovery) are changing the rules and responsibilities in civil and criminal court cases. Auditors and investigators should require a clear, written mandate from the appropriate authority to indicate that they have received lawful authorization before starting a forensic investigation.

There are four basic phases in the forensic life cycle—acquisition, examination, utilization, and review.

Acquisition

The acquisition phase deals with acquiring data from the best possible sources. Data may be recovered from *deleted files*, which are not actually erased by the operating system. The computer simply marks the file as being eligible for overwriting at any time. The actual data is still present.

Computer backups are referred to as *logical backups*. The logical backup copies the directories and files of the volume but ignores deleted files and residual data in *slack space*. The slack is the difference between space actually used by the file and the space allocated. Slack space refers to remnant areas on the hard disk. Physical disk imaging, known as *bitstream imaging*, creates a bit-for-bit copy of the original media, including the deleted files and residual data in slack space. A special *write blocker* is used to prevent the analyzed computer from writing to its storage media.

Without a write blocker, the evidence becomes altered (tainted), which destroys the chain of custody.

Data may be permanently destroyed on a hard disk by a *wiping utility*, which uses random values to overwrite portions of the media. Security professionals use wiping utilities to clear hard disks for redeployment. Hackers use wiping utilities to destroy the evidence, thereby covering their tracks.

Four important points to remember in the acquisition phase are volatile data, nonvolatile data, avoiding use of the keyboard, and creating multiple images of the files.

- *Volatile data* refers to information in memory that will be lost when the power is shut off. Prematurely shutting off power erases the evidence of an attack, which is stored in computer chip RAM. (We covered this in the hardware section of Chapter 4).

- *Nonvolatile data* is the information contained on the hard disk and flash memory devices. A graceful shutdown causes the operating system to clean up temporary files and clear the swap file before shutting down. A hacker may attach a utility in the shutdown process to erase the trail of their malicious attack. Abruptly removing power from the system can preserve swap files, temporary data, and other information that may have been deleted during a graceful shutdown. Some systems will create an automatic dump of all their contents into a special file, known as a *crash dump*. Unfortunately a sudden loss of power could also corrupt the data.

Preplan response procedures by conducting a review by a forensics expert before getting attacked. The best response will be different on different operating systems.

- *Keyboard remapping* allows for individual keys or a combination of keystrokes to perform a very different function than their standard purpose. Hackers frequently remap their keyboard so a simple keystroke such as Ctrl+Alt or F2 will start an automatic wiping of the hard disk to destroy evidence. The best way for the forensic analyst to acquire data is without using the keyboard. Special disk-imaging hardware has been designed specifically for this purpose.

- Multiple copies of the files should be created to avoid working with the originals. Integrity of the files is important. Logical backup is acceptable for informal collection from a live system. Physical bitstream imaging is required if preserving the file times is important.

Examination

Forensic analysts must work with read-only copies of the files, not the originals. Many files contain a header, which can identify the type of data it contains. File extensions are not trustworthy, because the user can assign any extension to a file. Examination should use a toolkit that is well recognized by law enforcement agencies. The de facto standard for prosecution is EnCase Forensic software. Examination includes at least the following files:

- Live data files and deleted files that can be recovered

- Contents of memory, network connections, network shares, strings, and directories

- Configuration files for OS, users, passwords, processes run, and jobs

- Log files of system events, audit records, command history, and previously accessed files

- Application files

- System swap files, dump files, temporary files, and hibernation files

Files may be examined from the computer system and the network traffic. Security event management (SEM) software is capable of importing log history from various devices and creating a correlation of events. This allows the reconstruction of events by replaying log and traffic data. Examination of forensic information has been helpful to prosecute espionage, theft of intellectual property, fraud, blackmail, hacking, spamming, murder, and child pornography. Policies and procedures are also needed in case the investigation creates an inadvertent disclosure of sensitive information.

 Forensics experts with prior law enforcement experience are preferred as investigators. The special training and experience as a police officer or special agent are well respected by the judge.

Utilization

Analysts should review the results of data from individual applications to determine how events will fit together during reconstruction. Correlating events is the most effective way to handle the situation. A detailed, methodical approach is required.

Review

Constant review of the processes can help identify procedural errors, skill gaps, and shortcomings in the plans. Changes and updates in the legal process must be incorporated into the process. Failure to prove the case with a successful conviction may backfire with a countersuit for damages.

Now we have covered the most important objectives for this chapter. We are ready to begin the chapter review.

Summary

The performance of information technology is ultimately interpreted by three fundamental business performance indicators: the IT budget, user satisfaction, and technical indicators. Technical indicators could include a combination of automated and manual metrics. You can gain a reasonable understanding of IT performance by reviewing these indicators.

IT management should conduct regular performance reviews of all the items discussed in this chapter. Management and staff should make provisions for an independent audit to review their work. The auditor's focus in IT service delivery will be to determine the effectiveness and efficiency of IT.

When reviewing IT service delivery, the paramount concern is that action items are identified, properly tracked, assigned to a competent individual, and resolved in a timely manner. IT's performance can be measured by a combination of metrics, budget performance, and user satisfaction.

The IT auditor evaluates the client's performance and effectiveness of their management techniques.

Exam Essentials

Know how to evaluate service-level management practices from internal and external providers. Service-level management is based on an understanding between the provider and the user as to system availability, service definition, personnel qualifications, security requirements, and data integrity requirements. Service-level agreements (SLAs) need to include performance reporting, right to audit, SLA change procedures, and the cost of service.

Understand the principles of IT operations management to ensure that the service meets the business requirements. IT operations management can be aligned to business requirements by using the traditional processes of mission, strategy, and metrics supported by policies, standards, and procedures. The alignment can occur by using the balanced scorecard methodology we discussed in Chapter 3.

Understand how the IT organization implements functional controls for service delivery. Controls are established for system access, data files, input, application processing, output, maintenance, change management, asset control, capacity management, and problem management.

Understand the issues surrounding software licensing.   Software licenses are assets that need to be controlled, inventoried, tracked, and managed. Unauthorized installation of computer software is a violation of copyright law, which carries stiff penalties.

Understand production change control, release management, and configuration control. Changes need to be carefully managed in a production environment to prevent an interruption or outage. Software may be released as a major release, an update, or an emergency fix. Emergency changes should undergo the standard change management process after implementation.

Understand the demands of ensuring processing integrity.   Data files must be protected from unauthorized access. Standing data is vulnerable to unauthorized copying. Application processing uses input controls, processing controls to ensure the completeness of processing, and output controls to ensure the confidentiality of the output.

Understand the purpose of valid backups and project management in maintenance controls. Data backups are used to ensure that two copies of the data exist in case a failure occurs during maintenance. Project management is used with risk analysis to manage maintenance changes. The goal is to ensure that the maintenance occurs with the least possible impact to the system's availability and integrity.

Know the issues in problem and incident management.   Problem and incident management requires a timely response via predefined procedures and a method for escalating problems. The purpose of problem response is to correct a condition. Incident response determines the impact and the steps necessary for resolution. A concern is that the location of an incident may be a potential technology crime scene.

Understand the issues of maintaining evidence integrity during forensic investigations. Forensics requires special handling procedures during the four phases of acquisition, examination, utilization, and review. Useful data may be scavenged from volatile RAM and nonvolatile temporary files on the hard disk in slack space or swap files. Data files should be obtained by using a write blocker to prevent the source media from being accidentally altered, which would taint the evidence.

Review Questions

1. Performance of a third party should be compared to the agreed-upon service-level metrics and must be

   A. Supplied by an independent employee of the service provider.

   B. Accepted at face value by the customer.

   C. Reviewed by management.

   D. Review is not necessary because it is a third party and outside the customer's control.

2. What is the most important responsibility of the IT security person?

   A. Controlling and monitoring compliance to data security policies

   B. Promoting security awareness within the organization

   C. Establishing procedures for IT and reviewing for legal accuracy

   D. Assisting in system administration of the servers and database

3. Segregation of duties may not be practical in a small environment. A single employee may be performing the combined functions of server operator and application programmer, for example. The IS auditor should recommend controls for which of the following?

   A. Automated logging of changes made to development libraries

   B. The hiring of additional technical staff to force segregation of duties

   C. Preventing the operator login ID from making program modifications

   D. Procedures verifying that only approved program changes are implemented

4. What are the four basic types of metrics that can be used to measure IT performance?

   A. Efficiency, implementation, impact, effectiveness

   B. Cost, quantifiable, qualitative, historical

   C. Process control, compliance, efficiency, cost

   D. Service definition, performance goal, cost, effectiveness

5. What type of control is representative of exception reporting?

   A. Processing

   B. Output

   C. Database integrity

   D. Service level

6. How should management act to best deal with emergency changes?

   A. Emergency changes cannot be made without advance testing.

   B. All changes should still undergo review.

   C. The change control process does not apply to emergency conditions.

   D. Emergency changes are not allowed under any condition.

7. What is one of the bigger concerns regarding asset disposal?

   A. Residual asset value

   B. Employees taking disposed property home

   C. Standing data

   D. Environmental regulations

8. Why is ongoing system monitoring important?

   A. For preventative control

   B. For historical logging and trend analysis

   C. To collect metrics for SLA reports

   D. To find inconsistencies and errors

9. What is the primary objective in problem escalation?

   A. Improve customer satisfaction

   B. Optimize the number of skilled personnel

   C. Ensure the correct response

   D. Prove that the IT staff is competent

10. Which of the following is a major issue facing incident response?

   A. The location may be a technology crime scene.

   B. Scheduling of personnel.

   C. Developing appropriate procedures.

   D. Compliance with IT policies.

11. Which of the following functions should be separated from the others if segregation of duties cannot be achieved in an automated system?

   A. Origination

   B. Authorization

   C. Correction

   D. Reprocessing

12. What is the primary concern regarding maintenance login accounts?

   A. Computer systems have default user accounts for system setup.

   B. Access to maintenance accounts must be restricted to a particular station address.

   C. Maintenance accounts must be configured to use the hardware that was selected by the organization.

   D. The default login ID used by maintenance accounts is often well known.

13. An IS auditor is auditing controls related to an employee termination. Which of the following is the *most* important aspect to be reviewed?

   A. Company staff are notified about the termination.

   B. All login accounts of the employee are terminated.

   C. The details of the employee have been removed from active payroll files.

   D. Company property provided to the employee has been returned.

14. What are the three layers for scoring IT performance according to ISACA?

   A. Policy, standards, established procedures

   B. Budget, service-level agreement, problem management

   C. Mission, strategy, metrics

   D. Definition of service, internal controls, change management

15. What is one of the first concerns that the IS auditor should have when reviewing service-level agreements?

   A. The vendor can provide evidence that security controls are present.

   B. The services in the agreement are aligned to actual business needs.

   C. The client received the absolute best price for services offered.

   D. The contract guaranteed the right to audit the outsource vendor.

16. Which of the following statements is *not* true concerning SLA performance reporting?

   A. Metrics are reported against qualitative measurement.

   B. Both parties need to agree on the content of metrics.

   C. Metrics are reported against quantitative measurement.

   D. Metrics must be developed to fill actual business objectives.

17. Which of the following statements about standing data is true?

   A. Standing data improves database performance. The data is standing ready for processing.

   B. Standing data is an operational requirement.

   C. Standing data is a security concern.

   D. Standing data is a normal occurrence in the database.

18. Which of the following is *not* an input authorization control?

   A. Signatures on source documents

   B. Sequence numbers

   C. Management review

   D. Separation of duties

19. What are three of the four key perspectives used to create the IT balanced scorecard for service delivery?

    A. Cost reduction, business process, growth

    B. Business justification, service-level agreements, budget

    C. Organizational staffing, cost reduction, employee training

    D. Service level, critical success factors, vendor selection

20. What is biggest advantage of using a lights-out operation?

    A. Reduced operating expense.

    B. The ability to run systems by remote control.

    C. Removing personnel from the data center reduces risk.

    D. Service personnel will occupy the room only during times of maintenance.

21. What is likely to be the biggest issue regarding log management?

    A. Systems need to be configured, and then someone needs to read the logs and respond to the findings.

    B. Log management is not required. It's considered a waste of time.

    C. Log files need to be configured, captured, read, and backed up.

    D. System log files consume valuable disk space and are used only by the auditor.

22. What is an applet compared to a servlet?

    A. An applet is mobile program running on the workstation, and a servlet is a server-side include (SSI).

    B. There is no difference, because both can run on the same computer.

    C. An applet is safer than a servlet.

    D. A servlet uses a Java Virtual Machine or ActiveX control to prevent crashing.

23. When separation of duties is not possible, what would be the terminology for forcing employees to take vacation, job rotation, reconciliation, and supervisor review?

    A. Preventative control

    B. Corrective control

    C. Compensating control

    D. Transaction control

24. Which qualification would be preferred in forensic investigations?

    A. Advanced Microsoft training and MCSE certification

    B. College degree in criminal science

    C. Masters degree in computer science

    D. Prior experience as a police officer or special agent

25. What is the purpose of a transaction processing monitor?

    A. Notify the operator or user of processing exceptions

    B. Verify the account totals for each job processed

    C. Provide limit checks so overly large transactions will not be processed

    D. Keep database activity from overloading the hardware

26. Which of the following statements is true regarding the programmer?

    A. Is responsible for maintaining the production software currently in use by the user

    B. Should never have access to the production software library

    C. Makes changes to the production version of software under the supervision of a computer operator

    D. Is responsible for reviewing user change requests and implementing approved changes to the production library

27. Which of the following refers to providing verification of data values during different stages of processing for the purpose of completeness of the transaction?

    A. Run-to-run totals

    B. Job cost accounting

    C. Limit checks

    D. Validation checker

28. Which of the following is the best definition of slack space on a hard disk?

    A. Unused space leftover after disk formatting

    B. Disk tracks and sectors marked as unusable

    C. Difference between space allocated and space actually used

    D. Uncompressed space remaining on the disk partition

29. Which of the following methods is used to make a backup copy of all the data files for a forensic investigation?

    A. Bitstream image backup

    B. Logical image backup

    C. Full disk backup

    D. Nonvolatile backup

30. Which of the following methods is designed to permanently destroy data on a hard disk?

    A. Reformatting the disk

    B. Deleting files

    C. Read blocker

    D. Disk wiping

31. Which of the following is the best description for a computer-generated report being printed during each processing run to indicate that no problems occurred during processing?

  A. Exception report

  B. Job audit log

  C. Run totals report

  D. Problem log

32. Which of the following is the best description of nonvolatile data?

  A. Contents of random access memory

  B. Data on the hard disk

  C. Data acquired by forensic recovery

  D. Data from logical disk backups

33. Which of the following is the most important component of customer satisfaction according to ISACA?

  A. External measurement

  B. System performance metrics

  C. Customer surveys

  D. Internal measurement

34. Who is responsible for the daily handling and tracking of physical media containing data files?

  A. System administrator

  B. IT manager

  C. Media librarian

  D. Business user

35. Why is a write blocker needed during the acquisition phase of digital forensics?

  A. To keep the hacker from changing or destroying evidence remaining on the hard disk, in order to preserve the chain of custody

  B. To prevent evidence from being altered, which destroys the chain of custody

  C. To disable the hacker's self-destruct utility from wiping the disk and destroying the chain of evidence

  D. To prevent activating a hidden keyboard remapping utility that the hacker installed to destroy evidence and cover their tracks

Answers to Review Questions

1.   C. All performance by a third party under the service-level agreement should be compared to the service levels that the provider and the user of the service agreed on.

2.   A. The primary responsibility of the IT information security person is to ensure the proper implementation of data security policies and to monitor the level of compliance.

3.   D. Compensating controls may be used when segregation of duties is not practical for a small staff. Procedures must exist to verify that only approved program changes are implemented.

4.   A. The four basic types of metrics are efficiency (which indicates timeliness), implementation (which demonstrates a comparative count or percentage attained), impact (shown as a qualitative measure of incidents sorted by type or represented as a dollar figure), and effectiveness (measured as a quantifiable number demonstrating satisfactory resolution).

5.   A. Exception reporting is a processing control used to capture input errors before processing occurs. The exception may be held in suspension until the errors are corrected or rejected.

6.   B. All emergency changes should still undergo the formal change management process after the fact.

7.   C. Any standing data should be purged from the equipment prior to disposal.

8.   D. Proper IT management focuses on proactive discovery of inconsistencies, errors, and processing failures. The results can be used for secondary value in trend analysis and SLA reporting.

9.   C. Problem escalation is used to ensure that the problem is analyzed by a competent individual with the proper training.

10.   A. The incident location may be a technical crime scene. The response should be preplanned and structured to ensure that the value of evidence is not diminished and confidentiality is maintained. The other points may be contributing circumstances but are not major issues.

11.   B. Authorization for changes should be separated from other work if separation of duties cannot be achieved. Additional compensating controls would be required.

12.   D. The default login ID used for maintenance accounts is frequently well known and commercially published. Login may be restricted to a particular station address. However, that is not the primary concern.

13.   B. Employee access to information systems should be promptly terminated. The accounts for contractors no longer employed by the organization should be suspended. All accounts should be reviewed before the account is deleted.

14.   C. ISACA defines the three layers for IT scoring as mission, strategy, and meaningful metrics for performance measurement.

15.   B. The services provided should fulfill the organization's business objectives. The second concern would be the presence of security controls, followed by the right to audit. The last concern should be the absolute best price. Price would not matter if the services provided did not fulfill an actual business requirement.

16. A. Service-level performance metrics should be quantitative measurements rather than qualitative. Qualitative measurements are too subjective. All other statements are true.

17. C. Standing data is a security concern that requires additional controls such as storage in an encrypted format.

18. D. Separation of duties does not grant input authorization. The other three answers represent valid input authorization.

19. A. The four perspectives on the IT balanced scorecard are the customer perspective, business process perspective, financial perspective, and growth perspective. Each of these seek to define the highest return by IT. The scorecard concept was introduced in Chapter 3. It's used to define the user's view for specifications of IT operations mentioned in this chapter.

20. C. Removing personnel from the data center reduces the risk to systems by reducing the risk of error, malicious attacks, and environmental contaminants.

21. C. Log files must be backed up. The best practice is to export log files to a Syslog. This helps protect the files from damage by moving them to another computer. Logs need to be configured to include the best possible data. Log files are used by IT operations staff for incident response. Auditors use log file data for audit evidence.

22. A. Applets are small programs that download to the user's computer. Applets are considered mobile code. The equivalent program running on the server is called a server-side include (SSI), named after the programmer's terminology.

23. C. Compensating controls are administrative controls used to detect problems that may be hidden by the person performing the work. Examples include audits, supervisor review, forced vacations, transaction logging, and account reconciliation.

24. D. Prior experience as a police officer or special agent is preferred because of their special training in crime scene management. Law enforcement officers are usually well respected by the court judge.

25. D. TP monitors are used to keep the database activity from overloading the available hardware.

26. B. Software developers (programmers) should not have privileged access to production libraries. A programmer may have the same limited access as the user, but should never be allowed to move programs into production. Doing so would violate change control and separation of duties. The system operator is responsible for moving approved programs into the production library.

27. A. Run-to-run totals are used to ensure the completeness of transaction during various stages of processing.

28. C. *Slack space* refers to the remnant areas of the hard disk. The slack is the difference between space actually used by the file and the space allocated. Remnants of data files often remain in slack space until overwritten or until the drive is defragmented.

29. A. Physical disk imaging (also known as bitstream backup) copies the entire disk by using every data bit, including deleted files and residual data in slack space. A standard computer backup would copy only.

30. D. A disk-wiping utility is designed to prevent data from being recovered from a hard disk. Disk formatting simply maps available storage locations. Reformatting the disk is equivalent to tearing the index section out of a book and leaving all the other original pages intact. Disk wiping writes random characters across every data bit location on the disk by using multiple passes to ensure that no data is leftover that may be readable.

31. A. Exception reports should be automatically created during all job processing. The report identifies any exceptions that occurred or indicates that no exceptions occurred. Exception reporting is a type of detective control.

32. B. Volatile data still remains on the hard disk, including temporary files and the contents of the system swap file.

33. A. External measurement represents the customer's perspective. Their interest is system availability, perception of the service received from the help desk, IT worker's attitude, and response time to get their problem fixed.

34. C. The media librarian is responsible for tracking all the media containing data. Proper tracking includes signing in and signing out physical backup media as it's transferred to and from offsite storage or elsewhere in the organization. The media librarian is usually a dedicated person in larger organizations or at least someone formally assigned in smaller organizations.

35. B. Write blockers are used during forensic bit-imaging backups to prevent evidence from being altered, which destroys the chain of custody.

Chapter 7

Information Asset Protection

THE OBJECTIVE OF THIS CHAPTER IS TO ACQUAINT THE READER WITH THE FOLLOWING CONCEPTS:

- ✓ Threats to security, perpetrators, and attack methods
- ✓ Administrative management controls used to promote security
- ✓ Implementing data classification schemes to specify appropriate handling of records
- ✓ Physical security protection methods
- ✓ Perimeter security designs, firewalls, and intrusion detection
- ✓ Logical access controls for identification, authentication, and restriction of users
- ✓ Changes in wireless security, including the robust security network
- ✓ Encryption systems using symmetric and asymmetric public keys
- ✓ Dealing with malicious software, viruses, worms, and other attacks
- ✓ Storage, retrieval, transport, and disposition of confidential information
- ✓ Controls and risks with the use of portable devices
- ✓ Security testing, monitoring, and assessment tools

In this chapter, you will study the implementation of access controls. These controls are implemented by using administrative, physical, and technical methods. The IS auditor is required to evaluate the implementation, processes, and procedures used by the client.

The goal of information asset protection is to ensure that adequate safeguards are in use to store, access, transport, and ultimately dispose of confidential information. The auditor must understand how controls promote confidentiality, integrity, and availability.

We will discuss a variety of technical topics related to network security, data encryption, design of physical protection, biometrics, and user authentication. This chapter represents the most significant area of the CISA exam.

Understanding the Threat

Protecting information assets is a significant challenge. The very subject of security conjures up a myriad of responses. This chapter provides you with a solid overview of practical information about security. The unfortunate reality is that concepts of security have not evolved significantly over the last 2,000 years. Let us explain.

The medieval design of security is still pervasive. Most of your customers will view security as primarily a perimeter defense. History is riddled with failed monuments attesting to the folly of overreliance on perimeter defenses. Consider the castle walls to be equivalent to the office walls of the client's organization. Fresh water from the creek would be analogous to our modern-day utilities. The castle observation towers provide visibility for internal affairs and awareness of outside threats. The observation tower is functionally equal to network management and intrusion detection. A fortress drawbridge provides an equivalent function of the network firewall, allowing persons we trust to enter our organization. The castle courtyard serves as the marketplace or intranet. This is where our vendors, staff, and clients interact. During medieval times, it was necessary for our emissaries to enter and exit the castle fortress in secret. Confidential access was accomplished via a secret tunnel. Our modern-day equivalent to the secret tunnel is a virtual private network (VPN). Consider these thoughts for a moment while you look at Figure 7.1, concerning the medieval defensive design.

It is possible that security has actually regressed. In medieval times, royalty would use armed guards as an escort when visiting trading partners. In the modern world, the princess is given a notebook computer, PDA, cell phone, and airline ticket with instructions to check in later. Where is the security now?

FIGURE 7.1   Medieval defensive design

Medieval castles fell as a result of infiltration, betrayal, loss of utilities such as fresh water, and brute force attacks against the fortress walls. This example should make it perfectly clear why internal controls need improvement. The only possible defensive strategy utilizes multiple layers of security with a constant vigil by management. Anything less is just another castle waiting to fall.

Let's take a quick look at some examples of computer crime and threats to the information assets.

Examples of Threats and Computer Crimes

There is nothing new about the threats facing organizations. History shows that these threats and crimes date back almost 4,000 years (over 130 generations). Therefore, none of these should be a surprise. We need to take a quick review of the threats and crimes that shall be mitigated with administrative, physical, and technical controls:

Theft   The *theft* of information, designs, plans, and customer lists could be catastrophic to an organization. Consider the controls in place to prevent theft of money or embezzlement. Have equivalent controls in place to prevent the theft of valuable intellectual property.

Fraud   Misrepresentation to gain an advantage is the definition of *fraud*. Electronic records may be subject to remote manipulation for the purpose of deceit, suppression, or unfair profit.

Fraud may occur with or without the computer. Variations of fraud include using false pretenses, also known as *pretexting*, for any purpose of deceit or misrepresentation.

Sabotage   *Sabotage* is defined as willful and malicious destruction of an employer's property, often during a labor dispute or to cause malicious interference with normal operations.

Blackmail   *Blackmail* is the unlawful demand of money or property under threat to do harm. Examples are to injure property, make an accusation of a crime, or to expose disgraceful defects. This is commonly referred to as *extortion*.

Industrial espionage   The world is full of competitors and spies. *Espionage* is a crime of spying by individuals and governments with the intent to gather, transmit, or release information to the advantage of any foreign organization. It's not uncommon for governments to eavesdrop on the communications of foreign companies. The purpose is to uncover business secrets to share with companies in their country. The intention is to steal any perceived advancements in position or technology. Telecommunications traveling through each country are subject to legal eavesdropping by governments. Additional care must be taken to keep secrets out of the hands of a competitor.

Unauthorized disclosure   *Unauthorized disclosure* is the release of information without permission. The purpose may be fraud or sabotage. For example, unauthorized disclosure of trade secrets or product defects may cause substantial damage that is irreversible. The unauthorized disclosure of client records would cause a violation of privacy laws, not to mention details that would be valuable for a competitor.

Loss of credibility   *Loss of credibility* is the damage to an organization's image, brand, or executive management. This can severely impact revenue and the organization's ability to continue. Fraud, sabotage, blackmail, and unauthorized disclosure may be used to destroy credibility.

Loss of proprietary information   The mishandling of information can result in the loss of trade secrets. Valuable information concerning system designs, future marketing plans, and corporate formulas could be released without any method of recovering the data. Once a secret is out, there is no way to make the information secret again.

Legal repercussions   The breach of control or loss of an asset can create a situation of undesirable attention. Privacy concerns have created new requirements for public disclosure following a breach. Without a doubt, the last thing an organization needs is increased interest from a government regulator. Stockholders and customers may have grounds for subsequent legal action in alleging negligence or misconduct, depending on the situation.

According to the U.S. Federal Bureau of Investigation (FBI), the top three losses in 2005–2006 were due to virus attack, unauthorized access, and theft of proprietary information. There is a trend of dramatic increase in unauthorized access and theft of proprietary information. So, the auditor may ask, who is doing this?

Real World Scenario

Examples of Legal Repercussions

Countless news stories have appeared about the criminal investigation concerning the use of pretexting at Hewlett-Packard during a political battle in upper management.

Morgan Stanley incurred sanctions from the Security Exchange Commission for failing to maintain auditable records of all emails between the brokerage and its clients, as required under SEC rule 17a-4.

Life Time Fitness is the target of investigation by the Texas attorney general for improperly discarding intact records with membership applications of its clients. Life Time Fitness membership records were found in the dumpster at more than a dozen of its fitness centers. This security breach exposed personal information, including driver's license data, credit card data, and other private information.

Identifying the Perpetrators

There is one fundamental difference between a victim and a perpetrator. The victim did not act with malice. The perpetrators of crime may be casual or sophisticated. Their motive may be financial, political, thrill seeking, or a biased grudge against the organization. The damage impact is usually the same regardless of the perpetrator's background or motive. A common trait is that a perpetrator will have time, access, or skills necessary to execute the offense.

Today's computer criminal does not require advanced skills, although they would help. A person with mal-intent needs little more than access to launch their attack. For this reason, strong access controls are mandatory. The FBI reported that the number of internal attacks were approximately equal to the number of external attacks since 2005. So, who is the attacker?

Hackers

The term *hacker* has a double meaning. The honorable interpretation of hacker refers to a computer programmer who is able to create usable computer programs where none previously existed. In this Study Guide, we refer to the dishonorable interpretation of a hacker—an undesirable criminal. The criminal hacker focuses on a desire to break in, take over, and damage or discredit legitimate computer processing. The first goal of hacking is to exceed the authorized level of system privileges. This is why it is necessary to monitor systems and take swift action against any individual who attempts to gain a higher level of access. Hackers may be internal or external to the organization. Attempts to gain unauthorized access within the organization should be dealt with by using the highest level of severity, including immediate termination of employment.

Crackers

The term *cracker* is a variation of *hacker*, with the analogy equal to a safe cracker. Some individuals use the term cracker in an attempt to differentiate from the honorable computer programmer definition of hacker. The criminal cracker and criminal hacker terms are used interchangeably. Crackers attempt to illegally or unethically break into a system without authorization.

Script Kiddies

A number of specialized programs exist for the purpose of bypassing security controls. Many hacker tools began as well-intentioned tools for system administration. The argument would be the same if we were discussing a carpenter's hammer. A carpenter's hammer used for the right purpose is a constructive tool. The same tool is a weapon if used for a nefarious purpose. A *script kiddy* is an individual who executes computer scripts and programs written by others. Their motive is to hack a computer by using someone else's software. Examples include password decryption programs and automated access utilities. Several years ago, a login utility was created for Microsoft users to get push-button access into a Novell server. This nifty utility was released worldwide before it was recognized that the utility bypassed Novell security. The utility was nicknamed Red Button and became immensely popular with script kiddies. Internal controls must be put in place to restrict the possession or use of administration utilities. Violations should be considered severe and dealt with in the same manner as hacker violations.

Employee Betrayal

There is a reason why the FBI report cited the high volume of internal crimes. A person within the organization has more access and opportunity than anyone else. Few persons would have a better understanding of the security posture and weaknesses. In fact, an employee may be in a position of influence to socially engineer coworkers into ignoring safeguards and alert conditions. This is why it is important to monitor internal employee satisfaction. The great medieval fortresses fell by the betrayal of trusted allies.

Ethical Hacker Gone Bad

The term *ethical hacker* or *white hat* is a new definition in computer security. An ethical hacker is one who is authorized to test computer hacks and attacks with the goal of identifying an organization's weakness. Some individuals participate in special training to learn about penetrating computer defenses. This will usually result in one of two outcomes.

In the first outcome, a few of the ethical white-hat technicians will exercise extraordinary restraint and control. The objective of ethical hacking is to exercise hacker techniques only in a highly regimented, totally supervised environment. The white-hat technician will operate from a prewritten test plan, reviewed by internal audit or management oversight. The slightest deviation is grounds for termination. This additional level of control is to protect the organization from error or personal agenda by the white-hat technician.

Separation of duties requires the white hat (ethical hacker) to operate under the management of internal audit or an equivalent audit department. Forced separation of duties provides evidence that protects both management and the technician. The ethical hacker must not have any operational duties or otherwise be involved in daily IT operations.

The second outcome is that a white-hat technician will direct their own efforts. Some individuals will demonstrate great pride in their ability to circumvent required controls. These self-directed hacking techniques create an unacceptable level of risk for multiple reasons including organizational liability. The series of movies about Jason Bourne, *The Bourne Identity* (2002), *The Bourne Supremacy* (2004), and *The Bourne Ultimatum* (2007) illustrate the risk of self-directed activity. After management loses control, there is no way back. These fictional movies are, in part, based on facts from real events.

As professional auditors, we've been engaged on several occasions to determine whether the internal staff has been using hacker techniques and tools without explicit test plans and approval. Proper test documentation requires keystroke-level detail combined with specific steps to capture corresponding evidence. In each event except one, the technician was fired for violating internal controls. Additional controls are necessary when a white-hat technician is employed by the organization. Honest people may be kept honest with proper supervision.

Third Parties

External persons are referred to as third parties. *Third parties* include visitors, vendors, consultants, maintenance personnel, and the cleaning crew. These individuals may gain access and knowledge of the internal organization.

You would be surprised by how many times auditors have been invited to join the client in a meeting room with internal plans still visible on the whiteboards. The client's careless disregard is obvious by the words *important— do not erase* emblazoned across the board. You can bet this same organization allows their vendors to work unsupervised. In the evening, the cleaning crew will unlock and open every door on the floor for several hours while vacuuming and emptying waste baskets. We seriously doubt the cleaning crew would challenge a stranger entering the office. In fact, a low-paid cleaning crew may be exercising their own agenda.

Ignorance

The term *ignorance* is simply defined as the lack of knowledge. An ignorant person may be a party to a crime and not even know it. Even worse, the individual may be committing an offense without realizing the impact of their actions. Management may be guilty of not understanding their current risks and corresponding regulations. The statement "We/I did not know" is the fastest route to a conviction. Every judge will agree that ignorance of the law is not an excuse. Every manager is expected to research the regulations bearing upon their business practice. There is no legal excuse for ignorance or apathy. Fortunately, ignorance can be cured by training. This is the objective of user training for internal controls. By teaching the purpose of internal security controls, the organization can reduce their overall risk.

Overview of Attack Methods

Your clients will expect you to have knowledge about the different methods of attacking computers. We will try to take the boredom out of the subject by injecting practical examples. Computer attacks can be implemented with the computer or against a computer. There are basically two types of attacks: passive and active. Let's start with passive attacks.

Passive Attacks

Passive attacks are characterized by techniques of observation. The intention of a passive attack is to gain additional information before launching an active attack. Three examples of passive attacks are network analysis, traffic analysis, and eavesdropping:

Network analysis The computer traffic across a network can be analyzed to create a map of the hosts and routers. Common tools such as HP OpenView or OpenNMS are useful for creating network maps. The objective of network analysis is to create a complete profile of the network infrastructure prior to launching an active attack. Computers transmit large numbers of requests that other computers on the network will observe. Simple maps can be created with no more than the observed traffic or responses from a series of ping commands. The network *ping* command provides a simple communications test between two devices by sending a single request, also known as a ping. The concept of creating maps by using network analysis is commonly referred to as *painting* or *footprinting*.

Host traffic analysis *Traffic analysis* is used to identify systems of particular interest. The communication between host computers can be monitored by the activity level and number of service requests. Host traffic analysis is an easy method used to identify servers on the network.

Specific details on the host computer can be determined by using a *fingerprinting* tool such as Nmap. The Nmap utility is active software that sends a series of special commands, each command unique to a particular operating system type and version. For example, a Unix system will not respond to a NetBIOS type 137 request. However, a computer running Microsoft Windows will answer. The exact operating system of the computer can usually be identified with only seven or eight simple service requests. Host traffic analysis will provide clues to a system even if all other communication traffic is encrypted. This is an excellent tool for tracking down a rogue

IP address. The Nmap utility provides information as to whether the destination address is a Unix computer, Macintosh computer, computer running Windows, or something else like an HP printer. This fingerprinting technique is also popular with hackers for the same reason.

Eavesdropping   *Eavesdropping* is the traditional method of spying with the intent to gather information. The term originated from a person spying on others while listening under the roof eaves of a house. Computer network analysis is a type of eavesdropping. Other methods include capturing a hidden copy of files or copying messages as they traverse the network. Email messages and instant messaging are notoriously vulnerable to eavesdropping because of their insecure design. Computer login IDs, passwords, and user keystrokes can be captured by using eavesdropping tools. Encrypted messages can be captured by eavesdropping with the intention of breaking the encryption at a later date. The message can be read later, after the encryption is compromised. Eavesdropping helped the Allies crack the secret code of radio messages sent using the German Enigma machine in World War II. Network sniffers are excellent tools for capturing communications traveling across the network.

Now let's move on to discuss the active attacks.

Active Attacks

Passive attacks tend to be relatively invisible, whereas active attacks are easier to detect. The attacker will proceed to execute an active attack after obtaining sufficient background information. The *active attack* is designed to execute an act of theft or to cause a disruption in normal computer processing. Following is a list of active attacks:

Social engineering   Criminals can trick an individual into cooperating by using a technique known as *social engineering*. The social engineer will fraudulently present themselves as a person of authority or someone in need of assistance. The social engineer's story will be woven with tiny bits of truth. All social engineers are opportunists who gain access by asking for it. For example, the social engineer may pretend to be a contractor or employee sent to work on a problem. The social engineer will play upon the victim's natural desire to help.

🌐 Real World Scenario

Real-Life Social Engineering

There is a wonderful movie about social engineering titled *Catch Me If You Can* (released in 2002), starring Leonardo DiCaprio with Tom Hanks and Christopher Walken. It is the story of teenager Frank Abagnale who successfully masqueraded for years as a doctor who actually practiced in a hospital, a commercial airline pilot who actually flew in the cockpit, and a lawyer with a genuine appointment to assistant district attorney. Abagnale at 19 was the youngest person to be on the FBI's most wanted list for forging over $6 million in fake checks passed worldwide.

Phishing   A new social engineering technique called *phishing* (pronounced *fishing*) is now in use. The scheme utilizes fake emails sent to unsuspecting victims, which contain a link to the criminal's counterfeit website. Anyone can copy the images and format of a legitimate website by using their Internet browser. A phishing criminal copies legitimate web pages into a fake email or to a fake website. The message tells the unsuspecting victim that it is necessary to enter personal details such as U.S. social security number, credit card number, bank account information, or online user ID and password. Phishing attacks can also be used to implement spyware on unprotected computers. Many phishing attacks can be avoided through user education.

Dumpster diving   Attackers will frequently resort to rummaging through the trash for discarded information. The practice is also known as *dumpster diving*. Dumpster diving is perfectly legal under the condition that the individuals are not trespassing. This is the primary reason why proper destruction is mandatory. Most paper records and optical disks are destroyed by shredding.

Virus   Computer *viruses* are a type of malicious program designed to self-replicate and spread across multiple computers. The purpose of the computer virus is to disrupt normal processing. A computer virus may commence damage immediately or lie dormant, awaiting a particular circumstance such as the date of April Fools' Day. Viruses will automatically attach themselves to the outgoing files. The first malicious computer virus came about in the 1980s during prototype testing for self-replicating software. Antivirus software will stop known attacks by detecting the behavior demonstrated by the virus program (*signature detection*) or by appending an antivirus flag to the end of a file (*inoculation*, or *immunization*). New virus attacks can be detected if any program tries to append data to the antivirus flag. Not all antivirus software works by signature scanning; it can also use heuristic scanning, integrity checking, or activity blocking. These are all valid virus detection methods.

Worm   Computer *worms* are destructive and able to travel freely across the computer network by exploiting known system vulnerabilities. Worms are independent and will actively seek new systems on their own.

Logic bomb   The concept of the *logic bomb* is designed around dormant program code that is waiting for a trigger event to cause detonation. Unlike a virus or worm, logic bombs do not travel. The logic bomb remains in one location, awaiting detonation. Logic bombs are difficult to detect. Some logic bombs are intentional, and others are the unintentional result of poor programming. Intentional logic bombs can be set to detonate after the perpetrator is gone.

Trapdoor   Computer programmers frequently install a shortcut, also known as a *trapdoor*, for use during software testing. The trapdoor is a hidden access point within the computer software. A competent programmer will remove the majority of trapdoors before releasing a production version of the program. However, several vendors routinely leave a trapdoor in a computer program to facilitate user support. The commercial version of PGP encryption software contained a trapdoor designed to recover lost encryption keys and to allow the government to read the encrypted files, if necessary. Trapdoors compromise access controls and are considered dangerous.

Root kit   One of the most threatening attacks is the secret compromise of the operating system kernel. Attackers embed a *root kit* into downloadable software. This malicious software will subvert security settings by linking itself directly into the kernel processes, system memory, address registers, and swap space. Root kits operate in stealth to hide their presence. Hackers designed root kits to never display their execution as running applications. The system resource monitor does not show any activity related to the presence of the root kit. Once installed, the hacker has control over the system. The computer is completely compromised.

Brute force attack   *Brute force* is the use of extreme effort to overcome an obstacle. For example, an amateur could discover the combination to a safe by dialing all of the 63,000 possible combinations. There is a mathematical likelihood that the actual combination will be determined after trying less than one-third of the possible combinations. *Brute force attacks* are frequently used against user logon IDs and passwords. In one particular attack, all of the encrypted computer passwords are compared against a list of all the words encrypted from a language dictionary. After the match is identified, the attacker will use the unencrypted word that created the password match. This is why it is important to use passwords that do not appear in any language dictionary.

Denial of service (DoS)   Attackers can disable the computer by rendering legitimate use impossible. The objective is to remotely shut down service by overloading the system and thereby prevent the normal user from processing anything on the computer.

Distributed denial of service (DDoS)   The denial of service has evolved to use multiple systems for targeted attacks against another computer to force its crash. This type of distributed attack is also known as the *reflector attack*. Your own computer is being used by the hacker to launch remote attacks against someone else. Hackers start the attack from unrelated systems that the hacker has already compromised. The attacking computers and target are drawn into the battle—similar in concept to starting a vicious rumor between two strangers, which leads them to fight each other. The hackers sit safely out of the way while this battle wages.

IP fragmentation attack   One of the common Internet attack techniques is to send a series of fragmented service requests to a computer through a firewall. The technique is successful if the firewall fails to examine each packet. For this reason, firewalls are configured to discard IP fragments.

Crash-restart   A variation of attack techniques is crash-restart. An attacker loads malicious software onto a computer or reconfigures security settings to the attacker's advantage. Then the attacker crashes the system, allowing the computer to automatically restart (reboot). The attacker can take control of the system after it restarts with the new configuration. The purpose is to install a backdoor for the attacker.

Maintenance accounts   Most computer systems are configured with special maintenance accounts. These maintenance accounts may be part of the default settings or created for system support. An example is the user account named *DBA* for database administrator, or *tape* for a tape backup device. All maintenance accounts should be carefully controlled. It is advisable to disable the default maintenance accounts on a system. The security manager may find an advantage in monitoring access attempts against the default accounts. Any attempted access may indicate the beginnings of an attack.

Remote access attacks   Most attackers will attempt to exploit remote access. The goal of the attack is often based on personal satisfaction for political gain. There is less personal risk involved in gaining remote access. The common types of remote access attacks are referred to as follows:

War dialing   The attacker uses an automated modem-dialing utility to launch a brute force attack against a list of phone numbers. The attack generates a list of telephone numbers that were answered by a computer modem. The next step of the attack is to break in through an unsecured modem. This is why it's necessary for modems to reject inbound calls or to be protected by a telephone firewall such as TeleWall by SecureLogix. Remote access servers (RASs) provide better authentication than a modem. RAS logging capability can be used to identify attacks, if properly configured. Using RAS modem pools combined with telephone-firewall products such as TeleWall will reduce the chance of an attacker making a successful penetration.

War driving/walking   Wireless access is known to be insecure. Wireless manufacturers have seriously compromised security in an effort to improve Plug and Play capabilities for users. The trade-off of fewer user support issues for less security provides casual attackers the opportunity to gain remote access by walking or driving past wireless network transmitters. Previous attackers use symbols to mark the unsuspecting organization's property, to show other attackers that wireless access is available at that location. This marking technique is referred to as *war chalking*. War chalk maps of insecure access points are available for download on the Internet.

> We discuss the latest standards in wireless security later in this chapter. Wired Equivalent Privacy (WEP) and Wi-Fi Protected Access (WPA) have been officially classified as insecure since April 2005 because of implementation failures. Existing equipment using WEP/WPA is designated as insecure. The current standard is IEEE 802.11i known as Robust Security Network.

Cross-network connectivity   Interconnected networks are effective in business. The connectivity across networks provides an avenue for more-efficient processing by the user. Computer networks are cross-connected internally, and even across the Internet. It is not uncommon for a business partner to have special access. All of these connections can be exploited by an attacker. Business partner connections can provide an opportunity for the attacker to remotely compromise the systems of a partner organization with little chance of detection. The purpose of internal and external firewalls is to block attacks. The implementation of internal firewalls is an excellent practice that dates back to the Great Wall of China. Better-run organizations recognize the need. Since 2005, the deployment of internal firewalls has accelerated. Figure 7.2 shows the threat of attackers entering through business partner connections.

FIGURE 7.2   Cross-network connectivity

Source routing   As stated earlier, useful system administration tools can be implemented as weapons. In the early days of networking, it was necessary to send data across a network without any reliance on the network configuration itself. Therefore, a special network protocol known as *source routing* was developed. Source routing is designed to ignore the configuration of the network routers and follow the instructions designated by the sender (the source). Source routing is a magnificent diagnostic tool for reaching remote networks. As you can imagine, source routing also is popular with hackers, because it allows a hacker to bypass routing configurations used for firewall security. For this reason, every firewall and most routers must be configured to disable source routing.

Salami technique   The *salami technique* is used for the commission of financial crimes. The key here is to make the alteration so insignificant that in a single case it would go completely unnoticed—for example, a bank employee inserts a program into the bank's servers that deducts a small amount of money from the account of every customer. No single account holder will probably notice this unauthorized debit, but the bank employee will make a sizable amount of money every month.

Packet replay   Network communications are sent by transmitting a series of small messages known as *packets*. The attacker captures a series of legitimate packets by using a capture tool similar to a network sniffer. The packets are retransmitted (replayed) within a short time window to trick a computer system into believing that the sender is a legitimate user. This technique can be combined with a denial of service technique to compromise the system. The legitimate user is knocked off the network by using denial of service, and the attacker attempts to take over communications. This can be effective for hijacking sessions in single sign-on systems such as Kerberos. We discuss Kerberos single sign-on later in this chapter.

Message modification   Message modification can be used to intercept and alter communications. The legitimate message is captured before receipt by the destination. The content of the message, address, or other information is modified. The modified message is then sent to the destination in a fraudulent attempt to appear genuine.

This technique is commonly used for a man-in-the-middle attack: A third party places themselves between the bona fide sender and receiver. The person in the middle pretends to be the other party. If encryption is used, the middle person tricks the sender into using an encryption key known by the middle person. After reading, the message will be re-encrypted using the key of the true recipient. The message will be retransmitted to be received by the intended recipient. The man-in-the-middle is able to eavesdrop without detection. Neither the sender nor the receiver is aware of the security compromise.

Email spamming and spoofing   You are probably aware of email spamming. *Spamming* refers to sending a mass mailing of identical messages to a large number of users. The current laws governing email allow a business to send mass emails as long as the recipient is informed of the sender's legitimate address and the recipient is provided a mechanism to stop the receipt of future emails.

Email spamming is a common mechanism used in phishing attacks. The term *spoofing* refers to fraudulently altering the information concerning the sender of email. An example of email spoofing is when an attacker sends a fake notice concerning your eBay auction account. The spoofed email address appears as if it were sent by eBay. Email spamming is illegal in some countries, and email spoofing is prosecuted as criminal fraud and/or electronic wire fraud.

A variety of other technical attacks may be launched against the computer. A common attack is to send to the computer an impossible request or series of requests that cannot be serviced. These cause the system to overload its CPU, memory, or communication buffers. As a result, the computer crashes. An example is the old Ping of Death command (`ping -l 65510`), which exceeded the computer's maximum input size for a communication buffer.

The first step in preventing the loss of information assets is to establish administrative controls. Let's begin the discussion on implementing administrative safeguards.

Using Administrative Protection

Throughout this Study Guide, we have discussed the importance of IT governance over internal controls. The first step for a protection strategy is to establish administrative operating rules. Information security management is the foundation of information asset protection. Let's discuss some of the administrative methods used to protect data: information security management, IT security governance, data retention, documenting access paths, and other techniques. We will begin with information security management.

Information Security Management

The objective of *information security management* is to ensure confidentiality, integrity, and availability of computing resources. To accomplish this goal, it is necessary to implement organizational design in support of these objectives. Let's discuss some of the job roles in information security management:

Chief security officer   The chief security officer (CSO) is a role developed to grant the highest level of authority to the senior information systems security officer. Unfortunately, this tends to be a position of title more than a position of real corporate influence. The purpose of the CSO position is to define and enforce security policies for the organization.

Chief privacy officer   New demands for client privacy have created the requirement for a chief privacy officer (CPO). This position is equal to or directly below the chief security officer. The CPO is commonly a position of title rather than genuine corporate authority. The CPO is responsible for protecting confidential information of clients and employees.

Information systems security manager   The information systems security manager (ISSM) is responsible for the day-to-day process of ensuring compliance for system security. The ISSM follows the directives of the CSO and CPO for policy compliance. The ISSM is supported by a staff of information systems security analysts (ISSA) who work on the individual projects and security problems. An ISSM supervises the information systems security analysts and sets the daily priorities.

IT Security Governance

The concept of IT governance for security is based on security policies, standards, and procedures. For these administrative controls to be effective, it is necessary to define specific roles, responsibilities, and requirements. Let's imagine that an information security policy and matching standard have been adopted. The next step would be to determine the specific level of controls necessary for each piece of data. Data can be classified into groups based on its value or sensitivity. The data classification process will define the information controls necessary to ensure appropriate confidentiality.

The federal government uses an information classification program to specify controls over the use of data. High-risk data is classified top secret, and the classifications cascade down to data available for public consumption. Every organization should utilize an information classification program for their data. International Standard 15489 (ISO 15489) sets forth the requirements to identify, retain, and protect records used in the course of business. It's the only method to ensure integrity with proper handling. Let's take a look at the typical classifications used in business:

Public   Information approved for public consumption. It is important to understand that data classified as public needs to be reviewed and edited to ensure that the correct message is conveyed. Examples of public information include websites, sales brochures, marketing advertisements, press releases, and legal filings. Most information filed at the courthouse is a public record, viewable by anyone.

Sensitive   There is a particular type of data that needs to be disclosed to certain parties but not to everyone. We refer to this data as *sensitive*. This data may be a matter of record or legal fact. However, the organization would not want to go about advertising the details. Examples of sensitive information include client lists, product pricing structure, contract terms, vendor lists, and details of outstanding litigation.

Private, internal use only   The classification of data for internal use only is commonly applied to operating procedures and employment records. The details of operating procedures are usually provided on a need-to-know basis to prevent a person from designing a method for defeating the procedure. Examples of private records include salary data, health-care information, results of background checks, and employee performance reviews.

Confidential   This is the highest category of general security classification outside the government. It may be subdivided into confidential and highly confidential trade secrets. Confidential data is anything that must not be shared outside of the organization. Examples include buyout negotiations, secret recipes, and specific details about the inner workings of the organization. Confidential data may be exempt from certain types of legal disclosure.

The overall purpose of using an information classification scheme is to ensure proper handling based on the information content and context. *Context* refers to the usage of information.

Two major risks are present in the absence of an information classification scheme. The first major risk is that information will be mishandled. The second major risk is that without an information classification scheme, all of the organization's data may be subject to scrutiny during legal proceedings. The information classification scheme safeguards knowledge. Failure to implement a records and data classification scheme leads back to our previous paragraph about ignorance and a speedy conviction.

Authority Roles over Data

To implement policies, standards, and procedures, it is necessary to identify persons by their authority. Three levels of authority exist in regard to computers and data. The three levels of authority are owner, custodian, and user.

Data Owner

The *data owner* refers to executives or managers responsible for the data content. The role of the data owner is to do the following:

- Assume responsibility for the data content
- Specify the information classification level
- Specify appropriate controls
- Specify acceptable use of the data
- Identify users
- Appoint the data custodian

As an IS auditor, you will review the decisions made by the data owner to evaluate whether the actions were appropriate.

Data User

The *data user* is the business person who benefits from the computerized data. Data users may be internal or external to the organization. For example, some data is delivered for use across the Internet. The role of the data user includes the following tasks:

- Follow standards of acceptable use

- Comply with the owner's controls

- Maintain confidentiality of the data

- Report unauthorized activity

You will evaluate the effectiveness of management to communicate their controls to the user. The auditor investigates the effectiveness and integration of policies and procedures with the user community. In addition, the auditor determines whether user training has been effectively implemented.

Data Custodian

The *data custodian* is responsible for implementing data storage safeguards and ensuring availability of the data. The custodian's role is to support the business user. If something goes wrong, it is the responsibility of the custodian to deal with this promptly. Sometimes the custodian's role is equivalent to a person holding the bag of snakes at a rattlesnake roundup or the role of a plumber when fixing a clogged drain. The duties of the data custodian include the following:

- Implement controls matching information classification

- Monitor data security for violations

- Administer user access controls

- Ensure data integrity through processing controls

- Back up data to protect from loss

- Be available to resolve any problems

Now we have identified the information classification and the job roles of owner, user, and custodian. The next step is to identify data retention requirements.

Identify Data Retention Requirements

Data retention specifies the procedures for storing data, including how long to keep particular data and how the data will be disposed of. All records follow a life cycle similar to the SDLC model in Chapter 5, "Life Cycle Management." The requirements for data retention can be based on the value of data, its useful life, and legal requirements. For example, financial records must be accessible for seven years. Medical records are required to be available indefinitely or at least as long as the patient remains alive. Records regarding the sale or transfer of real property are to be maintained indefinitely, as are many government records.

The purpose of data retention is to specify how long a data record must be preserved. At the end of the preservation period, the data is archived or disposed of. The disposal process frequently involves destruction. We will discuss storage and destruction toward the end of this chapter.

Now the authority roles and data retention requirements have been identified. So, the next administrative step is to document the access routes (paths) to reach the data.

Document Access Paths

It would be extremely difficult to ensure system security without recognizing common access routes. One of the requirements of internal controls is to document all of the known access paths. A physical map is useful. The network administrator or security manager should have a floor plan of the building. The locations of computer systems, wiring closet, and computer room should be marked on the map. Map symbols should indicate the location of every network jack, telephone jack, and modem. The location of physical access doors and locking doors should also be marked on the map. This process would continue until all the access paths have been marked. Even the network firewall and its Internet communication line should appear on the map.

Next, a risk assessment should be performed by using the map of access paths. Hackers can injure the facility via the Internet or from within an unsupervised conference room. Special attention should be given to areas with modem access. Modems provide direct connections, which bypass the majority of IT security. Computer firewalls are effective only if the data traffic passes directly through the firewall. A computer firewall cannot protect any system with an independent, direct Internet connection.

The purpose of documenting access paths and performing a risk assessment is to ensure accountability. Management is held responsible for the integrity of record keeping. Guaranteeing integrity of a computer system would be difficult if nobody could guarantee that access restrictions were in place.

The change control process should include oversight for changes affecting the access paths. For example, a change in physical access security may introduce another route to the computer room. Persons entering and leaving through the side door, for example, would have a better opportunity to reach the computer room without detection.

The next step to ensure security is to provide constant monitoring. Physical security systems can be monitored with a combination of video cameras, guards, and alarm systems. Badge access through locked doorways provides physical access control with an audit log. A badge access system can generate a list of every identification badge granted access or denied access through the doorway. Unfortunately, a badge access system will have difficulty ensuring that only one person passed through the doorway at a particular time. A mantrap system of two doorways may be used to prevent multiple persons from entering and exiting at the same time. A *mantrap* allows one person to enter and requires the door to be closed behind the person. After the first door is closed, a second door can be opened. The mantrap allows only one person to enter and exit at a time.

To support the increased security, it will be necessary to train the personnel.

Personnel Management

Everyone in the organization should undergo a process of security awareness training. Education is the best defense. Computer training and job training are commonplace. The organization should introduce a training program promoting IT governance in security to generate awareness. Let's consider the possible training programs:

- New-hire orientation, which should include IT security orientation
- Physical security safeguards and asset protection
- Reeducating existing staff about IT security requirements
- Introducing new security and safety considerations
- Email security mechanisms
- Virus protection
- Business continuity

Every organization should have a general IT security training program to communicate management's commitment for internal controls.

A good training program can run in 20 minutes or less. The intention is to improve awareness and understanding. This objective does not require a marathon event. Training can occur in combination with normal activities. A favorite technique of ours is to place a 20-minute video presentation on the back end of HR benefits and orientation sessions. This ensures that the audience will be present. HR will provide time and attendance reporting for the participants. Each person on staff will be tracked through a series of presentations, leading to cumulative awareness training. Other methods include a brown-bag lunch event, followed by a contest giveaway to promote attendance.

Physical Access

Physical access is a major concern to IT security. As an IS auditor, you need to investigate how access is granted for employees, visitors, vendors, and service personnel. Which of these individuals are escorted and which are left unattended? What is the nature of physical controls and locking doors? Are there any internal barriers to prevent unauthorized access?

The following is a list of the three top concerns regarding physical access:

Sensitive areas   Every IS auditor is concerned about physical access to sensitive areas such as the computer room. The computer room and network wiring closets are an attractive target. Physical access to electronic equipment will permit the intruder to bypass a number of logical controls. Servers and network routers can be compromised through their keyboard or service ports. Every device can be disabled by physical damage. It is also possible for the intruder to install eavesdropping access by using wiretaps or special devices.

Service ports   Network equipment, routers, and servers have communication ports that can be used by maintenance personnel. A serial port provides direct access for a skilled intruder. Shorting out the hardware can create a denial of service situation. Special commands issued through a serial port may bypass the system's password security. When security is bypassed, the contents in memory can be displayed to reveal the running configuration, user IDs, and passwords.

As auditors, we have observed senior maintenance personnel from the two largest router manufacturers. During one particular crisis, the skilled technicians successfully bypassed security and reconfigured a major set of changes to routers without halting network service and without knowing the actual administrator passwords.

Computer consoles   The keyboard of the server is referred to as the *console*. Direct access to servers and the console should be tightly controlled. A person with direct access can start and stop the system. The processes stopping the system may be crude and cumbersome, but the outcome will be the same. Direct access also provides physical access to disk drives and special communication ports. It would be impossible to ensure server security without restricting physical access.

Real World Scenario

Ensuring That Personnel Are Honest

Personnel in the organization are expected to be honest. Before access is granted, each person should undergo a formal hiring process complete with background checks. Some individuals in sensitive positions may be bonded to protect the company. The bonding process is a type of insurance that will pay the company for losses caused by the employee. *Fidelity bonding* protects the organization from employee theft. Unfortunately, most fidelity bonds will require the organization to successfully prosecute the accused before any money will be paid out.

Terminating Access

Administrative procedures are necessary to ensure that access is terminated when an employee leaves the organization. The access of existing employees should also be reviewed on a regular basis. In a poorly managed organization, the employee will be given access to one area and then to additional areas as their jobs change. Unfortunately, this results in a person with more access than their job requires. Access to sensitive areas should be limited to persons who perform a required job function in the same area. If the person is moved out of the area, that access should be terminated. The IS auditor should investigate how the organization terminates access and whether it reviews existing access levels. The concept of least privilege should be enforced. The minimum level of access is granted to perform the required job role.

Incident Handling

Incident handling is an administrative process we discussed in Chapter 6, "IT Service Delivery." Physical damage or an unlocked door at the wrong time should initiate the incident-handling process. Auditors will need to investigate how the organization deals with incident handling in regard to security implications.

Auditors need to ask the following questions:

- What are the events necessary to trigger incident response?
- Are the user and the IT help desk trained to know when to call?
- What is the process for activating the incident response team?
- Does the incident response team have an established procedure to ensure a proper investigation and protect evidence?
- Are members of the incident response team formally appointed and trained?

Violation Reporting

Policies and procedures in security plans are ineffective unless management is monitoring compliance. An effective process of monitoring will detect violations. Better control occurs when activity monitoring is separate from the person or activity performing the work. Self-monitoring is a violation of IT governance controls. The built-in reporting conflict of self-monitoring will seriously question the integrity of the reporting process. Separation of duties applies to people, systems, and violation reporting. The IS auditor needs to investigate how violations are reported to management:

- Does a formal process exist to report possible violations?
- Will a violation report trigger the incident response team to investigate?

The role of the IS auditor in personnel management is to determine whether appropriate controls are in place to manage the activities of people inside the organization. Now we will move on to physical protection.

Implementing Physical Protection

Physical barriers are frequently used to protect assets. A few pages ago, we discussed the creation of a map displaying access routes and locked doors. After risk assessment, the next step is to improve physical protection.

Let's review a few of the common techniques for increasing physical protection:

Closed-circuit television   Closed-circuit television can provide real-time monitoring or audit logs of past activity. Access routes are frequently monitored by using closed-circuit television. The auditor may be interested in the image quality and retention capabilities of the equipment. Some intrusions may not be detected for several weeks. Does the organization have the ability to check for events that occurred days or weeks ago?

Guards   Security guards are an excellent defensive tool. Guards can observe details that the computerized security system would ignore. Security guards can deal with exceptions and special events. In an emergency, security guards can provide crowd control and direction. Closed-circuit television can extend the effective area of the security guard. The monitoring of remote areas should reduce the potential for loss. The only drawback is that guards may be susceptible to bribery or collusion. It's a common practice for the guards to be monitored by a separate security staff in banks and casinos.

Special locks   Physical locks come in a variety of shapes and sizes. Let's look at three of the more common types of locks:

Traditional tumbler lock   An inexpensive type of lock is the tumbler lock, which uses a standard key. This is identical to the brass key lock used for your home and automobile. The lock is relatively inexpensive and easy to install. It has one major drawback: Everyone uses the same key to open the lock. It is practically impossible to identify who has opened the lock. Figure 7.3 shows a diagram of the tumbler lock.

FIGURE 7.3   Tumbler lock

Brass tumbler lock

Electronic lock   Electronic locks can be used by security systems. The electronic line is frequently coupled with a badge reader. Each user is given a unique ID badge, which will unlock the door. This provides an audit trail of who has unlocked the door for each event. Electronic locks are usually managed by a centralized security system. Unfortunately, electronic locks will not tell us how many people went through the door when it was open. To solve that problem, it would be necessary to combine the electronic lock with closed-circuit television recording.

Cipher lock   Cipher locks may be electronic or mechanical. The purpose of the cipher lock is to eliminate the brass key requirement. Access is granted by entering a particular combination on the keypad. Low-security cipher locks use a shared unlock code. Higher-security cipher locks issue a unique code for each individual. The FBI office in Dallas has a really slick electronic cipher lock using an LCD touchpad. The user touches a combination of keys in sequence on the LCD keypad. Between each physical touch, the key display changes to prevent an observer from detecting the actual code used. This is an example of a higher-security cipher lock.

Biometrics   The next level of access control for locked doors is biometrics. Biometrics uses a combination of human characteristics as the key to the door. We discuss this later in this chapter, in the section "Using Technical Protection."

Burglar alarm   The oldest method of detecting a physical breach is a burglar alarm. Alarm systems are considered the absolute minimum for physical security. An alarm system may be installed for the purpose of signaling that a particular door has been opened. Remote or unmanned facilities frequently implement a burglar alarm to notify personnel of a potential breach. Burglar alarm systems should be monitored to ensure appropriate response in a timely manner.

Environmental sensors   Technology is not tolerant of water or contaminants. Environmental controls are used to regulate the temperature, humidity, and airflow. The failure of air-conditioning or humidity control can damage sensitive computer equipment. All the servers in the computer room would overheat and crash without continuous air-conditioning. Environmental sensors should be monitored with the same interest and response as a burglar alarm.

Data Processing Locations

We have discussed the need for security to restrict physical access. The data processing facility requires special consideration in its design. Data processing equipment is a valuable asset that needs to be protected from environmental contamination, malicious personnel, theft, and physical damage.

The data center location should not draw any attention to its true contents. This will alleviate malicious interest by persons motivated to commit theft or vandalism. The facility should be constructed according to national fire-protection codes with a 2-hour fire-protection rating for floors, ceilings, doors, and walls.

Some locations in the building are not suitable for the computer room. Basements are a poor choice because they are susceptible to flooding. In 1960, computers were placed behind glass windows to showcase them as a status symbol. A series of riots in the mid-1960s made it apparent that computers needed to be rapidly moved into fortified rooms. The most expedient location was an unused basement with no windows. The standard over the past 50 years has been to place the data center on a middle floor in the building—preferably located between the second floor and one floor below the top floor.

> Basements are a poor choice for data centers. Ground-level floors are not a good choice because they are easy to access by both thieves and attackers. A top floor is not recommended because of the likelihood of storm damage and roof leaks. A floor just below the top floor may be acceptable. The second layer of concrete between the floors provides additional protection from roof leaks. Opaque windows are considered acceptable in some environments if the windows are shatterproof and installed by using a sturdy mount equal to the window rating.

Access to the data center should be monitored and restricted. The same level of protection should be given to wiring closets because they contain related support equipment. Physical protection should be designed by using a 3D space consideration: Intruders should not be able to gain access from above, below, or through the side of the facility.

The physical space inside the data processing facility should be environmentally controlled. Let's move on to a discussion of environmental protection.

Environmental Controls

The first concern in the data center is electrical power. Electrical power is the lifeblood of computer systems. Unstable power is the number one threat to consistent operations. At a minimum, the data center should have power conditioners and an uninterruptible power supply.

> You are expected to understand a few of the terms used to describe conditions that create problems for electrical power.

Figure 7.4 illustrates the different types of electrical power conditions.

FIGURE 7.4   Electrical power conditions

Emergency Power Shutoff

Electricity is both an advantage and a hazard. The national fire-protection code requires an emergency power off (EPO) switch to be located near the exit door. The purpose of this switch is to kill power to prevent an individual from being electrocuted. The EPO switch is a red button, which should have a plastic cover to prevent accidental activation. The switch can be wired into the fire-control system for automatic power shutoff if the fire-control system releases water or chemicals to disable a fire.

Uninterruptible Power Supply

The uninterruptible power supply (UPS) is an intelligent power monitor coupled with a string of electrical batteries. The UPS constantly monitors electrical power. A UPS can supplement low-voltage conditions by using power stored in the batteries. During a power outage, the UPS will provide a limited amount of battery power to keep the systems running. The duration of this battery power depends on the electrical consumption of the attached equipment. Most UPS units are capable of signaling the computer to automatically shut down before the batteries are completely drained. Larger commercial UPS systems have the ability to signal the electrical standby generator to start.

Standby Generator

The standby generator provides auxiliary power whenever commercial power is disrupted. The standby generator can be connected to the UPS for an automated start. The UPS will signal the generator that power is required, and the generator will start warming up. After the generator is warmed up, a transfer circuit will switch the electrical feed from commercial power to the generator power. The UPS will filter the generator power and begin recharging batteries. The standby generator can run for as long as it has fuel. Most standby generators run on diesel fuel or natural gas:

Diesel generator   A diesel generator requires a large fuel-storage tank with at least 12 hours of fuel. Better-prepared organizations will store at least three days worth of fuel and as much as thirty days of fuel. Simple power failures will typically be resolved within three days. Power failures due to storm damage usually take more than one week to resolve. Smart executives would never trust the business to hollow promises from a fuel delivery service. When power stops, attitudes will flare because the business has been shut down. More fuel storage is cheaper than the outage or expense of a court battle with your supplier over late fuel delivery.

Natural gas generator   Natural gas–powered generators have the advantage of tapping a gas utility pipeline directly or using a connection through a storage tank. The natural gas generator does not require a fuel truck to refill its fuel tank. The local natural gas pipeline provides a steady supply of fuel for an extended period of time. The natural gas supply is a good idea in areas that are geologically stable.

Air-conditioning equipment is the Achilles heel of generators. An enormous amount of fuel is consumed when running AC using generator power. It also takes a very big generator to run AC compressors. Realistic alternatives to AC include cycling cooler subsurface water from deep wells for convection cooling.

One alternate power-conserving method uses a stored tank of liquid nitrogen for temporary cooling over days or weeks. Liquid nitrogen is used by electronic manufacturers in environmental testing for component failure analysis. The same technique could be applied by venting small amounts of liquid nitrogen through a closed-loop condenser system. Air blowing across the condenser will keep the room cool without burdening the generator.

Dual Power Leads

The best way to prevent power outages is to install power leads from two different power sub-stations. It would be extremely expensive to just pay someone to run special power cables. Instead, the location of the building housing the computer room should be selected according to area power grids. Power grids are usually divided along highways. Careful location selection will place your building within a quarter-mile of two power grids. This makes the cost of the dual connection affordable. Dual power leads should approach the building from different directions without sharing the same underground trench. A construction backhoe is extremely effective in destroying underground connections.

Power Transfer System

The power transfer system, known as a *transfer switch*, provides the connection between commercial power and UPS battery power in the generator. The transfer switch may be manual or computerized. It is not uncommon for the power transfer switch to fail during a power outage. Therefore, manual power-transfer procedures should be in place. Automated power-transfer switches may not be able to react to a pair of short power failures occurring within the same 30-minute window. After the first power failure, the generator will come online to produce electrical current. After commercial electrical power is restored, the power switch will transfer back to commercial electricity. At the same time, the generator will receive a signal to begin cooling down and finally shut off. If another power outage occurs during the generator cooling period, the power transfer switch will cycle to generator power while the generator is not producing electrical current. This condition may be resolved by increasing the battery capability of the UPS and adjusting generator start and stop times.

Figure 7.5 illustrates the basic electrical power system used for computer installations.

FIGURE 7.5 Power system overview

Heating, Ventilation, and Air-Conditioning

The computer installation requires heating, ventilation, and air-conditioning. Electronic equipment performs well in cold conditions; however, magnetic media should not be allowed to freeze. Ventilation is necessary for cooling computer equipment. Physical damage occurs if the computer circuitry sustains extended use at temperatures of 104 degrees or higher. Physical damage will also occur if the internal electronic circuitry exceeds 115 degrees during operation.

Air-conditioning is also used to control humidity. Humidity will control static electricity that could damage electrical circuits. The ideal humidity for a computer room is between 35 percent and 45 percent at 72 degrees. This will reduce the atmospheric conditions that would otherwise create high levels of static electricity.

Fire, Smoke, and Heat Detection

The data center and records storage area should be equipped for fire, smoke, and heat detection. Unheated areas may need to be monitored for freezing conditions. There are three basic types of fire detectors, using smoke detection, heat detection, or flame detection:

Smoke detection   Uses optical smoke detectors or radioactive smoke detection

Heat detection   Uses a fixed temperature thermostat (which activates above 200 degrees), or rapid-rise detection (which activates the alarm if the temperature increases dramatically within a matter of minutes)

Flame detection   Relies on ultraviolet radiation from a flame or the pulsation rate of a flame

A fire-detection system activates an alarm to initiate human response. A fire-detection system may also activate fire suppression with or without the discharge of water or chemicals.

Fire Suppression

Fire suppression is the next step after fire detection. A fire-suppression system may be fully automated or mechanical. There are three basic types of fire-suppression systems:

Wet pipe system   The wet pipe system derives its name from the concept of water remaining inside the pipe. Most sprinkler heads in a ceiling-based system are mechanical. Each sprinkler head is an individual valve held closed by a meltable pin. A fire near the sprinkler head will melt the pin, and the valve will open to discharge whatever is in the pipe. This type of system can burst because of a freeze, or leak due to corrosion, which would create an unscheduled discharge. Figure 7.6 shows a wet pipe system.

Dry pipe system   The dry pipe system is an improvement over the wet pipe for two reasons. First, the pipe is full of compressed air rather than water prior to discharge. When the valve opens, there is a delay of a few seconds as the air clears from the line. The water will discharge after the air is purged. This leads us to the second advantage. The flow of rushing air can trigger a flow switch to activate the EPO switch to kill electrical power. Equipment will shut off during the few seconds before the water is discharged. This will reduce the amount of damage to computer equipment. Special computer cabinets are made to shed water away from electronic hardware mounted inside. Figure 7.7 shows a dry pipe system.

FIGURE 7.6   Wet pipe system

FIGURE 7.7   Dry pipe system

Dry chemical system   Dry chemical systems are frequently used in computer installations because dry chemicals avoid the hazards created by water. The dry chemical system uses a gas such as FM-200 or NAF-S-3 to extinguish fire.

> **NOTE**   Gaseous halon is no longer used because it is a chlorofluorocarbon (CFC) that destroys the Earth's ozone layer (1994 international environmental accord). The exception is aircraft and ships. Fires occurring while in flight or at sea could be devastating with tragic loss of life. All former halon installations in computer rooms should have been converted to FM-200 or an equivalent dry chemical.

When electronic sensors detect a fire condition, the dry chemical system will discharge into the room. Figure 7.8 shows the basic design of a dry chemical system.

FIGURE 7.8 Dry chemical system

Special administrative controls are necessary with dry chemical systems. Maintenance person-nel must never lift floor tiles or move ceiling tiles while the dry chemical system is armed. Floating particles of dust can activate a discharge of dry chemicals. Humans should not inhale the gas used in dry chemical systems because it may be lethal. A dry chemical discharge intro-duces a great deal of air pressure into the room within seconds. Fragile glass windows may shatter during discharge, creating a temporary airborne glass hazard.

You need to be aware that a water pipe system may be required even if a dry chemical system is installed. Fire safety codes can require wet pipe systems throughout the building, without exception. Some building own-ers will not allow the tenant to alter existing fire-control systems. The dry chemical system would then have to be installed in parallel to the existing water-based system.

Water Detection

Water is discharged from air-conditioning or cooling systems and usually runs to a drain located under the raised floor. Water-detection systems are necessary under the floor to alert personnel of a clogged drain or plumbing backup. Water-detection sensors also may be placed in the ceiling to detect leakage from pipes in the roof above. It is common for water pipes to be located over a computer room directly above the ceiling tiles or higher floors. Water can even cascade down inside the building from the roof.

Figure 7.9 provides a simple overview of a data processing center and the various environ-mental control systems.

To minimize risk, the organization should have a policy prohibiting food, liquids, and smoking in the computer facility. Now it is time to discuss safe storage of assets and media records.

FIGURE 7.9   Typical computer room

Safe Storage

Vital business records and computer media require protection from the environment, fire, theft, and malicious damage. Safe onsite storage is required. The best practice is to use fireproof file cabinets and a fireproof media safe. Standard business records are kept in the fireproof file cabinet. Computer tapes and disk media are stored in a special fire safe. The fire safe provides physical protection and ensures that the internal temperature of the safe will not exceed 130 degrees. Copies of files and archived records are transferred to offsite storage.

Offsite Storage

The offsite storage facility provides storage for a second copy of vital records and data backup files. The offsite storage facility should be used for safe long-term retention of records. The standard practice is to send backup tapes offsite every day or every other day. The offsite storage location should be a well-designed, secure, bonded facility with 24-hour security. This site must be designed for protection from flood, fire, and theft. The offsite vendor should maintain a low profile without visible markings identifying the contents of the facility to a casual passerby. Most offsite storage facilities provide safe media transport.

Media Transport

Business records and magnetic media should be properly boxed for transit. The contents in the box must be properly labeled. An inventory should be recorded prior to shipping media offsite for any reason. The tape librarian is usually responsible for tracking data media in transit. Backup tapes contain the utmost secrets of any organization. All media leaving the primary facility must be kept in secure storage at all times and tracked during transit. New regulations are mandating the use of encryption to protect the standing data on backup tapes. The tape librarian should verify the safe arrival of media at the offsite storage facility. Random media audits at the offsite facility are a good idea. The custodian must track the location and status of all data files outside the primary facility.

Disposal Procedures

Information and media will be disposed of at the end of its life cycle. This is the seventh phase of the SDLC model. A formal authorization process is required to dispose of physical and data assets. Improper controls can lead to the untimely loss of valuable assets. Let's review the common disposal procedures for media:

Paper, plastic, and photographic data   Nondurable media may be disposed of by using physical destruction such as shredding or burning.

Durable and magnetic media   Durable media may be disposed of by using data destruction techniques of overwriting and degaussing:

Overwriting   Data files are not actually deleted by a Delete command. The only change is that the first character of the file is set to zero. Setting the first character to zero indicates that the remaining contents can be overwritten whenever the computer system needs more storage space. Undelete utilities operate by changing the first character back to a numeric value of one. This makes the file contents readable again. To destroy files without recovery, it is necessary to overwrite the contents of the disc. A file overwrite utility is used to replace every single data bit with a random value such as E6X, BBB, or other meaningless value.

Degaussing   Degaussing is a bulk erasing process using a strong electromagnet. Degaussing equipment is relatively inexpensive. To operate, the degaussing unit is turned on and placed next to a box of magnetic media. The electromagnet erases magnetic media by changing its electrical alignment. Erasure occurs within minutes or hours, depending on the strength of the device.

As a CISA, you are required to understand the fundamental issues of physical protection. Advanced study in physical security is available from ASIS International, for the Certified Protection Professional (CPP) credential.

You're now ready to begin the last major section of this chapter, which covers technical methods of protection.

Using Technical Protection

Technical protection is also referred to as *logical protection*. A simple way to recognize technical protection is that technical controls typically involve a hardware or software process to operate. Let's start with technical controls, which are also known as *automated controls*.

Technical Control Classification

Technical protection may be implemented by using a combination of mandatory controls, discretionary controls, or role-based controls. Let's discuss each:

Mandatory access controls   Mandatory access controls (MAC) use labels to identify the security classification of data. A set of rules determines which person (subject) will be allowed to access the data (object). The security label is compared to the user access level. The comparison process requires an absolute match to permit access. Here is an example:

```
(User label "subject" = Data label "object") = ALLOW
Label does not match = DENY
```

The process is explicit. Absolutely no exceptions are made when MAC methods are in use. Under MAC, control is centrally managed and all access is forbidden unless explicit permission is specified for that user. The only way to gain access is to change the user's formal authorization level. The military uses MAC.

Discretionary access controls   Discretionary access controls (DAC) allow a designated individual to decide the level of user access. DAC access is usually distributed across the organization to provide flexibility for specific use or adjustment to business needs. The data owner determines access control at their discretion. The IS auditor needs to investigate how the decisions concerning DAC access controls are authorized, managed, and regularly reviewed. Most businesses use discretionary access control.

Role-based access controls   Certain jobs require a particular level of access to fulfill the job duties. Access that is granted on the basis of the job requirement is referred to as role-based access control (RBAC). A user is given the level of access necessary to complete work for their job. The system administrator position is an example of role-based access control.

Task-based access controls   Individual tasks may need to be performed for the business to operate. Whereas role-based access is used for job roles, task-based access control (TBAC) refers to the need to perform a specific task. Common examples include limited testing, maintenance, data entry, or access to a special report.

The type of access control used is based on risk, data value, and available control mechanisms. Now we need to discuss application software control mechanisms.

Application Software Controls

Application software controls provide security by using a combination of user identity, authentication, authorization, and accountability. As you will recall, *user identity* is a claim that must be *authenticated* (verified). *Authorization* refers to the right to perform a particular function. *Accountability* refers to holding a person responsible for their actions. Most application software uses access control lists to assign rights or permissions. The access control list contains the user's identity and permissions assigned.

Database Views

Data within the database can be protected by using database views. The database view is a read restriction placed on particular columns (attributes) in the database. For example, Figure 7.10 illustrates using a personnel file to create a telephone list. Data that is not to be read for the telephone list has been hidden by using the database view.

FIGURE 7.10   Database views for security

Restricted User Interface

Another method of limiting access is to use a restricted user interface. The restricted interface may be a menu with particular options grayed out or not displayed at all. Menu access is preferred to prevent the user from having the power of command-line arguments. The command line is difficult to restrict.

Security Labels

A major concern in security is the ability for users to bypass the security label. The security label is a control that specifies who may access the file and how the file may be used. The IS auditor should work with security managers to identify ways in which labels and security settings may be bypassed. Additional compensating controls are necessary to protect against the bypassing of labels and security.

Authentication Methods

The first step of granting access is identification of the user: A user presents a claim of identity. The second step is to authenticate the user identity claim against a known reference. The purpose of this authentication is to ensure that the correct person is granted access. Table 7.1 illustrates the difference between identification and authentication.

TABLE 7.1   Identification versus Authentication

Concept	Function
Identification	A claim of identity *or* a search process of comparing all known entries until either a match is found or the data list is exhausted. Identification is known as a one-to-many search process.

TABLE 7.1   Identification versus Authentication *(continued)*

Concept	Function
Authentication	A single match of the identity claim against reference information. If a single attempt fails, the authentication failed. Authentication is a single-try process, also known as a one-to-one process (compare only, no search).

Understanding Types of Authentication

Three types of authentication are possible using discrete information. The most common type of authentication is the user password. The user password is expected to be a secret known only to the user. Unfortunately, many user passwords are poorly constructed or suffer from ineffective protection. When a user logs in with a password, the only information known is that someone has logged in with the password. That is no guarantee of who that person is. Let's take a look at the three types of information, or factors, which can be used to authenticate the user:

Type 1: Something a person knows   The login ID and password should be unique to each user. Unfortunately, the password may be discovered by observation or insufficient security by the user. Passwords should be considered weak authentication. Passwords can be forgotten, shared, discovered by observation, and broken by technical means.

Type 2: Something a person has in possession   An improvement above the password is to authenticate the user based on a unique item in their possession. This requires the user to have a login ID with a password and the unique item at the time of login. Banks use type 2 authentication with your ATM card and PIN. Another example of type 2 authentication is the smart card. A smart card contains a microchip with unique information read by a card scanner. Figure 7.11 shows a drawing of a smart card.

FIGURE 7.11   Smart card with embedded microchip

It is possible to use type 2 authentication without specialized hardware. Common techniques include using a hard token, USB token, or soft token.

The hard token is a card or key fob read by the user during login. The user types a username and password combined with the number that appears on the token display screen. The number displayed by the token changes every 1 to 2 minutes, thereby making each password unique. The following shows a sample login and the password containing the code from the token:

```
Login ID = jmorris  Password = ******94328
```

Another method is to use a USB token. Authentication information is recorded in a microchip on a USB token device. The user plugs the USB token into the USB port when logging in to the computer. This type is popular in hospitals for use by doctors and nurse practitioners. Figure 7.12 shows a drawing of the two common types of hard tokens.

FIGURE 7.12   Hard authentication token

It is possible to use type 2 authentication without specialized hardware. Common techniques

Another method of type 2 authentication is the use of software tokens (soft tokens), also known as *digital certificates*. Soft tokens are relatively inexpensive. The software token captures unique information, including the CPU's electronic serial number during the initial certificate-signing request. The resulting digital certificate contains this embedded information to prove the identity of the computer. Soft tokens are not portable because each is assigned to a specific computer.

Unfortunately, hardware and software tokens can be stolen or lost, and some can be secretly duplicated. These problems are what bring us to the third type of authentication.

Type 3: Physical characteristic   The third type of authentication is based on a unique physical characteristic. The recording of physical characteristics and the matching process is known as biometrics. Let's investigate biometrics further.

Using Biometrics

Biometrics uses unique physical characteristics to authenticate the identity claimed by the user. This is accomplished by using either physiological characteristics or behavioral characteristics. You are expected to understand the different types of biometric data used for authentication.

Using Physiological Characteristics

These are considered strong authenticators of the user's identity because they are difficult to forge. A risk still exists in the management of the biometric sample and system implementation.

Fingerprint   Fingerprints have been used for many years to identify people, especially criminal offenders. In biometrics, the fingerprint is used to authenticate (not identify) the user. Information about the user's fingerprint is recorded into a biometrics database. Rather than the actual image, only summary lists of unique feature characteristics are recorded about the fingerprint. These features include curvature, position, ridge patterns, delta (separation), combined ridges (crossover), islands, and burification (ridge join). The feature data recorded in the database is called *minutiae*. When the user logs in, the minutiae are identified by the acquisition hardware and compared to the database. Authentication occurs when the acquired minutiae data from the biometrics scanner matches the minutiae from the database. Using fingerprint minutiae instead of capturing the image allows a smaller file size to be stored. Minutiae file size is usually 250 bytes to more than 1,000 bytes. Figure 7.13 illustrates fingerprint minutiae.

FIGURE 7.13   Using fingerprint data (minutiae)

Fingerprint recognition

Palm print   A person's palm print is as unique as a fingerprint. Like a fingerprint, the palm of the hand contains a significant number of unique minutiae plus additional wrinkle lines, blood vessel patterns, and scars. The palm offers a larger volume of data. Figure 7.14 illustrates the palm data.

FIGURE 7.14   Using palm print data

Palm of hand

Hand geometry   The concept of hand geometry is to measure the details of a person's hand in a three-dimensional image. The usual technique is to put your hand into a machine with your fingers spread between metal pegs. Another method in hand geometry is to grasp a metal knob or bar while sensors measure your knuckle creases or blood vessel patterns. Hand geometry is quite effective and inexpensive.

Retina scan   The retina, located at the rear of the eyeball, contains a unique pattern of tiny veins and arteries that reflect light. The red-eye in photographs is the reflection of the retina. Changes in the retina occur during a person's life. Some of these changes may signal the onset of a new medical condition, such as stroke or diabetes. Users may be concerned about physiological issues or the possible invasion of privacy. Overall, retina scanning is very reliable. Figure 7.15 illustrates retina scanning.

FIGURE 7.15   Retina scanning

Retina

Iris scan   Iris-scanning technology is based on visible features of freckles, rings, and furrows in the color ring surrounding the eye's pupil. The iris provides stable data from one year of age through a person's entire life. The visible features and their location are combined to form an iris-code digital template. To use an iris scanner, a person is asked to look into an eyepiece and focus on a displayed image. A camera records a picture of the iris and compares it to the biometric database to ensure that the viewer is a living person. Colored contacts would fail the iris scan. Iris scanning is very dependable.

Face scan   New face-scanning technology uses a series of still images captured by video camera. The technology uses three-dimensional measurements of facial features, including the position of eye sockets, nose, mouth openings, and heat pattern thermograph. The feature data is extracted from the image to form a digital facial template of 1,000 to 1,500 bytes. Major advances are occurring in facial recognition that reduce former problems of speed and accuracy. Figure 7.16 illustrates face recognition.

Using Behavioral Characteristics

Behavioral characteristics are considered a weak type of authentication because of concerns about their authenticity. Behavior is easier to forge than physical characteristics. For example, in my childhood, I taught my little brother how to speak. As a result, it's nearly impossible to distinguish even the slightest difference in our voices. My father's handwriting impressed me when I was learning to write in cursive. After much practice, my signature in sixth grade looked exactly like his. That illustrates the problem. Let's look at using signatures and voice patterns.

FIGURE 7.16   Face recognition

Face recognition

Signature dynamics   Signature dynamics is a behavioral form of biometric data. The user's signature is monitored for time duration, pressure, and technique. The advantage is the low cost of implementation. The disadvantage is that many individuals do not write their signature consistently. Some individuals, such as celebrities and authors of this Study Guide, refuse to allow their signature to be digitally recorded because it is still used as the primary means of authenticating legal documents.

Voice pattern   Voice pattern recognition is an inexpensive method of identifying a person by the way they talk. Voice pattern recognition is not the same as speech recognition. Speech recognition assembles sounds into words. Voice pattern analysis checks for characteristics of pitch, tone, and sound duration. A person's voice is analyzed for unique sound characteristics, tone, inflection, and speed. The typical method is to ask a user to repeat a particular pass phrase. The characteristics of the pass phrase are converted into a digital template. Voice pattern recognition is less expensive and less accurate than other types of biometrics. Voice authentication can be fooled by recorded audio playback of a person's voice. Figure 7.17 illustrates voice recognition.

FIGURE 7.17   Voice pattern analysis in biometrics

Voice recognition

    As a CISA candidate, you are expected to understand the older biometric techniques of signature dynamics and voice pattern analysis.

Management of Biometric Systems

Biometrics comprises technology-based systems and hence requires a disciplined approach. Each biometric system follows an SDLC life cycle. As an auditor, you will encounter a growing number of clients using or planning to implement biometric systems. Auditors don't need to be technicians. Our job is to witness whether management did their job of selecting the right system and how it is governed. Let's take a walk through the basic life cycle:

Phase 1: Biometric feasibility

Management determines their need, purpose, and function for biometrics. Are they interested in using biometric technology because it looks cool? Real planning considers the following points:

- Analysis of regulations and classification of their data to be protected.

- Physical environment, mission, and people. What problem is biometrics going to solve?

- Effect of biometrics on employees, customers, and business partners.

- Data collection may be difficult because of perceptions of intrusiveness, possible misuse, implications of system failure, and moral concerns.

- Return on investment (ROI) after analysis of initial cost, ongoing operation, maintenance, and comparison of alternatives.

The results of their feasibility study should be available for the auditor to review. Assuming that the decision was a good one, a formal review should occur to gain approval to proceed to phase 2.

Phase 2: Biometric requirements

Before rushing out to buy a product, you'll need to consider of the detailed requirements. These will come from a discovery exercise of intended use, unique needs, and the specific operating environment. Everyone knows you should not go shopping without a list. Doing so results in overspending or buying the wrong item. Independent consultants may assist with the requirements phase. The independent consultant shall be barred from bidding on or selling the biometric system to ensure that the consultant remains independent. Following the SDLC model, the requirements phase should include the following:

- Identification of the ownership roles, custodian duties, and users of the system.

- Executive support in the form of a signed biometrics policy, budget, and delegation of authority.

- Physical access restrictions covering both the biometric system and the area it will protect.

- Logical (technical) access needs to be restricted to prevent direct access into the data repository. Special methods such as single sign-on (SSO) are necessary for interfacing to other applications without risk of compromising the biometric repository.

- Solutions to design questions about biometric standards, data storage capacity, security, maintenance, backup, and restoration procedures.

- Functionality for the intended use. Will it do the job? Is additional functionality needed, such as the ability to export data for FBI background investigations? If so, the system needs to have that capability plus the implementation of a design using the Common Biometrics Exchange Format Framework (CBEFF) with the Electronic Fingerprint Transmission Specification (EFTS).

- Perform a risk analysis for what happens *when* this system fails. The two most common failures are rejecting authorized people and mistakenly accepting an attacker. One technique for compromising biometrics is to substitute the attacker's biometric data for that of a legitimate user. After access is granted, the attacker will reload the original biometric data to hide their intrusion.

Assuming that your client did a good job, it's time for the phase 2 review. All the research and planning is presented to determine whether this project should continue into phase 3, return to the drawing board to rerun the discovery process, or be cancelled. If all the issues are addressed, the project may be granted formal approval to proceed to phase 3. Evidence of phase 2 research and formal approval to proceed is expected to be available for the auditor to review.

Phase 3: System selection

We need to take a moment to explain the high-level technical concept of how a biometric system works. The two basic components in biometrics are the template generator and the template matcher. Everyone agrees that the vendor's product needs to be certified. The issue is how it's certified. Let's start with the template generator:

Biometric template generator   Biometric images are acquired during live enrollment of the user. A *template generator* converts images into a unique data template. This template becomes the user's biometric reference. A template generator must be laboratory tested by using very large data sets in repeatable evaluations. It will be tested offline to ensure that each unique user template is created by using the correct internal program procedures, so it is algorithmically correct and physically distinct from that of other users. Without this testing, the system would have no integrity and could accept the wrong person (false acceptance).

Biometric template matcher   A *template matcher* is used to compare images against the user's template. It may compare more than one image against more than one template. The goal is to determine whether the image and the template produce a similar score. A template generator is certified as a software library. Template generators and template matchers must be tested and certified separately. A match indicates Personal Identity is Verified (PIV).

Now let's return to the issues in phase 3 regarding system selection. A vendor's product has to be properly certified to be eligible for selection. Additional points to consider in this phase are as follows:

- Process for enrolling, re-enrolling, and removing users from the system
- Security protection to prevent tampering, sabotage, substitution of fake templates, and compromise of biometric data (templates)
- Available technical support and training materials
- Operational questions of user acceptance, maintenance, hygiene, backup, and restore functions
- Total cost of ownership (purchase, installation, maintenance) and the ROI
- Procurement method: bid, outsource, or straight purchase

Phase 3 concludes with a formal review. The selection criteria is presented along with alternatives. All the open issues need to be fixed, rejected, or withdrawn before formal approval can be given. With formal approval, the product may be purchased and the project proceeds into phase 4.

 It can be helpful to attend vendor-sponsored training during final selection, before making the purchase. The purpose is to learn the hidden points of your intended use that don't match the vendor's sales literature. Consider it a try-out before you buy.

Phase 4: System configuration

Some product training is helpful to ensure a proper installation. The auditee should be trained before the vendor sends the installation technicians out to configure the system. Too many times, the promise of knowledge transfer at a later date becomes just another failed promise. Points to consider in phase four include the following:

- Installing hardware and software
- Calibrating and recalibrating the system
- Operating procedures for enrollment, security, transmission, processing, backup, and restoration
- Using transaction controls
- Monitoring the systems and logs
- Detecting system compromise plus use of corresponding incident response procedures
- Connecting the biometric system interface to other systems

Additional points may be added to suit their intended use. Let's assume that everyone did their job. The next step is to certify the system for production use by testing the people and the procedures.

Phase 5: Biometrics implementation

Now the system is preparing to enter production. There are still a few steps to cover before announcing that the system is ready. Here's the short list:

- Formalizing configuration management and change control into a system baseline.
- Training users.
- Enrolling the user to populate the biometrics database.
- Managing the deletion of users removed from the system.
- User testing begins.
- Management determines whether the installed system met their objectives. Technical tests are run to certify system performance.

- Management determines whether the overall operation is acceptable. If so, formal accreditation is given in the form of a written sign-off to enter production. Management formally accepts the outcome and the responsibility for any possible failures. Accreditation may be for 90 days, 180 days, or annually.

- The biometric system may now enter production use.

This may seem like a lot of work because it is. The goal is to ensure that the right things happen for the right reason. This biometrics example is one of our first opportunities to demonstrate how a system goes through the SDLC life cycle process. Now it's time to look ahead into the system's future.

Phase 6: Biometrics post-implementation

Each year a system must be recertified and reaccredited. The purpose is to ensure that management has looked at its historical performance, ROI (if any), and changes in both regulations and attitudes. The question is whether the system is allowed to continue operation as is, is modified to keep up with changes, or is retired.

As auditors, we are interested in finding evidence of the postimplementation review, recertification process, and management's reaccreditation of the system for continued use in production for another 90 days, 180 days, or annually. The process repeats each year the system is in use.

Phase 7: Biometric system disposal phase

This is the same process as in Chapter 5. A review is held to determine the implications of shutting down the system. Topics considered include regulations related to the system, record retention requirements, and ways to archive the data. Formal approval is requested to shut down the system. The decision should be based on a risk analysis of the impact. After formal approval, the system is shut down, media is sanitized, and hardware is removed from capital inventory. Equipment is resold, donated, destroyed, or recycled.

As auditors, we would like to see the evidence that this disposal was authorized and properly handled. Biometric systems have several technical advantages that must be balanced against the known problems. Let's discuss some of the known problems with biometrics.

Problems with Biometrics

Using biometric systems has some drawbacks. How will the biometric results be used? Is the biometric system expected to provide identification or authentication?

Biometric systems face issues of social acceptability. The users may have concerns about sanitary health issues regarding physical contact or about invasion of privacy. Biometric data must be managed to ensure the security of initial data collection, data distribution, and processing. A biometric data policy is required to specify the data life cycle and control procedures. Biometric data must always be protected for confidentiality and integrity.

Error rates exist in all automated systems, and biometric systems are no different. It is possible for an error to occur during data collection or data processing. The following are various types of errors that can occur in a biometric system:

Enrollment   Every user provides a sample for the biometric system during the enrollment process. The sample may fail to be accepted by the system. The typical enrollment process should take only 2 to 5 minutes; any longer could lead to user dissatisfaction.

Failure to enroll   On rare occasions, the user's data will not be accepted by the system. This is referred to as failure to enroll (FTER). It could be due to image quality, calibration, system problems, or the scanner not interpreting a person's physical abnormalities.

False rejection   A legitimate person could be rejected and fail authentication; the correct user fails to authenticate. This failure to accept a legitimate user is known as the false rejection rate (FRR) or type 1 error. The biometric system rejects a legitimate user. This is considered a type 1 error because it is the most common type of error.

False acceptance   It is possible for the system to permit access to an individual who should have been rejected; the wrong person is authenticated. This is referred to as the false acceptance rate (FAR) or type 2 error. The biometric system accepts an unauthorized user.

Equal error/crossover error rate   Every system has a delicate balance of speed over efficiency. In biometrics, this balance is referred to as the equal error rate (ERR) or the crossover error rate (CER). The biometric system is not perfect. An acceptable error rate will always exist. Figure 7.18 illustrates the trade-off between speed and accuracy.

Throughput rate   How many people (samples) can the system process and still have reasonable accuracy? Lower throughput may be acceptable in situations of higher risk. Higher throughput may be better in low-risk situations such as the collection of visitors' fingerprints at turnstiles entering an amusement park.

We have discussed the methods for authenticating a user. Now it is time to discuss the types of access that could be granted on the network.

FIGURE 7.18   Crossover error rate

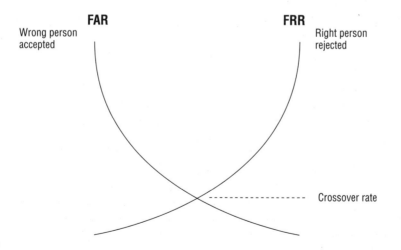

FAR
Wrong person
accepted

FRR
Right person
rejected

Crossover rate

Network Access Protection

All computer networks are prone to access control problems. It is an ongoing challenge to provide access to legitimate users while blocking access from all others. Several methods have been developed to accomplish this goal. Computer users demand ease of use, while computer custodians strive for tighter controls. Unfortunately, network access is predominantly a perimeter defense. Better controls are sorely needed at the application level.

In this section, we discuss several technologies including firewalls. We will start with single sign-on. The CISA is expected to understand the concept of single sign-on. Its purpose is to improve network access controls by implementing a higher-security system that is easier for the user. One of the most common examples is Kerberos, developed by the Massachusetts Institute of Technology.

Kerberos Single Sign-On (Shared secret authentication protocol)

The Kerberos single sign-on (SSO) system was developed to improve both security and user satisfaction. The name *Kerberos* refers to the mythical three-headed dog guarding the gates to the underworld. Kerberos provides security when the end points of the network are safe but the transmission path cannot be trusted—for example, when the servers and workstations are trusted but the network is not.

The concept of operation is for the user to log in once to Kerberos. After login, the Kerberos system authenticates the user and grants access to all resources. The process works as follows:

1. The user authenticates to the Kerberos workstation software. Authentication may be a password or a biometric method.
2. The *users* workstation software authenticates to the Kerberos server.
3. Shared encryption keys are used. A network access ticket is created by Kerberos.
4. A Kerberos access ticket is sent to the workstation, signed in the workstation's shared encryption key. All other network servers receive a similar ticket granting the workstation access to shared servers.
5. The user is automatically signed in to all servers.

The belief is that a user with a strong password and strong encryption will improve overall security. Unfortunately, Kerberos works only with specially modified versions of software designed for use with Kerberos. Merely installing Kerberos will not improve security. There are compatibility problems with different versions of implementation.

Special skills and experience are required to make a Kerberos installation successful. First, a knowledgeable installer will understand how to use separate domains to partition Kerberos access for better security. Second, restoring data from tape backup is quite involved. The Kerberos system must be shut down and the date rolled back to the timestamp of the file being restored. As soon as the file is restored, the time clocks must be rolled forward again with the system resynchronized for the users. Any compromise of the Key Distribution Center (KDC) means that the entire system is compromised and must be shut down. Using Kerberos requires highly experienced system administrators. Figure 7.19 illustrates the design of a Kerberos single sign-on.

FIGURE 7.19   Kerberos single sign-on

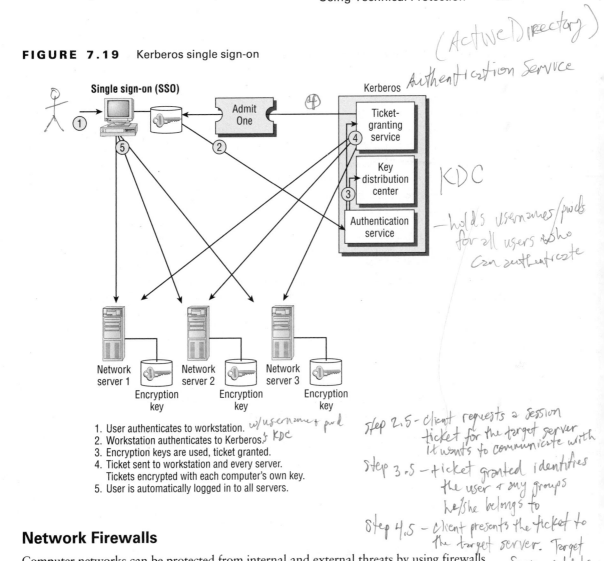

(handwritten) (Active Directory)

(handwritten) Authentication Service

(handwritten) KDC

(handwritten) — holds usernames/pwds for all users who can authenticate

1. User authenticates to workstation. *(handwritten) w/username + pwd*
2. Workstation authenticates to Kerberos. *(handwritten) + KDC*
3. Encryption keys are used, ticket granted.
4. Ticket sent to workstation and every server.
   Tickets encrypted with each computer's own key.
5. User is automatically logged in to all servers.

(handwritten) Step 2.5 — client requests a session ticket for the target server it wants to communicate with

(handwritten) Step 3.5 — ticket granted identifies the user + any groups he/she belongs to

(handwritten) Step 4.5 — client presents the ticket to the target server. Target Server validates ticket and grants or denies access to user

Network Firewalls

Computer networks can be protected from internal and external threats by using firewalls (FWs). The concept is that a specially configured firewall on the network will block unwanted access. However, this is a grossly misunderstood concept, and many organizations do not understand firewall capabilities and limitations. As a result, there can be a false sense of security. Let's consider the advantages and disadvantages of network firewalls:

Firewall advantages   Reduces external access to the network.

Firewall disadvantages   There is always a hole for traffic to pass through—either good traffic or bad traffic or both. A firewall can control only the traffic that passes directly through it. It does not protect modems or other access points. A firewall can be misconfigured or technically circumvented. There is no such thing as a completely safe firewall. The firewall concept creates a false sense of security.

(handwritten) Step 5.5 — ticket is stored on client workstation so it can be reused again later, until it expires. At which time it is purged.

Network firewalls have undergone several generations of improvement. The first generation was simply a router with a primitive access list specifying the *to* destination and the sender's *from* network addresses. Attackers became more sophisticated, and so did the need for better firewalls. The following are the different generations of firewall technology:

First generation: Packet filter   The first generation was a packet filter. Filtering is based on the sending and receiving address combined with the service port (a packet). The advantage of this design is its low cost.

The first-generation packet filter design was prone to problems. The design was plagued with poor logging and granular rules that were difficult to implement effectively. Hackers were still able to get in.

Second generation: Application proxy filter   A firewall application program was added to the first-generation design of packet filtering. The second generation uses an application proxy to relay requests through the firewall. The proxy checks the inbound request to ensure that it complies with safe computing in both format and type of request. Application proxies perform user requests without granting direct access to the target software. The application proxy is also referred to as a *circuit-level firewall*. This is because the application proxy is required to complete the circuit; otherwise, no connection exists. This design improved event logging; however, hackers were still able to get in.

Third generation: Stateful inspection   Hackers were able to trick second-generation firewalls by sending a request that was formatted to bypass the proxy design. Application proxy firewalls relied on open connections maintained with the user. Connectionless sessions such as the User Datagram Protocol (UDP) in IP were not protected. In the third generation, UDP connectionless requests are recorded into a history table. The historic "state" of connectionless requests is now controlled by the firewall for better protection. This is referred to as *stateful inspection*. Stateful inspection is the de facto minimum standard for network firewall technology. However, there's still room for improvement.

Fourth generation: Adaptive response   Improvements in technology allow the firewall to communicate with an intrusion detection system. This provides an adaptive response to network attacks. The firewall administrator can configure stored procedures designed to rebut many types of firewall attack. The firewall can reconfigure itself to block ports or reset connections. One drawback is that a skilled attacker may masquerade as a critical device such as a necessary server. The fourth-generation firewall could accidentally disable the critical device, which would create a denial of service problem.

Fifth generation: Kernel process   The fifth-generation firewall is actually an internal control mechanism designed into the operating system kernel. Individual processing requests are verified against an internal access control list. Those not on the list are rejected. Special military systems have been using fifth-generation firewalls for many years. Microsoft Windows XP has implemented a basic fifth-generation firewall.

The network firewall is the best defense for protecting a network. Each generation provides different levels of cost and protection. Figure 7.20 illustrates the firewalls by generation in relation to the OSI model. We covered the OSI model in Chapter 4, "Networking Technology."

FIGURE 7.20 Firewall generations compared to the OSI model

	Packet Filtering	Application Proxy w/ Packet Filter	Stateful Inspection w/ Proxy	Adaptive Response OS	Kernel
Application OSI layer 7	None	Varies	Varies	Varies	Π
Presentation OSI layer 6	None	None	Varies	Varies	Varies
Session OSI layer 5	None	Π	Π	Π	Π
Transport OSI layer 4	None	Varies	Π	Π	Π
Networking OSI layer 3	Π	Π	Π	Π	Π
Data-Link OSI layer 2	Π	Π	Π	Π	Π
Physical OSI layer 1	None	None	None	None	None

Network firewalls can be implemented by using one of three basic designs. The first method is the screened host implementation. The screened host protects a single host through the firewall. The host computer is strongly defended. It is expected that this host may be attacked. Technical manuals may refer to this as the *bastion host*. Figure 7.21 illustrates the screened host implementation.

The next method of firewall implementation is to install two interface cards in the same host. This method is referred to as to *dual-homed*. The host computer is configured with the routing disabled. A special software application such as an application proxy relays appropriate communication between the two interface cards. This is the configuration of many Internet firewalls. Figure 7.22 illustrates the dual-homed host.

FIGURE 7.21 Firewall-screened host

Screened host

WWW Internet

Router FW

ACL filter (choke router)

Bastion host

Computer

FIGURE 7.22   Dual-homed host

The third method of firewall implementation is known as the *screened subnet*, or DMZ design. *DMZ* is a term that refers to the demilitarized zone between enemy forces on a battle-field. The DMZ design allows for several computers to be placed in a protected subnet that is accessible from the outside and by systems inside the network. Any military veteran will tell you that it's possible to be attacked and killed in the DMZ. The same applies to computers located here. Figure 7.23 illustrates the DMZ concept.

Firewall systems should be implemented to support a separation of duties. Separation of duties is just as important for machines as for personnel. The intention is to provide additional layers of control. Separate firewalls allow tighter access-control rules. Selected data is mirrored from internal production servers to a DMZ server for access by business partners or clients. This eliminates the dangers of direct access to an internal server. In addition, the redundancy improves overall availability. An outage would affect a smaller audience. Figure 7.24 illustrates the separation of duties using a firewall.

FIGURE 7.23   Screened subnet, also known as DMZ subnet

FIGURE 7.24   Separation of duties with firewalls

Firewalls Supporting Separation of Duties

*Only reduced data within policy

Remote Dial-Up Access

Remote users can often access the network over standard telephone lines with modems. This method completely bypasses security mechanisms provided by the network firewall. The dial-up user may access the network through an access server modem bank or an individual modem on a networked computer. As an IS auditor, you need to determine whether the client has adequate safeguards to prevent this method of circumvention. Are the phone connections to modems properly managed considering the higher level of risk?

Remote VPN Access

Virtual private networks (VPNs) connect remote users over an insecure public network such as the Internet. The connection is virtual because it is temporary with no physical presence. VPN technology is cost-effective and highly flexible. A VPN creates an encrypted tunnel to securely pass data as follows:

- Between two machines

- From a machine to a network

- From one network to another network

[handwritten: Uses IPsec or SSL see next pg]

There are four types of VPN technology and protocol in use today. ISACA wants you to be familiar with the basic terms for each of the four types of VPN:

- Point-to-Point Tunneling Protocol, or PPTP

- Layer 2 Tunneling Protocol, or L2TP (OSI layer 2, Data-Link)

- Secure Sockets Layer, or SSL (OSI layer 5, Session)

- IP security, or IPsec, Internet protocol (OSI layer 3, Networking)

SSL and Transport Layer Security (TLS) are commonly used for confidentiality and integrity in the session between the user and the server. Both SSL and TLS operate in a similar manner. The design uses a digital certificate on the server to generate one-way authentication. A secure login to the server can be generated by using Secure Shell (SSH). Encryption occurs along the entire path between the sending and receiving computers. SSH provides end-to-end confidentiality and integrity in a terminal session with the host server.

Using the IPsec VPN

The IPsec design is the newest development in virtual private networking. IPsec uses ISP gateways with two modes of creating a VPN. Let's start with two important differences in operation of the VPN gateway:

- IPsec VPN gateways are used for data that is entering or leaving the organization's local area network. These gateways use an external address from their ISP vendor (AT&T, Deutsche Telekom, BT, Verizon, and so forth).

- VPN encryption is occurring between the gateways. Data transmitted between the local VPN gateway and internal computer is not encrypted.

In IPsec virtual private networks, there are two specific operating modes:

Transport mode is used when there is no need to hide the network address of the sender or recipient. The message payload is encrypted for security; the address header is not.

Tunnel mode is used to hide the identity of the sender and recipient. Both address header and payload (message) are encrypted. A new address header is added to data traveling across the Internet. This new address header will use addresses of the sender's VPN-ISP gateway and recipient's VPN-ISP gateway.

Security is managed by the *authentication header (AH)* and *security parameter index (SPI)*. The authentication header uniquely identifies each packet and provides sequencing information. AH provides authentication, integrity, and nonrepudiation.

The security parameter index provides information about encryption and special handling requirements. This design is based on the older X.25 communication standard you read about in Chapter 4.

Figure 7.25 illustrates the IPsec design.

FIGURE 7.25   VPN using IPsec transport versus tunnel mode

The goal of every VPN is to grant remote access to authorized users. Data can be shared across the Internet at a very low cost with relative safety if the proper internal controls are implemented. A VPN can be combined with a firewall DMZ by using a separation of duties between internal production servers and the external accessible server. Figure 7.26 illustrates a VPN with a separation of duties between servers.

Wireless Access

User demands for wireless access to network resources increase every day. When you read the vendor ads, it appears that wireless can provide security equal to wired access. However, wireless access to networks represents an additional level of threat. Wireless security has been completely compromised by vendors to improve Plug and Play capabilities.

Setting Up a Wireless LAN

It's relatively simple to construct a wireless LAN. A wireless network can be peer to peer, which is known as *ad hoc mode*. Another type of wireless LAN is *infrastructure mode* with the access points (APs) connecting various stations. Several vendors offer low-cost wireless AP that is similar to a wireless hub or router. Each AP is connected to a wired network and broadcasts connectivity to handheld devices.

FIGURE 7.26 VPN with separation of duties

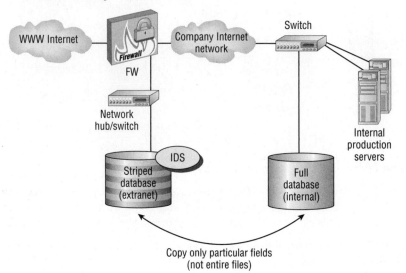

Usually the range of an AP is 300 feet, equivalent to 100 meters. Users can move freely within the 300-foot broadcast range without losing any connectivity. The individual broadcast area (range) is also known as a *cell*. This is comparable to the design of cellular telephone networks. Effective range can be increased by combining APs and their multiple cells (service range). WLANs are based on the IEEE 802.11 standard. Let's look at the basic components of a WLAN.

Station (STA) The station is a wireless device, such as a PDA, notebook computer, or mobile phone that is accessing the network.

Access point (AP) A wireless transmitter/receiver that provides basic network services, usually within 300 feet, equivalent to 100 meters. Higher-power transmitters with longer ranges are entering the marketplace. The AP and STA compose a basic WLAN.

Cell Individual AP broadcast range is known as the cell or span of coverage. Multiple AP cells are linked together to increase the range and to allow roaming within the building or between buildings.

Figure 7.27 shows the basic layout of a wireless network.

Usually the AP is connected to a distribution system such as the existing wired network to provide an infrastructure with greater services for the stations. This is the most common implementation of WLAN.

FIGURE 7.27   Basic wireless network

Obsolete IEEE 802.11 Wireless Standards

The original WLAN standard for wireless network was very slow, operating at only 1Mbps–2Mbps speeds. Three competing WLAN technology standards were established between 1999 and 2003. All three are considered obsolete due to security flaws:

802.11 a (1997)   Performance speeds were improved by increasing to 54Mbps with transmissions in the 5GHz frequency band.

802.11b (1999)   Transmitting at speeds up to 11Mbps using the 2.4GHz–2.48GHz frequency band.

802.11g (2003)   Provided for transmission at either the 2.4GHz or 5GHz band, with speeds up to 54 Mbps.

The lack of effective security is an enormous drawback in wireless networking. IEEE's original design of Wired Equivalent Privacy (WEP) proved to be practically worthless. In response, IEEE issued a revised wireless standard.

Updated IEEE Wireless Standards

Technology is a constant series of evolving standards. IEEE helps drive technology by issuing new wireless standards offering better security or longer transmission range. Let's start with improving wireless security.

802.11i (2005)   Introduced the concept of a robust security network (RSN) with better implementation of encryption keys.

Another IEEE standard worth mentioning is Worldwide Interoperability for Microwave Access (WiMAX) for metropolitan broadband wireless.

802.16 WiMAX (2003)   Mobile broadband using cellular-based networks. This standard allows roaming Internet access without any real data security. WiMAX is becoming increasingly popular because of its low-cost availability in metropolitan areas. WiMAX should always be considered an *insecure* network.

WLAN Transmission Security

Emerging demand for wireless connectivity is pushing the boundaries of information security. Moore's law states that computing power will double every 18 months, and at the same time the present methods of security will be reduced in effectiveness by 50 percent.

The challenge of protecting a WLAN can be solved only by a multilevel approach. Every subset of confidentiality, integrity, and availability (CIA) is at risk in WLAN implementations. There is no individual technology that will provide enough protection against the full spectrum of threats. WLAN security requirements can be summarized as follows:

Authentication   A third party must be able to authenticate the sender of a message as genuine. Authentication is the process of matching a claim to verify an exact match. There must be accurate methods of testing the claim to ensure that a legitimate match occurs. The worst method in WLAN authentication is the wireless device merely transmitting with the same shared key of the AP. The AP does not prove its identity to the wireless device, yet they are communicating to each other. This is why everyone should be worried about a rogue AP.

Three methods of WLAN authentication are as follows:

> **Shared key (poor cryptographic authentication)**   A wireless client device transmits a copy of the shared symmetric key belonging to the AP. Typical implementations use a 128-bit key in an RC4 stream cipher. It may be called a preshared key, wireless-PSK, or WPA-PSK by the vendor to gloss over the problem. Overall, this design is very weak and should be considered rudimentary. It is not safe unless a separate VPN is used during transmission over any form of shared-key wireless equipment.

> **Open system (default, no authentication)**   A wireless client device transmits the MAC address of the AP to establish communication. The open system method is notorious for falling victim to the infamous man-in-the-middle attack.

> **Robust 802.11i (strong cryptographic authentication)**   Uses 802.1x port-based access control with stronger key generation and authentication. Manual key management is still an important task to prevent compromise.

Only two methods are acceptable for security in wireless networks. The first choice is 802.11i (robust security networks). The second choice is a separate VPN implementation using strong authentication with digital certificates and tokens. All existing WEP equipment has been designated as unsafe under all conditions by current government standards and the information security industry at large.

Source: National Institute of Standards and Technology April 2005

Nonrepudiation   To deny involvement is equivalent to repudiation. Nonrepudiation means the other person will not be able to deny their participation. This is used to prove the sender and receiver messages or participants in a transaction. You must have strong authentication to provide nonrepudiation.

Accountability   Individual actions must be traceable back to each unique individual entity. Accountability is difficult or impossible without strong authentication and nonrepudiation.

Integrity   Both sender and receiver need a method to ensure integrity for messages transmitted between the wireless client and AP. We need proof that contents of a message have not been tampered with or changed in transit. All versions of IEEE 802.11a/b/g specifications provided poor authentication between wireless devices.

The IEEE design prior to version 802.11i used a simple cyclic redundancy check (CRC) approach. A CRC-32 frame check sequence is computed on each payload prior to transmission. Then, the CRC-32 frame check is encrypted by using the RC4 stream cipher to create a ciphertext message. The message recipient decrypts the CRC-32 frame check by using a shared key. The CRC-32 results are compared, and messages are discarded if the CRCs are not equal. Unfortunately, the intrinsic flaw is that CRC is not as cryptographically secure as a hash message authentication code (HMAC).

WEP's integrity scheme is still considered vulnerable to certain attacks regardless of key size. RSN 802.11i networks use *temporal keys* for much stronger authentication. RSN is a trusted technology approved for government use.

Privacy issues   Many misleading advertisements claim that wireless systems have privacy equivalent to a wired connection. As noted earlier in this chapter, the term used is Wired Equivalent Privacy (WEP). The concept of WEP is to use the RC4 symmetric key in a stream cipher to generate a pseudorandom data sequence. WEP's operating technique is simply an exclusive OR (XOR) function using modulo) 2 math for data transmitted in the Network layer and above. The XOR function is based on comparing two values for an equal match (for example 1 and 1 match so XOR will equal 0). Alternatively the values don't match (like 1 and 0 will XOR to equal 1). It's a simple binary comparison for the computer. Using XOR for security functions is a primitive design.

Standard WEP   The 802.11 standard uses a 40-bit cryptographic key for WEP. Individual vendors offer nonstandard extensions of WEP keys at 128 bit–256bits. The intention was based on a theory that larger key sizes would be more difficult to break. Unfortunately, several attacks have been identified, which makes WEP vulnerable regardless of key size.

Enhanced WEP   An enhanced version of WEP was created in an attempt to overcome the original 802.11 security shortfalls. The enhanced version is still susceptible to several of the WEP subversion attacks.

802.11i replaces WEP   All WEP implementations should be considered unsafe and obsolete. The current standard for wireless security is RSN. This may force the replacement of WEP/WPA products with newer RSN 802.11i equipment. The only acceptable alternative is using end-to-end client VPN.

Figure 7.28 provides a simple depiction of the difference between WEP and 802.11i using 802.1X. Notice the changes improving our CIA objectives.

FIGURE 7.28 Robust security compared to earlier versions

Achieving RSN Wireless Security

To secure wireless networks and their associated devices requires significant effort, coupled with proper resources and vigilance. It is imperative that management reassess wireless risks at least monthly. The only effective way to maintain security is by constant testing and evaluating systems security controls when wireless technology is being deployed.

Firewall Protection for Wireless Networks

All wireless access points should traverse a network firewall for security reasons. New regulations such as the joint Payment Card Industry (PCI) security policy governing Visa, MasterCard, Discover Card, and American Express have mandated that firewalls be used when merchant organizations process credit transactions on the network. The wireless firewall itself should be separate from the existing Internet firewall. It would be difficult or impossible to successfully combine the two functions into a single firewall. Figure 7.29 provides an overview of using a firewall with wireless access points.

We've spent quite a bit of time discussing firewalls and wireless access controls. It is time to discuss methods for detecting intrusion to the network. Intrusion detection systems have been in the marketplace for more than 10 years. Every organization should have intrusion detection systems in place.

Intrusion Detection

Network intrusion detection systems (IDS) function in a manner similar to virus detection or a burglar alarm. The objective is to inform the administrator of a suspected intrusion or attack occurring. Constant monitoring is necessary in order to receive the benefit of intrusion detection; otherwise, intrusion detection is no more valuable than an audit log of past history. An improved version of intrusion detection is the intrusion prevention system (IPS). The IPS concept is to ensure that the attack is blocked immediately upon detection. New standards refer to IDS and IPS systems as one combined *intrusion detection and prevention system (IDPS)*.

FIGURE 7.29   Firewall protecting wireless access points

There are two types of intrusion detection systems:

Host based   The host-based system monitors activity on a particular computer host or device such as a router. Attacks on other devices will not be seen by the host-based IDPS. To avoid confusion, the host-based IDS (HIDS) is now referred to as a host-based intrusion detection prevention system (HIDPS).

Network based   Network IDS systems observe traffic in a manner similar to a packet sniffer. Network-based IDS (NIDS) is referred to as a network intrusion detection prevention system (NIDPS). The network IDPS monitors activity across a network link. The IDPS can see attacks on promiscuous connections, but not across discrete switched network connections. The design of a network switch can prevent an IDPS system from detecting attacks occurring on systems connected to the other switch ports.

There are three technical methods of detecting a network intrusion:

Statistical   The statistical system uses a calculation of network traffic, CPU, and memory loading to determine whether an attack is occurring. Statistical systems are prone to false alarms because the traffic patterns of most networks are sporadic. The statistical system offers the advantage of being able to detect new attacks that might otherwise go unnoticed if a signature-based system were in use.

Signature   Signature-based IDPS relies on a database of attack techniques. The signature-based IDPS is similar in design to a signature-based virus scanner. The IDPS is looking for behaviors that indicate a particular type of known attack. Unfortunately, the signature-based IDPS cannot detect attacks that are not listed in its database.

Neural Neural-based learning networks are being implemented on intrusion detection systems. The objective is to create a learning system that is a hybrid between statistical- and signature-based methods.

Figure 7.30 illustrates an IDPS on the network.

FIGURE 7.30 Intrusion detection and prevention system

Intrusion detection systems are helpful for identifying network attacks in progress. Some of the more successful techniques are to make a server or subnet appear as an enticing target for the attacker. The purpose of the systems is to be a decoy target. An attack of the decoy provides early warning to the appropriate personnel. The decoy can be high interaction in a simulated production environment or low interaction of a static host. There are two basic styles of decoys:

Honey pot The honey pot is a sacrificial server placed in such a manner as to attract the interest of the attacker. The honey pot server has no legitimate business value other than alerting the organization of an attack. The honey pot utilizes host-based IDPS or network-based IDPS.

Honey net   A honey net is a sacrificial subnet with a few machines designed to attract the interest of the attacker. All traffic from the honey net is considered suspicious because no real production activity is taking place. The purpose of this design is to allow security personnel the opportunity for advance notice of a potential attack against real production.

We have discussed firewalls, remote access, and intrusion detection. Now it is time to discuss the encryption methods used to hide data from prying eyes. Encryption provides a method of hiding data from other people.

Encryption Methods

Encryption systems provide a method of converting clear, readable text into unintelligible gibberish. Decryption converts the gibberish back into a readable message. Encryption and decryption systems have been in use for thousands of years. As a CISA, you are expected to understand the two basic types of encryption systems: private-key systems and public-key systems.

Private Key

Private-key encryption systems use a secret key, which is shared between the authorized sender and the intended receiver. Private-key systems contain two basic components. The first component is the mathematical algorithm for scrambling and unscrambling the message (encrypting and decrypting). The second component is the mathematical key used as a randomizer in the encryption algorithm. The longer the key length, the higher the security it will generate.

A single secret key is carefully shared between the sender and receiver. This is referred to as *symmetric-key* cryptography (see Figure 7.31). Symmetric-key cryptography is very fast, because the same key is used on both ends. The drawback is that the key must be protected with the highest possible diligence. Anybody who has a copy of the secret key can read the message. Examples of symmetric-key (secret key) cryptography include Data Encryption Standard (DES), which is now obsolete, and the new Advanced Encryption Standard (AES) designed by two Belgian researchers, Joan Daemen and Vincent Rijmen.

Because of the secret-key design of symmetric cryptography, encryption and decryption is very fast and efficient. The drawback is that the secret-key design cannot be used for digital signatures. To do so would expose the key to outsiders. Exchanging the secret key in symmetric cryptography is a major problem.

Public Key

Asymmetrical cryptography is referred to as *public-key cryptography*. This design utilizes a separate pair of keys for encryption and decryption. The key pair is composed of a secret key protected by the owner and a second public key that is freely distributed. These two keys are mathematically related to each other. The secret key and public key are generated from a supersized prime number. It is practically impossible for a cryptographic hacker to derive the super prime number or related keys in use.

The strength of public-key cryptography depends on the algorithm used and the encryption key length. To encrypt a message, the sender would use their own secret key and public key, plus the public key of the intended recipient. Figure 7.32 shows the process of encrypting by using public-key (asymmetrical) cryptography.

FIGURE 7.31   Symmetric-key cryptography

FIGURE 7.32   Encryption using public-key system

The process of decrypting the message returns it to readable text. To decrypt, the recipient uses their secret key and public key, plus the public key of the sender. The basic concept is that you need only three keys to unlock the data (decryption). If two values were missing, decrypting the file would be impossible. Figure 7.33 shows the process of decrypting by using public-key cryptography.

Although there are more-complex systems, all it takes for confidentiality is to encrypt by using the sender's keys plus the receiver's public key (three keys). The receiver can decrypt by using the sender's public key with their own private key (both public keys plus their own private key). You never use, or need, all four keys to encrypt or decrypt.

Data in storage is seldom encrypted with public key systems because it is 1,000 times slower. Symmetric (same key) systems are used for storage. Public-key systems are used during data transmission.

The design of public-key cryptography eliminates the need to exchange a secret key between the sender and receiver. Public-key cryptography is designed to allow digital signing of files.

FIGURE 7.33   Decryption using public-key system

Control of Encryption Systems

The greatest vulnerability in encryption systems is the inherent lack of control. Encryption algorithms are well designed; however, their application or management may be poor. Encryption software and encryption keys should be managed as software applications under the SDLCS-DLC. Here are a few tips:

- Use of encryption should be implemented for intellectual property and regulatory compliance.

- Each application of encryption (use) must be formally authorized by management. A user must never be allowed to encrypt files that management cannot decrypt without the user.

- Encryption keys must be individually managed and unique to each task.

- The encryption keys need to be generated on a system that is physically and logically isolated from other systems (separation of duties). Key transfer is via read-only media.

- Encryption keys should be stored in a different encrypted format. The term *key wrapping* refers to encrypting an encryption key by using a different algorithm. This concept is intended to prevent threats to the encryption key itself being exposed as standing data.

- Encryption keys need to be tracked, similar to checking out books at the library.

- The users should never have direct access to encryption keys (separation of duties).

- The use of specific encryption keys should be limited to prevent overexposure or violating the separation of duties. For example, the encryption keys used for data backups cannot be used for encrypting email correspondence.

- The use, archiving, and destruction of encryption keys requires a formal review. Destruction of encryption keys cannot occur without formal approval of management.

Just imagine what would happen if the organization was backing up data using encryption, and the encryption keys were lost. It could get even worse when you consider the implications to business continuity. Heaven forbid that the backup was required for disclosure under a court order for electronic discovery. Each of these conditions indicates a management failure in which integrity of the organization is lost. Failure to control the use of encryption leads to dramatic consequences.

Digital Signatures

A digital signature is intended to be an electronic version of a personal signature. The purpose is to indicate that the message was sent by a uniquely identified individual. A digital signature created by running a hash utility against any size of file will generate a 120-bit or 160-bit output. Figure 7.34 illustrates the process of generating a hash file and digital signature.

FIGURE 7.34   Generating a digital signature

The digital signature is attached to the message file, and both are sent to the recipient. The receiver must use the message file, digital signature file, and the sender's public key to test the validity of the signature. Without testing the digital signature, there is no indication of its authenticity. Figure 7.35 illustrates the process of verifying a digital signature.

FIGURE 7.35   Verifying a digital signature

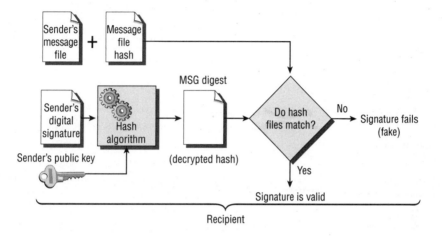

There is a new method for sending an encrypted message and the key along with it. This process uses a digital envelope. A message is encrypted along with a session key. The session key is encrypted a second time, using the recipient's public key. After transmission, the recipient can decrypt by using their private key, and then decrypt again by using the sender's public key. The double-step encryption ensures that no one else is able to decrypt the key in transit. Figure 7.36 illustrates the process of using a digital envelope.

FIGURE 7.36   Using a digital envelope

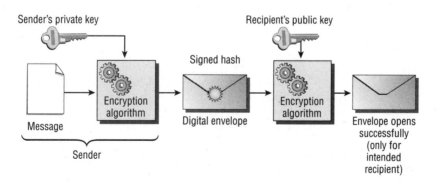

Elliptic-Curve Cryptography

The newest method for encryption algorithms is the elliptic curve. The concept of an elliptic curve is to generate a three-dimensional space. The encryption key refers to a reference point within those dimensions. It would be extremely difficult to calculate keys generated from an elliptic curve. A small elliptic-curve key is exponentially stronger than one generated by linear math.

Elliptic-curve cryptography is used with wireless encryption. The implementation within wireless encryption is completely compromised; however, the concept of the elliptic-curve algorithm is essentially strong. Unfortunately, a 97-bit elliptic-curve encryption has been cracked from the Web by the same people who cracked the RSA 512-bit encryption key. It took twice as long, but the cracking attack was successful.

Quantum Cryptography

Quantum cryptography is based on polarization metrics of random photon light pulses. This promising technology is not available as a commercial product yet. However, the overall design appears to be quite strong.

Public-Key Infrastructure

The process of sharing encrypted files between various parties is referred to as *public-key infrastructure (PKI)*. You should have a basic understanding of this process for the CISA exam. Public-key infrastructure is designed to provide a level of trust and authentication between users. This infrastructure is built by using the public-key encryption system we discussed earlier in this chapter. Public-key infrastructure comprises four basic components:

Certificate authority (CA)   A user contacts a certificate authority to procure a digital certificate. The digital certificate contains the user's contact information along with unique identifying characteristics. The certificate authority will vouch for the authenticity of the user after the certificate is issued. Certificate authorities typically follow the X.509 exchange standard.

Registration authority (RA)   Some big customers such as IBM, Novell, and Microsoft issue certificates from a block of certificates acquired through a certificate authority, such as Entrust, Trustwave or VeriSign. The RA is delegated bookkeeping and issuing functions from the CA. The certificate authority maintains the certificates that have been issued and verifies their authenticity.

Certificate revocation list (CRL)   Digital certificates are checked to ensure that they are valid at the time of use. A certificate revocation list is maintained by the certificate authority to indicate that certificates have expired or are revoked. This process allows invalid certificates to be cancelled.

Certification practice statement (CPS)   A certification practice statement (CPS) is a disclosure document that specifies how a certificate authority will issue certificates. The CPS specifically states how PKI participants will issue, manage, use, renew, and revoke digital certificates. It does not facilitate interoperation between certificate authorities, but rather the practices (procedures) of a single certificate authority.

Figure 7.37 shows the concept of registering and acquiring a PKI digital certificate from the certificate authority.

FIGURE 7.37   Getting a PKI digital certificate

1. Makes application   2. Certificate
                           application checked

Requestor   Certificate authority

Certificate repository (database)

3. Copy filed
   in database

4. Approval

After acquiring a digital certificate, the user will present it during a transaction. The receiver will check the certificate against the certificate authority's database. If the certificate is valid, the transaction will continue. Certificates can be checked against other authorities, using a cross-verification process. Figure 7.38 shows the concept of presenting and using a PKI digital certificate.

FIGURE 7.38   Using a PKI certificate

1. Sender info   2. Checks validity   3. Cross-certification process

Certificate holder   Recipient

Certificate repository (database)

External certificate repository

5. Completes
   transaction

4. Verifies as good

VeriSign, Entrust,
GEO, Thawte

Practical Example of Digital Certificates

Consider the process for flying on an airline. The airline issues an electronic ticket to the buyer. The electronic airline ticket is a digital certificate in a human-readable form, while the computer's digital certificate is not readable by humans. Let's walk though the amazing similarity between processing an airline e-ticket and the computer using a PKI digital certificate:

1. The airline issues an electronic certificate, as long as the tickets are paid for and the buyer can prove their identity. This means that the airline is the certificate authority (CA).

   A travel agent may handle the transaction to get an electronic airline ticket issued (certificate). The travel agent is acting as a registration authority (RA) for the airline (CA).

2. The buyer receives an electronic copy of their airline ticket (electronic certificate). The original data is held by the airline in their certificate repository (database of tickets sold).

3. Prior to boarding the aircraft, the electronic ticket code is verified against the airline's database repository to determine whether the ticket is valid. The certificate is checked by the CA to see whether it is valid. If it checks out as valid, you board the airplane.

   Tickets issued through other airlines can be verified by using cross-certification between the two database repositories.

Use of the electronic ticket is governed by the ticket revocation list and airline statement of policies. This is synonymous with the certificate revocation list (CRL) and certification practice statement (CPS).

Once again, the only real difference between the airline ticket example and your computer is the terminology—plus, a human can actually read an airline ticket. Now we need to move into email security.

Secure Multipurpose Internet Mail Extension

Secure Multipurpose Internet Mail Extensions (S/MIME) was developed so that people could send email across the Internet without having to worry about whether the recipient could read it. The original design was Privacy Enhanced Mail (PEM), developed in 1993. S/MIME was created in 1999 and incorporated several enhancements including support for the newer SHA-1 hash and MD5 hash. Additional support was added for the RSA encryption system and signing time attributes. S/MIME provides authentication of the sender and receiver and also verifies message integrity. S/MIME is the current standard for secure email and attachments. Figure 7.39 illustrates the reason why email security is so important.

FIGURE 7.39   Email security issues

Encryption-Key Management

Encryption-key management is critical to ensure confidentiality and integrity of encrypted data. There are several risks with regard to encryption keys. First, the key itself must be protected from theft or illegal copying. Second is a requirement to use several different keys—one for each purpose. It's important not to overuse a key. This is to ensure integrity of the encrypted files. Each use exposes the key to compromise. Unfortunately, this multitude of keys also creates a significant administrative burden, which if mishandled can turn into a catastrophe.

Every auditor needs to investigate how management is controlling and governing the use of encryption. The critical success factor in encryption is to physically and logically protect the secret key. All keys undergo a full seven-phase life cycle, just like application software.

Encryption keys must be stored with a great deal of care. The keys will need to be managed throughout their life cycle. At a future date, a key will be marked for destruction. Creating, managing, storing, and destroying the keys is of particular concern to the auditor. Few organizations do a good job.

Network Security Protocols

The world of safe e-commerce is built on a handful of network security protocols. These security protocols include the following:

- Pretty Good Privacy (PGP) for personal file encryption.

- Secure Sockets Layer (SSL), which is used by most Internet websites for HTTPS sessions. The newer implementation is called Transport Layer Security (TLS).

- Secure Hypertext Transfer Protocol (HTTPS), which uses SSL

- IP security (IPsec) protocol using the authentication header (AH) and encapsulated security payload (ESP).

Without these protocols, it would be impossible for businesses, individuals, and the government to conduct confidential transactions. Figure 7.40 shows where these protocols fall within the OSI model.

FIGURE 7.40   Security protocols and where they fall within the OSI model

E-commerce is becoming more important in today's IT landscape. Figure 7.41 illustrates several types of e-commerce in use today.

There is one special type of payment protocol that has been developed to protect credit card accounts. The Secure Electronic Transaction (SET) protocol provides a method for purchasing over the Internet without disclosing the credit card number to the merchant.

The merchant opens an account with a payment system such as PayPal's Payflow. A customer makes a purchase by using the merchant's shopping cart. At the appropriate time, the shopping cart passes the transaction to the SET payment gateway. The customer enters their credit card number on the SET gateway, completely out of sight from the merchant. The SET payment gateway sends to the merchant a transaction authorization to complete the purchase. The merchant uses the transaction authorization as authorization to ship the product. The SET gateway system deposits the funds into the merchant's bank account. This prevents a questionable merchant from being able to view a customer's credit card number. It also prevents credit card numbers from being retained in insecure shopping cart databases.

FIGURE 7.41   Types of e-commerce

Design for Redundancy

There is more to protecting information assets than just encryption. Communication networks must be designed for redundancy. One method of improving redundancy is to use alternate telecommunications routing. We discussed meshed networks in Chapter 4. Alternate routing provides multiple communication paths in case the normal path fails. Alternate routing can be used in a local area network or a wide area network.

Another technique to ensure availability and integrity of information assets is the use of mirrored servers. Two servers acting as one are said to be *mirrored*. Mirrored servers are also known as *high-availability servers*. One of the servers acts as a primary server. The second server is the failover server, which runs in the background until the primary server dies. The second failover server assumes all processing responsibilities if the primary should fail for any reason. Figure 7.42 shows the basic design of a mirrored, or high-availability, server pair.

Computer disk systems are known to experience failures. The loss of a disk system could result in the loss of valuable data. A tape backup system can restore the data at the cost of additional downtime. A solution to this problem is the implementation of redundant hard disks. A Redundant Array of Independent—or Inexpensive—Disks (RAID) provides an excellent method of protecting information assets. Special software drivers copy the data files onto different hard disk controllers on two separate sets of hard disks. Either set of hard disks is capable of running the system without data loss. Figure 7.43 shows the basic layout of a RAID system.

FIGURE 7.42 Mirrored, or high-availability, servers

FIGURE 7.43 RAID system

Telephone Security

The security of the telephone system is a major concern. Telephone hackers, known as *phreakers*, are notorious for attempting to steal telephone service.

The telephone PBX—which stands for Private Branch Exchange—needs to be protected by using the same techniques as those used to protect a network server or router. Care must be given to the life cycle controls of the PBX. Maintenance accounts and unauthorized access are major concerns.

Newer phone systems use voice-over-IP networks to save money. This introduces the problems of network security controls to telephone systems. As an auditor, you should be aware of the issues regarding IP networks for both data and voice.

Technical Security Testing

Clients should undergo a regular schedule of security assessment by using the control self-assessment (CSA) and technical tools such as port scanners. We discussed the issue of how all tests must be performed under controlled procedures. You should recall that access to testing tools and authority to run the test must be tightly controlled.

Management needs to promote a regimented approach to discovery and resolution of vulnerabilities. Several types of testing are needed to ensure that security weaknesses are corrected. Let's look at the common types of tests:

Network scanning   This is a fast method for discovering the hosts on the network, also called *host enumeration*. Most scanners are fully automated, yet they can also overload systems with service requests until they crash. Network scanning does not find all vulnerabilities. It should be conducted weekly.

Vulnerability scanning   Individual systems can be polled on all available service ports. This is known as vulnerability scanning. Versions of software are checked, and particular types of service requests are sent by the scanning software to the target computer. This type of test usually triggers an intrusion detection alarm. It also usually crashes the target computer or causes some software damage. This type of testing should be conducted monthly.

Password cracking   A special tool is used to test the strength of user passwords. It works by creating a large set of passwords from dictionaries printed in every language. The hash output is matched against the system password file. When a match is found in the hash file, the word used to create the match will equal the actual password. Password cracking utilities perform all the simple conversions, anagrams, palindromes, and common character substitutions just as a user would. Weak passwords can be easily identified. Care must be taken to ensure that the right people perform this test under totally supervised conditions. Otherwise, password abuse will become a problem.

Log review   All those great log files are useless if nobody reads the contents. Log reviews identify deviations in change control and security policies. This underrated jewel of data can be the auditor's best friend for determining whether operations are following their organizational policies. Unauthorized activities, security violations, and capacity problems can be quickly discovered. Log reviews should be continuous.

Penetration testing   Penetration tests are commonly used to uncover vulnerabilities that may be discovered by an attacker. It may take hours or days to penetrate the target. The U.S. National Security Agency has created a certification program for the level 1 Information Systems Assessment methodology (IAM) to be used for all systems depended upon by the government. This includes service providers and prime contractors. Use in smaller areas of private industry is recommended but not required. The NSA level 2 Information Evaluation Methodology (IEM) provides the planning details and software tools to run a penetration test, and then report the results against the government-approved NSA baseline. The NSA IAM and IEM techniques will be of significant interest to auditors specializing in regulatory compliance. The NSA certification is the only technical assessment method approved and endorsed by the U.S. government. Penetration tests should be run annually.

Summary

As an IS auditor, you should be extremely interested in the implementation of information asset protection mechanisms by the client. There are numerous threats that could compromise administrative, physical, and technical controls.

You should understand how these controls have been implemented by the customer and what level of monitoring is occurring. Implementing controls without constant monitoring would be a waste of effort. Without effective monitoring processes, the client would be negligent.

This chapter has covered several technical methods that the CISA is expected to know. Be sure to read this chapter at least twice and study the definitions carefully.

Exam Essentials

Be able to evaluate the effectiveness of technical (logical) access controls.   Technical controls include access control mechanisms, encryption, firewalls, and intrusion detection and prevention capabilities. Technical access control mechanisms include passwords, access control lists, and biometrics for authentication.

Understand the perimeter defense mechanisms.   The network security infrastructure must provide sufficient perimeter defenses along with mechanisms to minimize loss from hackers, viruses, and worms. But the network is susceptible to attack by hacking, spoofing, spamming, and denial of service, along with other threats such as social engineering.

Know the purpose of the environmental controls used in the IT environment.   Environmental controls are necessary to prevent an interruption to the system's availability and to protect assets from loss. Environmental systems include power, water detection, heating and air-conditioning, fire detection, fire control, and humidity to prevent the buildup of static electricity.

Recognize the different types of technical attacks.   Passive attacks collect information to be used later in an active attack. Active attacks are designed to break down the defenses and execute the will of the attacker.

Understand the different motives of the malicious attacker.   Internal controls are used to prevent or detect most crimes committed by strangers and internal personnel. Remain aware that most theft is committed by someone known within the organization, because of access, motive, and time. The police refer to this concept as MOM: motive, opportunity, and means.

Understand how biometrics are used to judge the authenticity of a user.   Physical access controls are used to prevent loss of assets during safe storage, retrieval, operations, transport, and disposal.

Understand the need to implement physical access controls.   The goal of all perimeter controls is to ensure that only trusted and honest individuals are allowed access. The weakest method of authentication is using a password (type 1 authentication). A better method is to use type 2 authentication unique physical characteristics such as the possession of a device (ATM card, smart card, hard token) and combine possession with a password (secret). It is possible for the legitimate users to be denied access by the system (type 1 error, or false rejection). Accordingly, illegitimate users may get access by mistake (type 2 error, or false acceptance).

Understand the differences between public-key and private-key encryption systems. The public key interchange (PKI) provides authentication, integrity, and confidentiality between parties. A public-key system uses asymmetric cryptography with a public key that is shared and a secret private key that must be protected for disclosure. Secret-key systems use symmetric cryptography with a single shared secret key. The symmetric system is faster but fails to provide authentication. A compromised secret key will destroy confidentiality.

Recognize that management must exercise control over encryption. Encryption algorithms do not manage themselves. It is the responsibility of management to control the use of encryption and encryption keys under a System Development Life Cycle (SDLC) model. Special handling is required with encryption keys, including methods of safe storage with separation of duties.

Recognize technical mechanisms. Technical mechanisms such as server mirroring and RAID disk systems can be used to increase redundancy in order to promote better system availability. The redundant hardware increases fault tolerance for conditions involving hardware failure and possibly intruder attacks.

Understand the purpose of different VPNs to protect remote access. Virtual private networks use encryption for secure communication between systems on different networks. Secure Sockets Layer (SSL) and Transport Layer Security (TLS) implement fully encrypted sessions running from the sending computer to the receiving computer. SSL and TLS require the use of digital certificates. IPsec VPN uses VPN gateways for transmission over a wide area network. With IPsec, the encryption is between the gateways, not individual systems. IPsec gateways use the address of their ISP provider on the external interface.

Understand intrusion detection and prevention systems. Intrusion detection and prevention systems are designed to function as a computer-based hacker alarm. The system can be implemented by using either a host-based method or network-based method. An IDPS will react to only those perceived attacks that occur on the system with host-based IDPS installed or that are transmitted down a network link that is actively monitored by a network-based IDPS. Attacks on all other systems are invisible to the IDPS. The IDPS identifies attacks by using one of three methods: comparing a database of known attack signatures, comparing changes to a statistical baseline, or using a neural network with knowledge-based rules.

Review Questions

1. What is the best method for an organization to allow its business partners to access the company intranet across the Internet?

    A. Shared virtual private network

    B. Shared lease line

    C. Internet firewall

    D. Network router with MLSP

2. Digital signatures are primarily designed to provide additional protection with electronic messages in order to ensure which of the following?

    A. Message deletion

    B. Message read by unauthorized party

    C. Sender verification

    D. Message modification

3. Internet communication requires more security. To audit Internet security and access control, the IS auditor will first need to examine what?

    A. Validity of password changes

    B. Architecture of the client/server application

    C. Network architecture and design

    D. Virus protection and firewall servers

4. Which of the following is the most appropriate method to ensure confidentiality in data communications?

    A. Secure hash algorithm (SHA-1)

    B. Virtual private network (VPN)

    C. Digital signatures

    D. Digital certificates with public-key encryption

5. What is the most effective method for preventing or limiting the damage caused by a software virus attack?

    A. Access control software configured for restricted setting

    B. Updated virus signatures

    C. Antivirus policies and standards

    D. Data download standards with administrative review

6. What is the primary purpose of a network firewall?

    A. Protect company systems from attack by external systems

    B. Protect downstream systems from all the internal attacks

    C. Protect all modem-connected systems from Internet attacks

    D. Protect attached systems from attacks running through the firewall

7. Which of the following is the least dependable form of biometrics?

   A. Hand geometry

   B. Facial recognition

   C. Signature analysis

   D. Iris scanning

8. The IS auditor has just completed a review of an organization. Which of the following weaknesses would be considered the most serious?

   A. Lack of separation of duties for critical functions.

   B. Weak password controls without effective policy enforcement.

   C. Business continuity plans include noncritical applications.

   D. Network server is not backed up regularly.

9. What is the purpose of the DMZ (demilitarized zone) concept for Internet communications?

   A. *Demilitarized* refers to a safe zone that is protected from all Internet attacks.

   B. Subnet that is semiprotected and allows external access.

   C. Protected subnet implemented using a fifth-generation firewall.

   D. Safeguard control for communication allowing access to internal production servers.

10. An e-commerce website needs to be monitored to detect possible hacker activity. What would be the best security component to perform this function?

   A. Third-generation firewall

   B. Honey net ACL router with built-in sniffer software

   C. Elliptic data encryption for privileged files

   D. Statistical or signature-based detection software

11. The auditee organization decided to implement single sign-on (SSO) for all their users. Their implementation will be using logon ID and passwords for access control. What situation should they be concerned about?

   A. Password aging must be set to force unique password changes every 30 to 60 days using alphanumeric characters.

   B. The user's system access will have protection; however, password changes will be more difficult because of synchronization issues between servers.

   C. Unauthorized login would have access to the maximum resources available on the network.

   D. The servers will need memory and CPU upgrades to handle the extra workload generated by SSO.

12. What is the primary purpose of intrusion detection protection systems (IDS/IDPS) when compared to firewall systems?

   A. A firewall blocks all attacks; IDS informs us if the firewall was successful.

   B. IDS will notify the system administrator at every possible attack that has occurred, whether successful or unsuccessful.

   C. A firewall reports all attacks to the IDS.

   D. IDS logs and notifies the system administrator of any suspected attacks but may not recognize every attack.

13. Which of the following statements is true concerning asymmetric-key cryptography?

    A. The sender and receiver have different keys.

    B. The sender and receiver use the same key.

    C. The sender encrypts the files by using the recipient's private key.

    D. Asymmetric keys cannot be used for digital signatures.

14. The IS auditor is auditing the controls related to employee termination. Which of the following is the most important aspect to be reviewed?

    A. Company staff is notified about the termination.

    B. All login accounts of the employee are terminated.

    C. Details of the employee have been removed from active payroll files.

    D. Company property provided to the employee has been returned.

15. Which is the most important responsibility of the IS security person?

    A. Controlling and monitoring data security policies

    B. Promoting security awareness within the organization

    C. Establishing new procedures for IT and reviewing their legal accuracy

    D. System administration of the servers and database

16. What method provides the *best* level of access control to confidential data being processed on a local server?

    A. Writing a history of all transaction activity to the system log for auditing.

    B. Processing of sensitive transactions requires a separate login and password.

    C. Application software uses internal access control rules to implement least privilege.

    D. System login access is restricted to particular stations or hours of operation.

17. What is the primary purpose for using database views?

    A. Allow the user access into the database

    B. Provide a method for generating reports

    C. Allow the system administrator access to maintain the database

    D. Restrict the viewing of selected data

18. Which of the following statements is true concerning an Internet worm?

    A. Able to travel independently through the systems

    B. Self-replicates and attaches itself to files during execution

    C. Uses a backdoor to access system resources

    D. Can be dormant until triggered by a particular date or time

19. What is the issue with regard to the use of source routing?

    A. Source routing is a diagnostic tool used with firewalls.

    B. No issue with compensating controls.

    C. Source routing can bypass network defenses.

    D. Is a desired feature for network monitoring.

20. The equal error rate (EER) or crossover error rate (CER) refers to which of the following?

    A. Firewalls

    B. Biometrics

    C. Encryption

    D. Separation of duties

21. Which of the following is the best definition of *minutiae*?

    A. Characteristics data

    B. Detailed log data

    C. High-definition scan

    D. Minutes of meeting

22. Complete the following statement with the best available choice: A _____ will subvert the kernel and bypass operating system security. This is _____ inside downloads and installs itself without the knowledge of the user.

    A. Denial of service, hidden

    B. Worm, impossible to detect

    C. Root kit, hidden

    D. Virus, impossible to detect

23. Which of the following represents a control failure of IT governance?

    A. Independent contractors

    B. External audit

    C. Internal audit

    D. Self-monitoring

24. Which of the following has the lowest correlation to the separation of duties concept?

    A. Change control

    B. Violation reporting

    C. Network firewalls

    D. Theft

25. Why should the transportation and tracking of backup media be given a high priority?

    A. Backup media has a limited shelf life.

    B. Backups should be transported in a locked storage box.

    C. Backup media contains the organization's secrets.

    D. Use of encryption eliminates transportation and tracking issues.

26. Which of the following techniques is used to prevent the encryption keys from being susceptible to an attack against standing data?

    A. Key wrapping

    B. Key generation

    C. Symmetric-key algorithm

    D. Asymmetric-key algorithm

27. Complete the following statement with the best answer. The _____ access controls are _____ managed with _____ approval requirements for the highest possible level of security.

    A. Mandatory, locally, manager

    B. Discretionary, centrally, formal

    C. Discretionary, individually, manager

    D. Mandatory, centrally, formal

28. Which of the following VPN methods will transmit data across the local network in plain text without encryption?

    A. Secure Sockets Layer (SSL)

    B. IPsec

    C. Transport Layer Security (TLS)

    D. Layer 2 Tunneling Protocol (L2TP)

29. Complete the following statement: The auditor can use _____ as a fast method for discovering the hosts on the network, and _____ to identify all available service ports.

    A. Vulnerability scanning, log review

    B. Penetration testing, host enumeration

    C. Host enumeration, vulnerability scanning

    D. File mount logs, vulnerability scanning

30. Which of the following VPN methods is used to transmit the payload and hide internal network addresses with encryption?

    A. IPsec tunnel

    B. Secure Sockets Layer (SSL)

    C. IPsec transport

    D. Transport Layer Security (TLS)

31. Which encryption system is primarily used in private industry for transportation rather than storage?

    A. Symmetric-key encryption

    B. Asymmetric-key encryption

    C. Secret keys

    D. Public keys

32. What is the best definition of *stateful inspection*?

    A. History and nature of connectionless requests

    B. Packet-filtering firewall with application proxy service

    C. Internal control mechanism designed into the operating system kernel

    D. History and nature of connection-oriented requests

33. Which of the following access control models is used for distributed management?

    A. Discretionary

    B. Mandatory

    C. Explicit

    D. Formal

34. What is the most important reason for management to control encryption by using a System Development Life Cycle model?

    A. To build better encryption algorithms.

    B. Poor management is the biggest threat.

    C. Encryption systems are complex.

    D. Cost overruns are common with encryption systems.

35. Which of the following situations is the most important topic for an auditor to spend extra time investigating?

    A. The system configuration is being dictated by security staff.

    B. A firewall is configured to disable source routing.

    C. Dual power leads are being installed to the computer room.

    D. An all-in-one device controls security and processes user requests.

Answers to Review Questions

1. A. The virtual private network (VPN) is the most flexible and least expensive solution for accessing company resources across the Internet.

2. C. Digital signatures provide authentication assurance of the email sender. Digital signatures use the private key of the sender to verify identity.

3. C. The IS auditor will need to understand the network architecture and design before being able to evaluate the security and access controls. Later, the architecture of the client/server application and virus protection will be of interest.

4. B. The virtual private network (VPN) would ensure data confidentiality. A secure hash algorithm would identify that a file has been changed but will not provide confidentiality. Digital signatures are used to assess the identity of the sender but do not provide confidentiality.

5. B. Maintaining updated virus signature files. Access control software is not directly responsible for limiting the virus attack. Antivirus policies and standards should require updated virus signature files in order to be effective. Data download standards will help; however, virus signatures is the best choice.

6. D. The network firewall can protect only those systems that route communication through the firewall. The firewall cannot protect systems attached via modem. Insecure wireless networks are also a major threat.

7. C. Signature analysis is the most undependable form of biometrics. Hand geometry and iris scanning are very dependable. Facial recognition is improving.

8. D. The network server not being backed up regularly is the most significant threat to data integrity and availability. Weak passwords would be a lesser concern. The lack of separation of duties may be offset by compensating controls.

9. B. The DMZ is a subnet that is semiprotected by the firewall and allows for external access.

10. D. An IDPS with statistical or signature-based detection software would be the best choice.

11. C. Any unauthorized logon would have access to all the server resources on the network. Password aging with unique passwords is a good idea anyway.

12. D. The IDS keeps the transaction log and alerts the system administrator of any suspected attacks. The IDS can use statistical behavior or signature files to determine whether an attack has occurred.

13. A. The sender and receiver each have their own public and private (secret) key pair. All the other statements are false. Asymmetric keys are definitely used for creating digital signatures. The sender would never use the recipient's private key, only the recipient's public key.

14. B. The system access and login accounts of the employee should be terminated immediately. Company property is important, but a lesser concern than system access.

15. A. Controlling and monitoring data security policies is the highest priority of the IS security person.

16. C. Application controls should use internal access control lists to implement least privilege. System login restrictions are of less importance by comparison.

17. D. Database views are used to implement least privilege and restrict the data that can be viewed by the user.

18. A. An Internet worm is able to travel independently through systems, unlike a virus. The virus self-replicates and attaches itself to files during execution.

19. C. Source routing should not be allowed to operate on network firewalls. It presents a significant risk by allowing a hacker to bypass router security settings.

20. B. In biometrics, the trade-off between the false acceptance rate (FAR) and the false rejection rate (FRR) is known as the equal error rate (EER) or crossover error rate (CER).

21. A. Minutiae is the collection of characteristics used in biometric data about a specific user (a user's biometric template). The process converts a high-resolution scan into a tiny count of unique characteristics.

22. C. Root kits are malicious software designed to subvert the operating system security. Root kits compromise system security and use stealth to hide their presence. After a root kit is installed, the system is completely compromised.

23. D. Self-monitoring represents a violation in separation of duties. A built-in reporting conflict exists without external monitoring by another individual. A person in the same job function cannot monitor their own work.

24. D. Theft is not part of the separation of duties concept because anyone at any level can commit crimes of theft. Separation of duties applies to computers, people, processes, and facilities.

25. C. Backup media must be tracked because it contains the utmost secrets of any organization. Media leaving the facility must be kept in locked storage boxes at all times. Tracking is required during transit to confirm its departure time and arrival. Some regulations require the use of encrypted backup tapes to protect the standing data. Remember, encrypting data increases security. Managing encryption requires more-involved handling procedures.

26. A. Key wrapping is used to protect encryption keys from disclosure. Otherwise, encryption keys would be susceptible to the same attacks as standing data.

27. D. Mandatory access controls are always centrally managed, with formal approval required to increase that individual's level of access.

28. B. IPsec uses encryption between the VPN gateways. Data transmitted from the gateway to the local computer is not encrypted.

29. C. Host enumeration provides a fast method for discovering all the hosts on the network. Vulnerability scanning will identify all the available service ports on the host computers. Neither of these processes should be performed during production hours. These scanning methods will activate intrusion detection alarms. Vulnerability scanning may crash the target computer.

30. A. Tunnel mode of IPsec will encrypt both the payload and local network addresses. This hides the messages and prevents identification of the sender and recipient while the messages travel across the public Internet.

31. B. Asymmetric-key encryption, also known as public-key encryption, is typically used for the transmission of data (electronic transportation). The other options are closely related distracters.

32. A. Connectionless UDP requests were almost impossible to track in older firewalls. Stateful inspection collects the history and nature of connectionless requests to determine whether the remote request should be transmitted to the destination computer or discarded as hazardous.

33. A. Distributed security uses discretionary access control. Decisions are based in the local assessment of requirements and intended use. Distributed security is notorious for having consistency problems.

34. B. The System Development Life Cycle is used to control the use of encryption and encryption keys. Poor management is the number one cause of failure.

35. D. An all-in-one device may be violating the separation of duties. This creates undue risk in the interest of cutting costs (greed).

Chapter 8

Disaster Recovery and Business Continuity

THE OBJECTIVE OF THIS CHAPTER IS TO ACQUAINT THE READER WITH THE FOLLOWING CONCEPTS:

- ✓ Distinguishing between disaster recovery and business continuity
- ✓ Understanding business process resumption
- ✓ Using the risk analysis to guide planning
- ✓ Using the business impact analysis for low-level mapping of existing processes
- ✓ Determining strategy based on time windows
- ✓ Creating a strategy without any dependency on the vendor's technology
- ✓ Introducing the international Incident Command System (ICS)
- ✓ Using invocation processes and known problems with leased alternate sites
- ✓ Developing a plan
- ✓ Understanding human resource management
- ✓ Improving plan-testing strategies
- ✓ Creating a communication and media plan
- ✓ Integrating with other plans

This chapter focuses on an organization's ability to recover from a disaster and to continue minimum acceptable operations. Your CISA exam maintains a very narrow focus of disaster recovery as it relates to an organization's ability to restore services to a predefined service-level agreement. However, we feel that to be a successful IS auditor, you should be taught a broader reference. Therefore, we're going to provide a brief introduction to the expanded scope of business continuity as well as the principles of disaster recovery.

We will compare the CISA exam's ISACA material to business continuity best practices. We will also introduce some of the terminology ISACA wants every CISA to know as it relates to disaster recovery and business continuity.

Defining Disaster Recovery

During the 1980s, the term *disaster recovery (DR)* became popular as a definition for rebuilding and recovery following a natural disaster. The entire focus of disaster recovery could be summed up with a one-word definition: *rebuilding*.

In 1988, the Disaster Recovery Institute International (DRII) was founded and set forth to produce a list of professional practices for disaster recovery planning. Its objective was to help organizations with their planning efforts to ensure that they could rebuild and recover their facilities and equipment following a natural disaster.

In 1992, Hurricane Andrew proved that disaster recovery lacked a critical element for survival. We could survive the storm, protect the people, and rebuild the facilities. However, without a steady stream of incoming revenue, organizations might recover only to find they were forced out of business by bankruptcy, or a lack of money. Granted, facilities and IT systems are important for an organization to conduct business. Unfortunately, those elements alone are not enough for any organization's existence to continue. The scope of disaster recovery needed to be expanded to include revenue and customers.

beyond [handwritten annotation]

Let's discuss the financial challenges that lead into defining business continuity.

Surviving Financial Challenges

The greatest threats to the survival of any organization center on financial concerns of continued existence. One needs to be sure that under all conditions special measures have been taken to ensure the following:

- The organization does not breach any significant contractual commitments.

- The banker does not call business loans due, rerate available credit lines, or increase the interest rate.

- Investors do not back out or dump their stock in a rapid sell-off.

- Clients continue to do business without hesitating, or canceling their orders.

- Business partners continue to perform under the original terms of contract without placing new demands or suspending services.

The loss of any of these items can structurally weaken the organization and management's ability to continue operation. In fact, the loss of any these items would probably be a showstopper. The organization would grind to a halt and cease to function.

Valuing Brand Names

Let's consider for a moment the subject of brand names. Brand names include well-known corporate names such as Gulf Oil, Frontier Airlines, and Holiday Inn. Few people realize that each of the aforementioned brands were once shut down or sold off. Brand names represent the recognition of goodwill established after years of successful advertising. If the advertising was successful, the brand name alone brings about recognition and a perception of value in the consumer's mind. Successful advertising generates revenue from 5 times to 30 times the cost of the advertisements. In fact, the established brand name may be one of the most viable assets of the organization.

You may ask, "What does this have to do with disaster recovery?" The answer is simple. Business continuity planning focuses on maintaining the public image of the corporate entity—in order to ensure survival of the organization.

 In 1994, a new airline was started by former Frontier Airlines executives. The Frontier brand name had reverted to public domain during eight years of disuse and was available again. Many consumers never realized that the original airline had ceased operation. The brand's value had continued to survive.

Rebuilding after a Disaster

Even the mightiest of organizations can be brought down by a variety of events. Every day in the *Financial Times* or *The Wall Street Journal*, you can find an example of operational failure, leadership failure, or a mishandled incident that became a man-made disaster.

If you recall, a simple definition of *disaster recovery* is *rebuilding*. Almost all activities under disaster recovery focus on rebuilding to match a previous historical configuration. It would be futile to rebuild without your customers and the flow of revenue created by their purchases. Most businesses are very sensitive to changes that reduce the profit margin. Increased operating costs or a reduction in sales will rapidly convert a profitable business into a nonprofitable mess. DR plans are departmental in nature. Cross-coordination between departments is necessary for survival. Even the greatest of businesses will be reduced to a fraction of themselves or be taken over by new management. Brands may survive, but the people will be different. Just look at the long delays in rebuilding New Orleans after Hurricane Katrina.

US Airways experienced a software problem in December 2004 that was created by a failure in change control. The programmers involved attempted to make a poorly timed change during the peak of holiday travel. The result was a logistical nightmare. US Air's manifest system could no longer coordinate flight schedules, airplanes, passengers, or their baggage. IT restored operations, but customers were furious. This problem became an unrecoverable disaster because of lost sales and spot increases in operating costs as a result of the original failure. Investors rapidly abandoned the airline within days. Regional competitor America West Airlines (AWA) took over US Airways for pennies on the dollar. AWA's first action was to discharge all the original executives and replace US Air managers with America West people. In its first year under new leadership, US Airways earned ½ billion dollars. The US Airways brand name continues under new ownership.

Both customers and investors are notorious for abandoning organizations during their rebuilding phases. People favor undamaged vendors. Few people will wait for the rebuilding to be completed; instead they take their money elsewhere. It doesn't take much of an interruption to cause layoffs, tumbling stock prices, and even permanent shutdowns. This leads us to the evolution from disaster recovery to business continuity.

Defining the Purpose of Business Continuity

Unlike DR, *business continuity (BC)* focuses on *revenue*. As long as the organization has time and money at its disposal, the organization can continue to function. Money can take the form of capital, credit lines, investors, and payments from customers. Business continuity focuses on putting more money in the bank, even if the business is not delivering a product. A perfect example is the age-old "fire sale." The objective of a fire sale is to increase the amount of capital on hand in order to allow the business time to continue operation and possibly fund their rebuilding activities.

The purpose of business continuity is to ensure that core business functions continue with minimal or no interruption. When focusing on business continuity, you may choose not to return to the past and to instead focus all endeavors toward new opportunities. The objective is to ensure that the organization will survive and continue to generate revenue. Uninterrupted revenue equals money that provides the luxury of time and opportunity.

An organization can use the principles of business continuity to accomplish the following:

Survive man-made or natural disaster   Survival means sustaining control while ensuring that enough money is flowing to the bank to keep the organization running during and after the event.

Acquire or divest business units   The business continuity planning process creates an incredibly valuable set of documents, including a current risk analysis and a low-level blueprint of business processes currently in use. This information would be invaluable for outsourcing or insourcing.

Organizations can be affected by events that disrupt the daily operation of their business. Consider, for example, AOL (formerly called America Online), which suffered a change management crisis in which the configuration of the routers and servers was lost. The result was an operational disaster in 1994 with a complete blackout of AOL's Internet services for more than three days. As a result, AOL suffered a negative public perception and negative publicity. This operational mistake ultimately led to the sale of the business. In 2003, while AOL was owned by Time Warner, AOL was again the subject of much controversy and rapidly falling stock prices. The issue this time centered on the management team refusing to sign for the integrity of the company financial statement. Their failure to sign created a legal requirement for the organization to notify the entire world that their record keeping was questionable and that there was no assurance of integrity in any statements made. AOL management was aware of the consequences but did not want to accept personal liability for signing a potentially false integrity statement. The resulting news stories led many investors to dump stock at a fraction of its previous value.

Change to a different market   Some markets are no longer profitable because of changes in consumer attitude, cost/competition, or increasing regulatory law. Management may find a more profitable market for their efforts. As an example, consider Daisytek International. Daisytek started business as a distributor of office supplies and later became a hardware manufacturer for Hewlett-Packard. After several years, the management team decided to quit manufacturing hardware and refocus on the more-profitable market of distributing office supplies. Recently the supplies portion of the business was sold because of low profit margin, and the remaining organization was renamed PFSweb. Now PFSweb operates as a contract fulfillment and distribution vendor, providing fulfillment services for other organizations. Many of the original executives and staff remain.

Improve market position by demonstrating a potential for surviving or profiting   One of the reasons an organization participates in business continuity planning is to attract better financial terms from investors and to attract more clients. A good business continuity plan could attract new contracts and revenue opportunities by demonstrating an organizational plan to fulfill contractual commitments.

Gain advantage over a competitor in the marketplace   An organization might gain advantage by demonstrating an ability to help their customers in spite of whatever may occur. We can use the example of FedEx and their "Absolutely positively overnight" reputation to demonstrate this point. Customers pay a premium for this level of commitment.

Other examples of gaining an advantage are as follows:

To service a surge in business   An organization may execute business continuity plans to undertake a higher than normal business volume. The organization sheds low-profit tasks to make resources available for the increased volume. An 80 percent surge in demand creates a survival challenge comparable to an equivalent reduction in capacity.

To lead an aggressive campaign against a faltering competitor   The competitor may be facing temporary delivery problems, an unfavorable media image, labor issues, or a man-made or natural disaster. Our client would unleash a marketing campaign with compelling offers to entice clients to abandon the competition. Customer swings have been recorded of 20 percent to 55 percent of market share during a 16-hour period.

Wow! incredible story!

To be available for your customer's needs   Consider the story of the Bank of Italy during the California earthquake of 1906. The earthquake lasted only 30 seconds, but the city of San Francisco was destroyed by the earthquake and subsequent fires. All the banks were ordered closed to prevent a run on the banks. The tiny Bank of Italy set up temporary oper-ations in a wooden horse cart at the wharf. While the other banks were closed, the Bank of Italy made small loans to help people rebuild. Many individuals wanted to make deposits to this little bank in a horse cart. The customers wanted their money from coffee cans and from under mattresses to be protected. Serving $10 depositors, the little Bank of Italy took in more than $800,000 during the next few years. This was an incredible sum of money during that period. Multiple divisions were formed under other names, and ultimately these were combined under one new name: Bank of America.

Survive a runaway marketing campaign   Do you remember the fabulously successful "Where's the beef?" campaign by Wendy's hamburgers? It is a marketing legend. It also illus-trates how a runaway marketing campaign can place excessive strain on an organization's resources. Dave Thomas, the founder of Wendy's, told the story as follows:

Wendy's had run a series of advertising campaigns which never really seemed to catch on. Other competitors were able to attract customers using lower-priced products with less meat. Wendy's "Where's the beef?" marketing campaign was based upon a commonsense observa-tion and was well timed to the marketplace. Wendy's advertisement caught on like wildfire. Aspiring politicians used the "Where's the beef?" slogan against competitors for coattail pub-licity during campaign rallies. The campaign was enormously successful beyond everyone's expectations. This one campaign created so much attention, new customers were lining up at their door. The ad also brought the attention of Wendy's larger competitors. Wendy's was forced into a rapid national expansion or face losing their marketplace. Wendy's opened over 500 new stores during a one-year period at the rate of two or more stores per workday. (Source: Discovery Channel)

Could your organization have done the same? Wendy's is not the only company facing this type of challenge. United Parcel Service (UPS) and FedEx are involved in the same type of competition for expansion. UPS purchased Office Depot. Next, UPS purchased the Mail-Boxes Etc. chain to increase the number of UPS drop-off locations. FedEx purchased Kinko's in a race to see who would dominate the market. FedEx Kinko's opened more than 250 stores in the first year of acquisition, with plans to open 2,000 additional stores over the next five years. This type of rapid expansion requires good continuity planning to ensure that your customers stay happy customers. It requires a strong leader like FedEx CEO Fred Smith to pull this off.

Uniting Other Plans with Business Continuity

As we have said, business continuity is the next level beyond disaster recovery. Business continuity is double-sided. One side protects what a business already has, while the other offers the opportunity to generate more revenue than ever before.

A good continuity plan defines a strategy and details for supporting a business with fewer resources. After the business has learned how to make more money, there is no need to wait for a disaster. The business can begin to execute the revenue-enhancement plans immediately, and will be prepared for both disaster and market opportunity.

Business continuity planning integrates and coordinates the narrow scope of smaller plans. It would be impossible for a single department to provide the broad-level support necessary to be successful. Figure 8.1 shows this integration.

FIGURE 8.1   Business continuity integrates smaller departmental plans.

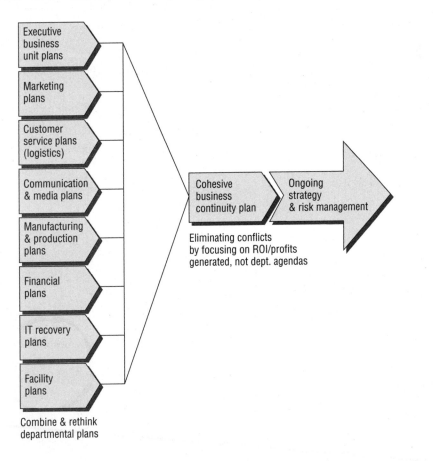

Business continuity spans departmental and political boundaries. While DR is based in facilities and IT plans, the BC plans focus on what it takes for the business to resume generating revenue. Business continuity is frequently led by the chief operating officer or program management office. Plans include media handling and campaigns to retain customers, vendors, and investors that would otherwise be tempted to switch to a competitor.

Identifying the Business Continuity Practice Areas

There are 10 practice areas in the business continuity model according to DRII and the UK's Business Continuity Institute (BCI). It is the job of the business continuity/disaster recovery planner to determine whether the focus will be disaster recovery for rebuilding or business continuity for revenue. This type of planning uses a very specialized version of project management. Each of these areas is a project unto itself.

The practice areas are as follows:

Initiation   Get a sponsor, authority, scope, and funding.

Risk analysis   Document and prioritize current risks. Risks include natural disasters and man-made events.

Business impact analysis   Develop a low-level business process blueprint; determine what is needed to sustain the business.

Strategy creation   Use the risk analysis and business impact analysis to formulate a possible strategy based on facts and assumptions in evidence.

Emergency response   Integrate the planned strategy with the first responder by using the Incident Command System (ICS).

Plan creation   Create and organize the plan, including personnel assignments and detailed procedures.

Training and awareness   Teach individuals the necessary roles and skills to perform the required functions of the BC/DR plan. Educate the organization about the plan's existence and anticipated areas of coverage.

Maintenance and testing   Nothing is out-of-date faster than a big book of plans. People have to practice their roles to gain proficiency, and a change control system will be needed to improve the documentation. It is impossible to keep plans current without structured exercises to improve skills and identify deficiencies.

Communications   Poor communications can be more damaging than the actual disaster. Clients, investors, partners, employees, and stakeholders need to be kept informed and feel comfortable with the information they receive. Internal and external messages need to be properly vetted to convey the intended message. A schedule of communications and scripted messages needs to be developed by the BC marketing team in advance. Misunderstood messages can be more damaging than the actual disaster. Plans need to include an uninterruptible communication system, which is not prone to outages as cell phones or land lines are.

Integration with other organizations   No organization can exist by itself. A good plan will integrate with plans of business partners, suppliers, clients, and government agencies. You may need to rely on them, or they may need to rely on us during critical functions. Often a prime contractor will incorporate the plans of a subcontractor into their own. Good integration adapts the relationship from one based on price to one based on being a true partner.

Figure 8.2 shows an overview of the 10 practice areas of business continuity planning.

FIGURE 8.2   The 10 areas of best practices in business continuity planning

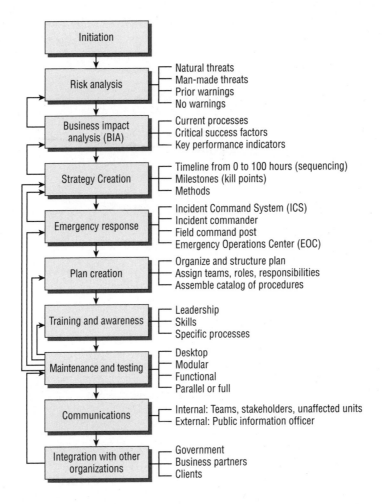

Real World Scenario

Best Practices Compared to the CISA Exam

The CISA exam and ISACA have a narrow view of business continuity and disaster recovery. The best practices for business continuity presented in this chapter are endorsed by the DRII and the BCI.

You are expected to know the terminology used by ISACA for the exam. Each organization uses similar terms of reference. You should also be introduced to an overview of best practices in business continuity to increase understanding of real-life situations. We have reduced the BCP class content to remain focused on the CISA exam. Each of the examples presented should help increase your value as an IS auditor.

The following shows the differences between business continuity best practices and the ISACA knowledge areas.

Business Continuity Best Practices	ISACA Knowledge Areas for CISA Examination
1. Initiate the process.	
2. Perform risk analysis (RA).	
3. Perform business impact analysis (BIA).	1. Analyze business impact.
4. Develop continuity strategy for all departments.	2. Develop business recovery strategy.
5. Establish emergency response and control using the Incident Command System (ICS).	
6. Write and design plan.	3. Develop detailed IT plan.
7. Train and increase awareness.	4. Implement the plan.
8. Maintain and test plan.	5. Maintain and test plan (IT focus).
9. Plan communications including marketing, scripts, and media-handling procedures.	6. Mention using public information officer (PIO).
10. Integrate plans of other organizations.	
11. Achieve certification as business continuity professional.	

automation is key

Some individuals are of the opinion that IT technology and facilities are the most important functions in business continuity. Although they have a signif- icant role, it is important to remember that the number one priority is your customer and your customer interface. Without the customer, there is no rev- enue. Without revenue, business continuity would be difficult or impossible. Without a steady stream of happy customers, the investors will bail out too.

Now let's explore the 10 practice areas of business continuity in a little more depth. Our goal is to provide you with a basic understanding that you can use in your audit work.

Practice Area 1—Initiation

See Business Process Reengineering, pg 150

Every project undergoes an initiation phase with the objective to secure the following:

- A sponsor to pay for the project
- A charter to grant responsibility and authority
- A defined scope (for a particular geographic site, division, product, or client)
- Specific business objectives (critical success factors, management direction)

We need to introduce the simple definition of two important terms:

Critical success factor (CSF)   Something that must function correctly every single time. A critical success factor represents an objective or task that absolutely must be accomplished. To fail a CSF would be a real showstopper. Let's use an example of a student in school. Scholar- ship requirements would be a type of CSF. If you don't meet all the requirements, you won't get the scholarship. Public corporations' timely filing of quarterly financial results is a CSF because failure to file will attract fines from the government. Worse yet, delayed filing will trig- ger stock analysts to spread a bad performance report that, in turn, drives down the stock value regardless of the truth.

Key goal indicator (KGI)   Identify the organization's goals and define the smaller departmental goals. Key goals are those objectives that are important, but not as threatening as failing a CSF. Goals can include customer satisfaction and quality levels. For comparison: KGIs can slip with- out creating a showstopper. Key performance indicators are used to determine whether the goal will be reached.

Key performance indicator (KPI)   Metrics are created based on a variety of sources. These lower-level metrics are similar to player statistics in sports (batting average, points scored, speed or distance covered). Unfortunately, KPIs may not indicate a problem until it's too late. Think of KPIs as comparable to report-card grades in school.

During the initiation phase, specific discussions are held between the BC/DR planner and executive management. The planner may use the technique of doom and gloom to threaten a variety of negative consequences. This technique is intended to intimidate executives with lia- bility if they fail to cooperate. A more favorable technique would be to provide clippings of related news articles to generate awareness. A person could ask, "If this event happened to us, would we have a similar outcome?"

The majority of BC/DR planners will use a shortsighted approach that business continuity or disaster coverage is similar to insurance. Their goal is to protect the business from a future loss. The problem is that many executives are more worried about generating revenue than they are about maintaining comprehensive insurance.

The BC/DR planner should develop a list of benefits that the enterprise would derive by developing and implementing a business continuity plan.

Brands and goodwill affiliated with a company name contain significant "real" value. Most marketing campaigns are built up year after year using anywhere from 15 percent to 25 percent of product gross revenue to pay for advertising. It is common to expect strong ad campaigns to earn returns that are 5 times to 30 times the cost of the campaign itself. Years of happy customers create brand loyalty. A hard-earned image can be destroyed by adverse publicity or disaster. Approach value by calculating the amount of money invested in advertising and public relations over the past years.

The BC/DR planner needs to communicate the multiple categories of risk that face the organization. Consider this to be the short and broad list in discussions with management. Each of these situations could rapidly surface and get out of control during a crisis or even cause a disaster.

The threat categories include the following:

Strategic (plans)   Poor marketing strategy, changes in laws, consumer attitudes

Financial (controls)   Fraud, poor record keeping, failed reconciliation, poor cash/credit management, treasury problems, Securities and Exchange Commission (SEC) reports, Gramm-Leach-Bliley bank performance rules

Operational (human)   Human error, apathy, wrong procedures, poor judgment, communications conflict, politics, lack of up-to-date training

Commercial (relationships)   Loss of key supplier/customer; supply-chain failure; scandal involving partner, supplier, or significant customer

Technical (assets)   Equipment breakdown, natural disaster, destruction, loss of use, other perils

Figure 8.3 shows that business continuity can be focused on protecting a variety of business processes.

An incredibly effective technique is to tie business continuity objectives into plans for revenue and market share. Earlier, we touched on a few examples of using business continuity planning to generate revenue. Funding is less of an issue when you include marketing plans in the objectives. This lends itself to acquiring a significant amount of funding from the advertising budget—far less money than advertising would miss and far more money than most DR plans would ever acquire.

Some of the possible deliverables from the business continuity/disaster recovery planning process include the following:

- Verification of capabilities (efficiency, inefficiency, deficiency, overreliance, unused capacity)

- Identification of new revenue opportunities

- Functional blueprint of current business processes with mapping of interrelationships and sequence

- Definition of risk and performance strategy

FIGURE 8.3   Selecting the business process to protect

- Documentation of specific required tasks for business survival
- Strategy to increase revenue
- Fulfillment of a business interest or executive business desire

People agree to fund and support projects for a variety of reasons. The goal of the initiation phase is to determine what the sponsor will pay for and why, and to document the desired result.

As an IT auditor, you will focus on whether the IT functions will be able to support the business objectives. Planning for business continuity/disaster recovery will be successful only when sponsored from the top down. It is the responsibility of senior executive management to ensure that this planning occurs. A business continuity/disaster recovery steering committee will be necessary to create an effective plan.

Practice Area 2—Risk Analysis   *- see pg 70 - Risk Management*

The second phase is to conduct a risk analysis. The business continuity/disaster recovery planner creates a list of all the threats known to face the organization—including both man-made and natural, those with prior warning, and those without. Many people see this phase as a well-known requirement but then proceed to skip right past it without any regard for its impact. In Chapter 2, "Audit Process," we provided a flowchart detailing the methods for performing risk analysis. *- pg 72 , 47 - PERT chart is a quantitative tool for performing Ris*

The starting point in risk analysis entails listing the threats and assigning a potential score. Risk managers are similar to gamblers: They want to calculate the present odds and see what can be done to improve them. Your goal at this stage of the planning process is to accurately document the present state of each threat. After you have identified all of the risks, the planner will focus their efforts on the threats of the highest priority. Priority may be determined by frequency, consequence, or dependency. *or impact*

A sense of order is necessary to manage the list of potential threats. Your sponsor and executive management team will have little interest in wading through volumes of spreadsheets. The easy way to deal with this is to create a summary sheet and related detail sheets. Each item on the summary sheet will relate to an entire page or pages of detail sheets.

Figure 8.4 illustrates risk assessment worksheets. Shown are the summary and related detail reports.

FIGURE 8.4   Risk assessment worksheets for summary and detail

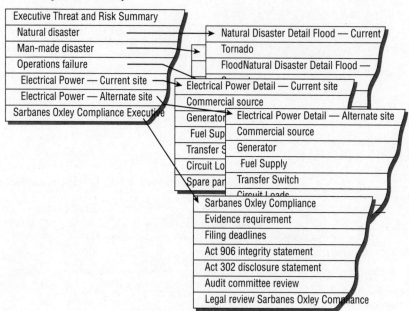

The higher-level summary sheet will include a list of threats related to the following:

- Various natural disasters
- Man-made disasters
- Operational and technology failures
- Vendor failures
- Current site failures
- Alternate site failures
- Relocation threats

Each of these line items will be broken down into individual components listed on a detail sheet. From the detail sheet, the planner will create a composite score that will appear on the summary sheet. Figure 8.5 shows the detailed ranking for each threat.

A well-documented threat listing will note where the evidence was acquired or where the evidence can be found. All risk analysis worksheets represent a tremendous value in time, effort, and informational detail. These worksheets should be preserved and protected. Every intelligent risk manager will review them on a regular basis. Finished worksheets may contain hundreds or thousands of line items.

FIGURE 8.5   A risk assessment worksheet

Threat	Likelihood (frequency)	Human Impact	Property Impact	Business Impact	Internal Resources	External Resources	Threat Score	Related Notes Archive (files)	Owner	Last Update
Labor Strike	1	3	1	4	4	3	16	strike.doc	VP hr	3/10/06
WTO protest	0.3	2	1	2	4	3	11.3	wto.doc	Facilities	9/9/07
Workplace Violence	0.7	4	1	2	5	5	14.7	wrkviol.rpt	HR	4/1/08

where's the beef? → *How to assess + score these?*

Let's take a moment to discuss the often neglected area of selecting an alternate site and potential threats to relocation. All too often the alternate site is selected by the service vendor providing the alternate facility for rent. In some cases, this could prove to be an absolute killer.

Suppose you were looking for an alternate site. What would be the geographic location requirements? Hopefully, the geographic selection process would include consideration of the following:

- General area hazards. Ask questions about the neighbors, crime rate, and previous events in the area.
- Downwind hazards from military targets and nuclear power plants.
- Known storm tracks for severe weather, including hurricanes and tornadoes.
- Potential flood areas.
- Geophysical data concerning potential earth movement.

- Access to telecommunications.

- Nearby airports, helpful for regular visits and necessary for rapid relocation.

- Roadway access. Remember September 11, 2001. Who says airplanes will be flying the day you need to fly? Some major city airports may be closed.

- Proximity. You need to be close enough to drive, yet not so close that you are affected by the same regional disaster. (Avoid collateral impact)

- Railway access for shipping heavy loads or volume goods.

- Municipal services, including fire, police, and hospital.

- Expedited services and mail services.

- Safe accommodations.

All this data is readily available, including maps of military targets and nuclear materials. Contrary to myth, worldwide military targets and nuclear materials maps are still available on the Internet at the time of this writing.

Figure 8.6 shows a simple map illustrating basic geographic threats for the state of Texas. Any country or state could have been used for this demonstration; however, the Texas map does a nice job of illustrating our objective. The northeastern United States is considered a more likely terrorist target; however, we still need to consider technical failure no matter where the business is located.

FIGURE 8.6   Geographic threat map for Texas

Notice how each of the elements of the selection process overlay the state. The major cities of Dallas, Fort Worth, Houston, Austin, and San Antonio contain multiple area threats. An upwind biological or nuclear hazard could affect each of the cities by carrying contaminants downwind.

Now take a look on the left side of the state. The Rio Grande River is the western border between Texas and Mexico. Notice the town of Del Rio, Texas, along the Rio Grande River. Del Rio is outside most of the severe weather zones. It has no significant upwind biological or nuclear hazard. The town is located within 175 to 300 miles of the major Texas cities. This is the recommended safe distance of separation from regional disasters. At a closer location, the same event or collateral disruption could impact both the primary and alternate sites.

The highway to Del Rio could fulfill the minimum access requirement. An organization could transport their staff by car, bus, or truck within 8 hours of normal driving time. Del Rio is a switching point along Union Pacific Railroad's main line. Rail access is good for heavy shipments but could represent a concern regarding possible transportation of hazardous materials. Amtrak provides regular passenger rail service. The Del Rio airport offers regularly scheduled flights and supports private aircraft operations. The organization can charter a full-sized commercial jet for about $8,500 an hour to move a large group of people in a hurry. The jet's cargo bay can be loaded with the freight needed for recovery. It is usually cheaper to charter rather than buy a handful of last-minute airline tickets.

All major air freight carriers operate from the Del Rio airport, including DHL, UPS, and FedEx. That will provide reasonable levels of logistical support. There are practically no geophysical concerns regarding earth movement. Fiber-optic access for communication is available. Land is relatively cheap. The crime rate is low. A seasonal rain may bring light flooding in low-lying areas, indicating the recovery site needs to be in an elevated area of town. Based on this information, Del Rio, Texas, scores well as an alternate site location.

Successful planners will go to this level of detail when selecting an alternate site.

Practice Area 3—Business Impact Analysis (BIA)   see pg 160

The *business impact analysis (BIA)* is the singular most important component of every business continuity plan. It is impossible to have a business continuity plan without performing a current BIA. Without the BIA, the best you could hope for would be basic disaster recovery.

The BIA process offers substantial benefits to an organization. The resulting information is invaluable for business process reengineering, outsourcing activities, resizing plans, acquisition or divestiture activities, and business continuity planning.

In Figure 8.7, you can see the relationships among business processes.

FIGURE 8.7   Relationships among business processes

just make an ERD for your business' data + processes

A BIA documents current low-level process dependencies and discovers new opportunities.

A BIA is a specialized project designed to uncover the inner workings and vulnerabilities of an organization. The value of this phase cannot be overstated. In Chapter 2, we discussed { pg 68 - 92 using both <u>qualitative</u> and <u>quantitative</u> assessment for planning. The same qualitative and quantitative techniques can be used in the BIA. Proper execution of the BIA process entails a series of discovery exercises, including the following:

see 193 141 }

- Asking a series of questions similar to those used in business process reengineering (BPR). - pg 150 These questions would focus on identifying trigger events and the current sequence of the organization's workflow.

- Interviewing key personnel.

- Reviewing existing documentation.

- Collecting data by observing actual processes.

- Possibly observing personnel performing actual tasks. The auditor should recall that using surveys can raise issues of accuracy and consistency.

- Looking for existing workarounds and alternate procedures. Many times, the client's personnel may be aware of workarounds that could prove valuable during a business continuity situation.

- Verifying critical success factors (CSFs). -see pgs 119, 261, 461

- Identifying vital materials and records necessary for recovery. This would include numerous items: data backups, vendor list, inventory records, customer lists, employee records with contact data, bill of materials, procedure documents, BC plan, banking information, copies of all contracts, and legal documents.

Collecting and organizing this information is a formidable task. All the disciplines of project management are invoked during the execution of the BIA. Later, during the business continuity planning process, the BC planners use the risk analysis and BIA information to guide the formulation of the BC strategy. Almost every organization would be unable to properly sequence business continuity activities if they failed to collect the correct information during the BIA phase.

All the data collected from the BIA and risk analysis should be properly archived and protected with the highest level of security available. This archive creates a central repository of all the organization's plans, secrets, and capabilities—hence effective security controls are paramount. The contents of this archive will be reused in subsequent planning sessions that should occur at the following times:

- At least annually
- Whenever the organizational structure changes
- Upon addition or loss of key customers
- Upon change of current business processes
- Upon change in the management direction

The business users must always be involved in the planning of business continuity. Without their input, it would be impossible to align the plans with real-world requirements.

Keeping users involved is the secret to attaining buy-in.

Practice Area 4—Strategy Creation

In using information from the first three phases, you can begin the process of selecting a business survival strategy. This strategy may be one of protection, growth, or change. It is unfortunate, but a number of uninformed individuals in all job roles may immediately jump ahead into technology solutions without having exercised a proper strategy selection process.

1) Strategy selection should take into account the management directives from initiation as well as the identified risks and documented process dependencies. Your risk analysis will allow the determination of the worst-case scenario. The BIA process will furnish a blueprint that can provide a critical path sequence. _— see PERT charts_

2) The next step in planning is to create a timeline sequence of activities necessary to support the critical path. A great deal of discussion and politics may enter into this otherwise simple process. Effective business continuity planners will categorize everything into one of three areas of interest:

Core process   Those activities that are specifically required in the critical path and related directly to production of revenue.

Supporting process   Supporting functions which are necessary to fulfill revenue direct activities. This may include an alternate mechanism for delivering invoices to the customer for prompt payment. Common examples include mail rerouting, invoicing and payment processing, regardless if it's done in-house or by an alternate contractor.

Discretionary process   Everything else that is not part of core or supporting processes. These activities are not used in critical business functions and do not feed or process data for critical or supporting systems. These activities would cost more to protect than the value of work that the system produces. Most of the IT service platforms are discretionary. For example, email is a supporting process but the system it runs on is discretionary since substituting Unix servers, mainframes or other mail platforms doesn't really matter as long as it works.

[handwritten: 3) Business Continuity metrics or SLAs]

With this information, the planner creates a working timeline for all BC/DR activities. This timeline references multiple levels of time and service delivery. We will identify these as follows:

- **Recovery time objective (RTO)**   The point in time at which a particular system is recovered to specific levels of operation. Consider a phone system that may be recovered in stages of increasing functionality. RTOs are assigned for each stage. RTOs are measured by when the business resumes use, not when IT restored the system. That's why it's called business continuity rather than IT continuity. Multiple RTOs will exist (RTO1, RTO2, RTO3, and so on).

- **Maximum acceptable outage (MAO)**   The maximum time the systems can be offline before breaching a deadline or causing damage to the organization. The MAO is factored into creating recovery time objectives (RTOs). This may also be referred to as *maximum tolerable downtime (MTD)*. It's simply that people with positive attitudes use the word *acceptable*. Both terms are similar in purpose.

- **Recovery point objective (RPO)**   The defined level of recovery for a particular item. Processing that occurs between the RPO and the incident will be lost work. An example is recovery of last night's backup tape or recovery to completed database transactions that occurred 5 minutes ago (based on a redundant high-availability system). Multiple RPOs may exist.

  Work in progress will be lost at the time of disruption. The business continuity/disaster recovery planner should review the risk and plan according to the criticality. Each RPO should take into consideration the following:

  Critical function   These must occur to fulfill the minimum requirements to accomplish *core processes* (mission). Critical functions will be very time-sensitive and might not be recoverable by manual operation.

  Vital function   These are less critical, with somewhat more time before recovery is necessary. Vital functions may be able to run manually depending on volume and duration of work.

  Sensitive function   These can be delayed for several days and might be performed manually or outsourced to another vendor.

  Noncritical function (everything else)   These may be discontinued for extended periods of time, and may or may not be restarted in the future. The recovery point objective (RPO) may be "none" for non-critical stuff.

- **Service delivery objective (SDO)**   The level of service available at a particular point in time. In the banking industry, an example of the first SDO (SDO1) may allow customers to deposit money, withdraw money, and check balances. The next SDO (SDO2) might allow the execution of financial trades. However, the customer may not be able to open or close new accounts until the account management SDO (SDO3) is reached. We use this reference to indicate the level of reduced or suspended service. Our final SDO (SDOx) would be full-service in normal operation.

At CertTest, we teach business continuity planners to organize and illustrate these objectives by using a visual timeline. Our timeline begins at 100 hours in the past and proceeds to 100 hours in the future. This will cover approximately four calendar days before and after the event. It is well documented that an organization that does not recover by the fourth day will likely fail during the coming year. Unfortunately, some organizations may fail in fewer than four days. Either way, our timeline will accomplish its purpose.

One of the most important objectives of business continuity planning efforts is to identify what constitutes the zero hour. In most organizations, nobody wants to be the person who cried wolf, nor the person who activated the plan before its designated time. Management see 89 477 holds the responsibility of identifying situations that would mandate activating the continuity plan. The senior manager on duty would be under orders to execute the plan whenever the predetermined conditions were met. Otherwise, the plan may be executed too early or too late to save the organization. The zero hour may be defined based on the level of physical damage, marketing failure, degraded media image, loss of production capability, or the runaway success of a marketing campaign.

By using this information, a variety of strategies may be selected. The IT strategy selection is based on the unique needs of individual departments, available personnel, facilities, capital management, technology, and business processes. An effective strategy will fit within the requirements of each RTO, RPO, and SDO. In highly regulated industries, the target objectives may be clearly defined by regulatory law.

4) After you identify the proper sequence of objectives, you need to decide the best method of implementation. Available options include the following:

Do nothing   This is often unacceptable and creates the potential for catastrophic liability.

Redundant hardware   A redundant hardware strategy may be used for equipment within the facility. The concept of redundancy could be to have spare systems online, or to stock an in-house supply of replacement parts. The following are examples of redundant hardware:

Mirrored servers   Mirrored high-availability servers are an example of redundant online systems. Two servers operate as one machine. If functioning correctly, a secondary server takes over processing when the primary server fails.

Mirrored disk drives   Using RAID technology, the date on disk drives can be mirrored. We discussed mirrored servers and RAID in Chapter 7, "Information Asset Protection."

Redundant communication   Network routers can be set up in a redundant configuration to ensure maximum uptime. This effective design utilizes communication services from more than one communication provider—for example, Internet connections from both AT&T and Verizon.

Alternate processing location   Alternate sites are used for processing in the event that the organization is unable to use a regular location. Alternate sites may be owned by the organization or leased by subscription. The leased site by subscription is rather expensive after calculating all the costs of usage and rehearsal exercises. Unfortunately, some leased sites have more customers than space available for recovery (oversubscription). Alternate sites are usually one of the following types:

Redundant site   This location contains either duplicate mirror facilities that are online at all times, or computing facilities of a reduced capacity that can process at the acceptable SDO requirement. The data is live—no delays waiting for files to be restored. All necessary personnel are already present and on the job. The redundant site is in full operation and able to take over processing within seconds or minutes. A redundant site can offer a competitive marketing and operational advantage. Redundant sites can be located in the same geographic region or across the country. A location should be selected that is not subject to disasters in the same proximity as the primary site. The two sites should be geographically separated. The dominant issue of operating a redundant site is the cost.

Hot site   This is similar to a redundant site except that it is offline when not in use. Hot sites can be obtained by subscription (rented) or by capital investment (owned). All necessary facilities, equipment, and communication lines are ready to go without delay or setup time. Basically, a hot site is fully operational and gathering dust until it is ready to be used. Data files will need several hours to load from backup tapes before the systems can go live. A hot site is fully equipped and capable of being in operation within hours. A delay may occur as personnel are traveling to the site. Hot sites may be elaborate for use in executive marketing to attract key investors and clients. Hot sites are ideal for supporting IT functions and live customer communication.

🌐 Real World Scenario

A Lesson in Hot Site Declaration Criteria

During the fall of 2005, several hurricanes impacted the southeastern United States. A handful of business continuity/disaster recovery planners complained that they were placed in a dangerous situation of being denied access to a hot site that they had paid to use by subscription. The vendor gave excuses that other customers from prior hurricanes were still using the facility. Another customer was told by the hot site vendor that they would not be allowed to declare hot site activation because their city had not been hit by the hurricane nor was it designated a disaster area. Their vendor allocated hot site space based on a *first to declare* criteria rather than guaranteed access. Stories verifying the situation appeared in newspapers and on the Internet.

Warm site   This location offers significantly less opportunity for success. Warm sites are typically shell buildings with basic utility services and require extra time to make ready. Computer equipment may not be onsite yet, or may require configuration before it is ready to use. After several hours of system configuration, additional delays will occur as data files are loaded. Communication lines will need to be activated and traffic rerouted before the voice and data can go online. This type of site will be operational in a matter of days or weeks. The location may be a branch office of the same organization.

Cold site   This option offers the lowest possibility of success. Cold sites are typically building shells without any computing equipment, and offer no more than a street address and basic shelter. Examples include a hotel conference room. A cold site is the cheapest of all alternate site options and is unacceptable for IT functions. A cold site may be acceptable for recovery of noncritical systems as time permits.

Mobile site   Very popular with vendors selling alternate site solutions, the mobile site is usually a trailer configured so that it is equivalent to the level of a hot site or warm site. These are popular for extended use onsite while buildings and facilities are reconstructed. Unfortunately, mobile sites may be restricted by building permit delays, mandatory evacuations, or inaccessible regions due to roadway damage or roadblocks. A handful of customers affected by hurricanes Charlie, Katrina, and Wilma reported that their mobile sites did not arrive as promptly as promised because of travel restrictions and fuel shortages. Many professionals consider the mobile site to be a derivative of the cold site, with no guarantee of timely service. If a mobile site can be reliably obtained, a practical application may be to use the site as an interim facility for the months after leaving a hot site, but before reoccupying a permanent site.

Table 8.1 shows the basic differences between the types of alternate sites.

TABLE 8.1   Comparison of Recovery Site Types

Type	Recovery Time	Basic Advantage
Redundant	Seconds	Always online and processing. Staff is in place and working. Perfect for high-priority processing that cannot be interrupted.
Hot site	Hours	Preconfigured, just restore data files. Designed for rapid 4- to 24-hour recovery of applications.
Warm site	Days	Cheaper. Will need to assemble equipment and activate communication lines.
Cold site	Weeks	Cheapest. Provides a building shell without equipment. Used for noncritical recovery or staging of salvaged assets.
Mobile site	8+ hours to days	Can supplement damaged facilities at original site. Can be configured with equipment equal to hot, warm, or cold site depending on customer's interest.

Fortification in place   It may be determined that an acceptable option is to create a fortress out of an existing facility. Fortifications can be made to compensate for minor natural disasters and varying degrees of man-made disasters. The fortification process requires a significant investment in structural reinforcement. Unfortunately, the fortification may not survive acts of terrorism, airborne contaminants of chemical or biological nature, flood, or mandatory evacuation. History is riddled with thousands of years' worth of failed fortifications.

Reciprocal agreements   This option is based on the belief that two organizations could render mutual aid to each other to save money. Unfortunately, often neither organization has the free space or excess capacity to support the other. Two organizations in the same geographic area could also be affected by the same event. Issues of security and noncompetition will also exist. Traditionally, reciprocal agreements are both unenforceable and unrealistic.

Cooperative recovery sites in banking are an exception for reciprocal agreements. Small banks in the financial industry frequently operate a shared hot site as a cooperative venture. Banking laws require even the smallest bank to prove its continuity strategy on a quarterly basis. Several smaller banks will form a cooperative to rent or purchase the necessary recovery site facilities. If a smaller bank fails to prove an effective recovery capability, federal regulators will reassign all of the small bank's accounts to a larger bank.

Use one of theirs as an example

Data backup strategy   Every recovery strategy requires data to be kept on backup tapes. The tapes need to be managed by a librarian, as discussed in Chapter 3, "IT Governance," and Chapter 6, "IT Service Delivery." The speed of recovery (RTO) is affected by the time needed for the restore process to run. The typical data backup strategy implements one of the following methods:

Full backup   Creates an entire copy of each file on the system. This is the most effective backup method and requires a significant amount of time. It's common for a full backup to be run at least once per week, but the frequency of your backup should depend on the value of your data. To restore data, the computer operator loads the latest full backup, usually from tapes. Next, the most current data is loaded by using files from a subsequent incremental or differential backup tape.

Don't assume the same backup strategy is the right approach for everyone. Listen to the RTO and RPO requirements from the BIA. For example, CertTest's internal servers run a full backup twice a day for everything related to our customers and seminar classes. CertTest's internal servers have an RPO of 4 hours with 2-hour RTO. Full backups will restore a complete system faster than any other method of restoration.

Incremental method   Copies only the files that have changed since the last backup. The incremental method is commonly used for backups on weekdays. This method requires less time than a full backup. Unfortunately, the file restoration process takes longer because it is necessary to restore the full backup and each version of incremental backup. An incremental backup resets the archive bit (backup flag) to indicate that a file needs to be backed up. If any of the tapes or disks in incremental restoration fails, the RPO will also fail. Incremental recovery requires using more tapes.

Differential method   Copies every file that has changed between full backup runs. Differential is the preferred method for business continuity. This method ensures that multiple copies of daily files should exist on multiple tapes. A differential backup is very fast on the first day after a full backup, and then takes longer each day as more files are copied. A differential backup works because the backup software does not change the archive bit (backup flag).

When selecting the data backup strategy, it is important to consider the time necessary for data restoration. Care should be given to ensure that the RTO and RPO are met.

yeah, right! Forget about it!

~~**Insurance**~~   Most business continuity/disaster recovery planners review insurance during the risk assessment phase. Insurance carries several risks, including significant delays in receiving payments, likelihood of claims being denied, and difficulties proving financial loss within the policy limitations. Insurance is commonly used for durable goods, property, and life or casualty. Most policies pay for only a percentage of loss and do not include lost income, increased operating expenses, or consequential loss.

Many

~~Some~~ insurance claims are never paid. Businesses in the World Trade Center at the time of the bombing in New York City for 1993 have yet to receive any financial settlements for damages or the extended utility service outages. Similarly it's doubtful any business will receive payment for Sept 11, 2001. Acts of war are excluded from insurance policies.

Insurance is available for a variety of situations. Let's look at a few of the types of insurance available:

Property insurance   Property insurance provides financial protection against the loss of or damage to physical property—for example, burglary, plate glass damage, and fire. It may include coverage for the loss of income-producing ability.

Casualty insurance   Casualty insurance revolves around legal liability *covers* for losses caused by injury to other people. Examples include robbery and workers compensation insurance.

Fidelity insurance or bonding   This protects the employer from theft caused by a dishonest employee. This type of insurance also covers embezzlement and fraudulent acts. To collect on this policy, the employer may need to prosecute the employee and win each court trial.

Omissions and errors insurance   A special policy covering administrative omissions and errors by corporate executives. This is commonly referred to as O&E insurance.

Machinery insurance (or boiler insurance)   Covers accidental loss to machinery and equipment. It is called *boiler insurance* for historic reasons from 100 years ago. This type of insurance can cover almost any mechanical or electrical device.

Business interruption (BI) insurance   A policy that covers consequential losses of earnings due to property loss. Business interruption insurance typically pays a historical average of earnings during the coverage period. This type of insurance typically covers the fixed operating cost while business operations are suspended. The cost of premiums may be high.

The number one concern with insurance is that potential loss decisions have been transferred to the insurance company. The insurance company may decide that salvage is inevitable. The cost of salvage is usually less than 15 percent of the cost of replacement. Salvage operations may take weeks and place the organization in a bind. Costs of salvage may be reimbursed for only a particular amount of services from a preauthorized vendor.

Stockpile of supplies   It is a common practice to stockpile supplies in preparation for recovery. These include common office supplies, items with long lead time, and spare parts. Stockpiling supplies is in direct conflict with just-in-time (JIT) inventory practices. A rule is to stockpile 30 days' worth of consumable supplies at the offsite or alternate storage facility.

Figure 8.8 shows the various recovery strategies compared to the amount of time it would take to resume processing.

FIGURE 8.8   Recovery options compared to time

Practice Area 5—Emergency Response   — See pgs 354-355 First

The emergency response phase is considered part of the "foundation" information that the business continuity/disaster recovery professional needs to know early in planning for the project.

An *incident* is defined as a negative or harmful event that involves people, property, or assets. After the event occurs, regaining control over the situation is a challenge. Advance planning is necessary to ensure that personnel are properly trained. Each response activity needs to be coordinated

See pg 5
for definitions
of assets, threats + vulnerabilities

to ensure timeliness and the safety of personnel. The number one priority in an emergency response is the safety of life. Nothing has a higher priority.

To develop emergency response procedures and document them as part of the plan, the business continuity/disaster recovery planner needs to understand how to fulfill the following objectives:

Set activation criteria   Management needs to create a set of criteria for declaring a business continuity emergency. The criteria should clearly state a set of conditions that would dictate activation of the plan. Nobody wants to be the one who is accused of crying wolf and activating the plan too early. As a result, management will delay activating a plan that compromises the recovery window. If you wait too long, it may become impossible to recover. Use easy-to-understand criteria. For example, set criteria to be based on the following:

- Major injury to persons.
- Time. If it appears that the business operation will be interrupted for more than 4 hours for any reason, the plan should be activated.
- Unknown severity. If you don't know the severity of the impact, it's time to declare.
- Management response using the activation criteria. A rule should be instituted that if the criteria are met, the senior manager is required to declare plan activation. This removes uncertainty from the process.

Identify potential emergencies   What are the types of emergencies and the appropriate responses necessary? Consider for example: fire, hazardous materials leak, collapse, terrorism, medical. Each event contains unique response requirements; however, all events will include the following:

- Reporting procedures for communicating information during the emergency. This information will be necessary after the event to justify actions taken and to provide evidence for legal challenges, insurance claims, and personnel training.
- Pre-incident preparation, making plans for responding to the crisis situation with equipment, planning, and training.
- Emergency actions to be taken to protect life, provide safety, minimize loss, and contain the situation.

Emergency response procedures   Identify the existence of, or develop, appropriate emergency response procedures. Most organizations have varying degrees of plans under different departments. Plans would include the following:

- Personnel protection procedures
- Emergency declaration process with procedures designed to contain the incident
- Procedures to assess the situation
- Procedures for communicating with responders, employees, customers, vendors, and the media

- Procedures for providing emergency response and triage
- Salvage and restoration procedures

Invocation procedures   Establish invocation procedures to activate the alternate site. The decision to activate the alternate site will cascade into a variety of tasks necessary for recovery or relocation. The hot site vendor will accept an activation request from only a list of preauthorized individuals. The activation process will cost the organization a significant sum of money for exercising the declaration. This is how the hot site vendor ensures that the client is serious about activation. Activation costs may be $50,000 to $500,000 each time. It depends on the scope of your need.

Use preplanned decision trees to minimize "on the spot" decisions   Establish written procedures with decision trees to lead management and others in determining the best actions to take in response to a specific situation. A decision tree is a logical process of questions and answers, often in the format of a flowchart. As you ask the question, the answer will lead you through the decision tree until a final decision is reached. If you can't agree before the stress induced by the emergency, you can bet that decisions during the emergency will be questionable. Now is the time to work out the decision criteria—before you need it.

see Decision Support Systems, pg 307

Integrate separate plans into one comprehensive plan   Integrate disaster recovery/business continuity procedures with emergency response procedures, creating one comprehensive plan. Everyone must be executing the same objectives and agreed-upon procedures in order to combat conflicting efforts and time delay in recovery. The last thing you need is someone attempting to push their own agenda ahead of predefined priorities. Changing sequence or emphasis is a sure sign of a pending failure by interrupting the recovery sequence.

Incident Command System   Identify the command and control requirements for managing the emergency. Learn the Incident Command System (ICS), the international command and control system used by first responders. The expanded version is called the Unified Command System (UCS). It would be unrealistic to expect public authorities to conform to your leadership method; therefore, you need to conform to theirs. ICS outlines roles and duties regarding the following:

Incident commander (IC)   The first person on the scene is the incident commander until relieved by a more qualified individual. The incident commander is in charge, leading on-scene activities in the field during the emergency response. All response team leaders report to the incident commander. A field command post is established to off-load logistical tasks from the IC. Incident commanders direct emergency teams and communicate to the field command post. Field command provides support services and coordination for the IC. Field command keeps the Emergency Operations Center (EOC) updated with the current status of the crisis control efforts. Figure 8.9 shows the roles and reporting structure of the Incident Command System.

Emergency Operations Center (EOC)   The Emergency Operations Center (EOC) serves as command headquarters for the emergency management team (EMT). This team of executives makes decisions and takes actions based on reports from the IC. The

EMT uses procedures outlined in the business continuity plan to provide crisis communication with stakeholders regarding support recovery plans. The EOC handles all
communications with the undamaged portions of the business still in operation. A designated public information officer (PIO) handles all media communications. Some key
investors may want to see the EOC in operation, and a degree of caution is urged before
you agree to allow financially interested observers in a crisis. Negative observations
could rattle investor confidence.

- Document command and decision authorities. Multiple authorities may respond to your
  emergency, and each will carry the full authority of their position. You can gain their trust
  and cooperation by demonstrating your ability to provide leadership. This can buy you
  time and grace to extend your business continuity efforts. You will be pushed aside if you
  fail to attain or maintain their confidence. This can get confusing, and the time to work
  out conflicts is before the crisis.

  sound familiar?

- Create procedures for opening the EOC and providing extra security. The media and
  competitors will likely have great interest in your situation. Details could make an
  interesting news story or competitive battle. To survive the situation, you must remain
  in control.

FIGURE 8.9   Roles in the Incident Command System

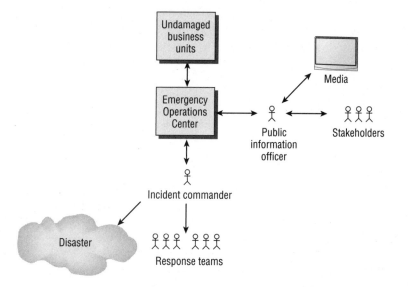

Explicit definition of authority roles   Recommend and develop command and control procedures to define roles, authority, and communications processes for managing an emergency.
These will become the structure of your plan in the next phase, developing and writing a
usable plan.

Practice Area 6—Plan Creation

Nothing goes out-of-date faster than a big book of plans. The written plan must be clear, intuitively organized, and easy to read. The business continuity plan is usually a multivolume set. The best practice is to use a modular design to enhance security and updating.

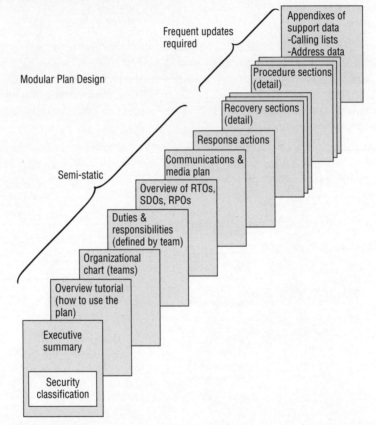

Full sets are kept at offsite storage and at the EOC. Security and version control are paramount concerns. This set of plans contains all the organization's secrets, process blueprints, and documented priorities.

Figure 8.10 shows the content outline for creating the plan.

The plan should be organized for quick and easy location of personnel duties and specific procedures. A suggested layout includes sections for the following:

- Executive summary to provide a brief overview of the plan's purpose, scope, and assumptions.

- Command and control instructions to identify who is actually in charge.

- Life safety procedures. Protection of life is the highest priority.

- Emergency response activities, including incident containment procedures and environmental protection plans.

- Asset protection strategy and procedures. A copy of inventory and vital materials will be useful.

FIGURE 8.10 Creating the plan structure and content

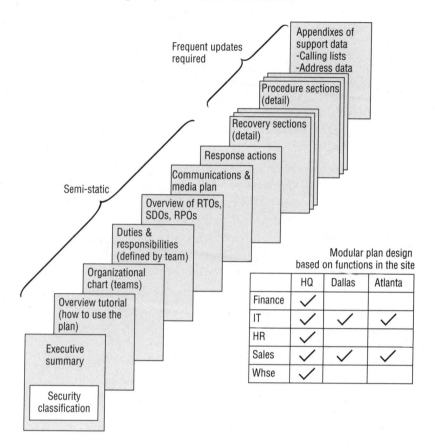

- Recovery plans to support restoration and resumption efforts. What are some alternate site provisions? Did you include a copy of the risk analysis?
- Administration and logistics designed to keep appropriate records of the event, maintain the emergency budget, and provide support to the recovery effort. Logistics include transportation requirements, relocation housing, meals, and sanitation needs.

The plan is intended to provide everyone with clear instructions on where each person is to report for work and what they will be working on at various time intervals. The business will not be running business as usual. All efforts need to focus on the predetermined priorities in assigned sequence.

Assigning People to Specific Teams

Alternate personnel may be necessary to accomplish all the tasks within the RTO and SDO requirements. The plans should account for the additional personnel. Procedures should contain easy-to-follow diagrams, photographs, maps, flowcharts, and step-by-step checklists. A significant number of concurrent activities will need to be coordinated.

The common practice is to divide into teams. The number of personnel is not as important as ensuring that all job duties are fulfilled. A risk management approach needs to be used. The following teams may be needed:

Emergency response team   The first responders internal to the organization. This team has the responsibility of accounting for personnel and rendering aid. The emergency response team includes fire wardens for each floor and those persons trained in administering first aid. The team may provide initial aid to victims and route injured personnel to the hospital. During a crisis, the injured will likely need to be routed to a hospital with available capacity, not necessarily the nearest hospital. The emergence response team needs to keep track of the location of injured personnel.

Emergency management team   Executives and line managers able to make tough decisions at the Emergency Operations Center. This team coordinates the managers still operating undamaged areas of the business. The EMT makes decisions about the allocation of personnel necessary to support the response and recovery effort. The leaders of each team report to the emergency management team.

Damage assessment team   Works with structural engineers to assess damage to the facility. This team is trained to provide accurate analysis and estimates of the impact. This team works with the safety team for matters of safe reentry to the facility.

Physical security team   This team addresses crowd control and security and operates 24 hours a day to protect individuals and organizational assets. This function may be provided by existing security staff and supplemental personnel. Physical security is needed at the original site and the alternate site. During a major disaster, a higher level of security is required.

IT recovery teams   May be deployed onsite at the incident and/or the alternate site depending on the situation. The IT recovery teams typically comprise several smaller teams, each with a unique specialty. Each of these functions would be operating in parallel to save time. The smaller teams include the following:

> **IT hardware recovery**   The hardware recovery team focuses on getting the hardware up and running as rapidly as possible in accordance with the RTO and SDO. Hardware recovery may be split into two categories: server hardware and user workstations.

> **Software loading**   As hardware is recovered, a software-loading process begins. This may be from a tape backup, disk image, or program CDs.

> **Server applications**   Application programs and data from tape are loaded onto servers as the hardware becomes available. This process may be dependent on the IT hardware recovery function. After software loading is complete, the systems administrator or database administrator verifies that the application is functioning correctly. After the application is up and running, users may log in and begin using it. Complex databases may require the dedicated attention of several technical personnel.

> **Network communications**   This group ensures that computer and telephone communication are back online. The process may entail verifying that redundant circuits are functioning correctly, installing new connections as needed, or working with a recommended vendor to expedite changes in order to restore service.

Data entry   The data entry personnel focus on reloading the most recent transactions and executing manual procedures during recovery. This may be an in-house or outsourced function.

User support   This team assists users in restoring individual workstations. It provides special assistance for workarounds to help persons with greatest impact on the recovery effort. Normal user support may be suspended during the recovery effort. The help desk focuses on finding user support necessary to achieve the stated RTO and SDO.

Marketing and customer support team   It is imperative to maintain communication with customers. The customer support team provides communication and reassurance to customers. Key customers will want to know that their needs will be met by the organization. Some customers may be impacted by the same event and may require the assistance of the organization—for example; customers may need to reschedule airline tickets because of a hurricane, while the airline is evacuating its own headquarters to a safer location. The customer support team may be a combination of in-house personnel and services contracted through an external vendor. The business does not want customers to switch vendors or cancel orders. The goal is to ensure that the organization continues to receive revenue even if they are not shipping a product.

Salvage team   The salvage team is responsible for onsite cleanup and recovery of assets. This team inventories, stages, and coordinates the salvage of assets. This team also is responsible for creating documentation to be used for insurance filings, legal actions (lawsuits), and future training exercises. The team will need provisions for site security during the salvage effort.

Communications and media relations team   This team provides communication via radio, phone, fax, and TV. The team uses preapproved scripts for communication to employees, stockholders, clients, and the media. Provisions are made for both inbound and outbound communication. All outbound communication to the media is handled by a designated PIO. Media relations involve issuing news releases, scheduling press conferences, and providing a controlled release of information to the news. News reporters will get the story one way or another, so stories should be released in a manner that demonstrates the organization's care, concern, and control of the situation. The media team needs to be aware of local and national broadcast deadlines. The plan will be needed to communicate with the appropriate personnel and each of the news agencies.

Logistics team   This team handles administrative support activities necessary to relocate personnel and equipment. The team facilitates resumption efforts by providing meals and rest locations for workers. The team also is responsible for transportation, mail rerouting, and a thousand other administrative details necessary to support the recovery effort.

Safe operations team (safety team)   The safety team supervises activities to ensure that nobody is placed in a hazardous work situation. This team can terminate any activity that is deemed to endanger personnel. The safety team ensures that workers are adequately protected from hazards, including potentially hazardous material or precarious work environments. The objective is to ensure that no additional injuries occur after the initial impact.

Finance team   This team provides budget control for recovery and accurate accounting of costs. It would be a shame to overspend on the recovery effort and later fail due to insolvency. The recovery costs may qualify for special financial aid. It is often necessary to file claims early, before recovery funding disappears. Special tracking may be implemented to identify the response and recovery costs.

Legal team   The organization's lawyers may be able to provide assistance and advice to the emergency management team. This advice could include dealing with regulators, government bureaucracy, extensions on filing deadlines, and confidential matters.

Personnel team   Human resources will be a busy place. Employees and their families will need assistance with benefits. Time and attendance tracking will be necessary for the workers. A process for rapid staff augmentation will be required.

Business unit recovery team   Each business unit will have its own recovery team to focus on restoring its operation. This team may comprise the power users in a particular business unit. The business unit plan may be a smaller or larger scale than the plan of the head office.

Property and insurance teams   The property team assists with locating or rebuilding the office. An inventory of each facility, including space requirements and furniture needs, is used to help guide the selection of suitable offices for the interim need and long-term requirements. The insurance team works to get claims processed and paid. Insurance loss consultants may be hired to help increase the dollar amount of the insurance settlement.

External agency team   This team coordinates with fire, police, the Federal Emergency Management Agency (FEMA), the FBI, and other government agencies. At least one dedicated liaison should be assigned for each agency expected to respond. Leaving a government official waiting is high on the list of bad ideas.

Vendor team   This team provides coordination with key vendors. The organization may need to make special requests of vendors to facilitate recovery. It will also be necessary to ensure that the vendor does not close the line of credit or delay shipment of product.

Practice Area 7—Training and Awareness

Training programs need to be implemented to educate staff about the plan, its limitations, and the procedures they will be expected to execute. Training can take many forms, including seminars, workshops, video presentations, and individual training sessions.

Training is designed to increase the proficiency of every individual. Some individuals will require specialized training for assertiveness, crisis resource management, and medical procedures. An individual who is unable to fill a role for any reason should be moved to another support area. If it is a senior manager, the best use may be to fulfill an advisory role. Some individuals will not be mentally capable to lead under the heavy burden of crisis command.

Successful planners know how to test components of the plan each week. The training is combined with modular testing to build both awareness and skills. Which do you think is better: a doctor aware of your condition or a doctor skilled in actually doing the work? Failing to train indicates a management failure.

Practice Area 8—Maintenance and Testing

Successful execution of the business continuity plan will depend on training and thorough testing. Without testing, the plan is sure to fail. Testing should begin with small processes and gradually build into testing larger functional processes. You need to focus on tests that support the core processes first. Every test should be timed and witnessed by a qualified observer. The objective is to record lessons learned and an estimate of the actual recovery time. By tracking these metrics, you will be able to benchmark improvement or reengineer the strategy:

Desktop review (paper exercise)   The simplest test is a desktop review. All the plans and documentation are laid out across the table and reviewed for obvious errors in consistency. Participants from each major area walk through the plans for a general review of accuracy. The purpose of the desktop review is to groom the document and eliminate obvious errors. After the errors are corrected, the next step is a functional test.

Functional (modular exercise)   In the functional test, actual procedures are executed by staff members. This provides an opportunity for hands-on training. During this training process, it is possible to view the effectiveness of both the procedure and actions by personnel. Functional testing is an extremely important component of preparedness. A functional test of the calling list, for example, could be used for notification of a company party. Another example is to use the business continuity procedures to train new staff members for their regular jobs. When you think about it, there are a number of opportunities for executing a small-scale functional test. An evaluator should grade the test exercise and make any recommendations for improvement. The first functional tests will start small, and then incorporate other functional tests with a growing scope. The final objective is to ensure that the full-scale business processes are properly supported.

Preparedness simulation   In the preparedness simulation, the staff is asked to react to a particular scenario as if it were a real event. The preparedness of each team is judged as well as the overall preparedness of the organization to respond. A preparedness simulation consumes resources and supplies. The objective is to carry out each activity to ensure that the staff is capable of responding properly. The next step after preparedness simulation is to perform a full operation test.

Full operation exercise   Testing should be planned and structured to ensure that the test does not create injury to persons or damage to the organization. Tests should be announced with warning to prevent panic. A well-known provision needs to exist to cancel the test if a real emergency occurs during the drill. Each drill needs to be preplanned, staged, executed, and subjected to a review. The lessons learned are recorded.

Figure 8.11 shows the life cycle of testing and exercising the plan.

It is strongly advised that all professionals adopt the terminology of *exercising* business continuity plans, rather than testing plans. The word *test* denotes passing or failing. A failing score will usually demoralize or alienate staff members. Nobody wants to be associated with a failure. A simple solution is to build on the concept of exercising for improvement. Athletes exercise before running marathons. The organization is no different.

The results of test exercises are used to gain support from management and buy-in from the team members. Testing is like auditing: You don't have to do it all at once. Failure to test indicates a management failure.

FIGURE 8.11 The life cycle of testing and exercising the plan

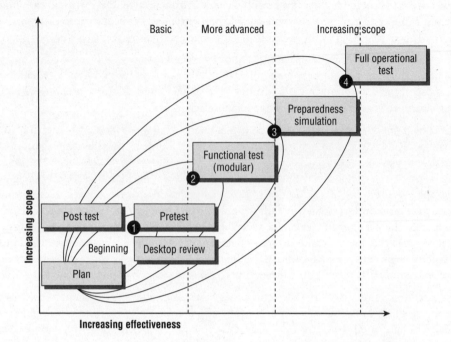

Practice Area 9—Crisis Communications

The public and stakeholders are always interested to hear how an organization has succeeded or failed miserably in their endeavors. The planner needs to design an uninterruptible communications system with access via multiple delivery methods. Controlling communications with the public and the company's stakeholders is essential to surviving a crisis.

Buy-in from the highest level of the company needs to be obtained to enforce a policy that improper and unauthorized communications during a declared disaster is a terminating offense with possible legal repercussions.

Support plans need to be created for employees and their families. Be aware that trauma counseling may be required for employees, their families, and even corporate management during a crisis.

The business continuity planner must make sure that all stakeholders, key customers, critical suppliers, and owners/stockholders are kept informed as appropriate during the crisis to avoid confusion or distrust. The time to build confidence is before the event occurs. During the event, the focus is to communicate status information and immediate needs. People need to feel that the situation is under control and being properly handled. Without timely communication, it is human nature to grow restless and distrustful. Let's look at some of the more common techniques for better communication.

Employee check-in aids   Provisions should be made for employee check-in after the declaration has been made. Individuals may attempt to check in and provide information concerning their status. Failure to account for personnel would be a serious problem. A common solution is to use 800 numbers answered by an operator in a message center. This could easily be outsourced to a telemarketing firm. The operator asks questions concerning the employee's status and whether the employee requires additional aid. Business travelers also can be accounted for through an 800 service. Another method is to implement a secure website database for check-in.

Prioritized calling list (call tree)   Outbound notification can be executed through a combination of live personnel and automated systems. Telephone numbers are sequenced according to the priority of the individual. Senior executives and recovery team leaders are, of course, a high priority. A scripted message is delivered to each individual with a short explanation of the situation. The message should conclude with instructions explaining what the organization is requesting the individual to do.

Alternate communications   All business continuity planning exercises incorporate a worse-case scenario. The loss of communications would definitely be the worst possible scenario. It is important to plan for alternate communication methods. Each communication method needs to be properly implemented and monitored during a crisis. Alternate methods can be accomplished via private radio, wired Internet access, cellular voice/data communications, and satellite voice/data communications.

A satellite phone with voice and data capability makes communication easy. For example, my satellite phone was purchased several weeks before the Florida hurricanes of 2005 for less than $300 on eBay. The satellite phone was the only dependable method of communication for several days. The satellite phone data kit made it possible to access the Internet in less than 1 minute.

Public information officer (PIO)   As previously discussed, controls are necessary to prevent damage or loss to the organization. A public information officer should be appointed as the sole media contact. This individual is the spokesperson for the organization through the entire crisis. A public information officer should be a well-spoken individual with a professional voice for radio and a presentable appearance for television. This role may be fulfilled by the vice president of marketing or another senior executive. Occasionally, the PIO is contracted through a public-relations vendor.

The time to communicate actions is before the crisis. Then the staff will face a lesser challenge of communicating the level of success or status attained under the plan. All communications should be based in prewritten templates that have been vetted for proper effect. Don't make the company look foolish to the public.

Communicating with external agencies and public authorities is a key element to this phase as well. It is essential that accurate information is available to the proper authorities.

Practice Area 10—Integration with Other Plans

After all this work, the organization needs to reach out to their clients, business partners, and government agencies to coordinate the organization's plans and strategy with theirs. No organization is an island. Every business depends on someone else for revenue, investment, and support. The business continuity/disaster recovery plans need to be reviewed and modified to incorporate cooperation between different organizations. The strategies may be different or priorities may conflict. Depending on the scale of the issue, this may require you to rerun the entire process in order to create the next generation of planning.

Summary

Business continuity planning is an involved process of preparation. The focus of this preparation could be to rebuild in response to a disaster. The organization may be more concerned about protecting a particular line of business or a highly prized customer.

Let's summarize with the points of interest that an IS auditor should look for. We have discussed the basic objectives to be fulfilled by management. It is the auditor's job to determine how well those objectives have been served. The auditor can use the following points for evaluation:

- Compare the results of the risk analysis and business impact analysis to the strategies selected. Does the BIA and risk assessment support management's strategy?

- Time delays are an absolute killer of business continuity plans. Has the client done a good job of documenting the RTO? Are the recovery time objectives well founded and realistic? Does the organization have the hardware and skills necessary to recover data in sufficient time to meet each RTO?

- Ask whether their document outlines a 0- to 100-hour timeline. This type of timeline sequences and prioritizes the recovery using RTO, RPO, and SDO. The presence of this document is a powerful statement in favor of the client. Absence of this document foretells a questionable future.

- Work backlogs exist every day in business. How does the organization intend to handle the backlog when the processing capability is significantly diminished? Manual methods are usually proposed because of the low cost; however, substantial testing would be required to prove that the organization could manually keep up with the volume of work.

- An audit of the vital records inventory will tell an interesting story. Well-organized vital records foretell the future of a successful recovery.

- When was the most recent exercise? It would be valuable to review the exercise plan, results, and the schedule of future exercises. Plans must be exercised regularly to remain effective.

This concludes this chapter on disaster recovery and business continuity. The subject is far deeper and broader than you will encounter for your CISA exam. Just remember that the next step after a control failure is a business continuity situation. According to the stories in the news, there is plenty of room for improvement.

Exam Essentials

Know the difference between business continuity and disaster recovery.   Disaster recovery is focused on rebuilding the organization. After obtaining the disaster recovery plan, the organization can upgrade plans to include business continuity. Business continuity ensures that critical revenue-producing processes continue.

Understand the requirements for business process resumption.   It is not necessary for all the business processes to be resumed immediately. The core business processes that generate revenue will be recovered first; supporting processes are recovered second. Noncritical, or discretionary, processes will be recovered last if they are recovered at all.

Know the business impact analysis and the value it represents.   The business impact analysis will generate a blueprint of the current business processes. The BIA is used to define the recovery priorities and sequence timing of activities in the plan. Without the BIA, it would be impossible to generate a business continuity plan. Without the BIA, the best one could hope for would be a disaster recovery plan.

Understand the key terms describing business priorities.   The recovery time objective (RTO) defines the target time when the system will be back online. The recovery point objective (RPO) defines the amount of acceptable data loss that will occur due to the interruption. The service delivery objective (SDO) specifies the level of service at a particular time in the recovery plan. The recovery plan will specify multiple RTOs, RPOs, and SDOs during the recovery timeline.

Understand how the business continuity plan is developed   The business continuity plan should be developed in a modular format. The business continuity planning exercise coordinates development of a clear and well-defined set of steps to accomplish the strategic objectives. Individual procedure plans will be created by the team leaders representing the key stakeholders. An ongoing series of revisions will groom the plan to become the best possible response to almost any event, whether it's a disaster or sudden surge in business volume. The plan will require special security controls because of the sensitive nature of its contents.

Understand providing for personnel management.   In the business continuity plan and the disaster recovery plan, it is imperative that procedures exist to ensure the direction and control of personnel. Temporary personnel and contractors will be joining the recovery effort. Human resources will need to provide support for employees and employee benefits.

Know the emergency plan invocation process.   The emergency plan needs to be designed with simple, easy-to-understand invocation criteria. The most effective method is based on the level of destruction or the estimated magnitude of the outage. A senior executive is responsible for invoking the recovery process.

Know the types of alternate sites.   A recovery strategy may include redundant sites, hot sites, warm sites, and cold sites. The redundant site is always parallel to normal production and available within seconds. The hot site is preconfigured, just waiting for the backup to be restored before resuming processing, and is available within hours. The warm site will require equipment to be set up and shipped in and is available for processing within days. A cold site is no more than the building and requires everything to be shipped in and set up. The cold site will be available for processing within weeks.

Understand how to control communications and the media during the emergency.   All communications must be predefined and vetted before distribution. The public information officer (PIO) should be the only spokesperson to the media. Stakeholder communication should occur in a confidential manner. All communication must occur at regular intervals to promote trust and confidence.

Review Questions

1. Which of the following acronyms refer to the expected level of service during recovery?

    A. RTO

    B. SDO

    C. RPO

    D. ITO

2. A critical success factor is defined as which of the following?

    A. A measure or score of efficiency

    B. An asset to be planned

    C. Something that must occur perfectly every time

    D. A factor that is calculated for insurance purposes

3. Which of these is the most significant issue to consider regarding insurance coverage?

    A. Salvage may be dictated rather than replacement.

    B. Premiums may be very expensive.

    C. Coverage must include all business assets.

    D. Insurance can pay for all the costs of recovery.

4. The ultimate obstacles to business continuity are threats that may include which of the following?

    A. Natural disasters

    B. Missed targets

    C. Loss of profit

    D. All of the above

5. When planning team assignments, it is more important to remember that

    A. Nobody should hold more than one team assignment.

    B. The number of people or number of teams is not as important as making sure all the duties are performed.

    C. A single key person can be assigned to all teams for consistency.

    D. The number of duties is the same for each team.

6. What is the principal reason you might use a hot site?

    A. Expensive, but already configured for our use

    B. May not be available during a crisis

    C. Expensive, but we will have to install and configure new equipment

    D. Expensive and prevents us from using other warm or cold site alternatives

7. What does the term *MAO* stand for?

   A. Minimum acceptable outage

   B. Maximum acceptable outage

   C. Minimum available on-hand

   D. Maximum available overnight

8. In business continuity, why it is important to replicate every process?

   A. To ensure 100 percent full operational capabilities

   B. Market pressures

   C. Not important, only select processes will continue

   D. To protect the company reputation

9. Name one of the purposes of creating the business continuity plan.

   A. To maximize the number of decisions made during an incident

   B. To minimize decisions needed during a crisis

   C. To lower business insurance premiums

   D. To provide guidance for federal regulations

10. What does the acronym *EOC* represent?

    A. Emergency Office Complex

    B. Evacuate Office Center

    C. Emergency Offensive Controls

    D. Emergency Operations Center

11. News media attention should be

    A. Directed to a single designated spokesperson

    B. Used to create awareness of the crisis and warn the public

    C. Restricted to prevent any information from being released

    D. Allowed full access to interview staff

12. Continuity planners can create BC plans without the business impact analysis (BIA) process when

    A. Business impact analysis is not required.

    B. Management already dictated all the key processes to be used.

    C. Not possible; critical processes constantly change.

    D. Risk assessment is acceptable.

13. What should signal that the business continuity plan needs to be updated?

  A. Time and market conditions

  B. Personnel changes

  C. Significant changes in business objectives or direction

  D. All of the above

14. What is the best example of why plan testing is important?

  A. To prove that the plan worked the first time

  B. To find and correct problems

  C. To show the team that is not pulling their own weight

  D. To verify that everyone shows up at the recovery site

15. What are the best examples of vital records and media?

  A. Specialized forms, financial records, how-to manuals, backup tapes

  B. Past annual reports, last year's cancelled checks, vacation forms, HR policies

  C. Preferred vendor lists, personal desk files, extra blank paper for copy machine

  D. Customer lists, office supplies, maintenance manuals, corporate seal

16. Which of the following should be considered when setting your business continuity strategy?

  A. Recovery time objectives

  B. Alternate sites available

  C. Testing time available at alternate sites

  D. All of the above

17. What is the process to activate the business continuity plan?

  A. Members of the organization call the recovery site to activate.

  B. Management designates decision criteria and appoints authorized personnel.

  C. The facility manager receives a severe threat warning.

  D. The senior manager on duty makes the decision.

18. What is the fundamental difference between disaster recovery and business continuity?

  A. Disaster recovery is focused on natural disasters; business continuity deals with man-made events.

  B. Business continuity is focused on ensuring that none of the services are interrupted; disaster recovery deals with restoring services.

  C. Disaster recovery is focused on rebuilding; business continuity deals with revenue to continue in the market.

  D. Business continuity is focused on protecting the IT investment; disaster recovery applies to the entire organization.

19. What indicators are used to identify the anticipated level of recovery and loss at a given point in time?

    A. RPO and RTO

    B. RTO and SDO

    C. RPO and ITO

    D. SDO and IRO

20. What are the five phases of business continuity planning according to ISACA? (Select the answer showing the correct phases and order.)

    A. Analyze business impact, develop strategy, develop plan, plan testing, implement

    B. Analyze business impact, develop plan, implement, plan testing, write the plan

    C. Analyze business impact, write the plan, test strategy, develop plan, implement

    D. Analyze business impact, develop strategy, develop plan, implement, plan testing

21. Which of the following best fits the description of *requires some assembly and can be operational within days*?

    A. Redundant site

    B. Warm site

    C. Hot site

    D. Cold site

22. What priority would the BC/DR planner at a manufacturing company place upon warranty repair services for clients during a recovery?

    A. Core process

    B. Discretionary process

    C. Critical function

    D. Supporting process

23. When can a warm site be used for recovery?

    A. When the downtime is acceptable to the business without breaching any legal requirements

    B. When it's not profitable to operate a hot site

    C. When the recovery is of high priority

    D. When the actual recovery exceeds the recovery time objective

24. Which of the following methods of testing BC/DR plans is not acceptable?

    A. Desktop

    B. Modular

    C. Full interruption

    D. Unannounced

25. Media updates and announcements should be _____ during the event.

    A. From the CEO when new events occur

    B. From the local disaster relief official in charge

    C. From the PIO at regular intervals

    D. From a senior manager or company officer

26. What is the best method for testing the effectiveness of specific recovery procedures?

    A. Ask the participants their opinion of the exercise

    B. Observe the procedure as it's being executed

    C. Time the procedure's execution and compare it to the RTO

    D. Follow the manufacturer/vendor's recommended procedures

27. Who is the incident commander?

    A. First person on the scene even if it's a five-year-old child

    B. Manager or executive of the organization

    C. Member of the police or fire department

    D. A person with special training

28. How does the term *oversubscription* relate to the response plans in business continuity and disaster recovery?

    A. Too much insurance coverage with overlapping policies.

    B. Using the same site for hot, warm, and cold recovery.

    C. More customers than the site can handle.

    D. Transportation is not available to the site.

29. What is the objective of the strategy planning phase?

    A. Select a vendor offering the best solution

    B. Pick a response to cover every situation

    C. Identify time windows and minimum service

    D. Satisfy all the stakeholders' interests to their satisfaction

30. Which of the following is *not* a recommended criterion for invocation of the BC/DR plan?

    A. Financial loss

    B. Duration of outage is unknown

    C. Cost of activation

    D. Scope of problem cannot be determined

31. Which of these is the primary output from the business impact analysis (BIA)?

    A. Identification of alternate revenue opportunities

    B. Analysis of dependencies and areas of overreliance

    C. High-level understanding of definitions

    D. Low-level blueprint of the business process

32. Which of the following definitions is the best example of an RTO?

    A. Target point of optimum data recovery

    B. Target time for the user to be processing again

    C. Target service level at a particular point in time

    D. Target for recovery to be completed

33. At a minimum, when should the BIA be updated and the BC/DR plan be exercised (tested)?

    A. Semiannually

    B. Annually

    C. When resources allow

    D. Every two years

34. Who should be the actual leader of business continuity planning?

    A. Chief executive officer (CEO)

    B. Chief financial officer (CFO)

    C. Chief information officer (CIO)

    D. Chief operating officer (COO)

35. What is the biggest difference between disaster planning and business continuity planning?

    A. Disaster plans are usually specific to a department.

    B. Business continuity plans are run by IT.

    C. Business continuity plans span department boundaries.

    D. Disaster planning is an extension of facility plans.

Answers to Review Questions

1.   B. The service delivery objective (SDO) illustrates the expected level of service during recovery. The organization may have several SDO targets based on the different phases of recovery. RTO is the recovery time objective, and RPO is the recovery point objective. ITO is a distracter.

2.   C. A critical success factor is also known as a showstopper. Critical success factors must go right every time in order for recovery to be successful. A key performance indicator (KPI) is a numerical score.

3.   A. The insurance company may dictate salvage to save money. Salvage will increase the delay before recovery. Any replacement purchases by the organization may not be covered under reimbursement.

4.   D. The concerns in business continuity include natural disasters, missed targets, and loss of profit. The goal of continuity is to ensure that important targets are not missed and revenue is not interrupted.

5.   B. The most important point to remember when planning team assignments is that all the duties are performed, regardless of the number of people. In major incidents, the organization may need to hire hundreds of extra personnel to ensure that all the duties are performed.

6.   A. The hot site is expensive but offers a better chance for recovery because it is already configured for use and ready to go.

7.   B. MAO is the maximum acceptable outage that can occur before critical deadlines are missed or recovery is no longer feasible because of the amount of time lapsed. May be referred to as maximum tolerable downtime (MTD).

8.   C. Only critical processes will continue. The other processes will be interrupted while the organization focuses efforts to restore critical processes. Plans will sequence recovery by using service delivery objectives (SDOs), recovery point objectives (RPOs), and recovery time objectives (RTOs). A noncritical process might be shut down and never restarted.

9.   B. The plan minimizes decisions needed during the crisis. Possible options would have been researched and decisions made in advance by management. The recovery staff is expected to follow the directions contained in the plan.

10. D. The EOC is the Emergency Operations Center, staffed by the emergency management team during a crisis.

11. A. All inquires and statements should be from the designated public information officer (PIO), the spokesperson for the organization. The PIO uses predefined scripts to deliver messages that have been vetted to ensure a positive image for the organization.

12. C. It is not possible to create business continuity plans without a current business impact analysis (BIA). The BIA will identify critical processes and their dependencies. The critical processes will change as the business changes with new products and customers.

13. D. The plan should be reviewed quarterly and updated at least annually. Updates should occur after each test, changes in personnel, or changes in business direction. Plans are often updated for changes in key customers and products.

14. B. Plans are tested to train the staff in carrying out their work. The intention is to find problems and correct any mistakes. A secondary benefit is to demonstrate improvement in the response and recovery efforts.

15. A. Financial records and backup tapes are extremely important. How-to manuals will help aid the recovery effort.

16. D. The strategy will be selected based on information obtained during the risk assessment and business impact analysis. All options should be considered when selecting the business continuity strategy.

17. B. The purpose of planning is to establish decision criteria in advance. After the criteria are met, the plan will be activated by the appointed personnel. The alternate site invocation process allows a preauthorized manager to activate the alternate site. Invocation of the alternate site will cost money and should occur only when it is required.

18. C. Business continuity is intended to ensure that critical processes are restored in a timely manner and that revenue is not interrupted. With revenue, the organization will acquire the money necessary to survive.

19. A. The recovery point objective (RPO) indicates the fallback position and duration of loss that has occurred. A valid RPO example is to recover by using backup data from last night's backup tape, meaning the more recent transactions have been lost. The recovery time objective (RTO) indicates a point in time that the restored data should be available for the user to access.

20. D. Notice that business impact is always the first step. Then criteria are selected to guide the strategy selection. A detailed plan is written using the strategy. The written plan is then implemented. After implementation, the plan and staff are tested for effectiveness. The plan is revised, and then the testing and maintenance cycle begins.

21. B. A warm site is a building preconfigured with utility services and may hold some equipment. Hardware will usually need to be shipped in and assembled. Telephone circuits will need to be switched over to the warm site and data loaded from backup tapes. Recovery time is measured in days.

22. B. Providing warranty repair services is discretionary and would be discontinued during recovery. Core processes, such as sales, generate direct revenue. Supporting processes such as invoicing also help the core process bring in money. Everything else may be discontinued or shut down during recovery.

23. A. The warm site is acceptable to the business when the downtime is acceptable without breaching any legal requirements. Making a profit is not the reason for using a warm site.

24. D. Unannounced testing is not acceptable because of the potential to create additional harm. Some people are not able to deal with the extra stress or may exercise the wrong response and create a real emergency.

25. C. All media updates and announcements should be handled by the public information officer (PIO) during the event. This is necessary to prevent misinformation or confusion. Providing information at regular intervals helps promote trust and confidence.

26. C. The best method from the options provided is to compare the elapsed time to execute the procedure against their stated recovery time objective (RTO). Participant opinions are important for buy-in; however, some opinions may be too optimistic or too pessimistic. Observing the procedure being executed will help determine its odds of being successfully completed. What really matters is that recovery occurs within its specific time window since other processes are depending on it.

27. A. The first person on the scene is the incident commander, even if it's a five-year-old child calling the police, ambulance, or fire department. The person on the scene directs all efforts until relieved by a more qualified person. Anyone can be an incident commander, and no special training is needed.

28. C. Oversubscription relates to the vendor overselling services to more customers than the recovery site can handle. To eliminate an oversubscription problem, the price consequences of failure and total cost of leasing an alternate site for 60 days can be used to help justify a cooperative venture to buy a dedicated site. The cooperative venture allows cost sharing with another organization, if both can use the site simultaneously.

29. C. The principle objective in strategy planning is to identify the available time window and minimum service necessary for recovery. This discussion should never involve a vendor or a specific product. The goal is to force the development of a well-defined specification, and then later look for solutions that fit that specification. Vendors and products are never, never, never a strategy.

30. C. Cost of activating is not an acceptable criterion for invocation of the BC/DR plan. The plan should always be activated if the conditions are met. Conditions requiring invocation of the plan include estimated financial loss, duration of outage, and the inability to determine the loss or scope of impact.

31. D. A low-level blueprint (or schematic) of the business process is the primary output from the business impact analysis (BIA). If performed correctly, the BIA will provide high-quality supporting detail for the other possible answer choices.

32. B. The recovery time objective (RTO) is the deadline for when the user must be processing again. IT is expected to have completed the necessary level of technical recovery. The user is able to resume processing work unless that RTO has failed.

33. B. Every organization should exercise the BC/DR plan at least once per year. Some regulations, such as Gramm-Leach-Bliley, require live recovery exercises at least once every 90 days (quarterly). The BIA should be updated at least annually or whenever a change occurs to the strategy, the organizational structure, or the business process protected by the plan.

34. A. The chief executive officer (CEO) should be the actual leader of business continuity planning. The second choice is the chief operating officer (COO) as the official delegate of the CEO function. The CEO and COO have the agenda of generating revenue. They can force the cooperation of all others in the organization. The CFO is the third choice. The CIO is the worst of these choices because of the CIO's distance from revenue activities and limited scope of authority.

35. C. Business continuity plans are focused on the processes for generating revenue. This is the biggest difference when compared to rebuilding in disaster recovery. Plans of the various departments such as IT, facilities, manufacturing, and sales may become smaller components of the final BC plan. All decisions and activities are determined by the revenue generated, not by the desires or goals of the department. The only agenda that matters is the CEO's agenda.

Appendix

A

About the Companion CD

IN THIS APPENDIX:

- ✓ What you'll find on the CD
- ✓ System requirements
- ✓ Using the CD
- ✓ Troubleshooting

What You'll Find on the CD

The following sections are arranged by category and provide a summary of the software and other goodies you'll find on the CD. If you need help installing the items provided on the CD, refer to the installation instructions in the "Using the CD" section of this appendix.

Some programs on the CD might fall into one of these categories:

Quick reference guide from National Institute of Standards. This summary guide identifies the major point for information security controls according to the NIST 800-53 standard. This is an excellent roadmap to help you be the best auditor your client has ever met.

Shareware programs are fully functional, free, trial versions of copyrighted programs. If you like particular programs, register with their authors for a nominal fee and receive licenses, enhanced versions, and technical support.

Freeware programs are free, copyrighted games, applications, and utilities. You can copy them to as many computers as you like—for free—but they offer no technical support.

GNU software is governed by its own license, which is included inside the folder of the GNU software. There are no restrictions on distribution of GNU software. See the GNU license at the root of the CD for more details.

Trial, demo, or evaluation versions of software are usually limited either by time or functionality (such as not letting you save a project after you create it).

Sybex Test Engine

For Windows

The CD contains the Sybex Test Engine, which includes all of the assessment test and chapter review questions in electronic format, as well as two bonus exams located only on the CD.

PDF of the Book

For Windows

We have included an electronic version of the text in PDF format. You can view the electronic version of the book with Adobe Reader.

Adobe Reader

For Windows

We've also included a copy of Adobe Reader, so you can view PDF files that accompany the book's content. For more information on Adobe Reader or to check for a newer version, visit Adobe's website at www.adobe.com/products/reader/.

Electronic Flashcards

For PC, Pocket PC, and Palm

These handy electronic flashcards are just what they sound like. One side contains a question or fill-in-the-blank, and the other side shows the answer.

System Requirements

Make sure that your computer meets the minimum system requirements shown in the following list. If your computer doesn't meet most of these requirements, you may have problems using the software and files on the companion CD. For the latest and greatest information, please refer to the ReadMe file located at the root of the CD-ROM.

- A PC running Microsoft Windows 98, Windows 2000, Windows NT 4 (with SP4 or later), Windows Me, Windows XP, or Windows Vista

- An Internet connection

- A CD-ROM drive

Using the CD

To launch the items from the CD to your hard disk, follow these steps:

1. Insert the CD into your computer's CD-ROM drive. The license agreement appears.

 Windows users: The interface won't launch if you have AutoRun disabled. In that case, choose Start ➢ Run (for Windows Vista, Start ➢ All Programs ➢ Accessories ➢ Run). In the dialog box that appears, type **D:\Start.exe**. (Replace *D* with the proper letter if your CD drive uses a different letter. If you don't know the letter, see how your CD drive is listed under My Computer.) Click OK.

2. Read through the license agreement, and then click the Accept button if you want to use the CD.

The CD interface appears. The interface allows you to access the content with just one or two clicks.

Troubleshooting

Wiley has attempted to provide programs that work on most computers with the minimum system requirements. Alas, your computer may differ, and some programs may not work properly for some reason.

The two likeliest problems are that you don't have enough memory (RAM) for the programs you want to use, or you have other programs running that are affecting installation or running of a program. If you get an error message such as "Not enough memory" or "Setup cannot continue," try one or more of the following suggestions and then try using the software again:

Turn off any antivirus software running on your computer. Installation programs sometimes mimic virus activity and may make your computer incorrectly believe that it's being infected by a virus.

Close all running programs. The more programs you have running, the less memory is available to other programs. Installation programs typically update files and programs; so if you keep other programs running, installation may not work properly.

Have your local computer store add more RAM to your computer. This is, admittedly, a drastic and somewhat expensive step. However, adding more memory can really help the speed of your computer and allow more programs to run at the same time.

Customer Care

If you have trouble with the book's companion CD-ROM, please call the Wiley Product Technical Support phone number at (800) 762-2974. Outside the United States, call +1(317) 572-3994. You can also contact Wiley Product Technical Support at http://sybex.custhelp.com. John Wiley & Sons will provide technical support only for installation and other general quality-control items. For technical support on the applications themselves, consult the program's vendor or author.

To place additional orders or to request information about other Wiley products, please call (877) 762-2974.

Glossary

A

Acceptable use policy (AUP)   A formal statement of policy signed by management and acknowledged by the user with their signature. This policy typically is enforced by the Human Resources department. The policy should state that computing resources are for company business only and noncompany activities, including those related to religion or topics of questionable use, are prohibited. The AUP should state that possession of administrative system utilities and related system tools not specifically authorized are prohibited as contraband. This eliminates any excuses or misunderstanding and enforces separation of duties.

Access control list (ACL)   A table of user login IDs specifying each user's individual level of access to computer resources.

Accountability   Responsibility, liability. To be accountable is to be liable for the final result or to be held responsible for one's actions.

Accreditation   A formal approval by management based on perceived fitness of use. Approval may be granted for a system, site location, or function. Accreditation occurs after system certification for a period of 90 days, 180 days, or one year. Systems must be reaccredited prior to expiration of their current accreditation period.

ACID principle   ACID stands for *atomicity* (write all or nothing), *consistency* (data is restored to its original state if the write fails), *isolation* (each transaction is independent), and *durability* (completed data is retained in the database).

Activation criteria   Conditions which, when met, dictate the activation of disaster recovery or business continuity plans. Any delay or failure to activate indicates negligence. Typically, the criteria are based on impact, anticipated duration of outage, or immediate lack of sufficient information to calculate the actual impact. It's always better to overreact when compared to the consequences of an inadequate response.

Active attack   An overt attack against the system or system data files. Active attacks are usually detected during routine monitoring.

ActiveX   A program applet designed by Microsoft with access throughout the entire system. ActiveX is more dangerous than Java applets. ActiveX applets can be digitally signed using authenticode, but this does not provide any protection from malware. Malicious programmers can design ActiveX programs to circumvent or defeat the security of Microsoft Windows. As a safeguard, firewalls should always be configured to prevent the downloading of ActiveX programs. Individual computers should have ActiveX disabled.

Address binding   Creating a software link (association) between the hardware MAC address of a network interface and the administratively assigned IP address.

Administrative audit   Verifies that appropriate policies and procedures exist, and that they have been implemented as management intended. This audit focuses on operational effectiveness and efficiency.

Administrative controls   The use of administrative policies and procedures in the implementation of preventative, detective, and corrective controls.

Advanced Encryption Standard (AES)   Symmetric-key encryption system designed by Belgian mathematicians. Also known as the Rijndael, Advanced Encryption Standard (AES) replaces the outdated DES data encryption standard used by the U.S. government.

After-image   Changes to data in the database are held in a temporary file called the after-image journal. The transaction can be reversed (discarded) until the program writes the change into the master file. Also see *before-image* and *ACID principle.*

Agile development   A micromanagement methodology to force development within a series of short time boxes. Agile is used for the development of prototypes. The focus is on tactile knowledge in a person's mind, rather than the use of formal SDLC design and development documentation.

Antivirus software   A specialized software program used to detect viruses based on a database of known behavior (signature) or an attempt to append to a file.

Applet   A small downloaded program using ActiveX, Java, XML, or a similar programming language.

Application   Computer software program designed for a particular purpose. Application software provides functions and stored procedures to solve a problem on behalf of the user.

Application controls   The lowest level of control, usually governing system use or internal program controls. Application controls are easily subverted if higher-level controls governing the operating environment are missing or ineffective. Higher controls include *general controls, pervasive controls*, and *detailed controls.*

Application layer   The highest layer of the OSI model is layer 7. The Application layer runs problem-solving software for the user. This layer provides the interface between the user and the computer program.

Application programming interface (API)   A software interface designed to allow communication between different programs. APIs are used to specify the procedural rules, type, and format of data to be passed between programs. Proprietary APIs are referred to as closed. Nonproprietary APIs are called open. The API design is used by programs in both open-system and closed-system architecture for cross-compatibility.

Artificial intelligence (AI)   An attempt to simulate human reasoning by using a computer program with a knowledge database and abstract procedures to measure cause-and-effect relationships.

Assessment   A less formal process used to determine value or relevance to the intended use. Assessments may be internal or external. The results of an assessment are of low to moderate value. The results are used for internal purposes only. See *audit* and *independent audit* to compare the differences.

Asset   Anything of value. May be tangible or intangible in the form of money, physical goods, products, resources, recipes, or procedures.

Assurance   A promise with supporting evidence given in a declaration or activity designed to instill confidence.

Asymmetric-key encryption   An encryption system using two different keys. Both keys are mathematically related. Asymmetric-key encryption is not time sensitive. The private key is kept secret by the sender, and the public key is freely distributed to anyone who desires to communicate with the owner. Also known as public-key cryptography.

Atomicity   A process used for database transaction integrity to ensure that the entire transaction is correctly processed or all the changes are backed out of the database.

Attestation   An affirmation by the signer that all statements are true and correct. The purpose is to certify that a declaration is genuine.

Attribute   In computer programming, an attribute is equivalent to a column in a database table. The attribute refers to a specific characteristic of a database entry.

Attribute sampling   A technique used to estimate the rate of occurrence for a particular attribute within the subject population. In compliance testing, attribute sampling answers the question, "How many?"

Audit   A formal and systematic process of collecting evidence to test or confirm a statement or to confirm a record of transaction. Also see *internal audit* and *independent audit*.

Audit charter   A formal document issued by management to designate audit responsibility, authority, and accountability. The absence of a formal audit charter document would indicate a control weakness.

Audit committee   A committee of the board of directors composed of financially literate executives. The purpose of the audit committee is to challenge the assertions of management by using internal and external auditors.

Audit objective   Specific goal(s) to be accomplished by the audit. This is the reason for the audit.

Audit risk   The possibility that material errors may exist that the auditor is unable to detect.

Audit scope   The boundaries and limitations of the individual audit. Normally, particular systems or functions that will be reviewed during the audit.

Audit subject   The target to be audited. The audit subject may be a particular system, process, procedure, or department function.

Audit trail   Evidence that can be reassembled in chronological order to retrace a transaction or series of transactions.

Auditee   The persons and organization being audited.

Auditing standard   The mandatory examination procedures to be executed during an audit to ensure consistency of findings. The auditing standard specifies a minimum level of performance. Any deviations must be well documented, with justification as to why the standard was not followed.

Auditor   The person(s) performing the audit by gathering evidence, testing, and reporting the findings. Auditors should not be related to the subject of the audit, to prevent bias. Also see *independence*.

Auditor's opinion   An overall score generated by the sufficient collection of evidence, effective testing, observations, and findings from the test results. It's actually a score based on the relevance of the test results rather than an opinion.

Authentication   The process of verifying a user's identity. The user's claim will be tested against a known reference. If a match occurs, the user is authenticated and allowed to proceed. A mismatch will deny the request.

Authentication header (AH)   Used in the IPsec protocol to provide integrity, authentication, and nonrepudiation by means of encryption. The authentication header contains the security associations (SAs), which are used for covert tunneling mode. The AH works with the encapsulated security protocol to both hide the internal IP address and encrypt the data payload.

Authenticode   Microsoft's technique for software developers to digitally sign downloadable ActiveX applets. The authenticode design fails to provide any security from poorly written programs and does not protect the user from malicious programs designed to intentionally cause harm.

Authorization   The granting of a right or authority.

Author's note. New terminology is created all the time by individuals wanting to portray an illusion of intelligence, by sales people attempting to make their product appear different from those of competitors, and by a very small number of people who actually have something new to convey. A person of intelligence and genuine understanding will have absolutely no trouble explaining concepts by using a handful of small words. A good explanation will include a simple test that the listener can duplicate to verify the meaning.

Availability   A term that refers to the accessibility and proper functioning of a computer at the time frame required by the user.

B

Backdoor   A hidden software-access mechanism that will bypass normal security controls to grant access into a program. A *root kit* creates covert access paths into the system. Synonymous with *trapdoor*.

Backup and recovery capability   The culmination of software, hardware, procedures, and data files that will permit timely recovery from a failure or disaster.

Balanced scorecard   A management tool that aligns individual activities to the higher-level business objectives.

Baseband   A single channel for data transmission. Coax cable is an example of a baseband technology.

Baseline   An agreed-upon reference point. Also see *software baseline*.

Bastion host   A gateway host exposed to an external connection such as the Internet.

Batch controls   Used to ensure the accuracy and correct formatting of input data. The batch controls include sequence numbering and run-to-run totals. The batch count will count the number of all the items to ensure that each transaction is processed. Batch totals can be used to verify the values within the transactions.

Before-image   A temporary record of work in progress. This database journal file contains the original data before a new transaction is written. A copy of the original data is retained in this "before" journal file in case the transaction fails. If the transaction fails, the change is discarded and the original data is kept. Related to the *ACID principle* and *after-image* transaction journal.

Benchmarking   A test to evaluate performance against a known workload or industry-accepted standard. Using the Capability Maturity Model (CMM) is a form of benchmarking.

Best evidence   Refers to evidence that specifically proves or disproves a particular point. The best evidence is both independent and objective. The worst evidence is subjective or circumstantial evidence.

Black-box testing   Tests the functionality of compiled software by comparing the input and output, without understanding the internal process that creates the output. The internal logic is hidden from the tester. The term *black box* refers to the software being in nonreadable machine format (compiled code). Almost all commercially available software is tested by using the black-box technique.

Blackout   The complete failure of electrical power.

Biometric management   Management isn't a policy; management is the enforcement/overseeing of the policy concerning the intended use of biometric data with corresponding standards and procedures. Management includes identifying how data is collected, stored, protected, transmitted, used, and disposed of.

Biometric template generator   The system sensor that acquires a biometric image and converts it into biometric minutiae for digital storage or comparison.

Biometric template matcher   Compares a biometric image template just acquired by the sensor to the biometric minutiae already stored inside the biometrics database. A match between the two templates will authenticate the individual, allowing access through the physical door or barrier.

Biometrics   A technical process to verify a user's identity based on unique physical characteristics.

Bitstream imaging   A special bit-by-bit backup of physical media, which records all the contents, including deleted files and current contents of swap space or slack space. Also known as physical backup. Bitstream backups are used in forensic analysis and may be used in electronic discovery. Also see *logical backup*.

Boot strapping (boot)   The initial loading of software to start a computer. Also see *initial program load (IPL)*.

Bridge   A network device or software process that connects similar networks together. Network switching is based on a bridging process to join users into logical network segments. A standard bridge will forward all data packets to the other users in the subnet. A bridge operates at the OSI Data-Link layer (layer 2).

Broadband   Multiple communication channels that are multiplexed over a single cable. DSL is an example of broadband transmitted on a different frequency and sharing the same physical wire with the voice telephone circuit.

Broadcast   A network transmission by one computer to all computers on the network. Ethernet uses broadcast technology to transmit data packets, which are seen by all the computers on the network.

Brownout   Low voltage for an extended period of time.

Brute force attack   An attempt to overpower the system or to try every possible combination until access is granted.

Buffer   A temporary memory location used to stage data before or after processing.

Bus   A shared connection used in common by other devices. Examples include the power bus and the computer data bus.

Bus topology   An early type of networking in which all the computers were connected on a single cable in a linear fashion.

Business continuity (BC) manager   A specific manager with the authority of a vice president or director assigned to lead planning and exercises. Usually this person reports to the chief executive officer (CEO), chief operating officer (COO), or holds a leadership position in the program management office. Unlike departmental managers, the BC manager has authority across departmental boundaries.

Business continuity plan (BCP)   An organizational plan to continue core revenue-generating operations following a crisis or disaster. The objective of business continuity planning is to ensure uninterrupted revenue for business survival.

Business impact analysis (BIA)   The process of determining the actual steps to produce the desired product or service, as in use by the organization. The intention is to provide management with accurate information about how the business processes are performed.

Business performance indicators   Business performance can be measured by a variety of indicators, including return on investment (ROI), gross profit margin (GPM), capital gains, market share, production cost, and debt ratio.

Business process reengineering (BPR)   The process of streamlining existing operations in an effort to improve efficiency and reduce cost. Benefits may be derived by eliminating unnecessary steps as the organization has progressed through the learning curve, or by expanding capability for more work.

Business risk   The inherent potential for harm in the business or industry itself, as the organization attempts to fulfill its objectives. Business risks may be regulatory, contractual, or financial.

Bypass label processing   An attempt to circumvent mandatory access controls by bypassing the electronic security control label. Examples include writing data to a read-only file, or accessing a file that would be off-limits because of its higher security rating.

Bytecode   See *pseudocode*.

C

Cable plant   A physical collection of network cables contained inside the building.

Cache   A high-speed buffer used to temporarily stage data before or after processing.

Candidate key   Rows of data used with search attributes to find all matching records within the database. For example, searching the database to find the name of every hotel in Grapevine, Texas.

Capability Maturity Model (CMM)   Developed by the Software Engineering Institute to benchmark the maturity of systems and management processes. Maturity levels range from 0 to 5. Level 5 is completely documented and optimized for continuous improvement.

Capacity monitoring   The process of continuously monitoring utilization in the environment against existing resource capacity. The objective is to ensure optimum use and expansion of services before an outage occurs.

Certificate   A written assurance or official record representing that an event has or has not occurred. Certificates can be stored as electronic records or physical documents, signed by the party providing a declaration of authenticity.

Certificate authority (CA)   The trusted issuer of *digital certificates* using public- and private-key pairs. The certificate authority is responsible for verifying the authenticity of the user's identity.

Certificate revocation list (CRL)   A list maintained by the *certificate authority*, of certificates that are revoked or expired.

Certification   A comprehensive technical evaluation process to establish compliance to a minimum requirement.

Certification practice statement (CPS)   A detailed set of procedures specifying how the *certificate authority* governs its operation.

Chain of custody   Refers to the mandatory security and integrity requirements used in the evidence life cycle. The custodian of evidence must prove that the evidence has been kept secure with a high degree of *integrity* and has not been tampered with.

Change control board (CCB)   A management review to ensure awareness and management control of changes in the IT environment. A change control board provides separation of duties.

Change control process (CCP)   A formal review of proposed changes using a systematic *methodology*.

Ciphertext   An encrypted message displayed in unreadable text that appears as gibberish. The message is displayed in cipher form.

Circuit-level gateway   Refers to a *proxy firewall*. No data packets are forwarded between the internal and external network, except by the proxy application. The proxy application is required to complete the data transmission circuit.

Circuit-switching   All communications are transmitted over a dedicated circuit such as a T-1 leased line telephone circuit. Circuit-switched is the opposite of *packet switching*.

Clear text   A message that is completely readable to a human. The message can be clearly read.

Client   A person or organization with the authority to request an audit. The auditor's report of findings is presented to the client at the conclusion of the audit. The client may be internal or external to the *auditee*.

Closed system   Software containing methods and programming of a proprietary design, which remains the property of the software creator. Most commercial software is closed system. Closed systems can exchange data to other programs by using a specific *application programming interface (API)*. Microsoft Windows is an example of a closed system containing proprietary design.

Cold site   A physical location that can be used for disaster recovery of noncritical processes. The cold site is no more than a street address with basic utility service. The entire computing environment must be shipped in and then assembled. The cold site will be ready for production use in weeks or months.

Common Criteria   An international standard (ISO 15408) for testing criteria of computer security controls. All ISO member countries are expected to use the Common Criteria standard with testing performed by an ISO 17025–certified laboratory testing facility. Common Criteria is currently in use by Canada, France, Germany, the Netherlands, the United Kingdom, and the United States.

Compensating control   An internal control that reduces the potential for loss by error or omission. Supervisory review and audit trails are compensating controls for a lack of separation of duties.

Compile   An automated process used by software developers to convert human-readable computer programs into executable machine language. Compiled computer software runs faster than interpreted program scripts. Compiled computer programs cannot be read by humans.

Compliance audit   A type of audit that determines whether internal controls are present and functioning effectively.

Compliance testing   The testing of internal controls to determine whether they are functioning correctly.

Computer assisted audit tools (CAAT)   The family of automated test software using a computerized audit procedure with specialized utilities.

Computer console   Physical access to the computer's primary input/output terminal, usually the video display and keyboard. Access to the computer console is a security risk that must be controlled.

Confidence coefficient   The quantified probability of error. The confidence coefficient of 95 percent is considered a high level of confidence in IS auditing.

Confidentiality   The protection of information held in secret for the benefit of authorized users.

Configuration management   An administrative process of being able to prove the documented design as built, by verifying the correct version of all the individual components used in final construction. The three elements of configuration management are control, accounting, and reporting.

Constructive Cost Model (COCOMO)   An early software project estimation technique used to forecast the time and effort required to develop a software program based on size and complexity.

Continuity of operations   Preemptive activities designed to ensure the continuous operation of core processes.

Contraband software   Any system utility or special software not required in the specific performance of a person's job duties. A tightly controlled software policy prevents any excuses for violating separation of duties. Examples of contraband software include password crackers, network discovery tools, CAAT software, traffic generators, disk-wiping utilities, or known hacking software. Violations should be grounds for immediate termination following the conclusion of an investigation.

Control   The power to regulate or restrict activities. IS controls are used as a safeguard to prevent loss, error, or omission.

Control environment   A space designed to protect assets by using sufficient physical and technical controls to prevent unauthorized access or compromise. The computer room is a control environment.

Control group   Members of the operations staff responsible for collecting data from users for input to the computer system.

Control risk   The risk that errors may be introduced, or not identified and corrected in a timely manner. The risk of losing control.

Control self-assessment   A formal review executed by the user to assess the effectiveness of controls. The purpose of the control self-assessment is to induce ownership by the user and to facilitate improvement.

Corrective control   A control designed to minimize the impact of an error by repairing the condition or executing an alternative procedure. Examples of corrective controls include data restoration from tape backup, hot sites, and automated failover systems.

Cost of asset   The capital expense of an asset may be measured as total ownership cost (TOC). The cost of the asset is the cumulative total expense based on purchase price, delivery cost, implementation cost, and effective downtime.

Cracker   A malicious computer attacker who attempts to break into a system. Synonymous with the term *malicious hacker*.

Crash dump   A special diagnostic file created when a computer system crashes. The contents represent the data being processed at the time of the crash, including contents of the memory registers and tasks running when the crash occurred. Crash dump files vary according to the operating system. Contents of this file are extremely valuable in forensic analysis.

Critical Path Methodology (CPM)   The path of execution that accomplishes the minimum objectives of the project. The critical path is the longest single route through a network diagram and the shortest time to accomplish the minimum objectives. Critical path items represent mandatory tasks which, if not accomplished, would wreck the project.

Critical success factor (CSF)   A process that must occur perfectly every single time in order to be successful. To fail a critical success factor would be a showstopper.

Crossover error rate   See *equal error rate (EER)*.

Cryptographic system   The implementation of a computer program using a cryptographic algorithm and keys to encrypt and decrypt messages.

Cryptography   The theories and methods of converting readable text into undecipherable gibberish and later reversing the process to create readable text. The purpose of cryptography is to hide information from other people.

Crystal-box testing   See *white-box testing*.

Cyclic redundancy check (CRC)   A simple error-detection process whereby the contents are divided by a number prior to transmission. After transmission, the process is rerun to determine whether an error occurred. A value of zero indicates that the transmission was successful.

D

Data classification   A process of ranking information based on its value or requirements for secrecy.

Data custodian   The individual charged with protecting data from a loss of availability, loss of integrity, or loss of confidentiality. The data custodian implements controls appropriate to the desires of the data owner and data classification.

Data dictionary   A standardized reference listing of all the programmer's data descriptions and files used in a computer program.

Data Encryption Standard (DES)   A cryptographic symmetric-key algorithm implemented by the U.S. government from 1972 to 1993. The DES standard was modified to use a triple process of encryption and decryption in an attempt to improve confidentiality (triple DES). DES was replaced by the *Advanced Encryption Standard (AES)*. DES is commonly used in older devices.

Data integrity controls   Procedures to ensure the appropriateness and accuracy of information.

Data mart   A group of data selected from a data warehouse for analysis. The data selected is of particular interest to a group of people.

Data mining   The process of analyzing volumes of data to determine correlations that may be useful.

Data owner   The individual or executive responsible for the integrity of information. The duties of the owner include specifying appropriate controls, identifying authorized users, and appointing a custodian.

Data retention   See *records management*.

Database   A collection of persistence data items that are maintained in a grouping.

Database schema   The data structure and design of the database that represents a logical layout or schema.

Data-Link layer   The transmit-and-receive protocol between networked devices. Data-Link operates on OSI layer 2.

Data-oriented database (DODB)   A data collection designed around relevant information in a known format. The database and the program methods operate separately from each other.

Data set   A set of related data files.

Decision support system (DSS)   A database information system with scenario models designed to convey important facts and details to aid the decision process.

Decryption   The process of reversing encryption to convert unintelligible ciphertext into human-readable clear text.

Default gateway   The address of a router used to communicate with systems located on a different subnet or different network.

Defense-in-depth (DID)   A process of building layers of defensive controls for protective assurance. Also known as a layered defense strategy.

Defuzzification   To sharpen the details of an average population by using a stratified mean (for example, demographics) to further define the data into small units.

Deleted files   Computer files remain on the hard disk after deletion. To conserve processing, space occupied by deleted files is simply marked as eligible for overwriting. Deleted files that have not been overwritten may be recovered by using a simple recovery utility or forensic analysis. Use of an overwriting utility or physical destruction is necessary to prevent unauthorized disclosure of deleted files.

Demilitarized zone (DMZ)   See *screened subnet.*

Denial of service (DoS)   An attack designed to prevent the user from accessing the computer system.

Detailed controls   Lower-level controls placed on specific procedures.

Detection risk   The risk that an auditor will not be able to detect material error conditions (faults) that exist.

Detective control   A control designed to report items of concern including errors, omissions, and unauthorized access.

Dictionary attack   An attack used to discover system passwords by loading all the words found in a language dictionary into a password-cracking utility. The password-cracking utility will encrypt each word by using the same method as the operating system. Matching encrypted passwords are identified, and the originating word is displayed to the attacker as the unencrypted password.

Differential backup   A file backup method that copies every file that has been added or changed since the last full backup. A differential backup does not set the final archive bit flag.

Digital certificate   An encrypted computer file containing unique information about the identity of the individual and the issuer of the certificate. Digital certificates are used to verify the authenticity of a remote system. Digital certificates are required to enable Secure Shell (SSH) and Secure Sockets Layer (SSL).

Digital signature   An encrypted hash of an electronic file. The subject file is processed by using a hash algorithm such as MD-5 or SHA-1. The resulting hash output file is encrypted with the sender's private key. This encrypted hash file is known as a digital signature that is related to both the sender and the subject file. The signature is verified by using the sender's public key to decrypt the hash.

Disaster recovery plan (DRP)   A set of procedures for providing an emergency response following a disaster. The objective is to rebuild the organization to a state equal to that prior to the disaster. Disaster recovery does not provide for losses of market share and revenue. Business continuity is the next step above disaster recovery.

Discovery sampling   The process of searching 100 percent of the available records for specific attributes to determine the probability of occurrence. Used when the likelihood of evidence is low or extreme accuracy is required. The intention is to discover whether a particular situation has occurred. Common examples include fraud, forensic investigations, and identifying correlations from unexpected events.

Discretionary access control (DAC)   A type of access control in which a person of authority decides to grant or revoke access for an individual. The decision may be based on need or desire.

Disk imaging   See *bitstream imaging*.

Disk mirroring   See *mirrored*.

Disk strings   The orderly connection of multiple disk drives in a storage array. Stings of individual disks are connected for use in *RAID* subsystems.

Disposal (SDLC phase 7)   The manner in which hardware and software assets are authorized for retirement without the loss of data records. Data must be archived according to legal commitments and regulations. No one in the organization should profit from the disposal process.

Distributed denial of service attack (DDoS)   A particularly vicious form of denial of service attack that is launched concurrently from multiple systems.

Domain   A kingdom or political territory of direct influence.

Domain Name System (DNS)   An Internet protocol that looks up the server's IP address by using the server hostname, such as www.CertTest.com. The Internet domain names and IP addresses are loaded into a server running the domain name service.

Downtime   A resource or system being unavailable to the user for any reason whatsoever. Downtime may be the result of a planned outage for maintenance or backups, or an unplanned outage due to a failure.

Dry pipe   A type of fire-suppression system in which the pipes remain dry until seconds after the release is required. Most dry-pipe systems utilize compressed gas to minimize the chance of leakage due to corrosion or freezing conditions.

Due care   The level of care that a normal, prudent individual would give in the same situation.

Dumpster diving   The process of digging through trash in a dumpster to recover evidence or improperly disposed-of records. The same process is frequently used by government agents and law enforcement to gather evidence; therefore, it's legal unless the person is trespassing. Trespassing is unnecessary if the refuse is going to be unloaded at the public waste dump. A hacker or investigator can pick through the trash after it's unloaded at the dump or recycler.

E

Electromagnetic interference (EMI)   Magnetic waves of interference generated by electricity. EMI generates interference with electrical transmissions.

Electronic Data Interchange (EDI)   Used for e-commerce communication between two organizations using the Electronic Data Interchange standard. EDI mapping converts the names of data elements (data fields) between two trading organizations. Traditional EDI transmits data through a value-added network (VAN) operated by a service provider. Web-based EDI transmits data across the Internet.

Electronic discovery (e-discovery)   Searching electronic records to gather evidence. The legal discovery process allows another party the right to investigate records for the purpose of compiling evidence relevant to their claim. Electronic discovery may include recovery of *deleted files* and the search of *standing data* on offline media, including backup tapes. Persons accused of obstructing the discovery process face serious criminal charges.

Electronic vaulting   A process of transmitting data to a remote backup site. This ensures that the most recent files are available in the event of a disaster. A common implementation is to transmit live data files to a remote server.

Elliptic curve cryptography   A new type of encryption using specific points on a three-dimensional random curve as the encryption key.

Emergency management team (EMT)   Senior executives with full delegation of authority to make decisions on behalf of the entire organization without additional delays or approval by other executives. During business continuity events or disaster recovery, this team will make the best possible decisions necessary for the survival of the organization.

Emergency Operations Center (EOC)   Alternate command post that houses the *emergency management team (EMT)* during business continuity events or disaster recovery.

Emergency power off (EPO)   A switch that shuts off computer room power in an emergency. The national fire protection act requires an emergency power disconnect to protect human life from electrocution. The EPO switch is located near the exit door.

Encryption   The process of converting human-readable clear text into decipherable gibberish. The objective is to hide the contents of the file from other people.

Encryption algorithm   A mathematical transformation procedure used to encrypt and decrypt files.

Encryption key   A unique randomizer used by the encryption algorithm to ensure confidentiality. Strength of *symmetric-key encryption* and the *PKI* private key is based on the absolute secrecy of the secret/private key. Secrecy is dependent on limiting use of the key, isolating the key, and regular rotation (changing the key). Also see *key wrapping*.

End state   A description of the anticipated final outcome. The end state explains the attributes of the finished product.

Enterprise resource planning (ERP)   An integrated database used for planning resource requirements of multiple departments.

Entity-relationship diagram (ERD)   A diagram of data elements and their relationship to other data. The ERD specifies data names and data attributes to be used by the software program being developed. The ERD is created in the requirements and design phase to build a database schema.

Equal error rate (EER)   A setting used in biometrics, which provides a compromise between the false acceptance rate (FAR) and the false rejection rate (FRR). Also referred to as the Crossover error rate.

Ethics   Discipline of following forthright and honest conduct without impropriety, deceit, or conflicting agenda.

Evidence   A collection of verifiable information that is used to prove or disprove a point. The best evidence is both independent and objective.

Evidence timing   The timely disclosure of evidence relevant to the situation. Evidence timing in computer systems also refers to the time window in which data is available before being lost or overwritten during normal processing.

Evolutionary development   See *iterative development*.

Exception report   A report identifying data and transactions that may be incorrect and may warrant additional attention. Exception reports can be manual or automated.

Expert   An individual with a significant amount of direct experience, or special training with direct experience, and the ability to deduce a correct conclusion when everyone else would form an incorrect conclusion.

Expert system   Specialized computer database software used to provide a recommendation based on the knowledge recorded from an expert. Expert systems possess between 50,000 and 100,000 discrete points of information. The system uses an inference engine to identify possible conditions relating to the problem and their meaning.

Exposure   The adverse consequence that will occur if a potential threat becomes reality.

Extensible Authentication Protocol (EAP)   A newer security protocol used in wireless networks with automatic encryption-key generation and authentication. EAP is a component of the new 802.11i standard known as *robust security network (RSN)*. EAP replaces the seriously insecure method of using a preshared encryption key in the outdated *Wired Equivalent Privacy (WEP)* protocol.

Extensible Markup Language (XML)   A universal program architecture designed to share information between different programming languages. XML uses three underlying programming specifications: Simple Object Access Protocol (SOAP) is used to define APIs; Web Services Description Language (WSDL) identifies the format to use; and Universal Description, Discovery, and Integration protocol (UDDI) acts as an online directory of available web services.

External audit   An audit performed by an external party, including business partners. External audits may be biased if the auditor is related to the auditee through a trading partner relationship (client, vendor, and subcontractor). Also see *independent audit*.

Extranet   An Internet communication server used to exchange files between the organization and external business partners.

F

False acceptance rate (FAR), type 2 error   An error condition in *biometrics* that allows an unwanted user to access the system by mistake. This is less common overall because of the lower volume of attempts.

False positive   Generating an alert by mistake or error.

False rejection rate (FRR), type 1 error   Used in *biometrics*, false rejection means to reject access to an authorized user by mistake. This is the most common type of biometric authentication error.

Failure to enroll (FTER)   An error in the collection of biometric data that prevents the information from being recorded.

Fault-tolerant   A system that can continue to operate after a single failure condition has occurred. RAID systems are designed to be tolerant of individual disk failures. The success of the fault-tolerant system depends on the system being able to identify that the fault has occurred.

Feasibility study (SDLC phase 1)   An initial study to determine the benefits that will be derived from a new system and the payback schedule for the investment required.

Financial audit   A review of financial records to determine their accuracy.

Fire-control system   A fire-suppression system using water or chemicals to extinguish a fire in the data processing facility.

Firewall   According to *The American Heritage Dictionary*, a fireproof wall used as a barrier to prevent the spread of fire. In information systems, the term refers to a combination of hardware and software used to restrict access between public and private networks.

Firmware   The solid-state memory chips on a circuit board containing a read-only program designed to operate the hardware.

Flowchart   A systematic diagram that details the procedures for data manipulation and data transformation in a computer program. The program flowchart is developed during SDLC design in phase 2.

Foreign key   Data in the database is stored in separate tables to improve speed. A foreign key is the link between data in different database tables. When the links are valid, the database has *referential integrity*.

Formal   Documented in writing and authorized by management.

Fourth-generation language (4GL)   An English-like programming language with integrated database support. 4GL programming tools allow the forms and database to be generated by using a drag-and-drop functionality. The 4GL does not create the data transformation procedures necessary for business functionality.

Full backup   The process of copying every file that exists onto backup media such as a tape cartridge. The full backup is used in combination with incremental or differential backup strategies to restore the most recent copy of data. The ability to restore files from a full backup is used to calculate the recovery point objective (RPO). Files that cannot be restored are lost.

Function Point Analysis (FPA)   A software estimation method used to forecast development, based on the number of system inputs, number of outputs, and complexity. FPA is used in the SDLC feasibility study to calculate resources and time required. FPA can be used as a baseline to measure the progress of software development.

Function testing   Tests run during software development to determine the integrity of specific program functions.

Fuzzification   Reducing the detail in an average by using an unstratified mean to roll the details into a larger lump-sum value.

G

Gateway   A device running software to transfer data between two networking protocols. The gateway is an OSI layer 7 application. Examples include a mainframe gateway converting TCP/IP to 3270 sessions.

General controls   Higher-level policies, standards, and procedures used across the entire organization to govern everyone's behavior.

Generally Accepted Accounting Procedures (GAAP)   A well-recognized set of agreed-upon procedures for auditing financial records and information systems.

Guideline   A list of recommendations to follow in the absence of an existing standard.

H

Hacker   A malicious attacker of a computer system. A secondary meaning in computer programming is a programmer able to generate usable applications where none existed previously.

Halon   A chlorine-based gas previously used in fire-suppression systems. Halon gas is now illegal because of the damaging effects of chlorine products on the earth's ozone. Halon is still used on aircraft because of the severity of fires while in flight. Computer room halon is replaced by FM-200, NAF-S-3 and other products.

Hand geometry   Used in *biometrics* to verify a user's identity based on the unique three-dimensional geometry of the human user's hand. Common examples include checking wrinkle patterns, measuring joints, and analyzing blood-vessel patterns.

Hashed Message Authentication Code (HMAC)   A hashed message file is used to verify message integrity (to prove no changes occurred) and is also encrypted to provide authentication of the sender. The more common hashing algorithms with encryption are MD-5 and SHA-1 (also known as SHA-160). Newer HMAC versions include SHA-256 and SHA-512. The format is [HMAC name] dash [output size]. SHA-512 means SHA algorithm with 512 output size.

Hashing algorithm   The mathematical formula used to reduce the contents of any size message file into a smaller output file representing a unique value that is very difficult to duplicate. The hash algorithm creates a unique output file that can be used like a tamper seal. If the source message is altered, the hashing algorithm generates a different hash value when regenerated by the recipient. Both sender and recipient must use the same hash algorithm.

Hash file   A mathematical value generated from the original message file for verifying integrity. The sender runs their original message through a hash algorithm to produce a unique hash value. The sender sends their message and hash file to the recipient. The recipient reruns the same hash process and compares the sender's hash file against the hash generated by the recipient. The purpose of a hash file is to determine whether any changes have occurred to the original message file. Matching hash files indicate that no changes occurred; different hash values indicate that the message has been altered.

Heuristics   Programmed rules inside the database used to evaluate data by sorting for possible correlations. Used in *expert systems*, *decision support systems*, email spam filters, and many common business applications. *Antivirus software* and *intrusion detection and prevention systems* use heuristics to determine which requests to accept or discard.

Honey net   A fake network created to entice a hacker to attack. The purpose is for the attack to generate an alarm signaling the early warning of a hacker's presence.

Honey pot   An individual system set up to entice a hacker and generate an early warning alarm of the hacker's presence.

Host based   Software that is installed on an individual host for the purpose of monitoring activity on that specific host.

Host enumeration   Automated software discovery of all the active hosts on a network.

Hot site   An alternate processing facility that is fully equipped with all the necessary computer equipment and capable of commencing operation as soon as the latest data files have been loaded. Hot sites are capable of being in full operation within minutes or hours.

Hub   See *network hub*.

Hybrid sourcing   A combination of using in-house workers and *outsourcing* selected processes.

I

Identification   The process of determining a user's identity based on their claim of identity. The identity claimed by the user must be verified with an authentication process before access is granted.

Ignorance   Lack of awareness or absence of knowledge. The fastest way to be convicted for violating a law or other obligation. Ignorance can be cured by education. Also see *stupidity*.

Immunization   See *inoculation*.

Impact   The level of damage that will occur.

Incident   Any disruptive event, especially those that may cause harm.

Incident Command System (ICS)   ICS is the internationally recognized, government-mandated standard for crisis command during disaster recovery and business continuity events.

Incident commander (IC)   Under the international Incident Command System (ICS), the incident commander is the first person to arrive on the scene regardless of training or experience. Even a four-year-old child calling 911 for help is the initial incident commander until relieved by a more qualified person. The incident commander directs the emergency response activities.

Incident handling   The systematic process of responding to an incident in order to determine its significance and impact. Proper incident handling will prevent negligent activities that could destroy meaningful evidence. A computer incident always has the potential of being a cyber crime scene.

Incremental backup   The process of backing up only the files that have changed since the last backup was run. An incremental backup uses the file archive bit flag to signal files that should be copied to the backup tape.

Independence   Independence in an audit refers to the auditor not being related to the audit subject. The desire is for the auditor to be objective and free of conflict because they are not related to the audit subject.

Independent audit   Independent audits are conducted by an auditor which is not related to the auditee and therefore represent a high value of assurance that can be used for external purposes, including regulatory licensing.

Information assets   Data that has a value.

Information processing facility (IPF)   The building that houses the data center.

Inherent risk   The natural or built-in risk that always exists.

Initial program load (IPL)   Computer systems are susceptible to compromise while the system is loading and before the security control front end becomes active. Computer software is vulnerable to configuration changes during the initial program loading. A system in IPL mode is in supervisory mode.

Inoculation   A technique used by antivirus software to replace the original end-of-file (EOF) marker with a new EOF marker generated by the antivirus program. Anything attempting to attach itself to the new EOF marker indicates a virus attack.

Integrated audit   A type of audit that combines financial records review with an assessment of internal IS controls.

Integrated development environment (IDE)   An advanced software development tool used for writing programs. The IDE provides built-in functions for capturing the software design, commands, and macros for creating program code and debugging testing.

Integrity   Unbiased honesty by a person dealing with other people or in the records of transactions.

Interface   A specification of physical characteristics, electrical signals, format, and procedures used to communicate between systems.

Internal audit   Internal audits are used to help the auditee improve their score. Reports from internal audits may be used only for internal purposes. The reports contain a known bias, which reduces their corresponding value of representations to low or moderate.

Internet   The shared public communications network.

Internet layer   The equivalent to OSI layer 3, the Networking layer, in the TCP/IP model.

Internet Protocol (IP)   The de facto communications protocol and addressing standard used on the Internet. IP is implemented with TCP for connection-oriented data transmission or UDP for connectionless transmission.

Interoperability   The ability for hardware and software systems from different manufacturers to communicate with each other.

Intranet   A private internal business network.

Intrusion detection and prevention system (IDPS)   A technical system designed to alert personnel to activity that may indicate the presence of a hacker. An intrusion detection system is a type of network hacker alarm. The *IDS* term has been officially updated by the government to *intrusion detection and prevention systems (IDPS)*. Preprogrammed response procedures activate stored commands to modify the IDPS to block an attack before it can penetrate (prevention activity).

Intrusion detection system (IDS)   See *intrusion detection and prevention system (IDPS)* for updated terminology.

IPsec   A security-based implementation of the Internet Protocol. IPsec offers encryption during data transmission or the tunneling of encrypted packets through network routing with an ISP.

Iris scan   A type of biometric technique that uses the unique characteristics found in the iris of the human eye.

Irrelevant   Having no significant bearing on the final outcome. Irrelevant, or trivial, information will not change the results.

IS steering committee   A committee composed of business executives for the purpose of conveying current business priorities and objectives to IT management. The steering committee provides governance for major projects and the IT budget.

IT governance   A clearly stated process of leadership to lead and control the performance expected from the IT function. The focus of IT governance is control over the technology environment.

Iterative development   The progressive development of software through a succession of multiple versions.

J

Java   A very portable object-oriented programming language created by Sun Microsystems. Java can run on cellular phones, iPods, and most computing devices. Java has very good security mechanisms.

Java Virtual Machine (JVM)   An internal processing environment for running a Java program inside of another Java program session, also known as a virtual machine. The partitioning of resources creates a secure environment to protect the rest of the computer system from harm.

Joint venture   Two or more obligators (persons or organizations) bind themselves without actual partnership or corporate designation in a specific venture with the risk, liability, and potential profits shared between the parties. All parties participating in the venture share a communal liability for the failure of the other party.

Just-in-time inventory (JIT)   A process of scheduling the minimum amount of inventory to arrive shortly before it is required in the manufacturing process. The objective is to reduce inventory on hand. The opposite of JIT is stockpiling inventory. JIT practices create a quandary with business continuity plans.

K

Key distribution   The safe process of exchanging keys to be used in a cryptographic system for encryption and decryption.

Key goal indicator (KGI)   The KGI identifies a specific goal to be reached. KPI (historical score) is used together with KGI (goal) in planning and forecasting.

Key performance indicator (KPI)   A historical score of business process performance. Unfortunately, the score may indicate a failure has occurred before corrective action can be taken.

Key wrapping   Encryption keys must be stored and transmitted in a different encrypted format to protect them from harm. A user should not have direct access to encryption keys. Encryption keys are re-encrypted with a different algorithm that uses a different key to obscure the original key. This key wrapping technique protects the real key from harm. It's extremely difficult to tell where the wrapping stops and the key inside begins.

Keyboard remapping   Changing the normal function of keys on the keyboard to execute different commands.

Knowledge base   A database of information derived from the knowledge of individuals who perform the related tasks. Knowledge-based systems are used for decision support systems.

L

Leased line   A dedicated communications line between two locations, such as a T-1 circuit. Also known as a circuit-switched connection. This type of connection is charged by distance covered regardless of volume of data transmitted.

Least privilege   Granting only the minimum access necessary to perform the job function or role. Least privilege is implemented to improve confidentiality.

Legal deadline (LD)   Used in business continuity and disaster recovery planning to identify potential violations that must be avoided or that require special handling to minimize penalties. Examples include mandatory government filings, required legal disclosures, specific performance, and contract breaches. Also see *lost work in process (LWIP)*.

Lessons learned   A best practice for recording the analysis of problems and improvements that worked. The purpose is to avoid repeating mistakes while improving the technique used.

Local area network (LAN)   A computer network with boundaries that match the physical building.

Logic bomb   A programmed function inside of a computer software application designed to damage the system or data files on the occurrence of a particular event, date, or time. Logic bombs are extremely difficult to locate.

Logical access   Electronic access to a system without being physically present.

Logical backup   The process of copying current data files for records retention (safe keeping). Logical backup will ignore *deleted files* and temporary system data in *swap space*. Also see *bitstream imaging*.

Lost work in process (LWIP)   Work tasks and data processing that were lost by a disaster, disruption, or failure. All work since the last backup is lost and must be re-created. LWIP may cause a violation of a *legal deadline (LD)*. LWIP needs to be calculated by the organization when planning their *recovery point objective (RPO)* and *recovery time objective (RTO)*.

M

MAC address   A unique serial number burned into the network interface card by the manufacturer. The Media Access Control (MAC) address operates in the Data-Link layer (layer 2) of the OSI model. The MAC address is used to tie the TCP/IP address to a particular computer.

Mainframe   A large-scale, traditional, multiuser, multiprocessor system designed with excellent internal controls.

Major software release   A new generation of software or a major design change resulting in a new version. Major releases tend to occur in 12–24 month intervals.

Malware   A family classification of computer programs designed to intentionally cause malicious damage.

Management oversight   A committee or reporting hierarchy to convey questionable situations involving management to the highest level of authority, often the board of directors.

Mandatory access control (MAC)   An access control system, based on rules that require the user to have an explicit level of access that matches the appropriate security label. The only way to increase access is by a formal promotion of the user ID to the next security level.

Mantrap   A physical location between doorway barriers that is designed to trap an unauthorized individual between the closed doors. Fully caged turnstiles can provide a mantrap to capture potential intruders.

Manual reconciliation   The process of manually verifying that records match.

Manufacturing requirements planning (MRP)   A computer database designed to schedule the requirements of manufacturing design, purchasing, scheduling, and the manufacturing production process.

Masquerading   Pretending to possess an identity under false pretense.

Materiality   Materiality applies to evidence. It is materially significant if the evidence will have enough bearing to change the final outcome.

Maximum acceptable outage (MAO)   The longest period of *downtime* that an organization can survive from a specific outage involving a system, process, or resource.

Maximum tolerable downtime (MTD)   Synonym for *maximum acceptable outage* (MAO) used as a negative connotation.

Meshed network   Connection of redundant links.

Message digest   A hash file of a fixed length created by a source file of any length. The purpose of the message digest is to indicate whether the source file has changed.

Message modification   The alteration of a message to change its contents.

Methodology   A systematic process of procedures to generate a desired outcome.

Metropolitan area network (MAN)   A type of limited-area network in which the boundary is equal to the city's metropolitan area.

Middleware   Utility software that operates on program interfaces and is invisible to both the user and the database server. Middleware performs an intermediary service between two programs.

Minor software update   Small corrective update issued by the software developer to fix problems found in a major version previously released. Also known as a software patch or minor software release. Also see *major software release.*

Minutiae   A special template of biometric data converted into a count of specific characteristics that is unique to each user.

Mirrored   Duplicate or redundant components operating in parallel.

Multicast   To transmit data across the network to several specific stations concurrently.

Multiprocessing   Using multiple processors.

Multitasking   Running multiple tasks concurrently in a time-sharing mode by allocating a specific amount of resources.

Multithreading   Running several instances of a program concurrently for multiple users.

N

Netmask   An overlay setting used to parse the IP address into two distinct portions representing the unique network address and unique host address. Without this setting, the computer will be confused and unable to communicate on the network.

Network based   A hardware or software device that is watching the communications traffic flowing across the network to other systems.

Network File System (NFS)   A method of sharing disk systems across the network by using remote procedure calls. NFS was invented by Sun Microsystems to share hard disks with multiple users across the network.

Network hub   An OSI layer 1 device designed to relay electrical transmissions and receive signals between computers.

Network layer   The OSI layer 3 functions of network addressing and routing.

Network monitoring   The process of monitoring communications, traffic, performance, and events by using packet analyzer (sniffer), *Simple Network Management Protocol (SNMP)*, and the Remote Monitoring Protocol (RMON).

Network switch   An intelligent bridge running on OSI layer 2. The network switch converts shared traffic from all ports into filtered discrete traffic for an individual port. The purpose is to reduce network congestion by eliminating traffic that does not involve the specific station.

Neural network   A type of decision-making system that uses weights and the simulation of human synapses to make a decision.

Nondiscretionary access control   A method of access control based on job role and required tasks.

Nonrepudiation   A technical process designed to eliminate the opportunity for a person to reject or renounce their participation. Intended to protect the recipient from claims of denial by the other party.

Nonvolatile data   Persistent data retained on the hard disk and other storage media after system shutdown.

Normalization   The process of removing duplicate, redundant data from a database.

O

Object   In object-oriented programming, the program object contains both data and procedural methods. Program objects are able to delegate to another program object.

Object class   An administrative grouping of program objects with similar attributes or related behavior. Similar to the classification of insects by their shared attributes, or classification of manned spacecraft versus unmanned spacecraft. Programming objects are classified by similarity of their attributes and operating methods.

Object code   The machine-executable instructions that are output from the programmer's compiling process. Object code is designed to run on the computer and is unreadable to humans.

Objective   A specific goal or target.

Objectivity   Impartiality, fairness. This term is used in relation to fair and unbiased information used in an audit. An auditor who acts in a manner that is fair and unbiased has objectivity.

Object-oriented database (OODB)   A database designed for data with an unknown format and structure. OODB is very flexible and may be quite complex. OODB is good for organizing information such as MP3 files with photographic images and other programs as items inside the database.

Open system   Software that is readily available by using nonproprietary programming methods in its design. The recipient receives the human-readable *source code* with the ability to make any internal changes they desire. An open system can exchange data with a *closed system* by using a specific *application programming interface (API)*. The Apache web server, Linux operating system, OpenOffice.org application, and SugarCRM software are examples of open systems.

Open Systems Interconnect (OSI)   An international reference model used to explain the functions in network communications.

Operating system (OS)   A computer software program that interfaces between hardware devices and the user's application. Operating systems provide the coordination of resources and the user interface.

Operational audit   A type of audit that reviews the internal controls used in daily operation.

Output controls   A combination of physical and administrative controls used to protect the confidentiality of system output. Examples of output controls include report distribution lists and physical security of specialized output such as payroll checks.

Outsourcing   The contractual arrangement to transfer ongoing operations to an external service provider.

P

Packet replay   An attack that replays a series of previously recorded legitimate network messages in an attempt to fool the recipient into believing that the attacker is a legitimate user.

Packet switching   A method of transmitting data through a variety of different paths en route to its destination. The user is billed by the data packets sent and not the route or distance traveled.

Packet-filtering firewall   A primitive type of network firewall that filters traffic based on source and destination addresses.

Paper test   A desktop review of printed documentation.

Parallel testing   Running two systems in parallel to verify the integrity of transactions and minimize risk during the system migration process.

Passive attack   Eavesdropping and other covert techniques used to collect information.

Password   A short sequence of characters used in single-factor (weak) authentication. Most user passwords are usually six to eight characters in length. Passwords should be changed every 30 to 90 days. The password itself should not be a word printed in any language, but instead a set of alphanumeric characters that is memorable to the user.

Patch   See *minor software update.*

Patch management   A planned method of testing and tracking *minor software updates* prior to implementation in production. Minor updates (or *patches*) are known to have unexpected consequences that can alter or disable other controls. All changes should be installed in a separate test environment and *regression tested* before being installed in production. The cost of separate testing can be justified by using the price of failure (*price of nonconformance*).

Patent   A public record of a unique design or function to which the author/inventor is granted exclusive rights for a limited period of time. Patents require the inventor to furnish a complete and functional blueprint of the design for anyone to reproduce a working replica with the exact same functionality. This is why intellectual trade secrets shall never be patented. Future patent applicants must show how their new design does not infringe on existing patents. Also see *trade secret*.

PDCA cycle   William Shewhart's quality planning cycle of Plan, Do, Check, Act. The PDCA model may be mistakenly referred to as the Deming PDCA cycle because Edwards Deming was a student of Shewhart.

Penetration testing   A type of test designed to gauge possible penetration through the system security mechanisms by exploiting known vulnerabilities. Penetration testing should be conducted only under the supervision of trained auditors with formal approval of executive management. Separation of duties must be enforced.

Pervasive controls   Specific mid-level controls over any technology shared across multiple departments. IT systems exist in almost all departments, and therefore IT-type controls must also exist in each department regardless of who is in charge.

Phishing   A social engineering technique designed to trick the user into divulging confidential information such as user ID, password, bank account information, and social security number.

Physical control   A type of control implemented by using barriers to prevent unauthorized access.

Physical layer   The lowest layer of the OSI model, which deals with physical cabling and electrical signals.

Ping test   Submarines detect other objects by using a single broadcast transmission and waiting for the sound reflection (ping) to bounce back. Similarly, computers use ping commands on the network to request that all machines on the same subnet respond with a ping-reply transmission.

Policy   A high-level statement by management specifying an objective that requires mandatory compliance for all persons of lower authority.

Portfolio management   Selecting projects based on the principles of "highest and best use" of available resources for generating the best return on investment (ROI). Projects are selected or cancelled according to which ones will generate the best return under the current circumstances. Similar to trading stock investments or baseball cards to improve the overall value of your collection.

Postimplementation review   A review of the system after it is placed in operation to determine whether it has fulfilled its original objectives. New objectives may be identified that require the system to be modified to attain compliance with the new requirements.

Presentation layer   This layer of the OSI model deals with screen formatting and display properties. Presentation runs on OSI layer 6.

Preventative control   A type of control that seeks to stop a particular type of event from occurring. Preventative controls may be implemented by using administrative methods, technical methods, and physical methods.

Price of conformance (POC)   The cost savings for doing it right the first time. Proper training and planning is a POC expense that conserves money and time by avoiding the additional costs of failure.

Price of nonconformance (PONC)   Represents the added costs of failure for not doing it right the first time. Added costs include penalties, redoing work, and uncompensated warranty repair. PONC usually exceeds the original profit margin.

Primary key   A unique entry into a database record that is required for the record to be valid. The primary key for user information might be the login ID. Without the login ID, the user's details would be invalid. Primary keys can be user ID numbers to prevent conflicts from using last names for people. Last names can change as users get married or divorced.

Private Branch Exchange (PBX)   The telephone switch that creates virtual private extensions for the users in the organization. The telephone switch is a technology resource that must be protected from hackers.

Private key   A file used as a randomizer in encryption algorithms. The private key must be kept secret from all other users in order to protect the confidentiality of encrypted files.

Procedure   A mandatory set of steps used as a cookbook recipe for a desired result. Procedures provide the day-to-day low-level execution necessary to support a standard.

Process audit   Evaluating the process method by measuring the inputs, sequence of activities, and output to determine whether the process meets the published requirements (specifications).

Product audit   Checks the product attributes against design specifications to determine whether the product meets the intended requirements. Attributes may include connectivity features, audit logging, security controls, and the quality of documentation.

Program Evaluation Review Technique (PERT)   A project management technique used to determine the critical path and to forecast the time and resources necessary to complete the most important elements of a specific project.

Program management   Managing a series of individual projects to create an ongoing operation, also known as a functional support program. Examples include maintenance, customer service, auditing for annual compliance, and new product development.

Project management   A management methodology used to plan and control the execution of a unique project to maximize its outcome based on limitations of time, resources, and scope.

Protection profile (PP)   A defined list of testing objectives applicable to the intended use of the system under evaluation (*target of evaluation*, or TOE). Different protection profiles exist in the *Common Criteria* (ISO 15408) depending on whether the system's role will be a workstation, file server, database, or security device.

Protocol   A formal specification of rules for interfaces and procedures used in communication.

Protocol stack   Different layers of services provided inside a communication protocol, also known as stack of protocol services.

Prototyping   A system development technique used to create initial versions of software functionality. The prototype is focused on proving a method or gaining early user acceptance. Prototypes seldom have any internal controls.

Provisioning   Administrative process of dividing services for allocation to the user.

Proxy firewall   A type of firewall that prevents direct access to network resources. The user request is rerouted through a proxy application that will filter the request for security compliance and present the filtered requests to the desired application on behalf of the user.

Pseudocode   A set of commands and macros developed into a custom template inside of an *integrated development environment (IDE)* programming tool. The software engineer designs the structure and function of the software inside the IDE for ease and maintainability. The IDE tool converts the pseudocode into actual programming code for the machine to use. Most fourth-generation programming tools use pseudocode templates to write programs.

Public key   A variable used in the encryption algorithm that is mathematically related to the private key. The public key is freely distributed by the sender to parties interested in communicating with the sender. A sender and recipient would exchange public keys in order to encrypt the files for transmission.

Public-key infrastructure (PKI)   See *asymmetric-key encryption*.

Q

Qualified opinion   The auditor has placed restrictions on the nature, use, or content of their findings. The audit may have encountered problems in scope, time, and thoroughness of tests, or content of available evidence. Also see *unqualified opinion*.

Quality   Development of well-defined specifications while ensuring adherence to those specifications. Quality is created in the planning and design phases, not by postinspection. Quality provides a cost savings when compared to the added costs of failure (*price of nonconformance*).

Quality assurance (QA)   A process of measurement standards designed to ensure product integrity.

Quality control (QC)   The process of planning, testing, and reviewing to ensure that the product meets the minimum acceptable performance specifications (level of quality).

R

Radio frequency identification (RFID)   Insecure method of reading radio signals to identify products, people, or physical items. Any RFID tag that can be read can also be duplicated.

Rapid Application Development (RAD)   A software development methodology that automates portions of the SDLC process. RAD does not provide the enterprise-level requirements planning necessary for a business system. RAD is designed to speed coding time in smaller software modules.

Reciprocal agreement   An agreement between two parties to help each other in the event of a disaster. Most reciprocal agreements are ineffective and unenforceable. The concept is popular because it does not bear any direct cost to either party. The reciprocal agreement ignores inherent conflicts that exist between two organizations. An exception exists regarding cooperative ownership of hot sites between financial organizations.

Records management   Collective process of classifying information to ensure proper safeguards and control with the goal of providing complete integrity. Records must be created, labeled for proper handling, kept in safe storage, have controlled distribution, and ultimately be retired with proper disposal. Records of real property transactions are required to be kept forever. All record management and criminal penalties are judged by comparison to the ISO 15489 standard for records management.

Recovered work in process (RWIP)   Work tasks and data processing interrupted by a disaster or system failure. Recovered work is reprocessed according to the designated *recovery time objective (RTO)*.

Recovery point objective (RPO)   Refers to a point backward in time to which the loss of data is acceptable. This means that work in progress since the last data backup will be lost.

Recovery time objective (RTO)   The estimated time to recover a system based on the organization's capabilities and maximum acceptable outage.

Redundant Array of Independent—or Inexpensive—Disks (RAID)   A technical method of providing redundant disk storage space by using multiple disk drives. Previously known as Redundant Array of Inexpensive Disks until hardware vendors discovered the opportunity for a price increase.

Referential integrity   When information contained in two or more data tables is valid across the links inside the database (*foreign key* relationship). A failure of referential integrity indicates a failed program or corrupt database.

Registration authority (RA)   A delegated representative of the *certificate authority* (CA) with the ability to issue a valid *digital certificate*. For example, a travel agent is the registration authority for selling airline tickets. The airline is the certificate-issuing authority and issues an electronic ticket (a type of digital certificate).

Regression testing   The process of retesting a system after changes to ensure that the change does not create any additional undesired complications.

Regulatory controls   Controls placed on industry by the government.

Relational database structure   A type of database that splits information between multiple tables while maintaining a link between the data for related entries. A relational database keeps a relation between different data elements.

Remote access server (RAS)   A service that provides security and authentication for remote users.

Remote procedure call (RPC)   A program method in client/server computing that allows a computer to request services from another computer without having to develop specific procedures for each program.

Residual risk   The amount of risk that remains after all controls have been implemented and mitigation efforts have been completed.

Retina scan   A biometrics technique that maps the unique pattern of veins in the back of the human eyeball.

Revenue objective (RO)   Used in business continuity planning to demonstrate the minimum revenue necessary for survival at various stages of recovery. Also used in business process reengineering as a claim of the expected benefit for reengineering a process.

Reverse engineering   An engineering technique used to steal the secrets of a competitor for the purpose of developing your own product. Reverse engineering is usually a violation of the software user license agreement.

Right to audit   The contractual rights of an organization to audit a third-party service provider. The right to audit must be clearly defined in the contract along with the expected terms of the audit.

Ring topology   A networking topology that creates two paths between the senders and receivers. The most common implementation is an IBM token ring for a local area network. The public telephone company uses a fiber ring topology for a redundant connection between central offices.

Risk   The likelihood that an unfortunate event will occur and cause a loss of assets.

Risk assessment   The process of reviewing risks, threats, and vulnerabilities to determine appropriate controls.

Risk management   The process of assessing risks in determining the organization's response. Acceptable responses could be mitigation, avoidance, acceptance, or transference.

Risk-based audit   The technique to determine the high-risk areas of an organization. Priority would be given to audit the high-risk areas first, before low-risk areas.

Robust security network (RSN)   A new 802.11i standard for security on wireless networks (2005). Mandated by the U.S. government to replace network equipment using the outdated and insecure *WEP* method of preshared encryption keys. RSN uses *Extensible Authentication Protocol (EAP)* with temporal keys and port-based access control.

Role-based access control (RBAC)   A type of nondiscretionary access control based on job duties.

Root kit   A malicious hacker program designed to unsuspectingly install a backdoor without the consent of the system user. A root kit will subvert the operating system kernel security and operate in stealth to hide its existence. Normal system utilities are usually unable to detect the presence of a root kit.

Router   A networking device that uses traffic routing to forward a message to its intended destination. Network routers operate on OSI layer 3.

Routing protocol   The procedure and formula used to direct communications across the available path. Static routing will always follow the same path. Dynamic routing will use a formula of metrics to redirect communications along the best available route at the present time.

Run-to-run totals   A process that tracks the total number of submissions to ensure that all transactions have been processed.

S

Scenario approach   Planning exercises center around solving the problems presented in a simulated event (scenario). This lends a credible purpose bearing on reality in the exercise. Scenario exercises are used in planning to uncover previous assumptions and interesting quirks used in the decision process. Assumptions may no longer be valid. You may discover additional defects in the decision criteria.

Screened host   A single computer host protected by a firewall and accessible by both internal and external users.

Screened subnet   A subnet of multiple computer hosts protected by a firewall and accessible by both internal and external users. A screened subnet is also known as a *demilitarized zone (DMZ)*. War veterans will tell you that you can still get killed in a demilitarized zone.

Script kiddies   Individuals who execute scripted programs or utilities without comprehensive knowledge of the internal mechanisms being executed. Your author is a script kiddy; every time I run a macro or setup script that I didn't write. Script kiddies also refer to novice hackers using automated attack tools downloaded from the Internet.

Secure Shell (SSH)   An encrypted terminal session providing additional security for the user.

Secure Sockets Layer (SSL)   Session-layer security and encryption between a user and a server. SSL is a common form of security for virtual private networks (VPNs). This method uses private-key encryption with a digital certificate on the server.

Security Parameter Index (SPI)   A security specification used in the header of the IPsec protocol to identify encryption keys used in communication.

Security policy   A formal statement by management of the importance in implementing proper security controls. A second definition is a set of rules implemented to protect the organization.

Security target (ST)   Security targets represent the chosen *Common Criteria* standard of performance acceptable from the system under evaluation (TOE). To fail this target would result in a lower assurance rating. Also see *protection profile (PP)* and *target of evaluation (TOE)*.

Segregation of duties   The separation of transaction authorization from other normal work activities. The purpose of segregation of duties is to ensure that no changes are executed without being observed by another individual. The purpose of the control is to minimize fraud, error, and omission.

Server mirroring   See *mirrored*.

Service delivery objective (SDO)   The level of service to be available at a particular point in time. This may be full-service for all users or service for a particular core process only.

Service-level agreement (SLA)   A contractual agreement between the user and the service provider that outlines an acceptable level of support for business processing.

Servlet   A web-based program that runs on the server, also known as server-side includes (SSI). This type of program does not download to the PC as an applet would. However, applets can access servlets for better performance by using distributed processing.

Session layer   Layer 5 of the OSI model, which manages service communication requests between systems.

Shell   A technical name for the user's display session on the computer.

Signature based   A technical method that relies on the database of known software behavior. Signature files indicate a particular type of attack for virus protection or intrusion detection.

Simple Object Access Protocol (SOAP)   Used in XML programming to define the *application programming interface* (API) being used.

Single sign-on (SSO)   A technical method that uses encryption to allow the user to simultaneously log in to all the network servers. The objective is to increase security with stronger passwords and to make the network easier for the user. Unauthorized access under single sign-on may allow the compromise of all network resources.

Single-factor authentication   A type of authentication that uses passwords alone or tokens alone to authenticate a user. There is no real assurance that the user is the intended party.

Single-factor authentication is known as weak authentication regardless of the constructive strength of passwords used. The password indicates only that somebody known or unknown has logged in by using that password string.

Skills matrix   An administrative planning tool used to ensure that each task is assigned to the right person with the correct skills. Data in the matrix will demonstrate skill gaps and help justify training needs. This discourages the assignment of untrained personnel, or warm bodies.

Slack space   Refers to the difference between space currently used by files compared to the remnant space previously allocated on a hard disk. Slack space is the leftover space that may contain old deleted data which has not yet been overwritten.

Sniffer   A packet analyzer that can decode data transmissions across the network. A sniffer can also display passwords in transit.

Simple Network Management Protocol (SNMP)   An automated process for managing devices across the network by transmitting remote commands with passwords. The SNMP passwords are referred to as *community strings*. The management value of SNMP is high, and security usually is very poor. If properly configured, SNMP version 3 contains some security, provided all the devices are using version 3 and not the older versions of 1 and 2. Running mixed versions SNMP indicates a security failure. SNMP can remotely reconfigure or reboot a device.

Simple Network Management Protocol (SNMP) console   A dedicated system used by IT operations to actively monitor all the SNMP alerts generated by all the network devices. Examples include HP OpenView and Open network management system (Open NMS). IS security usually has its own SNMP monitoring console for separation of duties.

Sociability testing   Software tests to determine how well a program can operate with other programs (social behavior).

Social engineering   The process of gaining access by tricking a user into cooperating.

Sockets   Special software buffer used for communication between programs across the network.

Software baseline   A document recording all the design features agreed to be included in the software. Progress and changes are reported against this baseline to indicate actual performance in the development phase. Any variance in the development needs to be approved by the user and management.

Source code   The original version of computer programs that are still in human-readable form. Programmers write program in source code. The source code is fed into a compiler that generates object code to run on the machine. Source code needs to be protected for integrity. The source code represents the original set of instructions and a tremendous amount of work.

Source lines of code (SLOC)   An older style of estimating the complexity of a program or of measuring progress of new development. SLOC is still used in software estimation. The value of this calculation is lost whenever you combine the SLOC count from different generations of programming tools.

Source routing   An old diagnostic protocol that allows the sender to specify the communications path to be used in spite of the network router settings configured by the network administrator. Source routing can circumvent firewalls and should be disabled on network devices.

Spamming   Replying to more people than necessary when you respond to an email message (also known as email flaming). It also refers to sending a large number of unsolicited email messages. Sending unsolicited commercial email advertisements is usually legal if the sender is fully identified and offers a working mechanism for the recipient to opt out of (stop receiving) future messages. Opt-out may be automated or offer the option of using a manual process.

Spiral model   A software development planning model that demonstrates the life cycle for multiple versions of software.

Split horizon   A network routing algorithm used to prevent communication loops by breaking the loop through the creation of an artificial horizon. Similar to the concept of creating the earth's international dateline.

Spoofing   Committing fraud by masquerading as a legitimate user or another system.

Standard   Specifies a minimum level of mandatory compliance to ensure uniform consistency with *integrity*.

Standing data   Information stored on the hard disk and other storage media. This information is "standing still" on the media and susceptible to attack, disclosure, or compromise.

Star topology   Uses a dedicated connection from the hub/switch to each node on the network. Star topology is the most flexible topology and has a higher cost due to the redundant use of cabling.

Stateful packet inspection   The technique used in third-generation firewalls to maintain a table of connectionless communications, also referred to as the state. Communication requests are monitored against the table to ensure that the request is in character with the transaction and is not a hacking attempt.

Statement on Auditing Standard (SAS)   A list of accounting standards put forth by the American Institute of Certified Public Accountants.

Stop-and-go sampling   A simple test used to prove that the likelihood of errors is low. It is used when errors are expected and allows the auditor to stop at the earliest possible opportunity.

Storage area network   A special type of network used to connect various storage devices to servers. Storage area networks are usually attached by fiber optics.

Strategic   Describes a fundamental method or change used to direct the organization toward an objective. Strategic objectives are usually in a time frame of three to five years.

Strong authentication   See *two-factor authentication*.

Stupid   Unknowledgeable person that is unable or unwilling to learn. Also see *ignorance*.

Subject   The target of the audit or control mechanism.

Subnet   A small group of computers and devices sharing the same broadcast domain. Subnets are connected to larger networks via routers. Also known as a subnetwork.

Substantive testing   A type of test that seeks to verify content and its integrity. Substantive tests include verifying count balances and performing physical inventory counts. Technical methods include executing detailed system scans to detect the effectiveness of a particular security configuration.

Swap space   A special area on the hard disk designated as a temporary location for data to be "swapped" out of RAM (electronic working memory). This improves system performance by moving selected tasks out of the way while other data is processed. Also known as *virtual memory*.

Switch   See *network switch*.

Symmetric-key encryption (secret key)   An encryption algorithm that uses the same secret key shared between the sender and the receiver. Symmetric-key encryption systems are time sensitive and will operate only while both ends are using the same key. Symmetric-key systems are faster than asymmetric encryption because the key does not have to be derived through mathematical calculation.

Syslog   A program designed to send system event logs to a remote system log server (also known as syslogging). A copy of all the log events is safely stored on a separate server. Log files are protected from the attacker, and the extra copy of log files enforces separation of duties.

System audit   Evaluates the management of a system, including its configuration. The purpose is to determine how well the system is managed by collecting evidence indicating its specific configuration settings.

System Development Life Cycle (SDLC)   A series of seven phases that represent the life cycle of software development. The phases are as follows: Feasibility Study, Requirements Definition, System Design, Development, Implementation, Postimplementation, and Disposal.

Systems Network Architecture (SNA)   Early hierarchical design created by IBM for connecting different computers.

T

Tactical   Describes the application of a procedure or method, hopefully in support of an organizational objective.

Target of evaluation (TOE)   A computer system or network device to be evaluated under the *Common Criteria* standard (ISO 15408). Also see *protection profile (PP)* and *security target (ST)*.

TCP/IP   Transmission Control Protocol running on the Internet Protocol. This has become synonymous with the Internet Protocol and accessing data across the network. Transmission Control Protocol is used for connection-oriented sessions on the Internet.

Temporal key   A temporary and uniquely generated encryption key. Also see *robust security network (RSN)*.

Threat   A potential danger that, if realized, will have a negative effect on assets.

Throughput   Effective speed metric for processing a complete set of specific transactions. Overall throughput speed usually varies according to the input, processing, and output requirements of particular transactions.

Top-down structured programming   A methodical design breaking down the high-level functions into an orderly design of smaller distinct program modules. Individual modules perform unique functions and can be updated or replaced with relative ease. Modules are linked together to form the finished program. In top-down programming, more time is spent on formal planning of functional specifications versus code development.

Trade secret   A unique process, tool, formula, pattern, or knowledge possessed by its creator and hidden from everyone else for the purpose of obtaining an advantage in the market. The owner must provide extensive protection to prevent disclosure, or risk forfeiting their claim. Trade secrets cannot be patented.

Transaction processing (TP) monitor   A software process that monitors the performance and health of the hardware running a database application. The purpose is to throttle back requests when necessary to avoid overloading the hardware. TP monitors help to prevent overloading or "crashing" the server with too much work.

Transborder data   Data crossing a political border. This data requires special handling. Transborder risks include legality of the data, differences in legal requirements, and extra protection necessary to prevent unauthorized disclosure. Examples include data transmission between countries or between trading partners in business.

Trapdoor   Secret point of entry into a system. Usually a hidden access technique left in the software by the developer for future use by the developer's technical support staff.

Tort damages   An injury or wrong inflicted upon another party and created by a violation of duty. It can be created by deprivation of a legal right, by violation of a private obligation with or without a contract, or by infraction of a duty to the public. Special damages will accrue. Examples include negligence or breach of an agreement in bad faith. The victim may be eligible for up to 20 times of the actual damages.

Traffic analysis   A technique used by an intruder to monitor communications and determine the most significant systems on the network. The objective is to build a map of network devices to be used for launching future attacks.

Transport layer   Layer 4 of the OSI model, responsible for the delivery of data transmissions across the network. Two common methods are the Transmission Control Protocol, which guarantees delivery, and the User Datagram Protocol, which does not provide any assurance of delivery.

Trojan horse   Malicious software that is intentionally hidden inside of a normal program. The concept is analogous with the Trojan horse story of ancient times.

Tuple   A row in a database, also known as the attribute of a particular data record.

Two-factor authentication   The processes of basing a decision regarding the user's identity on two pieces of information—usually, the user password and a unique physical characteristic of the user. Two-factor authentication is also known as strong authentication.

U

Unicast   A technical method used to transmit data to a single destination on the network.

Uninterruptible power supply (UPS)   An intelligent device that monitors commercial power and delivers supplemental battery power when necessary. The purpose of the UPS is to provide supplemental electricity for a brief period of time until the systems can be shut down. The UPS may have the capability to start an electric generator for extended runtimes during a power outage.

Unit testing   A testing technique to verify the functionality of an individual program module.

Universal Description, Discovery, and Integration (UDDI) protocol   An online directory used in XML programming to identify available web services.

Unqualified opinion   The auditor has no reservations about their findings, and there are no special restrictions on the use of the audit report. Also see *qualified opinion*.

Uptime   Refers to the system or resource being available for the user whenever they care to use it. Uptime is reported in simple comparison to all forms of downtime. Service-level agreements need to specify how uptime is reported and the specific operating hours that each system must be up and available for the user.

User acceptance testing (UAT)   A formal process of verifying that the system meets the user's requirements during the SDLC implementation phase.

User Datagram Protocol (UDP)   Provides for connectionless sessions with lower overhead by using Internet Protocol. UDP sessions are a best effort and will not ensure delivery to the destination.

V

Variable sampling   Used to designate a prorated dollar amount or weight of effectiveness to an entire subject population.

Version control   Tracking the details of tiny changes inside of software versions and revisions. Version control is the foundation of *configuration management*. Each change introduces the likelihood of unexpected consequences.

Virtual   Synonym for fake or not real.

Virtual local area network (VLAN)   An artificial grouping of systems into a common broadcast domain, also known as a subnetwork. Similar to a conference call between computers instead of people.

Virtual machine   A software partition simulating private processing, memory, and computer interfaces. The design was created for service bureaus using mainframes with different users running their own programs in time-sharing mode. Each partition is protected by isolation from the other partitions to prevent any disruption. The virtual machine concept has been copied for use in small computers by VMware, Parallels, and *Java VM*.

Virtual memory   See *swap space*.

Virtual private network (VPN)   The method of providing secure access to the network for a remote user by means of encryption.

Virus   A malicious, self-replicating computer program that spreads itself through the system as infected computer programs are executed. Viruses can destroy data or program files.

Volatile data   Information in the computer's working memory (RAM) that will be lost when power is shut off. Also see *nonvolatile data*.

Vulnerability   The weakness or path that can be exploited by a threat to damage an asset.

Vulnerability assessment   The process of reviewing risks and vulnerabilities to determine the organization's current level of exposure.

W

Walk-through testing   Used in disaster recovery testing to simulate the basic recovery process in order to clean any errors from the procedure.

War chalking   Process of physically marking insecure wireless access points to the Internet. Most war chalking has evolved into downloadable maps available on the Internet.

War driving   Process of driving through a neighborhood with technical tools to detect insecure wireless access points.

War walking   Similar purpose as *war driving*.

Warm site   A facility with basic utility services installed and some computer equipment but lacking all of the computer equipment necessary for recovery. A warm site needs to be built out before it can be used. It can be ready in days or weeks. A warm site offers a lower chance of success than a hot site.

Waterfall model   An early software development model that cascades the completion of each phase into the next phase.

Weak authentication   See *single-factor authentication*.

Web Services Description Language (WSDL)   Identifies the format used in the programming of XML objects.

Wet pipe   A fire-suppression system with water stored in the pipes at all times. This type of system is susceptible to corrosion and freezing.

White-box testing   Testing that checks the integrity of transactions while allowing the programmer to view the logical paths through the software. Also known as program code review. Internally developed software-programming scripts and *pseudocode* templates in human-readable form (not compiled) may be subjected to white-box tests. Conversely, compiled software is not readable and must use *black-box testing* techniques.

White hat   An honest software tester working in the security or audit department under a formal, structured test procedure to determine system vulnerabilities by using known hacker techniques. This individual never has any staff responsibilities in IT operations, to preserve the separation of duties.

Wide area network (WAN)   A computer network providing user access in multiple cities.

Wiping utility (memory wiping)   A special utility designed to overwrite the contents of storage media and RAM memory. This prevents any recovery of data from system memory or the hard disk. Wiping utilities can sanitize a system prior to redeployment, or be used by an individual to destroy evidence. Possession of wiping utilities should be a violation of the *acceptable use policy* unless specifically authorized in writing as a job requirement.

Wired Equivalent Privacy (WEP)   A *symmetric-key* (preshared key) encryption protocol originally designed to promote wireless security. The U.S. government published a declaration in April 2005 that all WEP installations are now considered totally insecure. Security was compromised by the industry vendor's poor choice of implementation that favors Plug and Play access over security. A radio beacon advertises the entire key to any listening device.

Wireless Application Protocol (WAP)   Loosely based on the OSI model and designed to display data on small screens with the limited resources of handheld devices.

Work in process (WIP)   Work tasks or data currently being processed at the time of disruption. Business continuity and disaster recovery plans need to identify how work in process will be recovered. The *recovered work in process (RWIP)* must be reprocessed in a timely manner to avoid violating a *legal deadline (LD)*.

Working papers   The auditor's notes, checklists, audit procedures, and results of audit testing. These documents must be kept secure via electronic file backup. The auditee is not permitted to see the working papers.

Worm   A malicious computer program that can travel independently through the network and infect systems.

Write blocker   A device used in forensic investigations to prevent any changes to the original data on the hard disk or media during *bitstream imaging.* Without a write blocker, the original media is considered tainted, tampered, or contaminated by any form of unintentional change that occurs during the investigation.

X

XML   See *Extensible Markup Language.*

Index

build vs. buy
decision making, 262

proactive controls, 82
problem management, 354
  acquisition phase,
      356–357
  digital forensic
      investigations,
      355–356
  examination, 357
  incident handling,
      354–355
  review, 358
  utilization, 357
problem state, 195
procedures
  description, 6, 7
  vs. work, 352
process technique, 68–69
processes
  auditing, 10
  in BPR, 159
      controls, 159
      documentation,
          158–159
      maps, 158
      understanding, 165
processing controls, 344–345
procurement management,
      44–45
product audits, 9
professional competence,
      ISACA standards, 14
program architecture, 309
program patches, 294
program scripts, 289, 290
programming languages,
      283–286, 285–286
progressive elaboration, 33
Project Communications
      Management knowledge
      area, 43
Project Cost Management
      knowledge area, 41
Project Human Resource
      Management knowledge
      area, 42–43
Project Integration
      Management knowledge
      area, 39
project management, 31–32
  approach, 265–266
  authority in, 36

defined, 34–35
diagramming techniques,
      45–48, 46–47
monitoring, 349, 350
planning and
      performance, 143
process framework,
      36–38, 38
project characteristics,
      32–34
quick reference, 38–45
requirements, 35–36
steering committee
      representation, 122
traditional, 266–267,
      267–268
Project Management Institute
      (PMI), 31–32, 36–38,
      38, 157
Project Management Office
      (PMO), 143
Project Procurement
      Management knowledge
      area, 44–45
Project Quality Management
      knowledge area, 41–42
Project Risk Management
      knowledge area, 44
Project Scope Management
      knowledge area, 39–40
Project Time Management
      knowledge area, 40–41
projectized organizations,
      authority in, 36
promotion policies, 148
property insurance, 475
property teams in business
      continuity plans, 484
proprietary information, loss
      of, 372
protection of assets.
      See information
      asset protection
protection profiles (PPs),
      295–296, 295
protocol analyzers, 239
protocol stacks, 215
protocols, 199, 201
  network security, 435, 435
  routing, 209–212,
      210–211

prototypes, 288–289
provisioning, 207
proxy filters, 414
pseudocoding, 285
Public Company Accounting
      Oversight Board
      (PCAOB), 13
public information
      classification, 383
public information officers
      (PIOs), 479, 487
public-key encryption,
      427–429, 428–429
public-key infrastructure
      (PKI), 432–433
  digital certificates,
      433–434
  encryption-key
      management,
      434–435
  S/MIME, 434, 434
public passwords in
      SNMP, 240
purpose
  auditing, 9
  business continuity,
      454–456
  metrics, 335

Q

qualifications of staff, 76
qualified opinions, 103
quality and quality control
  CMM for, 255–256
  Development phase in
      SDLC, 283–284
  ensuring, 77
  failures in, 280–281, 280
  ISO for, 256–260
  managing, 41–42,
      143, 255
  models, 31–32
  in project management, 34
  steering committee
      representation, 121
quantum cryptography, 432
questionable
      circumstances, 102
questionable payments, 101

Software quality, 258

T

Asset/Risk Mgmt triangle

Assets

Vulnerabilities   Threats

Wiley Publishing, Inc. End-User License Agreement

READ THIS. You should carefully read these terms and conditions before opening the software packet(s) included with this book "Book". This is a license agreement "Agreement" between you and Wiley Publishing, Inc. "WPI". By opening the accompanying software packet(s), you acknowledge that you have read and accept the following terms and conditions. If you do not agree and do not want to be bound by such terms and conditions, promptly return the Book and the unopened software packet(s) to the place you obtained them for a full refund.

1. License Grant. WPI grants to you (either an individual or entity) a nonexclusive license to use one copy of the enclosed software program(s) (collectively, the "Software," solely for your own personal or business purposes on a single computer (whether a standard computer or a workstation component of a multi-user network). The Software is in use on a computer when it is loaded into temporary memory (RAM) or installed into permanent memory (hard disk, CD-ROM, or other storage device). WPI reserves all rights not expressly granted herein.

2. Ownership. WPI is the owner of all right, title, and interest, including copyright, in and to the compilation of the Software recorded on the physical packet included with this Book "Software Media". Copyright to the individual programs recorded on the Software Media is owned by the author or other authorized copyright owner of each program. Ownership of the Software and all proprietary rights relating thereto remain with WPI and its licensers.

3. Restrictions On Use and Transfer.

(a) You may only (i) make one copy of the Software for backup or archival purposes, or (ii) transfer the Software to a single hard disk, provided that you keep the original for backup or archival purposes. You may not (i) rent or lease the Software, (ii) copy or reproduce the Software through a LAN or other network system or through any computer subscriber system or bulletin-board system, or (iii) modify, adapt, or create derivative works based on the Software.

(b) You may not reverse engineer, decompile, or disassemble the Software. You may transfer the Software and user documentation on a permanent basis, provided that the transferee agrees to accept the terms and conditions of this Agreement and you retain no copies. If the Software is an update or has been updated, any transfer must include the most recent update and all prior versions.

4. Restrictions on Use of Individual Programs. You must follow the individual requirements and restrictions detailed for each individual program in the About the CD-ROM appendix of this Book or on the Software Media. These limitations are also contained in the individual license agreements recorded on the Software Media. These limitations may include a requirement that after using the program for a specified period of time, the user must pay a registration fee or discontinue use. By opening the Software packet(s), you will be agreeing to abide by the licenses and restrictions for these individual programs that are detailed in the About the CD-ROM appendix and/or on the Software Media. None of the material on this Software Media or listed in this Book may ever be redistributed, in original or modified form, for commercial purposes.

5. Limited Warranty.

(a) WPI warrants that the Software and Software Media are free from defects in materials and workmanship under normal use for a period of sixty (60) days from the date of purchase of this Book. If WPI receives notification within the warranty period of defects in materials or workmanship, WPI will replace the defective Software Media.

(b) WPI AND THE AUTHOR(S) OF THE BOOK DISCLAIM ALL OTHER WARRANTIES, EXPRESS OR IMPLIED, INCLUDING WITHOUT LIMITATION IMPLIED WARRANTIES OF MERCHANTABILITY AND FITNESS FOR A PARTICULAR PURPOSE, WITH RESPECT TO THE SOFTWARE, THE PROGRAMS, THE SOURCE CODE CONTAINED THEREIN, AND/ OR THE TECHNIQUES DESCRIBED IN THIS BOOK. WPI DOES NOT WARRANT THAT THE FUNCTIONS CONTAINED IN THE SOFTWARE WILL MEET YOUR REQUIREMENTS OR THAT THE OPERATION OF THE SOFTWARE WILL BE ERROR FREE.

(c) This limited warranty gives you specific legal rights, and you may have other rights that vary from jurisdiction to jurisdiction.

6. Remedies.

(a) WPI's entire liability and your exclusive remedy for defects in materials and workmanship shall be limited to replacement of the Software Media, which may be returned to WPI with a copy of your receipt at the following address: Software Media Fulfillment Department, Attn.: CISA: Certified Information Systems Auditor Study Guide, Wiley Publishing, Inc., 10475 Crosspoint Blvd., Indianapolis, IN 46256, or call 1-800-762-2974. Please allow four to six weeks for delivery. This Limited Warranty is void if failure of the Software Media has resulted from accident, abuse, or misapplication. Any replacement Software Media will be warranted for the remainder of the original warranty period or thirty (30) days, whichever is longer.

(b) In no event shall WPI or the author be liable for any damages whatsoever (including without limitation damages for loss of business profits, business interruption, loss of business information, or any other pecuniary loss) arising from the use of or inability to use the Book or the Software, even if WPI has been advised of the possibility of such damages.

(c) Because some jurisdictions do not allow the exclusion or limitation of liability for consequential or incidental damages, the above limitation or exclusion may not apply to you.

7. U.S. Government Restricted Rights. Use, duplication, or disclosure of the Software for or on behalf of the United States of America, its agencies and/or instrumentalities "U.S. Government" is subject to restrictions as stated in paragraph (c)(1)(ii) of the Rights in Technical Data and Computer Software clause of DFARS 252.227-7013, or subparagraphs (c) (1) and (2) of the Commercial Computer Software - Restricted Rights clause at FAR 52.227-19, and in similar clauses in the NASA FAR supplement, as applicable.

8. General. This Agreement constitutes the entire understanding of the parties and revokes and supersedes all prior agreements, oral or written, between them and may not be modified or amended except in a writing signed by both parties hereto that specifically refers to this Agreement. This Agreement shall take precedence over any other documents that may be in conflict herewith. If any one or more provisions contained in this Agreement are held by any court or tribunal to be invalid, illegal, or otherwise unenforceable, each and every other provision shall remain in full force and effect.

The Absolute Best CISA Book/CD Package on the Market!

Get ready for the Certified Information Systems Auditor (CISA) exam with the most comprehensive and challenging sample tests anywhere!

The Sybex Test Engine features:

- All the review questions, as covered in each chapter of the book
- Challenging questions representative of those you'll find on the real exam
- Two full-length bonus exams available only on the CD
- An assessment test to narrow your focus to certain objective groups

Search through the complete book in PDF!

- Access the entire *CISA: Certified Information Systems Auditor Study Guide, 2nd Edition* complete with figures and tables, in electronic format.
- Search the *CISA: Certified Information Systems Auditor Study Guide, 2nd Edition* chapters to find information on any topic in seconds.

Use the electronic flashcards for PCs or Palm devices to jog your memory and prep last-minute for the exam!

- Reinforce your understanding of key concepts with these hard-core flashcard-style questions.
- Download the flashcards to your Palm device and go on the road. Now you can study for the CISA exam anytime, anywhere.